SCANDAL & CIVILITY

SCANDAL & CIVILITY

Journalism and the Birth of American Democracy

MARCUS DANIEL

OXFORD
UNIVERSITY PRESS
2009

OXFORD
UNIVERSITY PRESS

Oxford University Press

Oxford University Press, Inc., publishes works that further
Oxford University's objective of excellence
in research, scholarship, and education.

Oxford   New York
Auckland   Cape Town   Dar es Salaam   Hong Kong   Karachi
Kuala Lumpur   Madrid   Melbourne   Mexico City   Nairobi
New Delhi   Shanghai   Taipei   Toronto

With offices in
Argentina   Austria   Brazil   Chile   Czech Republic   France   Greece
Guatemala   Hungary   Italy   Japan   Poland   Portugal   Singapore
South Korea   Switzerland   Thailand   Turkey   Ukraine   Vietnam

Copyright © 2009 by Oxford University Press, Inc.

Published by Oxford University Press, Inc.
198 Madison Avenue, New York, New York 10016

www.oup.com

Oxford is a registered trademark of Oxford University Press

Library of Congress Cataloging-in-Publication Data
Daniel, Marcus Leonard, 1962–
Scandal & civility : journalism and
the birth of American democracy / Marcus Daniel.
p.   cm.
Includes bibliographical references and index.
ISBN 978-0-19-517212-6
1. Journalism—United States—History—18th century.
2. Press and politics—United States—History—18th century.
3. Journalism—Political aspects   United States   History   18th century.
4. Newspaper editors—United States—Biography.
I. Title. II. Title: Scandal and civility.
PN4861.D36 2008
071'309033—dc22   2008023724

1 3 5 7 9 8 6 4 2
Printed in the United States of America

For my parents,
John Turner Daniel and Judith Ann Daniel,
who helped teach me how much words matter
and how much more some things matter than words.

Acknowledgments

Like most first-time authors, I have a long list of people to thank for their witting and unwitting contributions to this book. Teachers first, for they really are the source of everything that follows. At Plymouth College of Further Education in Devon, England, Elizabeth Patel nurtured my enthusiasm for history and biography with her lectures on Disraeli and Gladstone, Bismarck and Garibaldi, and even more amazingly taught me to love the intricacies of diplomatic history when this still meant one damn treaty after another. Allan Insall (a student and staunch follower of the literary critic F. R. Leavis) taught me to wring meaning out of everything I read, from Alexander Pope to the daily press. As an undergraduate at Pembroke College, Cambridge, I was lucky enough to be taught by three remarkably dedicated teachers and scholars: Jay Winter, always exuberant and ready to talk; the late Mark Kaplanoff, who guided my first essays on American history in his own tartly conservative manner; and the late Clive Trebilcock, a fellow Plymouthian who tried hard to deter me from the life of an academic, but without success. At Oxford, John Rowett did the best he could with a difficult student at a difficult stage of his career, and when I wavered encouraged me to set out for the New World. For this I thank him.

At Princeton University, I encountered the most remarkable group of students and teachers I have ever known. And whatever the day-to-day drawbacks of graduate life in Princeton, they ensured it would be intellectually lively. Among the faculty (past and present) I'd especially like to thank Stephen Aron, Kathleen Brown, Gerry Geison, Gary Gerstle, Peter Mandler, Reid Mitchell, John Murrin, Dan Rodgers, Christine Stansell, and Sean Wilentz. My thesis committee at Princeton—Sean Wilentz, John Murrin, and Lawrence Stone—all left a deep imprint on the work that follows, although of course they bear no responsibility for its faults. It was the innovative scholarship of Sean Wilentz that first enticed me to Princeton, and he has remained an important influence on me ever since.

He helped shape my ideas about the early American Republic and showed great restraint and tolerance toward an often idiosyncratic and independent graduate student, quietly encouraging my interest in the political and cultural history of the 1790s, and patiently allowing a novice in the field of American history to find his own path. I hope his lenience has been repaid in the pages below. John Murrin's devotion to younger scholars in early American history is justly legendary and I've benefited immeasurably from both his example and his work. He's one of those rare scholars who raises everybody's game, and he certainly raised mine. The same was true of the late, great Lawrence Stone, who proved time and time again in his own life and work that scholarly rigor and intellectual generosity need not be mutually exclusive qualities. He kept me connected to eighteenth-century English history, and I will always remember him with fondness.

My fellow graduate students at Princeton were beyond compare, and I could have achieved nothing without them. In the blurred (often quite literally) line between seminar and bar, Jeff Freedman, Paul Smith, and Phil Katz played critical roles in my ongoing education, as did a larger cast that included Linda Lierheimer, Stephen Larsen, Brian Owensby, Walter Johnson, Steve Kantrowitz, Paul Lucier, Andrea Rusnock, Ben Alpers, Jonathan Berkey, Vivien Deitz, Kevin Downing, Vince DiGiralamo, Phil Harling, Laura Mason, April Masten, Gideon Rachman, Marla Stone, Emily Thompson, John Wertheimer, and Henry Yu. In long, midnight sessions at the home of Dror and Noa Wahrman many of the early ideas in this book were first thrashed out over endless cups of instant coffee. Heather Thompson's friendship and intellectual passion, and her capacity to keep life in perspective, were indispensable then, and I don't know how I've managed to get along without them since. Peter Thompson and Simon Newman, who both share my passion for eighteenth-century politics, have shaped my ideas and interests in ways I find hard to calculate or quantify. To them both I raise a "friendly glass."

My interest in the 1790s dates back a long way, but it was a course taught by the late Edward Thompson at Rutgers University that finally inspired me to work on this period. As a scholar, activist, and intellectual he had already influenced me profoundly, but as a teacher he was a revelation. Firing off notes to his students from his hospital bed, he demonstrated a commitment to our work that was genuinely awe inspiring. Always deeply conscious of the big issues at stake, he also taught me to pay attention to the small. "Generalization," he announced once in class, quoting one of his own heroes, William Blake, "is the idiocy of the age." It is a generalization I've tried hard to remember in my own work. Several other scholars have also helped me bring this work to fruition, including Alfred Young, who shares my passion for Thomas Paine and the radical past; Eric Foner, who gave me useful comments on an earlier version of this work; and Richard Bernstein and David Waldstreicher, both of whom provided much valued encouragement and support for this work at a critical juncture.

A number of institutions have helped support the research and writing of this book. A fellowship from Princeton University provided an environment almost free from the usual financial vexations of graduate life, and the Mellon Foundation provided a grant that helped me to write the thesis on which this book is based. Fellowships from the American Antiquarian Society, the Massachusetts Historical Society, the Library Company of Philadelphia, and the Historical Society of Pennsylvania not only provided financial support for my research but disclosed new wonders for me to explore. Many thanks to the staff at each of these institutions for their helpfulness and expertise, especially to the late John Hench and to Joanne Chaison of the American Antiquarian Society. I have also received support from the University Research Council at the University of Hawaii Manoa. My colleagues in the history department at the University of Hawaii have waited more or less patiently for this book to appear and have kept me entertained in the meantime, and I'd especially like to thank Ned Davis, Leonard Andaya, Mark McNally, Rich Rath, Matt Lauzon, Shana Brown, Danny Kwok, Bob McGlone, Dick Rapson, Dave Chappell, and Karen Jolly for their friendship and support.

My editors at Oxford University Press have been a pleasure to work with, although their own assessment of our collaborative enterprise may be somewhat different. Furaha Norton and Cybele Tom coaxed and goaded this book to life, and I thank them for their persistence and their faith in the final outcome. My production editor, Christi Stanforth, and my copyeditor, Merryl Sloane, have done an exemplary job guiding the final manuscript through the production process.

Finally, I would like to thank my mother, Judy Daniel, and my father, John Daniel, to whom this book is dedicated and who will be relieved to know it's finished; my siblings, Philip, Ivan, and Jessica, who always remind me that critical intelligence and intellectual creativity are to be found in plentiful supply outside the academy; and my kids, Owen, Will, and Miggy. But for their arrival this book might have been completed earlier, but its author would have been infinitely poorer. Patiently at times, impatiently at other times, Vina Lanzona has stuck by the author of this book, and although she's never read it, she's heard it described a thousand times over the breakfast table. To her I owe a debt of gratitude and love that will take a lifetime to repay.

Contents

SCANDAL & CIVILITY

The Other Founding Fathers

In a column for the *New York Times* published during the presidential primary campaigns of 2008, the conservative William Kristol declared that Senator Barack Obama's efforts to package himself as a man of unique political integrity and character had failed. "The more you learn about him," wrote Kristol, "the more Obama seems to be a conventionally opportunistic politician, impressively smart and disciplined, who has put together a good political career and a terrific presidential campaign." Behind the lofty rhetoric about the "audacity of hope," he argued, lurked more mundane interests: "the calculation of ambition, and the construction of artifice, mixed in with a dash of deceit—all covered with the great conceit that this campaign, and this candidate, are different." Kristol's comments revealed a deep skepticism about the reliability of words, as well as his belief that political "reality" was constituted not in the realm of language and ideas but in the realm of private interest and personal advancement. According to Kristol, Obama's "character" rather than his rhetoric was the key to understanding his political motives and behavior, and once this character was revealed by stripping away the carefully fashioned "construction of artifice" that concealed it, the spellbinding power of his oratory would be broken.[1]

Kristol's attack on Obama probably persuaded few readers of the liberal *New York Times*, but his emphasis on character and his skepticism about the self-presentation of political leaders extend across the political spectrum. Indeed, hardly a day goes by without a new example of the "hermeneutics of suspicion"[2] that dominates American public life. In election after election, candidates for office vie with each other to establish their own authenticity and sincerity and to impugn the authenticity and sincerity of their political rivals. Twenty-four-hour news channels like MSNBC, CNN, and Fox have created an entire industry devoted to tracking the slippage between public and private expression, speech and action, persona and self, and to exposing the true character of the men and women who

3

compete for our attention and political support. Blurring the boundary between news coverage and celebrity entertainment, this relentless cycle of revelation quite naturally generates political scandal and public cynicism, a cynicism that many believe undermines faith in the media itself and, ultimately, in our system of government.

In other words, the broad assumptions underlying Kristol's attack on Obama are widely shared in our political culture. Indeed, they have become so common-place in modern American politics that we scarcely question the validity of what political pundits constantly call the "character issue." The most basic of these assumptions is the understanding of character itself as a stable and coherent per-sonal identity that shapes and explains private and public behavior, a belief that has its roots in the intellectual developments of the Enlightenment and what one historian has called the "making of the modern self." Closely linked to this understanding of character is the belief that character has its origins in private rather than public life, is most clearly revealed in our private behavior, and there-fore is most easily exposed by the interrogation of our private affairs and asso-ciations rather than by the examination of our public words and acts. The most important measure of character, therefore, which Kristol equates with honesty and authenticity, is a clear and consistent—indeed, transparent—connection between private and public life. Men of character should appear to be what they truly are, and Kristol's indictment of Obama is not primarily that he is "oppor-tunistic" and "ambitious," although his self-interest is certainly troubling, but that he is inauthentic and dishonest, a "construction of artifice" and therefore unworthy of public trust and support.[3]

These assumptions about the role of character in public life and the relation-ship between private and public behavior lead naturally to a politics of intrusion and suspicion, of personal scandal and corruption, and to a personalization of political life—all of which I call the "politics of character." Many commentators believe that this obsession with the politics of character is a recent phenom-enon. Writing about the Monica Lewinsky scandal in the late 1990s, for example, Professor Carey Cooper, a social psychologist, described the scandal as a logical response to changes in social mores since the 1960s, in particular the wide-spread belief that "the personal is political." Americans had once believed that it was important to maintain a boundary between private and public life but now regarded the private lives of their political representatives as fair game for media scrutiny. Consequently, President Bill Clinton's sexual relationship with his former intern, Monica Lewinsky, provided fodder for a political drama of epic proportions and became a powerful symbol for the corruption and decay of the Clinton presidency. According to his critics, Clinton's behavior marked a new low point in the degeneration of American political leadership, while according to his supporters, the media's exploitation of the affair marked a new low point in the degeneration of American political discourse. All sides of the political spectrum, however, deplored the personalization and sensationalism of American politics, calling for a restoration of political "civility" and the election of "men of character" to restore public respect for the integrity of the political system.[4]

But the politics of character has a long history, a history that links the contentious democratic republic of our own day with the even more conflict-ridden republican democracy of the founding fathers.[5] A great deal of historical writing about the early Republic acknowledges this link, revealing a fascination with the character of the founders and a powerful sense of nostalgia for a lost eighteenth-century world of political civility and civic virtue, a nostalgia that tells us more about our disillusionment with our own politics than about the politics of the founding era. For there was no golden age of American politics when public-spirited men debated issues of great moment with a rationality as sharply honed as their classical rhetoric, when public debate was conducted within well-understood and widely accepted limits of civility, and when journalists deferred to their political betters and dutifully observed a sharp distinction between private and public life. On the contrary, scandal and incivility have always been a part of American politics and at no time was this more true than during the founding period.[6]

Far from being an age of classical virtue and republican self-restraint, political life in the postrevolutionary United States was tempestuous, fiercely partisan, and highly personal. And nobody was exempt, not even the founding fathers themselves. When George Washington retired from the presidency in 1796, his former revolutionary comrade-in-arms, Thomas Paine, denounced him publicly as a "cold hermaphrodite," and many of the leading Republican writers and editors of the day echoed Paine's words. And when Paine himself, author of *Common Sense* and *The Crisis Papers*, returned home to the United States from France in 1802, he was vilified in the Federalist press as a "lying, drunken, brutal infidel" who rejoiced in "confusion, devastation, bloodshed, rapine, and murder." Throughout the 1790s, American newspapers, which followed the political upheavals in revolutionary Europe extraordinarily closely, teemed with denunciations of bloodthirsty Republican "Jacobins" and power-hungry Federalist "Aristocrats," and the violence of the printed word often flowed off the page and into the streets, provoking verbal and physical assaults, duels, public demonstrations, and riots. Political emotions ran extraordinarily high in what was less an "age of reason" than what one historian has called an "age of passion."[7]

Then, as now, many Americans deplored this partisan passion, criticizing (and sometimes seeking to restrain by legal and illegal means) those they held responsible for fomenting these passions. Like many of us, they yearned for a more civil politics, projecting a lost moral unity and political consensus back into the revolutionary past and attacking the organized, self-interested agents of party politics. But as many of them recognized, and some even celebrated, scandal and incivility were closely linked to the creation of a more democratic and participatory political culture. Inspired by their own revolution and by the revolutionary upheavals of the broader Atlantic world, the 1790s were a remarkably creative period in American political life, and by helping to fashion a vibrant and iconoclastic culture of political dissent, American journalists contributed to the emergence of a more democratic social and political order.[8]

At the center of this volatile and turbulent postrevolutionary world were the partisan newspaper editors who are the principal subjects of this book. During the 1790s, these editors and journalists, new men with a new sense of vocation as political authors and activists, helped to create a new public for politics and to impart to it new ideas about national and partisan identity. In doing so, they played a critical role in the creation and expansion of an American public sphere and in what the historian Gordon Wood calls the "democratization of the American mind." Yet until fairly recently, they have received almost universally hostile treatment from scholars of the early Republic who, when they bother to notice them at all, dismiss them as mercenary hacks or as ciphers for more important political figures, like Thomas Jefferson and Alexander Hamilton. Frank Luther Mott, for example, the doyen of American journalism history, famously dismissed the political journalism of the 1790s and early 1800s as the "dark ages of partisan journalism," a less than heroic interlude between the nationalist triumphs of the revolutionary press and the rise of an independent, objective press in the nineteenth century.[9]

This book seeks to rescue these journalists from the condescension of both their own time and posterity and to restore them to their rightful place in the politics of the early Republic: center stage. It is organized around six biographical studies, each of which deals with an editor whom I consider to be among the most interesting and influential of the period. Three are Federalists: John Fenno, Noah Webster, and William Cobbett; three are Republicans: Philip Freneau, Benjamin Franklin Bache, and William Duane—although each of these men defined partisan identity in their own unique and fluid fashion, and their relationships to party organization and political discipline were often haphazard. All were fierce partisans and some were talented party organizers, but none of these journalists were simply party men. Most of them eventually quarreled with the professional politicians and party managers of their day, and they all possessed a strong sense of their own ideological independence, which they guarded jealously. All were men of political ideas as well as political activists, and that is how I've approached them in this book, taking their ideas seriously and giving them a degree of prominence not usually associated with the ephemeral character of newspapers and the generally low esteem in which the public (and many historians) hold their creators.[10] Their distinctive ideas and experiences shed light on different aspects and moments of American politics in the 1790s, but taken together I hope their stories also illuminate in new ways the broader story of American politics in the postrevolutionary period.[11]

In *A Brief Retrospect of the Eighteenth Century*, the Reverend Samuel Miller expressed astonishment at the rapid growth of partisan newspapers in the United States. "Never was there given to man a political engine of greater power," he wrote, "and never, assuredly, did this engine operate upon so large a scale as in the eighteenth century." The expansion of the press in the last quarter of the eighteenth century gave editors a central role in the politics of the 1790s. Between the Declaration of Independence in 1776 and the election of Thomas Jefferson to the presidency in 1800, the number of newspapers published each week in the United States increased from about 25 to approximately 230, creating for the first time a genuinely national public sphere. As the nation expanded and developed, newspapers formed a critical link between the new federal government and its citizens, and it was through the medium of the press that Americans (including many of those excluded from formal rights of citizenship, like women and African Americans) became steadily more conscious of their place in a broader but often distant national political debate.[12]

This quantitative revolution was accompanied by a qualitative revolution, a change in what Miller called the "form and character" of the press. Once regarded as vehicles for the conveyance of political "intelligence," by the 1790s, newspapers had become critical forums for the discussion of public life and a crucial influence on the formation of public opinion. Conscious of their new importance, editors who had once been regarded (and usually regarded themselves) as "meer mechanics," printer-artisans who published what others wrote and appealed to a reading public defined by proximity not politics, began to redefine themselves as editor-authors whose duty was to shape rather than to reflect or represent public opinion.[13] This transformation was part of a broader transformation in American print culture. Poised between the disintegration of a republican culture of print in the eighteenth century and the formation of a print culture in the nineteenth century characterized by the "rise of objectivity" and the growth of a mass circulation popular press, the 1790s presented unique opportunities to partisan editors and writers. The expansion of the literary marketplace and the low cost of producing newspapers, combined with the legal freedom of the American press, gave editors in this period unprecedented and unrivaled personal influence. Far from being party hacks, partisan editors during this period operated from a position of precarious but genuine economic and ideological independence.[14]

Their newspapers reflected this independence and were characterized by emphatic and powerful authorial voices. In the past, readers had expected responsible editors to keep their personal politics out of their newspapers and responsible political writers to pay homage to an ideal of authorial impartiality and anonymity. Authors were to be heard but not seen. And editors were to be neither heard nor seen. Newspapers were expected to function as passive and neutral media (literally, in the middle) through which independent writers communicated with equally independent readers. Although this "republican ideology of print" came under considerable strain during the American Revolution, when editors and political authors revised their ideas about impartiality and anonymity to permit the expression of their own revolutionary (or anti-revolutionary) commitments, it dominated the literary and political culture of colonial America and resurfaced vigorously in the postrevolutionary period.[15]

Partisan journalists in the early Republic broke sharply with the ideals of republican print culture, writing to persuade rather than to inform their readers and using their writings to fashion powerful representations of their own authorial personalities. The English émigré journalist William Cobbett, for example, made no effort to hide his authorial personality or to pretend he was the neutral arbiter of a rational and disinterested public debate. "Professions of impartiality," he declared in the very first issue of his daily newspaper, *Porcupine's Gazette*, "I shall make none. They are always useless, and are besides perfect nonsense, when used by a newsmonger." Rejecting the conventional pieties of American journalism, Cobbett placed his own distinctive persona at the center of his political writing, reconfiguring the idea of authorial independence not to affirm his own political impartiality but to justify his right to self-expression. With differing degrees of modesty, other partisan editors of the 1790s did the same.[16] Moreover, these editors not only represented themselves to the public in new ways, they also focused public attention on the public representations of others, developing an intrusive, ad hominem style of journalism dedicated to unmasking the characters and motives of public men. By asserting their own subjectivity and emphasizing the importance of character in their own writings and in the content of their newspapers, they helped to unleash a fierce public debate about the politics of character in the early Republic.[17]

This shift toward a more abrasive and personal style of political journalism was closely linked to developments in the 1790s, but it was also shaped by much broader changes in eighteenth-century American society. As Gordon Wood points out, issues of personal identity and public representation were a "source of continuing fascination in eighteenth-century Anglo-American culture," a fascination that reflected the spread of new ideas about the importance of human agency in the Enlightenment, ideas that placed human volition rather than divine providence at the center of the historical process.[18] These ideas about human agency manifested themselves in a fondness for conspiracy theories, which was common to both English and American political culture and which made the detection of true motives and character central to political discourse. As the English novelist and author of *Tom Jones*, Henry Fielding, wrote in "An Essay on the Knowledge of the Characters of Men," published in the 1740s, the art of reading and interpreting character was the key to that "excellent Art, called the Art of Politics." But there were other intellectual currents at work as well. One was the increasingly widespread belief that the world and its affairs were governed by "interest" rather than civic virtue (a development that was central to the new science of political economy), a belief that deepened public skepticism about the motives and intentions of political leaders. But even more important was the erosion of popular belief in the hereditary basis for social and political hierarchy. As ideas about social and political hierarchy were democratized (and relegitimized) in the eighteenth century by the idea of a "natural aristocracy," the task of identifying political leaders became increasingly difficult, fueling public concern about the identities of those who competed for public office.[19]

Anxiety about political identity acquired even greater potency because of the transformation and democratization of public life in the eighteenth-century Atlantic world. This transformation undermined the insular, aristocratic world of court politics, displacing it with what the German philosopher and sociologist Jurgen Habermas calls a bourgeois "public sphere." The creation of a public sphere in Britain and the British colonies of North America during the eighteenth century involved two central developments: the expansion of new forms of publicity, most important the newspaper press, and the growth of a new framework for public life outside the institutional boundaries of the political state, where citizens could meet to read the news (and other literary forms, like novels and poetry), exchange information, and discuss public affairs. These social institutions (coffeehouses, public houses, literary societies, and other voluntary organizations) created new forms of secular association and sociability, often based on a shared interest in commerce or politics.[20] The expansion of the newspaper press (fueled by the growing appetite for commercial and political information) reinforced this development but also reconstituted it at a more abstract level, connecting private readers and citizens through the impersonal medium of print. In this increasingly impersonal public world of politics and marketplace activity, personal identity was no longer always determined by direct acquaintance—the spoken word and the physical body—and the difficulty of determining identity became ever greater. Not surprisingly, explanations for political behavior became increasingly personal and conspiratorial.[21]

The transformation of public life in the eighteenth century also encouraged new forms of consciousness about the relationship between public and private and new ideas about the self. The eighteenth century was a period of cultural as well as political revolution, and at the heart of this cultural transformation was what one historian has called the "making of the modern self," an understanding of the self as a unique, stable, and identifiable subject. This new self-consciousness or subjectivity found its most creative and important expression in an entirely new literary form, the "novel." Although the novel had antecedents in earlier forms of fictional, autobiographical, and epistolary writing, what Habermas describes as the "domestic novel, the psychological description in autobiographical form," came of age during the eighteenth century and played a key role in the creation of a new reading public. By exploring in a literary form the psychological complexity of the self and the social complexity of private life, English novelists like Tobias Smollett, Henry Fielding, and Samuel Richardson linked the private, domestic world of the eighteenth century to the increasingly anonymous and impersonal public sphere.[22]

The authors of more explicitly public and political forms of writing, particularly satirical poetry and prose, shared the novelists' interest in personal character, in the relationship between private and public life, and in presenting the world in narrative terms. While the novel publicized private life, political satire personalized public life, and it was often hard to draw a boundary line between fiction, which always has a politics of its own, and political writing, which always generates its own fictions. Highly personal, satirical political writing thus linked private subjects and citizens to the new public sphere. Political satire was an ideal form for publicizing political life and connecting the hitherto insulated world of elite politics to the world of the common reader and the common man.[23]

Literary and political satire was an important part of American colonial culture and flourished despite the influence of republican ideas about impersonality. Although no colonial writers matched the satirical skill of Jonathan Swift or Alexander Pope, and few tried to match the rebarbative nastiness of their less celebrated "Grub Street" or "Hackney" counterparts, American writers nonetheless produced a healthy satirical tradition and helped to popularize writers like Swift and Pope. During the American Revolution, Patriot editors like William Goddard and Eleazar Oswald, poets like Philip Freneau (who was deeply influenced by

Pope), and the Tory editor of the *Royal Gazette*, James Rivington, yielded to none in the biting wit and partisan engagement of their writing. By the end of the century, this tradition was in the ascendant, manifesting itself in new forms of self-conscious literary activity: the production of the first American novels and plays, the creation of a tradition of American belles lettres, and the less lofty but infinitely more influential writings of American newspaper journalists. Although critics of the press often blamed British journalists like Cobbett and William Duane for the explosion of partisan invective and political satire, it had deep indigenous roots.[24]

Satire appealed to the tastes of Americans for the same reason it appealed to the British, because it was a literary form uniquely suited to unmasking and publicizing political hypocrisy. According to Henry Fielding, no mean satirist himself, the principal purpose of satire is forensic: to pierce what he called the "outer character" of men (he explicitly excluded women from his discussion) and to reveal their "inner character." Conceiving the political world in theatrical terms as a "vast Masquerade," Fielding argued that it was possible to detect the truth behind the "false Vizors and Habits" that men wore to disguise their true "nature" from the public. And the most infallible method for doing so was to observe

> the Actions of Men with others, and especially those to whom they are allied in Blood, Marriage, Friendship, Neighbourhood, or any other Connection.... Trace then the Man proposed to your Trust, into his private Family and nearest Intimacies. See whether he hath acted the Part of a good Son, Brother, Husband, Father, Friend, Master, Servant, &c. If he hath discharged these Duties well, your Confidence will have a good Foundation.

"The bad Man in private," declared Fielding, "can never be a sincere Patriot" nor a selfless guardian of the public interest.[25]

Fielding's assumptions about character were commonplace, and as a result eighteenth-century politics was dedicated to the art of political psychology, of reading words and bodies in order to read minds. At its most radical, this preoccupation with what Fielding called "inner character" fueled a politics of transparency and exposure that became one of the hallmarks of the Enlightenment. "Government, like dress," wrote Thomas Paine in *Common Sense*, "is the badge of lost innocence; the palaces of kings are built on the ruins of the bowers of paradise." Linking clothing with original sin, monarchical corruption, and the concealment of the self, Paine associated nakedness with natural innocence, republican virtue, and the unself-conscious display of the self. Thomas Jefferson expressed a similar series of assumptions in his response to attacks on George Washington in the Republican press during the 1790s. "Naked he would have been sanctimoniously reverenced," wrote Jefferson, "but inveloped in the rags of royalty, they can hardly be torn off without laceration." The value placed on political transparency justified and encouraged the development of intrusive forms of political writing. Even John Adams (who later complained bitterly about attacks on his own character) claimed that all men had a "right to that most dreaded and envied kind of knowledge—I mean of the character and conduct of their rulers."[26]

Issues of political character and identity were thus a central preoccupation of American politics well before the 1790s. Eighteenth-century America experienced rapid and bewildering social changes, and personal identity was a particularly troubling and problematic category in a society of such social and political flux and such constantly shifting boundaries and borders. Political insecurity was endemic among colonial elites, helping push them toward a revolutionary break with Great Britain in the 1770s.[27] The American Revolution, in turn, produced a radical redefinition of political citizenship, redistributing sovereignty (and patriarchal authority) to all white men and further destabilizing elites' control of political power.[28] Although such power remained closely linked to social status, elites now had to negotiate political legitimacy with an expanded and increasingly well-informed citizenry. And amid the rapid social and political changes of the postrevolutionary period, issues of political representation became highly contentious. While citizens were forced to decide how to embody their newly acquired sovereignty in political representatives, and who among them could be trusted to protect their interests and rights, elites weighed how to represent themselves to a newly enfranchised public and how to ensure that men like themselves rather than popular demagogues were returned to office. These issues lay at the heart of the debate about the adoption of the federal constitution, a constitution that many members of the political elite hoped would protect a republican government from the character flaws of its own citizenry by ensuring that only the "best of men" were elected to public office.[29]

Such hopes were quickly dashed. As the founding generation struggled to define the public policies and practices of the new nation, the unity created by their shared commitment to revolutionary nationalism dissolved. When an organized opposition to the Washington administration emerged in the early 1790s in the form of the Republican Party, Americans were forced to come to terms with systematic political conflict within the revolutionary nation, a development that challenged the hostility to party conflict and faction that was central to their republican ideology. Party conflict and the novelty and fragility of American political institutions led both Federalist supporters of the administration and their Republican opponents to question the durability of republican government in the United States and to predict the unraveling of American society. With the benefit of hindsight, these fears may seem exaggerated, but in a period when political revolutions and counterrevolutions were sweeping across Western Europe and the Atlantic world, they seemed all too justified. And in the context created by new forms of representative government, issues of character—personal identity and public appearance, transparency and hypocrisy, sincerity and artifice—that had long been central to Anglo-American political discourse became even more highly charged.[30]

The result was an increasingly vitriolic politics of character, a politics of personal exposure, that challenged and undermined the civility and polite sociability of elite political culture.[31] Not even Congress was immune. The personal abuse that characterized congressional debates, wrote one dismayed commentator, would "do honour to a society at Billingsgate." When Vermont congressman Matthew Lyon spat in the face of Connecticut Federalist Roger Griswold (earning lasting infamy and the sobriquet "Spitting Mat") during a debate on the floor of the House of Representatives in January 1798, Griswold exacted revenge by beating Lyon bloody with a hickory cane, and American public life descended to new depths of incivility. Contemporaries of all political persuasions were alarmed by the increasingly personal animosity of public life and the growing political animosity of private life. Writing to Edward Rutledge in June 1797, Vice President Thomas Jefferson, the organizer and leader of the Republican opposition, deplored the way that personal and political passions had become entwined in public controversy, eroding the ties of friendship and polite sociability that formed the basis of a civil society. "You and I have formerly seen warm debates and high political passions," he told Rutledge. "But gentlemen of different politics would then speak to each other, and separate the business of the Senate from that of society. It is not so now. Men who have been intimate all their lives, cross the street to avoid meeting, and turn their heads another way, lest they should be obliged to touch their hats."[32]

By the late 1790s, Jefferson's concern about the erosion of elite sociability was part of a broader public discussion about the social consequences of partisan conflict, one that focused increasingly on the role of the press. Again and again during the 1790s, observers of American public life equated the health and the vitality of the nation with the health and vitality of the press. "Whatever facilitates a general intercourse of sentiments, as good roads, domestic commerce, a free press, and particularly a *circulation of newspapers through the entire body of the people*," argued James Madison in an essay on "Public Opinion" published in 1791, "is equivalent to a contraction of territorial limits, and is favorable to liberty."[33] Madison's association of the expansion of the press, the preservation of political liberty, and the consolidation of American nationalism was commonplace. Newspapers were widely regarded as instruments of public education and

Congressional Pugilists. Unidentified artist, Philadelphia, 1798. Members of Congress watch and cheer on the fight between Republican Matthew Lyon of Vermont (brandishing the tongs) and Federalist Roger Griswold of Connecticut (wielding the cane) in January 1798. To many, the episode symbolized the personal animosity that characterized American political life by the late 1790s. Courtesy of the Library of Congress.

national integration whose free operation and subsidized distribution ensured the existence of an informed, virtuous citizenry. Their passion for reading and for reading newspapers, in particular, was what made Americans so well suited to republican government. This popular passion for news began early. Even before children had learned to read, they were *listening* to newspapers. One correspondent to the *Gazette of the United States* in 1790 observed that "children, very early in life, are eager for the sight of a newspaper," describing a family of his acquaintance that regularly "assembled around a large table" for family newspaper readings. Newspapers straddled the boundary between literate and oral culture and were not only read privately by their subscribers but also read aloud in public places: taverns and public houses, coffeehouses, marketplaces, and the steps of the county courthouse.[34] The Federalist writer Joseph Dennie satirized this popular thirst for news:

In America the impertinent eagerness for news should be scolded or laughed into moderation. The country gentleman, at peace on his farm, asks for translations from the Paris Moniteur, absurdly anxious for the welfare of Frenchmen skipping over the carcass of their King and country. Others are solicitous for the emperor Paul and the Grand Turk; and are not a little relieved to learn, that the first traverses St. Petersburgh [sic], at nine; and that the last uses more opium than sherbert. I have known profound calculators, so busy with Mr. Pitt and the Bank of England, that they utterly neglected their own debts, and, proving a national bankruptcy abroad, were thoughtless of their own, at home.

But Dennie's disdain for ordinary readers was not shared even by fellow Federalists, most of whom believed that the diffusion of political intelligence to the public was a source of political stability. "It is owing in a great degree to the want of information," argued Loring Andrews, the Federalist editor of the *Western Star*, "that the people are so often suspicious of their rulers." For Republicans like Philip Freneau, on the other hand, newspapers were an unqualified good and, without them, "a just knowledge of their rights, and indeed knowledge in general, can scarcely be attained by the mass of the human species." Newspapers made possible not only a stronger but a more democratic society.[35]

By the late 1790s, this optimistic consensus about the role of the press in a republican society was dissolving, and as Americans became more concerned about the growth of partisanship, they began to blame the press and the politics of character for the uncivilized and divisive nature of their politics. According to Thomas McKean, a signer of the Declaration of Independence, chief justice of the Pennsylvania Supreme Court, and a future Republican governor of Pennsylvania, the "art of libeling" and character assassination had become a "kind of national crime," distinguishing the newspapers of Philadelphia and the United States from the rest of the "civilized world" and fraying the ties of civility that bound the new nation together. By 1800, the Republican Samuel Miller also considered American newspapers to be the "most profligate and scurrilous public prints in the civilized world," a judgment echoed by many of his contemporaries. Both men exaggerated—American newspapers were no match for the personal and often pornographic venom of the most virulent English and French newspapers—but the perceived "licentiousness" of American journalism provides a crucial context for understanding the fierce debates about the liberty of the press that erupted in the late 1790s, the growing tolerance for civil and seditious libel prosecutions, and the passage of the Alien and Sedition Acts in 1798, which was an ill-judged and ill-fated effort to civilize political discourse as well as an attempt by Federalists to gain partisan advantage.[36]

Then, as now, for many Americans the desire to establish the virtue of their representatives warred with the desire to preserve the virtue of their Republic. Public alarm and constant jeremiads about the degeneracy of the press should be treated with skepticism (they constitute too great a part of our own public discourse for us to do otherwise), but McKean, Miller, and other critics were right to detect a sea change in the journalism of the 1790s and right to link this change to the increasingly personal tone of political discourse. As their great popularity attested, the journalists responsible for the development of a politics of character addressed issues that were deeply important to the reader-citizens of the new Republic. Their iconoclastic and personal style of journalism challenged the hitherto exclusive forms and forums of elite politics. And as the polite but restricted sociability of the republic of letters gave way to the contentious and increasingly anonymous public sphere of a lettered republic, the political journalism of the 1790s helped to connect citizens to the new nation-state and to create a more democratic and participatory public culture.

Although partisan journalists were important agents of this political transformation, they remain elusive and unfamiliar figures, confined to the margins (and footnotes) of books on the history of the early Republic. One reason for this is the moral piety of most conventional historians of journalism and their commitment to a profoundly teleological history of the press that emphasizes the growth of professionalism and the rise of objectivity, a perspective captured perfectly by the well-known motto of the *New York Times* (founded in 1802 by the highly partisan Hamiltonian editor William Coleman): "All the News That's Fit to Print." The unapologetically partisan journalism of the 1790s fits poorly into this progressive history. And, all too often, the history of American journalism has been left in the hands of historians of journalism. The recent expansion in the study of eighteenth-century print culture, for example, more or less avoids the uncharted ocean of print published in the popular press, choosing instead to explore the more easily charted boundaries of the book.[37] And although political historians and biographers make more use of partisan newspapers, they use them chiefly as sources for narrative color and information. Political historians who are more interested in the process of party formation have largely ignored the dynamic, creative role that journalists played in the growth of partisan ideology and their impact on popular political consciousness, wrongly assuming that political parties are formed from the top down.[38]

But the most important reason for the neglect of these journalists is the way that historians have conceptualized the political ideology and culture of eighteenth-century America. Since the late 1960s, historians have argued that eighteenth-century America is best understood within the framework, or paradigm, of classical republicanism, a world view organized around the belief that civic virtue, defined as the pursuit of the public interest, or res publica, was essential to the preservation of political liberty and that this virtue was perpetually threatened by both personal corruption and the influence of organized interests or factions.[39] The influence of this republican synthesis has been profound, but it has not gone unchallenged, and since the 1970s, historians have spilled a great deal of ink on the timing and nature of the transition from a republican to a liberal society.[40] Central to both sides in this increasingly sterile debate is a belief in distinct and definable political paradigms that we can categorize as "republican" or "liberal." But such categories create nonexistent boundaries, and their use reflects an approach to the history of political ideas and language that is highly structural and deterministic.[41]

Words are always political, and what gets lost in this approach to language is the politics, the realm of human contingency, action, and power within which language is used and interpreted by creative political agents like journalists and their readers. Consequently, political conflict often appears to unfold within a basic ideological consensus (whether republican or liberal) and with little sense that there is anything much at stake besides ideas. Usually relying on a restricted body of elite texts, this approach is sensitive to the changing historical meanings of words but shows little interest in the ways these constantly changing meanings are shaped and contested in public discourse. In contrast, I treat language as a field of ideological contention, a discourse that acquires meaning only as it is appropriated and used by particular social groups, classes, and individuals. I assume, in other words, that language is creative, dynamic, disruptive, and unstable—neither a reflex of social interests nor a structure that determines them. Political ideas are embedded in political practice, and in order to determine what they mean, we need to know as much as possible about who is using them, whom they are designed to persuade, and the political context within which they are being used.[42]

My emphasis on the rhetorical practices and strategies of individual journalists therefore reflects my belief that political ideas cannot be divorced from the specific political context within which they occur. Thinking about political language in this way compels us to rethink the stability and plausibility of the categories we use to think about politics in the 1790s and, particularly, categories of party identity. As I hope will become clear, party identity in the 1790s was extraordinarily fluid and unstable, and its nomenclature and definition were never fixed. Not only were the meanings of terms like "Republican" and "Federalist" hotly contested, but other labels of party allegiance and affiliation competed with them for primacy: "American," "Alien," "Aristocrat," "Democrat," "Jacobin," "Monocrat"— these and other terms, hurled as political epithets or embraced as badges of political honor, played a critical role in partisan debate. Paying close attention to shifts in language and meaning restores contingency and agency to the political history of the 1790s, a period that has long been dominated by overly rigid categories of partisan identity and an overemphasis on political modernization and the inevitable rise of Jeffersonian democracy. Labels like "Federalism" and "Republicanism" were never fixed, homogeneous, and transparent ideological or political categories that contemporaries or later historians could use to easily sort and decipher the politics of the 1790s, but fluid and elusive rhetorical categories that were themselves subject to political debate. Like all political language, they prescribed as well as described and were part of broader narrative strategies designed to persuade listeners and readers, to alter and change reality, and to do good political work. If we are unclear about this today, the political leaders and party polemicists of the 1790s were not. They understood that language was not a passive register of political reality but an active instrument of political persuasion, and they used it with a degree of self-consciousness that reflected their own expanded sense of importance in the political process.[43]

This is not to say that political parties were merely a rhetorical construction and did not exist in the 1790s. They did exist, and we know they existed because men and women at the time believed that they existed, said they existed, and acted as if they existed. But neither the Federalists nor the Republicans were a coherent, well-integrated political bloc. Like most political parties, they were a complex, fluid coalition of political, economic, social, and ideological interests, constituted and reconstituted in the conflict-ridden arena of American popular politics.[44] Parties were sharply defined in the political rhetoric of the day, but the distinction between Federalists and Republicans was the product of contemporary party warfare, and it is important not to reproduce this rhetoric uncritically in our historical analysis. All too often, this is the case, as historians reduce the history and politics of the 1790s to a Manichaean struggle between (democratic) Republicans and (reactionary) Federalists, with the supporters of one party cast as agents of the future (usually Republicans) and the other (usually Federalists) as guardians of the past.[45] This book sets out to challenge the facile narrative of economic modernization and political progress upon which such interpretations rest and to reimagine the inhabitants of the early Republic not as flat and predictable political caricatures but as "psychologically and politically complex, like the subjects of a good novel or a searching biography."[46] Neither the Federalists nor their ideas were destined to disappear as the ratchet of historical progress moved toward a predetermined liberal democratic future, and they did not. Rather, in a period of enormously complex economic, social, political, cultural, religious, and intellectual change, all Americans struggled to reconcile their visions of the future with their experiences of the present and their memories of the past. And in this supremely challenging task, there were no heralds of modernity.

CHAPTER I

John Fenno and the Constitution of a National Character

John Fenno was a man in a hurry. During the winter of 1789, the thirty-seven-year-old journalist left his wife and children behind in Boston and moved to New York City to establish what he hoped would become a new national periodical. In the spring, he worked feverishly to outfit and organize his small printing shop at 86 William Street, close to the busy mercantile offices and shipping wharves of lower Manhattan. In February, he traveled to Philadelphia to buy type for his printing press, consulting with Benjamin Franklin and his nephew Benjamin Franklin Bache about the pitfalls of the printing business and using all of his considerable energy and ingenuity to persuade politicians and businessmen of the Federalist persuasion in New York to lend him their support and their money. Now he was ready, and on Wednesday, April 15, 1789, he published the first issue of the *Gazette of the United States*, priced at six pence a copy and completely free of advertising. There were to be no commercial distractions in this newspaper. In his prospectus, Fenno promised to publish the proceedings of the new federal Congress and essays on "great subjects of Government," especially those touching "the *national* and *local* rights of AMERICAN CITIZENS," and to keep his readers abreast of any developments, domestic or foreign, concerning the "INTERESTS of the AMERICAN REPUBLICK." The newspaper, he declared, would be "A NATIONAL PAPER," dedicated to the propagation of "NATIONAL, INDEPENDENT, and IMPARTIAL PRINCIPLES."[1]

Publishing the *Gazette of the United States* was a risky venture for Fenno, who had left behind in his beloved Boston not only family and friends, but a budding career as a contributor to Benjamin Russell's *Massachusetts Centinel*. Newspapers, especially political newspapers like the *Gazette of the United States*, rarely turned a profit, and he had taken on a substantial personal debt just to get the paper up and running. To add to his difficulties, New York already had a thriving press. Each week, six newspapers were published in the city, and their editors generally shared Fenno's Federalist sympathies. Almost all of them had participated in the grand federal parade held in the city on July 23, 1788, to celebrate the ratification of the federal Constitution in New York, marching with other members of the New York printing trades alongside a "handsome stage, drawn by four horses" on which were mounted a "federal printing-press complete" and a flag inscribed with the name "Publius," the pen name used by the authors of the *Federalist Papers*, James Madison, John Jay, and Alexander Hamilton.[2]

But despite their support for the federal Constitution, none of the printers who marched in the federal parade was a standard-bearer for the new federal government in its own capital. The *New York Packet* and the *Daily Gazette* were both commercial rather than political papers, wary of alienating their mercantile advertisers and readers, and the *Morning Post*, run by the former Loyalist William Morton, also kept a low political profile. Francis Childs's *Daily Advertiser* was similarly nondescript and, after Childs hired the radical poet Philip Freneau to edit the paper in March 1790, it became "cautiously anti-federalist." The only vigorous Federalist newspaper in the city before 1789 was John Russell's *New York Museum*, and this expired when Russell returned to his native Boston.[3] The absence of a staunch Federalist newspaper in the city was compounded by the presence of Thomas Greenleaf, the only newspaper editor in New York who did not participate in the federal parade. Greenleaf was an implacable foe of the federal Constitution and had provided Anti-Federalists with ideological ammunition well beyond the boundaries of New York, and his dislike for the Constitution was not at all dampened by its passage. When a Federalist mob attacked his printing office after he published a satire on the recent "Grand Procession," Greenleaf confronted his antagonists with withering scorn and a loaded gun, and throughout 1789 and 1790, he maintained a steady barrage of criticism against the federal government in the pages of the *New York Journal*.[4] As Alexander Hamilton assured Fenno shortly after his arrival in New York, not only was there room for a newspaper strongly committed to the new federal government, there was a real need, and Fenno hoped to fill it.[5]

But there was another reason for Fenno's haste: to ensure that the first issue of the *Gazette of the United States* coincided with the arrival of the new government and its president, George Washington. He succeeded with only a week to spare. On Thursday, April 23, 1789, eight days after the first appearance of the *Gazette of the United States*, Washington arrived in New York. His progress from Mount Vernon to New York had been astonishing. At each stage of his journey, he was greeted by elaborate displays of public respect and affection. His reception,

Federal Hall, the Seat of Congress, by Amos Doolittle, New Haven, 1790. George Washington is taking the oath of office at his inauguration as president of the United States in New York in April 1789, a moment celebrated by John Fenno, who was overjoyed by the surge of popular nationalist feeling and his personal affection for Washington. Courtesy of the Winterthur Museum, bequest of Henry Francis du Pont.

writes his biographer Douglas Southall Freeman, was like "something from a page in Roman history, something very like the triumphal return of Caesar to his capital." But Washington entered New York as the freely elected leader of a democratic republic, not as a conquering classical hero. Already the embodiment of revolutionary virtue and national independence, as president of the United States, Washington now embodied national unity and political consensus. As the banners and speeches that greeted him along the road to New York declared, Washington was "the man who unites all our hearts," a figure who inspired public awe and reverence but also one who attracted public affection and love. "Never has a sovereign reigned more completely in the hearts of his subjects," declared the French minister, the Comte de Moustier, "than did Washington in those of his fellow-citizens."[6]

Overwhelmed by the emotion that Washington's arrival in New York created, Fenno was, at least metaphorically, lost for words. This "great occasion," he wrote, has "arrested the publick attention beyond all powers of description." But although the president's progress into the city was "sublimely great—beyond all descriptive powers of the pen," Fenno did his best to describe the occasion for the benefit of his readers outside New York and (one suspects) posterity. "THURSDAY last, between 2 and 3 o'clock, P.M.," he wrote solemnly, "the Most Illustrious PRESIDENT OF THE UNITED STATES arrived in this city." After a reception by U.S. senators and representatives at Elizabethtown, Washington was rowed across the Hudson River, amid a flotilla of brightly decorated sailing vessels, on a barge manned by thirteen pilots dressed in gleaming white uniforms, symbols of the thirteen newly united states. As he approached New York, he was greeted with thirteen gun salutes from the ships *Galveston* and *North Carolina* and the guns of the New York Battery. In lower Manhattan, "innumerable multitudes thronged the shores, the wharves and the shipping" to welcome him, and when Washington stepped ashore at Murray's wharf, Governor George Clinton greeted him and escorted him up Queen Street to his official residence. During this last stage of his journey, reported Fenno, Washington was accompanied by troops of dragoons, infantry and artillery, militia officers, members of Congress and the clergy, officers of the city and state of New York, the ambassadors of France and Spain, and "an immense concourse of Citizens." In the evening, the city was illuminated by brilliant "transparent paintings" that, Fenno declared, "did honor to the ingenuity and publick spirit of the parties concerned in their exhibition."[7]

But while Fenno was able to capture the events of the day, he struggled to express the intensity of the popular euphoria that Washington's arrival had created in New York. "All ranks and professions expressed their feelings, in loud acclamations, and with rapture hailed the arrival of the FATHER OF HIS COUNTRY," he wrote. "How *sincere*" these feelings were, he insisted, and "how *expressive* the sentiments of respect and veneration" that ordinary people felt toward Washington. As Fenno emphasized, these "spontaneous effusions of gratitude" were not confined to male citizens of the new republic. The elderly "could hardly restrain their impatience" to see the president, and neither could the "multitudes of children and young people" who turned out to follow him through the streets. Fenno was especially struck by the role that women and girls, as representatives of public sentiment and personal feeling, played in Washington's civic reception. "A lovely group of little girls," he reported, had gathered at Trenton Bridge to sing an ode to the president "while the beloved of all hearts was passing it," and a sloop containing representatives of the "Fair Daughters of Columbia" crossed the Hudson with Washington, enlivening "the scene by singing a number of expressive and animated airs." He envisioned the new republic not as a union of rational, independent, and disinterested male citizens but as an "immense concourse of Citizens" incorporating women, children, and the elderly in a union of emotional dependence, a sentimental union organized around filial and spiritual love for Washington, as the father and the "Saviour of his Country." As Fenno declared, Washington was not just the president of his country but the "PRESIDENT OF HER AFFECTIONS."[8]

To Federalist nationalists like Fenno, Washington's unique ability to arouse public affection and to forge an emotional basis for political union was the most important part of his popular appeal. While public veneration for Washington was legitimate and proper, expressions of popular adoration constituted something more significant: moments of public recognition and of self-recognition, moments in the constitution of a cohesive national culture and identity. Washington's journey and entrance to New York comprised one such moment, crystallizing national sentiment around the person of the new president. Declared Fenno:

> Merit must be great when it can call forth the *voluntary* honours of a free and enlightened people: But the attentions shown on this occasion, were not merely *honorary*, they were the tribute of gratitude, due to a man whose life has been one series of labours for the publick good.[9]

Public gratitude was a just reward for Washington's dedication to public service, but beneath this conventional rhetoric about the personal tribute due to the president, Fenno made a broader nationalist point that subordinated issues of personal character to issues of public and national character. What impressed Fenno about the popular affection for Washington was not what it revealed about Washington's character, but what it revealed about the character of the American people. As he argued in the first issue of the *Gazette*, only "Publick approbation" could "give stability and success to any undertaking which must ultimately depend upon public opinion," and the "undissembled testimonials of publick affection" for Washington were not only the "highest reward that virtue enjoys" but evidence of the emotional and sentimental bonds needed to preserve republican virtue and unite Americans in a new political union.[10]

These "undissembled testimonials of publick affection" had their origins in the heart rather than the head; they were "sincere" and "spontaneous," voluntary rather than coerced, and they found their most genuine expression in the popular demonstrations that greeted Washington wherever he went. According to Fenno, the most impressive manifestation of popular affection for Washington was his unanimous election. By electing Washington to the highest office in the nation without a single dissenting vote, Americans had shown an astonishing degree of political maturity, revealed the virtue of their own political character, and ushered in a new era in human history. "It is undoubtedly a new and astonishing thing under the sun," he wrote, "that the UNIVERSAL SUFFRAGES OF A GREAT AND VARIOUS PEOPLE, SHOULD CENTRE IN ONE AND THE SAME MAN." The election of Washington by the unanimous vote of "three million free citizens," declared Fenno, was "the happiest presage of the future greatness and respectability of our country." By recognizing Washington's worth, Americans had revealed their own. And by turning out in the thousands to welcome the president on the road to New York, they paid homage to both the person of the president and to the embodiment of their own political will. Washington's election demonstrated that the people of the United States had overcome the political factionalism and social disunity of the Confederation period, assumed a unified national character, and become a nation, giving real meaning to the motto of the new Republic: "E Pluribus Unum."[11]

For Federalists like Fenno, therefore, Washington's arrival in New York and the "unspeakable joy, with which he has been welcomed by all classes of people" was a pivotal moment in the constitution and maturation of American nationalism. But it was also a moment of restoration and recovery, as Americans once again rediscovered the collective virtue they had demonstrated in the struggle for independence, a virtue that had been lost during the 1780s with disastrous consequences. The stunning political achievements of 1788–1789: the framing of the federal Constitution, its successful ratification, the election of George Washington, and the upsurge of popular nationalism that accompanied the formation of a new national government were all signs of a renewal of revolutionary spirit and a vindication of America's "national character."[12] This national character had both a nationalist and a moral dimension, and Fenno used the term "character" to describe not only a unified and integrated sense of national identity but an identity rooted in moral virtue. He wrote optimistically:

America has discovered a superiority of genius in her sons, by a great variety of striking instances:—The whole course of the late glorious revolution, testifies to the truth of this observation. The adoption of the new Constitution confirms it in an eminent degree: It remains for her to complete the splendour of her character, by giving a successful operation to the new government.[13]

The prospects for the country were now bright, and "America from this day forward," he argued, "begins a new Era in her national existence." Only one obstacle remained to the creation of a powerful and independent republican empire: the novelty and fragility of the national government. "Reason and time," contended Fenno, would "concur in making the Americans reverence and love their government," but at present it enjoyed none of the popularity possessed by its beloved president. Until it did so, Fenno believed that his duty was to encourage public support and respect for the government and for those elected to represent and embody "popular sovereignty." He believed he had an active and important part to play in the formation of the new nation, not only by supporting the Constitution and the creation of national political institutions but by helping to constitute and strengthen a shared sense of national character. In the pages of the *Gazette of the United States*, Fenno hoped both to inform citizens of the new republic and to help form a national political culture.[14]

John Fenno was born on August 12, 1751, to an old but poor Boston family. The Fenno family had been in Massachusetts since the early seventeenth century, but his branch of the family had not prospered. Although he always spoke affectionately of his parents, Ephraim and Mary, his father worked for most of his life as a leather dresser and ale-house keeper, ending his days in a Boston almshouse.[15] Nonetheless, John was able to acquire an education at Abiah Holbrook's Old South Writing School, a free public school on Boston Common, and his good fortune made him a lifelong advocate of public education. "Discourageing the *free Schools*," he wrote later in his life with the raw emotion imparted only by personal experience, "is encouraging *private* [schools], & shutting the Door to learning, in the Face of the Poor." He was a bright boy and, after Abiah Holbrook died in 1769, Fenno became an instructor at Old South, where he taught until the eve of the American Revolution, although he and his closest friend, Joseph Ward, who also taught briefly at the school, tried unsuccessfully in the early 1770s to start their own "English grammar school" in Boston.[16]

During the revolutionary crisis that unfolded in Boston and the British American colonies in the 1770s, Fenno left Old South and abandoned his career as a teacher. As a young, unmarried man in his twenties, he must have witnessed many of the dramatic events that took place in Boston, and he probably participated in the local resistance to British policies and to the military occupation of the city that followed the passage of the Boston Port Act in June 1774. When war came in the spring of 1775, and the Boston public schools closed, there was no doubt about where his political loyalty lay. As New England militias mustered at Cambridge, encircling the British troops garrisoned in Boston, Fenno became an orderly on the staff of General Artemas Ward, commander of the fledgling American army. He probably secured the appointment, which placed him at the heart of the growing colonial resistance movement, through Joseph Ward, a kinsman and aide-de-camp to General Ward. On April 20, 1775, he attended a "Council of War" at Ward's headquarters in Cambridge, and he watched the disastrous British assault on Breeds Hill on June 17. As an orderly to Ward, who remained second in command after Washington arrived in Massachusetts to become commander in chief in July 1775, Fenno played an active part in organizing and imposing discipline on the ragtag colonial army.[17]

But his subsequent career in the Revolution was more mundane. He may have stayed on Ward's staff until the latter retired from the army in March 1777, and his brother and half brother both served as officers in the Continental army. But sometime after the British evacuated Boston in early 1776, Fenno resigned from the Continental army, marrying Mary Curtis, the daughter of local Loyalists, in May 1777, and, following the birth of his first child, John Ward Fenno, in March 1778, trying to earn a living for his new family in Boston. Exploiting his contacts in the Continental army (chief among them, Colonel Joseph Ward, now commissary general of musters), he went into the provision trade, supplying goods and equipment to American officers. It was a time that tried the souls of civilians as well as soldiers, and by the end of 1779, Fenno was heartily sick of the war and hoped a decisive American victory in the South would "prevent the necessity of another Campaign." But despite the privations and difficulties of wartime Boston ("Our regulating Measures have well nigh starved us—for weeks together hundreds of Families cannot purchase a pound of Meat"), his support for the American cause was unwavering. "Our Sufferings have been great," he wrote, but "for my part, I never tho't that we had paid half the price that Freedom ought to be estimated at." The grumbling of his fellow citizens provoked his scorn rather than his sympathy: "I live in the midst of a vile race who lust after the Leeks & Onions of Sodom—Eternally complaining of evils that are compara-tive blessings." "My happiness," he wrote loftily, "is that these wretches cannot set aside by their ingratitude the great designs of Omnipotence, which are fraught with Benignity to America."[18]

The postwar period was even harder for Fenno, who was responsible for a growing family (eventually, he had fourteen children with his long-suffering wife) without any stable means of support. His wife's parents, who had fled for Nova Scotia during the Revolution, were a hindrance rather than a help, and it's rumored that he ran a public house and livery stable in Boston in the early

1780s, following in his unfortunate father's footsteps. In the mid-1780s, however, his fortunes changed, and he became an assistant to Benjamin Russell, editor and proprietor of the *Massachusetts Centinel*. Fenno's intelligence and literary talent were quickly evident and within a few years he had become "in some sort an adjutant general to Russel [*sic*] in the printing way, particularly in the Poet's Corner." His apprenticeship to Russell was not only literary but practical, and during his time at the *Centinel*, he learned enough about printing to later publish the *Gazette of the United States* and to take on large government printing contracts.[19] But the turning point in Fenno's life was the controversy created by the ratification of the Constitution in Massachusetts in 1777–1778. According to Federalist Christopher Gore, it was Fenno, not Russell, who was the driving force behind the *Centinel* during this period. "The cause of truth, and federalism," Gore told New York Federalist Rufus King, "are much indebted to his pen for the various and honourable supports, they have reciev'd from the Centinel." "His literary accomplishments are very handsome," added Gore, and "his talents, as the editor of a public paper are unrivall'd in this Commonwealth." As Fenno planned his newspaper venture in New York at the end of 1788, the reputation he had already established at the *Centinel* enabled him to enlist the financial support of eight prominent Bostonians, including the former governor of Massachusetts, James Bowdoin.[20]

To Fenno, the chance to establish a newspaper at the new federal capital was irresistible. His financial prospects in Boston were limited. The *Centinel* had provided him with a vocation but not a living, and to survive he was forced to combine journalism with other business ventures, including a dry goods shop under the sign "John Fenno—English Goods," which failed in late 1788. It was probably this failure that prompted him to try his luck in journalism and in New York, and on New Year's Day 1789, he circulated proposals for "The Federal Oracle & the Register of Freedom" among a small group of friends and admirers in Boston, quickly raising £250 in loans, just enough to launch the newspaper and cover the first few months' operating expenses. In mid-January, he left Boston, promising to send for his family as soon as he could afford the expense, and set off for New York, "in hopes," wrote fellow Bostonian the Reverend Jeremy Belknap, "of retrieving matters in the printing way."[21]

Whatever aspirations Fenno had as a man of business, it was politics, not printing, that brought him to New York, and from the start, his aim was to create a newspaper devoted entirely "to the support of the Constitution, & the Administration formed upon its national principles." He designed the *Gazette of the United States* as much more than simply another Federalist, or even nationalist, newspaper, adopting the title *Gazette*, after rejecting the more commonplace *Federal Oracle*, to make clear to readers that his newspaper would be a quasi-official newspaper of public record, the voice of the new federal government.[22] In the first issue, he announced that the newspaper was "published at the SEAT of the FEDERAL GOVERNMENT," timing its appearance to coincide with the first session of Congress and Washington's inauguration. Fenno's desire to create a newspaper of public record also shaped his vision of the newspaper's content, readership, and circulation. As a "faithful register of publick transactions," he promised that the *Gazette* would publicize the affairs of the federal government, publishing nationalist essays for circulation "to all parts of the Union" aimed at both wealthy readers and "the MIDDLING AND LOWER CLASS OF CITIZENS." For a time, he also kept all advertising out of the newspaper, an innovation he was eventually forced to abandon. Advertising was both the lifeblood of eighteenth-century newspapers and the commercial tether that anchored them (in their circulation and politics) to local constituencies and communities. Excluding advertising cut this tether, extending the geographical appeal and circulation of the *Gazette*, affirming its nationalist credentials, and enhancing its official tone. The *Gazette of the United States*, wrote one subscriber approvingly, was the only newspaper which "goes upon a *continental* scale, and does not appear to be influenced by *local* politics."[23]

Why did Fenno believe that a newspaper like the *Gazette of the United States* was necessary? In his "Address" to Boston subscribers, Fenno celebrated the part that newspapers had played in "that general diffusion of knowledge" responsible for the "rise, progress, & honourable termination of the American Revolution." He also believed newspapers had helped to produce "that light, information and harmony of sentiment" that made possible the adoption of the federal Constitution, an "event unparalleled in the annals of mankind." But he warned readers against complacency. The task of American nationalists was far from complete. "The labours of the patriot in this important business," he wrote, "are not yet come to a period," and there was still much to be done to "strengthen and complete the UNION of the States." Powerful parochial forces existed in the United States, and neither the Constitution nor the political institutions it established were deeply rooted in the sentiments of the American people. "The merits of the Constitution," wrote Fenno,

> have notwithstanding many difficulties & obstacles to surmount. These must be encountered with spirit, & obviated with address, before the Constitution will be familiarized to the ideas, & habits of the people, and be considered by them, as it really is, the palladium of their Rights & Liberties.

The best way to familiarize Americans with their new Constitution and government was through the medium of a "well conducted press." By publicizing the activities of the new administration, including the proceedings of Congress and the federal judiciary, Fenno hoped to reassure anxious Americans, to "obviate ill-founded surmises, & jealousies," to encourage public support for "enlightened, upright Statesmen," and to "conciliate the minds of our citizens" to the new political order.[24]

But, as a newspaper editor, his responsibility went beyond providing the public with correct information. By circulating the *Gazette* throughout the country and creating a "chain of Domestick Intelligence," Fenno hoped to bring Americans and their government into a new "correspondence," closing the gap between local and national identity, tightening the bonds of common interest and sentiment, and drawing citizens into the orbit of their national government.[25] The *Gazette of the United States* thus had an important role to play in the formation of national identity. According to Fenno, the political crisis of the 1780s had been the result of a "scattered unproductive publick opinion" rather than "party spirit," and the most important task before Americans in 1789 was to preserve and encourage the public unity and sense of national character that had made the passage of the Constitution and Washington's election possible. Free public education and a free press could help to shape a nationalist consciousness, but an even more potent force for forging national identity and character was the new federal state. "The establishment of the new Constitution," wrote Fenno,

> will, with proper management, form a national character, and remove the evils we have so long suffered for the want of one. It will draw the clashing views and prejudices of the different parts of the union to a common center. The Court of the United States will be a respectable standard of national fashions.... The national court will give a tone, that shall pervade the whole.[26]

National character thus had its origins in a shared national politics as well as a shared national culture. As a "common center," the new national state could integrate the political and institutional life of the nation, while its members created what Fenno called rather carelessly "the Court," a national culture that transcended the provincial cultures of the United States and an equally provincial dependence on European culture. Like his fellow nationalist and New Englander Noah Webster, Fenno conceived of creating a national character as a political rather than social, cultural, intellectual, or moral task. A national state would create a nationalist political consciousness and culture.[27]

Newspapers had a pivotal role to play in the consolidation of this nationalist political culture. Fenno believed that public opinion was the basis for all stable and legitimate political authority, but he also believed that "men are, or may be, very much what the government pleases to make them."[28] And because Americans acquired their knowledge about politics by reading newspapers, the job of harnessing public opinion to the imperatives of nationalist politics rested with newspaper editors like himself. "It is an object of the greatest importance," declared Fenno,

> that an uninterrupted series of federal sentiments should be disseminated through the American nation—Our political connection with each other becomes daily more intimate and interesting: this will, in time assimilate our minds, our habits, our manners, our objects, till we become one great people, cemented by *national* ideas, *national* spirit, and *national* glory.[29]

Connecting Americans to their common government and to each other, the *Gazette of the United States* would operate as both advocate and agent for the federal government, a medium through which Americans would acquire a sense of familiarity with their government and a sense of shared national identity. Fenno's goal was to *represent* the federal government in the realm of public opinion and to *constitute* this public opinion on a new national basis: to create an American character. And it was this task, to create "one great people," that he announced to the public when he began to publish the *Gazette of the United States*.[30]

Fenno was one of a new breed of newspaper editors and journalists who emerged in the 1790s. "Men of ideas" fired by political ideology rather than political patronage, they possessed an almost limitless faith in the influence of the press and a determination to use this influence to reshape public life.[31] But unlike his more politically radical contemporaries, Fenno believed journalists should use their public influence to support rather than challenge the power of the federal government. Such views placed him at odds with most of his fellow journalists and with some of the central assumptions of American republican ideology. Ever since the trial of the New York printer John Peter Zenger for libel in the 1740s, newspaper publishers had justified expressions of political opposition by claiming to be mere mechanics, the impartial arbiters and agents of public opinion. This understanding of newspapers as neutral representatives of public opinion and civil society and as indispensable checks on the arbitrary and ever-expanding power of the state was part of a broader Anglo-American republican ideology that assumed state power was necessarily antithetical to civil liberty. Such assumptions about the inevitable and perpetual antagonism between power and liberty were greatly reinforced by the experience of the American Revolution and remained central to American political discourse in the postrevolutionary period. By describing himself as an agent of state power rather than public opinion, Fenno challenged the assumptions of this republican ideology, turning its conception of the press upside down. While most journalists regarded themselves as sentinels whose duty was to guard a vulnerable public against the constant threat of government tyranny and corruption, Fenno saw himself as the public advocate of a fragile democratic state, a state he had a duty to protect against the deeply engrained and corrosive suspicion of American political culture.

Fenno thus advocated a new and unconventional role for the press. In the first issue of the *Gazette of the United States*, he published a classic defense of the free press as a "palladium of liberty—the scourge of tyrants—the terror of Sychophants—and the detector of mock patriots and demagogues," a "powerful engine" with which to check the machinations of "aristocratical juntos."[32] And a series of early essays in the *Gazette* defended organized political dissent as "one of the main springs of political motion."[33] But while sentiments like these never completely vanished from the newspaper, Fenno believed his most important task was to nurture loyalty toward the federal government—"by every exertion to endear the general government to the people"—not to provoke popular antagonism toward the government.[34] At first, he combined lip service to the legitimacy of opposition with firm expressions of support for the government, but once rumblings of opposition to the federal administration became audible in the summer of 1789, he abandoned this balancing act and began to attack critics of the administration as opponents of the Constitution and the federal government.

These rumblings of discontent came almost entirely from the irrepressible Thomas Greenleaf and the *New-York Journal*, and although they posed almost no threat to Federalist political ascendancy, they prompted Fenno to warn readers about the dangers of press licentiousness. Constant railing against "our civil rulers," he argued, deterred men of ability and honesty from seeking public office, hastening the corruption and decline of republican politics.[35] But Fenno quickly pushed beyond predictable republican denunciations of scandalmongering, challenging conventional ideas about the press and the popular suspicion of government power, which he argued had plagued public life in the 1780s and which now threatened the fragile political consensus created by the Constitution.[36] Unreflective suspicion of government power, he argued, was corrosive and anachronistic. While the growth of liberty in colonial America had been the result of a struggle between the people (and their representatives in the press) and a corrupt British state, the creation of a republic based on the principle of popular sovereignty, "the most perfect republican system of Government the world hath ever seen," had resolved the perennial conflict between liberty and power. Now that the Constitution had established a system of popular election, the only "infallible remedy" for government corruption was a change of "REPRESENTATION." Elections had become "the last and only resort of freedom," making the government more responsible to popular authority but also endowing it with greater political legitimacy. In this new context, habits of political opposition borrowed from the English past—attacks on the government, commented Fenno, often appeared "to be copied from an English opposition print"—were neither appropriate nor legitimate. Indeed, all extraparliamentary protest and especially the creation of partisan organizations like the Democratic Republican societies (later denounced by Washington, Fenno, and many other Federalists as "self-created" societies that lacked the legitimacy conferred by popular election) were troublesome to Fenno, who dismissed attacks on members of democratically elected governments as insults to "the majesty of the people."[37] Habitual hostility toward the government played into the hands of men like Thomas Greenleaf and revealed an outdated conspiratorial mentality. Popularly elected members of the government now "bear the image of their constituents," argued Fenno, and signs of political malaise could no longer be blamed entirely on their personal shortcomings or on the "intrigues of small combinations." Since government was formed by the will of the people, the people themselves must accept responsibility for its character. "Among a free people," he wrote,

> it is not owing to the administration of bad men, that the state is not happy and flourishing. Those who attribute public miscarriages to the misconduct of a few individuals stop short of the mark....public opinion is the great hinge upon which public affairs must turn.[38]

By emphasizing the role of public opinion as the "great hinge upon which public affairs must turn," Fenno shifted attention from the character of public men to the character of those who elected them. This did not mean it was wrong to scrutinize members of the government, and he admitted that such scrutiny probably did "more good than evil," but it was important that the people "divide the blame with their rulers."[39]

Although Fenno's arguments could be used to challenge the legitimacy of political opposition and dissent, they should not therefore be dismissed as cynical and anti-democratic rhetorical ploys. Fenno's arguments mobilized widespread popular hostility to political faction, and his sense that the passage of the Constitution had altered the ground rules of American politics was irrefutable. Moreover, in a world of violent revolutionary transformation, such arguments made considerable sense, reflecting genuine anxiety about the durability and strength of the new federal government and respect for the powerful forces that besieged it, especially among citizens of a nation with a recent revolutionary past. It is easy but mistaken to read our own complacency about the survival of the American Republic into the past. Those who experienced the American Revolution knew better. "We have seen the beginning of our government," wrote Fenno. "[W]e have demolished one, and set up another, and we think without terror of the process." Faced with an anachronistic and irrational hostility toward government, Fenno asked his fellow citizens to adopt a new attitude toward the state. "Jealousy is called a republican virtue," he wrote, but "indiscriminate suspicion is the parent of those very evils, it pretends to detect, and expose to public indignation." Intemperate attacks on elected representatives corroded public trust in the political system and prevented the growth of popular loyalty to the new government. Americans, he declared, should recognize that their government was a public good, not a "necessary evil." "The revolution in America" was not based on the belief that republican government was antithetical to political liberty, "but on the reverse that it is the choicest blessing heaven ever has bestowed on the human race."[40]

John Fenno was deeply committed to the Federalist cause, but he was neither a political hack nor a government sycophant. His faith in good government was genuine and ideological and was anchored in a world view that equated social progress with man's capacity to control his natural and elemental desires. Human society and its gradual civilization, he believed, depended on the government and "self-government" of the "passions." Far from being born free, as Rousseau had declared in the famous opening sentence of *The Social Contract*, man was born enslaved to self-aggrandizing, antisocial passions. In primitive forms of civil and political society, these antisocial passions were controlled by arbitrary power and fear, but in more advanced and civilized societies, the passions were controlled by methods that went beyond the use of force: by formal and external constraints on individual behavior, primarily the authority and sanction of secular and religious law, or by informal and internal constraints, the capacity for self-control derived from social custom, personal religious belief, and enlightened self-interest. In the progress of civilization, formal constraints on behavior gradually gave way to informal constraints as human beings learned to curb their innate selfishness and to internalize the values of sociability and rationality upon which stable self-government depended. As the English politician and writer Edmund Burke put it in a passage reprinted in the *Gazette*:

> [S]ociety cannot exist unless a controuling power upon will and appetite be placed somewhere and the less of it there is within, the more there must be without. It is ordained in the eternal constitution of things, that men of intemperate minds cannot be free. Their passions forge their fetters.[41]

True freedom was the product of restraint. The fetters forged by the passions could be broken only by self-restraint, a self-restraint expressed both in individual terms, as government of the self, and in collective terms, as the self-government of society. Human *nature* might be fixed and corrupt (a view reinforced by the Calvinism of Fenno's native New England), but human *behavior* could be changed and improved. Civilization could advance. Forms of behavior were not inscribed indelibly in nature but learned, and the influence of the passions could be tempered by the influence of personal piety and habit, social custom, and good government. "Persons, who have lived long under the restraint of good laws," argued Fenno,

> and have been blessed with the refined regulations of civilized life, are changed into a different kind of beings.... the force of the passions is not only restrained, but their bent and direction becomes very different.[42]

But just as critical to the process of civilization as the "restraint of good laws," especially in a democratic republic like the United States, was public enlightenment. "Ignorance," wrote Fenno, "is the foundation of most of the political calamities which ever overwhelmed the world." Civilization and civil liberty rested ultimately on a broad diffusion of knowledge. This knowledge gave man a sense of himself as a social being, and when he became conscious of his social nature, he was willing to subject himself freely to the constraints of civil society. Only then could he be truly free.[43]

Like most of his contemporaries, Fenno thought newspapers were indispensable instruments of popular enlightenment, and in the United States, where so many of the "inhabitants generally know how to read," they had helped to create a uniquely enlightened citizenry. But a free press was not sufficient to create enlightened citizens, and the provision of free public education, an issue to which Fenno regularly turned in the *Gazette*, was crucial to the preservation of a republican society. Only education, he argued, could teach ordinary people to appreciate the virtues and advantages of controlling self-regarding behavior. In a natural state, man was selfish and antisocial, driven by crude desires and primitive instincts, and before it "can be safe living with him," argued Fenno, he must become "an artificial being," a process that required "the necessity of education." The failure of most states to provide free public education was thus deplorable. "Why," he asked, "do we neglect to provide for it? Why do we not enjoin it by law upon cities and districts of [the] country to support free schools?"[44]

Although Fenno's support for public education reflected his skepticism about the natural common sense of the citizenry and could easily curdle into a cynical justification for political paternalism, his ideas about education were surprisingly egalitarian. Knowledge, he argued, was a type of property that gave its owners the psychological independence they needed to be responsible citizens and should be as widely distributed as possible. "Knowledge is power," he wrote:

> By infusing knowledge into the body of the people, we remove them from the influence of the aristocratic few. Instead of being tools, they become partners,

perhaps the rivals, of men of wealth and education: we may consider that power as harmless which instead of being engrossed by an aristocracy is diffused among the people.[45]

The redistribution of knowledge was just as essential to the preservation of republican liberty as the redistribution of political sovereignty and real property. "The rich can buy learning," argued Fenno, but the benefits of education were often denied to the poor, making a mockery of republican attacks on inherited privilege. "It is tantalizing," he wrote tartly, "to say that there shall be no distinctions of ranks, or exclusive privileges—and that the avenues to the posts of honor and profit under the state and general governments, shall be accessible to all," but "while the paths of learning are not, and cannot be trodden by the poor," it was a cruel deception. By redistributing knowledge, free public education ensured economic and political mobility, as well as inoculating citizens against the arts of political demagogues. Only a virtuous and enlightened people, he argued, could appreciate and protect the virtues of enlightened republican government.[46]

Government therefore was not antithetical to freedom but essential to its realization, and the expansion of liberty required not less but more government. Fenno had little patience for those who thought that the peculiar moral virtue of Americans, or the operation of God's special providence, would protect them from moral degeneration and enable them to dispense with the "restraints of civil institutions." Americans had advanced further along the road to complete self-government than any other people, but even their virtues could not be relied upon. "Human nature is so selfish and corrupt," argued one writer in the *Gazette*, "that the legislator who depends on virtue alone for the support of a republican system, builds upon a foundation of sand." Good government was a "remedy against" the natural selfishness and corruption of human nature, and without its restraining influence, civil society quickly degenerated into a Hobbesian war of all against all. Morbid fear of government thus belonged to a primitive phase of political development when men "in a worse state of society" saw each other as evil and called "the government an evil, by way of a compliment to themselves." In a civilized society, however, men recognize the legitimacy and utility of government because "civilized, well-informed men are capable of being well-governed." Fenno's fellow citizens were mired in the past, suspicious of one another and of their own government, and oblivious to the fact that the federal government was an emanation of their own political will.[47]

Fenno's break with editorial orthodoxy was nowhere clearer than in his defense of the role played by panegyric in republican politics. As his treatment of Washington's election and inauguration revealed, he was by no means immune to the cult of personality that surrounded the president, and at first he reported every official ceremony and social function Washington attended as if he were compiling a court register, publishing details of his controversial weekly "levees," his visits to the playhouse, and his every public movement. But it didn't take Fenno long to realize that the new federal government (and the *Gazette* that aspired to represent it) required a more austere, self-consciously republican style.[48] And when Vice President John Adams launched a campaign in the Senate to confer a more dignified title on the president, a campaign that sparked strong criticism in Congress and the press, Fenno kept a discreet editorial silence. Privately, he sympathized with Adams, but sensing the public uneasiness that surrounded the use of "monarchical" titles, he published essays on both sides of the controversy and then quietly stopped using the term "His Excellency" to refer to Washington, adopting the simple form of "president" instead.[49]

But although Fenno was careful not to overstep the boundaries of republican decorum and insisted that his loyalty was to a government of measures not men, his enthusiasm for Washington was hard to restrain. When Washington toured New England in the fall of 1789, Fenno exploited the occasion to celebrate the popularity of the president, who had entered Boston as the "DELIVERER OF HIS COUNTRY," and "like the glorious luminary of Heaven...totally dissipated the fog of antifederalism."[50] When this lavish praise for Washington provoked scorn in the opposition press, he defended what he defined as a new right: the right to praise elected political leaders, the right to panegyric. Infuriated by critics who belittled popular demonstrations of respect for Washington, Fenno defended the people's right to "express their feelings, their respect and veneration...for the illustrious Saviour of their country." But he also defended demonstrations of affection for public men in more general terms. Criticism of public men, he admitted, had an important part to play in republican politics: "The sting of ridicule is sharp and piercing," wrote Fenno. "[I]t makes people ashamed of their follies, while reproach makes them fear to be vicious." But in a representative republic, the utility of political satire was limited, and while it could "restrain men from mean and perverse actions," it could never inspire them to undertake actions that are honorable and virtuous. Public exposure, the principal weapon of political satire, had a necessary but essentially negative role to play in public life. Acting alone, satire could never ensure good government, but when accompanied by more positive appeals to "expectations of fame and applause," which were the most powerful motives for "worthy and noble actions," it could help to preserve the public good. In other words, panegyric, or the public praise and celebration of virtuous men, was as essential to a healthy civic life as satire, although often regarded with greater suspicion.[51]

Fenno's emphasis on panegyric resonated powerfully in the minds of a revolutionary generation that believed "fame was the spur" that inspired good men to devote themselves to public service—and the only reliable source of virtuous public conduct.[52] "The practice of shewing respect to eminent characters by public addresses," declared Fenno, "is attended with more utility than is commonly imagined." Public praise rewarded past conduct and acted as a "spring to a patriotic line of conduct in future," stimulating a spirit of emulation among candidates for public office, who sought to win the same degree of public esteem already possessed by established political leaders. Without public recognition and praise, virtuous men would shun the "dangers and difficulties that are often to be encountered in the execution of public service," and the quality of political leadership would deteriorate, gradually transferring power to unscrupulous, self-interested men who cared nothing for the *res publica* and sought only their own advancement. Panegyric encouraged men of ability and integrity to enter public service and ensured their commitment to the commonwealth. It was a "cheap method of purchasing meritorious and distinguished services" that preserved public life from the corrupting influence of commerce and personal interest. Public eulogy and the desire of ambitious public men for present and future fame helped to guarantee a virtuous public sphere.[53]

Despite Fenno's ideas about panegyric, he published few political eulogies in the *Gazette* during its first few years, and usually treated even Washington with admiration rather than adulation. The president's birthday, for example, which became an occasion for elaborate national festivities in the 1790s, was not given much prominence in the *Gazette*. In 1790, Fenno published a discreet notice about upcoming public festivities in Philadelphia and Boston and an "Ode on the Birth Day of the President," but the next year he ignored Washington's birthday completely, noting briefly and belatedly that celebrations had taken place "in all parts of the union." When Washington turned sixty in 1792, his coverage was more punctual but equally brief. Although Washington's birthday assumed partisan significance for both Federalists and Republicans later in the decade, Fenno's coverage during the early 1790s gave little indication of this.[54]

Fenno had been quick to seize the chance to start a Federalist newspaper in New York and was quick to decide that his new home compared unfavorably with his old. "You must not hum a body about New York," he wrote to his friend Joseph Ward, now a businessman in Boston. "[I]t is well enough; no more." "After the Necessary is done here and that will be in less than ten years I hope," he wrote wistfully, he hoped "to come & spend many happy years with you." Alone in a strange city without family and friends, Fenno acquired a new sense of appreciation for his native state of Massachusetts: "the very dust of New England," he confessed, "is dear to me." Armed with the loan from his friends in Boston, a sum of about £250, and letters of introduction to prominent Federalists in New York, he struggled to make headway with the newspaper during the winter and spring

Gazette of the United States.

PUBLISHED WEDNESDAYS AND SATURDAYS BY JOHN FENNO, No. 69, MARKET-STREET, BETWEEN SECOND AND THIRD STREETS, PHILADELPHIA.

[No. 71, of Vol. II.]   SATURDAY, JANUARY 1, 1791.   [Whole No. 175.]

CONGRESS OF THE UNITED STATES.

AT THE THIRD SESSION,

begun and held at the City of Philadelphia, in the State of Pennsylvania, on Monday the sixth of December, one thousand seven hundred and ninety.

An ACT, Supplementary to the Act, intitled, "An Act making further Provision for the Payment of the Debts of the United States."

WHEREAS an export provision has been made for paying the aid, intitled, "An act to provide more effectually for the collection of the duties imposed by law upon goods, wares and merchandize imported into the United States, and on the tonnage of ships or vessels;" in the collection of the duties on the said goods, wares and merchandize imported into the United States, and on the tonnage of ships or vessels . . .

Be it enacted by the Senate and House of Representatives of the United States of America, in Congress assembled, That the act . . .

FREDERICK AUGUSTUS MUHLENBERG,
Speaker of the House of Representatives.

JOHN ADAMS, *Vice-President of the United States, and President of the Senate.*

APPROVED, DECEMBER TWENTY-EIGHTH, 1790.
GEORGE WASHINGTON, *President of the United States.*

(TRUE COPY)
THOMAS JEFFERSON, *Secretary of State.*

The following remarks are (self-evidently) copied from the New-York Daily Advertiser.

IT is a very honorable proof of the patriotism of the public creditors, that they did not in a hasty and general an acquiescence in the funding system . . .

. . . It is a favorable presage of the stability and wisdom of Congress, that the interest of the United States have passed their final consideration, with only one dissenting voice.

Public creditors! If ye be wise, be quiet where ye are.   CONSISTENCY.

BENNINGTON, Dec. 6.

Lately a ball at Windham, in Connecticut, was graced with the presence of about thirty young ladies, each of whom was decked in a handsome muslin gown, wrought by their own hands. A patriotic example worthy the imitation of every lady among us, who wishes well to her country, &c. on the advancement of the manufactures of America, depends her truest interest.

ALBANY, Dec. 20.

By a gentleman last evening from Quebec, we are informed of the arrival, at that place, of the Hon. Gen. Alured Clarke (late Lt. Governor of the Island of Jamaica) who is appointed to succeed Lord Dorchester in the government . . .

NEWBURYPORT, Dec. 11.

In this town, according to the late enumeration, the inhabitants number to 4837. The dwelling-houses are 616. According to an enumeration taken in 1784, the number of inhabitants was 3115 and the dwelling-houses 450.—The whole town numbers but 620 acres, about one of which are taken up for pasture, Green, &c. In general length is one mile and a half, and about half a mile in breadth.

Lately died, on the coast of Guinea, Captain WINGATE NEWMAN, of Philadelphia.

FOR THE GAZETTE OF THE UNITED STATES.

"FRANKLIN is gone," Columbia said,
"My sage is now no more!"
Then droop'd her head, and sorrowing bow'd,
She wist its dismal . . .

Before praise for wit or wind,
She droop'd her mournful head . . .
And thus the homage to some kind,
When the tribute was . . .

"Why weave Columbia? Franklin's good,
In Franklin lives the only . . .

Or here I saw my charming friend
. . . grandeur here to crown,
My foster'd ray rose shines in bright,
Thy fame improv'd has . . .

See Franklin! and let Reason with
. . . wisdom learning lore,
Columbia! give thy Sage a grave,
Which honor calls before . . .

. . .

CONGRESS.

HOUSE OF REPRESENTATIVES.

Sketch of the Debate in the MILITIA BILL.

FRIDAY, Dec. 24.

THE amendments of the committee of the whole to the militia bill, were further discussed this day by the house. The debate was continued on Mr. Madison's proposition in favor of persons conscientiously scrupulous of bearing arms. A majority of the Speakers appeared to be in favor of their exemption's being left to the several States in support of this idea.

Mr. Bourn observed, that if the general government should take up the matter, and subject the Quakers to a penalty as an equivalent for personal service, their situation would be rendered less eligible than it is at present—for, in several of the States, he observed they are not only exempted from militia duty, but from all fines and penalties in lieu thereof; he instanced the States of New-Hampshire, Massachusetts, Rhode-Island and Connecticut.

Another memorial from the society of Quakers on the Eastern shore of Maryland, against the 6th section of the bill, was presented by Mr. Smith, member from that State, and read.

A motion of Mr. Clymer, to amend the motion of Mr. Madison, after some discussion, was negatived, and the original motion being what was diligently to it, so first, on the bill was finally disagreed to: the whole question of persons religiously scrupulous of bearing arms, is to be provided for by the respective States.

Mr. Smith, (S. C.) then renewed his proposition respecting independent companies—which he informed the house he had to submit, as to avoid the objections before offered to it. It is to the following effect—

Whereas certain independent corps of artillery, infantry and dragoons, exist, and in their several States—it is hereby resolved, that nothing in this act shall be construed to the disbanding or incorporating said companies in the militia; they at the same time being liable to the performance of the military duties herein required.

It being understood that the bill should be recommitted to a select committee, it was moved that this proposition be referred, with the bill.

On motion of Mr. Livermore, the only section of the bill was expunged; a motion for the same amendment to strike out the 10th and 12th sections was negatived.

It was then moved that the bill be recommitted, which being past, passed to the committee to whom the business was referred, and Messrs. Wadsworth, Gilman and Tucker were appointed the committee.

MONDAY, Dec. 27.

In committee of the whole, on the State of the Union—Mr. Livermore in the chair.

The report of the Secretary of the Treasury on the establishment of land-offices, for the sale of the lands belonging to the United States, under consideration.

Mr. Scott offered the following relative to land—it is the basis of the resolution, that a land-office be established in the seat of the general government, under the direction of certain officers.

Mr. Scott wished the lands to take a general view of the business, before they went into the particulars of the resolution's report. Upon the whole it was placed with the great object in the plan, in short were for particular States...

Mr. White moved for the usual.

of 1789. Progress was slow. Although he quickly made contact with members of the city's political and financial elite, meeting privately with Alexander Hamilton and Rufus King (who soon afterward became a U.S. senator from New York) and dining with Henry Rutgers and the financier William Duer, these contacts provided little more than words of encouragement. His reception, he wrote, was "kind & flattering," and his plan for a Federalist newspaper met "with universal approbation," but enthusiasm for his plans was not matched by offers of specific financial support.[55]

The difficulties Fenno encountered raising money in New York were disappointing and led him to conclude that "the enterprise must depend upon my own exertions ultimately." "At the present my expectations of pecuniary assistance here, are rather problematical," he grumbled in late February. "I can depend upon only *one* Gentleman here, & on him only for Thirty Pounds." By this time, Fenno was thoroughly depressed about his prospects, homesick, lonely, and bowed down by the "weight of the undertaking." His lack of capital made it impossible to bring his family to New York, and the money he had raised so far was just enough "to push off with, & keep the boat afloat for a few months at farthest." His efforts to form a business partnership with an established printer in New York had come to nothing, and similar negotiations with John Russell, the former editor of the *New York Museum*, proved equally fruitless. By March, however, he had established himself at an office in William Street, and he was determined to persevere despite the obstacles he confronted. "I am now come to a Point," he wrote in early April, "and the appearance of the Paper will determine its fate."[56]

Once Fenno began to publish the *Gazette of the United States* in April 1789, his financial affairs went from bad to worse. Although his subscribers increased to about 600, by July he had collected only $90 in subscription payments, and his hopes of supplementing this income by securing government patronage and a "slice from the Printing Loaf" proved elusive. When Washington gave him a small publishing commission, Fenno hoped this would be the "entering wedge to the executive printing business," confessing that, without "auxiliary aid of this

Gazette of the United States, Philadelphia, January 1, 1791. Published twice weekly by John Fenno, the title and striking masthead of the newspaper announced Fenno's desire to make the newspaper the official gazette of the new national government. So did Fenno's bold decision to exclude advertising from the front page of the newspaper, leaving it free of local commercial clutter. Many contemporaries believed that his newspaper emulated too closely the royal gazettes issued by European courts and the Loyalist James Rivington's *Royal Gazette*, published in New York during the American Revolution. Courtesy of the Library Company of Philadelphia.

sort, I do not see how I can possibly get along." Working constantly, he left his office only to walk to Congress and back again, enjoying "no Company." This loneliness was relieved by the arrival of his wife and family from Boston in June, but supporting a family in New York only added to his rapidly mounting expenses. In a poorly calculated effort to turn a quick profit, he published a series of letters by John Adams on the American Revolution, a venture that turned sour when he priced the work too high and sold only a dozen copies, eating further into his diminishing capital.[57]

Fenno's financial difficulties flowed directly from his decision to publish an official gazette without advertisements, and he clearly hoped that members of the federal administration would find some way to support such an experiment. But he was smart enough to know that such support was unlikely. Americans were simply not accustomed to the idea of a government-supported press. "I wish to be an auxiliary to good government," he wrote to Ward:

> I should have one great object—and that object would confer dignity upon the Paper & give me a reputation upon a solid basis—but such a plan I fear can never be supported by public opinion.... it would be unpopular for Government to establish a State Paper or give a Printer a Salary.

But if expecting Americans to accept a newspaper supported directly by public funds was futile, raising money by subscription for an "official" newspaper like the *Gazette* was also difficult, and, as Fenno confessed to Ward, he was "puzzled to pioneer myself out of this dilemma." Moreover, while he was eager to get public and private printing contracts, he was reluctant to let this work compete with publishing the *Gazette*, which remained his "one great object."[58]

By August, "accumulating evils" and mounting debts forced him to consider relinquishing the idea of an official newspaper and running the *Gazette* on a more orthodox commercial basis. Casting about for alternatives, he kept "slaving on" and even toyed with a "general Scheme" for revamping the newspaper that would have opened it up to "every series of Speculations, public & private, serious, comic, satirical, personal & political." Fenno was annoyed by the failure of New York Federalists to provide him with direct financial support and by their failure to send lucrative federal printing contracts in his direction. As he quickly discovered, he faced "powerful competition in [his] attempts for publick business" from more well-established printers in New York, who "all have their eyes that way." But most irritating was that the lion's share of government printing had already been swallowed up by Francis Childs and John Swaine, who shared it with none other than Thomas Greenleaf. Fenno did receive a few "small Jobbs for the Treasury & War Office—also some for the President," but this trickle of patronage was woefully inadequate, and without the capital to expand his printing office and hire more journeymen, he had to "hire out" most of his government work to other printers, reducing his profit "to a pittance."[59]

By late 1789, Fenno's newspaper was on the ropes, and he had to borrow small sums of money from friends in Boston to keep it going. When subscriptions leveled off well below the number needed to support the newspaper (not to mention its editor's growing family), Fenno's debts grew to over $500. In a gloomy mood after the death of his youngest daughter, Caroline, from influenza in November, he was forced "with great regret" to bow to the inevitable and include advertising in the newspaper. But he still needed an "advance of 5 or 600 dollars" to get the newspaper back on a sound financial footing. Joseph Ward suggested that he "touch up" Federalist leaders like Henry Knox, the secretary of war, but although Knox and others were friendly to Fenno, he did not think they could provide such a large subsidy, and Hamilton in particular was "cautious, sage, *prudent & economical* as a public man to the greatest degree." "Is it not a pitiful business," remarked Fenno bitterly, "that one Paper upon this Plan cannot find support in the United States."[60]

Relying on "Hope & Loans" from his friend Royal Flint, a Boston merchant, to see him through the immediate crisis, Fenno managed to keep the newspaper afloat until Congress reconvened in New York in January 1790, at which point he declared, "my finances are o." But his fortunes then began to improve. By March, the *Gazette* had over 1,000 subscribers and his fellow Bostonian Samuel Otis, the new secretary of the Senate, had transferred publication of the *Senate Journals* from Greenleaf to Fenno, promising him more business in the future. When the new secretary of state, Thomas Jefferson, also decided to patronize the *Gazette*, Fenno was elated. "Mr. Jefferson," he wrote, "has given me the Publication of the Laws—my subscribers have greatly encreased—and I now do all the Senate business." Although his debts now totaled $800, and the $1,200 he was owed by subscribers was "scattered from Don to Beersheba," he thought he would be able to balance the books in the coming year, "after which, barring contingencies, my prospect will be flattering."[61]

Fenno sometimes expressed sharply conservative views in private, but he generally kept such candor out of his newspaper, and during the early 1790s, his public rhetoric mirrored the fluid political situation created by the constitutional settlement of 1789. His first aim was to establish the impartial, nationalist character of the *Gazette of the United States*, and he had no desire to create a campaigning, partisan newspaper. In fact, he criticized any "violation of impartiality" he detected in other newspapers, insisting that the printer who "can be made a tool of party…merits universal contempt." His ambition was to help create a sense of calm public authority and confidence around the federal government, especially as Congress was still establishing government departments, and for this reason he tried to avoid political controversy. The campaign for a Bill of Rights was thus, in his view, "unpropitious" because it would disturb the public mind, although he expressed respect for its chief congressional advocate, James Madison, and similar motives probably explain his failure to support John Adams's title campaign, which he worried would allow its opponents to raise a "popular Clamour."[62]

This determination to avoid public controversy changed abruptly when Congress began to debate how to repay the huge revolutionary war debt in the summer of 1790. The issue of the "Public Debt," predicted Fenno, "will be the most arduous & important business that ever came before Congress" and would "convulse the public counsels." He was right. According to Jefferson, the funding debate "created greater animosities than I ever yet saw take place on any occasion," providing former Anti-Federalist newspapers like Greenleaf's *New-York Journal*, Benjamin Ede's Boston *Independent Chronicle*, and Eleazar Oswald's *Pennsylvania Gazette* with a chance to take up cudgels against the secretary of the treasury, Alexander Hamilton. Fenno's *Gazette* gave unswerving support to Hamilton's fiscal program. "Great things are anticipated from Hamilton," wrote Fenno. "I think he considers his fame as much at stake as ever a General of an Army did.... he is one of those sort of men that consider wealth as less than nothing and vanity compared with Honor & Reputation." But not only Hamilton's honor and reputation were at stake. One of the most important tasks before the new federal government, believed Fenno, was to "explore and arrange the NATIONAL FUNDS" and "restore and establish the PUBLICK CREDIT."[63]

Fenno's mercantile background and close contacts with speculators like Christopher Gore and Joseph Ward gave him a strong personal interest in the financial affairs of the new government. In Boston, New York, and later Philadelphia, he moved in a "world of merchants, financiers, speculators and highly placed officeholders" and may have used his access to official information to advance the financial interests of his supporters and friends. But his interest in Hamiltonian finance had more to do with ideology than interest. Money was "the *nerve*—the *soul* of government," he wrote, and placing the financial affairs of the country on a sound basis was a matter of not just practical necessity but moral obligation. Just as Hamilton was inspired by personal honor and public reputation, Fenno believed that his financial program was inspired by a desire to restore public credit and confidence in the financial affairs of the United States. During the 1780s, the public character of the country had been tarnished by the failure of the states and the Confederation government to meet their financial obligations. Restoring public credit, argued Fenno, was critical to the restoration of "national character." "There is but one Sentiment with the Federalists," he wrote, "and that is to support the *Plighted Faith* of the Country at all possible events."[64]

Fenno's ideas about public finance closely reflected those of Hamilton, and Hamilton may have contributed to the newspaper directly or through intermediaries. In an article published a month before Hamilton became secretary of the treasury, Fenno gave readers a virtual preview of Hamilton's famous *Report Relative to a Provision for the Support of Public Credit*. With the restoration of political tranquility, insisted its author, it was "indispensably necessary to form a general liquidation of our domestic debt, consolidating the whole in one great mass." "Assumption," or the consolidation of state debts under the federal government, was the only way to preserve the "general equality of circumstances among the inhabitants of the Union" and prevent a "division of the public interests" that would pit the citizens of one state against citizens of another. More controversially, the author proposed preserving rather than paying off the national debt and creating a "national stock or capital" supported by the establishment of a national bank, which would provide a basis for the expansion of credit and economic growth.[65]

Hamilton's program was designed to encourage commercial development, and discussions about public finance in the *Gazette* placed great emphasis on the importance of winning support from the "wealthy part of the community." The "wealth of the industrious and prosperous citizen," argued Fenno, "is the wealth of the State," and it was the government's duty to create a legal system that would encourage the accumulation of wealth. But Hamilton's program was also designed to stabilize the new nation-state by ensuring the allegiance of its economic elite, and beneath Fenno's emphasis on private accumulation lurked a sense of skepticism about the public spirit of the rich. The creation of a national debt funded by federal taxes was one way to ensure that the wealthy remained loyal to the federal government, an argument used regularly by Hamilton. "Men, who bear the character of men of the world, must be managed some other way, than by appealing to their sense of publick duty," wrote one essayist in the *Gazette*, and the bonds created by economic self-interest could serve as "an equivalent for public spirit." Wealthy men usually pursued their own financial interests at the expense of the public good, and the only way to counteract this tendency was to give them a vested interest in the public good, by encouraging them to advance loans to the state. Securing the rights of property was thus a matter of public utility as well as a legal issue, ensuring that "advances to aid the public are always prompt, and liberal." When the "rich become the bankers for the public," the public possessed "an exhaustless source to draw upon." The creation of a national debt therefore would bind Americans to one another and bind the wealthy to the federal state, and as a "band of union" (as well as a stimulus to economic growth), it was a benefit rather than a burden to the country. In what proved to be an unfortunate excess of enthusiasm, Fenno pronounced the public debt a "NATIONAL BLESSING," words that would haunt Federalists for the rest of the decade.[66]

During the winter of 1789, Fenno published a flurry of essays and commentary echoing and amplifying these views, all of which placed great stress on the links between financial and political union. After Hamilton's report on public credit was presented to Congress in January 1790, a presentation Fenno described as "masterly," he made sure that its central arguments reached a broader public, maintaining a steady drumbeat of support for Hamilton's plans and calling on Congress to act expeditiously to "retrieve and establish the credit of the United States."[67] When Madison and others who were worried that speculators rather than soldiers and ordinary citizens would reap the benefits of a federally funded public debt proposed to distinguish or "discriminate" between the original and current holders of the debt, a position that had considerable public support, Fenno backed Hamilton and firmly opposed the idea. But although he reported the existence of a "great party opposed to the Funding System" in the House of Representatives in early March, he hardly mentioned the long and heated debates that took place in Congress during the summer of 1790.[68]

The silence of the *Gazette* was revealing. Despite delays in Congress, Fenno believed that Hamilton's proposals would be enacted without much alteration, and when the Funding Bill was passed in May, he predicted the "sun will break out" and Congress would pass an assumption bill before the summer. In an editorial written during the congressional debate on assumption in April, he observed that a "universal content pervades the union," and he may well have been right: despite opposition inside Congress, the public campaign against Hamilton was sporadic and uncoordinated, and public support for Hamilton's policies was widespread. Fenno's support for Hamilton did not distinguish him from other nationalist editors and politicians, some of whom later became political opponents of both men. The future Republican Tench Coxe was Hamilton's assistant at the treasury, and Benjamin Franklin Bache, who later denounced Hamilton as the architect of an American aristocracy, vigorously supported his work as treasury secretary in the Philadelphia *General Advertiser*. Even critics like James Madison did not yet see Hamilton's financial policies as a threat to republican government. Consequently, when Congress passed the Assumption Act in July, Fenno was not alone in hailing it as an act that "rivets the chain of union." "By this," he declared triumphantly, "the monster with thirteen heads receives his death wound."[69]

Fenno's support for Hamilton's financial program was emphatic, but it was not a sign of unswerving partisan loyalty. Party labels and political alignments remained in flux during this period, reflecting the political fluidity created by the constitutional settlement of 1789. Nothing illustrates this unsettled political situation better than the support Fenno and the *Gazette* received from Secretary of State Thomas Jefferson.[70] At this stage, Jefferson was happy to patronize Fenno, and Fenno was happy to secure his patronage, which provided him with a new source of income and the official imprimatur of the federal government. With great typological flourish, he published his first commission from Jefferson as "By Authority" under the heading "USA" in large, bold, scrolled letters. From the start, his relationship with Jefferson went beyond official patronage, and Jefferson clearly believed he could use Fenno's paper to convey his own views to the reading public.[71] Always careful to cloak his dealings with editors in secrecy, in this instance Jefferson was candid. As he later told Washington, he wanted an editor willing to republish reports from the *Gazette de Leyde*, a Dutch newspaper that supported the French Revolution and that Jefferson believed provided a "juster view of the affairs of Europe than could be obtained from any other public source." He hoped the *Gazette de Leyde* would be an antidote to less sympathetic accounts of the revolution in the British press, upon which American editors often relied. As he admitted to Washington, he circulated the *Gazette de Leyde* "through the press of Mr. Fenno while in New York, selecting and translating passages myself at first, then having it done by Mr. Pintard the translating clerk."[72]

But Jefferson's candor was only partial, and his desire to provide the public with more friendly accounts of the French Revolution seems peculiar at a time when the press was overflowing with enthusiasm for the revolution. Moreover, when he explained his subsequent negotiations with Benjamin Franklin Bache and Philip Freneau to Washington in the fall of 1792, he emphasized the same limited aims although his goals were by this time clearly more ambitious. What seems most likely is that Jefferson, who arrived in New York in April 1790 fresh from the turmoil of revolutionary France, hoped to use the wide circulation of the *Gazette of the United States* to establish his own official and personal influence over public opinion. Jefferson was not yet looking for an outlet for his own doubts about administration policies and still less looking to create an opposition newspaper, but his experience in France, where newspapers had played a conspicuous and critical part in the revolution, had made him deeply conscious of the role that the press and public opinion would play in the future politics of the new federal state, and he was determined to ensure that his own views found their way into the public sphere.[73]

Initially, he was pleased with Fenno's response, telling his daughter Martha that Fenno "promises henceforward to give his foreign news from the Leyden Gazette, so that it will be worth reading." Extracts from the *Gazette de Leyde*, which Fenno announced was "considered in Europe as the most authentic medium of intelligence," appeared regularly in the *Gazette of the United States* during the spring and summer of 1790 alongside other material on the French Revolution passed along by Jefferson. These efforts attracted the attention of the French minister, who wrote that Jefferson, "knowing the great influence of the gazettes continues to discredit those of England" by hiring a "writer to translate and have printed the most authentic news of France, especially that which can contribute to make the nation loved." But by the end of the summer, the budding political friendship between Jefferson and Fenno had fizzled out. According to Jefferson, passages from the *Gazette de Leyde* "found their way too slowly into Mr. Fenno's papers."[74]

Jefferson's about-face was a crucial moment for the *Gazette of the United States* and for the future of the American press. Disillusioned by Fenno, Jefferson searched for a suitable alternative, approaching a number of other editors before enlisting Philip Freneau to edit the *National Gazette* in 1791. Freneau's *National Gazette* quickly became the chief rival of the *Gazette of the United States* and a critical catalyst for the development of partisan politics in the early 1790s. Most historians have followed Jefferson's lead and interpreted his break with Fenno and the subsequent establishment of the *National Gazette* as a logical response to the arch-federalism of the *Gazette of the United States*.[75] The historian Julian Boyd, for example, suggests that the reason Jefferson abandoned Fenno was a "remarkable change" in the political complexion of the *Gazette of the United States* prompted by "some inducement or promise of material support" from Federalists. But there is no evidence for either claim. Federalist financial support for the *Gazette* remained negligible until late 1793, and the exact nature of the "remarkable change" that took place in the politics of the newspaper is unclear in Boyd's otherwise highly scholarly account. Aware that Fenno's enthusiasm for the economic policies of Alexander Hamilton was still widely shared, and in any case preceded his dealings with Jefferson, Boyd argues it was foreign, not domestic, issues that alienated Jefferson. Fenno's publication of John Adams's *Discourses on Davila*, which were critical of events in France, and extracts from John Courtenay's viciously reactionary, pro-Catholic, absolutist diatribe, "Philosophical Reflections on the Late Revolution in France," probably did upset Jefferson. The Courtenay essays were certainly startling, and Jefferson may have been so disgusted by their appearance that he decided to sever his connection with the *Gazette of the United States*. But the context in which these articles appeared suggests they may not have been signs of Fenno's hostility toward the French Revolution. Fenno had earlier published extracts from Edmund Burke's writings at Jefferson's request, possibly to discredit rather than celebrate Burke, a former supporter of American independence who had become a fierce critic of revolutionary France. When Fenno later published excerpts from Burke's *Reflections on the Revolution in France*, he also denounced Burke as a "madman," and he may have published Courtenay to expose rather than to express admiration for such virulent anti-French and anti-revolutionary political propaganda.[76]

This interpretation is certainly more consistent with Fenno's attitude toward the French Revolution. Even before Jefferson approached Fenno about publishing excerpts from the *Gazette de Leyde*, Fenno had expressed enthusiasm for the revolution in France, reporting the events of the French Estates-General in April 1789 diligently and sympathetically.[77] When news about the fall of the Bastille arrived in the United States in September, Fenno welcomed the event with all of the hyperbole he could muster. In a classic example of Enlightenment revolutionary fervor, he declared:

> Europe from America has caught the sacred flame of Freedom: It has kindled into a blaze—it has illuminated their darkness, and where tyranny erected her throne, and bigotry, ignorance and superstition supported her infernal reign, the sun of a glorious day has arisen—and liberty rejoices in the divine light and resplendent beams.[78]

Fenno expressed hope that the revolutionary blaze would spread rapidly to Spain and Great Britain, where the lower classes "shall ere long be completely delivered from every vestige of feudal tyranny." And like all zealous American Protestants and sons of New England Puritanism, he welcomed the French Revolution as a mortal blow to the temporal and spiritual power of the Roman Catholic church. Although he thought the French could learn much from the American Revolution, he had no doubt "but that mankind will be taught something *new*" by the revolution in France "on the subjects of *liberty* and the *rights of man*."[79]

The quantity and quality of information about France in the *Gazette* was astounding. Firsthand reports from well-disposed observers in France, accounts of debates in the national assembly, and articles translated from the French press made it possible for readers to follow the turbulent progress of the revolution in great detail. When he relied on English sources, Fenno culled material from radical, pro-revolutionary papers like the *Morning Chronicle*, glossing obviously slanted accounts with his own commentary and warning readers to exercise critical scrutiny. When Jefferson began to provide excerpts from the *Gazette de Leyde* in April 1790, they simply added to the profusion of pro-French material printed in the newspaper. Fenno's editorials revealed similar support for the revolution. Although he expressed concern about the slow pace of constitutional reform in 1790–1791, when the new French Constitution was approved his fears evaporated. Americans, he insisted, should have patience both with their French allies, who were "pursuing the work of reformation" with a steady sense of purpose, and with a revolution whose "objects are immense."[80]

When Louis XVI tried to flee France in the summer of 1791, Fenno argued that the popular response to the king's flight revealed "the new character of the people in a most respectable point of light." "Well might Louis declare," he wrote, "that he was now convinced that the people were in favor of the Revolution."[81] Endorsing the subsequent radicalization of the revolution, he reprinted Thomas Paine's *Letter to the Abbé Sieyès*, advocating the abolition of the monarchy and the creation of a republic, and declared the progress made by the French to be "truly astonishing." In October 1791, he published the following "Elegant Impromptu" by fellow poet and revolutionary enthusiast Joel Barlow:

> The French no more in stupid joy,
>   Torment the air, with "*Vive le Roi.*"
> A nobler wish expands the mind,
>   Let JUSTICE *live*—and *live* MANKIND.[82]

And when war broke out in 1792 between the French Republic and the combined powers, led by England, Fenno delivered the following stern (and prescient) warning to the monarchical leaders of Europe:

> On the whole, the French, united among themselves, and animated by the fervor of liberty, will be invincible, while their enemies will have to act with the utmost caution, lest while they attempt to extinguish the fire of freedom in a neighboring kingdom, their own houses should be involved in the flames.

Rallying to the cause of revolutionary France as fervently as any editor of the period, Fenno assured his readers that the outcome of the present struggle in Europe "must be favorable to the rights of man."[83]

Why then did Jefferson abandon the *Gazette of the United States*? The lack of testimony from Fenno himself makes it hard to explain exactly why his relationship with Jefferson deteriorated so suddenly, but Jefferson's charge that Fenno was slow to republish excerpts from the *Gazette de Leyde* is clearly unfair. In the end, it was Fenno's willingness to open his newspaper to critics, and particularly to Vice President John Adams, not his opposition to the French Revolution, that finally alienated Jefferson. The personal and political relationship between Fenno and Adams is hard to reconstruct, although Fenno always expressed respect for his New England compatriot, whom he once called "our American Lycurgus," and provided him with a public platform from which to express his idiosyncratic political views on a number of occasions. The first political pamphlet Fenno published in New York was Adams's *Twenty-Six Letters*, a series of letters from Adams to Dr. Hendrik Calkoen, a volume that left Fenno badly out of pocket. Then on April 27, 1790, Fenno began to publish the *Discourses on Davila*, and for a year (with a break of two months), they dominated almost every issue of the *Gazette of the United States*.[84]

The *Discourses* were a strange work, indeed, combining translations from the work of seventeenth-century Italian historian Enrico Caterino Davila with Adams's own reflections on avarice, ambition, fame, and emulation. In many respects, they simply popularized ideas that had long preoccupied Adams, but they also contained his response to the revolution in France about which he, like Edmund Burke, who published his *Reflections* at about the same time, expressed a deep sense of foreboding.[85] In the apotheosis of Enlightenment rationality, Adams too detected the violence of the Terror. "The spirit of enquiry," he wrote, "like a severe and searching wind, penetrates every part of the great body politic; and whatever is unsound, whatever is unfirm, shrinks at the visitation." This "searching wind," he warned darkly, might bring ideas that would "make mankind wish for the age of dragons, giants and fairies":

> If all decorum, discipline, and subordination are to be destroyed, and universal Phyrrhonism, anarchy, and insecurity of property are to be introduced, nations will soon wish their books in ashes, seek for darkness and ignorance, superstition and fanaticism, as blessings and follow the standard of the first mad despot who, with the enthusiasm of another Mahomet, will endeavor to obtain them.

The pursuit of equality, the animating principle of the revolution in France, would herald nothing but anarchy and chaos, and the "wild idea of annihilating the nobility" would leave French society without a "barrier against despotism." Enlightened citizens of the United States, Adams insisted, had nothing to learn from the revolution in France and everything to fear.[86]

This was not a popular message in 1790, and the *Discourses* did great harm to Adams's public reputation. His popularity "is falling lower and lower," observed the French minister, and "the public, tired of his diatribes, begins to harass him with lampoons and epigrams." When Adams included what was widely interpreted as a defense of hereditary monarchy in the *Discourses*, public protest grew so great that Fenno was forced to suspend publication.[87] The *Discourses* had "not been read by great Numbers," complained Adams, but they were treated "as full proof that he was an advocate of monarchy, and laboring to introduce an hereditary President and Senate in America," a misrepresentation that was made "the pretense for overwelming me with floods and Whirlwinds of tempestuous abuse, unexampled in the History of this Country."[88]

Even before Adams became vice president, Alexander Hamilton had feared that Adams would provide an easy target for political opposition to the federal government. He was right. Adams's quixotic campaign for a grander presidential title stirred up fears about the revival of monarchical government, which lay close to the surface in postrevolutionary American society, provoking one of the earliest published personal attacks on a member of the federal administration, *The Dangerous Vice*.[89] His taciturn manner and prickly independence isolated him from other major political figures of the day, and his political isolation was not balanced by popular support, a fact Adams himself acknowledged. "Popularity was never my mistress," he confessed to James Warren, "nor was I ever, or shall ever be a popular man." By the early 1790s, many of those who bothered to read his voluminous political writings suspected that he had abandoned his faith in republican government. Both Benjamin Rush and Jefferson thought he had renounced republican principles, and although he rejected the charge—"I am a mortal and irreconcilable enemy to Monarchy," he told Rush indignantly—it steadily gained popular currency, which the *Discourses on Davila* did little to dispel.[90]

Publishing the *Discourses* inevitably tarnished Fenno's political reputation as well, making it easier for his political opponents to portray the *Gazette* as the political mouthpiece of the vice president. In a satirical poem entitled "Pomposo and His Printer," Philip Freneau (who was editing Francis Childs's *Daily Advertiser*) portrayed Fenno as the simpering lackey of a puffed-up, conceited Adams:

> Have you a printing press—Pomposo cri'd—
> "I have not now"—the gaping Wight repli'd—
> "But if you'll promise work, I can, with ease,
> Provide a press, and play what tune you please."[91]

When Jefferson denounced the *Gazette* in May 1791 as a "paper of pure Toryism, disseminating the doctrines of monarchy, aristocracy, and the exclusion of the influence of the people," it was the *Discourses on Davila* he had in mind. But Fenno's support for Adams does not entirely explain Jefferson's alienation.[92] Despite publishing the *Discourses*, Fenno continued to support the French Revolution in the *Gazette*, and during the first few months of 1791 he became noticeably more sympathetic to Jefferson, perhaps in a belated attempt to mend his political fences.[93]

Jefferson's rift with Fenno had much more to do with his desire to create a party newspaper than with a dramatic alteration in the editorial policy of the *Gazette of the United States*. Jefferson dissolved the political partnership with Fenno in order to find an editor who reflected his own political views more faithfully and exclusively. Fenno's loyalty to Adams convinced Jefferson he had to look elsewhere, not because the *Gazette* was too partisan but because it was too promiscuous. As Jefferson's skepticism about the drift of federal policy increased, and as his opposition to Hamilton crystallized, he found the *Gazette*'s admiration and support for the administration more and more irritating. By early 1791, he was thoroughly alarmed and searching for a newspaper editor who would be willing and able to carry the battle he was waging against Hamilton inside the administration before a wider public. But for the time being, these maneuvers remained hidden from view.

Despite the criticism he attracted for publishing the *Discourses on Davila*, Fenno remained optimistic about the political state of the nation in the spring of 1791. The "transforming influence of the Constitution," he wrote, had created peace and prosperity and had laid the foundations of civil liberty "so broad and deep, as to resist the changes of human weakness, and the ravages of time." Americans were more united than ever before, thanks in large part to the salutary influence of a newspaper press that poured forth "a rich vein of information and instruction throughout the country." "Intolerance is universally reprobated," observed Fenno, "and Religion, Morals, politics, law and government, have fair play":

> The present posture of affairs in this Union, is as novel as it is pleasing: Envy, faction, and party are destitute of a subject—and except the pride of prophecy should be piqued at finding its anticipations totally illusory, our country must progress in freedom and happiness.[94]

This optimism was not confined to Fenno. Abigail Adams, no slouch when it came to detecting signs of factional intrigue and national decay, also thought that "our public affairs never looked more prosperous." Despite the attacks on her husband, she believed "the people feel the beneficial effects of the New Government by an increasing credit both at Home and abroad and a confidence in their rulers." By and large, the press reflected this sense of well-being and calm, but there were already signs of the political storms that lay ahead, notably the fierce controversy provoked by the publication of Thomas Paine's *Rights of Man*. At the end of 1791, the ever-astute and alert Federalist Fisher Ames observed that, although "tranquility has smoothed the surface" of political life for the past few months, "faction glows within like a coalpit."[95]

Even as Ames wrote, Philip Freneau was publishing the *National Gazette*, a newspaper that would quickly become the principal antagonist of the federal government and of the *Gazette of the United States*. At first, Fenno welcomed the *National Gazette* as a valuable addition to the ranks of the nationalist press, publishing passages from it in his own newspaper. But as Freneau's attacks on the government (and Hamilton in particular) escalated in the spring of 1792, Fenno became seriously alarmed that the "demon of slander" had been let loose and was eroding public confidence in the administration. Inspired by the *National Gazette*, the government was portrayed in the press as an oriental despotism rather than a republic, he complained, and "the newspapers are stuffed with licentious invectives as if they were aimed at the administration of Turkey or Tipoo Saib." These "new fangled federalists," he argued, went beyond the legitimate criticism of "men and measures" in their efforts to undermine the "frame of government itself." Nothing could be more absurd than the charges of "anti-republicanism" and "aristocracy" they hurled at a federal administration "freely chosen" by the people. Freneau's effort to appropriate the term "republican" to describe critics of the federal government particularly incensed Fenno, and he responded by vigorously defending his own republican credentials in the *Gazette of the United States*.[96]

But whatever differences existed between Fenno and Freneau about political definitions, by the summer of 1792, they agreed on at least one issue: two political parties now existed in the United States. As one writer in Fenno's *Gazette* thundered, the *National Gazette* was "established by a junto for electioneering purposes" whose "main design" was to overthrow the government. As conflict between the two newspaper editors erupted into full-scale partisan warfare, Fenno's efforts to remain above the partisan fray gave way to a more aggressive political strategy that propelled the *Gazette* into the orbit of Treasury Secretary Alexander Hamilton. In late July, Fenno began to publish a series of letters by Hamilton accusing Jefferson of hiring Freneau to run the *National Gazette*. These attacks on Freneau's editorial integrity provoked a furious response, and Freneau in turn accused Fenno of accepting Federalist largesse to finance the *Gazette of the United States*, a controversy that rumbled on through the summer and fall. By the end of the year, both Jefferson and Hamilton had become regular targets of personal abuse in the press. While the *National Gazette* accused Hamilton of secretly working to restore monarchical government, Fenno's newspaper denounced Jefferson as a political hypocrite whose efforts to prove the inferiority of black Americans belied his public image as a friend to the equal rights of man.[97]

Although Fenno sided with Hamilton in this war of words, he tried to preserve a sense of impartiality in the *Gazette* by republishing a series of articles defending Jefferson from the *American Daily Advertiser*.[98] But the growing intensity of the battle with Freneau left him dispirited and added to his other difficulties with the newspaper. His decision to follow the federal government from New York to Philadelphia in 1790 had not been the "ruinous derangement" he had feared, but it had forced him to suspend publication for a month and incur additional debts to cover his moving expenses. Although his subscribers then increased rapidly and he began to receive more government patronage, advertising income was still inadequate and delinquent subscribers owed him over $2,000. His budding partnership with Hamilton probably gave him new hope of financial assistance, but for the time being this was unrealized. Compounding his practical worries was a growing sense of disillusionment with political developments in Europe, where the outbreak of war between the French Republic and the rest of Europe was accompanied by the rise of Robespierre and the inauguration of the Terror. In April 1793, Fenno observed wearily that the "world appears full of commotion," and although he expressed faith in the eventual outcome of the revolution (while warning Americans not to emulate the French), privately he was much less optimistic. "With respect to french affairs," he told Ward, "I have long since lost all hope of them."[99]

Fenno's disillusionment may account for a new emphasis on religion both in his private correspondence and, more important, in the *Gazette of the United States*. In a letter to Ward written a few days before Christmas 1792 to express sympathy for the death of his friend's son, Fenno expressed his faith in divine providence. "*Faith* resolves all into the divine sovereignty & wisdom," he wrote:

> What a short period ere *all* will be over with us *all!* Time closes the tracks we make in our course—new ones are opened by our successors.... That we may estimate life on its true value, and learn the best lessons from all its *variety* is the only wisdom of our present existence—all else is delusory.[100]

This emphasis on "gracious providence" became more evident in Fenno's personal reflections after 1792 and began to shape his analysis of public events. The execution of Louis XVI had lost France "many friends in the U.S.," he believed, but this act of political violence was only the symptom of a deeper malaise. "The finger of Providence," he wrote, "was never more conspicuously displayed" than in the turmoil of the French Republic:

> [T]hat very being, whose government is neglected and despised, whose existence is called in question, is punishing in the most signal manner, a people, who by their acts & proceedings evince a total disregard to the true principles of truth justice & humanity.[101]

Fenno's anger was inspired by the Jacobin Party's policy of de-Christianization, a policy designed to abolish Christian worship in France and replace it with a civil religion dedicated to the goddess of Reason. In his view, the French had abandoned God, and in retribution, God had abandoned the French. French revolutionary leaders had betrayed the meritocratic and egalitarian spirit of 1789 and instead adopted a crude, materialist spirit of "levellism" in which "Philosophy without virtue—theory without experience & Speculation without Principle predominate." This "knot of Speculators," wrote Fenno, referring to the material "avarice & ambition" of French Jacobinism and its allegiance to an abstract, secular rationalism, were now trying to spread their infidel views to the rest of the world, and in the afflictions of the French people Fenno detected God's vengeance and the workings of a "Providence which is no doubt punishing the impiety of a most impious Age."[102]

This impiety, Fenno believed, now threatened the United States. The arrival of the flamboyant French minister, Edmond Charles Genet, in April 1793 galvanized Fenno's fears about the influence of the French Revolution and the growth of domestic opposition to the federal government. Citizen Genet's arrival marked the high tide of public support for revolutionary France. The declaration of the French Republic in 1792 and the stunning succession of French military victories that followed rekindled support for the revolution in the United States, and throughout the country civic festivals and feasts celebrated the revolution and the American alliance with France. In response to this outpouring of public support for revolutionary France, the federal government decided to clarify its own relationship to the belligerent powers, and shortly after Genet's arrival, Washington issued a proclamation reaffirming the neutrality of the United States. Critics of American foreign policy, on the other hand, worked hard to represent public expressions of support for the French Republic as expressions of "republican" opposition to the formal neutrality of the United States. These efforts to make foreign policy and the French Revolution central to domestic political debate increased Fenno's antagonism toward French influence, and while his fellow citizens toasted the rousing rhetoric of Citizen Genet, the *Gazette* was silent. "Truth, righteousness & common sense have but a scurvy time of it in these days," he complained privately, although in the end, he thought, "they must prevail." "The most intelligent & best of our citizens" deplored the popular clamor created by Genet, and despite the "arts used by the sons of mischief to stir up dissention," he was confident that the government would adhere to a "strict & decided Neutrality."[103]

He was right. Despite debate within the administration, the official policy of the United States remained unchanged, and when Citizen Genet appealed for help over Washington's head to the American people, hoping to exploit the widespread sympathy for France, the public mood soured. Popular disapproval of Genet's "Appeal to the People," argued Fenno, had dealt a "Death wound" to the "Hydra of Faction" and helped to revive a "true & genuine Spirit of Patriotism." But Fenno's optimism was short-lived. After a summer "hot almost without intermission," the outbreak of yellow fever in Philadelphia cut short public discussion about Citizen Genet and precipitated a more deadly crisis. By early September, the dead numbered 50 a day, and most able-bodied people had left the city. Unable or unwilling to leave the city himself, Fenno described the "Scene of Death" that surrounded his family. Hamilton had been taken ill—"I shall not be surprised to hear of his Death by Tomorrow," wrote Fenno—and his daughter Eliza fell ill in early October. Both recovered, but others were less fortunate, and by the middle of the month the death toll had risen to over 3,000. "There are a great many instances," wrote Fenno, "of whole Families being swept off," and the fever spread with ruthless efficiency "among the poor," especially among Irish immigrants, whose burial grounds were "like ploughed fields." Only the "protecting arm of Providence," thought Fenno, had spared his own family.[104]

The yellow fever epidemic left Fenno impressed by the bravery and self-sacrifice of his fellow citizens. "Whatever may be the issue of my career," he confessed, "whether my sun may set in splendor, or in clouds—my experience testifies that some of the brightest beams of divinity irradiate the human heart." But if his belief in the personal humanity of his neighbors was strengthened by the epidemic, he was concerned about the moral well-being of his community. Like many Americans, he was convinced that yellow fever was "an imported disease" brought in by French sailors and refugees from the West Indies, and he saw a close parallel between biological and political contagion. Both had their origins in the French Revolution, a link he made explicit in his discussion of the epidemic. "One of the earliest victims to the disorder," he wrote, "was a young man who dined aboard one of the [French] Frigates, at a feast made to celebrate the anniversary of the 10th of August," the anniversary of the overthrow of Louis XVI. The French had already been visited with God's wrath for their apostasy, and now he had delivered a warning to American supporters of French irreligion. Yellow fever was a "grievous visitation," argued Fenno, and when the governor of Pennsylvania, Thomas Mifflin, issued a proclamation calling for a day of "humiliation, thanksgiving & praise," Fenno expressed his hope that the "late visitation" would "prove the means of a radical & lasting reformation." Divine providence had not only protected his family from yellow fever, but used the epidemic to protect the country from revolutionary contagion.[105]

By the time the yellow fever abated, Fenno and the *Gazette* were on the edge of collapse. Although Fenno stayed in Philadelphia throughout the epidemic, he suspended publication of the *Gazette* on September 18, and it did not appear again until early December. During this time, delinquent subscriptions increased to about $4,000, and his debts reached ruinous levels. Without immediate assistance, Fenno told Ward, "my career as a Printer will be long suspended, if not closed forever." At this late stage, Federalist leaders finally stepped in to provide the *Gazette* with a direct subsidy. After Fenno submitted a schedule of "Debts and Credits" to Hamilton in November, warning him that without a loan of $2,000, "my career as a printer is closed," Hamilton quickly raised the cash needed to bail out and expand the newspaper. On December 11, 1793, the *Gazette of the United States* was reborn as a daily newspaper, and a week later Fenno and his family moved into spacious quarters at South Fourth Street, where he was able at last to "carry on the printing business extensively." At the end of 1794, he declared with satisfaction: "I am now better fixed in point of situation than I have ever been."[106]

The rebirth of the *Gazette of the United States* coincided with the demise of the *National Gazette*. The rash behavior of Citizen Genet allowed Fenno and his fellow Federalists to rally public opinion behind a policy of neutrality, peace, and independence and to seize the standard of American nationalism. Recognizing that opposition to the government was in disarray, Jefferson coolly cut his ties with Freneau, whose support for Genet had been unwavering, and let his newspaper expire. But opponents of the administration soon returned to the fray with renewed vigor and a new degree of organizational sophistication. Benjamin Franklin Bache's Philadelphia *General Advertiser*, rechristened as the *Aurora*, moved into the political vacuum left by Freneau's *National Gazette*. In January 1794, James Madison launched a new campaign in Congress to secure the passage of tariff measures designed to punish British attacks on American shipping, exploit public dislike for Britain, and galvanize opposition to the policies of the federal administration. During the course of the next year, a network of radical political clubs sprang up, the Democratic Republican societies, dedicated to preserving republican principles in the United States, defending the French Republic, and most important, providing opponents of the federal government with an organizational base for their political activities.[107]

These developments greatly alarmed Fenno, who denounced critics of the government as "self-plumed reformers" who "bawl for freedom—for a representative government and in the same breathe vent the gall of their souls against the freely elected servants of the people." The growth of political clubs modeled on the revolutionary societies of France and Britain, evoking memories of Committees of Correspondence during the American Revolution, greatly disturbed him. In his view, the Democratic societies were extraconstitutional bodies designed with only one purpose in mind: to mobilize resistance to properly constituted and elected political authority. When Washington denounced them as "self-created societies," Fenno immediately followed suit, condemning them as an insult to popular sovereignty and a threat to representative government. Composed of men who "possess neither public nor private confidence," he blamed them for the outbreak of the Whiskey Rebellion in the fall of 1794, an uprising of small farmers in western Pennsylvania who opposed the introduction of a federal excise tax on whiskey production, and used the occasion as an excuse to lecture his readers about the dangers of extraconstitutional politics. When disagreement about how to respond to the rebellion split the ranks of the Pennsylvania Democratic Society, Fenno was delighted.[108]

Fenno had hoped that the Terror, the antics of Citizen Genet, and the yellow fever epidemic would chasten Americans and that they would "learn a useful Lesson by the miseries of the European world": the need to cherish their own "Republican form of Government." But instead, the French Revolution was inspiring imitators: men who gathered in exclusive radical clubs, decried their own republican government as a conspiracy against the rights of man, encouraged armed resistance to democratically elected authority, and practiced the same kind of political fanaticism and intolerance as the French Jacobins. Although Fenno still refused to disown the French Revolution completely, calling the "subversion of the old despotism" a "good work," he condemned Robespierre as a "man of blood" and described the ascendancy of the Jacobins and the Committee of Public Safety as a revival of that "same lust for power & universal dominion" that had "actuated that execrable Tyrant Louis the Fourteenth." The execution of Brissot de Warville and other moderate Girondists in late 1793 was, in his view, a terrible blow to French democracy. "Democracy has not received so great a blow by all the Victories of the Allies, as by their death," he wrote, adding that "every species of merit was swept away by the guillotine." Continued support for revolutionary leaders in France was incomprehensible to him—"nothing else but submission absolute & unconditional to a succession of triumphing factions"—aiding those who were bent on the destruction of civil liberty and Christianity in France.[109]

But much as Fenno deplored popular support for the French Revolution, it forced him to confront a new possibility or possibly to revisit an old fear: that Americans themselves might be incapable of responsible self-government. Chastising New England clergymen for their "habit of praying for success to the french," he blamed them for "puffing up the worst characters in the universe" and undermining their own "civil & religious establishments." But he reserved his harshest criticism for the American press. In the years since the founding of the *Gazette of the United States*, he had remained remarkably optimistic about the influence of the press on public opinion. This optimism now evaporated. "If the enemies of this Country had chosen their agents of mischief," he wrote glumly in September 1794, "they could not have employed better, than the printers of News Papers in the U.S." During the constitutional debates of the 1780s, the press had been "generally engaged on the right side," he argued, but ever since newspapers had teemed with ideas "hostile to the government they before advocated, subversive of the principles on which civil liberty is founded, degrading to our character as freemen, and as an independent nation." Fenno blamed the decline of the press on "exiles from Europe," restless malcontents who used the press freedom of the United States to undermine its independence and poison its public life. This xenophobia, a xenophobia that found its way more and more often into the *Gazette* after 1795, was accompanied by faltering confidence in the judgment and maturity of his fellow citizens. Inspired by a "spirit of evil & malignity," foreign journalists had slandered respectable public men, but their slander had found a ready audience among Americans and its influence had "tinctured the public mind." Fenno had never exaggerated American virtues, but as his faith in the character and civic virtue of his countrymen waned, so did his allegiance to the kind of broad, inclusive political nationalism he had espoused in 1789.[110]

His growing pessimism about public life led him toward a more restricted, exclusive, and ethnic vision of national identity. Ever since the arrival of Citizen Genet, Federalists like Fenno and the editor of the *American Minerva*, Noah Webster, had been urging their fellow citizens to adopt a shared "American" identity, one defined not by politics but by birth, and to resist the centripetal pull of the French Revolution. But the darker side of this Americanism was a growing emphasis on the "alien" nature of the threat to the United States, and a tendency to blame alien ideas, alien journalists, and alien politicians for the political conflicts of American public life, a tendency that led to the passage of the Alien and Sedition Acts in 1798. For Federalists, this alien influence was almost entirely French (their opponents' anti-alien feeling took a different form: an aversion to the aristocratic and monarchical ideas that originated in European, and more specifically English, society) and was inextricably linked to the influence of the French Revolution and the growth of what they perceived as American Jacobinism. Just as the language of anticommunism would be used to define American identity in the mid-twentieth century, anti-Jacobinism was used to define American identity in the 1790s, and Fenno and the *Gazette of the United States* contributed greatly to this development.[111]

After he resumed publication of the *Gazette of the United States* in December 1793, Fenno edited the newspaper with a new partisan zeal. Publishing a daily allowed him to be less selective about the material he printed and gave him a "good pretext for introducing speculations in which the truth is more freely told, than has hitherto been the case," a pretext he intended to use "to take many rampant public errors by the Horns." During the long, drawn-out battle over congressional approval of the Jay Treaty in 1795–1796, the editorial style of the *Gazette* became noticeably more punchy and satirical and its content far more hostile to the French Revolution and its American supporters.[112] Typical was a column by "No Jacobin" published in the paper in early 1796, which traced the roots of American Jacobinism to the Genet mission. Argued its author:

> The seeds of Jacobinism were planted in the United States by a special missionary deputed for that express purpose by the parent Society at Paris and lest our soil might not prove favourable to the culture of this monstrous plant, the missionary was provided with one hundred thousand Guineas to defray the expense of erecting hot houses.—The success of the missionary was beyond his most sanguine expectations.—Nurseries for the cultivation of Jacobinism under the name of Democratic Societies were formed from New-Hampshire to Georgia. The plants invigorated by the influence of foreign gold grew apace.[113]

The sarcastic, conspiratorial tone of this political tale was quite different from Fenno's past discussions of French influence, probably reflecting the influence of a man who would soon become the embodiment of American anti-Jacobinism: William Cobbett. An English radical turned counterrevolutionary, Cobbett was not yet the infamous character assassin he became after founding *Porcupine's Gazette* in March 1797. But using the pen name "Peter Porcupine," he had already published several provocative pamphlets attacking "American Democrats," and his famous Blue Shop opposite Christ Church in Philadelphia had become a clearinghouse for the distribution of anti-Jacobin literature in the United States.[114]

Cobbett may simply have written for the *Gazette*. Many editorial paragraphs in the newspaper during this period bear the hallmarks of his distinctive style: biting, blustering, earthy prose that used italics to add emphasis and ellipses to channel the flow of polemic; serial lampoons of journalists like Benjamin Franklin Bache ("Huzza for Benny and the Hollow Ware Company") and politicians like Albert Gallatin ("the Gentleman from Geneva"); and a visceral hostility toward the French Revolution. But Cobbett also shaped the editorial tone of the newspaper through his protégé, John Ward Fenno. Commonly called Jack, Fenno's oldest son was born on March 29, 1778, and trained by his father as a printer. He was educated at a private academy in New York, graduated from the University of Pennsylvania in 1794, and although he wanted to study law in Boston, he was drafted to work on the *Gazette of the United States*. After his father's death in 1798, he edited the newspaper in close collaboration with Cobbett, defending the controversial Englishman and his views against a growing army of critics with unfortunate results for his own career and the political fortunes of the Federalists. Inspired by the powerful personality and prose of Peter Porcupine, Jack Fenno's presence on the *Gazette* from the mid-1790s onward accounts for its growing editorial combativeness. But it was Cobbett's unmistakable influence on the newspaper that transformed the *Gazette* into an anti-Jacobin newspaper and helped to make the language of anti-Jacobinism central to the political discourse of the 1790s.[115]

Unlike his son, John Fenno never fell completely under Cobbett's spell. Although Cobbett's personal invective gave a populist edge to Federalist political rhetoric, it had its risks. After one member of the Democratic Society of Pennsylvania was "pretty freely handled" in the *Gazette*, he threatened Fenno with a public flogging and assaulted him in the Philadelphia marketplace. Bloodied but unbowed, Fenno condemned his assailant as a "true blooded Jacobin" but privately expressed misgivings about Cobbett's relentless personalization of politics, roundly condemning its use by his opponents and denouncing the "outrageous attacks on the President" in the opposition press as the work of "abusive scribblers" without a "drop of American blood in their veins." Unlike Cobbett and his son, Fenno retained a residual faith in the good sense of the American public. Despite the attacks on Washington and other political leaders, he believed that most Americans supported the federal government and viewed the "revilers of our patriots" as "hollow hearted, bad hearted pretenders to republicanism" who wished to plunge the country into a costly and disastrous European war. He never seems to have doubted, for example, that the Jay Treaty would be ratified, despite the public opposition it aroused. "It is a glorious circumstance in favor of a free government," he wrote a few days before the final vote on the treaty in the House of Representatives, "that the people of the U.S. have not been seduced by the infernal lies & slanders of the antifederal horde." The approval of the treaty was a vindication of American government and the maturity and wisdom of the American people. "Surely as a people," he declared, "we are favored of Heaven beyond all that ever went before us."[116]

Ironically, the political storm created by the Jay Treaty revived and restored Fenno's faith in popular democracy and in the American national character. And when the storm began to dissipate—the *Aurora*, he noted with satisfaction in the summer of 1796, was the only newspaper "from which the few rivulets of anti-federalism that remain are supplied"—Fenno moved swiftly to reassert his editorial control over the newspaper. Although he kept publishing Cobbett's writings and the writings of the homegrown anti-democrat Joseph Dennie, his differences with Cobbett became increasingly clear, and Fenno never let his own anti-Jacobinism degenerate into general denunciations of democratic politics nor undermine his allegiance to American neutrality. In 1797, at a time when Cobbett was exploiting diplomatic tensions between France and the United States to create support for an alliance with Great Britain, Fenno reminded Americans that there were three parties in the United States: the French, represented by Bache and the *Aurora*; the British, represented by Cobbett and *Porcupine's Gazette*; and the American. And in this triangular struggle, his loyalty was clear. When Washington published his Farewell Address in September 1796, warning Americans to avoid "entangling alliances" with Europe, Fenno hailed it as a "true political creed" that captured the feelings of "every genuine and patriotic American." With Cobbett clearly in mind, he denounced those who wanted to drag the country into a war against France as pro-British "incendiaries." The United States, he wrote in response to public celebrations of the Fourth of July in 1796, "must be *independent* of *both* nations."[117]

The election of John Adams to the presidency gave Fenno even more faith in the country's prospects, as well as a new degree of access to political power. "I have had the honor of visiting the President several times," he reported to Ward in the spring of 1797. And although he was worried by the growing military power and belligerence of the French Republic, he was pleased that the crisis with France, and particularly French naval attacks on American shipping, had broken the "Virginia anti-federal Phalanx." Applauding the "patriotic state of the public mind," he urged his fellow citizens to "rally under the American standard." Despite congressional wrangling over war preparations and the increasingly poisonous tone of public debate, he remained loyal to Adams and convinced that he "spoke the language of independence." Hoping that a war with France could be averted, Fenno supported Adams's decision to send a diplomatic mission to Paris to negotiate with the French government, even suggesting Jefferson or Madison as envoys.[118]

When the XYZ Memorandum was published in the spring of 1798, exposing the efforts of the French foreign minister Talleyrand to elicit bribes from the American envoys, Fenno joined the outcry against France. Echoing the popular call to arms—"Not a Penny for Tribute and Millions for Defence"—he filled the columns of the *Gazette* with public memorials to President Adams, expressing support for his stand against the French Republic. Caught up in the war fever that swept the country, he welcomed Hamilton's return to public life as inspector general of the army and applauded the military parades that took place every day in Philadelphia. Anticipating "serious times," he hoped that the "great & glorious Spirit" that possessed the country would "not evaporate." But he would not live to find out. As political temperatures soared, so did the heat, and yellow fever appeared again in Philadelphia. Thinking of both politics and pestilence, Fenno placed his trust in God and divine providence. "As a people," he wrote, "we have great & many Mercies to be grateful for. The present impending Clouds may by gracious Providence be dissipated—in which Case, the prospects of our Country would brighten beyond any past experience."[119]

By late August, the city was deserted and the fever had made "tremendous ravages." Mercifully, his own family had so far been spared, and Fenno hoped the worst was past, determined to carry on "calm & unruffled." He believed it was his duty to stay "so long as other printers remain at their Posts," placing his trust in that "almighty power which has so graciously protected me & mine heretofore." Writing to his old friend Joseph Ward, he once again expressed cautious optimism about the course of events in Europe and hope that "universal peace, righteousness, justice & truth prevail thro' the Earth." It was the last letter he wrote before his death on September 14, 1798.[120]

CHAPTER 2

Philip Freneau and the Invention of the Republican Party

A few weeks after the launch of Philip Freneau's *National Gazette*, an essay appeared in its pages that set out to explain the current state of American politics. According to its anonymous author, it was important for all citizens to understand the true nature of party divisions lest "an opportunity is given to designing men, by the use of artificial and nominal distinctions," to divide "those who never differed." And in the interests of preventing such a division, the author provided his readers with a brief history of American political parties. During the "first period" of party organization, he informed them, Americans had divided sharply into two warring groups: those who supported and those who opposed the American Revolution. After the Revolution, although there were "parties in abundance," they were local rather than national in character, and it was the adoption of a new federal Constitution that "gave birth to a second and most interesting division of the people": into Federalists and Anti-Federalists. A "third division" arose after the formation of the federal government, and this division "being natural to most political societies," argued the author, "is likely to be of some duration in ours." It had created two irreconcilable camps: an "antirepublican party," consisting of those who believed that government could "only be carried on by the pageantry of rank, the influence of money and emoluments, and the terror of military force," and a "Republican party," consisting of those who believed that hereditary government was "an insult to the reason and an outrage to the rights of man." The question of the hour, concluded the author, was which of these parties would "ultimately establish its ascendance."[1]

The author of this essay, which according to one historian represented the "political christening" of the "Republican party," was James Madison. But

Madison's essay was more than a christening, the naming of something already born. As he knew, his belief that American public life was characterized by systematic party conflict and that this conflict took the form of a struggle between "enemies and friends to republican government" was neither self-evident nor uncontested. And his purpose in writing the essay was not simply to identify the existence of a "Republican party," but to literally conjure it into being, to give it birth. Through the act of writing, of inscribing the party divisions he believed *ought* to frame popular political discourse, Madison sought to bring such divisions to life. By appropriating the term "republican," he sought to define and legitimize a coherent sense of identity for an amorphous and illegitimate political opposition and, in doing so, to define and delegitimize the Federalist status quo as anti-republican. His genealogy was part of a broader effort to redefine the terms of party conflict in the 1790s and to convince Americans that the constitutional differences between Federalists and Anti-Federalists had been superseded by a more basic social and political conflict, a conflict between "republicans" and "aristocrats."[2]

Madison's attack on aristocracy had deep roots in Anglo-American political culture. Anti-aristocratic ideas, shaped by the political and religious iconoclasm of the seventeenth-century English Revolution, played a central role in the ideological conflict of the American Revolution. During the 1760s and 1770s, colonial leaders frequently used anti-aristocratic rhetoric to justify their resistance to British imperial policy, framing their struggle as a clash between the republican virtue of the American colonies and the aristocratic corruption of the British Empire. By challenging traditional political hierarchies and the deference upon which they were based, the Revolution and the formation of a republic encouraged the spread of anti-aristocratic ideas and, during the 1780s, politicians (and their allies in the press) deflected attacks on their own elitism by portraying their opponents as members of a "mushroom gentry" who were conspiring to reverse the egalitarian achievements of the Revolution. "Legislative halls and the press," writes historian Gordon Wood, "were filled with diatribes against aristocracy." The fierce public debate ignited by Aedanus Burke's attack on the Society of the Cincinnati as a "hereditary peerage" in 1783 showed how explosive such charges of aristocracy could be in the postrevolutionary United States. When partisan warfare erupted in Philadelphia in the mid-1780s between conservative critics of the Pennsylvania Constitution and its radical defenders (one of whom was Freneau), both sides used the language of anti-aristocratic denunciation to mobilize supporters. Anti-Federalists voiced similar concerns about aristocratic resurgence in the ratification debates of the late 1780s, although the success of the Federalists exposed the limits of this rhetoric and, for a time, subdued it almost completely.[3]

During the early 1790s, Philip Freneau and his literary collaborators on the *National Gazette* revived and reclaimed this anti-aristocratic rhetoric, making it a staple of republican propaganda and a central part of Republican "party" identity. As a result, during its brief existence, Freneau's *National Gazette* had a profound impact on the development of American partisan politics, transforming a diffuse and ideologically inchoate sense of opposition to the policies of the Washington administration into a purposeful and ideologically coherent opposition party.[4] But there was nothing inevitable about the emergence of the Republican Party, and its appearance was neither a logical democratic response to the reactionary policies of the Federalists, nor a natural political manifestation of broader processes of class formation in the postrevolutionary United States. Although historians often take republican charges of aristocratic subversion in the 1790s seriously, it is impossible to read the endless anti-aristocratic harangues of the period without a sense of skepticism. Did republicans take their own warnings of aristocratic and monarchical revanchism seriously? Or was this just a way to discredit and delegitimize Federalist opponents? And if they did genuinely believe that the Federalists were conspiring to reestablish an aristocratic political order, then how seriously should historians take such charges?[5]

By defining partisan conflict as a struggle between aristocracy and the people, the few and the many, Freneau and his Republican allies were mobilizing a language of class conflict. But as they knew, real aristocrats were thin on the ground in the postrevolutionary United States, and the Constitution explicitly barred the creation of a hereditary nobility. Although anti-aristocratic language was used during the 1790s as a vehicle for the expression of class conflict, it should not be used by historians to infer the existence of a real social formation, an American gentry. Indeed, when a southern slaveholder like Thomas Jefferson uses anti-aristocratic language to attack an *arriviste* lawyer from the West Indies like Alexander Hamilton, its usefulness as a term of strictly social classification seems almost negligible.[6] In fact, the language of aristocracy operated with relative autonomy, as a political signifier without a clear social referent. Its use in political discourse was not an inevitable response to the persistence and growth of class inequality in postrevolutionary American society, and it could easily be used to evade as well as to evoke such inequality. But if the growth of anti-aristocratic rhetoric was not simply an ideological response to a prior social and political reality, it would also be wrong to dismiss it as alien or anachronistic, as a discourse that reflected the influence of émigré journalists from Europe or of an anglicized colonial past.[7] Words like "aristocrat" and "monarchist" were political epithets, and whatever other resonance they possessed in postrevolutionary American political culture, it was impossible to use them after 1789 without invoking the French Revolution. In the context of the French Revolution, the word aristocrat

was a political rather than a social designation, attached (with often fatal consequences) to many unfortunate members of the Third Estate. Whenever American
republicans like Philip Freneau used the term aristocrat, they cast their Federalist
opponents as anti-republican apologists for the French Old Regime and as agents
of counterrevolution and monarchy in the United States.[8]

The revival of anti-aristocratic rhetoric in the early 1790s was therefore a
political act that required the creative work of political agents like Freneau, and it
was intended to legitimize political opposition in a culture that still viewed parties and organized opposition with a deep sense of distrust. By portraying themselves as heirs to the American Revolution and to the revolution in France, and
by recasting partisan conflict as a social and political struggle between the many

Philip Freneau. Engraving by Frederick W. Halpin, 1865. The only portrait of Freneau that
the author has been able to uncover but probably not from a life study. Courtesy of the
New York Public Library.

and the few, Freneau and his fellow republicans distinguished their opposition to the Washington administration from opposition to the Constitution and the nation. The emergence and growth of the Republican Party in 1792–1793 and the success with which Republicans redefined Federalists as members of an aristocratic and anti-republican party testified to the political skill and influence wielded by Freneau as the editor of the *National Gazette.* By late 1793, he and his contributors had convinced many Americans that the conflict between Federalists and Anti-Federalists was outdated and had been superseded by a far more significant struggle between the forces of republicanism and anti-republicanism. Their success literally shaped the history of the 1790s.[9]

Philip Morin Fresneau was born in New York City on January 2, 1752, and grew up on a small farm in Monmouth County, New Jersey. His mother, Agnes Watson, was from a prosperous Scottish yeoman family in Monmouth County, and his father, Pierre Fresneau, was a New York merchant and land speculator of French Huguenot origins, who led a checkered life as a merchant in the West Indies trade before dying in 1767 and leaving his wife and children little but debts. "Here ends," wrote his precocious fifteen-year-old son on the last page of his father's letter book, "a Book of Vexation, Disappointments, Loss and Plagues, that sunk the Author to his grave short of 50 years." Despite his father's business failures and early death, Philip Freneau (who changed the spelling of his last name after his father's death) acquired a sound education at a boarding school in New York and then attended a grammar school in nearby Manalapan, where he was outstanding enough to win admission to the College of New Jersey as a sophomore in November 1768.[10]

His timing was good. Freneau arrived at the college just a few months after its charismatic, intelligent, and dynamic new president, the Reverend John Witherspoon, and as part of one of the most distinguished classes in Princeton's history. Other members of his class included the future jurist and author Hugh Henry Brackenridge; Henry "Light Horse Harry" Lee; William Bradford, a future attorney general of the United States; a future vice president, Aaron Burr; and Freneau's closest friend and college roommate, James Madison. Inspired by this brilliant group of students and encouraged by the enlightened, liberal curriculum created by Witherspoon, a curriculum that included English composition and criticism as well as the usual instruction in the classics, Freneau flourished and quickly found his métier, English literature.[11] Inspired by John Milton and the eighteenth-century poets Alexander Pope and Oliver Goldsmith, he started writing poetry and prose of his own. In 1770, he and Brackenridge collaborated on a strange, picaresque novel entitled *Father Bombo's Pilgrimage to Mecca,* one of the first works of American prose fiction, and both earned an early taste of literary fame with *The Rising Glory of America,* an epic patriotic poem they composed for their college commencement in 1771, which was subsequently published by the Philadelphia printer Joseph Crukshank.[12]

As the title of this poem suggests, Freneau discovered politics as well as poetry at Princeton. His time at the College of New Jersey between 1768 and 1771 was a pivotal period in the development of colonial resistance to British imperial policy. The nonimportation movement, a response to the duties imposed on British goods by the Townshend Acts in 1767, made itself felt at Princeton after merchants in Philadelphia joined the trade boycott in 1769. To express their solidarity with the movement, Freneau and his fellow students wore clothes made of American homespun at the college commencement in 1770, an act of resistance applauded by President Witherspoon. Witherspoon, who according to John Adams was "as high a son of liberty as any man in America" and who was later a delegate to the Continental Congress and a signatory of the Declaration of Independence, wished to avoid turning the college into a place of "political contention," but he did little to discourage the patriotic feelings of his students and claimed proudly in 1772 that "the spirit of liberty has breathed high and strong in all the Members."[13]

Like most of his peers, Freneau was deeply influenced by the turbulent politics of the late 1770s. Closely related to the radical John Morin Scott, one of the founders of the New York Sons of Liberty, he probably opposed British colonial policy even before he arrived at Princeton, and once there he made his political loyalties clear, helping Madison, Bradford, and Brackenridge to revive the defunct college debating society, the Plain Dealing Club, as the American Whig Society and penning a series of "Satires Against the Tories" attacking the rival Cliosophic Society.[14] But despite his radical views, he did not yet envisage American independence. *The Rising Glory of America* praised colonial resistance to Britain—"the sons of Boston resolute and brave"—but celebrated the "golden tides" of British commerce that had carried civilization to America and rescued the land from Indian savagery. In other words, Freneau's support for the colonial cause jostled side by side with his enthusiasm for the British Empire, and like most colonists, the young patriot saw no conflict between his identities as an American and as one of the "sons of Britain." Poetry and politics had not yet converged to produce a vision of political independence.[15]

Freneau graduated from Princeton into a world that offered few prospects for a bright but penniless young poet. His family hoped that he would train for the clergy, and for the next few years he flirted with a religious career, but first he was forced to teach for his bread. Teaching did not come naturally. In April 1772, he took a position in Flatbush, Long Island, and survived only thirteen days, fleeing the school for Princeton and the study of theology. "Long Island I have bid adieu," he wrote to Madison after this debacle, "with all its brutish brainless crew." But theology inspired him even less than pedagogy, and in October 1772, he joined his friend Brackenridge at a school in Somerset County, Maryland. His second foray as a teacher was no more successful than his first, leading him to renounce "The Miserable Life of a Pedagogue." "This is the last time I shall enter into such a business," he told Madison. "[I]t worries me to death and by no mean[s] suits my 'giddy wandring brain.'" Briefly considering "reading Physic" and becoming a "quack," he spent his spare time sleeping and writing poetry. His hardships had left him "stiff with age" and looking like an "unmeaning Teague just turned out of the hold of an irish ship." After devoting himself to theology again, he decided that he was more interested in religious speculation than clerical life. "It was a vain notion," he confessed in his journal, to think "a Parson's life was the high road to wealth and independency in Life." The study of divinity was "the Study of Nothing," and "the profession of a priest is little better than that of a slothful Block head."[16]

After this spiritual epiphany, Freneau vanished from public view, reappearing on the eve of the American Revolution as the author of *American Liberty*, a poem "addressed to all lovers of this once flourishing country." His poem was a clarion call to combat:

> What breast but kindles at the martial sound?
> What heart but bleeds to feel its country's wound?
> For thee, blest freedom, to protect thy sway,
> We rush undaunted to the bloody fray;
> For thee, each province arms its vig'rous host,
> Content to die, ere freedom shall be lost.

Published in the fall of 1775, *American Liberty* captured the blend of defiance and irresolution that characterized the colonies just before the publication of Thomas Paine's *Common Sense* in January 1776. After Lexington and Bunker Hill, with the British general Thomas Gage bottled up in Boston, Freneau's hope that Britons would give up their effort "T'enslave their brethren in a foreign land" was widely shared. Freneau had grown more hostile to British commerce since his departure from Princeton. "The American Village," published the year after he left, described the corruption of American pastoral innocence by British commerce, but he still possessed a powerful sense of "brethren" identity with Britain.[17] His most popular poem of the time, *A Voyage to Boston*, excoriated British policy, but expressed hope for a reconciliation between empire and colonies: "Hear and attest the warmest wish I bring, / God save the Congress and reform the King! / Long may Britannia rule our hearts again, / Rule as she rul'd in George the Second's reign." Another poem of the same period, *General Gage's Soliloquy*, described a hesitant, conscience-stricken Gage expressing uncertainty about his own role in a fraternal conflict: "But did I swear, I ask my heart again, / To fight for Britons against Englishmen?"[18]

The conflict with Britain inspired Freneau to new levels of literary creativity, but the rupture created by independence precipitated an acute crisis of identity. As the breach with Britain widened, Freneau fled from participation in the revolutionary cause.[19] After becoming embroiled in a literary sparring match with Myles Cooper, the Tory president of King's College in New York and author of the satirical *Patriots of North America*, Freneau lost his appetite for political controversy. The poem *MacSwiggen*, a response to Cooper's work, started defiantly but lapsed into weariness and retreat:

> Sick of all feuds, to reason I appeal
> From wars of paper, and from wars of steel,
> Let others here their hopes and wishes end,
> I to the sea with weary steps descend,
> Quit the mean conquest that such swine might yield,
> And leave MacSwiggen to enjoy the field—
> In distant isles some happier scene I'll choose,
> And court in softer shades the unwilling Muse.[20]

True to his word, Freneau abandoned the battlefields of North America and pursued his muse to the Caribbean island of St. Croix, where he lived for the next two years. His flight—"O waft me far, ye muses of the west— / Give me your green bowers and soft seats of rest"—established a pattern of political engagement and literary retreat that continued throughout his life and his work.[21]

By the time he returned to the United States in 1778, Freneau had vanquished his reservations about the Revolution, and his movement from artistic seclusion to political participation was neatly captured in the title of a new volume of poetry, *The Travels of the Imagination: . . . To Which Are Added, American Independence, an Everlasting Deliverance from British Tyranny*. In keeping with his renewed political commitment, Freneau enlisted in the New Jersey militia and began to write regularly for Hugh Henry Brackenridge's *United States Magazine*. Two years later, he resigned from the militia and returned to sea, serving aboard privateers running goods past the British naval blockade.[22] In May 1780, the American privateer *Aurora* was shelled and boarded by a British frigate, the HMS *Iris*. Despite efforts to convince the British that he was a passenger and a "gentleman," the ship's third mate, Philip Freneau, was taken prisoner and transferred to the HMS *Scorpion*, a British prison ship anchored in the Hudson River. Conditions on board were appalling. "I expected to die before morning," Freneau later wrote, "but human nature can bear more than one would at first suppose." It was a pivotal moment in Freneau's war, an experience that left him with a deep and lasting hatred for Great Britain. His poem *The British Prison Ship* expressed this new and more visceral hatred:

> AMERICANS! a just resentment shew,
> And glut revenge on this detested foe;
> While the warm blood exults the glowing vein
> Still shall resentment in your bosoms reign.

Images of war in Freneau's previous poetry had been formulaic: "Drenched in her gore, Lavinia of the vale." No longer. During his six weeks in British captivity, Freneau experienced the violence of war at close quarters, and his poems were now filled with dark, sanguinary images of British slaughter and violence. The conflict from which he had once fled now assumed for him a grim reality.[23]

Freneau spent the next year recuperating at his family's home in New Jersey and published almost nothing except *The British Prison Ship*. Then, in the spring of 1781, he moved to Philadelphia to edit Francis Bailey's *Freeman's Journal*, a job that gave him a chance to support "the cause of the Revolution all the more." Bailey, who published Freneau's *British Prison Ship* as well as Paine's *Common Sense*, had served as a brigadier major in the Pennsylvania line at Valley Forge in 1777–1778. According to Freneau, he was "a good republican and a worthy honest man," and during the 1780s, he became Freneau's most important patron.[24] He launched the *Freeman's Journal* just as the tide of war turned decisively against the British, and from the start, Freneau's mark was "upon every page." In August 1781, Washington and Rochambeau entered Philadelphia en route to Yorktown and were welcomed with an outpouring of popular enthusiasm, a mood Freneau captured in his poem *To His Excellency General Washington*.[25] Although the *Freeman's Journal* promised to be a "Free Press," "open to all parties but influenced by none," Freneau made no attempt to disguise his allegiance to those "whose principles coincide with those of the Revolution," and the newspaper quickly became a vehicle for his rejuvenated patriotism, filled with satirical attacks on the Tory editor of the New York *Royal Gazette*, James Rivington.[26]

By 1782, British defeat seemed inevitable, and the *Freeman's Journal* began to pay more attention to domestic politics, particularly to the conflict between supporters and critics of the Pennsylvania Constitution, the most radical and democratic of the revolutionary state constitutions. Supported by both Thomas Paine and Benjamin Franklin, the Pennsylvania Constitution of 1776 had abolished the second legislative chamber of the old colonial assembly, creating a unicameral legislature with a Council of Censors and a president directly responsible to the legislature, essentially a parliamentary system without an upper chamber. Ever since its adoption, its Republican critics had waged a battle against its Constitutionalist defenders to transform the Council of Censors into a genuine second chamber and to make the president independent of legislative control. When Bailey founded the *Freeman's Journal* in 1781, he did so partly at the instigation of George Bryan and John Dicking Seargeant, both key figures in the Constitutionalist Party.[27] Freneau's involvement with the party and his opposition to constitutional revision are therefore highly revealing. As the editor of the *Freeman's Journal*, he aligned himself with the most radical wing of the revolutionary movement in Pennsylvania and demonstrated his commitment to the most egalitarian aspects of the American Revolution. A poem written for the *Freeman's Journal* in July 1782 expressed Freneau's egalitarianism unequivocally:

> Curs'd be the day how bright so'er it shin'd,
> That first made kings the masters of mankind;
> And curs'd the wretch who first with regal pride
> Their equal rights to equal men deny'd.[28]

This egalitarian radicalism shaped Freneau's response to the growth of Republican opposition to the constitution in Pennsylvania. The movement for constitutional revision, he argued, was an attempt to undermine the democratic advances of the American Revolution. His popular "Pilgrim" essays, published in the *Freeman's Journal* in 1781–1782, warned the citizens of Pennsylvania against reform and the growing influence of a "domestic aristocracy" and preached the virtues of an austere republicanism that would protect the interests of the common man, a theme that became a staple of his political writings in the 1790s.[29]

When the Republicans won a majority in the Pennsylvania House of Representatives in 1782, Freneau launched a "vitriolic newspaper crusade" designed to stem their popular influence. Francis Hopkinson, no stranger to fierce political satire, thought "calumny and slander were carried to a greater extent than was ever known, perhaps, in a civilized city," and Benjamin Franklin wrote from Paris that he never passed Pennsylvania newspapers along to others "till I have examined and laid aside such as would disgrace us."[30] The descent into gutter journalism was not all Freneau's fault; it also reflected the influence of another gifted editor, Colonel Eleazar Oswald, whose *Independent Gazetteer* was the standard-bearer of Pennsylvania Republicans. An undeservedly neglected figure, Oswald was a colorful and flamboyant man, a natural political controversialist, and without doubt the most important Philadelphia journalist of the 1780s. His patriotic credentials were impeccable. He had fought at Lexington in 1775, taken part in the invasion of Canada, and, after capture by the British at Quebec, served as a colonel in the Continental artillery. He later played a leading role in Anti-Federalist opposition to the federal Constitution and extended his military career into the 1790s, serving as an artillery officer in the French army and taking part in the Irish Rebellion. Trained as a printer by the fiery William Goddard, Oswald was a "gutsy and pugnacious editor" who paid no more than lip service to platitudes about the impartiality of the press. After establishing the *Independent Gazetteer* in April 1782, he lost no time in provoking a feud with Freneau and the *Freeman's Journal*, and the influence of his aggressive, populist journalism helps to explain how Republican critics of the Pennsylvania Constitution were able to fend off the anti-aristocratic rhetoric of their more radical Constitutionalist opponents in the 1780s.[31]

Unlike Oswald, Freneau's appetite for such partisan political combat was limited, and when exchanges between the *Independent Gazetteer* and the *Freeman's Journal* plumbed new depths of literary tastelessness, he conceded his position to the "scribblers" of the *Independent Gazetteer*: "Long may they write unquestion'd and unhurt, / And all their rage discharge, and all their dirt." Although he continued to contribute to the *Freeman's Journal* for the next eighteen months, his editorial role in the newspaper came to an end. Abandoning the battle with Oswald and the Republicans, Freneau sought refuge from the political fray by translating the Abbé Claude Robin's account of his experiences in the Revolution, *Voyage dans l'Amerique Septentrionale*, and a few weeks after the Treaty of Paris was announced in May 1784, he boarded a ship for Jamaica, where he spent most of the rest of the decade in self-imposed exile from American politics and public life.[32] When Washington arrived in New York in April 1789, Captain Freneau watched his progress across the Hudson from the deck of the schooner *Columbia*, just arrived from Charleston and "dressed and decorated in the most superb manner," commemorating the day in *Verses Occasioned by General Washington's Arrival*. But not until his return to New York in March 1790 to write for Francis Childs's *Daily Advertiser* did Freneau find his way back into the political life of the early Republic.[33]

The publication of Thomas Paine's *Rights of Man* in the United States in May 1791 marked a critical turning point in American political debate, reawakening an anti-aristocratic political discourse that had been slumbering since the ratification of the federal Constitution. Before the appearance of the *Rights of Man*, the use of anti-aristocratic political language was largely confined to critics of the vice president, John Adams, who was a lightning rod for concern about the revival of aristocratic and monarchical ideas almost from the moment he took office. The cranky Pennsylvania congressman William Maclay may have grumbled about the monarchical style of Washington's official conduct in the privacy of his diary, but it was Adams who attracted serious public criticism. Already viewed with suspicion for the aristocratic ideas contained in his *Defence of the Constitutions of Government of the United States*, his campaign to establish a more formal, ostentatious mode of address for the president in the spring of 1789 provoked widespread ridicule and the first real signs of public opposition to the new federal government. Even John Fenno, aware of the potency of the issue, abandoned Adams, while radical editors like Philip Freneau, who ridiculed Adams's title campaign and Fenno's "court sycophantism" in the New York *Daily Advertiser*, exploited the political opening the vice president had given to them. But at this stage, Adams's critics treated him largely as a political oddity—"The Dangerous Vice"—an idiosyncratic, eccentric figure whose views represented neither the American people nor their government.[34]

The appearance of Paine's work transformed this situation, and the political controversy it provoked in the summer of 1791, although nominally focused on Adams, signaled the first serious effort to organize opposition to the Washington administration around republican principles and what Jefferson called the "standard of Common sense."[35] Dedicated to George Washington, the *Rights of Man* was an unlikely source of political controversy in the United States. Written in response to Edmund Burke's *Reflections on the Revolution in France*, it was a brilliant defense of the principles of republican government and the French Revolution, both of which were enthusiastically supported by most Americans. Paine, who had returned to England in 1787, had supported the ratification of the federal Constitution and, in fact, had nothing critical to say at this stage about American government. It appeared in his work as a political abstraction: the "New World" that was to serve as a model for the regeneration of the Old. He gave no hint of political disagreements within the United States, and when the second part of the *Rights of Man* was published in 1792, he argued that the successful union of the American states proved that, by "constructing government on the principles of society and the rights of man, every difficulty retires, and all parts are brought into cordial unison." Nevertheless, when the *Rights of Man* was reprinted in Philadelphia by Samuel Harrison Smith and Benjamin Franklin Bache in May 1791, it "fell like a thunderclap on the quiet capital."[36]

The cause of this political storm was a foreword to Paine's work contributed by the secretary of state, Thomas Jefferson, expressing pleasure "that something is at length to be publickly said against the political heresies which have sprung up among us." Jefferson's remarks were taken from a letter he enclosed with the *Rights of Man* when he forwarded it to the printers for publication, and he quickly claimed that they had been published without his knowledge or consent. His disclaimers were less than convincing. The American publication of the *Rights of Man* was overseen by men close to Jefferson, chief among them John Beckley, clerk of the House of Representatives and one of the most important Jeffersonian republican operatives of the 1790s. It was Beckley who passed Paine's work along to Madison and Jefferson and arranged to have it republished by

Samuel Harrison Smith, future editor of the *National Intelligencer,* the official voice of Jefferson's administration after 1800, and Benjamin Franklin Bache, who was corresponding with Jefferson at that very moment about plans to make his *General Advertiser* a more effective political newspaper. It is hard to imagine any of these men publishing such a controversial preface by such a powerful patron without telling him and securing his tacit consent. One sign they had done so was the inclusion of Jefferson's inflammatory foreword in Smith's second Philadelphia edition of the *Rights of Man.*[37]

Whatever the exact circumstances surrounding its publication, Jefferson's foreword was a brilliant act of political appropriation, immediately giving Paine's work, which was most logically read as a ringing endorsement of American political institutions, a critical and polemical edge. And the target of his remarks was plain to all. While Jefferson maintained a discreet silence in public and privately professed his innocence, John Adams accurately observed that the foreword was "generally considered as a direct and open personal attack upon me." "The Question every where was What Heresies are intended by the Secretary of State?" fumed Adams, and "the Answer in the Newspapers was, The Vice Presidents notions of a limited Monarchy, an hereditary Government of King and Lords, with only elective commons." Jefferson's foreword, he complained, had skillfully hit its mark and "opperated as an Hue and Cry to all my Ennemies and Rivals."[38]

This "Hue and Cry" only increased in volume when a series of essays defending Adams appeared in Benjamin Russell's *Columbian Centinel* in June 1791. Widely reprinted and instantly attributed to Adams himself, the "Publicola" essays were actually composed by his son, John Quincy Adams, and their primary target was not the author of the *Rights of Man* but "the gentleman who has stood it sponsor in this country," Thomas Jefferson. As John Quincy Adams realized, Jefferson's foreword had transformed Paine's *Rights of Man* from a critique of counterrevolutionary politics in Europe into a critique of American politics, encouraging Paine's readers and admirers to draw invidious parallels between the politics of the United States and of revolutionary Europe. Jefferson's charges of "political heresy," argued the young Adams, were intended to make the *Rights of Man* a "Papal Bull of infallible virtue" with which to measure republican orthodoxy. And yet, as he pointed out, Paine's ideas about government clashed with widely held and well-tested principles of American constitutionalism, principles recently enshrined in the federal Constitution.[39] Adams's defense of American constitutionalism provoked a furious public response. Jefferson sent twenty-five published attacks on Publicola to his friend Paine and assured him that the newspapers were filled with a "swarm of anti-publicolas." The Boston *Independent Chronicle* devoted its entire front page for the next four months to reprinting the *Rights of Man* as an antidote to Publicola and published a series of savage attacks on John Adams and those who "sigh for monarchy and pant after aristoc-racy." Andrew Brown, editor of the Philadelphia *Federal Gazette*, applauded the fact that "an host of enlightened writers have arisen, in every part of the United States, to oppose the abominable *heresies of Publicola*."[40]

John Quincy Adams was astounded by the "torrent of abuse" that his writings unleashed, "not upon their real author nor upon the sentiments they express, but upon a supposed author, and supposed sentiments," and he challenged his critics to provide a single example of his "tendency to recommend either a monarchy or an aristocracy to the citizens of these States." But the debate was not being conducted in such measured, rational terms. Instead, opponents of John Adams seized on the Publicola essays to rehearse once again the political sins of their alleged author and to sound the tocsin about the growth of a domestic aristoc-racy. One measure of their success was the response of Federalist editors like John Fenno and Benjamin Russell, who were sympathetic to Adams. Although Fenno reprinted the Publicola essays in his *Gazette of the United States* and denounced the attacks on the vice president as sheer "Toryism," he was careful not to side too openly with Publicola and to provide readers with both sides of the debate.[41] Even more revealing was an editorial in Russell's *Columbian Centinel* in early July. "Aristocracy," the writer assured his readers, "is in deep and rapid decline":

> In the example of the United States, the world has seen, that the energy and dignity of government, may be combined with the just and equal Rights of Men. Power ought ever to spring from the People....the genuine principles of open and magnanimous Republicanism is every day growing more amiable and sal-utary. In this establishment, the annihilation of jealous Democracy as well as Aristocracy will be seen—and in their destruction, the world shall rejoice.[42]

The editorialist's struggle to accommodate and dismiss anti-aristocratic rheto-ric, to incorporate Paine's egalitarianism while deploring "jealous Democracy," reveals clearly the pressure exerted on the terms of political debate by the *Rights of Man*.

The most obvious victim of this debate was Vice President Adams, once again vilified in the press as an agent of aristocracy and, according to Edmund Randolph, rendered "irredeemable in public opinion." By contrast, Jefferson's political repu-tation was greatly enhanced. His political views, observed James Monroe, "if they had been previously question'd, are made known as well by the short note prefixt to Paines pamphlet, as a volume could do it," and he was now clearly identified in the public mind as a friend to the "rights of man" and a champion of republi-can ideas. Alexander Hamilton, who thought Adams was foolish to have "stirred the question" in the first place, tried to contain the controversy by discouraging other Federalists from attacking Jefferson. As he realized, although Adams was the ostensible target of Jefferson's political offensive, its principal target was the government. A few critics of the administration were already claiming that it was under aristocratic control, and if Jefferson and his allies in the press could persuade the public to see disagreements about federal policy as part of a larger struggle between republicanism and aristocracy, they would claim a critical political victory.[43] One small sign that Hamilton's fears were not misplaced is in the memoirs of Jonathan Roberts. He was nineteen when the *Rights of Man* was published and recalled reading it as a political awakening. "It's [*sic*] perusal," he wrote,

> broke up every tolerance for Kings, & old political institutions.... There remain'd in the country, a strong leaven of partiality for a policy of casts, and classes. [T]he rights of man (so Paine call'd his Book) had not less effect, in turning the popular feelings towards a free representative government, than his Common sense, had in severing those ties, that bound us to the English Crown.

In the next passage of his memoir, Roberts recalled that Paine's work appeared at the same time as Philip Freneau "establish'd a Democratic Paper, call'd the National Gazette." Like the *Rights of Man*, Freneau's paper had a profound impact on Roberts and his brother: "Our Democratic feelings were thus confirm'd and strengthen'd, & my Brother & I stood in the first rank of opposition, to the high ton'd measures of the Federal and State governments." Roberts later became a Jeffersonian republican senator in the Pennsylvania legislature.[44]

Reading Paine's *Rights of Man* also had an energizing effect on Philip Freneau. Since returning to the country in 1790, he had been editing Francis Childs's *Daily Advertiser* in New York, but although he gave the newspaper a more lively and radical editorial tone, most of his own contributions consisted of light satirical verse ("Nanny, the Philadelphia House Maid, to Nabby, Her Friend in New-York") that avoided politics altogether. The occasional foray into political verse was almost equally disengaged. *On the American and French Revolutions*, which praised Louis XVI as "the generous Prince that made our cause his own," was flat and uninspired rather than stirring and revolutionary. Perhaps Freneau, who was now thirty-eight years old and had been out of the country for almost a decade, was distracted by his upcoming marriage to Eleanor Forman. His political ennui only increased after the federal government moved from New York to Philadelphia in late 1790, and as subscriptions to the *Daily Advertiser* fell, he made plans to retire to New Jersey, began work on a new poem called *The Rising Empire*, and issued proposals for his own newspaper, the *Monmouth Gazette*. Then he read the *Rights of Man* and began to publish it in the *Daily Advertiser*. He recorded the dramatic impact of Paine's work in "Lines Occasioned by Reading Mr. Paine's RIGHTS of MAN." The first line of the poem,

Wha Wants Me, I Am Ready & Willing to Offer My Services to Any Nation or People under Heaven Who Are Desirous of Liberty & Equality. Unidentified artist, published by S. W. Fores, London, 1792. Thomas Paine, author of the *Rights of Man*, as the great anarchist, atheist, and advocate of popular rebellion. His work had a profound impact on Philip Freneau and the entire United States during the 1790s. Courtesy of the Library of Congress.

"Thus briefly sketch'd the sacred Rights of Man," sounds as if it was composed right after Freneau set the book down:

> *Rous'd* by the *reason* of his manly page,
> Once more shall *Paine* a listening world engage;
> From reason's source, a bold reform he brings,
> By raising up mankind he pulls down kings,
> Who, source of discord, patrons of all wrong,
> On blood and murder, have been fed too long:
> Hid from the world, and tutor'd to be base,
> The curse, the scourge, the ruin of our race.

The anti-monarchism of the poem contrasted sharply with his recent eulogy to Louis XVI and expressed a new sense of political purpose and determination:

> *Columbia*, hail!—immortal be thy reign;
> Without a king we till the fertile plain....
> So shall our nation, form'd on Reason's plan,
> Remain the guardian of the Rights of Man,
> A vast republic, fam'd thro' every clime,
> *Without a king, to see the end of time!*

From this moment forward, Freneau moved slowly but surely toward a central role in American partisan politics.[45]

The man who encouraged this movement was Thomas Jefferson. Still on the lookout for a reliable newspaper editor after abandoning John Fenno's *Gazette of the United States* in late 1790, Jefferson approached Freneau in February 1791, offering him the post of clerk of foreign languages at the Department of State. Avoiding any reference to newspapers, Jefferson's letter was a classic example of political circumspection. Probably aware that Freneau was planning to leave New York anyway (his plans for the *Monmouth Gazette* had just been published), Jefferson confessed that the position of clerk paid only $250 a year, but assured him that the post

> gives so little to do as not to interfere with any other calling the person may chuse, which would not absent him from the seat of government. I was told a few days ago that it might perhaps be convenient to you to accept it—if so, it is at your service.[46]

Of course, the "other calling" Jefferson had in mind was a newspaper. To Jefferson's surprise and chagrin, the irascible, middle-aged seafarer, poet, and editor was far from grateful for this "present," which he probably felt beneath his dignity, and Freneau responded to the offer "in dudgeon, as striking at his independence." After writing "a very insulting answer, which he showed to Mr. Childs," the proprietor of the *Daily Advertiser*, Freneau revised his draft, graciously declining the "generous, unsollicited proposal" of the secretary of state and announcing his plans to publish a weekly gazette in New Jersey. For the time being, Jefferson turned his attention to journalists closer at hand.[47]

Jefferson's association with Freneau and the foundation of the *National Gazette* created great controversy in the 1790s and has remained controversial ever since. Although he often expressed disdain for the press (a disdain demonstrated by his shabby treatment of Republican journalists in the 1790s), to a politician as perceptive and skillful as Jefferson, newspapers were an essential political tool. In fact, with the exception of Hamilton, who was a tireless newspaper polemicist, no other major politician of the period worked more closely with the press, and no politician was more careful to cover his tracks. When his relationship with the *National Gazette* became a political issue in late 1792, Jefferson was evasive, informing Washington that, despite his sympathy for Freneau's republican principles, he had done no more than pass along copies of the *Gazette de Leyde*, vehemently denying ("I can protest in the presence of heaven...") that he had played any part in the newspaper after it began publication. Partly to protect Jefferson and partly to protect his own reputation as an independent editor, Freneau also played down the relationship between the two men, claiming the *National Gazette* received no patronage from Jefferson.[48]

But no other newspaper of the period "received such powerful political patronage as the National Gazette." Jefferson claimed that his support for the *National Gazette* was inspired by his desire to support an editor who "looked only to the chastisement of the aristocratical and monarchical writers, and not to any criticisms on the proceedings of the government." But as the outcry against Publicola demonstrated, there was no lack of editors willing to denounce "the doctrines & discourses circulated in favor of Monarchy and Arastocracy" that so concerned Jefferson, especially in Philadelphia. Eleazar Oswald's *Independent Gazetteer*, Benjamin Franklin Bache's *General Advertiser*, Andrew Brown's *Federal Gazette*, Francis Bailey's *Freeman's Journal*, and John Dunlap's *American Daily Advertiser* were all reliable, republican newspapers. What these newspapers lacked was not hostility to the "doctrines & discourses" of aristocracy, but a sense of urgency about the flaws of government policy and the growing influence of Alexander Hamilton. When Jefferson approached Freneau in February 1791, he was looking for an aggressive, polemical newspaper that would provide a catalyst for the organization and unification of republican opposition to the Washington administration.[49]

But enticing Freneau to Philadelphia was not easy. After his initial rebuff, Jefferson turned for help to Freneau's old college roommate, James Madison. Madison, who regarded Freneau as a "man of genius" and "Republican principles," initially persuaded him to relinquish his plans in New Jersey and accept the job at the Department of State. But Freneau quickly changed his mind. "We have been trying to get another *weekly* or *half-weekly* [newspaper] set up," Jefferson wrote with exasperation to Thomas Mann Randolph in May 1791, "so that it might go through the States and furnish a *Whig vehicle* of intelligence. We hoped at one time to have persuaded Freneau to set up here, but failed." Still, Jefferson and Madison refused to give up on Freneau, and they met privately with him in New York during their controversial "northern journey" through the middle states and New England in the summer of 1791.[50] But despite their persistence, they could not persuade him to cooperate. Somewhat hopelessly, Madison approached Freneau again in July, this time accompanied by John Beckley and Henry Lee, and after a further series of hesitations, he at last agreed to establish a newspaper in Philadelphia. On August 4, he wrote to Jefferson announcing his intention to set up a "National Paper" in the capital, enclosing proposals for the paper, which he asked Jefferson to "glance your eye over, previous to its being printed." On August 16, Jefferson appointed him as clerk for foreign languages in the Department of State, and on August 25 a prospectus for the *National Gazette* was published in Francis Childs's *Daily Advertiser*.[51]

What explains Freneau's hesitancy and his subsequent change of mind? According to one biographer, he may have been struggling with his literary conscience, anxious that accepting Jefferson's patronage would undermine his independence. But the chief stumbling block was probably money. Freneau had no capital to invest in a newspaper, and with a wife and child to support (his first child, Helena, was born on September 20, 1791), he needed more than the meager annual salary of a clerk to survive in Philadelphia. Aware of this problem, Jefferson had promised additional patronage, "the perusal of all my letters of foreign intelligence and all foreign newspapers; the publication of all proclamations and other public notices within my department, and the printing of the laws." But Freneau was probably still reluctant to launch a political newspaper without secure financial support. It was Francis Childs, Freneau's employer and the owner of the *Daily Advertiser*, who broke this deadlock. As Freneau told Madison in July, he was willing to "sacrifice other considerations, and transfer myself to Philadelphia" if he could get "Mr. Childs to be connected with me on a tolerable plan." And his ability to persuade Childs and his partner, John Swaine, to underwrite the cost of publishing the *National Gazette* and to bear all losses with "myself in the mean time, to be considered as a third partner in that paper" was critical to the success of the entire venture.[52]

Why were Childs and Swaine willing to finance the *National Gazette*? Profit was an unlikely motive. As an experienced printer and publisher, Childs knew that political newspapers rarely made money, and Freneau virtually guaranteed that the paper would run at a loss by promising to limit advertisements to a single page. Ideological motives may have been significant, although Childs had a reputation as a political trimmer. Alexander Hamilton thought the explanation for Childs's support was simple: Childs, who was a "very cunning fellow" in Hamilton's view, was paid directly by Jefferson and Beckley to support the *National Gazette*. But the most likely explanation for the close involvement of Childs and Swaine was their virtual monopoly of congressional printing, a monopoly they possessed at the pleasure of two men, the clerk of the House, John Beckley, and the secretary of state, Thomas Jefferson. According to Douglas Southall Freeman, after Freneau moved to Philadelphia to start the *National Gazette*, Childs and Swaine received a "considerable share of Jefferson's departmental printing" as well as the printing of Congress, a privilege they preserved until Beckley was removed as clerk of the House by Federalists in 1797.[53]

It's unlikely there was any formal agreement among Freneau, Childs, Swaine, and Republican leaders to finance the *National Gazette* in return for government patronage, but Freneau suggested that there may have been an informal agreement. In a letter to Jefferson explaining his decision to move to Philadelphia, he wrote: "Upon recently talking over the matter with Mr. Madison and Col. Lee, I have proposed a concern (which they have accepted) with Messieurs Child[s] and Swain[e] in a press at the seat of Government." Although Freneau's statement is ambiguous, it suggests that his partnership with Childs and Swaine may have required the agreement of Madison and Lee. Perhaps they assured the New York–based printers that they would not lose out to rivals when the federal government moved to Philadelphia. Perhaps they promised more patronage. At any rate, when Freneau left New Jersey and arrived in Philadelphia in September 1791, John Swaine was there already, busily setting up a new printing shop for government work and the *National Gazette*. It was a perfect arrangement from Freneau's point of view, leaving him free to edit the newspaper without any of the financial burdens and printing problems usually experienced by eighteenth-century printer-editors. As he later admitted, the *National Gazette* would have sunk fast without the "complaisance and good will of Messrs. Childs and Swain[e], who furnished me with the necessary sums for carrying it on."[54]

Freneau's arrangement with Childs and Swaine at last gave Jefferson the newspaper he needed to organize opposition to Hamilton's policies, although this was not immediately evident to the public. When the *National Gazette* first appeared on October 31, 1791, its editor's address "To the Public" was a conventional affair, promising readers "the most important foreign intelligence," extensive coverage of affairs in Congress, "all decent productions of entertainment in prose and verse," and political essays with a "tendency to promote the general interests of the Union." This innocuous statement was hardly a rallying cry to opponents of the federal government, and Freneau staked out only a slightly more political position a few days later when he promised to support, "as far as a newspaper can with propriety be supposed to support, the great principles upon which the American revolution was founded, a faithful adherence to which can alone preserve the blessings of liberty to this extensive empire."[55]

In keeping with these timid declarations, for the first few months of its existence the *National Gazette* was uncontroversial, and Freneau printed a great deal of material from other newspapers, a clear sign that he hadn't yet established a voice of his own in political debate. Presenting himself as a conventional editorial arbiter, he

National Gazette

By *PHILIP FRENEAU.*

VOL. I. MONDAY, OCTOBER 31, 1791. NUMB. 1.

TO THE PUBLIC.

THE Editor of the *National Gazette* having found his proposals for establishing a paper of this kind attended with all the success he could reasonably expect, considering the short time that has elapsed since his first acquainting the public with his design, takes this opportunity in his first number, briefly to remind his subscribers, and others, of the plan upon which he originally intended, and still proposes to proceed.

The *National Gazette* shall be published on the *Monday* and *Thursday* mornings of every week, in the city of Philadelphia, and sent to the more distant subscribers by the most ready and regular modes of conveyance. Such persons, resident in the city of Philadelphia, as incline to become subscribers, shall be supplied early on the mornings of publication, at their own houses. The price will be *three* dollars a year; the first half-year's amount to be paid in three months from the time of subscribing, and for every payment after, in the same proportion.

The paper shall contain, among other interesting particulars, the most important news, foreign and domestic, principally from the British, French, and Dutch newspapers, a channel that has hitherto, but also from original communications, with which the Editor may have an opportunity of receiving from the usual authentic sources relative to the affairs of Europe.

The department for domestic news will be rendered as complete and satisfactory as possible...

Nortb-Carolina—John Steele, and Hugh Williams.

Soutb-Carolina—Daniel Shays, William Smith, and Thomas Tyler Tucker.

Georgia—Francis Willis.

CONGRESS

HOUSE OF REPRESENTATIVES, OF THE UNITED STATES.

MONDAY, *October 24th, 1791.*

TUESDAY, *October 25.*

published articles both critical and sympathetic toward the federal government, including Hamilton's entire *Report on Manufactures*. His response to General Arthur St. Clair's defeat by Native American forces in late 1791 is a good example of his early restraint. The humiliation of St. Clair's army sparked an angry public debate about the leniency of federal Indian policy, raising a chorus of demands for retaliation led by Freneau's old classmate Hugh Henry Brackenridge. Jefferson also favored giving Native Americans a "thorough drubbing." But rather than joining this outcry against the government, Freneau (perhaps restrained by his own sympathy for Native Americans) kept quiet, publishing a number of essays supporting Indian land claims and opposing an escalation of the war. Although the *National Gazette* was open to critics of the government, its editor remained uncommitted, and its readers were left to make up their own minds about political affairs.[56]

Freneau's caution made political sense. His first task as editor of the *National Gazette* was to distinguish his newspaper from the Anti-Federalist politics of the past and to reassure its prospective readers and supporters that it was genuinely nationalist in its outlook and allegiance. The title and format of the paper were designed to appeal to Federalists who were troubled by the drift of government policy but still committed to defending the Constitution and the federal government, and despite the rivalry to the *Gazette of the United States* implied in its title, Fenno greeted the *National Gazette* as a welcome addition to the ranks of the nationalist press.[57] But Freneau faced a tricky balancing act. Determined to forge a new political coalition, Freneau had to appeal to disaffected Federalists, who remained cautious about open opposition to the Washington administration, and former Anti-Federalists, who remained suspicious of the policies of a powerful federal state. This was no easy task, and the challenge that faced Freneau when he began to publish the *National Gazette* in late 1791 was to forge a party identity that united rather than divided critics of Hamilton's economic policies. Although the need to organize an opposition party, the animating idea behind the *National Gazette*, was already clear to Freneau and his political allies, the idea of the Republican Party had yet to crystallize, and until it did so they remained partisans in search of a party identity.

An essay by Madison on "Consolidation," published in December 1791, illustrated the difficulties that confronted them.[58] Often interpreted as an abstract dissertation on liberty and power in a republican society, Madison's essay was a highly practical effort to appropriate the language of consolidation and establish an ideological and rhetorical basis for cooperation between Anti-Federalists and Federalists. Expressing opposition to any further consolidation of power by the federal government, a position likely to appeal to Anti-Federalists, he argued that the best way to prevent such consolidation was to consolidate the "interests and affections" of the people on a national basis, an idea that closely reflected ideas about national character expressed by many Federalists. The idea of creating a national consensus, which Madison had dismissed as impossible in the *Federalist Papers*, was now resurrected as the only way to preempt "new and dangerous prerogatives from the executive" and to permit the people to "consolidate their defense of the public liberty." "Here then is a proper object presented," he wrote,

> both to those who are most jealously attached to the separate authority reserved to the states, and to those who are more inclined to contemplate the people of America in the light of one nation. Let the former continue to watch against every encroachment, which might lead to a gradual consolidation of the states into one government. Let the latter employ their utmost zeal, by eradicating local prejudices and mistaken rivalships, to consolidate the affairs of the states into one harmonious interest.[59]

This creative but unrealistic division of labor, which evaded rather than transcended the ideological division between Anti-Federalists and Federalists, was unlikely to provide the basis for a new political coalition, but it revealed clearly the political problem that confronted and preoccupied Madison.

Madison's argument also provided a raison d'être for the *National Gazette*. If the preservation of liberty depended on the consolidation of "public opinion," then the consolidation of public opinion depended on the circulation of newspapers. This conception of the press as an agent of national integration was one that Madison shared with many Federalists, including John Fenno, but it jarred uneasily with his famous contribution to the *Federalist Papers*. In *Federalist*, no. 10, he had argued eloquently that political conflict and the development of political parties or factions were an unavoidable part of all free societies. But unlike Hobbes, who believed the only solution to this problem was a strong state, or "Leviathan," and unlike classical republicans, who believed the only remedy for such conflict was the homogeneity of a small state, Madison argued that it was precisely the clash of interests in civil society that made possible the creation and preservation of an extensive republic.

Now, as he tried to find a political formula to bring together critics of the government, he fell back on conventional republican arguments about consensus and the creation of "one harmonious interest," invoking the power of the press to square the circle. Large republics, he argued, were possible not because the clash of interests in civil society prevented the emergence of a tyranny of the majority but because the circulation of newspapers created an identity of interest. "A circulation of newspapers through the entire body of the people," he wrote, "is equivalent to a contraction of territorial limits, and is favorable to liberty, where these may be too extensive."[60]

Madison's fertile political imagination enabled him to rework the rhetoric of consolidation and move beyond the parochial jealousies of Anti-Federalism, but his arguments sounded forced and full of unresolved tension, and despite his own impeccable Federalist credentials, they also sounded distinctly Anti-Federalist. Most of his early essays for the *National Gazette* emphasized the need to keep "every portion of power within its proper limits" and to preserve the constitutional balance between national and state governments, and although he also emphasized the importance of creating a national "public opinion," his nuanced and creative approach to consolidation easily degenerated into more conventional alarm about the perils of consolidation as "the high road to monarchy."[61]

Other writers for the *National Gazette* struck a more explicitly Anti-Federalist tone from the start. "Caius," for example, one of the first writers in the *National Gazette* to attack Hamilton's policies as anti-republican, was mainly concerned that the "consolidating idea of assumption" would "destroy the existence and independence of the states," and despite calling for a return to the "first principles of the constitution," he found it impossible to conceal his ambivalence about the federal government and his sense of alienation from its architects. "The government they have so recently reared," he warned, "however beautiful in theory, is calculated in its execution, to produce the ambitious sacrifice of the many to the aggrandizement of the few." In a series of articles that one historian calls the "earliest telling blow against Hamilton's influence," "Brutus" also condemned Hamilton's system of public finance for fostering a spirit of speculation that was intended to "aggrandize the few and the wealthy" and undermine republican government, but his main concern was that a "consolidation of the monied interest" would "encrease the energy and power of the general government." Hamilton's efforts to destroy the "little importance left to the state governments," he argued, confirmed the worst fears of those who had opposed the federal Constitution and "who prefer living under a confederation of free republics."[62]

By early 1792, Freneau had abandoned his initial neutrality and started to attack Hamilton and the Washington administration openly, but the problem of appealing to both Federalists and Anti-Federalists was still unresolved, and it was tempting, even for nationalists like Madison, to fall back on well-worn Anti-Federalist arguments about the dangers of federal consolidation. But as long as writers for the *National Gazette* continued to operate within a political framework defined by the issues of Federalism and Anti-Federalism, the message of the newspaper remained confused and defensive and its political effectiveness limited. Freneau was well aware of the problem and tried to fend off accusations of Anti-Federalism by occasional expressions of loyalty to the union and the "general government." But the constant attacks on consolidation and the political ambivalence of his contributors, who seemed unsure whether to attack Federalism or claim it as their own, made it hard to avoid such accusations. Exasperated by the effort, Freneau even flirted with embracing the label Anti-Federalist. In "Modern Explanation of a Few Terms Commonly Misunderstood," he defined an "Anti-Federalist" as a "republican of seventeen hundred and seventy six," and "Federalists" as "Stock-jobbers, scrip-mongers, and paper mongers of almost every description, exclusively." But although this defense of Anti-Federalism may have briefly amused Freneau, it was not a solution to the political problem he faced: how to forge a nationalist opposition to the federal government.[63]

There were some signs of progress. Caius, for example, denounced the "Myrmidons of speculation" created by Hamilton's policies, while Brutus condemned these policies for depressing "the great body of the yeomanry who are the ornament & support of their country." An article "On the Origin of Nobility" claimed that all hereditary power had its origins in wealth and that great accumulations of wealth inevitably paved the way for the introduction of hereditary power, an argument also developed by George Logan in a series of essays addressed "To the Yeomanry of the United States," which was reprinted from Eleazar Oswald's *Independent Gazetteer*. "The American aristocrats," wrote Logan, "have failed in their attempt to establish titles of distinction by law," but their efforts to achieve this goal indirectly "ought to be watched with the most jealous eye." But for all their alarm about aristocracy, most of these writers continued to emphasize the federal-state issues that constituted the fault line in their own political coalition, and as a result political commentary in the *National Gazette* was characterized by a confusing and dissonant array of voices. Freneau had not yet figured out how to move beyond the arguments that had filled the opposition press since 1787: that the Constitution and the federal government threatened the autonomy and sovereignty of the states. And until he found a way to do so, the *National Gazette* remained a political irrelevance.[64]

Shortly after the first essay by Caius was published in the *National Gazette*, Madison sent Freneau another essay on the subject of "Parties." Suddenly, the

Madison of the *Federalist Papers* reappeared. "In every political society," he wrote, "parties are unavoidable," arising "out of the nature of things" from the clash of interests within civil society. This clash of interests could be minimized by ensuring the political equality of all citizens and by preventing the growth of sharp inequalities of wealth, but conflict could never be completely eliminated. Indeed, argued Madison, the only effective way to manage party conflict was to make "one party a check on the other," which he called the "great art of politicians." Madison's essay, which is often interpreted as a warning against the dangers of party, was actually a declaration of political opposition. But although it announced the emergence of an opposition party and provided it with a theoretical justification, Madison was not yet able to define this party clearly nor endow it with any specific content. But he made a few suggestions. Since political parties were the product of "natural distinctions" within civil society, he argued, it was important not to increase these distinctions by encouraging the "inequality of property" and "an unmerited accumulation of riches," nor to create what he called the "artificial distinctions" of "kings, and nobles, and plebians." "This is as little the voice of reason," he wrote, "as it is that of republicanism." The implication of Madison's argument was clear: Hamilton's policies were encouraging the growth of economic and "artificial distinctions," and it was the duty of all genuine "republicans" to oppose them.[65]

During the spring of 1792, such arguments acquired new force. The rapid expansion of the economy since 1789 and the introduction of Hamilton's policies to fund the national debt had greatly increased the value of government securities and triggered a speculative boom. This economic boom, in turn, created widespread concern about the growth of economic inequality and, more generally, the impact of increasing economic prosperity on traditional social relations. Had "inequality in property," wondered one writer in a Boston paper, "ever before so suddenly took place in the world?" Surveying the frenzied financial scene from New York in the summer of 1791, Madison deplored the "daring depravity of the times" and predicted that "the stockjobbers will become the praetorian band of the Government—at once its tool & its tyrant." His fears about the political results of excessive speculation and his belief that this speculation had its source in Hamilton's economic policies were widely shared. And when the bottom dropped out of the securities market in February 1792 and stock prices fell precipitously, widespread anxiety and alarm exploded into full-blown financial panic, providing fertile soil for opponents of Hamilton's policies.[66]

Unfortunately for Hamilton, the central figure in this financial panic was his close friend and former assistant secretary of the treasury, William Duer. Duer, who lived a life of epic speculation and conspicuous consumption, symbolized the growing wealth of urban financial and mercantile elites in postrevolutionary

America. At the height of the speculative fever in December 1791, he and Alexander Macomb, a prosperous New York merchant, had formed a secret partnership to trade in government securities, and when the value of these securities suddenly fell, Duer was forced to suspend payments on debts of about a half million dollars. On March 23, 1792, he was imprisoned for debt, and his failure, followed closely by the failure of his partner, Macomb, precipitated a major financial crisis. Hamilton, who scrambled to restore public confidence in the financial markets, was stunned by the scale of the disaster, raging against those who had gambled with the "distresses of their fellow citizens." " 'Tis time," he declared, "there should be a line of separation between honest Men & Knaves." The problem for Hamilton was that many people regarded him as one of the knaves. Duer's dealings had brought the entire financial system "into odium," and as its principal author and a friend and patron of Duer, Hamilton was politically vulnerable, a vulnerability his critics were quick to expose and exploit.[67]

The financial crisis of March 1792 was a turning point in Freneau's conduct of the *National Gazette*. By April, the newspaper was filled with denunciations of "blood-sucking Brokers" and economic policies "which tend to raise the few into splendid opulence, and to generate monarchical and corrupt principles and habits." As the fallout from Duer's failure spread, Freneau shifted his attention from the issue of federal consolidation to the aristocratic consequences of Hamilton's funding system, infusing the *National Gazette* with a new sense of vitality and purpose. Once again, the clearest expression of this shift in strategy came from Madison's pen. In an article entitled "The Union: Who Are Its Real Friends?" he emphatically laid claim to the nationalist mantle, abandoning his previous efforts to appropriate the language of consolidation and arguing that it was the supporters of the federal government who "avow or betray principles of monarchy and aristocracy, in opposition to the republican principles of the Union, and the republican spirit of the people." This sharp distinction between the advocates of aristocracy and loyal republicans swiftly became the defining characteristic of the *National Gazette*, and writers in the newspaper assailed Hamilton's funding system for creating an American aristocracy and undermining popular sovereignty rather than the sovereignty of the states.[68]

Anti-aristocratic language resonated powerfully with Americans (both rich and poor) who were dismayed by the pace of economic growth and the emergence of a capitalist wage-labor economy in the late eighteenth century. But despite its radical and iconoclastic tone, the class correlates of anti-aristocratic rhetoric were never clear or predictable. Most critics of Hamilton's policies either ignored issues of economic inequality or subsumed them within a broader critique of economic corruption and the threat this posed to independent republican citizenship. Such rhetoric was quite compatible with contempt for the dependent poor, and on more than one occasion such views found expression in the pages of the *National Gazette*. But Freneau himself generally struck a more egalitarian and class-conscious note, distinguishing not only between the few and the many, between aristocrats and republicans, but also between the rich and the poor. In "Sentiments of a Republican," for example, he argued that Hamilton's funding system had introduced many evils:

> But the most alarming one is, it has produced so much inequality in point of property among our citizens, as to endanger the safety of our government. The most barefaced efforts have been made to substitute, in the room of our equal republic, a baneful monarchy in our country; and it is too evident these efforts originate with those states, and with those individuals, who are most interested in the funding system.[69]

Like Madison, Freneau argued that Hamilton wished to revive hereditary government in the United States. But unlike Madison and other political moderates, he expressed genuine concern about poverty and the political rights of the poor. Hamilton's financial policies not only laid the basis for the corruption of political life, but created economic inequality: "Poverty in the country—luxury in the capitals."[70]

Freneau's emphasis on economic inequality gave his critique of Hamiltonian finance a distinctly radical edge. Comparing Hamilton to British prime minister Robert Walpole and condemning his policies as a "servile imitation of British systems of finance" quickly became a cliché among opposition writers. Walpole was the architect of a vast system of ministerial patronage and "Old Corruption" in mid-eighteenth-century England, and Hamilton's critics accused him of grafting "all the weaknesses, vices, and infirmities of the decayed and expiring constitution of Britain" onto the robust, young, republican Constitution of the United States. According to them, Hamilton's goal was to establish a British system of ministerial government and install himself as first minister, using his financial patronage and influence to subvert the legislative independence of Congress. The "corruptions of the British funding system," argued "A Citizen of Philadelphia," were the "surest mode of preparing our country for British monarchy and aristocracy." Although Freneau shared these fears, he also drew attention to the role that the government's economic policies played in creating a society of vast economic inequality in Britain, where the desperation of poverty-stricken plebians was controlled by a penal code remarkable for its "frequency of human butchery." Although no counterpart to an English plebian class yet existed in the United States, Freneau warned that Hamilton's policies would inevitably produce such a class by excluding the poor from political power and eroding the government's capacity to ensure that the "division of property be made as nearly equal as possible." "Aristocracy," wrote one angry correspondent to the *National Gazette*, was a "hydra which is ever grasping to devour the defenseless poor man's rights."[71]

Money had already established a strong influence over public life, and if Hamilton had his way, Freneau stated bluntly, "money will be put under the direction of the government, and the government under the direction of money." Deeply disturbed by the spread of commercial values in American society, he was even more disturbed by the way such values had begun to seep into American public life. In a country where all men were "constitutionally equal," he argued, wealth was no distinguishing virtue, and "he who has no other quality to recommend him ought to be despised even in common life." But this was particularly true in public life and politics, where wealth should "have no weight in the scale of a representative":

> When we see men possessed of *this qualification* unacquainted with any other, stalking forth and offering themselves as *proper objects* of the confidence of the people, I would ask what heart throbs not within? who can contain himself?

"Let us sweep the legislative floors of such vermin," he thundered, and drive out of public life the speculators, stockbrokers, and bankers "who devour liberty in the bud, and suck the vitals of the honest industrious farmers, merchants, and tradesmen." The temple of the Constitution, he declared, had been "converted into a temple of mammon," and it was imperative for Americans to unite and "purge the tabernacle of all contamination by stock-jobbers."[72]

By the spring of 1792, the battle lines between republicanism and aristocracy were sharply drawn in the *National Gazette*. An editorial in late April argued that "two parties" had now "shewn themselves in the doings of the new government," one of which saw funding the national debt as a way to concentrate "vast wealth in the hands of the few," undermine the Constitution, and "divide and rule the many," and the other of which regarded the debt as "unjust and unrepublican." In the satirical "Plan for a Nobility in the United States," Freneau argued that the only obstacle now facing the friends of hereditary government in the United States was a dearth of noblemen. To overcome this scarcity, he proposed creating enough nobles to govern a "poor plebian country" by granting each financial speculator worth over $150,000 a title in one of three new orders of nobility: the "Order of the Leech," the "Order of the Golden Fleece," and at the apex of the new social order, the "Order of the Scrip."[73] In an essay published on the Fourth of July, he summarized for readers the political developments of the previous three years. Since 1789, Freneau argued, Hamilton had carefully prepared the soil for the planting of an American aristocracy. His "PUBLIC DEBT" had spawned legions of tax gatherers, a standing army, a "great incorporated bank," and a moneyed interest, "the readiest material that can be found for an hereditary aristocratic order." His goal now was to disguise his handiwork and to sow seeds of discord among ordinary Americans that would create "artificial divisions" and conceal

> the true and natural one, existing in all societies between the few who are always impatient of political equality, and the many who can never rise above it…between the general mass of the people, attached to their republican government and republican interests, and the chosen band devoted to monarchy and mammon.[74]

This "true and natural" division of society into the few and the many, the aristocracy and the people, the rich and the poor, had been concealed by Hamilton's political machinations and a false sense of economic prosperity, which had lulled Americans to sleep and given speculators a chance to forge "the chains of monarchy and aristocracy for them." But now that Hamilton's speculative bubble had burst, Americans were waking from their slumbers and were ready to inaugurate "A New Aera" when "Republicanism flourishes, and is again in fashion."[75]

Freneau's campaign against Hamilton and aristocracy caught supporters of the federal government off guard. John Fenno was dismayed that "the word republicanism seems to be snatched up as a weapon to knock an adversary down," and although he defended Hamilton's republicanism, he was put on the defensive by Freneau's aggressive tactics. In an editorial in the *Gazette of the United States* in late April, he tried to turn the charges of aristocracy back on the opposition. "What would a Frenchman think of a man who vilifies the National Assembly and their doings[?]" he demanded. "[W]ould he hesitate to say, that such a man was at heart an aristocrat, and an enemy to the revolution?" Attacks on the government had now gone well beyond legitimate opposition to men and measures to indict the "frame of government itself," and Fenno questioned the sincerity of critics who preached about republicanism and tried to "write down a republican government." Opposition writers portrayed the government as a "despotism," filling the newspapers with "licentious invectives as if they were aimed at the administration of Turkey or Tippoo Saib." Perhaps such critics could not accept a government "freely chosen" by the people, he speculated, reminding his fellow citizens that they had elected the federal government with their own votes. Those who were inclined to "chatter about the partizans of kingly power, and affect to consider the plan of subverting our republican government and free institutions as well matured," he wrote, deserved nothing but ridicule.[76]

But ridiculous or not, the charges of the opposition had to be answered. One way to do so was suggested by the *American Mercury* in Hartford, Connecticut. Parodying Freneau's own poetic inclinations, the editors described him as "Sinbat the author, captain, printer, tar, / The newsboy's poet and the dog of war, / The blackguard's pattern, and the great man's fool, / The fawning parasite, and the minion's tool," a clear reference to Jefferson's patronage of the *National Gazette*. An essay by "Crito" in the *Gazette of the United States* took a similar tack, condemning Freneau's slanders on the Washington administration and hinting that behind him lurked a political "junto" conspiring to overturn the government.[77] Although this junto believed that Americans were the "weak heedless dupes of a few, who have tricked them out of their property and liberties," in reality it was they who conjured up "evil spirits from the dark to haunt the sick imagination." "There never was a more barefaced attempt to impose on mankind," argued Crito, than the idea "that an aristocratic junto exists in the United States." "The Constitution of the United States," insisted Fenno, "is republican":

> [I]t is founded on the people, the only legitimate source of power—the friends of this Constitution are principled in republicanism—they imbibed republican sentiments with their mother's milk—they were nurtured and educated in the doctrines of equal rights and equal liberty—and yet so consistent is the junto, that they accuse those men who have fought to establish the freedom of this country (for these are the men who compose the administration of the government) as calumniators of republicanism; as agents to a faction (sometimes it is a faction itself) who are "paving the way to hereditary monarchy on the sly destruction of popular government."

"It is hardly possible," he concluded, "to conceive that the authors of such paragraphs can be so weak as to believe what they write." But whether they believed them or not, as Fenno's exasperation showed, their accusations were having an impact on public opinion, and the terms of political debate had shifted decisively in their favor.[78]

Alarmed by this shift, Fenno followed Crito's exploratory foray with a more incendiary attack. On July 25, he published a single paragraph in the *Gazette of the United States*, signed "T.L.," insinuating that Freneau received a salary for his editorial work from an officer of the federal government. "The Editor of the National Gazette," charged its author,

> [r]eceives a salary from the government. Quere—whether this salary is paid him for *translations*, or for *publications*, the design of which is to vilify those to whom the voice of the people has committed the administration of our public affairs—to oppose the measures of the government, and by false insinuations, to disturb the public peace? In common life it is thought ungrateful for a man to bite the hand that puts bread into his mouth; but if the man is hired to do it, the case is altered.

The author of this paragraph was Alexander Hamilton, who deeply resented Freneau's criticism of his conduct at the treasury and correctly believed that

Jefferson, "a man of profound ambition & violent passions," lurked behind him. Characteristically, his first response to Freneau's assault was to write a series of detailed and lengthy "Vindications of the Funding System" that contained veiled attacks on Jefferson and Madison. But shelving these, he decided to publish the T.L. note instead, directly attacking Freneau's editorial integrity and, more obliquely, Jefferson's patronage of the *National Gazette*. As he told Rufus King on the day the T.L. note appeared, "These things ought, in a proper way, to be brought into view."[79]

Hamilton's intervention provides further evidence of Freneau's political impact. Although Washington's position was still unassailable, the former Anti-Federalist governor of New York, George Clinton, had decided to challenge John Adams for the vice presidency in the fall presidential election, making it the first contested presidential election in American history. Rather desperately, Hamilton and Fenno decided that the only way to combat the growing influence of the *National Gazette* was to portray it as a "tool of faction, and the prostituted vehicle of party spleen and opposition" and to expose Jefferson's support for the newspaper. When Freneau retaliated by attacking Fenno's editorial integrity, accusing him of poisoning the "minds of the people" and "receiving emoluments from the government far more lucrative than the salary alluded to," Hamilton (this time, writing as "An American") immediately turned the spotlight on Jefferson. The secretary of state, he wrote, had undertaken "something new in the history of political maneuvers in this country; *a newspaper instituted by a public officer*" whose editor was "pensioned with the public money." Providing a detailed (and reasonably accurate) account of Jefferson's relations with Freneau, he identified him as the patron of the *National Gazette* and demanded his resignation. In response, Freneau published a carefully worded sworn affidavit denying that either "the Secretary of State, or any of his friends" had influenced the conduct of his newspaper, a tactic Hamilton curtly dismissed with the phrase "Facts speak louder than oaths."[80]

Hamilton's "American" essays effectively unmasked the secretary of state, portraying Freneau as Jefferson's pawn and Jefferson himself as a political dissembler who harbored deep reservations about the Constitution and had been "the declared opponent of almost all the important measures which have been devised by the government." But Hamilton's most damaging charge was that Jefferson had orchestrated public opposition to the government in which he served and used his official position to conceal his activities from the public. "As Mr. Jefferson is emulous of being the head of a party," he declared, "let him enjoy all the glory and all the advantage of it." This "virulent assault on Mr. Jefferson" took the opposition by surprise and shaped the terms of the fall election campaign. The "late insidious attack," John Beckley informed Madison, had been carefully calculated "as to time and manner, and is now industriously circulated thro' all the Eastern papers," and its "artful misrepresentation" was having a significant impact on public opinion. Rattled by his boldness, Hamilton's opponents did not regroup until September, when serious efforts to defend Jefferson and discredit Hamilton, spearheaded by Beckley and Madison, finally appeared in the *National Gazette*.[81]

The vice presidential contest gave the opposition another chance to renew its attacks on John Adams as a "decided adversary to republican government," and Adams complained that, in the southern backcountry, the *National Gazette* was "employed with great industry to poison the minds of the people." But Adams was no longer treated as an isolated, eccentric figure, and opposition attacks broadened to include Hamilton and the Washington administration. Significantly, few opposition writers now bothered to claim that they were real Federalists, and Freneau began to use the term "Monarchical Federalism" in the editorial columns of the newspaper. An editorial in early December declared, "The mask is at last torn off from the monarchical party who have, with but too much success, imposed themselves on the public for the sincere friends of our republican constitution." Whatever the outcome of the current election, declared Freneau, it showed that "the name of Federalism" had been assumed by men who saw the Constitution as merely "a promising essay towards well-ordered government; that is to say, as a step towards a government of king, lords and commons." A couple of months later, "Franklin" developed this argument to its logical conclusion, stating that Hamilton's policies had already created a government that "constitutes the essence of monarchy."[82]

Throughout the fall of 1792, Hamilton waged a tireless campaign against the Jeffersonian opposition, aided only by the publication of *The Politicks and Views of a Certain Party Displayed*, an anti-Jeffersonian pamphlet by William Loughton Smith. Even Beckley (with the grudging admiration of one skilled political operative for another) admitted that Hamilton's "efforts direct & indirect are unceasing and extraordinary."[83] Although his influence on public opinion is hard to gauge, the reelection of Adams as vice president in November 1792 suggests that Hamilton had the better of the public debate and "spiked or silenced the cannon of the most effective contributors to the National Gazette." But his campaign against Jefferson came at a cost. Exhausted and possibly constrained by the discovery of his adulterous affair with Mrs. Maria Reynolds in December 1792, he lapsed into silence.[84] His attack on Jefferson had given his opponents a perfect opportunity to portray a hitherto abstract debate about economic policy as a struggle between two men: Jefferson, "the decided opponent of aristocracy, monarchy, hereditary succession, a titled order of nobility, and all the other mock-pageantry of kingly government," and Hamilton, who had "opposed the constitution in the Grand convention, because it was too republican, and advocated the British Monarchy as the perfect standard." As Hamilton himself observed contemptuously, Jefferson now stepped forward as a "plain and simple unambitious republican," a rallying point for public opposition to the aristocratic designs of the treasury secretary. Moreover, Hamilton's attempt to expose Jefferson's political maneuvering allowed opposition writers to blame Hamilton for the descent into the politics of personality. His attacks on Jefferson, they argued, had distracted public attention from serious political debate and undermined political civility. But most alarmingly, Hamilton's personal intervention made it easier for opposition writers to confront the entire administration. "Certain it is," wrote James Monroe to Madison in September, "that the field is open for a general discussion of the measures of the gov[ernmen]t," and he urged Madison to "turn your attention to it."[85]

One week later, Madison published his "A Candid State on Parties" in the *National Gazette*, announcing the existence of a "Republican party" and driving home the nature of domestic party divisions with unprecedented force. While Fenno continued to insist that republicanism was a political term that "excludes all party ideas" and referred to "every friend to the equal rights of man," the Jeffersonian opposition relentlessly politicized the term. One sign that Republican writers were growing more confident about their political identity was their repudiation of the term Anti-Federalist. "It does not appear to me to be a question of federalism or antifederalism," argued Brutus in the *National Gazette*, but of the "Treasury of the United States against the people." Although "the word antifederal will be artfully used to prejudice the uninformed," predicted Freneau,

> no such party as the antifederal exists in the United States. It is a word without a representative in society, and only to be found in the mouths of interested characters, or their humble servants, who fear a change in certain measures, in which they suppose the ruin of their own importance will be involved.

This argument quickly became commonplace. "A Republican Federalist" observed that, "for some time past, great pains have been taken to revive the exploded names of federalist and antifederalist, and turn them at the present crisis into signals for electioneering purposes," an "artifice" that had met with some success. But "the question in America," concluded another author, "is no longer between federalism and anti-federalism, but between republicanism and anti-republicanism."[86]

When news about the declaration of the French Republic arrived in the United States in late 1792, it reinvigorated American enthusiasm for the French Revolution and gave opposition arguments about republicanism and aristocracy even more potency. "The popular tide in this country," wrote Hamilton to William Short, "is strong in favor of the last revolution in France." The dramatic French military victories at Valmy and Jemappes had "caused a great sensation here," observed British diplomat Edward Thornton, and increased popular support for the opposition. "The anti-federalists do most assuredly gain ground daily," he wrote in February 1793:

> [T]he doctrines of liberty, and equality gain daily proselytes; public din-ners, congratulations, civic feasts in honor of the French victories are given throughout the United States, and the appellation of citizen is used on all these occasions....the open and joyful applause bestowed on French affairs by the majority of the newspapers here...form in my opinion conclusive evidence that the sense of this country goes in the same direction.

According to Thornton, this popular euphoria coincided with a sharp increase in attacks on George Washington "for his levees and other appendages of Monarchy and Aristocracy." As public support for the French Revolution intensified, so did Republican attacks on the "monarchical" character of the Washington adminis-tration and even on George Washington himself.[87]

The radicalization of the French Revolution in 1792–1793 reinvigorated the egal-itarian and anti-monarchical character of Republican political rhetoric. But the connection between political rhetoric and political reality was complex, and the connection between American support for the French Revolution and American partisan politics reflected this complexity. Most historians assume, like the British minister Edward Thornton, that popular support for the French Revolution was closely linked to the growth of political opposition in the 1790s and distinguished pro-revolutionary Republicans from anti-revolutionary Federalists. But although the ideological cleavage created by the revolution played some part in determin-ing partisan identity, the assumption that partisan identity (which was highly fluid throughout the 1790s) mapped neatly onto differences about the French Revolution is an oversimplification. In the first place, this argument assumes that the revolution was a single, indivisible event rather than a process: a series of radical changes and reactions that unfolded over time, to which Americans, who were well informed about events in France, responded in a complex and fluid way. Moreover, it fails to distinguish carefully between private responses to the revolution, generally although not always more negative among Federalists, and popular support for the revolution, which was strong into the late 1790s. As a result, many historians have interpreted the relationship between the French Revolution and American politics in a way that reflects rather than interrogates the political rhetoric of the day and fails to account for the ways that the revolu-tion was *used* in American partisan debate.[88]

Popular divisions about the French Revolution were negligible until the late 1790s, and almost all Americans welcomed the French Revolution in 1789 as an extension of their own revolutionary struggle against Great Britain. What is striking about the subsequent popular response to the September massacres, the executions of Louis XVI and Marie Antoinette, the Jacobin dictatorship, the Terror, and even Robespierre's campaign against Christianity is how little these events diminished popular enthusiasm for the revolution. As David Brion Davis argues, American support for the revolution persisted "well after the reign of Terror" and crossed rather than defined party lines. Outright Francophobia or anti-Jacobinism of the kind later associated with the English journalist William Cobbett was rare. And after the overthrow of Robespierre and the Committee of Public Safety on July 27, 1794 (9 Thermidor), conservative critics like Noah Webster renewed their support for the revolution and welcomed the establishment of the directory as a return to stable constitutional government. When New England's clergymen, who greeted the revolution as a mortal blow to the temporal and spiritual power of the Roman Catholic church, finally grew disaffected with the revolution in the mid-1790s, it was Thomas Paine's *Age of Reason* that was to blame and not events in France. At a celebration for Washington's birthday in New England in 1796, participants saw no contradiction between celebrating the president's birthday, toasting Federalist leaders, and extending good wishes toward the "people of France: a speedy termination of their toils, glorious as the hopes of their patriots, and splendid as their victories."[89]

Because of popular support for the revolution, Republican activists worked tirelessly to politicize the issue. When the *National Gazette* first appeared in October 1791, its most striking characteristic was its attention to affairs in Europe and revolutionary France. Freneau promised readers a "constant and punctual supply" of news from European newspapers like the *Gazette de Leyde* and *L'Argus Patriote*, and the *National Gazette* was crowded with reports from Europe. From the start, however, this coverage had a sharply polemical tone, and the French Revolution quickly became a weapon of partisan warfare. It was well known, claimed one author in Freneau's paper, "that there is a very considerable party in the United States, extremely inimical to the principles of the American and the French Revolutions," and its secrecy only made it more sinister. "The most zealous enemies of French republicanism," argued another essayist, disguised their views from the public, concealing the fact that the "true contest at present in France is between liberty and tyranny; between republicanism and royalty—or, in a word, between the people and the enemies of the people" and that the same conflict existed in the United States.[90]

Republicans quickly made support for the French Revolution a litmus test of both republican politics *and* American patriotism. Loyalty toward the revolution, argued "William Tell," was a "touch stone by which you may try the attachment of men to your freedom—suspect the man that attempts to dampen the ardor of your friendship to France." Whatever the outcome of events in Europe, argued another contributor to the *National Gazette*, the situation revealed that those who "wished well to the despots employed in overturning the new republic, are at heart inimical to liberty and the rights of the people in their own country." It was impossible to imagine, he believed, that critics of the French Revolution could be "in their hearts either true Americans or sincere republicans." By linking the two revolutions so closely—"whoever owns the principles of one revolution must cherish those of the other," argued James Monroe—Republicans also made the fate of "either dependent on the other." This point seemed obvious to Monroe, writing as "Aratus" in the *National Gazette* in December 1791. The politics of revolutionary Europe, he believed, had already begun to replicate itself in the United States, and the battle between republicans and Hamiltonian aristocrats was directly linked to the struggle between revolutionaries and counterrevolutionaries in Europe. Ignoring its warm public reception in his own country, Monroe believed that the French Revolution had ignited a "flame" that had "been communicated like an electric shock across the Atlantic." "The terror which this wonder-working spirit" had created among European monarchists, he wrote, had produced a "kindred panic" in the United States, where Federalists had already laid the groundwork for an aristocratic counterrevolution. Americans, insisted Monroe, must aid their French republican allies and defend their own republican institutions against an aristocratic counterrevolution or both would perish. "Every good republican," he warned, must "stand on his guard."[91]

If Monroe was right, Americans had little to celebrate and much to fear, and his argument quickly became a critical constituent of Republican political identity. Madison and Jefferson also believed that a battle against aristocratic resurgence had to be fought and won in the United States, and both thought that republican success at home was directly linked to its fortunes in France. "Symptoms of disaffection to Republi[can go]vernment," wrote Madison in 1793, "have arisen & subsided among us in such visible [cor]respondence with the prosperous and adverse accounts of the French Revolution, that a miscarriage of it would threaten us with the most serious dangers to our present form & principles of our Governments." Jefferson also emphasized the interdependence of politics in France and the United States, and he thought recent events had shown that "the form our own government was to take depended much more on the events of France than any body had before imagined." In the *National Gazette*, "Sidney" welcomed the overthrow of Louis XVI as a triumph for republicanism in France and as an event that severed "the only sinew of hope to the American monocrats of establishing a limited monarchy in the United States." "On the same ground our fortunes rest," wrote Freneau, "and flourish, or must fail."[92]

Conceiving their opposition to Federalists as part of a transatlantic struggle against aristocracy, Republicans were fiercely critical of the American political system. Brutus, for example, who believed Europe was convulsed by the consequences of "loans, funding systems, monopolies, bounties and perpetual taxes," not surprisingly concluded that government policies in his own country were "controuled by the avarice and ambition of the few" and "seem to be following the same course and to be leading to the same evils." "Our republican governments," he wrote, "are passing away like a shadow." "Alcanor" also believed that the United States had made "rapid strides toward aristocracy" since the end of the Revolution, and to "arrest her progress" must renounce "ministerial splendour" and "luxurious effeminacy." Preserving liberty required manly sacrifice and support for the French Republic, argued "An Old Soldier," who warned Americans not to be lulled to sleep by the "anodyne of aristocracy." "We have too many of the follies of monarchy in our country, and it is high time we purge ourselves of them," he declared:

> [L]et true republicans form a centre of union, let them determine to exterminate the political heresies which have sprung up among us; let them, from this moment, declare war against every aristocratic and monarchical principle and fashion, and happiness and liberty will be perpetuated.

In contrast to American corruption, An Old Soldier regarded France as a source of political renewal, a country that had "remounted to the source of reason," whose "purity of...creed is greater than ours." Another correspondent to the *National Gazette* urged Americans to emulate the "resolute, determined, and impetuous steps which the French have taken to divest themselves of every remnant of aristocracy." Such determination to emulate French republicans could have revolutionary overtones. The "artifice and deception" practiced in American politics, wrote Brutus on July 4, 1792, had already brought about a "revolution in favor of the few"; now, "another revolution must be brought about in favor of the people."[93]

Ironically, the parallels that Republicans drew between French and American politics (parallels that Federalists later duplicated in their denunciations of American Jacobinism) grew out of a deeply rooted popular hostility toward the Old World. "It is curious to observe," commented one writer in the *National Gazette*, "how the ideas of your American monarchy-mongers have flowed-altogether in corrupted European channels." Republicans may have emphasized continuity between America and Europe, but their goal was to preserve the purity of the New World from the corruption of the Old, and behind their expressions of republican internationalism lurked antipathy for Europe and a nostalgia for the unity and virtue of their revolutionary past. It was a nostalgia that their

Federalist protagonists sometimes shared, although their views were based on a more optimistic assessment of American politics and society. As one critic of the French Revolution argued, the United States had advantages unknown to "any European nation," especially the "superior knowledge and information which is possessed by the great body of the people," and in his view, the less Americans had to do with Europe the better.[94]

But even Federalists who supported the French Revolution rejected Republican arguments about the relationship between American politics and the politics of revolutionary Europe. In their view, the French Revolution was simply an extension of their own Revolution, and if Americans had yet to bring this Revolution to a conclusion (and Federalists like Fenno believed that more work was needed to instill a sense of national character), they had little to learn from France. "A Freeman" in the *Gazette of the United States* ridiculed the idea that "Americans are to be taught the lesson of freedom by the French nation." Americans, he argued, deferred to none in "the honor of setting an illustrious example in the field of liberty, civil and religious." Fenno, who welcomed the formation of the French Republic enthusiastically, dismissed the idea that the United States had to be "revolutionized," or that "we are now left in the rear by our Gallic allies, in the glorious race of Liberty." Although often described as reactionary pessimists, for most of the 1790s, it was Federalists who were buoyantly optimistic about American public life and Republicans who composed gloomy jeremiads on the degeneration of the Republic.[95]

Freneau's campaign to halt the spread of aristocratic corruption in the United States was dampened only slightly by the news of Louis XVI's execution, which reached the United States in early March 1793. Despite the king's support for the American Revolution, public expressions of grief were restrained. A broadside entitled *The Tragedy of Louis Capet*, which was "published at the request of many true Republicans," condemned the "barb'rous Mob" responsible for his execution, but Jefferson, who hoped his execution would eradicate "that aegis of insolence and oppression, the inviolability of the king's person," was surprised that his death had not "produced as open condemnations from the Monocrats as I expected." While many Americans expressed sympathy for the king, few condemned the revolution that had killed him. In Virginia, reported Edward Carrington, support for the revolution remained strong even though the execution of Louis XVI was widely regarded as "an Act of unprincipled Cruelty." James Monroe found the same. Despite regret about the execution of the king, he found scarcely "a man unfriendly to the French revolution as now modified." Widespread public sympathy for Louis XVI, observed Madison, was for the "man & not the Monarch."[96]

Freneau's reaction to Louis XVI's execution was less restrained. After the overthrow of the French monarchy, he had demanded that the U.S. Senate remove portraits of Louis XVI and Marie Antoinette from its walls, and his response to the king's death was equally iconoclastic. "Had no royal blood flowed in the veins of Louis," wrote "A Republican" in the *National Gazette*, "his fate, in all probability, would neither have called forth a sigh nor a tear, from those who are so ready to bewail the fall of royalty." Those who felt sorry for the king (and the author admitted there were many) were slaves of superstition, who believed he was the "Lord's Anointed... something above the common run of mankind." Freneau even mocked his death and those who mourned with the headline "Louis CAPET Has Lost His CAPUT." Louis XVI, he argued, had betrayed his people and the revolution; he was a corrupt and debauched king who (echoing the misogynist propaganda aimed at Louis and Marie Antoinette in France) was the "mere engine of A Woman! Full of VICE, INTRIGUE, DECEPTION, and DUPLICITY." There was no better proof of the "strong propensity to aristocracy" in the United States, argued Freneau, than the "lamentable effusions on the decapitation of Louis the XVI, and the unqualified abuse that is lavished upon those who refuse to join in the melancholy condolence." Sympathy for the dead king, he insisted, was nothing more than an effort to "alienate the good wishes of America from the cause of liberty in France."[97]

Freneau need not have worried. When the fiery young minister plenipotentiary of the French Republic, Edmond Charles Genet, arrived in Charleston in April 1793 on *L'Embuscade* with two captured British ships in tow, the public response left no doubt about the strength of American support for France. Genet's arrival coincided with the outbreak of war between Great Britain and the French Republic, news of which created a surge of public sympathy for France and renewed antagonism toward the British, reviving the "old spirit of 1776." "Newspapers from boston to charleston" declared their support for the French Republic, wrote Jefferson, and "even the Monocrat papers are obliged to publish the most furious Philippics against England." Freneau's Anglophobia escalated sharply, and he filled the *National Gazette* with attacks on Great Britain and British influence in the United States. War between Britain and France had revealed the existence of a band of American Tories, claimed one writer, "bawling, ferociously, against the glorious revolution of our magnanimous friends, the French." It was this "black band of tories," speculators, and aristocrats who bewailed the fate of Louis XVI and attempted to "blast, with their venomous execration, the whole Gallic Nation." Charges like this grew in frequency and intensity as Republicans accused Federalists of treacherously collaborating with the British against the United States and the French Republic.[98]

But war between Britain and France posed problems for the Republicans. The Treaty of 1778 between France and the United States allowed French ships to use American ports, but closed them to enemies of France, a provision that infuriated the British and threatened Anglo-American mercantile interests. And the actions of the new French minister immediately placed great pressure on the Washington administration to clarify American policy. Almost as soon as he arrived in Charleston with his British prizes, Genet commissioned four French privateers and manned them with American sailors. As he made his way from Charleston to Philadelphia, greeted by wildly enthusiastic demonstrations of popular support for the French Republic, Washington's cabinet met to consider its response. Despite some disagreement between Hamilton and Jefferson about the details of American policy, on April 22, 1793, Washington issued a formal Proclamation of Neutrality, prohibiting American citizens from engaging in pri-vateering on behalf of the French Republic and instructing them to "adopt and pursue a conduct friendly and impartial toward the belligerent powers."[99]

As Jefferson realized, "tho' necessary to keep us out of the calamities of a war," this policy of "fair neutrality" was a "disagreeable pill to our friends." As secretary of state, he supported the official policy, but privately he was pleased to see Freneau and others reminding the Washington administration of its fraternal duty to the French Republic. Having made support for the French Revolution a sine qua non of Republican political identity, Freneau refused to alter his position to protect the United States from involvement in a European war. "Neutrality," he wrote simply, "is desertion," a betrayal of France and a betrayal of Republican politics. In the spring of 1793, he and other Republican political activists in Philadelphia sug-gested that "committees be appointed, in proper places, throughout the union" to raise money for the French Republic, and after the establishment of a German Republican Society in Pennsylvania in April, Freneau broadened this call, demand-ing the creation of a network of political societies to serve as "powerful instru-ments in support of the present system of equality, and formidable enemies to aristocracy in whatever shape it might present itself." Clearly envisioning political organizations that did more than collect money for France, Freneau's call inspired the formation of more political clubs. The Patriotic French Society was founded in late April and, a month later, the Democratic Society of Pennsylvania, which was christened by Genet himself. Widely copied in the rest of the country, these Democratic Republican societies formed an organizational basis for the growth of the Republican Party in the 1790s and provoked a significant public debate about the nature of representative and participatory democracy.[100]

But more immediately, they prepared for Genet's arrival in Philadelphia. Working closely with Benjamin Franklin Bache, editor of the *General Advertiser*, and John Dunlap, editor of the *American Daily Advertiser*, Freneau turned the offices of the *National Gazette* into a hive of activity for the Patriotic French Society, raising money for the French Republic and organizing a grand public reception for its minister. Americans, urged A Freeman, should demonstrate their loyalty to republicanism and the French Revolution by giving Citizen Genet a "proper and joyful reception." When Genet arrived in Philadelphia on May 16, Freneau greeted him with unrestrained enthusiasm, and at a civic banquet in his honor at Oeller's Hotel on May 22, he translated and read an ode "a la liberte" by Citizen Louis Pichon, a French diplomat, which was published in the *National Gazette*. Genet's welcome by the citizens of Philadelphia was a "genuine display of affection for the cause of France," and it silenced the advocates of aristocracy. Captivated by Genet's revolutionary élan, his "noble simplicity," and his "genuine republicanism," Freneau attached himself to the cause of the French minister and immediately launched an attack on his own government. While war with Great Britain was undesirable, he argued, it was better to "let America join in the combat with France than forfeit her honor and her virtue." The Proclamation of Neutrality was not only a mistake but was "unsanctioned by preceding laws," and the use of such monarchical forms to overawe the "swinish multitude," wrote Freneau, violated the constitutional limits on executive authority. Addressing Washington directly, he warned him that "sovereignty still resides with THE PEOPLE" and that "neither proclamations, nor royal demeanor and state can prevent them from exercising it."[101]

This incendiary article provoked a violent response from Washington, who was usually a model of self-control, and brought to a boil the simmering controversy in Washington's cabinet about Jefferson's role in the *National Gazette*. During a cabinet meeting on May 23, wrote Jefferson:

> [President Washington] adverted to a piece in Freneau's paper of yesterday; he said he despised all their attacks on him personally, but that there had never been an act of the government…which that paper had not abused….He was evidently sore and warm, and I took his intention to be, that I should interpose in some way with Freneau, perhaps withdraw his appointment…but I will not do it.

Enraged by such personal attacks from a clerk serving in his own government, Washington clearly believed that his secretary of state had the power to stop Freneau, but Jefferson refused to intervene, insisting that he had no control over the *National Gazette* and even defending Freneau's conduct. The *National Gazette*, he told Washington, "has saved our Constitution, which was galloping fast into Monarchy, and has been checked by no means so powerfully as by that paper." Writing in the privacy of his political diary, Jefferson expressed a strong sense of distaste for what he saw as Washington's efforts to limit a "free press," and he showed no desire to restrain Freneau's attacks on either Washington or the government's neutrality policy. His support for the *National Gazette* was unwavering.[102]

If Freneau knew that his words were creating such high-level turbulence, this knowledge did nothing to restrain him. Following another civic banquet for

Genet on June 1 ("I live here in the midst of perpetual fetes," commented the French minister), at which Freneau read his new poem *God Save the Rights of Man*, he began publishing the controversial "Veritas" essays in the *National Gazette*, the first breach in the wall of public decorum that had previously protected Washington from public criticism. Freneau had already attacked the president's neutrality policy, but attacking the president himself was more risky. Shrewdly, he made this risk the central issue of his campaign against the "superstitious veneration" and "infallibility" of the president, reminding readers (and Washington himself) that "a first Magistrate in every country is no other than a public servant, whose conduct is governed by the will of the people." When the will of one man, argued Veritas, "whether founded on popularity or power," usurped the popular will and dictated government policy, freedom itself was in jeopardy. A "manly investigation of public measures" was essential to keep public servants in check, and if Washington were regarded as infallible, then "in the name of heaven, under what sort of government do we live?" "Infallibility is a species of tyranny," he argued, and "no public character ought to be so sacred as to make it dangerous or criminal to arraign it; this is a species of inviolability which royalty lays claim to, and where it obtains, the government is no longer free."[103]

By late August, Freneau was publishing denunciations of the president's "inviolability" side by side with justifications for the execution of the French king, and articles in the *National Gazette* reached a new level of rhetorical violence.[104] "A Citizen of Georgia" stated bluntly that the federal government was "not republican." "Ye demi-gods of federalism," thundered its author,

> do no visions haunt your slumbers of the distresses endured on our frontier?—Surrounded by minions, sycophants and parasites (the first ostensible marks of royalty) the glare of your borrowed plumes has so dazzled the eyes of the astonished multitude, that it has, in fact, become difficult to persuade them that you are not infallible....Solomon slept with his fathers—Rehoboam ascended his throne—he took bad counsel, which Jereboam availing himself, rent the kingdom in twain. It is possible, nay it is more than probable, that a duplicate of the transactions of those days may be copied in to the pages of American history, when certain heads, which are now warm, are reposing in the dust.[105]

Attacks like this sought and drew blood. According to Jefferson, Washington lashed out at Freneau again during a cabinet meeting in early August, complaining "that *by god* he had rather be in his grave than in his present situation":

> And yet that they were charging him with wanting to be a king. That that *rascal Freneau* sent him 3 of his papers every day, as if he thought he would become the distributor of his papers, that he could see in this nothing but an impudent design to insult him.

Washington's outburst was provoked partly by the Veritas essays and partly by the circulation of an anonymous pamphlet, *The Funeral Dirge of George Washington and James Wilson, King and Judge*, describing the president's execution by guillotine, a pamphlet he believed had come from the pen of Philip Freneau.[106]

By this time, Freneau's hostility toward Washington and loyalty to Genet had begun to alienate even the leaders of his own party. Despite Jefferson's best efforts to mollify Genet, by June relations between the French minister and the Washington administration had cooled sharply. On June 22, Genet sent a letter to Jefferson as the secretary of state protesting government policies, which Hamilton called "the most offensive paper, perhaps, that ever was offered by a foreign Minister to a friendly power." Even more seriously, in defiance of the Proclamation of Neutrality, he outfitted a privateer in Philadelphia, the *Petit Democrat* (formerly the *Little Sarah*, a British merchant ship captured by *L'Embuscade*), and refused to assure Pennsylvania's secretary of state, Alexander James Dallas, that the privateer would not leave port. His refusal to give such assurances forced Jefferson to intervene personally, and after an interview with the French minister that Jefferson believed had produced such assurances, he wrote to Madison denouncing Genet's conduct and character. "Never in my opinion, was so calamitous an appointment made, as that of the present minister of F[rance] here," he declared:

> [He is] [h]otheaded, all imagination, no judgement, passionate, disrespectful & even indecent towards the P[resident] in his written as well as verbal communications, talking of appeals from him to Congress, from them to the people....If it should ever be necessary to lay his communications before Congress or the public, they will excite universal indignation.

Jefferson immediately informed Washington about Genet's threats, and when the cabinet learned a few days later that Genet had given the *Petit Democrat* permission to sail, it decided to request his recall.[107]

But even before the rift between Genet and the Washington administration became public knowledge, Federalists had realized that Republican opposition to the Proclamation of Neutrality gave them a political opening. Once again, it was Hamilton who exploited this opportunity most effectively. Keen to fend off Republican charges that the Federalists were an "English party," Hamilton argued in an unpublished essay written in April that neutrality was the policy of an "American party." "A dispassionate and virtuous citizen of the U[nited] States," he noted, "will scorn to stand on any but purely American ground," and only a policy of impartiality toward all the European powers would prevent the country from the "destructive vortex of foreign politics." The "Pacificus" essays conveyed this argument to a wider public. Published in the *Gazette of the United States* in June and July 1793, they provided a detailed, scholarly justification for the government's policy of neutrality, but underlying this legal pedantry lay a far more persuasive argument about the need for the United States to pursue an independent foreign policy. Neither filial obligation nor gratitude justified subordinating American national interests to the interests of the French Republic, argued Hamilton, and he warned Americans that such sentimental attachments "introduce a principle of action, which in its effects, if the expression may be allowed, is anti-national." "Foreign influence," he insisted, "is the GRECIAN HORSE to a republic. We cannot be too careful to exclude its entrance." As "An American" wrote in the *Federal Gazette* shortly after these essays appeared, Americans had to defend their own interests and "national character," a theme that was the central leitmotif of Noah Webster's new political daily, the *American Minerva*, established with Hamilton's aid in December 1793.[108]

Hamilton's Pacificus essays, which mobilized American patriotism, the popularity and prestige of President Washington, and a widespread desire for peace all deeply troubled Jefferson, who felt that the whole drift of political events favored the administration. After the first two essays appeared, he dashed off a panic-stricken note to Madison, imploring him to respond to Hamilton. "Nobody answers him," he wrote, "& his doctrines will therefore be taken for confessed. For god's sake, my dear sir, take up your pen, select the most striking heresies, and cut him to pieces in the face of the public. There is nobody else who can & will enter the lists with him." But Madison was reluctant to confront Hamilton once again, predicting wearily that the "business will not be terminated by a single fire." It would be hard, he told Jefferson, to challenge the arguments of Pacificus without challenging Washington's policy of neutrality, a prospect neither he nor Jefferson relished. He was right. When his "Helvidius" essays finally appeared in the *Gazette of the United States*, they reflected both the difficulty of his task and his reluctance to enter the political fray. At first rancorous and rebarbative, they quickly degenerated into a dry, legalistic treatise on the war- and treaty-making powers of the executive.[109]

In the meantime, Hamilton was busy exploiting Genet's quixotic behavior to undermine the credibility of the opposition. Once the Washington administration decided to demand Genet's recall, Hamilton archly suggested that his inflammatory correspondence with Jefferson should be made public "by way of appeal to the people," a move that Jefferson correctly interpreted as an effort to "declare war on the Republican party." Probably suspecting that his suggestion would be stonewalled by Jefferson, Hamilton had already taken steps to publicize Genet's diplomatic indiscretion. Writing as "No Jacobin" in the *American Daily Advertiser*, he reported that it was "publicly rumoured in this City that the Minister of the French Republic has *threatened to appeal from the President of the United States to the People*." Shortly after this report, a letter from Rufus King and John Jay appeared in the New York press testifying to the truth of this statement, and Hamilton used their "corroboration" to press his advantage. Genet's outrageous behavior, he argued, again writing as No Jacobin, showed that the French minister regarded the United States "more like a dependent Colony than like an Independent Nation!" His threat to appeal to the people over the head of an elected government was an insult to national pride and honor and "to the feelings of every man whose feelings are truly American."[110]

Jefferson was appalled by this turn of events. Genet's reckless behavior had caused a dramatic shift in public opinion, and he now sensed real danger for the Republicans. "He will sink the republican interest," warned Jefferson in a coded message to Madison in early August, "if they do not abandon him." The "desire of neutrality is universal," he wrote, and Republicans must not be caught criticizing Washington in matters "where he will be approved by the great body of the people." Jefferson urged Madison to ensure that Republicans in Congress "approve unequivocally of a state of neutrality" in order to deflect the Federalist campaign against them. But he was deeply concerned that not all Republicans would fall in line and wondered if "some of the more furious republicans may not schismatise."[111] He was right to worry. Although he and other members of the opposition abandoned Genet, Freneau stood faithfully by the French minister. By the summer of 1793, he had turned the *National Gazette* into a quasi-official mouthpiece for Citizen Genet and the French. A series of essays by "Juba," probably written by Freneau himself and published after Genet's recall, even encouraged the French minister to defy the federal government, assuring him that the American people were on his side. When Rufus King and John Jay published their statement on Genet's "appeal to the people," Freneau dismissed their testimony and tried to justify Genet's appeal, accusing the Washington administration of conducting a campaign of vilification against Genet in the press and of conspiring to subvert the will of the American people. In a government of the people, he argued, "they alone ought to determine every momentous question," and if there was a difference of opinion between the administration and the French minister, "who ought to determine this difference but the people?"[112]

On September 14, 1793, Freneau mentioned the outbreak of a yellow fever epidemic in Philadelphia. As other editors fled the city, he sent his wife and daughter home to New Jersey and continued to publish the *National Gazette*, determined to defend Genet against his Federalist detractors. But the newspaper's coffers were dangerously depleted, and more significantly Childs and Swaine had grown weary of losing money on a newspaper that had alienated its most valuable political patron, Thomas Jefferson. When the yellow fever epidemic and Freneau's unpopular defense of Genet led to a sharp decline in circulation, they delivered the coup de grâce. On October 11, in a terse, business-like letter to Jefferson, Freneau tendered his resignation, virtually ending correspondence between the two men. On October 26, he issued the last edition of the *National Gazette*, promising his readers that the newspaper would resume publication when Congress reconvened in the New Year, a promise he left unfulfilled. Instead, he returned to his family's farm in New Jersey, where he spent the next two years publishing an almanac and an edition of his collected poems. But he did not completely retreat from political life, editing the *Jersey Chronicle* and leading local opposition to the Jay Treaty and "monocratic" government in the strongly federalist state. Resigned to obscurity, he told Madison that he intended to stay in this "crude barbarous part of the country" and "pass the remainder of my days on a couple of hundred acres of an old sandy patrimony."[113]

This was not to be. In the late 1790s, Freneau was drawn back into partisan politics, returning to New York City to edit the *Time-Piece* in 1797–1798 at the height of the Federalist campaign against the French Republic. After leaving the *Time-Piece*, he wrote a column for William Duane's Philadelphia *Aurora* under the pen name "Robert Slender, O.S.M.—One of the Swinish Multitude." These brilliantly satirical letters, which he published as a pamphlet in 1799 and dedicated to the "Freemen, the Lovers of Liberty, the Asserters, Maintainers and Supporters of Independence throughout the United States," were the most effective and fluid writing of his political career, but they also marked its end. Their gentle humor and iconoclasm seemed out of place in the brave new world of Jeffersonian party politics, and so was Freneau, who was by now almost fifty years old. Writing as Robert Slender, he contributed significantly to Jefferson's election in 1800, but when he was offered a post in the new administration, he declined, determined never again to "meddle with the public or their business."[114]

Despite his disillusionment with public life, Freneau never lost his faith in Thomas Jefferson. His opposition to neutrality and his support for Citizen Genet had cost him dearly. When Jefferson and other Republicans scurried for cover during the political storm unleashed by Genet, Freneau was caught out in the open and left to fend for himself, a pattern that recurred again and again in the 1790s when the ideological zeal of partisan editors like Freneau outran the strategic caution and political maneuvering of party leaders like Jefferson. But unlike the later victims of Jefferson's finely developed sense of political discretion, Freneau never harbored any sense of bitterness. Despite the abrupt termination of their relationship, he continued to celebrate Jefferson as a great champion of republican equality, the man who had wrested the country from the grip of "Brittannia's tools": "Him, whom Columbia her true patriot calls; / Him, whom we saw her codes of freedom plan, / To none inferior in the ranks of man."[115]

CHAPTER 3

Benjamin Franklin Bache
and the Desacralization
of George Washington

On the occasion of George Washington's retirement from the presidency in 1796, the editor Benjamin Franklin Bache published a commentary in the Philadelphia *Aurora*. "If ever a nation was debauched by a man, the American nation has been debauched by WASHINGTON," declared its author:

> If ever a nation has suffered from the improper influence of a man, the American nation has suffered from the influence of WASHINGTON. If ever a nation was deceived by a man, the American nation has been deceived by wa sh ingt on. Let his conduct be an example to future ages. Let it serve to be a warning that no man may be an idol, and that a people may confide in themselves rather than in an individual. Let the history of the federal government instruct mankind, that the masque of patriotism may be worn to conceal the foulest designs against the liberties of a people.

This savage indictment of Washington was the final salvo in a Republican campaign against him that was waged with implacable intensity in the *Aurora* throughout 1795 and 1796, a campaign orchestrated by Bache. Over fifty years later, John Prentiss, who had been an apprentice working in the printing office of the Boston *Independent Chronicle* at the time, vividly recalled how President Washington was "bitterly attacked in Bache's Phila. Aurora." And Bache is still remembered primarily as a scurrilous newspaper editor who slandered the father of his country, George Washington.[1]

The American Revolution, unlike its predecessor the English Revolution and its successor the French Revolution, created a republic without killing a king.

109

Instead, American revolutionaries enacted his death metaphorically, and the crucial moment in this symbolic patricidal drama was the publication of Thomas Paine's *Common Sense* in January 1776. Rejecting the patriarchal claims of George III—"the wretch, that with the pretended title of 'FATHER OF HIS PEOPLE' can unfeelingly hear of their slaughter"—Paine called on the power of the Crown to be "demolished, and scattered among the people whose right it is."[2] Patriarchal sovereignty, embodied in the person of the king, was to be replaced by fraternal sovereignty, embodied in the person of the republican citizen. The Sons of Britain (and of George III) became the Sons of Liberty as political sovereignty was stripped of its personal character and became disembodied, impersonal, and abstract. "In America THE LAW IS KING," wrote Paine, "for as in absolute governments the King is law, so in free countries the law *ought* to be King; and there ought to be no other."[3]

Paine's act of textual decapitation and his belief that sovereignty should be "scattered among the people" represented a profound challenge to the patriarchal assumptions of eighteenth-century Anglo-American society, and the rapidity with which Americans rejected monarchical government was truly startling. "Idolatry to Monarchs, and servility to Aristocratical Pride," declared John Adams in 1776, "was never so totally eradicated from so Many Minds in so short a Time." The transformation of American colonists from subjects to citizens seemed complete and almost instantaneous. But it was not. Paine's vision of fraternal sovereignty was itself deeply patriarchal. A republic of citizen-brothers, who redistributed rather than dispensed with patriarchal power, appealed greatly to those who hoped that patriarchal power in colonial households would be strengthened rather than weakened by declaring independence from Great Britain. While many Americans after the Revolution rejected conventional patriarchy and adopted more benign ideas about patriarchal responsibility and obligation, many remained more orthodox, especially those whose support for independence had been less than enthusiastic. Despite the changes in political culture wrought by the Revolution, the patriarchal ideas that sustained support for the British monarchy before 1776, ideas deeply embedded in the social relations, cultural practices, and consciousnesses of ordinary Americans, persisted well after 1776.[4]

The clearest evidence of such persistence was the popular apotheosis of General George Washington. Although Americans reclaimed the sovereignty of the British Crown in 1776, "the sons of the Revolution soon lapsed into acclaiming their staunchest leader as the Father of His Country." As the leader of the American cause, Washington was both George III's principal antagonist and his symbolic successor, harnessing quasi-monarchical respect to the goals of revolutionary nationalism. In the midst of the Revolution, he became a symbol of political consolidation and order, the epitome of the conservative revolutionary. Even before the nation was formed, writes Gary Wills, Washington was "steadying the symbols, lending strength to them instead of drawing from them." His importance to the nation, states Wills, "lay in his capacity for eliciting veneration not yet given to less personal symbols of republican order. He was the embodiment of stability within a revolution, speaking for fixed things in a period of flux."[5] Whatever the truth of this argument—and it may be time to unveil a more revolutionary George Washington—there is no doubt that popular reverence for Washington reflected a deep need to personalize the revolutionary struggle with Great Britain. But even during the Revolution, Washington's immense popularity worried skeptics like John Adams, who (painfully aware of his own lack of charisma) denounced the "superstitious veneration that is sometimes paid to General Washington." And while revolutionary leaders exploited his prestige to advance their cause, they limited the scope for personal, charismatic leadership. Throughout the war, Congress employed a cumbersome and inefficient committee system rather than risk vesting too much political power and influence in individuals.[6]

This tension between personal and impersonal political authority continued into the postrevolutionary period. Indeed, the creation of the American Republic and the hostility of many Americans toward the conventions and forms of monarchical government created an important political problem for its citizens: how to represent or embody political sovereignty once it had been redistributed to the people. And fear of personal executive power remained strong. The president of the U.S. Congress in the 1770s and 1780s wielded little power and was replaced every year to ensure that he acquired none. Not everybody approved of such wariness. The secretary of Congress, Charles Thomson, found the absence of a head of state troubling. "A government without a visible head," he wrote in 1784, "must appear a strange phenomenon to European politicians and will I fear lead them to form no very favourable opinion of our stability, wisdom or union." Writing in the early 1790s, John Adams thought that a government without strong executive power vested in a single individual was vulnerable to political faction and disorder. When citizens had no single point of focus for their political loyalties, he argued, "when they look up to different individuals, or assemblies, or councils, you may expect all the deformities, eccentricities and confusion, of the Polemick System."[7]

By the late 1780s, enough Americans agreed with Adams to ensure the passage of a federal Constitution that created a powerful, highly personal form of executive authority subject to more or less democratic control: the presidency. But most Americans remained ambivalent about such personalized authority, and the phrase "founding fathers," which came into use in the 1780s, captured this ambivalence: the desire to both reconstitute patriarchal authority and avoid its traditional political form, monarchy. Federalists hoped that Washington's popularity would defuse public anxiety about the role of the presidency. Abigail Adams believed that only Washington was capable of binding the new nation and its people together: "no other man could rule over this great peopl[e] & consolidate them into one mighty Empire but He who is set over us." Like most other Americans, she saw Washington's popularity and prestige as indispensable to the success of the new federal government. But his popularity could also intensify opposition, as Washington himself was well aware. "I greatly apprehend that my countrymen will expect too much from me," he wrote to Edward Rutledge shortly after his first inauguration:

> I fear, if the issue of public measures should not correspond with their sanguine expectations, they will turn extravagant (and I may say undue) praises which they are heaping upon me at this moment, in to equally extravagant (though I will fondly hope, unmerited) censures.[8]

Washington was right. From the start of his tenure in office, critics worried that the presidency, and Washington's demeanor and behavior as president, were too dependent on monarchical precedents, and his great personal influence only heightened their sense of alarm. By the mid-1790s, Republicans were denouncing Washington as a traitor to his country who had usurped popular sovereignty and replaced a republican with a monarchical government. These attacks on Washington were highly personal and reflect the explosion of personal abuse that characterized the politics of the 1790s, but they were inspired by profound political differences. Loyal to Paine's vision of a fraternal citizenry and energized by the execution of Louis XVI and the triumph of revolutionary *fraternité* in France, radical Republicans rejected not only Washington's Federalist politics but the patriarchal assumptions that underpinned the presidency and were sustained by his great popularity. They regarded the embodiment of popular sovereignty in a single figure like Washington as tantamount to a restoration of monarchical government, hence their use of the term "monocrats" to characterize their Federalist opponents. Washington's efforts to remain above the political fray only fueled such fears, and political opponents like William Maclay viewed Washington's self-consciously aloof style and professions of political "impartiality" as part of a systematic effort to transform the presidency into a quasi-monarchical office. Their fears were not entirely unfounded. Washington himself believed that the role of the president was to preside over the political system, to create political unity rather than to advance partisan objectives. Radical Republicans like Benjamin Franklin Bache rejected this conception of the presidency and by the late 1790s were proposing its replacement by a collective or plural executive, like that which existed in the French Republic.[9]

Born in Philadelphia on August 12, 1769, Benjamin Franklin Bache (at that time pronounced Beech) was the eldest son of Richard and Sarah Bache. Richard Bache was a genial, competent, but rather unlucky Englishman who emigrated from Yorkshire to Philadelphia in 1760, hoping to make his fortune in the colonial trade. After a series of unsuccessful business ventures, he lost all of his money in a disastrous shipping speculation in 1766, a setback from which he never completely recovered. His one stroke of good fortune was his marriage in 1767 to Sarah Franklin, the only daughter of the most celebrated American of the eighteenth century, Benjamin Franklin. Sensing the limitations of his prospective son-in-law, Franklin, who was in England at the time of the courtship between Richard and Sarah, did all he could to discourage the match. When the couple presented him with a fait accompli, he refused to acknowledge the union, accusing Bache of marrying his daughter with "not merely nothing beforehand, but being beside greatly in debt." But he eventually came to like his affable son-in-law, regarding him as honest and reliable enough to entrust with the administration of his own complex financial affairs. Benjamin Franklin Bache's mother, Sarah, was made of sterner stuff. A woman of "unusual intelligence and wit," she had the courage to marry Richard Bache against the will of her formidable father, gave birth to seven children, and played an active part in the American Revolution, organizing an association of Philadelphia women to raise funds and equipment for the Continental army and winning Washington's praise for her "female patriotism."[10]

But Benjamin Franklin, rather than Bache's parents, was the formative influence on Bache's early life. Even before he returned to America, Franklin formed a sentimental attachment to his grandson, hosting a second birthday celebration for him in London and expressing his longing to be "at home to play with Ben." When he returned to Philadelphia in 1775, Franklin quickly developed a fondness for the dark-eyed young boy, who his grandmother called her "little kingbird," and when he returned to France a year later, he took Benjamin and his other grandson, William Temple, with him, partly to provide himself with company and partly to protect them from the war that was engulfing the newly independent United States. At Passy, the suburb outside Paris where Franklin and his household lived in considerable elegance, Bache was enrolled in a local boarding school, Le Coeur's (with John Quincy Adams, who was two years older), and began to acquire the accomplishments of polite French society, learning to draw, dance, and speak fluent French. After the boy spent three years at Le Coeur's, Franklin became alarmed that his grandson was turning into a young Frenchman and packed Bache off to school in Geneva, the home of John Calvin and Jean-Jacques Rousseau, hoping to turn him into "a good Presbyterian, and a good Republican." Largely ignored by his grandfather for the next few years,

Bache spent a miserable two years at the Pension Marignac, but by the time he left in mid-1783, he had developed a sense of quiet self-sufficiency that impressed even Franklin.[11]

After the Treaty of Paris in 1783, Bache returned to Passy, where he basked in the reflected glory of his illustrious grandfather, met many of the greatest figures of the age, and learned typecasting and printing from Franklin's master printer, Maurice Meyer, and more briefly, François Didot, the greatest printer of his day. His encounters with the many luminaries and men of affairs who visited Franklin's household did nothing to turn his head. Franklin himself praised Bache's diligence and intelligence, and his surrogate daughter, Polly Hewson, who met the fifteen-year-old Bache in 1784, was also impressed by his work ethic and described him as "one of the most amiable youths I ever knew…sensible and manly in his manner without the smallest tincture of the coxcomb." In May 1785, Bache watched a review of the Swiss Guards by Louis XVI and participated in the festivities surrounding Marie Antoinette's return to Paris after the birth of the dauphin; and on July 12, he left Passy with Franklin, sailing from Le Havre to Southampton, where they boarded the "London Packet" for Philadelphia. When they arrived home on September 13, they were welcomed with great public jubilation. In the last entry of the diary he kept during his time at Passy, Bache wrote simply: "We are arrived at Philadelphia. The joy which I felt at the acclamations of the people, in seeing a father and mother, and many brothers and sisters may be felt and not described."[12]

But despite the joy of being reunited with his family, Bache returned to a country he knew only through his memories of childhood. Although he felt American and adapted quickly to his new home, after nine years he had developed a sense of attachment to France that would last until his death in 1798.[13] Bache's sense of divided and displaced identity was probably familiar to his grandfather, who had spent years outside America and shared his experience of life in France, and the two became almost inseparable during the last years of Franklin's life. Although Franklin sent Bache to the University of Pennsylvania to complete his studies, when Bache graduated in 1788, Franklin urged his grandson to follow in his own footsteps, informing a correspondent that Bache had "finish'd his Studies at our University, and is preparing to enter into Business as a Printer, the original Occupation of his Grandfather." To assist him and provide for the rest of his family, Franklin undertook an ambitious building program to expand and remodel Franklin Court, adding more living space and constructing a new printing office and typecasting foundry. By the late 1780s, Bache was working closely with his grandfather, casting type, undertaking printing jobs, collecting debts, and, in his spare time, copying Franklin's unpublished *Autobiography*.[14] Not surprisingly, he aspired to be a man of learning, wealth, and public renown like Franklin. "My principal object," he wrote,

> shall be to be esteemed virtuous, reputed learned, & to be useful thro' their means to my Country & Mankind. Ambition is I think my strongest passion. To be great, truly great, by my virtues, I want sufficient money to shew those virtues in their most brilliant appearance, & a Wife who may by partaking increase the Bliss I expect by their exercise. I shall aim at being a public character to shew how I could choose the good of my Country in opposition to my private interest, which is a rare thing now a days.[15]

At this stage, the only politics in his life was the politics of genteel local society and the clashes between partisans of "Cotillions & Country dances." Even the drama of the Constitutional Convention in Philadelphia, in which Franklin played a dignified if largely symbolic role, made little impression on Bache. His interests were largely restricted to the family printing business and to courting Margaret Hartman Markoe, the daughter of a West Indian planter whom he met in the summer of 1788. As the federal Congress in New York debated how to fund the revolutionary war debt in 1790, Bache confessed to her that he had enjoyed a "gay winter" and "been to almost every Party we have had."[16]

Franklin's death in April 1790 was a sobering blow. Although he had absorbed his grandfather's lessons in self-reliance, Bache had hoped Franklin would live long enough to help him launch a business career "not only by the pecuniary Help he may afford me, but much more by his Advice." Describing his grandfather's loss as "irreparable," and determined to marry Margaret Markoe, Bache was forced for the first time to assess his prospects and to make concrete plans for the future. His inheritance from Franklin was modest, roughly £1,500, "chiefly in Tools that his Industry are to put in Motion," and Bache quickly decided to establish a daily newspaper, hoping to profit from the removal of the federal government to Philadelphia from New York. But even with his printing pedigree, it was a risky venture for someone of his youth and inexperience, and at least some of his acquaintances thought the job of a newspaper editor was beneath his station. The banker Robert Morris thought the city already had too many newspapers and that Bache's request for government patronage was unlikely to succeed, "for early as you think your application, others have been before you." He was right. When Bache petitioned the secretary of state, Thomas Jefferson, for permission to publish the laws of the United States, his offer was politely declined. Bache might be "more Honourably & lucratively employed by the Printing of Books," suggested Morris, warning him that it would be difficult to maintain a "Character of Freedom and Impartiality" as a newspaper editor, a warning borne out by subsequent events.[17]

Undeterred by Morris, Bache circulated his *Proposals for…the Daily Advertiser, and Political, Commercial, Agricultural & Literary Journal* in July 1790, and arranged to have Benjamin Vaughan send him the latest commercial and international news from the London coffeehouses. But, possibly in deference to Morris and his grandfather, who had despised the Philadelphia press, Bache conceived the *Daily Advertiser* as a respectable alternative to the political press in Philadelphia, a genteel "miscellany" that would appeal to men of business and what he called "the man of leisure," distinguished from its rivals "by the more particular attention he proposes paying to the literary division of his publication." Although Bache announced that the paper was open to politics "and any other interesting subjects," he promised that he would observe the "strictest impartiality" and warned contributors they must "deliver their sentiments with temper & decency" and with the intention of contributing to the "public good." These proposals for a polite, commercial newspaper with literary aspirations attracted about 400 subscribers, and after a last-minute change of name, Bache published the first issue of the *General Advertiser, and Political, Commercial, Agricultural and Literary Journal* on October 2, 1790, under the motto "Truth, Decency, Utility," a declaration of his newspaper's utter respectability to the world.[18]

For the first few months, this respectability was undisturbed by political controversy, and the only topic in the *General Advertiser* that aroused heated discussion was the future of the theater in Philadelphia. Bache claimed that the absence of political debate in the newspaper was simply a sign of the times, that there were no party disputes to generate copy and "raise the printer's drooping spirits," and there was some truth to his claim. But the newspaper also reflected Bache's conventional political views and his general complacency about the state of American politics. As he made clear to readers, the task of the *General Advertiser* was not to criticize either the Constitution or the Washington administration. "No country in the world," he wrote, "can boast a constitution so wisely constructed, or whose various departments are conducted by men of more ability and integrity."[19] He was especially enthusiastic about the economic policies of the Washington administration, hailing the Bank of the United States as an institution that would "encrease the circulating medium—facilitate business in every line and profession—enhance the value of real property—and enable the government to reduce the public debt." Its establishment, he insisted, "must, and will meet the approbation of every friend to his country." When Hamilton's *Report on Manufactures* was published in December 1791, he praised the treasury secretary as the architect of economic stability and prosperity. With men like Hamilton at the helm, he asked readers, "What evils have we to fear…or rather what blessings may we not hope for?"[20]

Like his fellow nationalist John Fenno, Bache thought that the press had a responsibility to assist in the consolidation of the new political order, and the carping of opposition journalists drew a chilly response from the young Federalist editor. A few months after the launch of Freneau's *National Gazette*, he wrote, "how jaundiced must be the eye which views the systems of Congress as pernicious to the honour, interests, and happiness of our country!"

> Although the impartial foreign world resounds with applauses for the revival of our public credit—for the maintenance of honesty between man and man—for the restoration of commerce and the advancement of manufactures—though the resulting prosperity of our increasing agriculture is attracting the attention of the most intelligent nations of Europe—though our government is the frequent topic of the eulogies of the struggling patriot of the old world, the tongue of prejudice and error is incessantly recounting a different tale to the happy people of the United States.[21]

Such criticism, he believed, was unfounded and irresponsible. The leaders of the United States were "the choicest patriots, men of long experience and unshaken firmness" whose conduct was guided by "liberal, just, independent and successful principles." To find fault with them was simply incomprehensible. "Can it possibly be considered as a criterion of patriotism," he demanded, "to excite jealousies and suggest suspicions respecting the general government?"[22]

Bache's views closely mirrored those of John Fenno and, not surprisingly, he borrowed freely from the *Gazette of the United States*. According to one of his correspondents, he clipped most of his copy from other newspapers:

> The other day I was at Mr. Franklin's Vendue, and there you was sitting in your room, by your desk—there was an inkstand on the table, to be sure, and a pen stuck behind your ear; but that was all; you never took it out; but the way you did, I'll tell you how it was. There was a great heap of newspapers laying on the table, and on the floor all about you, and you had in your hand a large pair of taylor's shears, and there you cut out of other papers as much as you thought would fill your's. The young man would come down and ask for more copy. You tumbled over the papers and measured it off in half a minute.[23]

Bache's literary cannibalism was hardly unique at a time when most newspaper editors were compilers of "information" rather than partisan journalists. But his dependence on a single source made the *General Advertiser* little more than an echo of the *Gazette of the United States*. His brief flirtation with Jefferson in the spring of 1791 only underscored Bache's loyalty to the federal government. By this time, Jefferson was actively seeking an editor willing to challenge the growing influence of Fenno's *Gazette of the United States*, and after his failure to recruit Freneau, he turned to Bache, whom he had met at Passy in 1785. At first, Jefferson's confidence in the nationalist principles, republican beliefs, and political discretion of the young editor appeared justified, and excerpts from the *Gazette de Leyde*, Jefferson's distinctive calling card, began to appear regularly in the *General Advertiser* in March 1791.[24] Bache helped Samuel Harrison Smith and John Beckley publish the first American edition of Thomas Paine's *Rights of Man* in May 1791, playing an active part in the subsequent controversy between "Publicola" (Bache's former classmate at Le Coeur's, John Quincy Adams) and his adversaries. During the summer of 1791, the *General Advertiser* acquired a new anti-aristocratic tone, and Bache even published an article attacking the national debt, the first sign of political opposition to appear in the newspaper.[25]

But if Jefferson believed he'd found a newspaper to rival the *Gazette of the United States*, he was quickly disappointed. One problem was the limited circulation of the *General Advertiser*, a problem he raised in his customary indirect manner. Writing to Bache in the third person, he suggested that the *General Advertiser* might be transformed into a "paper of general distribution, thro the states" by omitting advertising from its country edition, making it less bulky and expensive to deliver. Perhaps the advertising, wrote Jefferson,

> could be thrown into the last half sheet which might be torn off or omitted for distant customers. Mr. Bache will be so good as to excuse these officious hints, which proceed from a wish to serve him, and from a desire of seeing a purely republican vehicle of news established between the seat of government and all it's [*sic*] parts.

Bache ignored these "officious hints." In fact, he had already decided to concentrate on expanding his readership in Philadelphia, dropping "Agricultural" from the masthead of the paper and abandoning a weekly edition for rural subscribers, and he made no move to modify his decision after Jefferson's plea.[26] Preoccupied by the arrangements for his marriage to Margaret (which took place in November 1791) and starting his own family, Bache was not keen to alienate existing subscribers by announcing a sudden change in the complexion of the *General Advertiser*. But most important, although he had been willing to help publish Paine's work and to enter the lists against Publicola, Bache saw no connection between these activities and more general opposition to the Washington administration. Frustrated once again, Jefferson continued his dogged pursuit of Freneau, commenting after the founding of the *National Gazette* that "Freneau's two papers contain more good matter than Bache's six."[27]

Once established, however, the *National Gazette* exerted a strong gravitational pull on Bache, drawing the *General Advertiser* slowly into its orbit. The financial panic in the spring of 1792 marked a turning point, sending shock waves through the country and shaking Bache's faith in Hamilton's fiscal policies. Just days before the crisis, he had praised Hamilton lavishly; now, he qualified his praise:

> That there is wisdom displayed in our public councils, no one can deny—that we enjoy a considerable share of prosperity is evident; but that some measures have produced evils, experience testifies,—that a change of measures might bring about a change of circumstances is clear.—Then while there is room for improvement, why be satisfied with our present progress toward political prosperity.

For the first time, Bache expressed concern about the policies of the treasury secretary, although his criticism was still tentative. But when Freneau began to exploit the panic to attack Hamilton's economic policies, Bache quickly followed his lead. In early April, he reprinted a series of attacks on the excise system by "Sidney" that had appeared in the *National Gazette*, and he defended critics of the government against the charges of subversion and disloyalty leveled at them in the *Gazette of the United States*. But almost immediately, Bache retreated, discontinuing the Sidney essays and ignoring the Duer scandal completely. While Freneau denounced "paper aristocrats" as products of the "treasury system," Bache conspicuously refused to link Hamilton's policies to the speculative collapse, and his criticisms of the government remained muted. No longer willing to play the part of government panegyrist, he was not yet willing to join the ranks of the political opposition.[28]

What propelled Bache into the ranks of the political opposition was not the slow unfolding of Hamilton's economic policies but the sudden plot turns of the French Revolution. Right from the start, Bache was fascinated by events in revolutionary France. Writing to his father in September 1789, at a time when he showed little interest in American politics, he discussed the "late & direct accounts" from France with a sense of easy familiarity:

> The Queen and Comte D'Artois heads of the Nobles have fled, probably to her brother the Emperor.... Great Disorder by the mob in Paris, Bastille pulled down, Govr. Beheaded.—Foulon for a Day Minister, beheaded & his Body abused the next.—Neckar new Minister.—the Caisse d'Escompte seized by the *Mobility* as well as another considerable Bank, that of Poissy.... The Mob is not only enraged but drunk they have broken open the Cellars of the Nobility and are drinking their best Wines, they must be lost upon their coarse palates.

His disdain for the mob was revealing. Before the creation of the French Republic in 1792, Bache supported the constitutional monarchy established by the 1791 Constitution, attacking its critics as "Mad Democrats." But when Girondists in the national assembly declared war on monarchical Europe in 1792, precipitating the overthrow of Louis XVI, he abandoned his former moderation. War in Europe would lead to the "universal reformation" of mankind, he declared, dismissing the mob violence that accompanied the overthrow of Louis XVI and the "dreadful massacre of the 2d of September" as no more than the birth pangs of a "Nation emerging from the horrors of Despotism." When news about the declaration of the French Republic arrived in the United States, Bache was delirious.[29]

He was not alone. In early 1793, American enthusiasm for the French Revolution reached its zenith, and Bache began to argue that the French had now outstripped their American revolutionary predecessors. The revolution in France, argued one writer in the *General Advertiser*, had rekindled the spirit of political equality in the United States and revealed the incomplete nature of the revolution in America. "Turn your eyes, my brethren to France," urged "Mirabeau":

> She will afford you an example well deserving of your imitation—there you will see none but citizens, nothing but equality, the substance and not the shadow of democratic spirit—are there any levees since the downfall of the monarchy? Are there any birthday celebrations and titles of office there? Does any officer of her government refuse to mix with the citizens? Does the pomp and splendor and distance of royalty cloath any officer acting under the republic?

"Condorcet" also thought that the French now surpassed Americans "in the spirit of true republicanism" and were busy uprooting aristocratic influence while Americans allowed it to flourish. Earlier in the year, Bache had been reluctant to follow Freneau into battle against Hamilton, but the radicalization of the French Revolution alarmed and emboldened him. Now, he was convinced that Americans faced the same reactionary forces as those ranged against the French Republic. Echoing the arguments developed in the *National Gazette*, Bache stated that "the question in America is no longer between federalism and anti-federalism, but between republicanism and anti-republicanism." Those who "passed under the name federalists," he claimed, wished to create a political system based on "anti-republican orders and artificial balances," and "all true friends of liberty ought to be on their constant guard." By the end of 1792, the rhetoric of the *General Advertiser* had become fiercely anti-aristocratic, and in the presidential elections Bache campaigned hard against the reelection of Vice President Adams, aligning himself closely with the *National Gazette*. But Adams was not his only target, and both Freneau and Bache began to explore more explosive political territory, for the first time publicly criticizing the political conduct and character of President George Washington.[30]

After the formation of the federal government in 1789, public criticism of Washington was rare. Writing in the early 1790s, the French minister, Louis Guillaume Otto, was impressed by the respect shown to Washington in the press despite the fact that American newspapers were "often very licentious." The *General Advertiser* was no exception. Despite his later attacks on titles of distinction, Bache usually referred to Washington as "his Excellency the President," assiduously reported his official movements and activities, and treated him with unqualified admiration. In a eulogy to the administration published in November 1790, he exulted in the fact that "A WASHINGTON presides over us with as much dignity and wisdom as man is capable of exerting." Bache was especially conscientious about the celebration of Washington's birthday, which even Fenno treated with restraint, warmly endorsing the festivities surrounding the sixtieth birthday of "our beloved PRESIDENT" in 1791. The following year, he helped to organize a ball in Washington's honor under the auspices of the New City Dancing Assembly, applauding the president's decision to attend this event as well as a more socially exclusive gathering at the City Dancing Assembly, as the act of a truly "republican magistrate" who recognized "no distinction between citizen and citizen." Observing the president's birthday, he argued, responding to critics of the celebration, was simply an act of public gratitude. "The anniversary of our President's birthday," he wrote,

> is the most suitable occasion for demonstrations of the sense entertained of his services, by marks of manly joy and decent festivity. As long as Americans feel the blessings of Liberty, and of a pure republican government this day will be remembered as one of the most auspicious in their calendar. Should American republicanism be crampt by aristocratical encroachments, still the remembrance of the day will live in the bosoms of every freeman.

Such expressions of public gratitude, argued one correspondent, were "the most pleasing of all possible incense, when proceeding from the voluntary ardor of independent citizens."[31]

The publication of "Forerunners of Monarchy and Aristocracy in the United States" by Mirabeau in December 1792 was the first sign of a dramatic shift in Bache's attitude toward Washington. Although the essay did not mention Washington by name, its tone and argument were unmistakably hostile to the president. Official titles ("Excellency, Honourable and Esquire"), "Levees," and presidential birthdays, argued Mirabeau, were sure signs of monarchical corruption, and in a clear reference to Washington's famous equipage and fondness for public display, the author condemned "parade of every kind in the officers of government, such as pompous carriages, splendid feasts and tawdry gowns." Underlying this catalog of "monarchical" sins was a powerful and coherent critique of the political culture that sustained the presidency, a critique that was central to Republican ideology in the 1790s. Mirabeau, for example, objected not only to the "monarchical" rituals surrounding Washington but to all forms of ritual that created a "ceremonial distance between officers of the government and the people." Rituals of subordination, he argued, preserved and perpetuated habits of popular deference and encouraged the "crime and folly of idolatry." They represented "an inversion" of the political order in a republic, "for in a republic, officers of the government are the political servants of the people, and therefore are entitled only to universal civility, and in no instance to awful and distant respect."[32]

Any elected representative who sought to create such "awful and distant respect" and to distinguish himself from his constituents by a "fastidious distance," declared Mirabeau, had usurped popular sovereignty and "should be displaced." In other words, elaborate public ceremony by its nature enacted and reconstituted hierarchical and patriarchal relations of power, mystifying and undermining the proper relationship between citizen and representative. Republican citizens were not children governed "by their senses and imaginations," insisted Mirabeau, but rational and responsible adults who shared in the exercise of political sovereignty and had no need to be "looking up to heads of departments, and praising or blaming them for the good or evil things which flow from the government." But the author's hostility toward patriarchal authority was not absolute. Like Thomas Paine, Mirabeau believed that the American Revolution had redistributed the authority of a single political father to a nation of political fathers, who possessed collective responsibility for the preservation of the state. "Liberty will never be safe or durable in a republic," he argued, "till every citizen thinks it as much his duty to take care of the state, as to take care of his family." This conception of patriarchal democracy, or the democratization of patriarchy, directly echoed the arguments of Paine's *Common Sense*. Republicanism was not incompatible with patriarchal authority but required its dispersal among a male citizenry. Similarly, monarchy was not defined by patriarchy but by its concentration in the body of a single man, ideological assumptions that were extremely hostile to the position that Washington and the presidency occupied in postrevolutionary American political culture.[33]

The religious character of Mirabeau's argument is striking. His hostility toward the exterior nature of ritual and the way ritual functioned to create "ceremonial distance," his insistence on the "fallibility" of political leaders, his denunciation of the "incense" of public praise, and his contempt for popular "idolatry" drew on a Protestant (and, to a lesser extent, deist) language of anticlericalism and anti-Catholicism. While Fenno and the Federalists tried constantly to encourage greater reverence in public life, Republicans insisted on the primacy of irreverence. And the chief litmus test for such irreverence was the sanctity surrounding George Washington. According to "Cornelia," popular reverence for the president had its roots in habits of servility and deference inherited from the monarchical past: "To homage any one is to destroy the equality which constitutes the essence of our sovereignty."

> No character or place ought to be so sacred in a republican government as to be above criticism. Inviolability and infallibility are royal qualities, which *slaves* only can comprehend: It is the inalienable prerogative of freemen to scrutinize the conduct of their rulers, and if derogatory to just and equal principles, it ought to meet their severest reprehension. To elevate any character, however meritorious, beyond the level of scrutiny, is to establish a precedent, big with the most destructive consequences—it is to lay out the turnpike of slavery.

Behind this critique of political deference lurked an even more powerful argument for the separation of religious and political life. In a system based on popular sovereignty, nothing could be safely regarded as sacred, and the preservation of political freedom and equality depended on the desacralization of public life. As Cornelia argued, issues of personal character were irrelevant because no member of an elected government was anything more than a temporary embodiment of popular sovereignty. Reverence for even the most deserving and "meritorious" of elected leaders therefore involved an alienation of political sovereignty that reduced the citizen to the position of a subject or slave.[34]

It also reduced the independent male citizen to the position of the dependent female subject, and it is significant here that the author selected a female pen name, Cornelia. Implicit in the author's discussion of reverence and idolatry was a highly gendered understanding of public life as a realm of male authority and power. Reverence constituted an alienation of patriarchal power that emasculated the male republican citizen, and Cornelia explicitly linked political deference with aristocratic society and the insidious influence of women. While it was true that women formed the "political character of men," the author inverted more progressive arguments about "Republican Motherhood" that were becoming common during the 1790s, arguing that it was in the female world of the drawing room (a dangerous and aristocratic blend of domestic and public space) that "anti-republican distinctions" were first encouraged. Mirabeau made the same connection between political reverence and emasculation, deploring the decline of "manly republicanism" and the growth of servile, fawning "effeminacy." "A freeman," he declared, making the religious implications of his position clear, "ought to homage no one but his God—the evening of idolatry ought to vanish before the morning of reason." Republican citizens, like those in search of religious truth, required no intermediaries, only a free and independent will, and to argue that they should be governed by the wisdom of their political leaders was political blasphemy. In the language and symbolism of Republican politics, Federalists were cast as a political priesthood and George Washington as a political pope.[35]

The primary target of Mirabeau and other Republican writers was the political culture of the presidency, but by early 1793 their attacks on Washington himself had grown more personal. Sidney, for example, described him as a political "puppet" and hoped "for a reform of his good sense," and Mirabeau, sounding an even more iconoclastic note, questioned his conduct as both a general and a president. "Even the President's character," commented the Federalist politician Oliver Wolcott, Jr., to his father, "no longer remains inviolable." But by the time of Washington's second inaugural in March 1793, attacks on him in the *General Advertiser* had subsided, and after a series of hostile essays on plans to celebrate his birthday, Bache let the inaugural day pass quietly. When Washington's Proclamation of Neutrality was published in April and the *National Gazette* began to attack him for betraying republican France, Bache stayed silent. What explains this sudden shift in the attitude of the *General Advertiser*? Bache's attacks on Washington were inspired by the formation of the French Republic and the spectacular military victories at Valmy and Jemappes, reflecting the atmosphere of republican idealism that these events created in the United States. Bache made this link himself in a letter to his father in February 1793. "Since the news of the success of the French," he wrote,

> our politics in general have taken a very different turn, from the course in which they were gliding. The spirit of republicanism is reviving, and the President, of whom no one, six months ago would have thought disrespectfully, is now freely spoken of, and in *print* found fault with, his livery, his six horses, etc. etc., are generally censured.

Events in Europe had opened a "critical period in our politics," he argued, and "the national character" was now "refermenting & will no doubt take a shape less inauspicious to liberty & equality." As a result, a new division had taken place in American politics, and Bache hoped that he would be found "on the right side of it."[36]

But when the news of Louis XVI's execution reached Bache on March 15, he was profoundly disturbed. Even at the height of popular enthusiasm for France, Bache had expressed misgivings about the direction of the revolution in France. In response to a letter from his father questioning the conduct of "blood-thirsty characters such as Robespierre & Marat," Bache replied:

> I dont know what to think about Robertspierre or Marat. I begin to dislike these fellows since Condorcet no longer keeps company with them. I have great hopes that the French for humanity sake, not for the sake of royalty, will forbear sacrificing Louis & Antoinette to their just vengeance.

In January 1793, he had published an essay by Condorcet attacking Robespierre to show "what the men of sense of Paris think of Robesspierre." And when he learned of Louis XVI's death, he reacted with sadness, not enthusiasm. The king's treachery was clear, he argued, but "the loss of a crown would have been considered as a sufficient punishment" and "the fate of that unfortunate king must be deeply lamented" by those who recalled his contribution to American independence. Several days later, he published a sympathetic "Elegy on the Death of Louis XVI," and although he acknowledged the right of the national convention to execute the king and even printed one or two essays supporting its decision, most of the commentary he published in the *General Advertiser*, including essays by Thomas Paine, Brissot de Warville, and Condorcet, opposed the execution of Louis XVI.[37]

Bache's response to Washington's Proclamation of Neutrality demonstrated the sobering influence of Louis XVI's execution. Earlier in the year, he had grumbled about the way "this ungrateful republic" had treated France, urging Americans to rouse themselves from their "ignoble torpidity." But now, his tone became cautious and conservative. In an editorial criticizing the king's execution, he advised Americans to "keep aloof from the storms of Europe" and "let strict neutrality be our aim." Several days later, he discussed the outbreak of war in Europe, arguing that "policy incontestably dictates a strict neutrality on our part," and when Washington's Proclamation of Neutrality was published, he greeted it with unqualified enthusiasm. "The public mind," he wrote, was greatly relieved by the proclamation of the executive, "which informs us it is the duty, as well as interest of the United States, to act toward the belligerent powers with perfect impartiality." This did not stop Bache from organizing support for the French Republic. Like Freneau, he helped to arrange the public reception for Citizen Genet in Philadelphia in late May, and he turned the offices of the *General Advertiser* into a center for relief efforts in France. But unlike Freneau, his support for the administration's policy of neutrality remained firm.[38]

The contrast between Bache and Freneau is striking. The execution of Louis XVI tempered Bache's hostility toward Washington at the same time as it galvanized Freneau, who linked his campaign against Washington and the Proclamation of Neutrality explicitly to support for the execution of the French king. By mid-1793, Freneau's iconoclasm was widely shared in radical Republican circles and was part of a broad resurgence of egalitarian, anti-aristocratic language, symbolized by the growing use of the term "citizen." The unfolding political revolution in France did more than heighten sensitivity to vestiges of monarchical government in the United States. The desacralization of the French monarchy—made definitive by the execution of Louis XVI on January 21, 1793—provoked renewed criticism about the way political power and popular sovereignty were embodied in the American Republic. Freneau and other radicals welcomed Louis XVI's execution as a measure that annihilated the body of the king and the king's body, the embodiment of sovereignty in the person of the king. By refusing to sacrifice the "freedom and happiness of twenty-six millions of his fellow creatures" to the life of "one man," argued Freneau, Robespierre had established the primacy of principles over men and revolutionary egalitarianism over divine right. And by creating the collective revolutionary leadership of the Committee of Public Safety, the French had made the principle of impersonality central to republican government. In contrast to this revolutionary break, Americans remained wedded to the personal, monarchical form of political authority embodied in the presidency.[39]

This idea of impersonality was expressed in many of the public celebrations and civic festivals organized by Americans to demonstrate their solidarity with the French Republic in 1793. At a banquet at Oeller's Tavern in Philadelphia, "friends of equality and of the French Revolution" celebrated French military victories with a series of toasts, including one to "All who are governed by principles and not men," and the phrase "principles not men" quickly became a rallying cry and article of faith for radical partisans of the French Revolution. Of course, the phrase usually referred to one man in particular—George Washington—and at gatherings where participants toasted "principles not men," they often omitted the conventional toast to the president or added a qualifying phrase like "because he is a friend to the rights of man." Members of the French Society in Philadelphia demoted rather than ignored the president, quaffing thirteen bumpers before raising their glasses to the "virtuous Washington." Participants at a civic feast in Massachusetts used the phrasing of their toast to demonstrate their radical principles, drinking to plain "Citizen Washington," and French partisans in Charleston drank to the simple "George Washington," a form that became increasingly common.[40]

After the arrival of Citizen Genet and the publication of Washington's Proclamation of Neutrality, toasting the president became almost unacceptable among hard-line supporters of the French Republic. Members of the French Patriotic Society (which included Bache and Freneau) celebrated the Fourth of July by drinking to the French Republic, the United States, the French National Convention, and the U.S. Congress, acknowledging Washington's significance only by toasts to "Principles not men" and "Liberty, Equality, and no King." A banquet held to honor Genet and the French alliance "in the true republican style, and to regard principles and not men, as the objects of commemoration" underlined this message with the toast: "May Principles and Not Men be the objects of Republican attachment." And the next day, Freneau drove home the importance of this toast in the *National Gazette*, congratulating those who attended the banquet for breaking the "fetters of idolatry" and emancipating

A Peep into the Antifederal Club. Unidentified artist, New York, 1793. After Washington denounced them as "self-created," the Democratic societies that had sprung up in 1793–1794 subsided almost as quickly. Here, Jefferson (inspired by Hamlet and by Milton's Satan) addresses the membership of a club that includes the devil and James Monroe. Its anarchist principles ("Liberty is the power of doing any thing we like") also appeal to the African American on the right, who declares, "our turn nex." Courtesy of the Library Company of Philadelphia.

"themselves from their superstitious veneration for individuals." Genuine republicans, he argued, should have "no other idol than liberty" and should place their faith in "the whole body of the people" rather than a single person. In a remarkable discussion of the relationship between principles and personality, he warned readers that past efforts to embody principles of religious and political freedom in men had corrupted both men and principles. The only solution was to separate the two. "But strip religion and liberty of men," he declared, "behold them in their naked and abstracted simplicity, and our adoration and affection will be eternal."[41]

Despite his support for France, Bache avoided the controversy stirred up by Citizen Genet and ignored the attacks on Washington that filled the *National Gazette*. After Genet's "Appeal to the People" in August 1793, he expressed strong support for the Washington administration. Although Americans wished to preserve their alliance with the French Republic, explained "A Citizen," they "revere the President, and are firmly united in supporting the government, and preserving peace." As Bache realized, in a contest between the political power and personal influence of Genet and of Washington, the result was a foregone conclusion. Nonetheless, the Genet mission marked a turning point for Bache and the *General Advertiser*, and his public support for the Washington administration was more tactical than heartfelt. "Our Federal Executives carry things with a high hand," he wrote privately in August, and "the British interest has by far outweighed the French with government. The commercial, the monied interests carries all before it."[42] In September, he fled Philadelphia to escape the yellow fever epidemic, suspending publication of the *General Advertiser*. And when he returned in late December, he was in a new, more defiant mood. On New Year's Day, he published the following short but significant declaration:

> In politics, the violence of parties, and the severe duties of the Editor of a free press leave him to regret some friends lost and some friends made.... The editor, however, never will shrink from what he conceives his duty. Public men are all amenable to the tribunal of the press in a free state; the greater, indeed, their trust, the more responsible are they.[43]

Both his friends and enemies understood this declaration of political independence. Jettisoning his previous commitment to impartiality, from this moment onward, Bache edited the *General Advertiser* as an unapologetically partisan newspaper.

By early 1794, the *General Advertiser* had replaced Freneau's defunct *National Gazette* as the leading voice of the Republican opposition. The backdrop to this development was the diplomatic crisis provoked by British attacks on American shipping in 1793–1794. Jefferson's *Report on Privileges and Restrictions on the Commerce of the United States in Foreign Countries* and the retaliatory resolutions introduced in the House of Representatives by Madison in January signaled the start of a belligerent Republican campaign against Britain and its alleged allies in the United States. Bache took an active role in this campaign, maintaining a steady drumbeat of support for Madison's resolutions in the *General Advertiser*, as well as joining the Democratic Society of Pennsylvania, one of the many political societies that sprang up to organize petitions against British attacks. By March, war with Britain seemed unavoidable, and in this highly charged political atmosphere Bache's support for American neutrality evaporated. Repudiating the Proclamation of Neutrality as a "declaration of our fears," an editorial in late March argued that, far from ensuring peace, it had invited British injury and insult. "Had a revolutionary energy been displayed," argued the editorial, "instead of the effeminacy of a funding system, respect and tranquility would have been the reward."[44]

Bache's growing hostility toward Britain was accompanied by a hardening of his support for the French Revolution. In early 1794, despite his previous misgivings about Robespierre and Marat, he defended their execution of Brissot de Warville, Condorcet, and other Girondin leaders. A toast in the *General Advertiser* to "the Courageous and Virtuous Mountain" (the members of the Jacobin Club in the national convention who supported Robespierre) caught the new, militant tone: "may it crush the moderates, the traitors, the federalists and all Aristocrats, under whatever denomination they may be dignified." When he learned of the Girondin leader Georges Danton's death, Bache blamed it on the "maneuvers of the aristocrats" and published a nauseating account of the charges against him that praised Robespierre as the embodiment of public virtue. He dismissed rumors of Thomas Paine's death (he was actually rotting in a Paris prison) as an "aristocratic fabrication," and when Robespierre suffered the same grisly fate as Brissot and Danton, Bache briskly assured his readers that the death of one man would not halt "the grand cause" of the revolution nor "the immutable force of principles which no opposition can check."[45]

He began to employ the same aggressive rhetoric in his discussions of domestic policy and politics. Until 1794, the constant barrage of abuse aimed at Hamilton by the Republican press had found no support in the *General Advertiser*, and Bache shared none of Freneau's anti-commercialism, his concern about aristocratic revanchism, and his contempt for Hamilton.[46] But by 1794, he was ready to change tack. An editorial in early February called the national debt "subversive of public liberty," and a few days later, Bache attacked Hamilton for creating a "system of inequality and instrumentality which has long been the darling idol of our mushroom gentry and their supporters." From this point onward, a steady parade of "paper noblemen" and "knights of the funding system" cantered through the pages of the *General Advertiser*. One explanation for Bache's newfound hostility to Hamilton was the influence of a Scottish émigré journalist, James Thomson Callender, who began to contribute to the *General Advertiser* in early 1794. Callender, the author of the *Political Progress of Britain*, an indictment of British economic imperialism, was a violent Anglophobe who despised Hamilton, and his satirical pen is clearly evident in the new editorial emphasis on the "knights of the funding system." But Bache was also becoming concerned about the way that Hamilton's economic policies were shaping the foreign policy of the Washington administration and, in particular, its approach to the French Republic.[47] An editorial linking the funding system to British influence on American foreign policy argued that Britain had at last "thrown off the mask" and attacked the "national interest and honor." "And to whom are we indebted for this?" asked the author:

> To those men who begin to speak of the people and their opinions with disdain, and whose creed contains the doctrine, that a public debt is a public blessing. To a monied aristocracy.... To those men who have...studiously endeavoured to cement our connection with Great Britain and detach us from the Republic of France. In a word to the knights of the funding system.

The "hero of their order, the arch corrupter of our government" was Hamilton, who worked tirelessly to undermine the French alliance by encouraging dependence on British financial and commercial interests. Earlier in the 1790s, Freneau had argued that the growth of a domestic aristocracy required Americans to make common cause with their French revolutionary brethren. Now, Bache's sense of common cause with revolutionary France led him to acknowledge the existence of a domestic aristocracy. But France, not Alexander Hamilton, remained the touchstone of his politics.[48]

Nothing demonstrates this more clearly than his response to the Whiskey Rebellion in 1794. When news of an armed uprising in western Pennsylvania against Hamilton's excise tax on whiskey reached Philadelphia, Bache immediately condemned the revolt. Whatever the injustice of Hamilton's tax, he declared, "we have a government of our own choice and those abuses can be removed, for the people have all power in their hands." At first, his denunciation of the whiskey rebels was tempered by criticism of the government. When the Democratic Society of Pennsylvania (with Bache presiding as chairman) passed a resolution condemning both the excise tax and the rebellion, Bache endorsed the resolution in the *General Advertiser*, urging the government to show restraint toward the small farmers involved in the protest and suggesting that the "knights of the funding system" should form the vanguard of any army sent to quell them.[49] But as the crisis developed, Bache became less sympathetic toward the rebels. In early September, he described the "excise mobs" as pawns of "British gold" and praised the "manly and calm decision of our government." And when the government mobilized an army to suppress the uprising, he assured readers that "an universal ardour for military exertion seems to pervade every rank of citizens in Philadelphia," an ardor inspired by the "deliberate and just conviction that every thing dear to the commonwealth is at stake." Promoting and publicizing the formation of McPherson's Blues, a volunteer militia of "true republican principles," he reported the progress of the militia through western Pennsylvania, even expressing alarm at the number of liberty poles they encountered.[50]

Other members of the Democratic Society of Pennsylvania shared his military zeal. After a debate on September 11, the society passed two resolutions, one approving the "moderate, prudent and republican conduct of the President of the United States," and a second recommending that the "strength of the state ought to be exerted should the power of reason prove inadequate." A more strongly worded resolution describing the revolt as an "outrage upon order and democracy" was approved by a single vote but withdrawn when the defeated minority stormed out in disgust. Bache was part of the majority. His support for the suppression of the Whiskey Rebellion tempered his opposition to the federal government. When Washington condemned the Democratic societies as "self-created societies" in November 1794 and blamed them for the outbreak of the Whiskey Rebellion, Bache reacted with patriotic indignation. "I firmly believe," he wrote, that "were the muster rolls of the army, which has turned out against them [the whiskey rebels] to be printed, that more members of Democratic societies in proportion to their numbers would be found upon the lists, than of any class of citizens." The Democratic societies, he declared with pride, had proved themselves "friends to good order."[51]

In early 1794, the editor of the *American Minerva*, Noah Webster, had claimed that public respect for George Washington had "hitherto restrained the violence of parties." "Whatever be the difference of opinion on subjects of government," he wrote, "all parties agree to confide in the president." As Webster's comment suggests, he sensed a change in the political atmosphere, and so did Vice President John Adams, who traced this change to the *General Advertiser*. "Bache's paper," he wrote, "which is nearly as bad as Freneau's, begins to join in concert with it to maul the President for his drawing rooms, levees, declining to accept of invitations to dinners, tea parties, his birthday odes, visits, compliments, & etc." But even Republican firebrands like Freneau confined their criticism largely to Washington's public self-presentation and policy and avoided direct attacks on Washington's private or personal character. Much as Republicans deplored his personal influence over American public opinion, before the mid-1790s, they did little to challenge it, and Washington remained a symbol of political unity and impartiality in an increasingly factionalized political culture.[52]

The clearest signs of Washington's continued popularity were the public celebrations of his birthday each year in February. Although Washington's birthday and the Fourth of July became increasingly politicized in radical Republican circles after the Genet mission in 1793, popular politicization of these celebrations was much less evident. Washington remained a central figure in most public celebrations of the Fourth of July, while radical, pro-French sentiments often found their way into celebrations of Washington's birthday. Although some Republicans denounced the celebration of Washington's birthday as "monarchical," contrasted it unfavorably with the Fourth of July ("the birth-day of a nation" rather than the "birth-day of an individual," wrote one critic), and used the two occasions to rehearse the conflict between "men" and "measures," most Americans continued to celebrate both events enthusiastically and without much sense of political contradiction. A celebration of Washington's birthday in Massachusetts in 1793, for example, saluted Washington, Adams, the Marquis de Lafayette, and "The People of France" before concluding with a rousing chorus of the French revolutionary song "Ça Ira." The Tammany Society of New York, which was considered a stronghold of Republican politics by the mid-1790s, nonetheless held a banquet in honor of Washington's birthday in 1795 and toasted "George Washington, President of the United States, and the father of his country."[53]

Challenging this widespread public affection for the president was politically hazardous, as Thomas Greenleaf, editor of the *New-York Journal*, had discovered in December 1793. Greenleaf had already published a series of essays on the new French Constitution by "A Citizen," attacking the existence of a "single executive head" as despotic and tyrannical, an "elected limited monarchy," and accusing Washington's supporters of elevating "*their* beloved President *above* the People—*above* the Constitution, and *above* the Representatives of the Union." But when he published a "letter from a gentleman in Virginia" that contained a lengthy examination of the "character of ——," making clear that his subject was Washington, Greenleaf broke new ground. Drawing attention to the royal blood that flowed in Washington's veins, the author described his education as typical of the rich and well-born, "gambling, reveling, horse racing, and *horse whipping* constituted the essentials of it," and attributed his support for the American Revolution and the Constitution to wounded pride and avarice. The attack went well beyond public policy:

> Is —— munificent in private transactions? No, —— is most infamously niggardly. Does ——, in —— public declarations put on the mask of religion? In private life —— is a most horrid swearer and blasphemer. Is —— apparently tender of public opinion? In private life —— is a severe tyrant. Is —— a lover of liberty? No —— hates it from his —— birth; —— never knew what it was.

"Is not ——," raged the author, "among that groupe of vultures which are eternally yelling *federalism, federalism* when in their hearts they mean royalty and despotism?" This public assault on Washington's private character was too much for respectable public opinion in New York. At the Tontine Coffee House, members passed a series of resolutions condemning Greenleaf's "infamous libel against the President" and summoned him to appear before a committee of the members to account for his outrageous conduct. Despite Greenleaf's fury about this effort to censure him, he immediately disowned the offending letter as a "series of villainous observations and innuendos" and assured Tontine members of his "personal respect for the President." At their request, he issued a public apology in the *New-York Journal* assuring readers, "the character intended to be calumniated must be sacred to every true American."[54]

Greenleaf's experience revealed the limits of partisan politics. No matter how defiantly he and other Republicans defended the freedom of the press against the Tontine Coffee House, they had no wish to associate themselves with public attacks on Washington's character. This sense that Washington's character remained "sacred to every true American" was shattered during the next two years by ferocious public debate about the Jay Treaty. Negotiated by Chief Justice John Jay in 1794, the Treaty of Amity, Commerce and Navigation with Great Britain resolved the crisis with Britain but created widespread opposition in the United States, especially among Republicans who saw it as a betrayal of the alliance with France.[55] From the start, Republicans interpreted the negotiation of a treaty with Britain as a battle between the will of the people and the will of the president. When Noah Webster suggested strengthening executive powers to deal with the British crisis, the *General Advertiser* denounced the idea as an attempt to create "a virtual King in our President." And when Washington announced Jay's appointment as a special envoy to Britain in April 1794, Bache attacked it as an unconstitutional exercise of executive power. In his view, the sole purpose of the Jay mission was to placate Great Britain and to "prop a tottering minority" in Congress who would rather "submit to a monarch, or dissolve the Union, than that the present majority should dictate the measures of government." When this "tottering minority" defeated Madison's embargo resolutions and approved Jay's appointment as special envoy, Bache accused the Washington administration of trying to "govern the proceedings of the legislative," an argument that would later become central to Republican arguments against the ratification of the Jay Treaty.[56]

This focus on the executive meant that attacks on Washington in the *General Advertiser* became steadily more personal, a development that also reflected Callender's influence on the paper. When Washington entered a theater in Philadelphia through the back door, he was attacked as a "horrible-imitator of a British crown-bearer," and another editorial suggested satirically that he should be declared dictator forthwith so "every man, beast and thing would be obliged to bow to his sovereign will." Bache also began to campaign against high government salaries, which he alleged allowed public officials to live in "dazzling splendour," an issue that Republicans exploited effectively for the rest of the 1790s. "No Aristocrat" argued that high salaries were another of those "capital errors, which we have sucked in from the breasts of monarchy," and demanded that Washington's official salary be cut from $25,000 to $15,000. Simultaneously, Republicans introduced a series of resolutions to Congress to reduce the civil establishment and cut the president's pay to $12,000 a year. The desire for "Economy and Simplicity" toasted by members of the Democratic Society of Pennsylvania on the Fourth of July 1794 clearly reflected this latest campaign against executive privilege and influence. During the summer and fall of 1794, Bache was preoccupied with the Whiskey Rebellion, and his attacks on the Jay mission and Washington subsided. When Washington denounced the Democratic societies in November, Bache responded coolly, steering clear of direct attacks on the president. But when news about the conclusion of the Jay Treaty arrived in January 1795, he abandoned all former restraint. "The success of Mr. Jay will serve peace abroad," predicted Fisher Ames, "and kindle war at home. Faction will sound the tocsin against the treaty. I see a little cloud, as big as a man's hand in Bache's paper that indicates a storm."[57]

Ames was right. Even before the provisions of the treaty were made public, popular opinion was hostile to a treaty with Britain, and opposition to the president and the administration revived almost at once, with Bache's newspaper, rechristened the *Aurora* in November 1794 under the motto "Surgo ut Prosim" (I Rise That I Might Serve), leading the charge. Realizing that the fate of the otherwise unpopular Jay Treaty depended on the personal prestige of the president, Republicans urged Americans not to let their admiration for Washington silence public debate. Carefully avoiding any suggestion of an attack on the president, Madison attacked those who made use of his name in the *Aurora*. "Do arguments fail?" he wrote, "is the public mind to be encountered? There are not a few ever ready to invoke the name of Washington; to garnish their heretical doctrines with his virtues, and season their unpalatable measures with his popularity." "Franklin," the author of a series of essays on the treaty first published in Eleazar Oswald's *Independent Gazetteer*, was less cautious. "Let not your reverence for any individual," he wrote, "blind you to the great interest of your country." Washington's decision to negotiate the Jay Treaty was totally irreconcilable with the "wishes & sentiments of the people," he argued, and where a "public measure dare not be arraigned, because it is the offspring of a public character; there liberty lies prostrate; there is despotism."[58]

The secrecy surrounding the provisions of the treaty in the first few months of 1795 intensified and legitimized such attacks, making it easier for Republicans to portray conflict about the treaty as a struggle between the popular will (expressed by "public opinion" or the people's "immediate representatives" in the House of Representatives) and the will of the president and fueling charges that the government was now a monarchy in all but name. In this sense, the Jay Treaty debate was not only a debate about a treaty, or even a debate about the power of the executive to negotiate and conclude foreign treaties, but a struggle to define the relationship between popular sovereignty and the Constitution. Although Republicans constantly expressed devotion to the Constitution, there

Aurora General Advertiser, Philadelphia, December 14, 1794. Published daily by Benjamin Franklin Bache, the newspaper had recently been rechristened the *Aurora*, with the addition of the rising sun and the motto "Surgo ut Prosim" (I Rise That I Might Serve) to the masthead. Although the *Aurora* began life as a commercial newspaper with polite Federalist politics, by this time it had become the leading Republican newspaper in the country, a position it held until 1800. Courtesy of the Library Company of Philadelphia.

was a great deal of ambiguity about it in their writings, and they usually identified popular sovereignty with the House of Representatives, refusing to acknowledge the democratic legitimacy of the executive. Sidney, for example, condemned Washington's "open war with the legislature and the People," warning that, if he persisted, the people "must either crouch to a will not their own, or wade thro' the blood of a civil war, to the horrors of anarchy or the gloom of despotism." Such denunciations of Washington's "unconstitutional" conduct were difficult to distinguish from simple hostility toward the constitutional role of the presidency, and some Republicans acknowledged this difficulty, arguing that the presidency and the Constitution were inherently anti-democratic. An editorial published in the *Aurora* soon after news of the Jay Treaty arrived confronted the issue boldly:

> The Constitution of the United States is said to be the perfection of human wisdom, and although emanating from the people, they dare hardly question its delivery from Mount Sinai. According then to this perfection of human wisdom, the people can be legislated for without the consent of their immediate representatives; indeed the laws made by their representatives can be superseded by the decrees of the President and the Senate. By this perfection of human wisdom, treaties are declared to be the supreme law of the land, and the President, by and with the advice and consent of the Senate, can make treaties—this is, the supreme law of the land.[59]

This was an unusually candid attack on the democratic credentials of the Constitution, but its underlying assumption—that the powers of the presidency were antithetical to the preservation of popular sovereignty—informed almost all Republican discussions of the Jay Treaty.

When the provisions of the Jay Treaty were finally made public in July 1795, criticism of Washington momentarily subsided while anger about the treaty itself exploded. Bache played a pivotal role in these events. After the Senate (whose sessions were still conducted in secrecy) approved the treaty in late June, Washington decided to release it to the public. But Bache beat him to the punch. Acquiring a copy from Republican senator Stevens Thomson Mason, Bache printed an abstract of the treaty in the *Aurora* on June 29, and on July 1 announced that "Authentic Copies of the Treaty" were for sale at his office. This scoop could not have been better timed to benefit the Republican cause. "The inestimable treaty with Britain," crowed an editorial in the *Aurora* on July 4, "is at last entrusted to the perusal of the public." "The whole transaction," charged Bache, invoking the democratic spirit of July Fourth, "has been conducted with a studied contempt for the sentiments of the people."[60] Eager to exploit his good luck and to rally public opposition to the treaty, he set out at once from Philadelphia to distribute copies of the treaty in New York and New England.

After a successful public meeting in New York City and a chance breakfast encounter with John Adams in Worcester, Massachusetts (Adams thought "the generality of the people" would approve the treaty), on July 6, Bache reached Boston, where he attended a hastily organized public meeting in Faneuil Hall. "The voice of the toad-eaters of government," he declared triumphantly, had been "drowned in the universal disapprobation of the treaty." "I hope every city thro' out the Union will follow their example," he wrote to his wife, Margaret; "this is a momentous crisis in our affairs, and much depends on our exertions at this instant."[61]

As Bache hoped, the public reaction to the terms of the Jay Treaty was sensational. In Philadelphia, July Fourth celebrations turned into angry protest meetings against the treaty, and an effigy of John Jay was paraded through the streets and burned. Similar protests occurred throughout the country. Several thousand people attended a tumultuous demonstration against the treaty in New York City on July 19, and a few days later an even larger protest meeting passed a series of fiery resolutions condemning the treaty. Republicans lost no time in channeling this flood of popular emotion into a petitioning campaign against the treaty. "From north to south," observed Bache, "there appears to be but one common sentiment, that of reprobating the treaty."[62] He hoped that Washington would now be persuaded not to sign the treaty, or would "think it prudent to suspend, at least, the ratification." The Democratic Society of New York expressed the same hope at its Fourth of July celebration, calling on Washington to "comply with the unanimous wishes of every friend of his country" and prevent the Jay Treaty from becoming the "supreme law of the land." Such a deed would be further proof, declared a gathering of citizens in New Hampshire, that Washington was entitled to the "appellation of FATHER OF HIS COUNTRY."[63]

Washington's decision to sign the Jay Treaty on August 18 stunned Republicans, and after a period of disbelief, Bache reacted to the president's action with fury. The central issue, he argued, was no longer the treaty (discussion of which disappeared from the pages of the *Aurora* for the next few months) but the president himself. "Blind obedience is the doctrine now preached up," he thundered. Supporters of the Jay Treaty had "set a name in opposition to the constitution, to reason and republicanism" and had exploited Washington's popularity to force through an unpopular measure against the will of the American people. "The people," wrote "Hancock" in the *Aurora*, "have been treated with a superciliousness & arrogance which ought to kindle indignation in every bosom not dead to manly sentiment." Louis XVI, wrote one furious correspondent, had shown less disdain for his subjects than Washington did for his fellow citizens. The president's contempt for public opinion, argued the author, "would lead us to suppose, that he was the omnipotent director of a seraglio, instead of the first magistrate of a free people."[64] By signing the Jay Treaty, argued Bache and other writers in the *Aurora*, Washington had revealed his contempt for the will of the people and for the Constitution, which they regarded as synonymous. "The constitution supposes, and the principle of every free government supposes that the voice of the people ought to govern," argued Hancock, yet Washington had ratified the Jay Treaty "in opposition to the almost unanimous voice of America!" If he could defy the voice of the majority in such a brazen manner, argued "Pittachus," "we certainly do not live in a Republic."[65]

To Republicans, Washington's signing of the Jay Treaty was an act of usurpation and a betrayal of American interests, an act that cast doubt on his claims to patriarchal reverence and respect. In opposition to the "general will of an enlightened nation," claimed one commentator in the *Aurora*, he had assumed a "tone of majesty and superiority"; consequently, he was no longer the father of his country but its "master." In the same vein, "Atticus" instructed Americans to rally around their "immediate representatives" in the House of Representatives, promising "we shall not find in them the step fathers of their country." An almost insurrectionary article by "Valerius" warned Washington that the powers of the president and the Senate "may be reclaimed by the people," reminding him that "THE SAFETY OF THE PEOPLE IS THE SUPREME LAW." "The American People, Sir," declared the same author defiantly, "will look to death, the man who assumes the character of an usurper." These acts of patriarchal repudiation marked the beginning of a relentless campaign in the *Aurora* against Washington's popular influence. It was time, asserted Bache, to shatter public confidence in the president by subjecting his character to public scrutiny. If Washington wished to use his great personal influence to give the Jay Treaty "the force of *irrevocable* law," argued Valerius, then his critics were entitled "to enter into an exposition of your public character." Any lingering sense of obligation toward the "feelings of an INDIVIDUAL," he argued, was more than outweighed by "the interests, the happiness, the existence of a NATION." It was now necessary to "rend the veil of superstition" surrounding Washington and demolish the myth of presidential infallibility.[66]

The arguments of Valerius were a turning point for Republican propagandists and for the *Aurora*. Rather than blaming the Jay Treaty on the machinations of an "aristocratic junto" or the secret influence of Washington's advisors, Valerius argued that Washington was personally responsible for the passage of the treaty and for the political problems facing the country. Despite promising to restrict his criticism to Washington's "public character" and to disregard personal failings—"While therefore we contemplate the political degeneracy of the President, let us be blind to the transgressions of the man"—he and other Republican polemicists quickly abandoned any effort to retain such a distinction.

Had Americans undertaken a revolution, asked Atticus, to make Washington a monarch, to "establish a political infallibility, and consecrate a political pope in our country?" If so, then he would "preach up a reformation, and dare to be a Luther in politics." "I will unmasque the idol we have set up," he promised, "and shew him to be a man, and a man too, not fashioned according to the model of liberty." The fiery iconoclasm of Atticus was shared by "Belisarius," who thought that Washington should be "stript of the mantle of infallibility" and shown to be "a frail mortal, whose passions and weaknesses are like those of other men." Accusing him of visiting "upon his country deep and incurable public evils," Belisarius assured him that his name would descend with Hamilton's—"the chief promoter of all your measures"—"to oblivion." By defying the "voice of the people," charged Pittachus, Washington had relinquished any claim to public gratitude and respect. "A change," declared the author, "must be the consequence."[67]

The issue of "popular gratitude" raised by Pittachus signaled a further development in Republican attacks on Washington. Atticus, for example, deplored the way that public gratitude for Washington's past service to the nation had "put a seal upon our lips" and silenced debate about the defects of his policies. Gratitude was a "living virtue," argued one writer in the *Aurora*, and Washington's past achievements should not deflect criticism from his present failures. "Portius" went even further, and wondered if Washington was entitled to public gratitude at all. His contribution to the American Revolution had been much exaggerated, argued the author, and he challenged Washington to identify "one single act which unequivocally proves you a Friend to the Independence of America." As Portius understood it, public faith in Washington rested on his ability to represent and embody the achievements of the American Revolution, and to discredit him, Republicans had to discredit his contribution to the American Revolution and his status as a founding father. This they now attempted. Far from being the "Father of His Country," wrote Portius, Washington was a man of "childish ambition" whose military service had been inspired not by manly honor but by an effete desire for the "Garter of St. George or the Cross of St. Louis." "Exalted into a demigod" by the American people, "merely because he was not an open traitor," he had been merely cowardly, and would have seized power after the Revolution, argued Portius, if circumstances had been more favorable and if America had offered "the opportunity of imitating monarchical splendor, or of exercising regal power."[68]

This attempt to discredit Washington's revolutionary past was a central theme in the *Aurora* and inspired Bache to compile and publish *Letters from General Washington* in October 1795 as an "interesting appendix to the official Letters of George Washington, which have lately made their appearance." Designed to exploit the recent publication of Washington's *Official Letters* in London, they were in fact clever forgeries, first published as Loyalist propaganda by the editor of the *Royal Gazette*, James Rivington, in 1778, which cast doubt on Washington's support for the American cause and his confidence about the outcome of the war with Great Britain. In an ironic twist, they now reappeared, circulated by radical Republicans to discredit Washington's record in the revolutionary war. Although they probably had little influence on public opinion, Republican writers put them to good use in the *Aurora*. Valerius invoked them in his description of Washington as "neither a Briton nor an American, a whig nor a tory," a man of "insipid uniformity of mind" and "diminutive soul." Whether they were genuine or not, argued Pittachus, the letters had "the cast of Presidential character about them," revealing Washington's affection for George III and his "frigidity, if not repugnance to the declaration of independence." The ambition, arrogance, and despotic inclinations they displayed, he argued, "all correspond exactly with the genius of the man."[69]

The Republican campaign against Washington was not confined to personal abuse and the rewriting of revolutionary history. Republicans also began to call for the impeachment of the president. While earlier opposition writers referred briefly to the issue of presidential impeachment, it was first raised unequivocally by "Casca" in October 1795. The article by Casca intensified the attack on Washington and raised significant constitutional issues. In the first place, the author called on the House of Representatives to use its "sublime power of chastising ambition, of saving the Constitution, and of rescuing Liberty" to impeach the president, listing seventeen separate charges against him, which included patronizing the "enemies of the people," dismissing Thomas Jefferson from office, maintaining a standing army, displaying "cowardice" and "haughtiness" in office, and undermining the Constitution by signing the Jay Treaty. "The people are not sanguinary," stated Casca. "[T]hey only demand that those should be removed from office who abuse power," including "the man they once styled the father of his country."[70]

As Casca knew, the Senate, not the House of Representatives, controlled the power of impeachment, and as long as it was dominated by Federalists, it would not use its power to impeach Washington. The laundry list of charges provided by Casca was intended largely for rhetorical effect. But the threat to the president appeared less rhetorical when an article by "A Calm Observer" appeared in the *Aurora* a few days later. Official salaries had been a target of Republican criticism since 1794, but A Calm Observer went much further than earlier critics. Rather than attacking official ostentation and the high level of official salaries, he flatly accused Washington of overdrawing his presidential salary, condemning this as an outrage "upon the laws and constitution of our country." Such common theft from the public purse, he argued, made a mockery of Washington's image of disinterested public service.[71] As Bache realized at once, charges of financial corruption not only represented a threat to Washington's reputation, but gave force and substance to demands for his impeachment. After a blustering, unpersuasive attempt to refute these charges by the comptroller of the treasury, Oliver Wolcott, Jr., that one observer admitted made things "ten times worse" for the president, A Calm Observer renewed his offensive. Pressing home the case for Washington's impeachment, he wrote: "I know of no crime or misdemeanour against the constitution and the laws greater or higher than that which you have severally committed." The article of the Constitution dealing with powers of impeachment, he insisted, "was not made in vain, or is to be regarded by the people of the United States, as a mere dead letter." Other Republicans immediately took up the issue. "The opinion that the President ought to be impeached is gaining proselytes daily," wrote Pittachus. "[T]he people have no remedy left but in their immediate Representatives or a Convention." "Scipio" demanded Washington's immediate resignation, advising him to "let no flatterer persuade you to rest one hour longer at the helm of state." And Bache informed the *Aurora*'s growing chorus of critics that Republicans would not be "deterred from persevering in their noble and praise-worthy undertaking, by the barking of American aristocrats or the yelping of English curs."[72]

These demands for Washington's impeachment quickly subsided, but they show how ambivalent many radical Republicans were about the federal Constitution in the mid-1790s. Republicans could have used the impeachment campaign to emphasize their loyalty to the principles of the Constitution, but they did not. As Casca admitted, he hoped that the demand for Washington's impeachment would encourage people to "abhor a Senate" and generate a public groundswell for the constitutional reform of both the Senate and the presidency. Inspired by the example of the French National Assembly and the Jacobin Committee of Public Safety, Casca advocated "one legislative assembly and an executive composed of many persons possessing few powers and no splendor." Such a constitutional arrangement, he believed, "will soon form the favourite articles of every enlightened politician's creed." It would be wrong to dismiss Casca as a political eccentric. In a letter written to James Madison in 1795, Thomas Paine hoped that Americans would soon see the "necessity of shortening the time of the Senate and new modelling the Executive Department," and he expressed the same view publicly in his *Letter to Washington*, which was published by Bache in 1797. By the mid-1790s, there was widespread support for constitutional reform among Republican activists who believed that the passage of the Jay Treaty had exposed a serious imbalance between executive and legislative power. And there are a few signs that this radical Republican hostility to the Constitution was more widely shared. Militia officers of the Philadelphia County Brigade drank the following toast at a Fourth of July celebration in 1795: "To the Constitution of the United States—May it contain a remedy against its violators, or be so modified as to prevent the assumption of unlawful power and give greater security against usurpation." And in December 1795, the Virginia General Assembly debated and passed a series of resolutions supporting constitutional amendments to limit the power of the Senate and the presidency. Although these amendments were not as sweeping as the constitutional changes demanded by Casca, they were widely debated in the Republican press and endorsed by state legislatures in Kentucky, South Carolina, and Georgia. At the very least, the debate about these resolutions reveals a broader public interest in questions of constitutional revision from which the radical proposals of Casca emerged.[73]

That radical ideas about constitutional reform circulated in Republican circles is shown clearly by John Beckley's *Remarks Occasioned by the Late Conduct of Mr. Washington*, which was published by Bache in early 1797. Written by a Republican activist deeply involved in partisan organization, Beckley's work rehashed the personal attacks on Washington that had filled the *Aurora* for the past two years and was not distinguished for its political creativity or novelty. "We avow freely," he wrote, "that our chief object here is to destroy undue impressions in favour of Mr. Washington." However, in the course of rehashing standard Republican attacks on Washington, Beckley also demanded constitutional reform to limit the powers of the presidency. In Beckley's view, the presidency was far too powerful, and Washington's central role in the passage of the Jay Treaty made clear the need to reform the federal Constitution as well as those state constitutions which "partake of its defects." Drawn up and ratified before Americans had "unmonarchized" their ideas and habits, the Constitution "had dismissed the name of King" but "retained a prejudice for his authority," embodying executive power in a single man, a phenomenon Beckley believed was inherently monarchical. The framers of the Constitution, he argued, had created a "monocrate president," and this "exclusive" and "solitary president" should be replaced with a "plural directory, gradually renewed." Like their republican counterparts in France, American republicans would benefit from a collective form of leadership that would "no longer exhibit the fluctuating character of an individual, but approach nearer to the fixed abstract of the American nation." Although such ideas had little chance of realization, they show how vehemently Republicans like Beckley and Bache disliked the patriarchal political culture surrounding Washington and the presidency and how skeptical they were about the constitutional settlement of 1789.[74]

The essays of A Calm Observer were the high-water mark of the Republican campaign against Washington. By early 1796, the vilification of Washington in the Republican press had clearly become counterproductive. Although Federalists raised a subscription to defend the president against libelous attacks in the press, and threatened to bring civil lawsuits against Republican editors who printed them, the majority of Federalists were unfazed by Republican attacks. Writing at the height of the Republican campaign at the end of 1795, John Fenno thought that the public had seen through the "the late outrageous attacks on the President," and "this being the case, the constituted Authorities will receive the firmest support of the people." Despite the abusive treatment of Washington in Bache's newspaper, argued Federalist Elias Boudinot, "the generosity of the People in every state is undoubtedly firmly attached to him, and would risque their lives to serve him." Alexander Hamilton's responses to the charges of A Calm Observer began to appear in the *Aurora* on November 18 and continued for the next four days. Patiently and persuasively, Hamilton demolished the arguments of A Calm Observer, instantly silencing controversy about Washington's salary. After this reversal, criticism of Washington in the *Aurora* became increasingly threadbare and desultory. While Casca continued to demand Washington's impeachment, other Republicans changed tack and called on Congress to impeach those "who advized the President to this fatal decision." When Congress reconvened in December, Republicans focused on persuading the House to reject financial appropriations for the Jay Treaty, and their attacks on Washington lost energy and momentum.[75]

But Washington's personal influence remained an important political issue. If members of Congress were not seized by a "frenzy of idolatry," argued "Codrus" in the *Aurora*, they could prevent the growth of a "practical monarchy" in the United States and ensure that "tyranny will not establish its bastile in our Country." According to Bache, the nation faced a critical moment in its history, one that would decide the future of American republican government, and he filled the *Aurora* with firsthand accounts of the congressional debates on the Jay Treaty, which he then published and circulated as a pamphlet. The issue before the House of Representatives was not just the Jay Treaty, he argued, but whether the "immediate representatives of the people" had a right "to legislate on those subjects specifically delegated to them by the constitution" or whether this right was to be usurped by the executive. "The democratic part of the constitution" hung in the balance, believed Bache, and if the House capitulated to the president, "we had better at once change the name of our government" and admit that "America resisted and subdued one tyrant to make room for another." When Washington refused to provide Congress with official documents covering Jay's negotiations, Bache was apoplectic. Comparing him to Louis XVI and Oliver Cromwell, he applauded the resistance of the House of Representatives to "the torrents of Presidential and Senatorial usurpation," urging citizens to rally behind their elected representatives. The issue confronting Americans, he wrote, was "shall the people or the President be the sovereign of the United States?" If the treaty were approved, "the President will be as sovereign and omnipotent as the Demi-God of a Turkish Seraglio."[76]

But victory was slipping from the grasp of Bache and the Republicans. As Federalists successfully organized public opinion behind Washington and the Jay Treaty, Republican opposition to the treaty collapsed, rhetorically and politically exhausted, and Republicans began to turn against public opinion, dismissing popular support for Washington and the administration as the work of "banks, British agents, old tories &c." Defeat fueled cynicism, and Republicans now blamed Americans themselves for what Casca called the "despotic popularity of George Washington." "How long are the freemen of America to be the dupes of an administration and the sport of Great Britain," Bache fumed in an editorial that made his disillusionment with, and even contempt for, public opinion all too clear. "Can it be that one man can have palsied the principles of free born souls…converted men into eunuchs, and have substituted the distaff for the sword?" Like sentimental women, Americans had been seduced by Washington's popularity. Only those with "childish minds," he wrote with disgust, "would be persuaded our constitution and liberty means nothing more than the gratification and the aggrandizement of Washington."[77]

The final approval of the Jay Treaty by the House of Representatives left Republicans completely demoralized. "In vain have we seceded from the arbitrary power of Great Britain," lamented one writer in the *Aurora*, "if we are to substitute the will of an individual for the constitution of our country." But despite his hostility toward Washington, Bache did not revive the personal abuse that had filled the paper since 1795, and new subjects began to find a place in the *Aurora*: the spectacular French military victories in Italy and Germany, the exploits of a brilliant young French general called Napoleon Bonaparte, and the shenanigans of an English journalist called William Cobbett. By the spring of 1796, rumors of Washington's retirement were already in the air, and with one eye on the upcoming presidential contest between Adams and Jefferson, a few contributors to the *Aurora* even began to express support for the president. An essay reprinted from the Boston *Independent Chronicle* insisted: "Washington is a Republican" who is hostile to the monarchical party supporting Adams, and another writer in the *Aurora* claimed that Republicans rather than Federalists were the "real friends to the President." Bache echoed these sentiments. Depleted and dejected by his recent political exertions, he fought the presidential elections of 1796 without energy or enthusiasm, wearily repudiating his past attacks on Washington and identifying Thomas Jefferson with the political legacy of "our much loved President."[78]

But this was not Bache's last word on Washington. Once the presidential elections were over and the Republican campaign against John Adams was clearly lost,

The Times: A Political Portrait. Unidentified artist, Philadelphia, 1798. This cartoon may contain the only graphic depiction we have of Benjamin Franklin Bache. The caption reads: "Triumph Government: perish all its enemies. Traitors, be warned: justice though slow, is sure." It shows Washington at the head of an American army of Volunteers, ready to repulse the invading French "cannibals" as Republican Albert Gallatin tries to halt his progress and "stop de wheels of de gouvernement," aided by Thomas Jefferson. The figure being trampled underfoot by the marching Volunteers is probably Bache, who looks on as a dog urinates on the *Aurora*. Courtesy of the New-York Historical Society.

two advertisements appeared in the *Aurora*, one for *A Letter to George Washington* authored by one "Jasper Dwight of Vermont," the pen name of an Anglo-Irish radical called William Duane, and the other for *A Letter to George Washington* by Thomas Paine. After a series of memorable remarks of his own on the occasion of Washington's retirement, Bache also published John Beckley's *Remarks Occasioned by the Late Conduct of Mr. Washington*. These three pamphlets and Bache's remarks were the last salvos of a campaign that had a far greater impact on the reputation of the editor of the *Aurora* than on the reputation of their subject, George Washington. The best illustration of the failure of the Republican campaign to discredit Washington was Bache's decision to delay the publication of the pamphlets until after the election of 1796, when they might have harmed the presidential prospects of his favored candidate, Thomas Jefferson.[79]

But the efforts of Bache and other Republican journalists may have left some mark on popular political consciousness. Fisher Ames observed that, among his "plain neighbours" in Massachusetts, those who read the *Independent Chronicle* "will not commend the President." When Isaac Weld toured the country in 1796, he was surprised by the number of people who were "either so insensible to [Washington's] merit, or so totally devoid of every general sentiment" that they refused to celebrate the president's birthday. But the silence of Republican journalists was eloquent, and after 1796 they abandoned their efforts to discredit Washington entirely. The publisher and printer Matthew Carey, a firm but not fanatical supporter of Jefferson, thought the *Aurora* campaign had been a political disaster that had damaged rather than aided the Republican cause and created unnecessary division among Republicans themselves. He was probably right, and by the late 1790s, Republicans were scrambling to appropriate Washington for their own political cause, a shift that reflected a broader transformation in Republican political rhetoric. As Republicans began to present themselves as guardians of political order, constitutional principles, and the "constituted authorities," they also began to participate in the deification of Washington, challenging Federalists for the right to define and claim his political legacy. At the funeral procession for Washington held in Philadelphia on December 26, 1799, Federalists and Republicans marched separately, each competing to pay their final respects, and Republican eulogists paid tribute to Washington as extravagantly as did Federalists. Even "that rascal Freneau," once a thorn in Washington's side, published a poem praising him in the Charleston *City Gazette*.[80]

What influence, if any, did the Republican campaign against Washington have on American public life? Most obviously, it angered Washington himself, who blamed attacks in the press for his retirement from the presidency. Both Federalists and Republicans frequently claimed that the growth of personal political scurrility in the press drove good men from office and deterred others from seeking it, undermining the quality of political leadership. And once Washington had been subjected to forensic personal examination by Republican journalists, the boundary between the legitimate censorship of public character and public men and the assassination of private character and private men disintegrated, a phenomenon most spectacularly encouraged and exploited by the English émigré journalist William Cobbett after 1796. The explosion of personal partisan journalism that accompanied the rise of the infamous "Peter Porcupine" in turn fueled widespread disillusionment with the press. During the late 1790s, the belief that newspapers could be impersonal and impartial arbiters of public opinion gave way rapidly to a belief that they were irresponsible vehicles of personal and partisan advantage, sowing the seeds for the growth of more intolerant and repressive public attitudes toward the press and, eventually, to the passage of the Alien and Sedition Acts.

For Bache, the campaign against Washington created instant notoriety and lasting infamy. But while his campaign against Washington was a failure, his campaign against the presidency was more successful. By the late eighteenth century, the Second Great Awakening had begun to transform American culture in ways that were profoundly democratic and egalitarian. At the heart of this revolt against religious authority was what historian Nathan Hatch describes as a "populist hermeneutics" that replaced the authority of clerical elites and church doctrine with an internalized conception of religious conscience, what Hatch calls the "individualization of conscience." The intersection between the religious ideas of the Second Great Awakening and the ideology of radical Republicans like Bache is striking, and the ideological convergence between deist political radicals like Bache and radical evangelicals would help to propel Jefferson to the presidency in 1800. Republican attacks on the popular reverence for Washington sought not only to discredit Washington himself but to desacralize the presidency and secularize American public life. By the second half of the 1790s, provoked by Federalist accusations of religious infidelity, their ideas about the separation of religious belief and public life found a direct counterpart in the ideas of radical evangelicals who wished to preserve religious freedom from the encroachment and control of the state. If nothing in political life should be sacred, nothing sacred should be part of political life.[81]

Although Bache and other Republicans failed to convince Americans to revise the Constitution and diminish the powers of the presidency, they challenged the aura of sanctity and personal reverence with which Federalists tried to surround the presidency after 1789. After 1796, the presidency was firmly anchored in the profane world of American politics, as Washington's successors, John Adams and Thomas Jefferson, both quickly discovered. "Measures," argued a writer in the *Aurora* at the height of the Republican campaign against Washington, "ought to be considered in themselves and not in connection with men who are the author of them." One irony of American politics in the 1790s was that the Republican Party, a party that vociferously advocated a politics of impersonality, of "measures not men," played a central role in the personalization of political debate. And in a further irony, although Washington's deification had no place in the impersonal world of Republican ideology, their commitment to the separation of church and state was embodied in the emergence of a new political icon, the author of the Virginia Statute of Religious Freedom, Thomas Jefferson.[82]

CHAPTER 4

Noah Webster and the Demoralization of the Body Politic

In 1841, the eminent British geologist Charles Lyell visited the New Haven home of the equally eminent author of *An American Dictionary of the English Language*, Noah Webster. During his visit, Lyell expressed great interest in the work of the aging lexicographer, and as he was leaving asked Webster how many words he had personally contributed to the language he had taken such pains to document and define. Only one, replied Webster, "to wit, demoralize," a word he had first used in a pamphlet on the French Revolution published "about the year 1793." Webster was eighty-three years old at the time, but his memory was sharp. He had first used the word "demoralize" in his pamphlet *The Revolution in France*, published in New York in 1794. But although he was the first writer to use the word in English, the term demoralize was an anglicization of the French verb *demoraliser*, a neologism coined in France in the 1790s and recognized by the Academie Français in 1798. Webster probably ran across the word in the many French pamphlets and newspapers that crossed his desk at the *American Minerva*, the newspaper he edited in New York. But why did this particular word catch his eye, and why did he use it in his essay on the French Revolution?[1]

By the time Webster wrote *The Revolution in France* at the end of 1793, he was profoundly disillusioned by events in France, and although he still expressed support for revolutionary principles, he had become sharply critical of revolutionary practices. He was especially incensed by the efforts of Robespierre and the Committee of Public Safety to replace Christianity with a civil religion devoted to the worship of Reason and denounced the materialist doctrines of

148

the Jacobins and their "atheistical attacks on christianity." Robespierre's policy of de-Christianization, he believed, had eroded the moral foundations of civilized society in France, propelling the country into a state of amoral barbarism and primitive political violence. The terrorism of the Committee of Public Safety was a direct consequence of the moral degeneration, or demoralization, of French civil society and was destroying a revolution that Webster had once judged "the noblest ever undertaken by men."[2]

Webster's use of the term demoralize signaled an important shift in his understanding of the French Revolution and the problem of political order. In the past, he had dismissed morality and religion as irrelevant to issues of political order and state formation. Men were innately corrupt and self-interested, he believed, and consequently it was absurd to make their political virtue the basis for political institutions. Before writing *The Revolution in France*, Webster had regarded social cohesion and consensus as the result rather than the source of wisely framed political institutions. But by 1793, he had come to question this assumption. Deeply troubled by the chaos and violence he saw in revolutionary France, he now argued that these developments were symptoms of a profound moral malaise. He had once believed that there were no limits to the process of political renewal and reformation; now, he emphasized the limits and dangers of political reform. The French Revolution had exposed these limits. By trying to fashion the world anew and to transform subjects into citizens with such speed, the Jacobin government of France had shattered the moral and religious framework upon which the stability of civilized society depended. Without moral order and religious belief, he now believed, it was impossible to preserve political liberty and the health of the body politic.

Webster's loss of faith in the French Revolution was also a turning point in his relationship with American political life, and by the mid-1790s, he was drawing similarly pessimistic conclusions about the faction-ridden and intemperate character of American party politics. His publication of *The Revolution in France* thus marked the beginning of his own political demoralization: his loss of faith in republican and democratic politics and in the capacity of his fellow citizens for personal and collective self-government. By the early years of the nineteenth century, Webster had relinquished his faith in the possibility of radical political renewal and retreated into the past, returning literally and figuratively to his place of origin in Connecticut. There, he sought consolation in the prerevolutionary world of his childhood and youth, constructing an idealized vision of New England patriarchy within which he could shelter from the brash egalitarian iconoclasm and boisterous partisan passions of Jeffersonian and Jacksonian America.

In a memoir written in the 1830s, Noah Webster recalled the trauma of departing from home after graduating from Yale College in 1778:

> The subject of this memoir was now cast upon the world, at the age of twenty, without property, without patrons, and in the midst of a war which had disturbed all occupations; had impoverished the country; and the termination of which could not be foreseen. He remained some time at his father's house; and while there, his father put into his hands an eight dollar bill of continental currency, then worth three or four dollars; saying to him "take this; you must now seek your living; I can do no more for you."

It's possible that Webster recalled this moment in his life exactly as it occurred, but it's more likely that his recollection was shaped by the prejudices of time and the tricks of memory. It resembles too much the opening scene of a picaresque novel to be treated as wholly reliable. But however we interpret the passage, it captures brilliantly the tension produced by the revolutionary transformation through which Noah Webster lived. When Webster left home in 1778, he stood on the threshold of a revolutionary world, a world in which the knowledge and experience of fathers were no longer reliable guides for the actions and ideas of sons. His account of his departure from home reveals the contrast between this new world, a world of adulthood, independence, and uncertainty, an uncertainty symbolized by the fluctuating value of Continental currency, and the security of the patriarchal household within which he grew up, a world of childhood, dependence, and certainty. It reveals also Webster's ambivalence about this critical transition in his life and the revolutionary turmoil that surrounded him.[3]

But Webster's story also captures the ambivalence of an old man longing for a world he had lost. Situated at the start of his autobiography, this account begins a saga of self-creation very much in keeping with early nineteenth-century middle-class culture. Webster portrays himself as a man of independence and self-reliance, one of a new breed of self-made men, merging his own moment of youthful independence with the independence of the new nation and placing his own departure from the patriarchal fold against the backdrop of a revolution against the patriarchal authority of the British Crown. The emphasis on independence from both family and patrons reveals a man completely attuned to the dogmas and assumptions of a new age. But the elderly Webster describes his parting from his father as a moment of exile rather than an act of youthful rebellion, and in doing so reveals his own longing for patriarchal dependence. Looking back from the vantage point of the 1830s, he presents his independence as a condition imposed on him by his father and the circumstances of the Revolution, and he describes his departure with a palpable sense of loss.[4]

Noah Webster, by James Sharples, 1795–1801. This portrait from life captures Webster as a serious and intelligent man, with a hint of self-importance, during his tenure as editor of the *American Minerva*. Courtesy of Independence National Historical Park.

Noah Webster was born in West Hartford, Connecticut, on October 16, 1758. His mother, Mercy Steele, was descended from William Bradford and his father, Noah Webster, Sr., counted a governor of Connecticut among his ancestors. Not surprisingly, Webster recalled being raised "in the religious principles of the first planters of New England" and remembered "his father, mother, & most of his family relatives, paternal & maternal, being pious."[5] There was little in his rural Connecticut upbringing to disrupt this atmosphere of family piety. Although Connecticut was influenced by the Great Awakening, the religious revival of the 1740s, the Fourth Church of Hartford, to which Webster and his family belonged and where his father served as a deacon, was left almost unscathed. When the Reverend Nathan Perkins, later a prominent evangelical preacher and the author of *The Benign Influence of Religion on Civil Government and National Happiness*, became the pastor of the church in the early 1770s, he found a congregation that was apathetic and orthodox. Webster's education reflected this conventional piety. At the common school he attended, no books were used "except a spelling book, a psalter, testament, or Bible," and instruction in the catechism was required by law. His early education was not an inspiring experience. "It is my serious opinion," he wrote,

> that, when I was a school-boy, the greatest part of the scholars did not employ more than an hour in a day, either in writing or reading; while five hours of the school time was spent in idleness—in cutting the tables and benches to pieces—in carrying on pin-lotteries, or perhaps in some more roguish tricks. The reason of such mispense [*sic*] of time was, that they had nothing to excite them to application.

Despite the inadequacies of the local school, the young Webster acquired a taste for learning and by his early teens had decided on a "collegiate education." Reluctantly, his father agreed to release him from the drudgery of farm work, and in 1772 he began to study classics under the Reverend Perkins, who prepared him for admission to Yale College.[6]

When Webster entered Yale in 1774, it was a stronghold of Calvinist orthodoxy, shaped by the long presidency of the Reverend Thomas Clap, a "firm supporter of the established religion." Clap's resistance to religious innovation had led Jonathan Edwards, Aaron Burr, and others to abandon New Haven and found the College of New Jersey at Princeton in 1746, leaving Yale, in the words of one historian, "close to becoming a narrowly sectarian college." But Clap also introduced a number of important changes to the Yale curriculum, placing a new emphasis on mathematics, science, and classical learning, reforms extended by his successor, the Reverend Naphtali Daggett. Daggett's most important innovation was to introduce English grammar and literature in 1767 and to appoint Timothy Dwight and John Trumbull, both talented writers, as college tutors in 1771. Dwight and Trumbull did much to raise the intellectual tone of the college before the Revolution, and in 1776 Dwight introduced the study of history, rhetoric, and belles lettres for the first time, an innovation that may have encouraged Webster's early interest in the English language.[7]

How much influence did Yale have on Webster? According to one biographer, Webster's time at Yale transformed his "values and his life," eroding the intellectual core of his Calvinist upbringing and leaving only the husk of his religious belief intact. "Yale introduced Noah Webster to the Enlightenment," writes Rollins, and exposed him to new ideas about social progress and the malleability of human nature. Such ideas were certainly in the air at Yale in the 1770s, and

Webster himself admitted that the intellectual climate of the college undermined his early religious beliefs.[8] But it is easy to exaggerate the iconoclasm of Yale, and the dominant tone of the college under Daggett remained staunchly Calvinist. Dwight, who later became president of Yale, is best remembered as the scourge of Jeffersonian deism and the author of "The Triumph of Infidelity." Both Daggett and his successor, Ezra Stiles, combined religious orthodoxy with a deep interest in Enlightenment ideas, and while Webster may have abandoned the Calvinist pieties of his youth at Yale, his commitment to the philosophical optimism of the Enlightenment was always tempered by Calvinist skepticism about the limits and imperfections of human nature.[9]

In any case, it was the American Revolution rather than Calvinist New Haven that had the greatest impact on Webster's intellectual formation. In his memoir, he hardly mentions Yale at all, and then only in disparaging terms, and although his class was one of the most distinguished ever to graduate from the college, their education was so disrupted by war "that it may be wondered if they got much more from college than their diplomas." The opening shots of the Revolution were fired just a few months after Webster arrived at Yale and, according to a contemporary, "rendered it impossible for us to pursue our studies to any profit." College authorities suspended classes once in 1775 and twice in 1776, and Webster spent his entire third year in Glastonbury, Connecticut, because of fears the British would invade New England, returning to New Haven in 1778, his last year, only to collect his degree. His experience at Yale, he wrote later, was "much inferior to those enjoyed before and since the Revolution."[10]

Nonetheless, Yale gave Webster a number of important friendships and placed him at the center of the revolutionary struggle. The college may have been religiously orthodox under Daggett's leadership, but it was a "nursery of sedition, of faction, and republicanism," according to one Tory graduate. Some students were drawn directly into the military conflict. Webster's classmate and friend Joel Barlow served with the Connecticut militia at the Battle of Long Island, and Webster himself "shouldered a musket" and joined his father and brother in the Connecticut militia when they were mustered to repel the British invasion of New York. Although he experienced no military action—before they reached Albany, General John Burgoyne had surrendered and Webster encountered nothing more hazardous than hordes of mosquitoes—these events loomed much larger in his life than parsing Latin and Greek.[11] In 1776, the revolutionary spirit spilled over into the life of the college when students petitioned for President Daggett's removal, and there were a number of other college rebellions in the late 1770s. According to Joseph Buckminster, Webster's class was especially intransigent and exhibited an "independent spirit" that made them difficult to "instruct and lead."[12]

This spirit of independence animated Webster's intellectual development in the late 1770s and early 1780s. The first sign of it was the essay he submitted for his master of arts at Yale in 1781, "Dissertation on the Universal Diffusion of Literature as Introductory to the Universal Diffusion of Christianity." Here, Webster defended Christianity as "the most rational system of religion ever published to mankind" and as a religion favorable to "equality and independence." But as his language suggested and as his argument made clear, his belief in Christianity was no longer based on the authority of revelation but on "the impartial voice of reason." This emphasis on rationality led Webster toward an understanding of Christianity that was essentially moral and ethical in character. This is clearest in his discussion of classical culture. Forced to explain the cultural achievements of pagan Greece and Rome, his response was interesting. "We must allow," he stated, "that they entertained as rational ideas of the Deity, and of human obligations, as the modern christians, in proportion to their improvements in literature." He suggested, in other words, that moral progress was not dependent on Christian revelation but on the development of literary culture. "Setting aside all regard to revelation," argued Webster in a revealing passage, "and supposing morality to be a part of religion…the progress of religion, will naturally be proportioned to improvements in literature." This is a remarkable statement. In Webster's view, Christianity was no longer the basis for the progress of civilization and enlightenment; instead, civilization and enlightenment had become the basis for the progress of Christianity. Literature was the new source of revelation.[13]

Webster outlined in this essay the ideas that inspired his early interest in education. If the diffusion of secular knowledge was the sine qua non of social progress, then where better to start than with children? In a letter discussing the production of his famous blue-backed speller in 1783, Webster acknowledged the importance of "sacred writings" but went on to argue that secular rather than sacred literature "must be the principal bulwark against the encroachments of civil & ecclesiatical tyrants." For this reason, the final version of his speller contained no mention of God and presented religion largely as a matter of moral precepts and examples. Webster's attitude toward the Bible was also unorthodox. Although he expressed respect for its teachings, he criticized its use in the classroom. The Bible, he argued, was not an instructional manual but a sacred text, and its use as a mere reader threatened this sanctity: "Let sacred things," he declared, "be appropriated to sacred purposes." Pious as this sounded, it was hard not to detect in Webster's ringing defense of sacred texts an effort to smuggle in secular texts. More than a few observers believed that his revolutionary new speller was intended to replace the Bible rather than Dilworth's English grammar as the principal source of instruction in American schools. And they were right.[14]

From this perspective, Webster's subsequent commitment to the cultural and linguistic independence of the United States makes sense. If literature was the engine of moral progress, then it was imperative for Americans to develop their own literary culture and their own language after the Revolution. This was not just a matter of national pride and cultural self-assertion, of competition with the cultural aegis of Europe, but a moral imperative necessary in order to detach the wellsprings of literary culture in the New World from the poisoned channels of the Old World. Webster's speller was intended to begin this work of moral reformation and to expunge the corrupting moral influence of the "English" language. It is in this context that Webster's famous concluding remarks to the first part of his *Grammatical Institute* should be understood. "The author," he wrote, "wishes to promote the honor and prosperity of the confederated republics of America":

> Europe is grown old in folly, corruption and tyranny—in that country laws are perverted, manners are licentious, literature is declining and human nature debased. For America in her infancy to adopt the present maxims of the old world would be to stamp the wrinkle of decrepit old age upon the bloom of youth, and to plant the seed of decay in a vigorous constitution.

While Webster's moral position grew less secular with age, his commitment to cultural nationalism (and his aversion for European culture) never faltered. "America," he declared to his friend John Canfield in January 1783, "must be as independent in literature as she is in politics."[15]

Webster's own quest for independence was more halting. After graduating from Yale in 1778, he returned home to contemplate his future with apprehension. When his father, who had mortgaged the family farm to send his son to Yale, told him that he could help him no further, Webster experienced the first in a series of intellectual and emotional crises. "I knew not what business to attempt nor by what way to obtain subsistence," he wrote. Significantly, he did not consider becoming a minister, a logical occupation for a farm boy educated at Yale, but took to his room instead, his mind "embarrassed with solicitude, and overwelmed with gloomy apprehensions," and read Samuel Johnson's *Rambler* essays. The importance of this episode has escaped most writers on Webster. But it is enormously significant that Webster turned to the worldly Johnson rather than to the Bible for support and guidance. Webster later chastised himself for this decision:

> I now perceive that I ought to have read my Bible first, but I followed the common mode of reading, and fell into the common mistake of attending to the duties which man owes to man, before I had learned the duties which we all owe to our Creator and Redeemer.

But at the time, Webster felt no such qualms. As he admitted even later, it was the secular moral content of the *Rambler* essays that attracted him, and he was deeply impressed by what he read. Johnson's essays had "a visible effect upon my moral opinions" and "when I closed the volume, I formed a firm resolution to pursue a course of virtue through life, and to perform all moral and social duties with scrupulous exactness."[16]

This critical reference to the greatest English lexicographer is fascinating. Johnson had published his famous *Dictionary of the English Language* in 1755, and his career was a model of the new literary professionalism made possible by the expansion of the reading public in the eighteenth century. He embodied the new status of the writer as an independent intellectual, a model that clearly appealed to the young Yale graduate. But Johnson's appeal to Webster and the affinities between the two men did not end there. At a time of confusion and uncertainty in his life, Webster found in the *Rambler* essays an emphasis on intellectual control and order, a "moral discipline of the mind," in Johnson's words, that was profoundly compelling.[17]

Like Webster, Johnson was a rationalist and a moralist who harbored a deep sense of skepticism about the worthiness of human nature. In his writings and particularly in the *Rambler* essays, he argued that social progress and moral order were only possible when individuals practiced self-restraint and the pursuit of enlightened self-interest. Deeply influenced by the sensationalist psychology of John Locke and the writings of Bernard Mandeville, Johnson believed that human self-interest—the desires to avoid pain and to seek pleasure—was an inevitable part of the calculus of a moral life. Human behavior, he argued, was shaped by the conflict between passion and reason, and it was the task of all rational people to "govern our thoughts, restrain them from irregular motions, or confine them from boundless dissipation."[18]

Although Johnson's emphasis on the role of rational self-interest linked him to the philosophers of the Scottish Enlightenment—like them, he had no patience for arguments based on the idealization of "nature"—unlike Scottish common-sense philosophers, Johnson did not believe in the existence of an innate "moral sense." Instead, he argued that social progress depended on the ability of individuals (endowed with the use of reason and free will) and of social custom to channel and control deeply embedded human impulses. In other words, human nature was neither benign nor evil but amoral and self-interested, driven by animal appetites that could be shaped and civilized by cultural institutions and social practice.[19]

Johnson's ideas had a significant impact on Webster. He echoed Johnson's emphasis on rational thought—he that "would govern his actions by the laws of virtue," wrote Johnson, "must regulate his thoughts by those of reason"—in his master's thesis, written only a year or so after reading the *Rambler* essays. Like Johnson, Webster also believed that self-interest was the primary motive for human behavior, and this belief provided the basis for a broader pragmatism that reflected Johnson's own political position. In Webster's essay, as in Johnson's writings, religion played a secondary role to reason in the creation of moral order. But Johnson's appeal lay deeper than this. His emphasis on self-restraint and psychological independence in the *Rambler* essays galvanized Webster to action at a time when he felt isolated and uncertain and reassured him about his own moral worth at a moment when he felt alienated from his family and his Calvinist upbringing. At the same time, Johnson's ideas allowed him to conceive the pursuit of his own interests as legitimate and morally justifiable. Johnson's emphasis on both restraint and release was intellectually liberating for Webster. The skepticism about human nature and the belief in progressive social change that Webster discovered in Johnson's writings disclosed a role for him. In Samuel Johnson, Webster found not only a model for the professional writer, but a didactic moralist who believed that "the end of writing is to instruct."[20]

Reading Johnson was an intellectual inspiration to Webster, but it did not solve his immediate problems. He may have experienced some sort of nervous breakdown in 1779, and several years later he still "suffered extreme depression and gloomy forebodings." His intention in this period was to study law. But revolutionary New England was not an ideal place to practice law, and he was forced instead to teach. For someone remembered as a pedagogue, Webster's teaching career was surprisingly brief and unhappy. After teaching in and around Hartford for a while, he opened his own school in Sharon, Connecticut, in the summer of 1781. It survived for only a single term, and although a subsequent effort to start a school in Goshen, New York, was more successful, Webster was no more content. Teaching, he grumbled, left his health impaired and no time to advance his legal career. But he had no idea how to "find [a] business better suited to his inclination."[21]

Much as Webster disliked teaching, it inspired his first published work as an author. During the summer of 1782, he completed the first draft of a spelling book designed to replace the standard work by the English author Thomas Dilworth. Published in Hartford in 1783, Webster's *A Grammatical Institute of the English Language* was an instant publishing success. The first edition sold out in nine months, and a further two editions followed quickly. By 1800, according to one estimate, more than 1.5 million copies of Webster's speller had been sold. The impact of Webster's famous blue-backed speller on American education was profound, but its impact on American politics may have been even greater. Although Webster conceived the speller as part of a scholarly assault on the grammatical principles of Thomas Dilworth, and hoped it would make reading and writing easier for children, his principal motive was more ambitious. Published just as the war against Britain was coming to a conclusion, the speller was intended to lay the basis for a distinctively American literary culture—and moral order— independent of European cultural influence, and its appeal was explicitly nation- alistic and propagandistic. The speller was a "revolutionary broadside" brimming over with radical political sentiments and excerpts from writers like Thomas Paine. Its purpose was twofold: to spread the principles of American revolutionary nationalism and to begin the process of creating a national language.[22]

Webster wrote the speller for children—"the only practicable method to reform mankind, is to begin with children," he wrote a few years later—but he also had a broader audience in mind. In a letter to John Canfield discussing its composition in January 1783, he argued that American liberty depended not only on the progress of literature but on the progress of popular literature:

> A folio on some abstruse philosophical subject might, at first thought, appear to be a work of some consequence and attract the public attention; but this would be read only by a few, and its utility seldom reach further than the philosopher's head, while a fifteen-penny volume, which may convey much useful knowledge to the remote, obscure recesses of honest poverty, is overlooked as a matter of trivial notice. The former like a taper gives light only in the chamber of study. The latter like a star casts its beam equally upon the peasant and the monarch.

In petitions to the legislatures of Connecticut and New York soliciting support for his project, Webster reiterated this desire to reach a broad reading public. He wanted, he said, to "diffuse a political knowledge of this grand confederation of republics among that class of people who have not access to more expensive means of information." This democratic conception of his audience was an essen- tial aspect of Webster's cultural nationalism; his aim was to create "Americans," and in order to do so, he had to reach as many of them as possible.[23]

The *Grammatical Institute* articulated the nationalist cultural agenda that absorbed much of Webster's time and energy in the 1780s and launched him into the mainstream of American public life. Although he continued his study of law in Hartford, his real interest was now the promotion of linguistic reform and the creation and dissemination of a national language. If Americans were to "assume a national character," he wrote, a national language was indispensable. "A national language is a national tie," he wrote to Timothy Pickering, who shared both his nationalism and his zeal for things grammatical, "and what country wants it more than America?" In March 1784, Webster published the second part of his *Grammatical Institute*, a dry but innovative work that opposed the use of Latin as a model for English grammar, and in February 1785, he completed the third and final part of his *Institute*, a reader.[24] Neither work was a bestseller, but combined with the speller, they gave Webster an entrée to American intellectual life, which he was quick to exploit. His decision to tour the newly formed United States in 1785 was inspired by a variety of motives—his interest in copyright reform, a desire to increase book sales, a thirst for publicity, and a desire to make connections with the most eminent men of his day—but Webster also used the tour to promote his ideas about language reform. After a successful series of public lectures in Baltimore in September and October 1785, he delivered similar lectures in Virginia, Maryland, Delaware, New Jersey, Pennsylvania, New York, and Connecticut.[25] When he returned to Baltimore in 1786, he wrote optimistically, "there is no longer a doubt that I shall be able to effect a uniformity of language and education throughout this continent."[26]

Webster's enthusiasm for the creation of a national language was inspired by politics rather than pedagogy. With its emphasis on cultural formation—the creation of a national character and an American identity—his *Grammatical Institute* is best seen as part of a broader nationalist project upon which Webster embarked in the 1780s. Although he genuflected toward the improvement of youth—his speller was designed to "inspire youth with an abhorrence of vice and a love of virtue and religion"—his true concerns were political rather than moral or didactic. He was more interested in creating citizens than saints. At a time when concerns about social cohesion and national unity were prompting renewed jeremiads about the need for moral discipline, Webster's approach to the postrevolutionary problems of American society remained resolutely secular. "Our political harmony," he wrote, is "concerned in a uniformity of language." To Webster, the creation of a common identity and a common culture—carefully distinguished from that of Europe—remained the key to political stability and union.[27]

But it was not the only key. While cultural identity and language were critical to the broader task of nation building, Webster regarded state formation as the sine qua non of a successful and unified American empire, and he repeatedly emphasized the importance of political institutions to the formation of the American national character and the preservation of a democratic, republican political order. Not surprisingly, he was one of the leading public supporters of the Constitutional Convention and the ratification of the Constitution. The passage of the Constitution, he argued in true Enlightenment fashion, would establish an "empire of reason," a nation based on political wisdom and rationality rather than the coercion of its citizens. The centralization of power in a strong national state, argued Webster, was essential. Without the creation of a "Federal Sovereignty," he stated, "we can have no union, no respectability, no national character."[28]

The publication of the *Grammatical Institute* gave Webster an entrance to American intellectual life, but it also propelled him into his first political engagements. In the summer of 1782, prior to its appearance, he traveled to New York, New Jersey, and Pennsylvania to lobby for the passage of state copyright laws, but with little success. He had more luck in Connecticut, where a copyright law passed the general assembly in January 1783, and this success was followed by similar legislation in New York, Massachusetts, and Maryland. In May 1783, the Confederation Congress (at Webster's instigation) passed a resolution favoring the establishment of copyright laws in each of the states, and by the end of the year New Jersey, New Hampshire, and Rhode Island all had copyright legislation on the books. When Webster set out on his tour of the country in the spring of 1785, one of his chief aims was to "make application to the legislatures of several states for the enactment of laws to secure authors the copyright of their writings."[29]

At about the same time, Webster made his debut as a political journalist. The occasion was the controversy aroused by the issue of commutation in early 1783. The decision of Congress to grant officers of the Continental army five years' full pay created a public uproar in New England. In September 1783, a "General Convention" met in Middletown, Connecticut, to organize resistance to the measure, which was known as commutation. Writing as "Honorius" in the *Connecticut Courant*, Webster led opposition to the Middletown Convention, denouncing its organizers as a "nest of vipers, disturbing the tranquility of government, to answer selfish purposes." The Honorius essays, which were followed by a series on "The Policy of Connecticut," made a convincing case for commutation, for the creation of a national tax to meet this obligation, and for the nationalization of the revolutionary war debt, establishing Webster's reputation as a skillful polemicist and one of the leading advocates of political centralization in the United States. The strengthening of the federal state, he argued, was essential to prevent any relapse into the kind of anarchy represented by the Middletown Convention, and he set out to "convince his fellow citizens of the inefficiency of the Confederation for the government of the United States, and the preservation of the union."[30]

Webster's *Sketches of American Policy*, which was published in March 1785, captured brilliantly the tension latent in his radical nationalist vision. He wrote the work "shortly after reading Rousseau's *Social Contract*, from which [he] imbibed many visionary ideas," and *Sketches* was deeply influenced by both Jean-Jacques Rousseau and the English radical Richard Price, although the final product was very much Webster's own creation.[31] By the time he wrote *Sketches*, Webster had concluded that state sovereignty was incompatible with representative democracy. The "body politic or state," he argued, echoing Rousseau, was the result of a social compact whereby each individual, in return for protection, "consents to obey the general voice." But under the Articles of Confederation, the "general voice" was obstructed by the power of each state to veto the policies of the other states, a situation that invited the ridicule and contempt of the rest of the world but, even more important, violated the principle of popular sovereignty. "All power is vested in the people," argued Webster, and the legitimacy of the state rested on its ability to represent and embody the popular will. The best way to ensure the legitimacy of the state was therefore to grant the greatest number of people control over the creation of laws and the smallest number control over their execution. "A representative democracy," concluded Webster, "seems therefore to be the most perfect system of government that is practicable on earth."[32]

Webster's defense of radical democracy thus advanced and legitimized his defense of radical political centralization. According to him, a free government could survive only if the states were united, and they could only be united by a national legislature "composed of representatives from all the states, and vested with the power of the whole continent to enforce their decisions. There is no alternative." State sovereignty, in other words, had to be entirely dissolved and replaced by a national government that derived its legitimacy directly from the people. Nothing but the creation of a strong federal state could prevent the country from lapsing into anarchy and ultimately monarchy. And nothing but a strong "sovereign power at the head of the states" could overcome the cultural fragmentation of the new nation: "We ought not to consider ourselves as inhabitants of a particular state only," said Webster, "but as *Americans*; as the common subjects of a great empire."[33]

Given his later conservative views, it's tempting to see Webster's defense of radical democracy and popular sovereignty as a cloak for the advancement of a conservative political agenda. But this would be a mistake. Thomas Paine, whom Webster met and admired greatly, used similar arguments during the 1780s (and later in the *Rights of Man*) and, like Webster, supported constitutional revision and a stronger federal union. In the 1780s, radical democracy and federalism were not incompatible, and our understanding of this period (and of American politics) is seriously distorted if we assume that there is some necessary correlation between democracy and decentralization. Webster's ideas were potentially coercive—he reminded readers slightly ominously that they were all "subject" to the sovereign power as well as part of it—but his political radicalism was beyond dispute. He denounced "aristocratic" government in the harshest terms, demanded the abolition of slavery and primogeniture, called for a system of progressive taxation to finance public schools and social benefits, and supported a broad equality of property.[34]

But the most striking aspect of Webster's *Sketches* was his secular understanding of the connections between religion, moral life, and political order. The establishment of religion, he argued, had been a disaster for humankind. "Religion, by which I mean superstition, or human systems of absurdity, is an engine used in almost all governments," wrote Webster, and ought to be expunged.

His animosity toward religion went far beyond conventional Protestant hostility to religious establishments and clerical orders. In an article in the *Freeman's Chronicle*, he lashed out at clergymen who "joined the terrors of eternal damnation to the iron rod of civil magistrates" and made it clear that his target was the theocratic traditions of his native New England. His hostility toward religion was not restricted to denominational involvement in political life. Although Webster applauded the liberal religious practices of the American states, he branded as one of the "badges of bigotry" the belief that "a profession of Christian religion is necessary...to entitle a man to [public] office." As Webster himself later confessed, at this stage of his life, his religious ideas were far from orthodox.[35]

But most important, he did not believe that political stability and order depended on the state of public morality and religion. Centralization and state formation were the cures for the ills of the body politic, not moral reform or religious revitalization. In one of the most interesting passages in *Sketches*, Webster discussed the belief, which he associated with Montesquieu, that virtue is the indispensable foundation of republican government. He emphatically rejected this idea. Republican government, he argued, did not depend on virtue but self-interest. "Public spirit" was nothing more than "self-interest...the aggregate sum of the individual interests in a state." Anticipating some of Madison's later arguments about self-interest in the *Federalist Papers*, Webster's political realism made the state crucial to social integration. In a country as large as the United States, he argued, concentrating political power in the state was essential to check the self-aggrandizing nature of civil society. In other words, political virtue was less important than political institutions. Moral order was not the guardian of the state; the state was the guardian of moral order.[36]

The political arguments that Webster developed in *Sketches of American Policy* appeared frequently in his writings of the late 1780s. In a defense of the Constitution written in 1787, he again rejected the idea that virtue is a stable foundation for republican government. "Equality of property," he stated, not political virtue, is the "soul of a republic." He made the same point in an essay written the following year, insisting that the solution to the new nation's problems was the passage of the Constitution, not a revival of public spirit or virtue. If public virtue had ever existed, it "has long ago subsided, and is absorbed in the general steady principle, private interest." "That enthusiasm," he concluded dryly, "is not to be rekindled." The social unrest of the period—especially Shays's Rebellion in 1787—made him more skeptical about popular government and encouraged his authoritarianism, but he did not abandon his basic political position. Indeed, Webster's skepticism and disenchantment strengthened rather than diminished his commitment to political reform. Revealing his early Calvinist influences, he believed that neither human beings nor governments could be perfect. Even the Constitution was flawed, he admitted, and if every objection to it were removed, "not a syllable…will survive the scrutiny." "Perfection is not the lot of humanity," he argued, and to preserve the political union, it was vital to accept this truth. As Webster's concern about social political disorder in American society mounted during the late 1780s, he placed more, not less, emphasis on the need to forge powerful political institutions and a powerful federal state. In the essay "On Government," published in 1790, he argued that members of a national legislature were not bound by either the Constitution or the Bill of Rights and were answerable only to the popular will expressed through regular elections. Popularly elected legislatures were permanent conventions, he declared, which possessed "all the power of the state."[37]

Webster's early demands for a "National Constitution" were finally realized in the work of the Philadelphia Convention, which met in 1787 to revise the Articles of Confederation. After moving to Philadelphia in the fall of 1786, he had accepted a position as an English instructor at the Episcopal Academy, and as members of the convention deliberated in secret during the summer of 1787, Webster played an active role in the events. But his most important contributions to the passage of the Constitution were literary, first as the author of *An Examination into the Leading Principles of the Constitution*, a pamphlet written at the request of Thomas Fitzsimmons, a Pennsylvania delegate to the convention, and second as the editor of the short-lived *American Magazine*.[38] After the Constitution was ratified in New York, Webster took part in the federal procession of July 1788 with fellow members of the newly established Philological Society of New York, a society founded for the purpose of "improving the American tongue." Dressed in black, members of the Philological Society marched alongside representatives of the city's trades and professions, led by their secretary, who held aloft a scroll inscribed with the principles of a "Federal Language." The librarian of the society carried a copy of John Horne Tooke's *Diversions of Purley* (a work that had a formative influence on Webster), and the dramatist William Dunlap brought up the rear, carrying a standard emblazoned with "the arms of the society." Among other esoteric symbols inscribed on the standard was

> [t]he Flag, embellished with the Genius of America, crowned with a wreath of 13 plumes, ten of them starred, representing the ten States which have ratified the Constitution. Her right hand pointing to the Philological Society, and in her left, a standard, with a pendant, inscribed with the word, CONSTITUTION.

Amid this triumphant celebration of American nationalism, Noah Webster's hopes for the new republic reached their zenith.[39]

His hopes for his own future were less sanguine. On his thirtieth birthday in October 1788, he lamented, "30 years of my life gone—a large portion of the ordinary age of man! I have read much, written much and tried to do much good, but with little advantage to myself. I will now leave writing and do more lucrative business." The *American Magazine* had been a dismal flop, and his efforts to revive it met with little success. After leaving New York at the end of 1788, Webster went to Boston to supervise the publication of his *Dissertations on the English Language*. It, too, lost money. These setbacks and his desire to marry Rebecca Greenleaf, whom he had met in March 1788, led Webster to consider abandoning his literary career for a more stable and respectable livelihood. In February 1789, he announced that he was "done with making books" and intended to return to Hartford and resume his legal career. "I have relinquished forever all little projects," he wrote a short while later, "& determined upon my profession as a permanent business."[40]

In May 1789, Webster returned to Hartford, took up residence with his friend John Trumbull, and resumed his legal studies. On October 22, 1790, he became an attorney and counselor-at-law in the U.S. Circuit Court at Hartford, but he found it hard to make a living and was forced to rely on his brother-in-law James Greenleaf to keep his growing family afloat.[41] But his problems were not confined to money. Although Webster declared himself unconcerned "with the bustle of public life," he couldn't resist it. During his four years in Hartford, he joined the Abolition Society, was a moving spirit of the Charitable Society, and was elected a member of the Hartford Common Council. He also played an active role in local literary circles—as a member of the Friendly Club, which included Trumbull, Lemuel Hopkins, David Humphreys, and Timothy Dwight. And he began to write political essays again, composing a pamphlet on excise laws in Connecticut and producing a stream of articles for the local press, including the immensely popular "Prompter" essays, and a series of articles on education for the newly established *Gazette of the United States*. He published some of these essays in 1790 in *A Collection of Essays and Fugitiv Writings* and produced an important edition of John Winthrop's *Journal*.[42]

By early 1793, he was ready to abandon his legal practice, this time permanently. But the alternatives were unclear. "All I ask (or ever wished)," he wrote to James Greenleaf, "is business, and whether on a large or a small scale, I will be satisfied with it." Relying once again on the financial assistance of his brother-in-law, Webster decided to enter the book trade, convinced that bookselling "will be profitable if well conducted" and would complement and promote the sale of his own works. This scheme failed to materialize, but at some point Webster caught wind of another opportunity, the chance to edit a new Federalist newspaper in New York. Although nothing was firmly settled, Webster sold his law books and set out for New York.[43]

Webster was not the moving force behind the *American Minerva*. The money and the inspiration for the newspaper came from a group of Federalist politicians connected to the secretary of the treasury, Alexander Hamilton. According to Webster, "Mr. James Watson...first suggested the plan, and a number of the principal characters in New York furnished me with capital for the purpose." These men were troubled by the weakness of the Federalist press in New York, especially after John Fenno's *Gazette of the United States* moved to Philadelphia in 1791, and they were tired of the relentless partisan battering they received from Thomas Greenleaf's *New-York Journal*. They were also deeply concerned about the growing influence of Philip Freneau's *National Gazette*, whose attacks on Hamilton and support for Citizen Genet made them determined to establish a newspaper that would muster public support behind the Washington administration and American neutrality. After a series of meetings with Webster, a small but prominent group of Federalist politicians, including Hamilton, John Jay, Rufus King, James Watson, and James Greenleaf, each subscribed $150 "for five years without interest" to support a new Federalist daily paper. Armed with this capital, Webster moved swiftly. On August 30, 1793, he formed a partnership with printer George Bunce to publish the newspaper; in November, he moved his family from Hartford to New York; in early December, he issued proposals for a new daily newspaper; and on December 9, 1793, the first issue of the *American Minerva* appeared before the reading public.[44]

Webster's nationalism made him the ideal spokesman for a policy of American neutrality in the early 1790s, and he quickly made this clear in the pages of the *American Minerva*. The goals of the newspaper were well defined from the start: to counteract the influence of Citizen Genet and the French Republic, to combat the efforts of the Republican press (led by Freneau's *National Gazette*), to make the French Revolution a touchstone of party identity, and to defend Washington's policy of neutrality. But underlying these goals was a significant shift in Webster's political concerns. In his first "Address to the Public," he presented the *American Minerva* as a means to extend and realize the nationalist objectives he had pursued throughout the 1780s. The goal of the newspaper, he told prospective readers, was to support the national government—"This Paper will be the Friend of Government," he wrote—and to contribute to the creation of a national culture. These objectives were not new, but Webster now feared that their realization was impeded by a dangerous new obstacle: the factionalization of American politics and the development of political parties.[45]

In earlier political writings, Webster had argued that the primary obstacle to national unity was the localism of American life. Citizens of the new Republic, he believed, remained mired in local cultures and tied to the political institutions of provincial life. Although he discussed political parties in some of his work—in

American Minerva: An Evening Advertiser, New York, January 1, 1796. Published daily by Noah Webster and George Bunce, the *Minerva* was Webster's newspaper during the successful battle to secure the ratification of the Jay Treaty. The title of the newspaper made clear Webster's uncompromising nationalism and his determination to advance "American" interests, but the front page of the paper has a strongly commercial feel. Courtesy of the Library Company of Philadelphia.

the *Grammatical Institute*, he quoted Alexander Pope's verdict that "party is the madness of many for the gain of a few"—the issue did not interest him much before 1793. By that time, the growth of political factions had become an obsessive concern to Webster, a concern that rapidly grew to dominate his conduct of the *American Minerva*. This development was not completely surprising. Party distinctions had begun to crystallize when he launched the *Minerva* in late 1793, and hostility toward political parties was deeply rooted in American political culture. But the conventional critique of faction—that it was a vehicle for the pursuit of private interest at the expense of the *res publica*, or public interest—was one that Webster had specifically rejected in the past. Previously, he had believed that political conflict and self-interest were inevitable features of public life and that no stable political order could depend on the virtue and disinterestedness of its citizens. "Montesquieu has declared *virtue* to be the principle of Republican governments," he wrote in the first issue of the *Minerva*, but "it may be doubted whether such a principle ever existed." Nonetheless, he insisted, the growth of parties represented a threat to the "unity of character" that was needed to preserve American independence.[46]

As this comment suggests, Webster's hostility to political parties reflected his commitment to national integration and the creation of a national identity, not his commitment to the primacy of the public interest. In fact, far from representing the triumph of private over public interest, parties represented a descent into irrationality that was the antithesis of self-interest. Parties, declared Webster, had their origins in the passions, not the interests. "It is a notorious truth," he wrote,

> that people very often quarrel with each other without knowing the reason why. It is equally true that in politics, violent parties originate in trifles; and when persons have taken sides, the same parties continue on other questions, which have no kind of relation to the cause which first divided them.

By creating irrational loyalties, parties undermined rational political debate and the rational pursuit of private interest, and inevitably led to the displacement of the impersonal by the personal—"a dissatisfaction arising from *things*," observed Webster, "is afterwards transferred to *persons*"—a development that was a serious threat to republican social and political order. The obsession with personalities encouraged by the growth of factional loyalty undermined public and private life. "One of the greatest evils resulting from a difference of political opinions," wrote Webster, "is the ill will and dissocial passions which they create in the intercourse of private life." By giving these "dissocial passions" a permanent form, parties enabled them to seep deeply into the social fabric, disrupting the civility and natural sociability of public and private life. "A party spirit," declared Webster, is as great a curse to society as can befall it; it makes honest men hate each other, and destroys a good neighborhood.... Examin[e] the detached clubs at the Coffee-House; there you see persons of the *same party* associated. Go into private families, at dinners and evening visits, there you find none but people of the *same party.*

By factionalizing private life, "party spirit" eroded the basis for social cohesion and destroyed civil society from the bottom up.[47]

In Webster's view, the politicization of private life was closely tied to the personalization of public life. As parties developed, partisan identity was increasingly defined by personality rather than political substance, and political rhetoric became more and more heated and irresponsible, transgressing further and further into the private lives of public figures. Slander was therefore a natural consequence of party conflict, easily overwhelming rational political debate. "If a man is held up as a candidate for office," wrote Webster, "the men who oppose him endeavour to depreciate his worth, by publishing his private faults and even his weaknesses." These personal attacks were both illegitimate—"Everything should be kept out of sight which does not affect his *public* character"—and deeply harmful to the body politic, undermining popular confidence in political leadership and deflecting attention from more important issues of public policy.[48]

The growth of political parties also struck at the roots of national solidarity and independence. By sowing the seeds of personal antagonism and alienation, parties corroded what Webster called "social affection," disrupting the domestic unity of the family and the "natural" domestic unity of the nation. Not surprisingly, Webster saw parties as a product of "unnatural" external influences rather than as genuine social or political conflicts of interest. Domestic disagreements, he believed, were aggravated and exploited by the "artful emissaries of foreign nations" and "emigrants from Europe, who have been but a few years in this country." According to one essayist in the *Minerva*, party conflict was an "imported distemper," the result of foreign influence that was "as inevitably fatal to the liberties of the state, as the admission of strangers to arbitrate upon the domestic differences of man and wife is destructive to the happiness of a private family." As a result of foreign influence, wrote the author:

Americans, equally patriotic and republican, and equally interested in the welfare of their common country, become open enemies to each other. Thus, instead of uniting in the means of serving our own country, we become the dupes, the tools of foreign nations, quarreling with each other, about foreign politics in which we are very little interested. It is thus we are split into factions and intrigued out of our good harmony and good fellowship.... reject foreign influence, and be what you ought to be, independent Americans.

In their eagerness to take sides in foreign political squabbles, argued Webster, his fellow citizens revealed a fatal irrationality and lack of self-respect, subordinating their own national interests to the interests of other nations and undermining the political unity and independence of the United States.[49]

Nobody who read the *American Minerva* could fail to notice that it was the influence of the French Republic that most worried Webster. But he was no more favorably disposed toward other European powers. He was harshly critical of the monarchical coalition against France, condemning British participation in a "vile league of tyrants," and in his coverage of British reform movements, he sided with radicals like Horne Tooke, Thomas Hardy, and John Thelwall, denouncing British prime minister William Pitt as "an enemy to freedom and to this country." He discounted British influence on American politics not because he was an Anglophile, but because he thought "the British have as little influence on the politics of this country, as the Chinese." "The British government," he declared, "has treated Americans so ill that a general and rooted detestation of that government prevails throughout the U[nited] states. We are therefore in no danger from any English influence in this country." British policy, especially the recent attacks on American merchant shipping, had only exacerbated this "general and rooted detestation."[50]

In contrast, Webster believed that France possessed great influence in the United States, whose citizens viewed that nation as a valued ally and a "sister republic." "Almost every man who espoused the cause of America, in her struggle for independence," he maintained, "is now friendly to the revolution in France." This included Webster himself, who described the French Revolution in May 1793 as

> the most interesting spectacle ever exhibited on the theater of this earth; a great enlightened people struggling, not only to break down the feudal and hierarchical systems of despotism, but to exterminate their very principles, remove the gothic rubbish from their extensive territory, and prepare the soil for the more generous plant of liberty.

But the French had exploited this natural sympathy to advance their own interests and to bring the United States to the brink of a disastrous war with Great Britain. And although Webster blamed "foreign emissaries" like Genet, he also blamed Republicans like Freneau, who exploited an "undue partiality" for France to advance their own partisan objectives. As he realized, challenging their ideological appropriation of the revolution required fostering doubts about the revolutionary movement in France, and its relevance to American politics, without repudiating the revolution itself. "At the present critical juncture of our political affairs," he wrote to George Washington in April 1794, it appears to be the duty of every good citizen to use his influence in restraining the violence of parties and moderating the passions of our injured fellow-citizens. For this purpose a just estimate of the Revolution in France and the danger of faction may not be without its effects in this country, in determining the people to resist any intrigues that may be hostile to our government. The enclosed is intended to aid the cause of government and peace. Should it have the least influence for this purpose, I shall be satisfied.

The enclosure to which Webster referred was his recent pamphlet, *The Revolution in France.*[51]

The Revolution in France marked an important turning point in the evolution of Webster's political ideas. As he told Washington, his goal was to convey to Americans a "just estimate of the Revolution in France and the danger of faction." Like most of his countrymen, he had greeted the French Revolution with joy and "felt nearly the same interest in its success, as he did in the establishment of American independence." But the present course of the revolution required a more critical response:

> A just estimate of things, their causes and effects, is always desirable and it is of infinite consequence to this country, to ascertain the point where our admiration of the French measures should end, and our censure begin; the point, beyond which an introduction of their principles and practice into this country, will prove dangerous to government, religion and morals.

Webster described himself as a "historian" interested only in the "causes of great changes in the affairs of men." But although this judicious tone masked highly partisan objectives, it would be wrong to characterize his essay as a counter-revolutionary tirade or an American counterpart to Burke's *Reflections on the Revolution in France.*[52]

As Webster was well aware, an indiscriminate attack on the French Revolution would be counterproductive, and the first part of his essay was devoted to an optimistic survey of events in France. Throughout the essay, he distinguished carefully between the worthy principles of the revolution and the despicable practices of the revolutionary leaders. "Let us then separate the men from the cause," he wrote, "and while we detest the instrument, let us applaud the end to be accomplished." This nuanced approach to the revolution was not just tactical. Webster still supported the goals of the revolution, "the noblest ever undertaken by men," expressed optimism about its eventual success, and was even impressed by some of the achievements of the Jacobin government. Although war and domestic violence had ravaged France, he wrote, it was still possible to detect signs of regeneration and rebirth, to see "roses growing among thorns."[53]

But Webster made no effort to disguise his disgust for the "sanguinary proceedings of the Jacobins" and their "atheistical attacks on christianity." "Under pretence of guarding the public safety," he wrote, the revolutionary tribunal "together with its executive instrument, the guillotine, have filled France with human blood and swept away opposition." Under the guise of republicanism, the Jacobins had established a dictatorship, and under the guise of reason, they had revived a spirit of religious fanaticism and persecution. "With professions of the most boundless liberality of sentiment and with an utter abhorrence of bigotry and tyranny," he argued, the Jacobins "have become the most implacable persecutors of opinion." And in this, they resembled nothing so much as their Catholic predecessors:

> The Jacobins differ from the clergy of the dark ages in this—the clergy persecuted for heresy in religion and—the Jacobins, for heresy in politics....the object may change, but the imperious spirit of triumphant faction is always the same.

The Jacobins had even waged war on fellow revolutionaries, executing republicans like Danton and Brissot merely because they "*belonged to another party.*" The violence they had unleashed, wrote Webster, "displayed a rancor of malice and cruelty, that reminds us of savages." France was not governed by republicans but by a "military aristocracy" of unparalleled ruthlessness. "What," he demanded, did such government have to do with "*liberty and the rights of men?*"[54]

According to Webster, the fratricidal violence in France was the logical consequence of party politics, "that scourge of almost every free government, and the disgrace of the French Revolution." Political violence, he argued, had its origins in the inexorable progress of "party-spirit" and its institutionalization in "private societies" like the Jacobin clubs, which eroded personal independence—"The moment a man is attached to a club," he wrote, "his mind is not free"—creating an exclusive "aristocracy" that abridged "the rights of fellow-citizens." Such "private societies" required an irrational abdication of personal autonomy, and the habits of association they fostered encouraged an irrational "bigotry and illiberality" toward those with different opinions.[55] Far from representing private interests, they represented the negation of rational interest (which could be determined only by the autonomous individual), and their growth undermined rational, self-interested political debate. Violence was the inevitable consequence. Parties mobilized the passions needed to destroy but not the moderation needed to preserve. The quest for power was their only raison d'être; they made sense only in a revolutionary context and, while "useful in pulling down bad governments," were "dangerous to good government and necessarily destroy liberty and equality of rights in a free country."[56]

The triumph of the Jacobin Party in France illustrated this process perfectly. But Webster also had in mind some private societies closer to home: the Democratic Republican societies. "The principal danger to which our government is exposed," he wrote, was neither "consolidation" nor "the disorganizing tendency of state jealousy" but the "spirit of party, which is now taking the form of a system." The rise of parties was a disastrous development, which he blamed on naive popular enthusiasm for the politics of the French Republic. But while the French, who were struggling to establish political liberty, had some justification for creating revolutionary organizations like the Jacobin clubs, there was no such justification in the United States. Where a republican government already existed based on "principles of liberty and equal rights," there was "no necessity for private societies to watch over the government." The Democratic societies, alleged Webster, were "laying the foundation of factions" that would end in the "destruction of liberty and free government" and in "open hostility and bloodshed." Americans should be more skeptical about revolutionary France and demonstrate greater faith in their own political institutions. "Americans be not deluded!" he declared in the last paragraph of his pamphlet:

> In seeking liberty, France has gone beyond her. You, my countrymen, if you love liberty, adhere to your constitution of government. The moment you quit that sheet-anchor, you are afloat among the surges of passion and the rocks of error; threatened every moment with ship-wreck. Heaven grant that while Europe is agitated with a violent tempest, in which palaces are shaken, and thrones tottering to their base, the republican government of America, in which liberty and the rights of man are embarked, fortunately anchored at an immense distance, on the margin of the gale, may be enabled to ride out the storm, and land us safely on the shores of peace and tranquility.

But even as Webster warned Americans to shun the influence of republican France, he smuggled analogies with France back into the political debate.[57]

Running through the essay was an analogy between the Jacobin clubs and the Democratic societies, an analogy Webster developed further in the *Minerva* and which quickly became a staple of Federalist propaganda. His comparison between Jacobinism and Republicanism had obvious partisan motives: to undermine the credibility of the Democratic societies and to challenge the way that Republicans used the French Revolution to define their party's identity. By challenging the standard narrative of the French Revolution—and casting the Jacobins as enemies rather than as agents of a republican revolutionary tradition—Webster sought to turn Republican efforts to identify themselves with the French Revolution to his own advantage. Although he urged Americans to shun the French example, like his Republican counterparts he encouraged readers to view American politics through the prism of the French Revolution.[58]

The Revolution in France was a thus a sustained polemic against the Democratic societies, employing a sensational analysis of Jacobin politics to discredit the activities of the Republican opposition. But Webster's essay also signaled a turning point in his political thinking. He had always regarded "self-interest" as the principal motive for political behavior, but the behavior of Jacobin revolutionaries defied the idea of rational interest altogether. What rational explanation could there be for the political success of the Jacobins, who had created a new inquisition to root out "heresy in politics"? Or for the deification of a "bloodthirsty wretch" like Marat, who "lived by publishing libels"? How could one explain the recrudescence of superstition, idolatry, and fanaticism that characterized the revolutionary political culture in France? The absurdity and pomposity of Robespierre's cult of Reason? The brutal massacres in Paris, Lyons, and Toulon; the bloodshed of the Vendee; or the merciless work of the Committee of Public Safety?[59]

As he struggled to comprehend the chilling violence of the French Revolution, Webster's faith in the influence of political institutions faltered. While it was true that the French Constitution was "sown thick" with the "seeds of faction," the irrationality of party politics in France was clearly not sufficient to explain the Terror. The outrages in France could "admit of no excuse but a political insanity." But what, he asked, had caused the most civilized nation in Europe to sink into political insanity? The French Revolution had been "attended with a total change in the minds of the people":

> They are released, not only from the ordinary restraints of law, but from all their former habits of thinking. From the fetters of a debasing religious system, the people are let loose in the wide field of mental licentiousness; and as men naturally rush from one extreme to another, the French will probably rush into the wildest vagaries of opinion, both in their political and moral creeds.

This "mental licentiousness" was, to some extent, the natural result of revolutionary upheaval and war, but it was dramatically compounded by the anti-Christian policies of the French Convention. Like most Protestant Americans, Webster welcomed the anti-Catholic policies of the revolution, including the disestablishment of the Catholic church in France, as a blow against "papal domination." But he was deeply angered by the anti-Christian policies of the Committee of Public Safety after 1793: the abolition of the Christian calendar, the replacement of the Sabbath with a *Decadi*, the creation of temples and festivals dedicated to the worship of Reason, and the persecution of Christian believers. Fusing anti-Catholicism and Christian hostility to "atheism and materialism," Webster denounced the Jacobins as "modern idolators" who were waging "an inveterate war with christianity." Instead of encouraging religious tolerance and rational religion, they had revived the spirit and practices of their native Catholicism, creating new objects of idolatry (a "goddess of reason" and a "stupid veneration" of "canonized Jacobins") and a new pretext for fanaticism and persecution.[60]

The results of Jacobin de-Christianization were profound. The French Revolution, argued Webster, had unleashed a torrent of violent passions that swept away the rotten debris of the Old Regime. But restoring calm and chanening these destructive passions required the restraining moral influence of civil society, and reconstructing the moral order of French society had been made impossible by Jacobin attacks on the "sublime truths of christianity." Their efforts "to exterminate everything that looks like imposing restraint upon the passions, by the fear of a supreme being and future punishments," he wrote, "are a most extraordinary experiment in government." "Atheism and materialism," he argued, could never support a stable social and political order, and the assault on Christianity had left French society "totally demoralized" and subject to chronic instability and violence. The Terror was the logical result of a society in which primitive political passions had extinguished reason and the moral life, a society in a state of utter "demoralization."[61]

Webster's concept of demoralization represented a decisive shift in his understanding of politics. Before writing *The Revolution in France*, he had argued that morality was irrelevant to problems of political order and state formation. Human behavior was governed by the passions and rational self-interest, and the role of the state was to control these passions and direct this self-interest, to create civility and moral order. But events in France had demonstrated to him that rapid political change could undermine the moral foundation for civil society and a civilized polity. And once destroyed, this moral foundation was hard to reconstruct. Reforming political institutions could have only a limited influence, argued Webster, because the stability of political society did not depend on institutions but on the "moral character of men." Without the restraining influence of morality and religion, he concluded, it was impossible to preserve the health of the body politic.

One startling consequence of Webster's new sensitivity to moral reform was his advocacy of patriarchal government. In his essay on France, he blamed the demoralization of French society partly on the abolition of patriarchal government and the erosion of respect for "old age and wisdom," and he subsequently took up this idea in the *Minerva*. Conflating the idea of an aristocracy of talent with an aristocracy of age (and gender), he pronounced "patriarchal government" to be the "most natural, as well as the most useful species known in society." This form of government, he argued (with a new sensitivity to historical precedent), "was the first mode of governing men, and wherever it exists in any tolerable degree of purity, men are, in a great degree, happy." "Let me live," he declared, "where the councils of old men are deemed wisdom, and experience, the most venerable instructor." Like most supporters of patriarchy, Webster believed that the basis of political order lay in family government. Where natural relations of authority and deference existed within the family, the family provided a stable foundation for social and political order. But where they did not, all was chaos. "The father of a family is the natural governor of his children and domestics," wrote Webster. "[W]here he is loved and respected there is peace, order, subordination, and harmony." But "where the pater-familias, the father is hated or despised, we see in the family disorders, angry passions, discord and every evil." Similar principles govern the good order of the wider community. "Where we find an old man of virtue and talents, whose grey hairs command respect, and whose opinions influence the people," he argued, "there we find peace, harmony, few vices, and great social felicity."[62]

Webster thus linked moral disorder to the erosion of "natural" forms of patriarchal authority in the family, "the nursery of the virtues," and the community as a whole. As his arguments reveal, he had shifted his focus from government and political institutions to family life and civil society, and at the heart of this shift was his growing sense of alarm about the intrusion of politics into family life, a development that one writer in the *Minerva* called a "solvent of the moral system." Webster's defense of patriarchy and gerontocracy, an aristocracy of age, gender, and experience, was clearly a response to Republican attacks on George Washington. The vilification of Washington and other founding fathers profoundly disturbed Webster. Writing to his friend and political ally Oliver Wolcott, Jr., during the Jay Treaty debates in July 1795, he worried that the unpopular treaty would harm the "popularity of the President, whose personal influence is now more essential than ever to our Union."[63] But he also regarded Republican attacks on Washington as part of a more general descent into a politics of personality (or "private character"), a development that appalled Webster. As he now believed, attacks on private character not only dissolved the natural relations of authority that created a stable domestic and civil life, but the natural relations of authority that created a stable political life. Ironically, Webster's anxiety about the personalization of American politics explained his newly discovered enthusiasm for patriarchy and his emphasis on the role played by "personal influence" in the preservation of social and political order.[64]

As long as Webster remained optimistic about American politics, these ideas remained an undercurrent in the *Minerva*. Indeed, when news of Robespierre's execution reached the United States in early 1795, he even recovered some of his earlier enthusiasm for the French Revolution. "Nothing can give more pleasure to all true friends of liberty and a republican government," he wrote in response to the news, "than the late revolution in France." Although he continued to document French atrocities in the *Minerva* and to denounce signs of French influence on American politics, he praised French efforts to frame a new constitution and welcomed the improvement in Franco-American relations that occurred in 1795. "Even the villainies of the Jacobins," he confessed, "have never detached Americans from their love of the revolution."[65] The divisive struggle to ratify the Jay Treaty presented a greater challenge to his political equilibrium. But even this highly partisan conflict ultimately reinforced his optimism about public affairs. Despite obvious flaws in the treaty, popular hostility to the British, and the tireless efforts of the Republican press, by early 1796 public opposition to the treaty had subsided. The Republican campaign against Washington, commented Webster, had "fallen before the power of reason and mature reflection, into general contempt," and the passage of the Jay Treaty vindicated his faith in the good sense of the American people and in republican government. Confident that public opinion was firmly behind the Washington administration and the Federalists, he declared, "Republicanism, that is, government formed by the free choice of the people to be governed, is everywhere admitted to be the only legitimate government on earth."[66]

On July 4, 1796, Webster celebrated the preservation of American independence and expressed guarded optimism about the future. "We have safely steered between Scylla and Charybdis," he wrote:

> Let us rejoice that the clouds that overspread our political horizon are, in a degree, dissapated [*sic*]; that our free and excellent Constitution has weathered the adverse shocks of faction and treachery; and acquired new energy by a wise and pacific administration. Let us, at the same time, rejoice at the extension of light and freedom in Europe and the prospect of a speedy regeneration of the monstrous despotisms of the old world. Let us rejoice at the prospect of the downfall of all monarchies & aristocracies, and the establishment of *governments by elections*.

The election of President John Adams and Vice President Thomas Jefferson in 1796 gave him further cause for celebration. And he hoped that, contrary to the "views and expectations of both parties," the election would be a "means of reconciling discordant opinions, of moderating the asperity of party, and uniting, in the administration, the confidence of men of different political opinions." But his hopes for political consensus were unrealized. Even as he wrote, a diplomatic crisis between France and the United States was brewing, provoked by French hostility toward the passage of the Jay Treaty; it reenergized the partisan conflict between Republicans and Federalists and created a rift in the Federalist ranks that left Webster disillusioned and embittered with public life. The first sign of this rift was an editorial in the *Minerva* in March 1797, urging members of the Tontine Coffee House to take down a French flag on display there. "Give the flag to the bar keeper to be removed forever out of sight," wrote Webster, "then resolve never to suffer any flag but the American to be displayed on the territories of the United States." The French tricolor was taken down, but to his dismay it was immediately replaced by the British Union Jack. "When will the honor of the American name be vindicated by discarding such badges of faction?" he demanded the following day. "When will Americans unite under their own flag, and learn to be a Nation?"[67]

This attack on the British flag did not go unnoticed. Webster's remarks were reprinted in the pages of a new Philadelphia daily, *Porcupine's Gazette*, and dismissed as a sign of his poor political judgment and "vulgar prejudice." The editor of the newspaper, William Cobbett (better known by his nom de plume, Peter Porcupine), then proposed an alliance between Britain and the United States. Although Webster had praised Porcupine's work in the *Minerva* and welcomed the establishment of *Porcupine's Gazette*, there was tension between the two Federalist editors from the moment *Porcupine's Gazette* appeared before the public. The day after his editorial on the British flag, Webster scolded Cobbett for printing an attack by Edmund Burke on the Marquis de Lafayette, warning him not to attack "the principles or the friends and defenders of our independence and republican government." Cobbett's support for an Anglo-American alliance against France was clearly designed to provoke Webster, and it succeeded. Brandishing his own political principles, Webster declared war on Peter Porcupine:

> Such, Peter, is my political creed—I know of no party, but that of MY COUNTRY. My country is INDEPENDENT; it is for our interest…that it should be so; and the man who seeks to tack it onto *any* foreign country, to involve it in European broils or make its independence the sport of European policy, is conceived to be an ENEMY.

Cobbett took Webster at his word, and the two Federalist editors were soon embroiled in a bitter newspaper feud. From the start, Webster was on the receiving end. He had no stomach for the vitriolic newspaper warfare that Cobbett conducted with such relish, skill, and inexhaustible energy. And he had no answers to Cobbett's relentless sarcasm and endlessly inventive abuse. Within two months, Webster was considering stepping down as editor of the *Minerva*.[68]

The significance of this feud was not only personal; it symbolized political differences among Federalists that would tear the party apart over the next three years. Cobbett's popularity and influence exposed a fault line in the Federalist

ranks about American neutrality, a policy that Webster had defended unswerv-
ingly in the *Minerva* and regarded as the touchstone of Federalist political
identity. But, as popular opinion turned against the French Republic, many
Federalists abandoned neutrality and embraced an aggressive Anglophile version
of Federalist nationalism. Although Cobbett's blatantly pro-British politics and
support for a British alliance attracted few Federalists, his belligerence toward
France and his fiercely anti-revolutionary writings had a much broader appeal.
These tensions between Webster and Cobbett and within the Federalist coalition
became even clearer when President John Adams proposed diplomatic negotiations with France in mid-1797. While Webster supported neutrality and "manly"
negotiation, Cobbett became the chief spokesman for Federalists who believed
that war with France was inevitable and even desirable.[69]

During the period of Federalist ascendancy that followed the Jay Treaty's
ratification in 1796, Webster's political skepticism was muted. But even before
divisions in his own party became clearly evident, his confidence was shaken by
events in Europe. Although he was angered by French attacks on American shipping in 1796, it was Bonaparte's conquest of Italy in 1796 that finally transformed
Webster from an alienated critic of the French Revolution into an irreconcilable
opponent.[70] In a series of essays on "Political Fanaticism," Webster revisited the
themes of his earlier work on the French Revolution, explaining that although his
belief in republican government remained intact, he was now more concerned
about popular virtue and education than political institutions. "Neither liberty
nor tyranny," he argued, "results necessarily from a particular form of government." In France, revolutionary leaders had imposed republican government on
a people who had "not been *educated* republicans—they do not know how to
govern themselves." And the result was disorder and dictatorship. According to
Webster, there was no easy solution to this problem. "Books and schools teach a
few theories," wrote the man who had once argued that literature was the source
of all moral order, but "manners descend from age to age by imitation." Political
change takes time, and sudden changes in religion or government inevitably produce violence and despotism.[71]

Webster's retreat from revolutionary politics was complete. Political change
depended on slow changes in custom and habit, on the transformation of deeply
rooted social attitudes, not on the creation of new political institutions. And he
blamed "visionaries" like Rousseau, Godwin, and Condorcet—"who, sit down in
their closets to frame systems of government, which are as unfit for practice, as a
vessel of paper for the transportation of men on the troubled ocean"—for the violence that had engulfed France and Europe. His emphasis on "republican habits"
rather than republican political institutions clearly drew on his own New England
origins in the "land of steady habits." "No man can understand," he wrote,

[w]hy the eastern people are *good republicans*, unless he sits down to reside a year or two among them. He must begin to learn, where children do, in families. He must observe the strict discipline that prevails there—he must then enter the school houses, where the teacher has his pupils under such subordination, that they pass hours without almost a whisper or a smile; and where they are instructed and compelled to be respectful to superiors. He must attend their churches, observe the silence and decorum that prevail not only there, but in private families on Sunday.

This culture, focused around the patriarchal family, the discipline of the school-house, and the authority of the church, produced those "regular habits of self-government" that were the "surest basis of republican government." Webster had once used the natural depravity of mankind to argue against a politics of morality. Now, he used it to support such a politics.[72]

As he fought a war on two fronts against Republicans and the indefatigable William Cobbett, his disillusionment curdled into disgust. "Porcupine," he argued, was "attempting to create or rally an English party in our country as violent and devoted to foreign government as the French party." Cobbett's influence left Webster bitter about the apostasy of fellow Federalists, and the popularity of Cobbett's savage, personal journalism left Webster disturbed about the sanity of the public mind. Writing just after James Thomson Callender had exposed Alexander Hamilton's affair with Maria Reynolds to the world, he condemned the "squadrons of liars and defamers, who vomit forth, from the public presses, the poison that saps the foundations of government and moral virtue." "Foreign" journalists like Cobbett and Callender, he argued, were responsible for the spread of scurrilous political journalism; they were men "with low vitious minds, but some talents and education," who established themselves as "pimps of faction, English or French" and abused "the officers of our government, the government itself and the most respectable Americans." Webster's nationalism, formerly characterized by an inclusive and principled support for national independence, now became darker and more xenophobic. In July 1797, he produced the following jeremiad in the *Minerva*, deploring the influence of immigrants in American politics and demanding that the government take action against them. "From the days of Adam, to this moment," he wrote,

no country was ever so infested with corrupt and wicked men as the United States. Imported "patriots," bankrupt speculators, rich bankrupts, "patriotic" Atheists, and other similar characters, are spread over the United States without number, deceiving the people with lies, gaining their confidence, corrupting their principles and debauching their morals. We see in our new Republic, the decrepitude of Vice; and a free government hastening to ruin, with a rapidity without example.[73]

By this time, Webster had already begun to abandon the role of Federalist editor and agitator and turn his mind to other pursuits. In October 1797, he changed the name of the *Minerva* to the bland *Commercial Advertiser* and turned the newspaper over to his nephew Ebeneezer Belden just as it reached the zenith of its commercial success. After publishing proposals for "An Inquiry into the Origins of Epidemic Diseases" in March 1798, he left New York for New Haven with his family to escape the "bustl of commerce and the taste of people inquiring for news." But in reality, he was fleeing the political fray. As editor of the *Minerva*, he wrote shortly afterward, "I found myself exposed to so many personal indignities from different parties that retirement was essential to my happiness, if not to my life." "Few men of honour and feeling," he explained, "can consent to take charge of public papers—they must generally be superintended by men who are callous."[74]

In a letter to Federalist secretary of state Timothy Pickering in July 1798, Webster poured out his complaints about Cobbett and the "English in New York" and declared himself unwilling "to be thus abused by the subjects of foreign nations." Reproaching Pickering and other Federalists for their lack of support, he announced his withdrawal from national politics:

> I shall withdraw my exertions for the support of government, and as I shall be its advocate in private, I shall only support it by my single suffrage. When *aliens* assume such a tone and abuse honest, faithful men, it is time for native citizens to retire and seek peace and quietness in more private occupation. I could raise a flame even now about the heads of the English, but it would be against the public interest. I, therefore, choose to retire and be the victim of party rancor.

Wounded by his experiences, Webster warned his fellow citizens in Connecticut to protect their patrimony. In a Fourth of July oration in 1798, he described the United States as a "sequestered region, where religion, virtue and the arts may find a peaceful retirement from the tempests which agitate Europe" and where the "seeds of a pure church and excellent constitutions of government" could be preserved for transplantation to the Old World. But Americans must not relinquish their "civil and religious institutions for the wild theories of crazy projectors" or abandon "the sober, industrious habits of our country, for experiments in atheism and lawless democracy." "*Experience*," he insisted, "is a safe pilot; but *experiment* is a dangerous ocean, full of rocks and shoals." Looking out over the restless ocean from his home in New Haven, Webster had found himself a harbor from the storm.[75]

True to his word, he did not pick up his pen to defend either Federalism or the Adams administration again until the presidential elections of 1800. Between April 1798 and late 1799, he devoted himself almost exclusively to his study of epidemics, producing the two-volume *A Brief Study of Epidemic and Pestilential Disease*, which was published in both England and America to almost complete public indifference. And when he returned to journalism in 1800, the break had done nothing to restore his political zeal or his faith in popular democracy. Torn between dislike for Hamilton, who was maneuvering to replace John Adams, and a belief that party unity was necessary to secure victory, his contributions to the public debate were minor and lackluster.[76] His ineffectiveness was not entirely his own fault. The breach between Adams and Hamilton hampered the entire Federalist Party in 1800, but Webster's waning enthusiasm was also due to his growing conservatism and alienation from party politics. His election pamphlets were self-absorbed and politically maladroit, adopting an anti-democratic, elitist rhetoric that must have alienated even Federalist sympathizers. Repudiating the language of democratic politics, Webster defined "Democrat" as synonymous with "Jacobin" and defined the United States as a "Representative Republic" not, as he had once argued, a "representative democracy." Most significantly, for the first time he supported franchise restriction and even the introduction of hereditary political institutions.[77]

Webster had previously endorsed the idea of a "natural aristocracy" based on hierarchies of gender, age, and talent, but his beliefs were prescriptive, not coercive, and did not yet represent a complete break with democratic politics. By the end of the 1790s, however, he was prepared to use coercion as well as persuasion to ensure that government remained in the hands of a natural elite. This shift explains his support for the Alien and Sedition Acts in 1798, which he believed would protect political leaders from character assassination and protect public opinion from the misinformation of the partisan press. But even his support for these measures was based on a residual faith in the rationality of the American public. By late 1800, with the Republican Party clearly in the ascendant, his faith in popular democracy evaporated altogether, and Webster concluded that there was no alternative but to impose his vision of patriarchal order. "As to mankind," he wrote to Benjamin Rush, "I believe the mass of them to be *copax rationis*":

> It would be better for the people—they would be more free and more happy—if all were deprived of the right to suffrage until they are 45 years of age and if no man was eligible to an important office until he is 50, that is, if all the powers of government were vested in our old men who have lost their ambition chiefly and have learned wisdom by experience, but to tell the people this would be treason. We have grown so wise of late years as to reject the maxims of Moses, Lycurgus, and the patriarchs: we have, by our constitutions of government and the preposterous use made of the doctrines of *equality*, stripped *old* men of their dignity and *wise* men of their influence, and long, long are we to feel the mischievous effects of our modern policy.

This is an extraordinary statement. But it was not yet a doctrine of hereditary aristocracy or class rule. Webster was proposing a democracy of old men.[78]

Issues of class, however, loomed ever greater in Webster's mind. In his writings of the 1780s and early 1790s, he had treated economic inequality as a grave threat to republican government, but by the early 1800s he considered the preservation of property and economic inequality as the raison d'être of republican government. In an oration delivered on the Fourth of July 1802, he argued that all men were not "free, independent and equal":

> Government is chiefly concerned with the rights of person and the rights of property.... Now if all men have an equal right of suffrage, those who have little and those who have no property, have the power of making regulations respecting the property of others; that is, an equal right to control the property of those who own it.

It is hard to imagine a more revealing statement about capitalism, property rights, and democracy. Webster's earlier democratic, egalitarian vision of republican government had been replaced by fears of class expropriation. Political equality was an infringement of the rights of property, he now argued, and democracy "a monstrous inversion of the natural order of society, a species of oppression that will ultimately produce a revolution."[79]

Despite his hostility to popular democracy, Webster's response to the election of Thomas Jefferson in 1801 was surprisingly conciliatory. Thoroughly disillusioned with his own party, the publication of his scathing *Letter to General Hamilton*, which blamed Hamilton for the destruction and defeat of the Federalist party and denounced him as the "evil genius of this country," left him completely isolated.[80] But his tolerance for the new administration was short-lived. When Jefferson began to replace Federalist officeholders with Republican appointees in 1801, Webster was furious. As he explained to Benjamin Rush, Jefferson's system of political preferment would debase public life: "Bad men begin to scramble, and compel the good to resort to the same means in their own defense, till the whole machine of government is managed by money and favor." After trying to convince Jefferson of his folly, Webster composed and published a rebarbative *Letter to the President*, revealing how much his views had changed since the early 1790s. Before writing *The Revolution in France*, Webster had believed strongly in the formative influence of political institutions. Republican government, he had argued, would create a republican citizenry. After 1794, he began to place more faith in moral habits and patriarchal political leadership than in political institutions, and by the time he wrote his *Letter to the President*, political institutions were largely irrelevant to his understanding of politics. Government, he wrote, should be judged "by its effects on public happiness," not according to an infatuation with forms and names; it was not the form of the government that mattered most but the character of the governors. What use was republican government, he asked, if it were controlled by "fools and knaves?"[81]

Political patronage, believed Webster, made a mockery of enlightened government by failing to protect those who were dedicated to the public good from the irrationality of public opinion. Jefferson's indifference to "the moral character of a candidate for office" not only elevated unqualified, corrupt party hacks to public office but inverted the "whole order of society":

> The natural sentiment of man is, to respect virtue, religion, grave manners, eminent talents, the wisdom of experience and the hoary head. Your practices tend to depress eminence of talents, to point the finger of scorn at a veneration for religion; to exalt the young over the head of the old; [and] to discard solid worth.

By sacrificing the *res publica* to the interests of the Republican Party and by appointing those who did the same to public office, Jefferson's policy undermined the authority of the entire government and the political elite, transforming the state from a bulwark against faction into its instrument. The executive branch, railed Webster, had become an "engine of corruption" that would turn the body politic into a "morbid, cadaverous corpse." Expressing savage contempt for Jefferson—"Wretched man! exalted by the popular breath, only to add force to your fall, to sink more deeply into future oblivion"—and profound disillusionment with American politics, Webster wrote:

> Gracious Heavens! Is that a successful experiment, which, in twelve years, has spread discord over our peaceful country, planted the thorns of animosity and rancor in the bosoms of neighbors and former friends; which has converted our printing presses in to the convenient instruments of slander and malice, and the right of suffrage into the means of corruption—which has substituted jealousy for confidence, private views for public good, and for wise and venerable statesman, aspiring demagogues and scramblers for office?

The whole machinery of government, Webster argued, had been turned over to "money and factions, so that the people have lost their free agency and liberty." And because they were no longer able to identify virtuous political leaders, the only solution was to create a ruling body "independent of popular suffrage," a kind of republican peerage.[82]

By now, Webster was close to despair. Deeply disillusioned with public life, he also faced the failure of the *Commercial Advertiser* and financial ruin. In the fall of 1801, Hamilton established the *New York Evening Post* and installed the fiery William Coleman as editor. It was a logical response to divisions in the Federalist

Party and to the feeble conduct of the *Commercial Advertiser*, but it was also designed to ruin Webster and exact revenge for his pamphlet on Hamilton. After a halfhearted effort to revive his newspaper, Webster tried to sell it to Coleman, who responded by ridiculing him mercilessly in the *Evening Post*. And as Federalist support ebbed away, Webster grew bitter. "Such gross and cruel ingratitude to a man who has spent the largest part of 18 years in opposing Democracy," he wrote to Oliver Wolcott, Jr., "cannot be overlooked or forgiven." But Webster had few retaliatory weapons left at his disposal, and a few months later he announced his retreat into the world of "private affairs." "I have no hope of the duration of the Union," he wrote, with weary finality.[83]

In the winter of 1782, Webster's father had written to him, inquiring about his welfare. He was especially concerned about Webster's spiritual condition. "I wish to have you serve your generation & do good in the world," he wrote,

> & be useful & so behave as to gain the esteem of all virtuous people that are acquainted with you & gain a comfortable subsistence, but especially that you may so live as to obtain the favor of Almighty God & his grace in this world & a saving interest in the merits of Jesus Christ, without which no man can be happy.

These remarks were an admonition to the young Webster, who had strayed far from his father's Calvinism during his years at Yale, to return to the religion of his forefathers. But he could not. Deeply committed to the primacy of reason and skeptical about some of the central tenets of Christianity, Webster's religious beliefs in the 1780s and early 1790s were shaped by a thoroughgoing rationalism. As his hostility toward New England's religious establishments made clear, his political views were also thoroughly secular.[84] It is difficult to know exactly when his beliefs began to change. Although Webster had abandoned any early deist inclinations he possessed by the time he wrote *The Revolution in France*, his Christianity remained highly rationalist in the mid-1790s, inspired more by fear of French Jacobinism and irreligion than of everlasting perdition. Religion, to Webster, was a form of social control rather than a source of spiritual solace and personal salvation. But by the turn of the nineteenth century, his writings revealed a growing interest in religious issues, and his conception of politics was much less secular. He even began to revise his opposition to religious establishments. Only the principles of Christianity, he argued in 1802, were "compatible with rational freedom and calculated to maintain a republican constitution."[85]

By compelling a "return to his Heavenly Father" and the religion of the patriarchs, the Second Great Awakening restored a sense of unity to Webster's private and public professions. When the Awakening reached New Haven in 1807, his attitude toward Christianity was still ambivalent. As he informed his brother-in-law Thomas Dawes, he still had "doubts respecting some of the doctrines of the Christian faith, such as regeneration, election, salvation by free grace, the atonement and the divinity of christ," and these doubts prevented him from making the confession of faith "required in Calvinistic churches as the condition of admission to their communion." Not surprisingly, his first response to the Awakening was one of skepticism and distrust. "I felt some opposition to these meetings," he recalled,

> being apprehensive that they would, by affecting the passions too strongly, intro-
> duce an enthusiasm or fanaticism which might be considered as real religion.
> I expressed these fears to some friends and particularly to my family, inculcating
> on them the importance of a *rational religion* and the danger of being misled by
> the passions.

But despite his discouragement, Webster's wife and two daughters were among the first to be swept up in the revival.[86]

The participation of his wife and daughters in the Awakening challenged Webster's control over the life of his family as well as his religious beliefs. At first, he tried to reassert control over his family by suggesting that they attend Episcopal services together, a suggestion the women firmly rejected. Forced to choose between his doubts about the "articles of the Calvinistic Creed" and an "extreme reluctance against a separation from my dear family in public worship," Webster was plunged into intellectual and spiritual crisis. After several weeks of mental agitation and struggle, during which he tried to quiet his mind "by a persuasion that my opposition to my family and the awakening was not a real opposition to a *rational religion* but to enthusiasm and false religion," he was finally led "by a spontaneous impulse to repentance, prayer and entire submission of myself to my Maker and Redeemer." His conversion and "confession of faith" enabled him to reclaim his paternal role in the family. Accompanying his two daughters to church for the first time, he wrote: "It was with heartfelt delight I could present myself before my Maker and say 'Here I am, with the children which thou hast given me.'"[87]

Webster's conversion was a genuine watershed in his life—"the most solemn and affecting of all transactions of my life," he wrote—and provided a "new Christian foundation for his thinking," resolving the complex and contradictory aspects of his political ideology in the idea of a Christian republic. After his conversion in 1808, Webster argued that republican government depended not on human ingenuity but on the acceptance of divine inspiration. Political reform was therefore synonymous with religious conversion. "Men may desire and adopt a new form of government," he argued in the 1830s, "but there *is*, there *can be* no effectual remedy, but obedience to divine law." In an essay published in the 1840s, he blamed the corruption of American politics on the founders' failure to acknowledge the existence of a "Supreme Being" in the Constitution. A government formed by men who treated Christianity with contempt, he argued, "can not be a good government; it is not possible":

> It is the irreversible decree of heaven, that in all governments founded by human wisdom, and conducted only by human reason, corruption and disorders must ultimately compel men to resort to physical force for the execution of law and the preservation of public peace. These facts and principles may be considered as unalterable, so long as the throne of the Almighty and his moral government remain unshaken.

Good men produced good government, and only Christianity could produce good men. Therefore, only individual religious conversion could lay the basis for a genuinely republican government. Americans must renew their covenant with God, and until they did so, they could expect nothing more than the continued degeneration of the body politic, "for certain it is that if we abandon the God of our fathers, the God of our fathers will abandon their [sic] children."[88]

Webster's life had come full circle. Born into the patriarchal, Calvinist world of colonial Connecticut, he was baptized in the principles of the radical Enlightenment, joined a revolt against patriarchal government, and identified himself as a citizen of an independent democratic republic. Rejecting the religion of his fathers and the cultural values of his colonial ancestors, he broke with tradition and tried to forge a new national character and culture. With his religious conversion, he returned to the political and cultural traditions of his Connecticut past. It was an admission of disillusionment and defeat. Born into a revolutionary generation that believed it could master and control public life, Webster's conversion marked a moment of renunciation. "I am taught now," he wrote, "the utter insufficiency of our own powers to effect a change of the heart, and am persuaded that a reliance on our own talents or powers is a fatal error." His intellectual odyssey illuminates the shift from revolutionary and secular civic activism in eighteenth-century America, to reformist and religious individualism in nineteenth-century America. By the early nineteenth century, for respectable citizens of the early Republic like Noah Webster, the pursuit of happiness had shifted from public to private life.[89]

CHAPTER 5

William Cobbett and the Politics of Personality

In the first issue of his new daily newspaper, *Porcupine's Gazette*, published in March 1797, William Cobbett called on his rival Benjamin Franklin Bache to observe a political truce. In the future, Cobbett promised, he would "avoid all personality whatever" in his discussion of politics, provided that Bache agreed to do the same. "I do not wish to fill my paper with personal satire and abuse," he wrote:

> Our readers, especially those of this city, know already every thing that is worth knowing about you and I. Nothing that we can say will alter their opinions of us; and as for altering our opinions of one another, that is a thing not to be thought of.... It is therefore useless, my dear Bache, to say any more about the matter. Let us disappoint them; let us walk arm in arm: many a couple, even of different sex, do this, and at the same time like one another no better than we do.[1]

As regular readers of *Porcupine's Gazette* knew, this conciliatory gesture was simply another installment in a long-running feud between the two newspaper editors. But Bache was not the only object of Cobbett's mockery. Cobbett's tongue-in-cheek invitation also satirized the conventional pieties of American journalism, in particular the expressions of editorial impartiality and respectability that appeared in the inaugural issues of most newspapers.

To Cobbett, such pious intentions were trite and hypocritical. But his mockery of them was inspired by more than outraged honesty. Such commonplace statements of political impartiality and editorial decency expressed an ideal of "impersonality" that was deeply embedded in American print culture and remained highly influential throughout the 1790s. This desire to exclude issues of personality from the press (and the public sphere more generally) had two facets: the suppression of editorial and authorial personality and the avoidance of personal, or ad hominem, journalism. Regardless of their politics, most newspaper editors paid lip service to these ideals, defending impartiality as the cornerstone of editorial independence and the free circulation of ideas in a rational public sphere. As the masthead of Anthony Haswell's *Herald of Vermont* declared in 1792, "Let sentiment Flow Free, and candour guide—We own no party and espouse no side." Editors who subscribed to this ideal saw themselves as simple purveyors of political intelligence and their newspapers as impartial forums for restrained, rational political debate. They believed that it was their duty to take no active part in this debate and to remain invisible to the reading public. Whether or not they realized these editorial ideals in practice—Haswell, for example, was a partisan Republican who was prosecuted for seditious libel—this tradition of literary and political impersonality had a powerful legitimizing role

Mr. William Cobbett, by Francesco Bartolozzi after John Raphael Smith, London, 1801. This portrait of Cobbett was executed just after his return to England from the United States. Courtesy of the National Portrait Gallery, London.

in the world of late eighteenth-century American journalism. Most editors and journalists used pseudonyms to present their political views and to disguise their personal identities, and even highly political journalists like Philip Freneau and Benjamin Franklin Bache preferred to present themselves as agents of public opinion rather than admit their own political agency.[2]

William Cobbett broke sharply with this tradition of literary self-effacement, belligerently asserting his own political views and developing a powerful and distinctive editorial persona. In his first editorial for *Porcupine's Gazette*, he scoffed at the pretensions of supposedly impartial political editors. "Professions of impartiality," he wrote with characteristic bluntness, "I shall make none":

> They are always useless, and are besides perfect nonsense, when used by a news-monger.... He that does not exercise his own judgement, either in admitting or rejecting what is sent him is a poor passive tool and not an editor. For my part, I feel the strongest partiality for the cause of order and good government, such as we live under, and against every thing that is opposed to it.

As Cobbett makes clear here, he conceived *Porcupine's Gazette* as a vehicle for his own political views, not a forum for free and disinterested public debate. But although he was an uncompromising partisan, he was not a reliable party man, and his first loyalty was to political ideas rather than party politics. Denouncing those editors who concealed their political prejudices behind fraudulent declarations of impartiality, he also denounced political "trimmers" who sacrificed their political beliefs to expediency or party policy. Just as committed to the idea of editorial independence as any other journalist of the 1790s, he rejected the idea that independence required the adoption of an impersonal or anonymous authorial voice. To Cobbett, the injection of personality into political debate guaranteed rather than compromised his integrity and independence as an editor and a journalist.[3]

Public hostility toward ad hominem journalism, or journalism directed toward the person and personality, was part of the same ideal of political impersonality. Almost all newspaper editors and journalists professed to believe that personal attacks were scandalous and unjustified, and this belief attracted broad support among the reading public. Journalists and readers distinguished sharply between public character and private character and between public life and private life, and although these distinctions were disputed, in practice there was widespread agreement that private character and private life lay beyond the legitimate reach of the press. Newspaper attacks on men in private life were generally condemned, as were almost all attacks on women, who were associated with the protected sphere of private life. The most contested and ambiguous terrain was public life. While criticism of public men and their policies was considered legitimate, attacks on the private character of public men were not.

These distinctions were often difficult to negotiate and subject to much discussion, but most newspaper editors nonetheless tried to observe them. Cobbett's writings, however, continually oscillated between the personal and the political, the private and the public. "No man has a right to pry into his neighbour's private concerns," he acknowledged,

> and the opinions of every man are his private concerns, while he keeps them so; that is to say, while they are confined to himself, his family and particular friends....but, when he makes these opinions public; when he once attempts to make converts; whether it be in religion, politics, or anything else; when he comes forward as a candidate for public admiration, esteem or compassion, his opinions, his principles, his motives, every action of his life, public or private, become the fair subject of public discussion.

Cobbett's belief that the press had a right to interrogate the private lives of public men challenged the conventional boundary between public and private life. But it also challenged a more significant boundary, the boundary between the liberty and the licentiousness of the press. The transgressive, iconoclastic quality of Cobbett's writing explains both its enormous appeal and the enormous hostility it provoked. As the most skilled practitioner of what Republican editor Charles Holt called "the new English style," Cobbett was one of the most popular and influential journalists of the 1790s. In a language that spoke clearly to ordinary readers, he contributed greatly to the democratization of American politics in the late eighteenth century, helping to create the political space within which a vigorous democratic press could develop. His role in the Federalist politics of the late 1790s was critical, and his colorful writing left a lasting impression on the journalism and literary culture of the early Republic. But as the "self-taught master of the art of Billingsgate," Cobbett also became a lightning rod for public anxiety about partisan politics and the partisan press, and by the end of the 1790s, he symbolized the political degeneracy and disorder that many Americans believed had engulfed public life. His spectacular success, and his equally spectacular failure, reveal a great deal about the uneasy relationship that existed between Americans and the newspaper press in the early years of the Republic.[4]

When William Cobbett arrived in Philadelphia in October 1792, he was a political refugee, a republican, and an ardent admirer of the United States. Although he was twenty-nine years old at the time, he had spent little of his adult life in England. The son of a small yeoman farmer and publican, Cobbett was born in Farnham, Surrey, in 1763 and later recalled his rural childhood with fondness. But he demonstrated an early desire to escape the charms of country life. At the age of nineteen, he decided he wanted to be a sailor and "sighed for a sight of the world," and the following year he ran off to London (while on his way to a country fair) and became a clerk instead, working "like a galley-slave" for a barrister at Gray's Inn. After several months of joyless labor, Cobbett tried to enlist in the marines but instead found himself in His Majesty's Fifty-Fourth Regiment of Foot, where he spent the next six years, 1785–1791, stationed at a garrison in Nova Scotia.[5]

His education began after he joined the army. Cobbett was a classic autodidact. His father had taught him to read, write, and do basic arithmetic, but when he arrived in London in 1783, his literary skill did not extend much beyond an ability to "write a good plain hand." During the year he waited to embark for Nova Scotia, he devoured the contents of the local circulating library, reading many books "more than once over" and undertaking a systematic study of English grammar that enabled him to "write without falling into any very gross errors." He continued this program of self-education after his arrival in Canada, reserving "an hour or two to read" every morning before he went on duty. His hard-won accomplishments paid off. After becoming a clerk in the regiment, he earned rapid promotions, and by the time he left the army in 1791, he was a regimental sergeant major, the highest rank attainable by a noncommissioned officer.[6]

Cobbett disliked the barren, rocky landscape of Nova Scotia, which he described as a place of "bogs, rocks, and mosquitoes and bull-frogs." And he was no fonder of the Loyalist political elite in St. John's, New Brunswick, where he was stationed, "thousands of Captains and Colonels without soldiers, and of Squires without stockings or shoes." He had nothing but contempt for the officers of his regiment, whom he called the "epaulet gentry," and their casual corruption and ineptitude had a radicalizing impact on the bright and proper young sergeant major. But his hostility toward officers and the local elite did not preclude sympathy for ordinary Loyalists, and his work on the Loyalist Claims Commission of 1785–1787 made him familiar with their problems and concerns. The most significant relationship of his early adult life was with a family of "Yankee loyalists," whom he recalled many years later with affection. His first impressions of American life were formed through the eyes of American Tories.[7]

When Cobbett returned to England in 1791, he was immediately caught up in the political ferment created by the French Revolution and the publication of Paine's *Rights of Man*. Its influence on Cobbett is unclear. He claimed that he was "a perfect novice in politics" when he arrived back in England, although he admitted that he "took up the book of Paine (just then published) with my mind full of indignation at the abuses" he had encountered during his military service. What is clear is that, after receiving his discharge from the army in December 1791, he brought corruption charges against several officers in his old

The Life of William Cobbett—Written by Himself, 2nd plate, by James Gillray, published by Hannah Humphrey, London, 1809. This is part of a series of engravings by Gillray to illustrate an English edition of Cobbett's *Life and Adventures of Peter Porcupine*. The cartoon shows the young Cobbett abandoning his "agricultural pursuits" for the British army. Courtesy of the National Portrait Gallery, London.

regiment, and this action brought him into contact with political radicals and reformers in London. Perhaps alone but more likely in collaboration with others, he produced a pamphlet called *The Soldier's Friend*, attacking army corruption and assailing "the close connection that exists between the *ruling faction* in this Country and the military Officers." It was a dangerous moment to call attention to the deficiencies of the British army, and Cobbett quickly found himself in trouble. Stonewalled by the War Office and facing accusations of treason against the Crown, he fled to France in March 1792 after spending only three months in his native land.[8]

According to his own account, he had already decided to return to North America. "My determination to settle in the United States was formed before I went to France," he wrote, "and even before I quitted the army":

> A desire of seeing a country so long the theatre of a war of which I had heard and read so much; the flattering picture given of it by Raynal; and, above all, an inclination for seeing the world, led me to this determination. It would look a little like coaxing for me to say, that I had imbibed principles of republicanism, and that I was ambitious to become a citizen of a free state; but this was really the case. I thought that men here enjoyed a greater degree of liberty than in England; and this, if not the principal reason, was at least one, for my coming to this country.

Events in France hurried him along. Although he had planned to spend a full year there, the downfall of the French monarchy and the prospect of war between England and France forced Cobbett and his new wife, Nancy, to leave after only six months—"the six happiest months of my life," he later recalled. In September 1792, they sailed for the United States and after a voyage of about six weeks arrived in Philadelphia.[9]

Cobbett arrived optimistic about his prospects and life in the new Republic. After a short stay in Philadelphia, he and his wife moved to Wilmington, Delaware, where Cobbett decided to "keep school." He may have regarded this situation as temporary. While in France, he had procured a letter of introduction to Secretary of State Thomas Jefferson, and in early November he sent this letter to Jefferson, probably hoping for an offer of government employment. He was disappointed. Jefferson replied that "public offices in our government are so few, and of so little value, as to offer no resource to talent," but Cobbett's cover letter reveals his sense of hopefulness about life in the United States. "Ambitious to become the citizen of a free state," he wrote, "I have left my native country, England, for America: I bring with me youth, a small family, a few useful literary talents and that is all." He was, he wrote later, "brimful of republicanism."[10]

Although Cobbett prospered in the United States, he never became an American citizen. Like many immigrants, his expectations of life in the United States were disappointed. After settling in Wilmington, he found he could make a living teaching English to French refugees from Santo Domingo who had fled the Haitian Revolution in 1791, and he started work on an English grammar for French speakers, which he eventually published. But America was not the land of natural bounty and republican virtue he had been led to expect by the Abbé Raynal. "This country is good for getting money," he wrote caustically to an English correspondent, but only if a person were "industrious and enterprising." "The land is bad-rocky—houses wretched—roads impassable after the least rain.—Fruit in quantity, but good for nothing" and "the seasons detestable." Americans themselves were "worthy of the country—a cheating, sly, roguish gang." "In short," he concluded, "the country altogether is detestable."[11]

Disparaging remarks like this were common among political émigrés, but usually their republican ideals survived the reality of a republican society. Not so with Cobbett. His disillusionment with the country was accompanied by disillusionment with its politics. During his first year in Wilmington, however, teaching and family occupied most of his time and his interest in politics was minimal. As he wrote to his friend James Mathieu in the summer of 1793, he was content to observe the partisan quarrels of the community from a distance:

> Every time the newspapers arrive the aristocrats and democrats have a decent quarrel to the admiration of all the little boys in the town. My dear good Mathieu, God preserve you from the political pest. Let them fight and tear one another's eyes out; mind take care of your business and let the devil and them decide their disputes.[12]

But by the time he moved his family to Philadelphia in January 1794, his indifference toward American politics had vanished and his views had undergone a dramatic transformation. The scourge of political radicalism had replaced the republican refugee.

The first sign of this was his anonymous attack on the British scientist and political radical Joseph Priestley. Like Cobbett himself, Priestley had fled political persecution in Britain and arrived in New York in June 1794, in the middle of a major diplomatic crisis with Great Britain. The addresses of welcome he received from the Democratic Society in New York and other radical political organizations were published in the American press together with Priestley's replies, and their hostility toward Britain infuriated Cobbett. He described his reaction in his first political pamphlet, *Observations on the Emigration of Dr. Joseph Priestley*:

One of my scholars, who was a person that we in England should call a Coffee-House Politician, chose, for once, to read his newspaper by way of lesson; and, it happened to be the very paper which contained the addresses presented to Doctor Priestley at New York, together with his replies. My scholar, who was a sort of republican, or, at best, but half a monarchist, appeared delighted with the invectives against England, to which he was very much disposed to add.

Provoked by a Frenchman who was "half a monarchist," Cobbett decided to "write and publish a pamphlet in defense of my country" and in this way became a "writer on politics."[13]

This account, which attributes his pamphlet to the discovery of his own *amor patriae*, captures perfectly the way that Cobbett wished to present his own political activity during the 1790s and the way his activities have been presented by others. Cobbett always portrayed himself as a simple British patriot, inspired by dogged devotion for his native country. During his years in the United States, he wrote with characteristic hyperbole, "I lived not for myself or my family, but exclusively for my country and my king." Rarely missing a chance to display the strength and fearlessness of his patriotic ardor, this display could assume comic proportions. A good example of this was the opening of his famous Blue Shop in Philadelphia in 1796. Cobbett established his printing shop and bookstore on Philadelphia's Second Street, a busy thoroughfare opposite the largest Episcopal church in the city. Despite the threat of mob violence, he painted the front of the shop a provocative royal blue and filled his windows with pictures designed to provoke local Republicans:

> I put up in my windows, which were very large, all the portraits that I had in my possession of Kings, queens, princes and nobles. I had all the English Ministry; several of the Bishops and Judges; the most famous Admirals; and, in short, every picture that I thought likely to excite rage in the enemies of Great Britain....Early on the Monday morning, I took down my shutters. Such a sight had not been seen in Philadelphia for twenty years. Never since the beginning of the rebellion, had anyone dared to hoist at his windows the portrait of George the Third.

The intensity of Cobbett's loyalty to Great Britain during these years is beyond question. The French political émigré Moreau de St. Mery knew Cobbett well and described him as the most patriotic man he had ever met. And most historians have accepted this assessment, treating him as an interloper, an English Tory in America. But this point of view fails to account for Cobbett's strong links to the Federalists and his enormous contribution to Federalist politics in the late 1790s, and it obscures the central motive for his involvement in American political life as well as the reason for his political influence and popularity with the reading public.[14]

Most writers on Cobbett's American career have overlooked the degree to which his political persona was the product of rhetorical self-fashioning, the creation of an unusually intelligent and self-conscious man. The image of Cobbett as the embodiment of John Bull, the archetypal English yeoman, rooted in the soil, honest, practical, hard working, instinctively loyal to his country, and unshakably independent, assumed mythical proportions by the end of his life. But it appeared only gradually in his political writings. The first clear articulation of this image is in his brilliant *Life and Adventures of Peter Porcupine*, published in 1796. Here, readers encountered for the first time Cobbett as a young man, decked out in his "smock-frock" and laborer's hat, toiling in the hop fields of a prelapsarian England untouched by agricultural, industrial, or political change. "I was bred at the plough-tail, and in the Hop-Gardens of Farnham in Surrey," wrote Cobbett. "[A]ll there is a garden":

> I do not remember the time when I did not earn my living. My first occupation was, driving the small birds from the turnip seed, and the rooks from the peas. When I trudged afield, with my wooden bottle and my satchel over my shoulders, I was hardly able to climb the gates and stiles, and, at the close of day, to reach home was a task of infinite labour. My next employment was weeding wheat, and leading a single horse at harrowing barley. Hoeing peas followed, and hence I arrived at the honour of joining the reapers in harvest, driving the team and holding the plough.[15]

This is timeless stuff, saturated with the pastoral romanticism of eighteenth-century English literary culture (one can hear the echoes of Oliver Goldsmith and of Thomas Gray's "Elegy Written in a Country Churchyard"). But these memories were not straightforward autobiography, if such a thing exists, and if we treat them this way we risk reducing a complex and sophisticated man to a political caricature.

The triumph of Cobbett's caricature has enabled historians to dismiss him as an English eccentric and to banish him to the margins of American political life. But even those who take him seriously have trouble explaining his influence. If Cobbett was simply a British Tory, then why was he so popular? His own explanation is interesting but insufficient. By displaying an image of George III in his shop window and expressing his unswerving devotion to Great Britain, Cobbett believed that he had reawakened loyalties that had been dormant in the United States since the Revolution. "I untied the tongue of British attachment," he declared, and "broke the shackles in which the public mind had been held from the commencement of the revolutionary war." This explanation reinforces the view that Cobbett's popularity was based on his British identity and Tory politics, but this was only part of his appeal. Cobbett's carefully constructed public persona has deflected attention from a far more significant and influential aspect of his American writings: his violent anti-Jacobinism.[16]

The dramatic shift in Cobbett's political sympathies between his arrival in the United States and the publication of *Observations on the Emigration of Dr. Joseph Priestley* is puzzling. Cobbett himself claimed, "the change in my way of thinking was produced by experience. I had an opportunity of *seeing* what republican government was," and he was not impressed. The failure of the republican future threw him back upon his English past. "From this perspective," argues David Wilson, "Cobbett's conversion to conservatism is not as puzzling as it first appears. The powerful patriotism that had been invisible at home was brought into sharp relief in America." But whatever Cobbett's disillusionment with American society in the period from 1792 to 1794, it paled in comparison to his sense of horror about the course of events in France since his departure. And it was these events—the Terror, the execution of Louis XVI, the establishment of the cult of Reason—rather than his experiences in American society that undermined his radicalism in the period from 1792 to 1794, and it was anti-Jacobinism rather than patriotic indignation that propelled him into American partisan politics.[17]

Cobbett was deeply interested in French culture. While in the army, he had begun to teach himself French, and his experience in France during his stay in 1792 was an extremely happy one. This identification with France was reinforced by his close relations with the French émigré community in Wilmington and, later, Philadelphia. Cobbett made his living teaching English to French refugees, had French lodgers during his time in Wilmington, formed his closest acquaintances with "French merchants from St Domingo and Martinico," and found his closest friendship with a Frenchman, James Mathieu. The refugees, who had fled the slave revolution that took place in the French colony of Santo Domingo in 1791, formed a hotbed of anti-revolutionary sentiment and reinforced Cobbett's hostility toward the French Revolution. Shortly after his arrival, he translated a French pamphlet for the Philadelphia printer John Parker that attacked Republican critics of the Marquis de Lafayette in the national assembly, and he may also have had a hand in a sympathetic account of the trial of Louis XVI published by Parker in March 1793.[18]

Observations on the Emigration of Dr. Joseph Priestley, a response to a French student "who was a sort of republican," reveals the importance of the French Revolution to Cobbett's political evolution. As he pointed out, it "said not a word in praise of Great Britain, generally," and although it was partly a defense of British justice and law, the pamphlet was first and foremost an anti-Jacobin tract.[19] Cobbett disliked Priestley not because he supported political reform in England, about which Cobbett was himself ambivalent, but because he supported the revolution in France. Portraying Priestley as an apostle of the French Revolution, Cobbett used his arrival in New York to launch an attack on the revolution that was unparalleled in the United States. Here is how he described the arraignment of the Princess de Lamballe before the revolutionary tribunal in Paris:

> When this much-lamented unfortunate lady was dragged before the villains that sat in a kind of mock judgement on her, they were drinking *eau de vie*, to the damnation of those that lay dead before them. Their shirt sleeves were tucked up to their elbows; their arms and hands, and even the goblets they were drinking out of, were besmeared with human blood! I much question if the assassin's stab, or even the last pang of death, with all its concomitant bitterness, was half so terrible as the blood-freezing sight of these hell-hounds.

This lurid account—the literary equivalent of the English artist James Gillray's famous anti-revolutionary political cartoons—captures the style of the entire pamphlet. Again and again, Cobbett returned to the same sanguinary themes, portraying the revolutionaries as a "*a gang of bloodthirsty cannibals*" who had "drenched the country with the blood of the innocent." By taking part in celebrations of the French Revolution and accepting "the *honour* of becoming a French citizen," Priestley made clear his desire to create "a revolution in England upon the French plan" and to spread the gospel of the French Revolution to the United States. His public recognition of the Democratic societies was designed to encourage the growth of a network of revolutionary clubs "in perfect conformity to that of the Jacobin clubs in France," argued Cobbett, and if his "infidel Unitarian system" and doctrines of political regeneration were allowed to take root in America, they would create the same anarchy and bloodshed that existed in revolutionary France. The lessons for Americans were clear.[20]

Cobbett's *Observations* shows his sharp understanding of American politics and political sensibilities in the mid-1790s. At the time he wrote the *Observations*, support for the French Revolution in the United States was becoming more ambivalent and more divided. Although there was still a great deal of popular good will toward France, the events of the revolution had unsettled even avid supporters and provoked the first signs of public opposition since 1789. More significantly, the Genet crisis, the growth of the Democratic Republican societies, and the outbreak of the Whiskey Rebellion had begun to fuel alarm among supporters of the federal government about the popular influence of French revolutionary ideology. As Cobbett was aware, the revolution had become a key symbolic issue in American partisan politics, and the purpose of the *Observations*, like Webster's *Revolution in France*, was to challenge "prejudice in favor of the French Revolution" and to inoculate Americans against French influence.[21]

Like Webster, Cobbett did this by raising the specter of religious infidelity and revolutionary violence, including the bloodshed associated with the abolition of slavery in Santo Domingo. And he was careful not to make invidious comparisons between Britain and the United States, admitting that a prejudice against Great Britain was "not only excusable, but almost commendable in *Americans*." He was also careful not to challenge American republican ideals and pointed out that the French themselves had locked up the author of the *Rights of Man* in a "dirty dungeon, not a hundred paces from the *sanctum sanctorum* of liberty and equality." Above all, Cobbett presented himself as a champion of the American government and people against the influence of ungrateful foreigners and their deluded American supporters.[22]

Cobbett said nothing in the *Observations* about his own origins. The image of Cobbett as "Peter Porcupine," the indefatigable advocate of Great Britain, emerged only slowly. Not until the publication of *A Kick for a Bite* in 1795 did he use this more combative nom de plume, and although his support for British political institutions was obvious from the start, his point of comparison was always France, not the United States. As he knew, his success as a political propagandist depended on his ability to balance loyalty to Great Britain with loyalty to the federal government and to not alienate readers by launching savage attacks on the American government. Until his break with John Adams in 1798, he balanced these loyalties with great success. Although he believed that his greatest achievement in the 1790s was to have "untied the tongue of British attachment" in America, his remarkable political influence rested on another achievement: his revival of a robust and deeply rooted tradition of American anti-Gallicanism.[23]

Cobbett's anti-Jacobinism had a profound impact on American politics. After the establishment of his bookshop on Second Street in early 1796—"which I looked upon as being at once a means of getting money, and of propagating writings against the French"—he became a crucial intermediary in the Anglo-American book trade, disseminating the products of British anti-Jacobin propaganda to an American reading public. In addition to importing volumes from booksellers like John Wright, whose London bookshop was the headquarters of British anti-Jacobinism, he reprinted anti-Jacobin standards like Burke's *Letters on a Regicide Peace*, John Robison's *Proofs of a Conspiracy*, William Playfair's *History of Jacobinism*, and Anthony Aufrere's *Cannibal's Progress*. Aufrere's work in particular, published at the height of the quasi war with France in 1798, was a spectacular success that Cobbett claimed sold over 100,000 copies in the United States.[24]

But Cobbett's most important contribution to American anti-Jacobinism was his own writing. Realizing that the anti-revolutionary tone of the *Observations* had struck a popular chord, he lost no time fusing his anti-Gallicanism with hostility toward the political opposition within the United States. His next pamphlet, *A Bone to Gnaw for the Democrats*, was inspired by the indictment of British imperialism contained in James Thomson Callender's *The Political Progress of Britain*, but Cobbett quickly broadened his attack on Callender into a wide-ranging attack on the Jeffersonian opposition and "American sans-culottism." *A Bone to Gnaw* bears all of the hallmarks of Cobbett's distinctive satirical style. Callender, wrote Cobbett, suffered from the "*mania reformatio*," a malady that if not cured at once "by the help of a hempen necklace, or some other equally efficacious remedy…never fails to break out into Atheism, Robbery, Unitarianism, Swindling, Jacobinism, Massacres, Civic Feasts and Insurrections." His *Political Progress* was a collection of "Whiskey-boy Billingsgate libels" designed to drum up support for the Whiskey rebels and cash for its impecunious author. But Cobbett's real target was the Jeffersonian opposition, especially Bache's *Aurora*, which he accused of disloyalty toward the federal government. By ridiculing "Civic Feasts, Cockades *a la Tricolor*, and such like buffoonery" and reprinting Joel Barlow's song "God Save the Guillotine," Cobbett made opposition to the federal government seem both demonic and comic. Above all, he made it seem French. The "Democrats," he argued, had been thoroughly infected by the "Carmagnole system," and their hostility toward Great Britain merely cloaked "their enmity to the Federal government."[25]

With *A Bone to Gnaw for the Democrats*, Cobbett hit his stride as a political journalist, and in his next pamphlet, *A Kick for a Bite*, he found his political persona: Peter Porcupine. Although he took a slight detour in this work to attack the feminism of the English dramatist and writer Susanna Rowson, Cobbett quickly returned to his greatest concern: the French and their supporters in the United States. Just before the publication of the Jay Treaty in July 1795, he published an account of the destruction of Lyons, which described the murder and rape of Lyonnaise women and contained the sensational claim that over 2 million people had been slaughtered in France since 1792. With compendiums of political violence like his own *Bloody Buoy* and Aufrere's *Cannibal's Progress*, Cobbett hoped to convince Americans that the bloodshed occurring in revolutionary France was no accident but the inevitable result of French democratic principles.[26]

Cobbett referred constantly to the "sanguinary ferocity" of the French Revolution and the orgiastic character of revolutionary violence. This was not only effective anti-French propaganda, but it also cast a sinister shadow over his otherwise humorous and satirical treatment of the Jeffersonian opposition in works like *A Little Plain English* and *A New Year's Gift to the Democrats*. American supporters of France appear in Cobbett's writing as ludicrous denizens of a world turned upside down, "citizen-sovereigns and sovereign-citizens" who ape French customs and political practices. The public theatricality of eighteenth-century American political culture gave Cobbett a great deal of ammunition for such satire. Here

Property Protected (a la Francoise). Unidentified artist, published by S. W. Fores, London, 1798. In this English cartoon satirizing the XYZ Affair, "America" tries to protect her rights from the "hug Fraternal" while being fleeced by the five members of the French directory as John Bull (Great Britain) roars with laughter from his perch atop Shakespeare's cliff. At this point in time, Cobbett was at the height of his public influence in the United States. Courtesy of the Library of Congress.

is his account of a civic fete held in Philadelphia in 1794 to celebrate the anniversary of the French Republic. After the usual artillery salvos, parade, speeches, and patriotic hymns, the crowd began to dance around "the altar of liberty":

> These dances were the finest fun I ever enjoyed. The patriotic hymns were well enough; four hundred fellows howling out French bombast, without understanding a word of it, was not a bad specimen of fraternal dissonance; but to behold fifty or sixty groupes, promiscuously formed, whistling, singing, and capering about they knew not why nor wherefore; and to see the "*chiefs civil and military of Pennsylvania*," heaving up their legs and endeavouring to ape the light-heeled mounseers, was a spectacle which, I trust, has seldom been equalled.

The "bloody" choruses of French revolutionary songs like "Ça Ira"—"*Ah! ca ira, ca ira, Les Aristocrates a la Laneterne*"—the "Carmagnole," and the "Marseillaise" "seemed to issue from the lungs of twenty infernals."[27]

Cobbett's richly comic and evocative writing suggested that there was a more sinister side to the absurd revolutionary mimicry of his opponents and linked them to the bloodshed taking place in France. Although American "democrats" were more cautious than their Jacobin counterparts, their goals and methods were identical. While opposition newspapers like the *Aurora* disseminated the ideas of the French Revolution, the Democratic societies, "dark caballing clubs," organized insurrection, and opposition members of Congress attempted to "stop the wheels of government" and to concentrate power in the House of Representatives. When the House hesitated to ratify the Jay Treaty in April 1796, Cobbett warned readers that a war with Great Britain would lead to the creation of a "revolutionary state" and the ascendancy of "our Brissots and our Robespierres."[28]

Cobbett made this equation between Jacobinism and Jeffersonianism even more explicit in his *History of American Jacobinism*, which was published in November 1796. By this time, his writings were openly anti-republican, full of denunciations of the "rights of man" and "the popular doctrine of *equality*," although he continued to express his support for Washington and the federal government. The *History* contained little that had not already appeared in his previous writings. But the aim of the pamphlet was clear: to identify the political opposition with the bloody legacy of the Jacobins and to warn about their clandestine political influence in the United States. By this time, the Republican opposition was on the defensive. Popular opposition to the Jay Treaty had collapsed, John Adams had been elected president (despite his monarchical views), and a diplomatic crisis with France was brewing. But Cobbett warned against complacency. "Let not the friends of the General Government, of order, of peace and of general happiness and prosperity," he wrote at the conclusion of the work, "imagine that the sect is annihilated."[29] His message was widely heard. By early 1797, Peter Porcupine was enjoying unprecedented popularity and political influence. His literary output in the previous two years had been prodigious, and during the public debates on the Jay Treaty in 1795–1796, he had established himself as a major Federalist propagandist. In March 1797, he founded a new daily newspaper, *Porcupine's Gazette*, that quickly became one of the most important and widely read newspapers in the country. In a broadside poem to the "Friends" of *Porcupine's Gazette* on New Year's Day 1798, Cobbett recalled the days of "Gallic frenzy wild" and assured his readers they would not return. "The worst is past," he wrote, "I hope to see, at no far distant day, / All sansculottish jargon done away."[30]

As the leading anti-Jacobin journalist in the United States, Cobbett played a reactionary part in American politics during the 1790s. Unlike Federalist editors like John Fenno and Noah Webster, he expressed undisguised contempt for the "sovereign people" and their doctrines of political equality. As an "Englishman," he declared, "I shall be excused for not thinking myself upon a level with every patriot, every negro, and every democrat, that pleases to call me fellow citizen." But despite his conservative politics, Cobbett was an instinctive iconoclast, and his abrasive, coarse satirical prose posed a challenge to the decorum and civility of elite political culture. Best known as the scourge of American Democrats, his writings contributed greatly to the creation of a more democratic American political culture. In a culture that valued classical restraint, politeness, and impartiality, his unrestrained, abrupt, and personal style was deeply disturbing. He drew continuously and repetitively on his own personal experiences and constantly intruded into the narrative flow of his own political writings. (He also intruded into the writings of other authors, developing a unique interrogatory style of political commentary.) His authorial presence was unmistakable and unapologetic. Rather than establishing his independence *before* the reader by adopting an impartial and impersonal authorial style, he asserted his independence *against* the reader by insisting on his right to say whatever he wished. Entitled to exercise their own independent judgment, readers could take it or leave it. As he declared at the end of *A Bone to Gnaw for the Democrats*: "As for myself, reader, I most humbly beseech you to have the goodness to think of me—JUST WHAT YOU PLEASE."[31]

Cobbett presented himself as the common man, the plain-spoken yeoman farmer who knew his mind and had the independence and spirit to speak it. He expressed pride in his humble, rural origins—"All that I can boast of in my birth, is, that I was born in Old England," he wrote in the opening passage of *The Life and Adventures of Peter Porcupine*—and his common origins were the origin of his common sense. Unlike Bache, he was not descended from a speculative philosopher: "Everyone will, I hope, have the goodness to believe that my grandfather was no philosopher. Indeed he was not. He never made a lightening [*sic*] rod nor bottled up a single quart of sunshine in the whole course of his life." His style of argument reflected this practical, self-sufficient literary persona. He made no use of the historical precedents and classical allusions that weighted down so much eighteenth-century political prose. But he also rejected the appeals to rationality and natural law that permeated the work of that other brilliant popular political writer and advocate of common sense, Thomas Paine. Cobbett drew on his own experiences, recycling them endlessly in his writings and wringing from them the political lessons he wished to convey to readers. His writing was closer to dramatic representation than abstract argument. He persuaded readers by impression rather than logic, piling detail upon detail in an exhausting and apparently arbitrary fashion. At his worst, he is tedious, repetitive, and predictable. But at his best, reading him is like listening to an opinionated, fascinating raconteur in the local public house. It is this concreteness and immediacy, what the English master of prose William Hazlitt called the "coziness" of Cobbett's style, that made his writing so appealing and so accessible to readers of the early Republic.[32]

Cobbett's writing may have lacked the "smoothness of Addison," as one contemporary reader noted, but his apparently artless prose was carefully crafted and crackled with the energy and wit of popular speech. Readers at the time recognized how well his style suited popular tastes. "Porcupine's paper," wrote Federalist politician William Loughton Smith, was widely circulated among the "middle and town classes," and in his view, Cobbett's "blunt vulgar language suits them and has a great effect." The Republican journalist Samuel Harrison Smith commented that, although Cobbett's views were far from radical, he wrote like a Democrat. As these contemporary comments reveal, judgments of Cobbett's prose were invariably political as well as aesthetic, and the accents of his later radicalism were already evident in the writings of the anti-Jacobin crusader. In his classic work on English working-class radicalism in the early nineteenth century, the historian E. P. Thompson also emphasizes the politics of Cobbett's prose style:

> It was Cobbett who *created* this Radical intellectual culture, not because he offered its most original ideas, but in the sense that he found the tone, the style, and the arguments which could bring the weaver, the schoolmaster, and the shipwright, into a common discourse....in tone, will be found at least one half of Cobbett's political meaning.[33]

Cobbett's use of language demonstrated his determination to challenge the exclusiveness of elite political discourse and to address his arguments to a broad political audience. Making use of the colloquial language of the street and the rhythms of ordinary speech, of dramatic characterization and political "gossip," of political fables and folktales, Cobbett created a popular audience for his writing by addressing the people in their own terms. His writings, which are best understood as installments in a political serial rather than as self-contained and discrete works, created a narrative spectacle of American political life that was more accessible to ordinary readers than the restrained, classical style of conventional political discourse. Reactionary but never exclusive, Cobbett set out to expand rather than limit the audience for political debate by connecting the politics of everyday life to the world of political power.[34]

The most characteristic and transgressive aspect of Cobbett's journalism was his enthusiasm for ad hominem argument. "I never could see," he wrote,

> how abuses were to be corrected, without attacking those to whom they were to be attributed. If swindling and debauchery prevails, how are you to check it without exposing the *swindler* and the *debauchee*? And how are you to expose them without attacking their private characters?

Almost all of his writing was constructed around particular political or literary figures, often chosen for their comic potential as much as their prominence, whom Cobbett subjected to merciless sarcasm and used as a foil to develop his own political views. This emphasis on private character was the hallmark of his style. In the *Philadelphia Jockey Club*, an attack on a number of prominent Philadelphia Federalists published in 1795, the author claimed that the "precedent of the infamous Peter Porcupine" justified his own lack of regard for "individual reputation."[35] But to fully appreciate the subversive quality of Cobbett's exposure and interrogation of private character, it is necessary to examine American conceptions of press freedom before the 1790s.

Shortly after he arrived in Philadelphia, the radical Scottish journalist James Thomson Callender declared that it was "the happy privilege of an American that he may prattle and print in what way he pleases, and without anyone to make him afraid." Callender was right. In comparison to their counterparts in Europe, American writers and publishers were free from official regulation and censorship, the heirs of a tradition of press freedom that was well established in colonial America and Great Britain. Prepublication censorship ended in England with the expiration of the Licensing Act in 1695, and although these controls remained formally intact in the American colonies, by the 1730s colonial printers had established de facto freedom from the licensing powers of colonial governors. The chief threat to press freedom in colonial America was the common-law doctrine of seditious libel, which enabled colonial governments to bring official prosecutions against those responsible for "seditious" publications, and this threat also evaporated after the unsuccessful prosecution of the New York printer John Peter Zenger in 1735. After the Zenger trial, American printers and journalists enjoyed the freedom, in practice, to publish anything they pleased.[36]

Legal restrictions on the press in eighteenth-century America were thus virtually nonexistent. But this freedom remained conditional. As Alexander Hamilton argued in the *Federalist Papers*, the final arbiter of press freedom was public opinion, and throughout the eighteenth century, Americans remained ambivalent about the meaning and limits of liberty of the press. As Jeffrey Smith and others have argued, America possessed a strong libertarian tradition that viewed the press as the "palladium of all our liberties." And most Americans opposed prior restraint of the press and common-law prosecutions for seditious libel. But there were few advocates of unqualified press freedom, and few believed that the press should be entirely immune from legal prosecution and control. The distinction between the "liberty" and the "licentiousness" of the press was a real one during the eighteenth century, which left open the possibility that the press could be held legally liable for its transgressions.[37]

In practice, the distinction between liberty and license was difficult to make, and Americans made no effort to define such a distinction in statute before the passage of the Sedition Act in 1798. But there was considerable informal agreement about where this boundary lay. In keeping with their libertarian traditions, most

Americans believed that the discussion of government policy and public affairs in general was the rightful prerogative of a free press. But the right of the press to scrutinize political authority did not extend to the private character of the men who embodied and wielded this authority nor to the character of other prominent public figures. This desire to protect the private character of public men from the scrutiny of the press stemmed from a more general disapproval of attacks on private citizens in the press. In his "Directions for Conducting a Newspaper in Such a Manner as to Make It Innocent, Useful and Entertaining," Benjamin Rush instructed the editor Andrew Brown to acknowledge this right to privacy and not "suffer your paper to be a vehicle of private slander or of personal disputes." While newspapers had a right and a duty to expose the faults of public officers "with decency," argued Rush, "no man has a right to attack the follies or vices of private citizens in a newspaper." Attacks on private character in the press constituted an invasion of domestic life and a dangerous intrusion into the world of female honor and virtue. "Public measures" were fair game and, to a more limited extent, so were "public men," but women, private men, and the private character of public men were off limits.[38]

Benjamin Franklin's "An Account of the Supremest Court of Judicature in Pennsylvania, viz. the Court of the Press," published in Andrew Brown's *Federal Gazette* in 1789, is a good example of these widely held reservations about press freedom. Franklin was no enemy of press freedom, but he was dismayed by the tone of the press in Philadelphia in the late 1780s and equated its growing "licentiousness" with its taste for personal slander. Contrary to popular belief, he argued, the press was not an impartial court of public opinion but an arbitrary "Spanish Court of Inquisition" before which a citizen could be dragged and "sentence pronounc'd against him, that he is a *Rogue* and a *Villain*." The liberty of the press, worried Franklin, was being abused to destroy reputations:

> If by the *Liberty of the Press* were understood merely the Liberty of discussing the Propriety of Public Measures and political opinions, let us have as much of it as you please: But if it means the Liberty of affronting, calumniating, and defaming one another, I, for my part, own myself willing to part with my Share of it when our Legislators shall please so to alter the Law, and shall cheerfully consent to exchange my *Liberty* of abusing others for the *Privilege* of not being abus'd myself.

The press, he fumed, was irresponsible and unaccountable. "Any Man," he wrote, "who can procure Pen, Ink, and Paper, with a Press, and a huge pair of BLACKING Balls" could go into business and pillory his fellow citizens. And anyone who objected was branded "an *enemy to the liberty of the press*" and became the next victim of this arbitrary tribunal. The only solution, he suggested facetiously, was to restore the "*liberty of the cudgel*": "Thus, my fellow-citizens, if an impudent writer attacks your reputation, dearer to you perhaps than your life, and puts his name to the charge, you may go to him as openly and break his head." Franklin's heavy-handed humor concealed his seriousness. Although he was not encouraging his fellow citizens to assault irresponsible journalists, he was concerned about the way that press licentiousness encouraged physical violence, and not only did he believe that verbal assaults often led to physical assaults, but he believed that assaults on personality and public reputation were analogous to assaults on the person. Both were symptomatic of a primitive and "rude state of society prior to the existence of laws." And Franklin was much more disturbed by this decline in political civility than by the prospect of modest legal restraints on the press. The preservation of liberty depended on self-restraint and, in its absence, on the sanctions of the law. A civilized society, argued Franklin, must "secure the person of a citizen from *assaults*" and "provide for the security of his *reputation*."[39]

Cobbett's journalism not only ignored such widely accepted distinctions between liberty and license but openly challenged them. By infusing his attacks on private men (and, occasionally, women) with political content and his attacks on public men with personal content, he deliberately undermined the informal boundaries that preserved the civility of public debate. This did not mean that Cobbett rejected the distinction between public and private (as we shall see, his understanding of the distinction was in some ways more rigid than that of many of his political opponents), but he refused to let this distinction limit the range of political discussion. In his view, anyone who chose to participate in public life relinquished their right to privacy, providing the press with complete justification for scrutinizing both their public and private lives. Nothing illustrates Cobbett's approach to the boundary between private and public life more clearly than his attitude toward women's participation in public life. Cobbett was never shy about himself, but his personal and family life remained hidden from the curious reader. Although he was a devoted father, he never mentioned his children, and on the rare occasion he mentioned his wife, it was to praise her domesticity. His sense of privacy was accompanied by a strong belief that the proper role of women was in domestic and private life. Acknowledging that his writings had a female readership, in the preface to *A Bone to Gnaw*, he told them "to proceed no further":

> **Politics** is a mixture of anger and deceit, and these are the mortal enemies of Beauty. The instant a lady turns politician, farewell the smiles, the dimples, the roses; the graces abandon her, and age sets his seal on her front. We never find **Hebe**, goddess ever fair and ever young, chattering politics at the table of the gods; and though **Venus** once interposed in behalf of her beloved **Paris**, the spear of **Diomede** taught her "to tremble at the name of arms."

Although it was "a little singular for an author to write a preface to hinder his work from being read," he admitted, "all I wish to do, is to confine it within its proper sphere."[40]

The threat implicit in the reference to the "spear of Diomede" was not idle. Convinced that women had no legitimate place in public life, Cobbett went out of his way to attack women who assumed a public role. The best example of his hostility was his unprovoked attack on the English novelist and playwright Susanna Rowson. Rowson, who emigrated to the United States in the early 1790s, was the author of *Charlotte Temple* (America's first bestselling novel) and *Slaves in Algiers; or, A Struggle for Freedom*, a play about the Barbary pirates that opened to public acclaim in Philadelphia in 1794. She was also an actress, a staunch republican, and a feminist—all characteristics that inflamed Cobbett's misogynist sensibilities. Attacking her savagely in *A Kick for a Bite*, Cobbett argued that Rowson was representative of "the whole tribe of female scribblers and politicians." Although he despised her sentimental style and republican politics, it was her presence in public life and her assertions of female superiority in *Slaves in Algiers* that most disturbed him. Such ideas, he sneered, could only be well received in a degenerate country like the United States where "the authority of the wife is so unequivocally acknowledged" and "*reformers* of the *reformed church*" had struck "the odious word *obey* from their marriage service." "I almost wonder," he quipped, "they had not dispensed with the ceremony altogether; for most of us know, that in this enlightened age, the work of generation goes hummingly on, whether people are married or not." To Cobbett, Rowson's feminism, declining patriarchal authority, sexual disorder, and the growth of republican politics were all linked, and the popularity of her work, which he believed was feeble and pornographic, led him to believe that "the whole moral as well as political world is going to experience a revolution."[41]

Cobbett's attack on Rowson, delivered in a tone of mock gallantry, was immediately condemned as a violation of female honor. In a spirited defense of Rowson, the Philadelphia merchant and Republican politician John Swanwick called the author of *A Kick for a Bite* "as base a poltroon as ever trembled; for what can be a more incontestable and unequivocal pusillanimity, what can portray the coward in more vivid colors than your virulent and unprovoked attack upon a woman." This outrage was as conventional in its assumptions about gender as was Cobbett's abuse. While both men identified women with the private sphere, Swanwick believed that this shielded Rowson from public attack and Cobbett believed that it justified such an attack. By playing a public role and defending such a role for women, Rowson relinquished her right to the protection of male honor. In a phrase borrowed from the title of a pamphlet later published by Cobbett, she had "unsex'd" herself and exposed herself to public scrutiny. But Cobbett's eagerness to subject her to such scrutiny and his coarse insinuations about her sexuality show just how ready he was to ignore the conventional boundaries between public and private life in his political writing.[42]

Again and again in his writing, disputes that had their origins in political differences degenerated into personal abuse and character assassination. Poor John Swanwick's defense of Rowson and support for women's rights, as well as his patronage of a ladies' academy in Philadelphia, made him a constant butt for Cobbett's lampoons. "My imagination cannot form to itself any thing more perfectly comic," he wrote,

> than to see a diminutive superannuated bachelor, cocked up upon a stool, and spouting out compliments to an assembly of young Misses.... "Phillis the fair, in the bloom of fifteen," feels no more emotion at your fine speeches, than she would at the quavers of an Italian singer: for they are both equally soft and smooth... but, take heart, citizen: all men are not made for all things.

Cobbett's crude sexual banter equated Swanwick's political radicalism with sexual impotence, and it quickly became a standard part of his literary repertoire. In the congressional elections of 1796, he attacked Swanwick, who was running for reelection, as an "omiccuolo (for the Italian diminuitive [sic] suits him best on every account)" who decorated his bedroom with lascivious pictures of "*Leda and her Swan*, and such like stimuluses," and made up for his sexual deficiencies by lecturing to "young Misses." Swanwick, wrote Cobbett, was more absurd than "poor Gulliver astride the nipple of the Brobdignagian maid of honour."[43]

Even for Cobbett, these attacks were extreme. But they show his refusal to respect the boundary between Swanwick's public and private lives. Indeed, the point of Cobbett's ad hominem style was to connect private character with public conduct, and for this reason, although he occasionally singled out prominent political opponents like Madison and Jefferson ("a man as much fit to be President as I am to be an Archbishop"), his ridicule was usually reserved for familiar local figures like Swanwick. The effectiveness of his style depended on his familiarity with his victims, a familiarity he shared with his readers. Thus, the drinking habits of the governor of Pennsylvania, Thomas Mifflin, whom Cobbett dubbed "Tom the Tinker," provided him with an endless stream of colorful and amusing anecdotes. Whatever Mifflin's real character, he appears in Cobbett's writings as a drunken sot whose personal immorality was of a piece with his politics and who was most commonly to be found "toping, bawling and dancing *a la canibale* round the altar of *La Liberte*."[44]

Not all of Cobbett's victims were public figures, and he also had an uncanny knack for turning personal squabbles into conflicts charged with deeper political significance. After quarreling with the Philadelphia printer Thomas Bradford in early 1796, for example, Cobbett vilified Bradford as an "abominable sharper" and pornographer whose books were mere "*literary panders,*" "pimping for the eyes" that encouraged readers to indulge in more scandalous transgressions. But in addition to accusing Bradford of running a "bawdy-book-shop," Cobbett transformed the unfortunate printer (a moderate Federalist) into a symbol of republican hypocrisy. Bradford, he disclosed, possessed a lively interest in heraldry and great pride in his own allegedly aristocratic origins, failings that Cobbett lampooned mercilessly in a mock "Last Will and Testament" that he published in March 1797:

> To Thomas Lord Bradford (otherwise called goofy Tom), bookseller, printer, newsman, and member of the Philosophical Society of Philadelphia, I will and bequeath a copy of the Peerage of Great Britain, in order that the said Lord Thomas may the more exactly ascertain what probability there is of his succeeding to the seat which his noble relation now fills in the House of Lords.

This "Last Will and Testament" exemplifies the strengths of Cobbett's journalism and the difficulty of distinguishing personal from political motives in his writing. It included attacks on his favorite villains, Thomas Bradford, Noah Webster, Thomas Mifflin, Benjamin Rush, John Swanwick, and Benjamin Bache, as well as attacks on prominent Republicans like Albert Gallatin, James Monroe, Tench Coxe, Michael Leib, and Edmund Randolph. Here is his bequest to "Thomas Jefferson, philosopher":

> I leave a curious Norway spider, with a hundred legs and nine pairs of eyes; likewise the first black cut-throat general he can catch hold of, to be flayed alive, in order to determine with more certainty the real cause of the dark colour of his skin; and should the said Thomas Jefferson survive Banneker the almanack-maker, I request he will get the brains of said Philomath carefully dissected, to satisfy the world in what respect they differ from those of a white man.

This is savage and effective satire, evoking both horror and humor in the reader. Without any formal argument, Cobbett conjures up a damning picture of Jefferson as a cold-blooded racist, Republican zealot, and abstract scientist dissecting the remains of Toussaint L'Ouverture and Benjamin Banneker, two black men who could challenge his claim to be an advocate of universal liberty and equality.[45]

The transgressive, iconoclastic nature of Cobbett's journalism was highly political. But this should not blind us to its other purpose. His sensational journalism was also designed to arrest public attention, generate controversy, and create a market for the products of his literary labor. Never a paid party hack writing scandalous paragraphs to measure, Cobbett was an astute, professional writer and printer who realized that his autonomy as an author depended on his survival and success in a volatile and ruthless literary marketplace. He had a genius for generating publicity. As he later admitted, his decision to single out the celebrated figure of Joseph Priestley in his first work (which he first proposed calling *The Tartuffe Detected*)[46] was a deliberate attempt to promote his literary fortune. And in his subsequent pamphlets and *Porcupine's Gazette*, he developed this strategy by attacking those political opponents most likely to answer back: fellow journalists and writers.

These tactics were strikingly successful. His *Observations on the Emigration of Dr. Joseph Priestley* immediately provoked an anonymous champion for Priestley, who condemned Cobbett's work as "vitiating trash," although he was forced to admit it was widely read: "If you wrote for Fame…your object is most marvelously secured." His diatribe against James Thomson Callender in *A Bone to Gnaw for the Democrats* inspired the Scotsman to devote an entire pamphlet, *British Honour and Humanity; or, The Wonders of American Patience, as Exemplified in the Modest Publications, and Universal Applause of Mr. William Cobbett*, to a hostile evaluation of his work and influence, and his attacks on Rowson and Swanwick provoked the latter to compose *A Rub from Snub; or, A Cursory Analytical Epistle: Addressed to Peter Porcupine*, which was neither cursory nor analytical, excoriated Cobbett's "mental sterility," and promised to pursue him "till I scald him out of his hole."[47]

The desire to give Cobbett a taste of his own medicine inspired a steady stream of hostile and satirical pamphlets, including Samuel Bradford's *The Imposter Detected*, James Carey's *A Pill for Porcupine*, Joseph Hopkinson's *Congratulatory Epistle*, Santiago Felipe Puglia's *The Blue Shop*, and Matthew Carey's *Porcupiniad*, mainly from the pens of Republican opponents.[48] These productions were all grist to Cobbett's mill. When Benjamin Franklin Bache published a scurrilous account of Cobbett's life in the *Aurora*, Cobbett promptly sat down and wrote his classic *Life and Adventures of Peter Porcupine*. When a political cartoon picturing Peter Porcupine trampling on the works of Republican writers at the urging of the devil and the British lion was published, he was not offended but pleased. In a letter to his father (which he printed in his *Political Censor* of September 1796 but probably never sent), Cobbett wrote with an inimitable sense of self-satisfaction:

> Dear Father, when you used to set me off to work in the morning, dressed in my blue smock-frock and woolen splatterdashes, with my bag of bread and cheese and bottle of small beer swung over my shoulder on the little crook that my old god-father Boxall gave me, little did you imagine that I should one day become so great a man as to have my picture stuck in the windows, and have four whole books published about me in the course of a week.

The responses that his work aroused were a source of relish to Cobbett as well as celebrity and profit, testifying to his political influence and the provocative skill of his writing.[49]

See Porcupine, in Colours just Portray'd, Urg'd by old Nick, to drive his dirty trade, Veil'd in darkness, acts the assassins part, And triumphs much to stab you to the heart, published by Moreau de St. Mery, Philadelphia, [1796]. This shows William Cobbett as Peter Porcupine sowing the "seeds of discord" with his quill. Probably published during the Jay Treaty debates, Columbia weeps over a memorial to American independence as the devil ("More scandal, let us destroy this Idol, liberty") and the British lion ("I will reward you") encourage Porcupine's work. Courtesy of the Historical Society of Pennsylvania.

His success as a printer and as the editor of *Porcupine's Gazette* clearly demonstrated his popularity as an author. Just how popular and influential his journalism was by the late 1790s is difficult to determine. Naturally, he claimed enormous popularity and influence, and on the eve of his return to England in 1800, he declared, "there was not, in the whole country, one single family, in which some part or other of my writings have not been read." This was characteristic hyperbole, but Cobbett was a far more important figure than most studies of American politics and journalism in the 1790s have recognized. The volume and distribution of his writings suggest that he was one of the most widely read and influential political writers in the early Republic. His political pamphlets sold well from the start. His first pamphlet, *Observations on the Emigration of Dr. Joseph Priestley*, went into four editions and was reprinted several times between 1794 and 1798. *A Bone to Gnaw* also went through four editions by 1797, and *A Kick for a Bite* was published in two separate editions in 1795–1796. The first edition of the second part of *A Bone to Gnaw* "sold off in the space of six weeks," which was brisk, and at least two further editions appeared before 1798. Other pamphlets sold equally well, and collected editions of Peter Porcupine's work were published by Thomas Bradford in 1795 and 1796 and by Cobbett himself in 1797.[50] Sensational, anti-revolutionary pamphlets like *The Bloody Buoy* sold in the thousands. Pennsylvania Federalist Jacob Hiltzheimer helped to distribute a German edition of 3,000 copies that Cobbett claimed sold out in two weeks. The first print run of Anthony Aufrere's *Cannibal's Progress* numbered 25,000 copies, and in June 1798, Cobbett sent 2,000 to one New York bookseller alone.[51] After he returned to England, Cobbett claimed he had sold over a half million pamphlets in the United States between 1794 and 1800, an extraordinary and probably exaggerated number. While he was still in the United States, he claimed more modestly that "of each pamphlet, published under my assumed name of Peter Porcupine, about six thousand copies, upon an average, have been printed and sold in America." On this basis, Cobbett published about 200,000 copies of his own pamphlets in the period from 1794 to 1800, a figure which is both impressive and plausible.[52]

Cobbett realized that the key to expanding his audience was the creation of "that cut and thrust weapon, a daily paper," and after founding *Porcupine's Gazette* in March 1797 and the *Country Porcupine* in 1798, he greatly enhanced his political influence. Starting with 1,200 subscribers, Cobbett had acquired over 2,000 subscribers by April, and by November he was turning out 3,000 copies of the *Gazette* every day. Even allowing for some exaggeration, this is an impressive number, twice that claimed by other comparable political newspapers.[53] Not only was the circulation of *Porcupine's Gazette* high, it was also surprisingly broad. Although exact figures are hard to come by, Cobbett's paper probably circulated most widely in Pennsylvania, New York, and New England, but it also penetrated Republican strongholds in the South. A list of "country subscribers" to the *Gazette* indicates about 300 subscribers in Virginia, and according to one correspondent to the *Charleston State Gazette* in September 1797, the local mail was clogged with cart loads of *Porcupine's Gazette* "and other trash of a similar kind."[54]

While there are no subscription figures available for Philadelphia and the northern states, *Porcupine's Gazette* probably circulated more widely in the middle and northern states than in the South, despite the competition Cobbett faced from Federalist editors like Noah Webster and Benjamin Russell. In March 1797, just after the first issue of *Porcupine's Gazette* appeared, Cobbett sent 150 copies a day (or about 15 percent of his entire subscription) to New York City alone. Webster's claim that *Porcupine's Gazette* did not circulate at all in New England has to be balanced against his own admission that it appealed greatly to those

Porcupine's Gazette and United States Daily Advertiser, Philadelphia, March 4, 1797. This was the first issue of William Cobbett's new daily newspaper, which became extraordinarily influential between 1797 and its demise in 1799. Preserving his celebrated pseudonym only in the title of the paper, Cobbett made his editorial approach clear in his announcement "To the Public": "Professions of *impartiality* I shall make none." Like Fenno and Freneau, Cobbett placed his politics on the front page. Courtesy of the Library Company of Philadelphia.

"fond of low wit and scurrility," and that "in the course of a journey of eight hundred miles through the eastern states," he "everywhere heard the writings of Cobbett spoken of with the utmost contempt and abhorrence." Cobbett may have been unpopular, but he was not unread. The Republican politician William Branch Giles, who detested Cobbett, thought his newspaper was extremely influential and "too much countenanced" by readers throughout the country. Cobbett claimed that the success of *Porcupine's Gazette* "in point of extensive circulation, over all others, in this country, has long been universally known and acknowledged." And he was probably right to do so.[55]

Republican opponents never underestimated his influence and political importance. Writing as early as 1796, James Thomson Callender described Cobbett as the "literary favorite of the American public," and although Cobbett's influence waned at the end of the 1790s, Joseph Priestley still thought he was the most popular political writer in the country. In a letter of congratulation to Jefferson in 1801, Benjamin Rush welcomed the resurgence of Republicanism in a country that until recently had been "so much under the influence of the *name* of [Washington], the *plans* of [Hamilton], and the *press* of Peter Porcupine." The election of Jefferson, according to Republican journalist Benjamin Austin, had cut short a "reign of terror" conducted by the Federalist press in which "Corporal Porcupine" had been the "chief director…the orb around which the Federal satellites moved."[56]

Cobbett's use of ad hominem argument also had an important place in the political culture of eighteenth-century Anglo-America. Enlightenment ideas about causality placed great emphasis on the role of human agency, and Cobbett's tendency to place the individual actor at the center of his political narrative, to personalize politics, reflected these ideas. But this emphasis on the centrality of individual actors and the importance of personal psychology created a new sense of anxiety about political "representation" in eighteenth-century political culture. How was it possible to tell an honest politician from a dishonest one? A corrupt minister from a virtuous one? A leader who sought his own interests from one who sought the interests of the *res publica*? Issues of political dissimulation and deceit were hardly new, but they took on new, public significance in the eighteenth century, and the problem of determining the relationship between political rhetoric and political reality, of evaluating the public self-representation of political leaders, became one of the obsessions of the age, according to historian Gordon Wood, "a source of continuing fascination in eighteenth-century Anglo-American culture."[57]

One reason for this obsession with self-representation was a more secular understanding of social causality and human agency, but the other was the structural transformation of public life. The transformation of the public sphere in the eighteenth century created a new audience for elite politics at the same time as it eroded the face-to-face relationships on which local politics had traditionally been based, giving public life a new anonymity. Knowledge about public affairs, exchanged like the latest shipping news in coffeehouses, was gleaned from a rapidly expanding periodical press that created a politically conscious public and forced political elites to consider their own public reputations as valuable political capital. In the context of expanding publicity and popular involvement in public life, issues of political identity became more problematic and more urgent. While power remained firmly in the hands of the few, elite conflicts were played out before an increasingly assertive popular audience that possessed little knowledge about elite politicians or the factional intricacies of elite political culture. The result was the development of an intrusive and interrogatory politics "dedicated to the unmasking of hypocrisy."[58]

Ironically, as the expansion of the public sphere made public life more impersonal and anonymous, the discourse of politics became more personalized. Public anxiety about political identity and representation was linked to a fascination with the parallels between theater and politics, and by the eighteenth century, Anglo-American political discourse was saturated with metaphors of the stage. The author of an anti-revolutionary pamphlet called *The Sham Patriot Unmasked*, published in New York in 1802, neatly summarized arguments that recurred again and again in eighteenth-century politics:

> The world is a stage, and life is a drama. Successive generations are acting over the same parts, which had been frequently acted before....In every age a variety of tragi-comic scenes have been exhibited on this great stage, by knaves disguised in visors, and bearing on their front a label, upon which are written in capitals, the words, Honesty, Benevolence, Patriotism; while the multitude, never attempting to look under the mask, are seen stupidly staring at the label— reading the inscription with the gape of wonder, and uttering their applauding shouts in extacies of joy and veneration.

In a series of essays on political radicals like John Wilkes, Marat, and Robespierre, the author probed the gap between their hidden private motives and their public rhetoric, warning his readers to beware of political seduction, of those "who speak to you in the whining cant of a lover, and profess unbounded affection for you—'Their hearts mean not so'—Beware of men who are ever proclaiming their patriotism. It is the hypocrite's trumpet, that they sound."[59]

But how could a citizen-reader determine the true heart of a man? If political rhetoric was unreliable and appearances were always deceptive, then how could the public distinguish men of virtue from "knaves disguised in visors"? And if politics resembled a drama, then the best actors rather than the best men were the most likely to win popular favor. Almost by definition, suggested the author, those most worthy of public approbation were those least likely to court popularity, and as a result, "the most deserving characters are hissed off the stage." Americans, he warned, must look beneath the surface of those who compete to guide their political affairs, placing faith only in those "who in their personal characters are known to be men of talents and integrity." But this simply restated the problem of the relationship between rhetoric and reality. How were citizens to determine men of worthy character? If the public world was a stage and public men were actors, it was crucial to catch them without their costumes on, naked to the public eye. And if they hid their genuine motives behind rhetorical masks, then "unmasking" and exposing them to public view was a civic duty. In this politics of public exposure, Cobbett's ad hominem journalism acquired its raison d'être.[60]

In a public sphere constituted by the expansion of print culture, the problem of political representation, of determining the true nature or character of a politician, was ultimately a problem of political language. As Cobbett argued, the elusive language of the revolutionary enlightenment, what he called the "tasteless, turgid, hyperbolical" language of the French Revolution and the "canting jargon of modern republicans," made its true meaning impossible to determine. The abstraction of republican rhetoric was a source of mystification that concealed rather than revealed the true intentions of its users. Words like "liberty" were floating signifiers without political significance, and phrases like the "rights of man" incantations that served as little more than symbols of partisan identity. Part of Cobbett's self-appointed role was to police the language of political life, to insist on the need to use language with precision, clarity, and concreteness— A Little Plain English, as he called one of his pamphlets—and to expose the emptiness of the "new-fangled vocabulary" used by his Republican adversaries. Always eager to present himself as the guardian of good prose, Cobbett warned his opponents that "though patriots are permitted to talk nonsense with impunity in all other republics, they have not, nor ever will have, any such privilege in the Republic of Letters."[61]

Cobbett mocked not only the "sansculottish jargon" of republican writers and politicians, but what he regarded as their absurd reverence for words. Although republican France had assumed "the language, and put on the garb, of liberty," he argued, it had slaughtered over 2 million of its own citizens and was "no more a Republic in reality than Turkey or Morocco, or any other despotic state." Yet Americans continued to believe "notwithstanding the terrible example before their eyes, that men cannot be enslaved under a form of government that is called republican." Why, he wondered (in a passage that captures brilliantly the solidity, shrewdness, and persuasiveness of his prose), were French attacks on American shipping tolerated while those of the British were condemned:

Is it because one is a monarchy, and the other calls itself a republic? I have heard, or read, of a fellow that was so accustomed to be kicked, that he could distinguish, by the feel, the sort of leather that assailed his posteriors. Are our buttocks arrived at this perfection of sensibility?

"What more stupid doltish bigotry can there be," he asked, "than to make the sound of a word the standard of good and bad government?" Americans should attach themselves "to things and not to words; to sense and not to sound."[62]

Cobbett's approach to language was shaped by his desire to maintain a stable relationship between words and things, politics and character, measures and men. And his enthusiasm for dismantling the rhetorical façade of modern republicanism was matched by his desire to ground this rhetoric in the reality of private life. As the English eighteenth-century novelist Henry Fielding argued in "An Essay on the Knowledge of the Characters of Men," the interpretation of character was the key to that "excellent Art, called the Art of Politics," and the best way to assess the character of a man was to examine his private life:

> Trace then the Man proposed to your Trust into his private Family and nearest intimacies. See whether he hath acted the Part of a good Son, Brother, Husband, Friend, Master, Servant, &c. if he hath discharged these duties well, your confidence will have a good foundation.

Because character has its origins in private life, the only way to establish the authenticity of a man's public character was to examine his private life. A similar emphasis on the connection between public and private life also pervaded the work of a writer who had a decisive influence on Cobbett's thinking in the 1790s, Edmund Burke.[63]

In his *Reflections on the Revolution in France*, Burke argued that all forms of human association, including political association, had their origins in private life and the family. "We begin our public affections," stated Burke, "in our families." Here, men first transcended the limitations of self-regarding behavior and developed an awareness of others, acquiring those habits of private virtue and self-restraint that were an indispensable basis for social life and the preservation of public liberty, what Burke called "*social* freedom." As Burke explained in one of the many famous passages from *Reflections*:

> To be attached to the subdivision, to love the little platoon we belong to in society, is the first principle (the germ as it were) of public affections. It is the first link in the series by which we proceed towards a love to our country, and to mankind.

According to Burke, society was not a compact created by self-interested, rational individuals but a complex, interdependent organism held together by irrational bonds of affection and loyalty, by sentiment. These ties of sentiment originated in the affections and loyalties that characterize family life, and to violate them was an act of unforgivable hubris and treachery. This link between private and public lay at the heart of Burke's critique of the French Revolution. By reconstructing society around a series of political abstractions, revolutionaries had destroyed that "mixed system of opinion and sentiment" that held Old Regime France together, and in their "new conquering empire of light and reason," he warned, only force or self-interest could ensure social cohesion. "All the decent drapery of life is to be rudely torn off," he wrote:

> A king is but a man; a queen is but a woman; a woman is but an animal; and an animal not of the highest order. . . . Nothing is left which engages the affections on the part of the commonwealth. On the principles of this mechanic philosophy, our institutions can never be embodied, if I may use the expression, in persons; so as to create in us love, veneration, admiration, or attachment.

The result was a world of "cold hearts" and callousness. "Without opening one new avenue to the understanding," argued Burke, revolutionaries in France had "succeeded in stopping up those that lead to the heart." By banishing from public life the "sentiments which beautify and soften private society," they had made social chaos and violence all but inevitable.[64]

Burke's influence on Cobbett was enormous. "When Cobbett wrote," states David Wilson, "it was as if Burke had crossed the Atlantic" and adopted the "plain style." Cobbett shared his belief that society was held together by natural bonds of affection that originated in family life, and he believed, like Burke, that the "nakedness and solitude of metaphysical abstraction" threatened such natural bonds. In his view, the impersonality of republican political rhetoric, the cry of "measures not men," sought to deny this organic connection between private and public character, an evasion that Cobbett viewed as a source of political hypocrisy and political violence. Like Burke, Cobbett's sentimentalization of private life was accompanied by a fascination with the "unnatural" ferocity (much of it sexual) that characterized the "family romance" of the French Revolution.[65] Revolutionary violence reflected the impersonal, dehumanizing character of revolutionary language and the false character of the revolutionaries themselves. Unlike Webster, who attacked the disparity between revolutionary principles and revolutionary practices but condemned only the latter, Cobbett believed that principles and practices were intimately linked, and he dismissed "the cant of the enslaved French and American democrats" who blamed revolutionary violence on the personal failings of men like Robespierre. Bad men, he argued, were attracted to bad principles; public character was a reflection of private character. Modern republicans made bad husbands—"See if there be one among the yelping kennel of modern patriots who is not a bad husband, father, brother, or son," he wrote—and bad husbands made modern republicans. As he pointed out, Thomas Paine had left his wife behind him in England when he came to America. "Paine's humanity," sneered Cobbett,

> like that of all the reforming philosophers of the present enlightened day, is of the speculative kind. It never breaks out into action. Hear these people, and you would think them overflowing with the milk of human kindness....They stretch their benevolence to the extremities of the globe: it embraces every living creature— except those who have the misfortune to come in contact with them. They are all citizens of the world: country and friends and relations are unworthy [of] the attention of men who are occupied in rendering all mankind happy and free.

"The good citizen or subject, the good husband, parent and child, and the good christian," declared Cobbett, "exist together or they exist not at all."[66]

As his attack on Paine's universal "benevolence" shows, Cobbett believed that disloyalty to people and disloyalty to place were intertwined, and his British patriotism was as much a matter of political ideology as personal identity. Like Burke, he believed that patriotism had its origins in sentiment rather than rationality and was analogous to the family loyalty from which it derived. In a passage that probably reflected feelings of guilt about abandoning his own father, family, and country, he wrote:

> A man, who is not dead to every sentiment that distinguishes him from the brute, feels himself attached to his native land by ties but very little weaker than those which bind him to his parents....Who would not regard as a monster the ungrateful wretch that should declare that he was no longer the son of his father.

Cobbett's reverence for patriarchal genealogy, a reverence that also lay at the heart of Burke's political theory, explains his hostility toward immigrants like Joseph Priestley, who attacked their native land after arriving in America. When Robespierre threw Paine into a Paris prison, Cobbett viewed his fate as a lesson to all those "who change countries every time they cross the sea." "A man of all countries," he declared, "is a man of no country."[67]

Like familial loyalty, patriotism expressed fidelity to a series of human relationships structured by place and the past rather than political principle. According to Cobbett, a world of abstract, transferable loyalties was a world without loyalty. If personal and political allegiances could be changed at will, he argued, "there could be no such thing as a *traitor* in the world" and nothing to hold society together but raw power and the pursuit of crude self-interest. Without obligation and attachment, declared Cobbett, "the barriers of society would be broken into shivers." But Cobbett was not simply a plebian version of Burke, and the differences between the two men are instructive and important. While both men viewed public life in theatrical terms, for Burke political leaders occupied the public stage and the people composed a more or less passive audience. Politics was a rhetorical art designed to win public approval for the government of a political elite, and Burke had no wish to let citizens see what was going on backstage. For Cobbett, on the other hand, personal attacks were designed to rattle the performers, tear off the "decent drapery of life," and expose his political opponents to public view. Burke deplored such invasive tactics, while they show how much Cobbett had in common with his more radical Republican opponents. While Burke wished to privatize public life, Cobbett sought to politicize private life, and his writings had a demystifying, iconoclastic quality that disturbed those who thought public affairs should remain the province of a select and self-selecting few. If Burke spoke for those who strutted the public stage, Cobbett spoke for those who packed the Gods.[68]

Cobbett was one of the most popular and widely read journalists of the 1790s, and he was also one of the most vilified. A typically nasty reaction to his writing appeared in the *Boston Mercury* in late 1797. Warning Americans that personal slander threatened the health of "our young country," the author left readers in no doubt:

> Peter Porcupine, possessing talents peculiarly adapted to this base business, seems to have distinguished himself above all the other editors and newspaper scribblers, in the cruelty of his indiscriminate and wanton attacks on private character....Nature and a low education, seem to have united their powers, in fitting him for his present profession, that of the *arch butcher of reputation.*

Attacks like this became commonplace by the late 1790s. "No name is secure," wrote one newspaper correspondent, "against the unbridled licentiousness and scandalous aspersions of this *pugilistic scribbler*" and "Billingsgate Hero." Peter Porcupine was an "ever bubbling spring of endless lies," according to another critic, "a foul murderer of fame." The author of *A Twig of Birch for a Butting Calf* denounced Cobbett's pamphlet on Priestley as a "mere gasconade of scandal," and Philip Freneau published a whole series of satirical verses addressed to Cobbett, condemning *Porcupine's Gazette* as a "sink of scurrility" funded by the British to attack American Republicans. According to Matthew Carey, "the style of Porcupine's Gazette is unquestionably the most base and wretched of any newspaper in Christendom."[69]

Predictably, most of these attacks were by Republican opponents, but even Federalists echoed the charge that Cobbett was a "foul murderer of fame." Some of these attacks were also politically inspired. Noah Webster, for example, who suffered directly at Cobbett's hands, denounced him as a "mere bully," deploring his abuse of "honest, faithful men." Benjamin Russell, another New England Federalist who disliked Cobbett's pro-British politics, thought Peter Porcupine was merely a "suitable beast" with which to hunt down "Jacobinic foxes, skunks, and serpents." One Connecticut writer thought that his attacks on "virtuous and honest American patriots" had done the Federalists more harm than good and that, by introducing a "practice of indecent railing and scurrility into our public papers which far outgoes the dirtiest democratic paper in the country," Cobbett had destroyed public respect for character and morality. Political allies also had reservations about the personal savagery of his journalism. The British ambassador, Robert Liston, tried unsuccessfully to persuade him to avoid the "gross personal abuse" in his writings "which has frequently marred their complete effect." And although Abigail Adams believed that he wrote "very handsomely," she also thought he could "descend & be as low, and vulgar as a fish woman." Federalist sympathizers were often apologetic about Cobbett's tactics and style. It was true, admitted one New England correspondent, that his prose lacked decorum and restraint, but this was the price of his unique vigor and effectiveness. Besides, added the writer, the subjects of his venom—"such *virtuous* characters as Jefferson, Randolph, Mifflin, Blount, McKean, Genet, Dallas, Monroe, Coxe, and the whole horde of political knaves who are for selling this country to the wicked rulers of France"—deserved no better.[70]

Hostility toward Cobbett was part of a broader sense of dismay about the degeneration of the American press, and Cobbett was only one of the "masters of scurrility" whose editorial tactics rekindled public debate about the proper limits of press freedom in the late 1790s. Until this time, public controversy about freedom of the press had been episodic, and most Americans, although probably sympathetic to the criticism expressed by Benjamin Franklin in 1789, were content to let the press regulate itself. But by the mid-1790s, faith in self-regulation had begun to falter, and many Americans had come to believe that greater legal regulation was needed to preserve a respectable, republican press. The catalyst for this sharp shift in public opinion was the spread of the ad hominem journalism most closely associated with *Porcupine's Gazette*. Instead of exercising self-restraint, partisan editors like Cobbett and Bache were exploiting the unique freedom of the American press to fill their publications with personal slander. The rapid expansion of the newspaper press in this period heightened fears about the consequences of this practice, eroding confidence in the corrective power of a free market of ideas. As newspapers like *Porcupine's Gazette* and the *Aurora* acquired more and more influence, it seemed naive to think that their scandalmongering could be easily refuted. By encouraging personal scurrility, partisan editors had intensified political conflict and threatened the fragile unity of the new nation-state, and if they refused to check their licentiousness, argued Samuel Miller, "we may anticipate the arrival of that crisis in which we must yield either to an abridgement of the press, or to a disruption of every social bond."[71]

The Reverend William Linn, a staunch Federalist, addressed public anxiety about personal scandal in a sermon delivered and published in 1795. Infuriated by the incessant Republican attacks on President George Washington, Linn told his congregation that these attacks not only overstepped the boundaries of public decency but had a corrupting influence on political leadership. Pointing out that Jefferson and Hamilton had already retired from public office, Linn asked fellow citizens to consider "who will serve us if obloquy be the reward?" This was not just a question of political civility. In a culture saturated with classical republican ideas, the pursuit of public recognition and respect rather than private self-interest was supposed to be the primary motive for public service. But if fame were the spur that inspired men of the founding generation to accept the burdens of public office, defamation was the spur that drove them back to the seclusion and tranquility of private life.[72] According to critics like Linn, if elected leaders were not protected from abuse in the partisan press, disinterested men would be driven from public office or deterred from seeking it altogether. In other words, slander undermined the basis of republican civic life, ensuring that political power gravitated into the hands of self-interested, ambitious men. The preservation of republican government, argued one Federalist, depended on how "a free people treat their public servants." If they subject them to constant abuse, "none will accept appointments but those who have no characters to lose."[73]

This decline in the integrity and quality of political leadership was a prelude to more general social and political degeneration. "A republican government," stated Judge Samuel Chase during Thomas Cooper's trial for seditious libel in 1800, "can only be destroyed in two ways; the introduction of luxury, or the licentiousness of the press." While he acknowledged that opposition to the government was legitimate, Chase condemned efforts "to injure the characters of those to whom you are opposed." Chase was a Federalist, but his concern about the spread of personal abuse in the partisan press was shared by some of his political opponents. According to Republican Samuel Miller, the tendency of people to "defame their personal and political enemies" was universal, but democratic electoral politics exacerbated the problem:

> Where the supposed provocations to this are numerous, and no restraints are imposed on the indulgence of the disposition, an inundation of filth and calumny must be expected. In the United States the frequency of Elections leads to a corresponding frequency of struggle between political parties; these struggles naturally engender mischevious [sic] passions, and every species of coarse invective.

Democratic politics thus encouraged a politics of personality that undermined rational political debate. The "prostitution of the press" to the interests of party, wrote one dejected correspondent to *Porcupine's Gazette*, had led respectable men to "lament the invention of printing." A writer in the Philadelphia *Courier François* believed that party conflict threatened to divide the nation in two and "break down all the barriers which guard private character in a social state." Partisan intolerance had destroyed any regard for personal character or merit. "The most immaculate and respectable men of one party are loaded with all the billingsgate epithets by the other," he observed, and while members of each party portrayed themselves as uniquely virtuous, "those who differ from them, are represented as villains, scoundrels and devils." Personal slander, he concluded, was "one of the most dangerous poisons in civil society."[74]

A lengthy disquisition on the dangers of slander in the *Boston Mercury* came to the same conclusion. The scurrility of the newspaper press, argued its author, had become a "secret poison in the public mind." Political scribblers and newspaper editors, in particular the infamous editors of "the CHRONICLE, the ARGUS, and the AURORA, on the one side, and PORCUPINE'S GAZETTE on the other," had raised the art of character assassination to its "utmost pitch," excluding "no reputation, however virtuous and unsullied," from "the shafts of their envenomed malice." The consequences were a calamity for the American people and republican government:

> The effect of this vile practice, upon the moral habits of a people are, in a high degree pernicious. Continual attacks on the private characters of men, lead not only the defamer himself, but his readers also, to a habit of disrespect for all character. Let a man be accustomed for any length of time to write or read private slander, and he loses not only his respect for the characters attacked, but also that nice regard to reputation, from which proceed half the decency of behaviour and the civilities of life, and which alone can preserve the peace and harmony of society.

The "continual torrent of invective" that flowed from the press destroyed the feelings of sociability and self-restraint, "that nice regard to reputation," which made civilized life possible. Without these civilizing forces, society would be overwhelmed by the forces of anarchic individualism and descend into violence. "The man who deals in scandal and personal abuse," argued the author, "loses his sensibility to the value of reputation and takes from his neighbour his good name, with as little feeling and remorse as the butcher takes the life of an ox." "Murdering characters," he implied, was not far removed from more literal kinds of murder.[75]

Like this writer, by the late 1790s, many Americans blamed partisan newspapers for the growing animosity of public life, and their discussions about personal slander were suffused with fears of physical violence and civil unrest. Benjamin Rush compared the "bitter and unchristian spirit" that divided Americans to divisions in revolutionary France: "We have not, it is true, erected a guillotine in our country, but we enjoy similar spectacles of cruelty in the destruction of public and private characters in our newspapers." The poison of party conflict, he warned, consumed "the best feelings and noblest charities of life" and might yet ignite the "flame of civil discord." John Adams made similar predictions, telling fellow Bostonians in 1798 that the "obloquy which you have observed in your newspapers" was a graver threat to the United States than the possibility of a French invasion. War with France, he argued, would create political unity, but the scandalous practices of the press would lead to "divisions, seditions, civil war and military despotism." The conflation of verbal and physical violence in discussions of the partisan press was only partly metaphorical. Underlying hostility to the press lurked fear of a more profound social cataclysm.[76]

Just before Cobbett launched *Porcupine's Gazette* in March 1797, one of his most avid readers, the Federalist Henry Van Schaack, predicted that his attacks on Republicans would never be forgiven: "He must rely much on the strength of the laws of this country, as I hope nature has formed his body sufficiently strong to resist any manner of attacks on him." Van Schaack's fears and hopes were well founded. Despite threats to his person and livelihood, the burly Cobbett escaped all but verbal retaliation until the fall of 1797. But at this point, Pennsylvania Republicans launched a campaign of systematic legal harassment against Cobbett that destroyed his political influence and drove him from the country. Both legal and political historians have overlooked the significance of this Republican campaign.[77] Cobbett was the first newspaper editor to be prosecuted for seditious libel by the federal government, the first to be prosecuted by both federal and state governments, and the first to be subjected to crippling damages in a civil libel suit. His successful civil prosecution was a harbinger of the future. The verdict against him was not only unprecedented in size but constituted a model for the future prosecution of public speech. After 1800, private libel suits rather than public prosecutions became the preferred and highly effective legal method for dealing with unruly, irresponsible political journalists.[78]

Cobbett's legal difficulties originated in a dispute with the Spanish ambassador to the United States, the Chevalier Don Martinez d'Yrujo. The background to this dispute was Spain's alliance with France in October 1796 and the subsequent breakdown in negotiations between the United States and Spain over the implementation of Pinckney's Treaty, a treaty between the two countries concluded in 1795. By July 1797, relations between Secretary of State Timothy Pickering and the Spanish minister, d'Yrujo, were so poor that the latter launched a blister-ing public attack on Pickering in Bache's *Aurora*. Cobbett, who was close to Pickering, had commented caustically on the controversy in *Porcupine's Gazette*, but when d'Yrujo's "impudent letter" appeared, his criticism grew savage. The next day, he demanded the expulsion of d'Yrujo (whom he dubbed "Don Sans-Culotta de Carmagnola *minor*") and attacked the Spanish king as an ally of French regicides.[79]

The response was almost immediate. Within a fortnight, d'Yrujo had writ-ten to Pickering demanding Cobbett's prosecution for libels against himself, the king of Spain, and the Spanish nation. After Pickering forwarded this request to President Adams, the attorney general of the United States decided to pros-ecute Cobbett, and Pickering instructed the U.S. attorney general for the District of Pennsylvania, William Rawle, to commence a libel prosecution in the federal courts. On August 8, Cobbett was bound over to appear before the next session of the U.S. Circuit Court for Pennsylvania, charged with publishing libels on d'Yrujo and the Spanish king.[80] Not content with this, d'Yrujo demanded that Pickering transfer the case to the Pennsylvania courts, a request he refused. On August 18, however, Cobbett was arrested and brought before the chief justice of the Pennsylvania Supreme Court, Thomas McKean, who charged him with further libelous publications against the Spanish minister and king and com-pelled him to post a bond of $2,000 for his future "good behaviour." The motives behind this second prosecution in the state of Pennsylvania were transparent, and there is strong evidence of collusion between d'Yrujo and McKean. "The little Don," wrote Cobbett, who got wind of the impending state indictment in early August, "has, for some time past, been extremely assiduous in his addresses to Miss M'Kean, the amiable daughter of poor Pennsylvania's Chief Justice." D'Yrujo was a close friend of McKean's, was courting his daughter Sally, and became his son-in-law in April 1798. According to McKean's biographer, it is not clear whether d'Yrujo or McKean made the decision to prosecute Cobbett in the Pennsylvania courts, but the two men clearly acted in close concert.[81]

In any event, the indictment by the state of Pennsylvania delivered Cobbett into the ruthless hands of Chief Justice Thomas McKean, a central figure in Pennsylvania Republican politics, a man Cobbett had attacked personally in *Porcupine's Gazette*, and a judge whose views on liberty of the press were famously reactionary. It was McKean who had presided over the trial of Eleazar Oswald for seditious libel in the 1780s, and he had not moderated his views in the years since. When Cobbett's case was heard on November 27, 1797, McKean delivered a charge to the grand jury that must have shocked even Republicans by its sweep-ing defense of legal orthodoxy. Defending the idea that attacks on public men were "an aggravation" of libel that bred "faction and sedition," McKean rejected altogether the idea of a critical press. Printing presses were free, he claimed, as long as they "take care in their publications, that they are decent, candid and true; that they are for the purpose of reformation and not for defamation; and that they have an eye solely to the public good." "Every one who has in him the sentiments of either a Christian or gentleman," he continued,

> cannot but be highly offended at the envenomed scurrility that has raged in pamphlets and newspapers, printed in Philadelphia for several years past, insomuch that libeling has become a kind of national crime, and distinguishes us not only from all the States around us, but from the whole civilized world. Our satire has been nothing but ribaldry and Billingsgate; the contest has been, who could call names in the greatest variety of phrases; who could mangle the greatest number of characters; or who could excel in the magnitude and virulence of their lies. Hence the honour of families has been stained; the highest posts rendered cheap and vile in the sight of the people, and the greatest services and virtue blasted. This evil, so scandalous to our government, and detestable in the eyes of all good men, calls aloud for redress. To censure the licentiousness is to maintain the liberty of the press.[82]

This extraordinary charge, which, legal historian Leonard Levy observes, "might have been issued under the name of Hutchinson, Blackstone or Mansfield," left the grand jury unmoved. Despite McKean's prejudicial remarks, they refused to indict Cobbett.[83]

But Cobbett was now a marked man. Even before the Pennsylvania grand jury dismissed his indictment, he faced a new legal threat: civil libel suits brought by two other prominent Philadelphia Republicans, Benjamin Rush and Matthew Carey. These cases quickly became entangled in the more general campaign against Cobbett. Both cases were heard before the Pennsylvania Supreme Court in December 1797 with Chief Justice McKean presiding, and in March 1798 Cobbett's request to have the cases removed to the federal courts was refused. The Carey suit was apparently abandoned at this stage, but the Rush suit went ahead. And in a move that made clear how closely intertwined this libel suit was with a carefully orchestrated political campaign against Cobbett, Rush was persuaded to drop a similar libel suit against John Fenno by his legal counsel, the attorney general of Pennsylvania, Jared Ingersoll. Ingersoll then requested a motion for continuance that was granted by McKean and kept the case hanging, like the sword of Damocles, over Cobbett's head until December 1799.[84]

As if this were not enough, in December 1797, Ingersoll, acting in his official capacity as attorney general, initiated an action for debt against Cobbett, demanding that he forfeit the $2,000 bond for "good behaviour" that he had given in August. In his charge to the grand jury, McKean had argued that libels were tantamount to a "breach of the public peace." Now, ignoring the decision of the Pennsylvania grand jury, Ingersoll claimed that Cobbett's continued publication of libelous materials violated his bond. Once again, Cobbett tried to have his case removed to the federal courts, once again McKean and the Supreme Court rejected his request, and once again judgment in the case was postponed from session to session until December 1800. At this point, Chief Justice Edward Shippen, who had replaced McKean when the latter was elected governor of Pennsylvania in 1799, found in favor of the prosecution, accepting the alarming argument of the new state attorney general, Joseph McKean, Thomas McKean's son, that a magistrate could levy fines and initiate prosecutions for libel without the assent of a grand jury.[85]

These legal proceedings did not silence Cobbett. He continued to vilify Benjamin Rush as a bloodthirsty quack and used the opportunity provided by his own persecution to portray himself as a champion of press freedom. In October 1797, he announced the publication of a series of essays in *Porcupine's Gazette* on "American Liberty of the Press." Although American freedom of the press had always been compared favorably with freedom of the press in Great Britain, he declared, circumstances had now arisen "which will put this *literary liberty* to the test; which will prove to every one ... what is the precise meaning of 'the *unrestrained* liberty of the American press.'" His most important statement on liberty of the press, however, was his vicious attack on Thomas McKean—the "Fouquier Tinville of America"—in his pamphlet *The Democratic Judge*, which was published in March 1798. Although this work was highly polemical and self-exculpatory, nonetheless it was an important, serious, and persuasive defense of press freedom. As Cobbett rightly argued, under the doctrine of libel set forth in McKean's charge to the Pennsylvania grand jury, "there is no book sacred or profane, which might not be construed into a libel." "If these are libels," he asked, "who is safe?" But Cobbett's target was broader than the chief justice. He believed that the reactionary views and high-handed conduct of McKean were part of a much wider public hostility toward press freedom. While American law offered important legal protections to the press, argued Cobbett, there was a difference between "*real* liberty of the press" and formal press freedom.[86]

According to Cobbett, the real liberty of the press had been "most shamefully and disgracefully *restrained*" in the United States by a combination of popular prejudice and official tyranny. This intimidation had produced a press of fawning insipidity whose "cowardly guise of *impartiality*" was a "disgrace to literature, a dishonour to the country, a clog to government, and a curse to the people." Part of the reason for this lay in the structure of American government. As Cobbett pithily put it, everyone "must be obnoxious to one of the two governments under which he lives." But the real obstacle to an uninhibited and free press was not government intimidation but public opinion. Although he thought that few Americans supported McKean's belief that public figures were entitled to greater legal protection from the press than were private citizens, most accepted the view "which has been, for evident motives, inculcated by artful men, that no *private character* ought to be publically censured." Cobbett contrasted this sharply with the spirit of irreverence that he believed inspired the English press. "Only compare one of the London papers with an American paper," he wrote,

> and you will soon see which comes from the free-est press. Is there a crime, is there a fault or folly, which the editors and print-sellers in London do not lash? They dive into every assembly and every house; they spare characters neither public nor private; neither the people; the gentry; the clergy; the nobility, nor the royal family itself are sheltered from their ridicule or their censure.

Compare this, he demanded, to the "leaden sheets" produced in the United States. Were these so dull, he asked, because no "such thing as drunkeness, adultery, swindling, corruption or blasphemy" existed in the United States, or because "we wish to keep these things hidden from the world?"[87]

Leonard Levy has argued that "not until after 1798 did Americans rival the libertarianism of their English counterparts." But he is wrong. Without so much as a reference to Milton's *Areopagitica* or Cato's *Letters, The Democratic Judge* demolished the distinction between private and public character that provided the rationale for all libel prosecutions. Indeed, Cobbett treated the demolition of such a distinction as a precondition for public enlightenment and the creation of a critical public sphere. His position, however modified in his own fluid, opportunistic political rhetoric, could not have been more firmly rooted in his practice as a political writer. His successful prosecution by Republicans in Pennsylvania established the limits of American press freedom in the late 1790s and the limits of Republican commitment to a free press. But just as important, his writings constituted a direct and crucial link between American ideas about press freedom and the robust libertarianism that developed in the combative world of eighteenth-century English political journalism.[88]

Shortly after he published *The Democratic Judge*, Cobbett's federal indictment was laid before a grand jury and returned "ignoramus." The Rush lawsuit, however, did not come to trial until December 13, 1799. But even before the verdict, Cobbett had decided to fold his tent and move on. McKean's election as governor in October 1799 made Cobbett's continued residence in Philadelphia both unbearable and foolhardy, and Cobbett had promised his readers that he would "*never live six months under his sovereign sway.*" Besides, the election of McKean signaled a shift in the political winds, including a decline in public support for the bellicose anti-Gallic Federalism that had dominated political life in

1797–1798, which Cobbett had represented so forcefully. The *Country Porcupine* ceased publication right after McKean's election, and on October 21, 1799, the last Pennsylvania edition of *Porcupine's Gazette* appeared. In mid-November, Cobbett decided to move to New York, and on December 9, he took flight, leaving his suit with Rush in the hands of his lawyers.[89]

These hands proved less than capable. When the case finally came to trial, Cobbett's lawyers excused rather than defended his actions, and none of them raised basic issues of press freedom. In contrast, Rush's lawyers conducted an aggressive case against Cobbett, portraying him as an alien and a slanderer driven by partisan hatred and personal animosity. The presiding judge, Chief Justice Edward Shippen, then instructed the jury to consider exemplary damages, and after a two-hour recess they returned a verdict against Cobbett, awarding Rush damages of $5,000. As Cobbett's biographer Mary Clark observes, nobody can read the account of this trial and fail to detect "the determination to punish Cobbett heavily for the part he had played in the political scene." But more than this, nobody can read these proceedings without feeling that the establishment, both Republican and Federalist, was ganging up on Cobbett. It was not an inspiring sight. As Mahlon Dickinson, a Republican lawyer, observed tersely in his diary: "a ruinous verdict, and therefore a rascally one."[90]

Cobbett assured the English printer John Wright: "I am not cast down. I will fight as I retreat to the water's edge." But the Rush verdict delivered the coup de grâce to Cobbett's American career. He remained in New York, where he was warmly received by local Federalists, including Alexander Hamilton, until June 1800, but psychologically he had already left the country. The campaign against Rush and McKean in his new publication, the *Rush-Light*, was as skillful as ever but utterly without relevance to American politics. In his public writings, Cobbett did not once mention the presidential elections of 1800 and, even more striking, expressed sympathy for his fellow Britons Thomas Cooper and Joseph Priestley, both radicals who were suffering political persecution at the hands of the Federalists. In April 1800, he urged Priestley to repent his sins and return to England, assuring him that "you have a country that ever stands with open arms to welcome her wandering sons." Cobbett's romantic vision of his native land had by now overwhelmed any lingering attachment to the New World. On the first day of June 1800, he left New York for England, commenting acidly that, "when people care not two straws for each other, ceremony at parting is mere grimace."[91]

CHAPTER 6

William Duane and the Triumph of Infidelity

When Thomas Paine returned to the United States in 1802, William Duane was one of the few American editors who welcomed him publicly. "Thomas Paine, the early and uniform asserter of the *Rights of Mankind* [*sic*], and author of the immortal revolutionary papers called COMMON SENSE and the CRISIS," wrote Duane, "arrived at Baltimore on Saturday last." "The arrival of this interesting man," he continued,

> was as might be expected, an object of interest and curiosity to the old who knew his services, and to the young who had heard of his fame in all the opposite modes which political sympathy or hatred could employ to express their respect or abhorrence of the asserter of freedom.

Duane's oblique reference to Paine's notorious *Age of Reason* was followed by a brief acknowledgment of the religious controversy that swirled around the great patriot-author of the American Revolution. "The writings of Mr. Paine on religious subjects," he added, "were not even mentioned, and the right of private opinion was neither assailed, nor brought into question."[1]

Duane had already expressed his own views on Paine's religious writings:

> The pretended crime of Thomas Paine, is his *Age of Reason*. We do not mean to defend that work. That has been undertaken by hundreds, and the book itself is now thrown by among other lumber. We assert however that the writing of that book, is not a proof of his impiety, nor can it be a justification of any person in attempting to asperse the man.

Duane's tone was defensive and apologetic. Like most Republicans, he was worried that the return of the old revolutionary and author of the *Age of Reason* would tarnish the public image of President Thomas Jefferson and give Federalists a chance to reopen the debate on Jefferson's religious "infidelity," a debate that had played a central role in the elections of 1800. But Duane wasn't willing to abandon Paine completely. He defended Paine's right to his religious views and attacked the Christian piety of Paine's assailants who, he claimed, were using religion "as in all former ages, as a MASK, to cover the attacks made on the man, whose writing vindicated *America* and the *Rights of Mankind*." But this was as close as he was willing to get to an outright defense of Paine's radical deist ideas.[2]

Duane was a brave man, a courageous journalist, and a deist himself, but even he was unwilling to defend Paine's hostility toward Christianity in public by 1802. And other Republicans were even more reluctant. While Paine was being vilified in the Federalist press as a "drunken atheist" whose return was an "insult to the moral sense of the nation," Republican editors and politicians kept silent and kept their distance.[3] Although Jefferson himself, who had helped to arrange Paine's return, met with him shortly after his arrival, he was acutely aware of the political hazards of his association with Paine and keen to dampen rather than aggravate the continued Federalist attacks on his religious beliefs. In January, he had issued his famous letter to the Danbury Baptists, defending the "rights of conscience" and the "wall of separation between Church and State." But he was also at work on his "Syllabus of an Estimate of the Merit of the Doctrines of Jesus, Compared with Those of Others" in which he rejected the "Deism of the Jews," endorsed the idea of a future state, and declared his own qualified faith in Christianity. Privately, he and Paine may have had much to discuss, but in public Jefferson was keen to display his respect for Christian orthodoxy.[4]

Religion had been a major issue in the presidential elections of 1800, pitting Jefferson as the author of the 1786 Virginia Statute of Religious Freedom and the representative of religious freedom and freedom of private conscience against Federalists who argued that his election would herald the triumph of religious infidelity and the moral corruption of the Republic. This conflict about personal religious belief was part of a broader conflict about the connection between Jefferson's private religious views and his public and political character, a conflict that ranged those who believed in a secular public sphere against those who believed religion and public life were indissolubly linked and that "Civil Magistrates are the chosen of God."[5] But after 1800, Federalist fears about Jefferson's election and the "triumph of infidelity" over Christianity went unrealized. Republicans had never embraced Paine's politicized deism and his belief that Christianity and all systems of belief based on religious revelation should be extirpated, and neither did most Americans, as the virulent public reaction to Paine's return in 1802 demonstrated all too clearly.

Mad Tom in a Rage. Unidentified artist, [1802–1803?]. Sometimes misidentified as Thomas Jefferson, the figure pulling down the federal edifice built by Washington and Adams is Thomas Paine, fueled by brandy and infidel ideas. This cartoon probably dates from Paine's controversial return to the United States in late 1802 and shows how politically threatening his radical deism had become by the turn of the century. Courtesy of the Huntington Library.

What triumphed in 1800 was not Paine's radical political deism but the depoliticized Christianity of the Jeffersonian Republican Party, a Christianity based on the strict separation of church and state, religion and politics, and a Christianity that became especially influential in the slaveholding regions of the South during the course of the nineteenth century. Ironically, the election of Thomas Jefferson did not establish the right of "infidels" to hold public office but the need for all candidates for public office to express their belief in Christianity—and for candidates like Jefferson, whose ideas about Christianity were far from orthodox, to mask their real religious views behind a public commitment to Christian orthodoxy. Federalists may have lost the election, but Republicans were forced to acquiesce in the creation of a new culture of religious commitment in American public life. Jefferson paid homage to this by his own religious evasion, and in this respect only, the election of 1800 witnessed the triumph of a different kind of infidelity, the sacrifice of public honesty to the demand for public religious conformity.[6]

William Duane was a true son of the British Empire. Born on the New York frontier on May 17, 1760, he was raised in colonial British America and Ireland, came of age in London, and spent his thirties in British India before returning to the United States at the age of thirty-six. Each of these places shaped his sense of identity and his understanding of politics. He was born in a cauldron of imperial politics. Lake Champlain, where his Irish Catholic father settled the family in the late 1750s, was on the frontier of British settlement but at the epicenter of the conflict among France, Britain, and Native Americans for control of North America. As a Catholic, his father supported the French and was wounded fighting the British during the French and Indian War. After his death in 1765, his wife, Anastasia, decided that the frontier was too dangerous for a widow and a young child, and Duane grew up roaming the streets of Philadelphia and New York during a period of intense political ferment. In these urban crucibles of the American Revolution, Duane witnessed much of the prerevolutionary drama of the 1760s and 1770s firsthand. These early experiences left a deep impression. Although he was only fourteen when he returned to Ireland with his mother in 1774, he retained a lasting affection for his native country. He loved America "from my first reasoning hour," he later wrote, and for the rest of his life considered himself to be an American.[7]

But he was also Irish by descent and upbringing. When his mother moved back to Ireland with her adolescent son, she also returned to her family, the Sarsfields, a Catholic land-owning family from Clonmel in County Tipperary, the birthplace of Laurence Sterne. Here, Duane was educated by Franciscans and raised by a family with a long and distinguished history of resistance to British rule in Ireland, a history he always refused to disown. "I am proud to say both my parents were Irish," he wrote later, "and to Ireland I am indebted for my education, and every qualification of heart and head (such as they are) that I do not owe to nature, my parents and a varied course of extensive experience in different parts of the world." Nobody could wish for the "emancipation of Ireland from the horrid yoke of Britain" more than he did. Duane's anticolonialism was partly a result of his experiences in America, and after his return to Ireland, he continued to support the American cause, claiming that his basic political principles were "inculcated from the declaration of Independence." But his Irish identity and commitment to Irish independence were also the result of political developments in Ireland, particularly the growth of the Volunteer movement in the 1770s. Established in 1778 in response to fears of a French invasion, the Volunteers rapidly became a focus for a resurgence of Irish nationalism. As support for the American Revolution grew and British authority in Ireland grew more precarious, the movement became a significant force in Irish politics. In 1779, the Dublin Volunteers, led by James Napper Tandy, organized public demonstrations and a trade boycott that forced the British to repeal restrictions on Irish trade, and the Volunteers played a key role in the political reform movement that developed in the early 1780s. Although the Volunteers drew their greatest strength from Presbyterian Ulster, their nonsectarian aims—greater political autonomy for Ireland, a more democratic franchise, economic reform, and the lifting of civil disabilities against Protestant dissenters and Catholics—appealed greatly to members of the Catholic middle class like Duane. In the same year that Tandy led demonstrations in Dublin against British policies, Duane took his first job as an apprentice to the printer of the *Clonmel Gazette*, a newspaper dedicated to the new politics of constitutional and economic reform.[8]

But it wasn't only politics that drew Duane toward the world of newspapers. He also needed a job. After his marriage to Catherine Corcoran, the daughter of a wealthy local Protestant family, his mother disinherited him, and his first child was born in 1780. Duane worked on the *Clonmel Gazette* for two years, but by 1782 the Volunteer movement was in decline, divided by the issue of Catholic emancipation, and prospects in Ireland for an ambitious, young Catholic seemed poor. Taking his wife and son (William Duane, Jr., a future secretary of the treasury under Andrew Jackson), he moved to London and took up residence with his paternal uncle Matthew Duane, a successful lawyer, fellow of the Royal Society, and trustee of the British Museum. "The most unexceptionable man in England," according to his client and neighbor Horace Walpole, Matthew Duane was also very honest, very rich, and a strict Roman Catholic. With no children of his own, he welcomed his young nephew into his home, and Duane quickly came to rely on his support. Determined not to follow his uncle into the legal profession, he found work in London as a parliamentary reporter for John Almon's *General Advertiser*, probably through Matthew Duane's connections with Walpole and the Whig political opposition.[9]

Working on the *General Advertiser* was a formative experience for Duane. Almon was a colorful and important figure in the world of London printing and politics, and he held strong views on the rights of the press. "The liberty of exposing and opposing a bad Administration by the pen," he wrote, "is among the necessary privileges of a free people, and is perhaps the greatest benefit that can be derived from the liberty of the press." A central figure in the opposition politics of the 1760s and 1770s, an ally of the radical politician John Wilkes, an opponent of the American war, and the publisher of the famous *Letters of Junius*, Almon's willingness to confront press censorship helped to bring about important changes in English libel law and gave the English press greater freedom to report parliamentary debates. By the time Duane went to work for him in 1782, Almon was at the end of his career but had lost none of his former combativeness. The *General Advertiser* was a fiercely anti-administration newspaper. After accusing Prime Minister William Pitt of pocketing £150,000 by speculating on the outcome of peace negotiations with the Dutch, Almon was found guilty of seditious libel against George III and forced to flee the country. His iconoclasm and commitment to press freedom taught Duane the qualities of character needed by a first-rate opposition editor.[10]

But Almon's example also taught Duane the costs of opposition. Parliamentary reporting was a hazardous profession in late eighteenth-century England. Although debates in Parliament were widely published by the 1780s, publication was still considered a "breach of privilege" under English law. As a reporter for the *General Advertiser*, Duane thus occupied a position that was to become familiar to him: at the heart of the political system and on the margins of political legality. Learning from experienced reporters like William "Memory" Woodfall of the *Morning Chronicle* (famous for his ability to reproduce parliamentary speeches accurately from memory), Duane received a rapid education in the rigors of parliamentary reporting and the factional intricacies of late eighteenth-century English politics. But as he moved through the newspaper offices, printing shops, and bookstores of the metropolis, he also grew familiar with a less visible political world: the world of London's radical artisans. Duane would encounter this world again as a member of the London Corresponding Society in the 1790s, when the activities and ideas of these artisans, deeply influenced by Thomas Paine's *Rights of Man*, would shake English society to its foundations. But his acquaintance with them now, while he was working for the more conventional *General Advertiser*, added the accents of English radicalism to the Irish and American inflections of his youth.[11]

Almon's legal problems with William Pitt may have contributed to Duane's sudden decision to leave England for India in late 1786, but it's more probable that the death of Matthew Duane in the previous year and the transfer of his substantial estate to another nephew, Matthew Bray, left Duane and his family once again dis-inherited. After trying unsuccessfully to secure passage to the United States, Duane enlisted as a lowly private in the military service of the East India Company, sent his wife and three children back to Clonmel, and boarded the *Rodney* bound for Calcutta, where he lived for the next nine years in the "luxurious and seducing climate" of British India. Calcutta was the center of British power and influence in India and was dominated by the British East India Company. Until 1785, the governor general, Warren Hastings, presided over a system of such legendary corruption that it inspired the passage of the India Act in 1784, the first concerted effort by the British government to wrest power from the East India Company and create a colonial state in India. In a campaign that mobilized widespread anxiety about British involvement in India and the corrupting influence of "Asiatic" wealth on English society and politics, Hastings was vilified by Edmund Burke and the Whig opposition and tried by Parliament in 1787.[12]

As a parliamentary reporter, Duane probably followed this political drama firsthand, and he knew that the new governor general of Bengal, Lord Cornwallis (of Yorktown fame), was charged with implementing the India Act and replacing the private authority of the East India Company with the public authority of the British Crown. After Duane's expulsion from India in 1795, his American friends argued that he was expelled for "attempting to disseminate the democratic principles of Tom Paine in his paper," and Duane himself later wrote that the "British entered India by fraud, proceeded by corruption, conquered by treachery, and established their dominion by the basest and most barbarous means." But when he first arrived in 1787, he was a loyal subject of the British Empire. His first brush with the authorities underlined this loyalty. In May 1791, rumors circulated in Calcutta that Governor Cornwallis had died on a military expedition to Bangalore. By this time, Duane had resigned his position as a clerk in the East India Company and become the editor of the *Bengal Journal*. Despite his American origins, he defended Cornwallis and the British, praising them as "among the most ardent advocates of freedom" and attributed the rumors to the French governor, Colonel Canaple, a monarchist "whose politics I detested and reprobated." When Canaple lodged a formal complaint with the British authorities, they insisted that Duane apologize and issue a public retraction. He agreed, but his subsequent actions further inflamed the situation. Convinced that he was defending British interests and the freedom of the press, he blamed the "despotic" character of French government in India for the entire incident, defending himself as someone "born and bred on the bosom of America and confirmed in my love of freedom by a long residence under the British Government."[13]

His loyalty didn't appease the Governor's Council, which ordered his immediate arrest and imprisonment at Fort William, site of the dreaded Black Hole of

Calcutta, until he could be "packed off to England." The experience was devastating for the idealistic young editor. After two months in solitary confinement and several futile appeals to the British administration and the courts, Duane was saved only by Canaple's sudden death and the intervention of a new French agent, who was more sympathetic to his politics. Chastened but undeterred, Duane quickly raised 10,000 rupees to start a new weekly paper, the *Indian World*, proclaiming in its first issue his right as a "citizen of the World" to discuss "all subjects whatever." But despite this radical declaration, the *Indian World* remained a good Whig newspaper, enthusiastic about the French Revolution, the *Rights of Man*, and the necessity for an alliance with the French Republic and friendly toward Lord Cornwallis, the British administration in Bengal, and British colonialism in India. Britons, among whom Duane still counted himself, may have lost an empire in America, he wrote, but they had "laid the foundation for civilization and the extension of science" in India and created a "new Empire of our own happy and secure to the nations of India and valuable to ourselves."[14]

Duane's effort to balance support for the French Revolution and the British Empire became harder to sustain after the outbreak of war between Britain and France, but it was local rather than international politics that landed Duane back in trouble, this time for airing the grievances of officers serving in the East India Company Army. Although the new governor general, Sir John Shore, was sympathetic to the officers, warning the British government that "the Temper of the Army is not disposed to bear with harsh resolutions," he was equally sure that the army could not bear the continued agitation of editors like Duane. In March 1794, Duane was served with an arrest warrant for debt, and a few days later he was dragged through the streets to the law courts "by a body of persons armed with clubs and chubdar sticks." His efforts to bring charges against those responsible proved futile, and a correspondent warned Duane that he now had the "whole influence of Government opposed to you." In late May, Shore asked the Governor's Council to expel Duane from India, and a few weeks later a group of armed sepoys ransacked his house. Reading the writing on the wall, Duane began to arrange his affairs and booked passage on the American ship *Hercules*. On December 26, 1794, the final issue of the *Indian World* appeared. "*Englishmen*," he wrote, drawing a new distinction between himself and his British readers, "I have experienced the blessings of Liberty in your country and for a time I wished to be as one of you." But now he wished only to return to his native land, America, where he trusted God he would find the freedom to "forget if possible that Slavery exists anywhere."[15]

Duane's trial was not over, however. Afraid that he would be detained before he sold his property, he wrote to the governor general, pleading for delay and threatening to publish "the state of Grievances which I have sustained under this

Government" unless Shore agreed to see him. Shore's response was swift. When Duane appeared the next day, expecting an audience with Shore, he was met by thirty sepoys who "sprung instantly from an inner apartment, and presented their bayonets to my breast." After clapping him in irons, they took him to Fort William. "I never expected to have seen Constantinople epitomized but on the Theatre," wrote Duane. "[I]t wanted but the Bowstring and the poisoned bowl to complete the Asiatic Costume Completely." Sir John Shore saw things differently. "Our newspapers in Calcutta have of late assumed licentiousness, too dangerous to be permitted in this Country," he told the colonial secretary, Henry Dundas:

> I have ordered one of the Editors to be sent to Europe; his name is William Duane, and I think You will agree with me, that his Conduct did not entitle him to the protection of the Company; he addressed a Letter to me, in terms of Intimidation, and as he had long been ordered to return to Europe, he was apprehended & confined to the Fort by my directions.[16]

On New Year's Day 1795, still not formally charged with any crime, Duane left India in the hold of the *William Pitt*. "I have lost all," he wrote, "for I know nothing of what has become of the fruits of seven years of industry." Taking with him only a few personal belongings: four containers of clothes, table linen, a few books, a chest of wine, three small cases of liquor, a sea cot, and some bedding, he was mystified by the "extraordinary violence" with which he had been treated. The voyage back to England took six months, made worse by the hostility of a captain who treated him as the "vilest of felons" and confined him aboard ship even during a month-long layover at St. Helena. Nonetheless, Duane still expressed hope that the "Honorable E. India Company will be too just to suffer the property of my children to be ruined and wasted," and when he arrived in London in July, he petitioned the company for redress, calculating his losses at about 100,000 rupees. "Without a resource but in your justice," he wrote, "I seek but the fruit of a meritorious labor wrested from me" and implored the company to take his "unsullied character" into account. After they referred his petition to their lawyers, Duane recognized the futility of his position and dropped the case. Penniless, embittered, and unemployed, he was quickly sucked into the vortex of English politics, and turning to the political radicals he had befriended since his return from India, he took a job as editor of the *Telegraph*, the journal of the London Corresponding Society.[17]

The importance of this period in Duane's life has been overlooked. When he returned to England in 1795, the country was in a state of deep political crisis. These were momentous and turbulent years in the history of English radicalism, and Duane was quickly caught up in the popular political agitation of the period. Fresh from his experience of persecution and humiliation in India, he plunged into the radical politics of the metropolis, breaking with the respectable, constitutionalist politics of Whig reformers like Charles James Fox and embracing the much less respectable republican politics of Thomas Paine. He was not alone. Paine's influence on Duane and his entire generation of British radicals is hard to overstate. "Paine dominated the popular radicalism of the early 1790s," argues the historian E. P. Thompson, and the publication of the *Rights of Man* in 1791–1792 was a decisive moment in the transformation of radical politics in Britain and the broader Atlantic world. "Hey for the New Jerusalem!" wrote the radical playwright Thomas Holcroft. "The Millen[n]ium! And peace and eternal beatitude be unto the soul of Thomas Paine."[18]

Paine's work injected a new revolutionary, republican tone into the discourse of British politics. His ringing conclusion to the first part of the *Rights of Man* captured brilliantly the political optimism inspired by the American and French revolutions. "From what we now see," declared Paine, "nothing of reform in the political world ought to be held improbable. It is an age of Revolutions, in which everything is to be looked for." Ordinary English men and women devoured copies of the *Rights of Man* when it appeared, and its author quickly became a household name. Part 2 was even more successful. Paine's powerful denunciation of economic inequality, his proposals for reforming the hated Poor Laws, and his hostility to idle wealth—"Ye who sit in ease, and solace yourselves in plenty...have ye thought of these things?"—struck a deep chord among working people struggling to cope with the industrial revolution. Hawked on street corners for six pence each, over 200,000 copies were printed in its first year. "Even children lisp the Rights of Man," wrote the Scottish poet Robert Burns in November 1792, and middle-class radicals like Benjamin Vaughan, who thought Paine's work was a "dangerous book for any person who does not share in the spoil," were forced to admit that the *Rights of Man* "is now made as much a standard book in this country, as Robinson Crusoe and the Pilgrim's Progress."[19]

But Paine's ideas not only created a "new rhetoric of radical egalitarianism," they also created a new plebian political movement, and the most important manifestation of this movement was the London Corresponding Society. By the time Duane joined the LCS in the summer or fall of 1795, the society was almost four years old and had become, under the leadership of Thomas Hardy and John Thelwall, the most important radical organization in Britain, the hub of a network of corresponding societies that extended throughout England, Scotland, and Ireland. Its first rule—"That the number of our members be unlimited"—reflected a membership of "shopkeepers, artisans, mechanics and laborers" that may have numbered 10,000 by 1795. Although the society was committed to radical political reform—universal manhood suffrage and annual parliaments—

rather than republican revolution, according to the Irish radical John Binns, "the wishes and hopes of many of its most influential members carried them to the overthrow of monarchy and the establishment of a republic."[20]

It may have been Binns, with whom Duane became "warm personal and political friends," who introduced him to the LCS and encouraged him to edit the *Telegraph*. Binns, a former participant in the Dublin Volunteer movement and a member of the United Irishmen who had fled repression in Ireland in 1794, became chairman of the LCS Executive Committee in 1795 and was part of a strong and extremely radical Irish contingent in the society. When a Loyalist mob attacked Thomas Hardy's house in 1795, Binns defended it with "about 100 men, chiefly members of the society, many of them Irish, armed with good shillelahs." Duane may have been among them. His decision to become editor of the *Telegraph* was certainly a brave one. After the declaration of war with France in 1793, government repression became severe. Terrified by the popular influence of Paine's work, the Crown issued a proclamation against seditious publications in 1792, tried and outlawed Paine in absentia, and ordered his work burned by the public hangman. In 1794, the Pitt government moved against the popular political societies, suspending habeas corpus and putting Hardy and Thelwall on trial for high treason. Although they were both acquitted, radical journalists like Duane were highly vulnerable to government prosecution, and by the mid-1790s "the political wing of Newgate prison could have been mistaken for a press corps club."[21]

By joining the LCS, Duane aligned himself with the most radical wing of the British reform movement, and as editor of the *Telegraph*, whose offices were a meeting place for LCS members, he placed himself at the heart of this movement. Here, he rubbed shoulders with agrarian radicals like Thomas Spence, author of *Pig's Meat* and *The End of Oppression*, and Citizen Richard Lee, whose pamphlets, published at "the TREE OF LIBERTY, No. 444, STRAND," included *The Happy Reign of George the Last* and *Citizen Guillotine; or, A Cure for the King's Evil*. Lee's publications captured the quasi-insurrectionary spirit of the LCS at this time, a spirit also expressed at the great public meetings convened by the society, the first of which was chaired by Citizen John Binns at Copenhagen House in Marylebone in October 1795 and attracted upward of 150,000 people. Duane almost certainly attended this meeting and was probably present in the streets three days later when crowds shouting, "Bread! Bread! Peace! Peace!" "No Pitt!" "No War!" and "No King!" stoned George III on his way to open Parliament. Binns thought that England was on the verge of revolution and so did the government. Blaming the disturbances on the LCS, the king immediately issued a proclamation against "Seditious and Unlawful Assemblies," and the government introduced the Two Acts, making it treasonable to "incite or stir up the people" against the Crown or the Constitution and placing the right to public assembly under close government supervision.[22]

E. P. Thompson describes the interval between the introduction and passage of the Two Acts as "the last, and greatest, period of popular agitation" in eighteenth-century England, and Duane was literally at its center. In November 1795, he was elected to chair a protest meeting against the Two Acts and the "unjust and ruinous war with France" that attracted "nearly four hundred thousand Britons." Attacking the royal proclamation as a violation of British rights, Citizen Duane expressed his belief in "the right to public Meetings and private deliberations; the necessity of private and public opinion, and free discussion on all topics which could interest or affect men." Citizen Jones more bluntly expressed his hope that the ministers responsible for such an "arbitrary measure against the long-established rights of the people, would answer for it with their heads." But rather than a prologue to the rising of radical England, this outburst of popular discontent was the final act. The passage of the Two Acts and the political repression instituted by the Pitt government drove the LCS and the English radical movement underground. In March 1796, Binns was arrested in Birmingham trying to rally the forces of provincial resistance, and the LCS entered a period of terminal disintegration and decline. By this time, internal divisions in the society were also undermining its unity and political effectiveness.[23]

The most important division was religious. If Paine's *Rights of Man* inspired the foundation of the LCS, his *Age of Reason* hastened its dissolution. Paine wrote the work in the shadow of the Terror—"My friends," he told Sam Adams, "were falling as fast as the guillotine could cut their heads off"—expressing his fear that the French were "running headlong into atheism" and that "in the general wreck of superstition, of false systems of government and theology, we lose sight of morality, of humanity, and of the theology that is true": a belief in one God. Like Noah Webster, Paine saw the Committee of Public Safety as a modern incarnation of the "intolerant spirit of church persecutions," but unlike Webster, he blamed Christianity rather than Catholicism. Although Paine had long been a deist, his open hostility toward Christianity was a new departure. Previously, his anticlerical rhetoric and belief in religious freedom had made his views indistinguishable from those of most American Protestants and British dissenters. When he had announced in the *Rights of Man* that the "present age will hereafter merit to be called the Age of Reason, and the present generation will appear to the future as the Adam of a new world," rational Christianity still had a place in his paradise.[24]

With the publication of the *Age of Reason*, Paine's revolutionary deism parted company with radical Protestantism. Paine's previous religious pluralism had been based on his belief that all religions were originally "kind and benign, and united with principles of morality" but became corrupted by their entanglement with political power. Now, he argued that all forms of revealed religion were inherently corrupt and oppressive and that the only reliable source of religious knowledge was the natural world—the "Bible of the Deist"—and the only reliable interpreter of this source was the individual consciousness. "My mind," wrote Paine, in a statement that captures perfectly the belief in radical intellectual autonomy that was the cornerstone of his thought, "is my own Church." Jettisoning his commitment to religious freedom, he claimed that he had long hoped that the American Revolution would inaugurate a "revolution in the System of religion" and restore "an unadulterated belief of one God." But the French Revolution had forced him to reconsider the relationship between religion and revolutionary politics. He had once believed that a revolution in the principles of government would lead to a revolution in the principles of religion; he now believed that a revolution in religion must come first. To ensure political freedom, Christianity had to be extirpated and its superstitious absurdities exposed. "Of all the systems of religion that ever were invented," he wrote in the *Age of Reason*, "none is more derogatory to the Almighty, more unedifying to man, more repugnant to reason, and more contradictory in itself, than this thing called Christianity."[25]

When the *Age of Reason* appeared in the spring of 1794, it was a sensation, spawning dozens of replies from Christian apologists in both Britain and the United States. Stung by this "war whoop of the pulpit," Paine then published part 2 of the *Age of Reason*—which he called his "two-and-six-penny Bible purge"— in late 1795. His assault on Christianity completed the alienation of middle-class dissenters like Joseph Priestley and moderate Whigs like Richard Watson, the Anglican bishop of Llandaff, who believed that Paine's "extraordinary performance" had "unsettled the faith of thousands" and spread its "poison through all the classes of the community." As Watson and others rightly feared, the *Age of Reason* found an enthusiastic audience among plebian radicals and marked the start of a "new and important aera" in which the "doctrines of infidelity…extensively circulated among the lower orders." The radical shoemaker Francis Place recalled reading the *Age of Reason* "with delight" in April 1794 and discussing it with his Irish landlord, who then introduced him to the LCS. According to Place, "nearly all its leading members were either Deists or Atheists," and W. H. Reid, a member of the society who wrote a sensational account of Paine's impact on the LCS, claimed that to hold a position of responsibility in the organization, a man had to be a "good Democrat and a Deist."[26]

This was not entirely true. Many LCS leaders were Christians, including Thomas Hardy and Citizen Richard Lee, and as subsequent events would show, so was much of the membership. Radicalism and religion were closely intertwined, both inside and outside the LCS. Richard Brothers, the millenarian radical who predicted that an earthquake would destroy London on the king's birthday in June 1795 and that French republican armies would triumph over their monarchical enemies, was the prophetic voice of plebian London in 1795–1796, and even the deist John Binns fell under his spell for a time. At first, the LCS leadership prevented religion from becoming a subject of controversy in the society, but the fierce public debate provoked by the *Age of Reason* made this increasingly difficult. Finally, in September 1795, Christian radicals in the LCS proposed a motion to the General Committee recommending the expulsion of "Atheists, Deists & other blasphemous Persons" who propagated "the most horrible doctrines, contrary to every principle of liberty, & which frighten all good Christians from the society." When the supporters of expulsion found they were outnumbered, they withdrew from the society; created a new organization, the Friends of Religious and Civil Liberty, whose members pledged to "believe in Scriptures"; and took a substantial minority of LCS members with them. The LCS founding principle of "members unlimited" had been tragically compromised by the influence of Paine's work.[27]

When this religious schism occurred, Duane sided with the majority. While he may not have been a radical deist when he arrived back in England, his exposure to infidel London and Paine's *Age of Reason* made him one. During 1795–1796, deist clubs and debating societies sprang up all over the city, and there was even a short-lived Temple of Reason in Whitecross Street where lectures were delivered "distinguished for their rancour or prejudices against Christianity." This lively deist culture clearly had an impact on Duane, and reading the *Age of Reason* strengthened his commitment to the sanctity of private conscience and the creation of a secular public sphere. But although he sided with the deists in the LCS, he also learned a valuable lesson about the divisiveness of religious controversy, and although he never repudiated the radical religious ideas of the *Age of Reason*, he never publicly embraced its hostility to Christianity. Duane's participation in the LCS and his brief but intense exposure to popular politics transformed him into a radical Republican but not a religious doctrinaire, and as he and other radical exiles helped to build the Republican Party in the 1790s, infusing it with the egalitarian spirit of Paine and the LCS, he kept his deism to himself, remembering that not all good democrats were deists.[28]

When Duane's boat docked in New York harbor on the Fourth of July 1796, he was thirty-six years old and a stranger to his native land. He arrived with his family virtually penniless and was forced to rely on his traveling companion, Thomas Lloyd, to help pay the cost of their passage to the United States. Duane had met Lloyd, a fellow Catholic and a former officer in the revolutionary army, while Lloyd was languishing in Newgate Prison, serving a three-year term for seditious libel. Duane may have played a role in securing Lloyd's release, but in any case the two men became good friends and later found work together on Thomas Bradford's *Merchant's Daily Advertiser*. Lloyd helped Duane and his family find their feet in New York, and helped him to make contact with the

William Duane, 1760–1835, by Charles B. J. F. de Saint-Mémin, 1802. This portrait of Duane was done as he reached the height of his political influence and importance as editor of the *Aurora*. Courtesy of the National Portrait Gallery, Smithsonian Institution; gift of Mr. and Mrs. Paul Mellon.

Republican press in Philadelphia, where Lloyd had worked for John Dunlap's *Pennsylvania Packet* in the 1780s. Less than three weeks after Duane's arrival, Bache's *Aurora* advertised for an experienced printer and editor interested in producing a "public Newspaper, conducted on pure republican principles," and invited those interested to apply to "W.D. at the Aurora office."[29]

Duane's connection with Bache may have existed even before his arrival in the United States. A paragraph in the *Aurora* in June 1795 publicized Duane's expulsion from India, and in March 1796, Bache reprinted the "Declaration of the Principles and Views of the London Corresponding Society" from the London

Telegraph, material that probably came from Duane. Although his advertisement suggests that he was in Philadelphia in July, Duane remained in New York until the fall, picking up hack work from the printer John Stewart, who asked him to write an additional volume for an American edition of John Gifford's *The History of France*. He may also have contributed to the *Aurora*. An article in August attacking Cobbett and British cruelty in Bengal bore all of the hallmarks of Duane's style. In any case, hoping to nurture his budding relationship with Bache and take advantage of the opportunities that existed in the capital city, Duane moved his family to Philadelphia in the winter of 1796, where he occupied a "room with his family, in a small frame house, in an alley" just off Fifth Street. Although William Wood Thackara described Duane as "wretchedly poor and friendless" when he arrived in Philadelphia, he quickly worked his way into the circle of Republican activists who gathered at the printing offices of the *Aurora*. By the end of 1796, according to the printer Matthew Carey, an "association" of Republican activists existed whose "Prime Leaders" included Bache, John Beckley, James Reynolds, Michael Leib, and William Duane, and it was these men who led the assault on George Washington and the Jay Treaty in 1796. Shortly after his arrival in Philadelphia, Duane must have sat down and composed his own contribution to this debate, *A Letter to George Washington, President of the United States*, which was published on December 6, 1796, under the pen name "Jasper Dwight, of Vermont."[30]

By the time Duane wrote his *Letter to Washington*, the debate on the Jay Treaty had been fought and lost. Nonetheless, his pamphlet was an important contribution to a barrage of Republican attacks on Washington provoked by his retirement from public office. Publishing the *Letter* was an astute move by Duane, establishing his political reputation and attracting just the kind of public notice and notoriety he needed to advance his career as a journalist. But, as he confessed, it was hastily planned and executed, somewhat rambling and disconnected, and revealed his basic lack of familiarity with American politics. Unlike many other attacks on Washington, however, the essay had a well-defined target, the Farewell Address, and a coherent and well-developed message: "to expose the PERSONAL IDOLATRY into which we have been heedlessly running" and to reveal to Americans "the fallibility of the most favored of men, [and] the necessity of thinking for themselves." With brilliant political instincts (instincts he displayed again and again in the late 1790s), Duane picked up the religious themes that had run submerged through public debates about Washington since 1793. But the *Letter* was not a crude exercise in political iconoclasm. His approach to Washington was restrained and respectful rather than scurrilous and vituperative, presenting the president as a man of ruined magnificence and venal self-importance.[31]

At the heart of Duane's argument was his attack on the cult of personality that surrounded Washington and the political and ideological conformity that sustained this cult. Directly challenging one of the central arguments of Washington's Farewell Address—his belief that morality was the "necessary spring of popular government" and that "religious principle" was indispensable to its preservation—Duane detected in his views an effort to establish uniformity of opinion and "dogmas repugnant to free government, [and] subversive of the right of private judgment." He also detected a veiled attack on the principles of Thomas Paine, and the entire essay reflected Paine's powerful influence. Counterposing the figure of Paine to that of Washington, Duane declared: "I cannot suffer the spirit of party rancour under the mask of religion to overturn and annihilate the gratitude which this nation owes to that great man THOMAS PAINE." Although he declined to defend "his writings on the subject of revelation," Duane vigorously defended Paine's right to produce them:

> Alas! What is belief if it is not free!—what must become of the Jew, the savage, the Mahometan, the Idolator, upon all of whom the sun shines equally, whom the same heart warms and the same cold chills, must I allow no virtue, no right of opinion on matters which divide and have divided all mankind in all periods and times, upon which even we ourselves are split into countless sects.

"Are we," asked Duane, "to close up the doors of discussion against him, who desires every man only to think for himself?"

Washington's emphasis on the connections among religion, a moral life, and political liberty, believed Duane, contained the seeds of a "design to erect a national church among us." "Religion should be kept apart from politics," he wrote. "[T]emporal establishments are never bettered by spiritual influence; they have always corrupted each other, and slavery has been the fate of all who have fallen within their united jurisdiction." And Washington's hostility toward faction and political parties betrayed a similar desire to impose a stultifying orthodoxy on Americans. "Who are they," demanded Duane, "that the constitution appoints to restrain private deliberation and mark the line beyond which freedom becomes sedition." Political beliefs, like religious beliefs, were best left to the "opinion of every free citizen," and just as personal religious beliefs found legitimate expression in religious institutions, so personal political beliefs could be legitimately expressed in party organizations. The "spirit of party" was not an unfortunate sign of man's innate depravity, argued Duane, but an expression of his "spirit of resistance to oppression, the spirit of philanthropy, the spirit of benevolence, of humanity."[32]

By the time Duane published his *Letter to George Washington*, religion was very much in the air. The catalyst for this development was once again Paine's *Age of Reason*. Between late 1794 and the end of 1796, at least seventeen editions of the *Age of Reason* (parts 1 and 2) were published in the United States, making it the most widely circulated religious work of the eighteenth century. It also provoked a flood of hostile religious polemic. American clergymen like Jeremy Belknap and Elhanan Winchester rushed into print against Paine, and major British critics like Hannah More and Bishop Watson were reprinted in America. Boston merchants distributed 200 copies of Watson's *Apology for the Bible* to students at Harvard College, who drank a toast to "the learned and worthy *Bishop of Llandaff*, and his unanswerable letters to the scoffer at *christianity* and villifier of *Washington*." In the year 1794 alone, five editions of Thomas Williams's *Age of Infidelity* and four editions of Gilbert Wakefield's *An Examination of the Age of Reason* were published. Joseph Priestley, who had already published a reply to the first part of the *Age of Reason*, was so concerned by the "torrent" of unbelief that Paine's work had unleashed that he produced a reply to the second part as well. By 1801, when Elias Boudinot published his *Age of Revelation; or, The Age of Reason Shown to Be an Age of Infidelity*, more than fifty pamphlet-length responses to the *Age of Reason* had rolled off American presses, and Thomas Paine had come to personify the issue of religious infidelity.[33]

But the impact of the *Age of Reason* on American politics was even more profound than its impact on American religion. Prior to its publication, religion had not been a major public issue, and religious divisions had not been a major source of partisan identity. Although the *Age of Reason* did not transform the religious landscape of the United States, it politicized the issue of religion itself, giving the clergy an opportunity to reassert their traditional role as guardians of public virtue. It also gave Federalists a chance to portray Republicans as agents of infidelity and themselves as defenders of Christian orthodoxy and to make belief in Christianity a litmus test for holding public office.[34]

Among radicals, enthusiasm for Paine's work was divided. Bache, a deist like his grandfather, who sold copies of Robespierre's "Report on the Principles of Public Morality" at the *Aurora*, received 10,000 copies of the *Age of Reason* directly from Paine and sold them to the public at a price that Cobbett alleged would "hardly pay the cost[s] and expenses." Although the book sold well and circulated widely, it didn't spark a popular deist movement like that in Britain, and according to one scholar, Paine's militant anti-Christian deism "never spread beyond a half-dozen committed societies." The most well known of these, Elihu Palmer's Society of Theophilanthropists, founded in New York City in 1795, had little popular influence.[35] Most supporters of Paine's politics were disappointed by his attack on Christian revelation and felt he had "wounded the warm and tender feelings of more than a million of his real friends." A few were actively hostile. Thomas Greenleaf, the fiery editor of the New York *Argus*, whose masthead declared, "We guard the Rights of Man," printed attacks on Paine and pronounced his abhorrence of "all Deistical and every other anti-Christian tenet," but most Republican editors passed quietly over Paine's work or presented it to readers in a way that emphasized their own religious impartiality.[36]

While the *Age of Reason* created few deist disciples and alienated Christian Republicans, it provoked a strong backlash among Christian Federalists that propelled its clerical opponents to the center of the political stage in the late 1790s. Before the mid-1790s, most American clergymen welcomed the French Revolution as an extension of the revolutionary principles of 1776 and as a blow against their traditional religious enemy, the Roman Catholic church. The growth of religious infidelity was an unfortunate but inevitable part of the destruction of French Catholicism, they argued, and they believed that a purified Protestant France would eventually emerge from the religious rubble of the French Revolution.[37] These millennial expectations were dampened slightly by the Terror and the inauguration of Robespierre's civil religion, but most clergymen remained optimistic. In his Thanksgiving Day sermon in 1794, the Reverend Jedediah Morse, who later achieved notoriety as an implacable foe of French infidelity, delivered a sermon to his congregation in which he called the French Revolution "unquestionably good" and described its anti-Christian policies as part of a divine plan to rid the world of papal tyranny.[38]

The *Age of Reason* shattered this religious consensus, undermining support for the revolution among Federalist clergy and conservative Christians, especially in New England. "Tom Paine," wrote the Massachusetts Federalist Fisher Ames with delight, "has kindly cured our clergy of their prejudices." Having assumed that American Protestantism would redeem France, they now feared that French infidelity would corrupt the United States. And as Federalists began to equate support for the French Revolution with opposition to Christianity, they also began to blame Republicans for what they believed was a rising tide of infidelity. Ever since the appearance of the *Age of Reason*, complained one Republican, Paine's religious beliefs had been attributed to everybody who shared his politics "and hence to be a Republican, a Frenchman, or an admirer of the French Revolution, was supposed to be synonymous to a disorganizer, and an infidel, anxious to overthrow every vestige of the Christian system."[39]

Paine's work served as a catalyst for the emergence of Christianity as a partisan issue in national politics and for the emergence of the Federalist clergy as key political spokesmen. There was more at work here than fear about the spread of deism. Underlying partisan debate about religious infidelity was a more wide-ranging debate about the relationship between religious belief and political order. Americans had long regarded Christianity as an indispensable basis for civil and political order, and the creation of a republic only reinforced this belief. As Washington warned in his Farewell Address, public virtue was impossible to sustain without religious belief, and without public virtue, responsible citizenship, political leadership, and national cohesion were impossible to sustain. "Feeble indeed would be the guardians of virtue, slender the fences that policy might erect against transgression," argued John Fenno in the *Gazette of the United States*, "did not man feel a dread of that Being from whose eye not a spot in the universe lies concealed":

> A belief in his superintending providence—that he is the detector of the heart, and the punisher of human wickedness, alone creates the sanctity of an oath, fixes the basis of virtue, and preserves inviolate the laws of justice....religion is the soul of duty—it forms the intrepid soldier, the conscientious legislator, the faithful magistrate, and the upright judge; it is the great basis of civil government and of society.[40]

Republican government could never be based on the pursuit of self-interest, and because a belief in the "superintending providence" of God was the only way to prevent men from pursuing their own interests to the exclusion of the public good, unbelief eroded the moral basis of republican government. Paine's individualism, argued his conservative critics, who dubbed him "Citizen Ego," eroded the self-restraint upon which a republican social and political order depended.[41]

By the mid-1790s, many Federalist clergymen blamed Paine and infidel ideas for the rampant materialism and violent partisanship of American life. What else could explain the growth of systematic political opposition and the degeneration of American political discourse? The lack of reverence for leaders elected by the people themselves? The vicious attacks on the character and reputation of George Washington and the general animosity and scurrility of the party press? The ominous spread of politically inspired mob violence, assault, and dueling? Weren't these signs of a deeper crisis that had its origins in the corruption of private and personal life? Wasn't corrosive self-interest eating away at the sources of private sociability, domestic relations, and the inner recesses of family life? The Reverend Ashbel Green thought so. He believed that the "infidelity" of American society was revealed not only by its "contempt of gospel institutions" but also by

> the neglect of family government and family religion, the dissoluteness of youth, the wanton and wicked reviling of magistrates, the exciting of hatred against them, the cherishing of seditious practices, the opposition to the laws of the country, the prevalence of dueling, the open practice of adultery and fornication, the multiplied instance of fraud and swindling, the gross and abusive attacks on private character and reputation, [and] the devotedness of thousands to the covetous pursuit of wealth.[42]

To clergymen like Green, support for Paine and the French Revolution were symptoms of a society that had lost its moral and religious bearings, signs of an age of infidelity in which self-assertion and self-interest had replaced the natural deference toward familial, religious, and political leaders, corroding the bonds of amity, kinship, and interest that held Americans together. They reacted to the *Age of Reason* by launching jeremiads against what Webster called the "demoralization" of American society. Linking the threat of French infidelity to the divisiveness of domestic politics and casting both in a language of moral and religious crisis, Federalist clergy successfully reasserted their waning influence over American public life and mobilized a growing sense of public alarm behind a defense of Christian orthodoxy and Federalist politics.

The Federalist crusade against infidelity made religion a central political issue in the late 1790s. But rather than discrediting and dividing Republicans, the Federalist campaign ignited a fierce public debate about the relationship between religion and politics that ultimately benefited and unified them. As guardians of religion and moral order, Federalist clergymen believed that they had a right and a duty to participate in public life. They had always done so, especially in New England, where Fast Day and Election Day sermons were an integral part of the public culture. But as the clergy began to reassert their public role in the mid-1790s (partly in response to the growing influence of the press), Republican journalists challenged their right to participate in public life. As the author of "Press versus Pulpit" argued, clergymen should cease "substituting *political polemics* for lessons of practical Christianity and benevolence." Clerical interference in politics not only injected religion improperly into public affairs but undermined the pastoral role of the clergy, distracting them from their most important task, preaching the lessons of the gospel, lessons that had nothing to do with politics.[43]

Underlying this debate lay radically different views about the relationship between religion and politics, church and state. While Federalist clergymen believed that religion should play a central role in public life and that civic engagement was an important part of religious life, Republican commentators argued exactly the opposite: religion had no legitimate role to play in public life, and politics had no legitimate part to play in religious life. Religious belief was a matter of private conscience, not public morality, they argued, and just as the state had no right to regulate religious belief (or any other expression of private conscience), so personal religious belief had no place in the regulation of an impersonal, secular public sphere. Clergy should restrict themselves to the spiritual needs of their congregations and stay out of public life. Religious and political freedom required a sharp separation of church and state, an idea that received its classic formulation in Jefferson's Virginia Statute of Religious Freedom, the touchstone of Republican religious policy in the 1790s. While Federalists tried to identify Republicans with Paine's radical deism and French infidelity, Republicans insisted that their commitment to Jeffersonian ideas of religious freedom made them the true guardians of American Christianity.

By the spring of 1797, Duane and Lloyd had found work in Philadelphia editing Thomas Bradford's *Merchant's Daily Advertiser*, possibly with Duane's old comrade from the London Corresponding Society, Citizen Richard Lee. But after a public brawl with Bradford over a pay dispute in July, Duane was bound over by the mayor for disturbing the peace and found himself once again unemployed. According to Cobbett, he immediately found work on James Carey's *Daily Advertiser*, but when Carey's newspaper folded in September, Benjamin Franklin Bache recommended Duane to Andrew Brown, Jr., the owner of the politically moderate *Philadelphia Gazette*. Once again, Duane found it hard to get along with the proprietor, and in the summer of 1798, he parted ways with Brown and was forced to look for work as a journeyman printer. This was a humiliating and difficult time for him. His wife, who was expecting their fourth child, contracted cholera, and Duane experienced a series of "petty embarrassments," the most serious of which was his inability to pay the rent. Consequently, in June his landlady, "an unconscionable foul mouthed Dutch woman," seized his belongings and evicted the entire Duane family. Then, in mid-July, his wife died. Amid these tragic circumstances, fortune finally favored Duane. On July 13, James Thomson Callender, Bache's chief editorial writer and assistant, fled to Richmond, Virginia, afraid he would fall victim to the Sedition Act that President Adams was due to sign into law the next day. Bache hired Duane to replace Callender on the *Aurora*, and the penurious writer found himself working for a newspaper that was virtually a national daily.[44]

When Duane started working for the *Aurora*, the Republican opposition had reached a nadir. Their efforts to defeat the Jay Treaty by rallying the country behind conflict with Great Britain and challenging Washington's prestige and popularity had failed, inaugurating a period of Federalist political dominance symbolized by John Adams's election to the presidency in late 1796, the revival of popular anti-Gallicanism, and the influence of *Porcupine's Gazette*. "Porcupine's Gazette," wrote Duane in July 1797,

> is the universal source and topic of conversation—it is the inseparable companion of the country house and ornaments the morning toilette of modesty—it furnishes refined sarcasm for the tea-table, and the want of ideas to the evening lounger....among its patrons are to be found men of high trust in government, members of the legislature, members of philosophical and literary societies, and a great number of the clergy of all denominations!

The source of Cobbett's popularity was the sharp deterioration in diplomatic relations with France caused by the passage of the Jay Treaty, which France regarded as a violation of its treaty agreements with the United States. By early 1798, retaliatory attacks on American merchant shipping and the refusal of the French to negotiate had brought the sister republics to the brink of war. This tense political atmosphere was made even more explosive by the publication of the XYZ letters in April, which exposed the efforts of the French foreign minister, Talleyrand, to solicit bribes from the American negotiators, unleashing a storm of public protest against France and a wave of popular support for President John Adams. Rallying the public around the cry "Millions for defense but not one cent for tribute," Federalists organized public meetings throughout the country, which issued patriotic addresses to the president, and organized public subscriptions to finance warships, military defenses, and militia companies. "The President and his Ministers," wrote an astonished Fisher Ames in June 1798, "are decidedly popular."[45]

As war with France loomed and Federalists fueled popular fears of a French military invasion, the volatile war of words that had previously been waged in public assemblies and the press spilled into the streets. When John Adams declared a national Fast Day on May 9, 1798—"to engage [the] Powers above against the French," complained the cranky Republican Nathaniel Ames—and Cobbett instructed Federalists to demonstrate support for the government by wearing black cockades, partisan conflict assumed a new ferocity and public visibility. Provoked by Cobbett, Republicans donned tricolor cockades, and the Fast Day, which some had hoped would be a day of quiet prayer and national unity, degenerated into "a day of riot and disorders." Similar disturbances punctuated the spring and summer of 1798. In July, a group of boatmen singing a French revolutionary song, "Ça Ira," assaulted a group of Federalists singing the new patriotic anthem "Hail Columbia" on the Battery in New York, and the next night hundreds of rowdy, young partisans gathered on the Battery to do battle, in the end without serious incident.[46]

Federalists exploited public alarm about this political disorder and the surge of anti-Gallican nationalism produced by the confrontation with France to enact a legislative program of military preparedness and domestic political repression. In April, they began to "press for an alien & sedition law," and by the end of July, Congress had passed the Alien and Sedition Acts, giving the federal government sweeping new powers to arrest and deport "alien" subversives without trial and to prosecute expressions of political sedition, both measures designed to limit the influence of Republican journalists, especially the group of Anglo-Irish radicals (including Duane) gathered around the *Aurora*. These legislative measures were accompanied by a series of well-orchestrated public campaigns against Irish immigrants, partisan violence in the press, and French infidelity, issues that resonated powerfully with the public and put Republicans on the political defensive. Although Bache kept the tone of the *Aurora* upbeat and denied Federalist claims that he was losing subscribers, events favored the Federalists. In March, Bache had thought "the people begin to see their madness

The Cinque-Tetes; or, The Paris Monster. This violently anti-revolutionary cartoon illustrates American hostility toward the French Republic by 1798. A commentary on the XYZ Affair, it juxtaposes three honest and gentlemanly American commissioners with a rapacious five-headed monster that represents the French directory and demands "Money, Money, Money" from them. The figures on the right are clearly designed to remind Americans about the horrors of the Terror and the threat posed by the slave rebellion in Haiti. Such a cartoon was intended to have broad popular appeal. Courtesy of the Huntington Library.

in preferring John Adams and a French war to Thomas Jefferson and a French peace," but after the publication of the XYZ letters, these hopes were dashed. "LOST—by the Editor of the Aurora, THE PEOPLE," crowed John Fenno in the *Gazette of the United States.* Even Bache was forced to admit that public opinion had abandoned the Republicans and the country was on "the eve of war, if not actually at war with the French Republic."[47]

Bache's support for the French Republic and his opposition to war made him a prime target for unofficial and official Federalist repression. During the Fast Day riots in May, a crowd of young Federalists, outraged by his opposition to the Fast Day, attacked his house and terrorized his family, and in August he was assaulted by John Ward Fenno, the son of the editor of the *Gazette of the United States.* More seriously, the Federalist press hounded him as an agent of France and a traitor to his country. On June 26, just as the sedition bill came before Congress, the federal government arrested and charged him under the common law with "libelling the President & the executive Government." Bache was unbowed, promising to uphold the "cause of truth and republicanism" despite being made a "victim to the dark rage of the worst enemies of our government and liberties." The *Aurora*, he declared, would always be "a scourge to Tyrants of every denomination." As the worst yellow fever epidemic since 1793 swept through Philadelphia in the summer of 1798, Bache refused to suspend publication of the *Aurora*. On September 4, he advertised for a new pressman, describing the atmosphere at the newspaper as "airy and healthful." Two days later, he fell ill with yellow fever, and on September 10 he died, and the *Aurora* ceased publication.[48]

The political crisis of 1798 transformed Republican political rhetoric. Confronted by a fierce popular backlash against the French Republic and growing dismay about partisan political violence, which Federalists blamed on Irish immigrants, irresponsible journalists, and French infidelity, Republicans were compelled to adapt to a more conservative public mood. Signs of this shift were quickly apparent. Commenting on the partisan violence in New York, Thomas Greenleaf blamed it on Federalists like Cobbett, who claimed that "unless the throats of the Jacobins are cut, the blood of the Federalists will soon run down the gutters of Philadelphia." "In truth," wrote Greenleaf, it was the Federalists who posed a threat to peace and public order and had "become the Jacobins of this country." After his house was attacked in the Fast Day riots, Bache had warned darkly that the "work of blood once begun, who will say where it will stop." Urging magistrates to ban partisan cockades in the interest of national unity, he argued that the riots "should be a warning and teach our citizens to discard a badge, which can only tend to mark division among us, and increase the heat of party spirit." Another writer in the *Aurora* evoked the bloodshed of the French Revolution, warning readers that partisan uniforms and the creation of "hostile corps" were a prelude to "ruin and murder" and civil war.[49]

These arguments revealed a subtle but critical shift in the terms of Republican political discourse. Despite their continued support for France, Bache and other Republican journalists began to use the language of anti-Jacobinism against Federalists, adopting a rhetorical strategy that exploited rather than challenged popular discontent with France and popular disillusionment with the French Revolution. Accommodating themselves to a political environment that was increasingly hostile to revolutionary politics, Republicans began to place new emphasis on the virtues of public order, social integration, and political harmony. "It is a serious source of regret to the real friend of his country and of alarm to the friend of peace and quiet to find the spirit of party bursting forth in acts of violence," Bache had written after the disturbances on the New York Battery in July. By insisting that everyone who refused to wear a black cockade was a "disorganizer, a Jacobin, a pensioned tool of the French," he argued, Federalists were trying to "excite a civil war in our country," and it was the duty of the authorities to "repress this party heat." A memorial to the government from Republicans in Caroline County, Virginia, took up the same theme, condemning the alarmist writings of Peter Porcupine and demanding that the government indict him under the Sedition Act for "Jacobinism." Republican rhetoric had taken what turned out to be a permanent lurch to the right.[50]

The turning point for this rhetorical volte-face was the passage of the Sedition Act in late July, just a week or so after Duane joined the *Aurora* as Bache's new editorial assistant. While Federalists argued that the Sedition Act was necessary to rescue the country from Jacobin Republicans, Republicans argued that the act expressed the political intolerance and Jacobinism of the Federalist Party. Writing in the *Argus*, "Brutus" interpreted the act as a prelude to political revolution and a sign that Federalists intended to introduce "into this country, the system of Jacobinism." Republicans, he warned, should "arm and discipline themselves without delay, to defend their persons and property against every illegal violence," and he advised them to create armed Republican militias to defend their country against foreign invasion and the "Jacobinical mob." Bache, who had earlier described Federalists as bloodthirsty advocates of the guillotine, condemned the Sedition Act as part of a "system of terror" employed by Federalists to crush political opposition.[51]

The Sedition Act not only gave Republicans a chance to castigate Federalists as Jacobins, it allowed them to portray themselves as a party of political order and constitutional orthodoxy, and they seized the opportunity with relish. Citing the First Amendment liberally in their discussions of the Sedition Act, Republicans attacked Federalists as dangerous innovators who had betrayed the first principles of the Constitution. "Our motto and principles," trumpeted the author of "The Spirit of the Press" in the *Aurora*, "are, *an attachment to the* CONSTITUTION." "To the laws of our country," he continued sententiously,

> we owe that profound submission, which a Republican will never withhold. But to the *constitution* upon which alone those laws must be founded, and to the *people* for whose security it was established, we owe duties still more sacred, and these we will never violate.

A toast condemning the Sedition Act at a Republican Fourth of July celebration in Newburgh, New York, in 1798 put the matter more succinctly: "The Constitution; the Constitution; no deviation from the Constitution."[52]

This new enthusiasm for the Constitution did not go unnoticed. Those same Republicans who had been "cursers and opposers of the Constitution for the last nine years," pointed out John Fenno, were now its most ardent advocates. But such logic was easily turned back on Federalists themselves, whom Bache accused of violating their "*solemn oaths*" to preserve and defend the Constitution. The Sedition Act even allowed Republicans to portray themselves as guardians of the religious status quo. Writing in the *Aurora*, "Obadiah" (who sounded a lot like William Duane) claimed that he had quit the Federalist Party in disgust when the Sedition Act was passed. Within the confines of the law, he argued, "each man was free to think for himself," but the Sedition Act showed that the Federalists wished to impose "one standard of opinion" on the whole society, and such "persecution for political opinions" could easily "terminate in persecution for religious ones." While Federalists claimed that Republicans were immoral agents of French infidelity, Republicans claimed that Federalists were religious inquisitors and fanatics, casting themselves as apostles of religious tolerance and pluralism. The new mood of the Republican Party was captured perfectly at a public banquet to protest the Sedition Act and the prospect of war with France. After toasts attacking Federalist encroachments on the Constitution and applauding "liberty of *speech*—the *pen*—and the *press*," those in attendance drank to "National unanimity" and a spirit of "True and genuine federalism." Two years before Jefferson's first inaugural speech would declare "we are all republicans, we are all federalists," the spirit of party conciliation was already in the air.[53]

When the *Aurora* appeared again on November 1, Bache's widow, Margaret, was its proprietor and William Duane was its editor. Both Duane and the newspaper were in bad shape. In early September, Duane had fallen ill, complaining about a mercury cure that left his "gums inflamed, teeth loose, and my face swelled." Responsible for Bache's young widow (whom he married in 1800) and her four children, in addition to his own four motherless children, money was a daily problem. After selling a gold watch for $50, he begged Tench Coxe, the *Aurora*'s unofficial "fiscal manager," for a further $100 to cover the expenses of "my late friend's funeral," pay the wages of two apprentices who worked at the *Aurora*, and meet his family's expenses. He also asked Coxe to approach Alexander James Dallas for another $50–100. But despite these personal and financial problems, Duane showed a steely determination to reestablish the *Aurora* and to prevent the spirits of the "friends of liberty as much as possible from drooping." Fortunately, public support for the newspaper was still strong, although delinquent subscribers owed the *Aurora* between $15,000 and $20,000, and as Duane told Coxe, "*Newspaper debts are the worst of all others.*" Nonetheless, with the help of Dr. Michael Leib, he quickly regained his own health, and with the help of Coxe and other Republican donors, he quickly restored the health of the newspaper.[54]

Duane took over the *Aurora* at a critical moment in the history of the Republican Party. By the end of 1798, the Republican press was in disarray, and the *Aurora* stood almost alone as a standard-bearer for the political opposition. The crisis with France had created a new and more challenging context for Republican politics, and the close association that Republicans had cultivated with the French Republic now returned to haunt them. The Federalist counterattack of 1798—the campaign against alien immigrants, political sedition, and religious infidelity—attracted support across partisan lines, and Republicans were compelled to adapt. A Fourth of July toast in 1797, praising "The DEMOCRATIC PRINTERS throughout Republican America," also warned them not to abuse "the influence they hold over the public mind" and to remember their responsibility for the "political and moral character of the nation." In their efforts to reconstitute the Republican coalition, journalists like Duane could not ignore such sentiments. Ironically, although it was Federalists who helped conjure into being a new "politics of order," it was the Republicans who exploited this political atmosphere most imaginatively and successfully, and William Duane's *Aurora* led the way.[55]

Because the partisan rhetoric of the day shapes our understanding of the late 1790s, it is hard not to see this period as one of Federalist terror. But although this phrase captures the political dominance of the Federalists in 1798–1799, it reflects an understanding of the period fashioned by Republican editors and journalists like Duane. His first opportunity to portray Republicans as supporters of "Order and Good Government" was a controversy created by an alleged riot at St. Mary's Church in Philadelphia on February 9, 1799. Duane had gone to St. Mary's, a Catholic church with a largely Irish congregation, accompanied by Samuel Cummings, a journeyman at the *Aurora*, Dr. James Reynolds, and Robert Moore, both recent Irish immigrants and former members of the United Irishmen, to collect signatures for a petition demanding the repeal of the Alien Act. Cobbett claimed that, after the service, Reynolds harangued the crowd from a tombstone, and when church trustees tried to disperse the crowd, he "pulled from his pocket a loaded pistol." Mathew Carey, on the other hand, claimed that Reynolds had been peacefully collecting signatures and was "severely handled" by the crowd before he pulled his pistol. But in any case, when Reynolds pulled the pistol (later claiming he had been warned of a possible attempt on his life), the crowd seized what Cobbett called "REYNOLDS and his gang" and hauled them through the streets of Philadelphia to the mayor, who refused to release them until they had posted a bond of $4,000 each.[56]

At the trial two weeks later, Reynolds was charged with attempted murder and the other defendants, including Duane, with riot and assault. Francis Hopkinson, the state prosecutor, made their foreign origins a central part of his case against the defendants, attacking them as a "foreign junto" and an "imported gang of discomfited seditious [men]," who brazenly meddled in the political affairs of a country of which they were not citizens and who fomented party divisions and political violence. However, the jury disagreed, and after an eloquent address on behalf of the defendants by Alexander James Dallas, they dismissed the charges against Duane, Reynolds, and the others. Nonetheless, the Federalist press had a field day. The "riot," argued Fenno with considerable exaggeration, was the "most daring and flagitious riot that we remember to have outraged the civil law and the decorum of the society for more than forty years," proving that the threat to political order posed by the growth of the United Irishmen in the United States, a threat Cobbett had been warning about since 1798, was real. "That there is such a banditti," wrote Fenno, "organised for the subversion of government, and the establishment of a system of anarchy and terror, cannot longer be doubted by the most incredulous."[57]

Naturally, Duane interpreted the "riot" quite differently. To him, the entire episode symbolized the campaign of official and unofficial intimidation that Federalists had waged since the passage of the Sedition Act. Only the calm, independent "verdict of an honest jury" had saved the peaceful petitioners from the "unprincipled measures" of the Federalists. Using arbitrary legal power and the violence of the mob, Federalists had tried to silence those who opposed the Alien Act. "Could it be believed," wrote Duane after the trial, "that in civilized society, four men should be attacked with violence, taken into custody, laid under an enormous sum of 4000 Dollars bail each to appear to stand trial…for the peaceable pursuit of obtaining signatures to a petition?" Federalists, not Republicans, were responsible for the partisan violence that was undermining the civility of public life. The "spirit" of what he called "disappointed faction" lay behind the prosecutions, "faction palsied in a daring effort to pervert the laws to its purposes, and to oppress men who are assailable by no other means, than by the means of tyrants and assassins."[58]

Duane's reference to "disappointed faction" was significant. Two days before he wrote these words, President John Adams had announced his desire to resume diplomatic negotiations with France. His decision stunned Federalists and cut the ground from beneath the war hawks in the party. At first, Cobbett refused to believe that Adams had executed such a dramatic policy reversal, but as the truth became clear, he reacted with characteristic savagery.[59] So did his protégé John Ward Fenno, who published a lengthy essay in the *Gazette of the United States*, pouring out his disgust with American society and politics. Part political jeremiad, part resignation letter, his essay proved to be a political epitaph for the pro-war wing of the Federalist Party. Perhaps out of respect for his dead father, who had supported Adams throughout the 1790s, the younger Fenno did not attack Adams directly. But he made clear the four principal failings of American public life:

1. The imbecility of our frame of government
2. The general depravity of morals
3. The influence of newspapers and the dearth of literature
4. The absence of national character & public spirit

The Constitution, he argued, was a "system of shifts and expedients" that failed to ensure the "organization of regular government." "Religious and moral institutions," which had a far greater influence on "character and conduct than the wisest political systems," had also failed to ensure national integration. But at the root of all of these problems was the partisan press.[60]

His father, John Fenno, had once believed that the "powerful influence of the press" could create a national culture, but now John Ward Fenno declared that vision to be "hopeless." The "formidable *propagande*" of the press had established an ascendancy over the public that kept the country in a constant state of "insurrection and revolution." American newspapers, he argued, edited by "ignorant, mercenary and vulgar automatons," were a national disgrace, a "mass of corruption" that had "stained with superlative and indelible reproach, the name, forms and character of republican government." The malign power of the press, government weakness, and the "*desolating force of the demoralizing principles that prevail*" had produced a "perfect non-entity of national character." The young Fenno had hoped that an energetic war against the French Republic would restore a sense of national unity and purpose, strengthen the national government, and check the corruption of the press. Now, all hope was lost. "I no longer behold," he announced, "any thing of much moment to struggle for!" Patriotism, argued Fenno, was the "fountain of national life, and the germ of every virtue," and "where this spirit is wanting, no efficient barrier can ever be directed against the inroads of decay." Renouncing all "interest or concern in the Gazette from this day," he concluded that the "sun of federalism is fast retiring behind the clouds of turbulence and treason," and "in a little while it may be seen no more."[61]

The cause of Fenno's gloom was the cause for Duane's celebration. Warmly applauding the wisdom of President Adams in the *Aurora*, Duane immediately shifted his polemical focus from Adams to those who surrounded him, particularly the "arch-fiend" Alexander Hamilton, casting disgruntled Federalists as enemies of American neutrality, the "constituted authorities," and the president. John Ward Fenno's ill-judged jeremiad made Duane's task even easier. "Expired…of a Malignant Distemper," he wrote in a mock obituary for the *Gazette of the United States*, "The Oracle of Toryism—the mouth-piece of Monarchy—and the disgrace of America." By publishing his "confession," argued Duane, Fenno had "thrown off the masque," revealed the "true character" of Federalism to the public, and "declared war on the Constitution." Through its champion, the "federal party boldly and audaciously avow[s]"

> that the constitution is like an effeminate grenadier, wanting courage, literally good for nothing; that the state governments ought to be annihilated; that there ought to be an established religion in the United States; and that the people are unfit to be anything more than asses to a British faction.

Americans should be outraged by such unmanly and anti-republican views and be prepared to defend American honor against traitors like Fenno. Let true republicans, he declared, "answer like *men*" with conviction and, if necessary, "with *the point of their bayonets*."[62]

Duane's martial defense of the status quo increased in stridency after he was assaulted and beaten by Federalist militia officers in May 1799. This assault had its origins in the tax revolt led by John Fries in Pennsylvania in March 1799. Unlike the Whiskey Rebellion, Fries's Rebellion attracted little support in Philadelphia, and by April the state militia had restored order and imprisoned Fries. But in May, the *Aurora* published a letter from a resident of Northampton, the center of the revolt, accusing the militia of abusing local inhabitants. In response, about thirty militia officers led by Joseph McKean, son of the chief justice, marched to the *Aurora* offices (after a morning of calm deliberation in Hardy's Tavern) and demanded an explanation from Duane. When he refused to clarify the charges and chastised McKean for aiding his father's political enemies, McKean struck him and called him a "damned liar." When Duane retaliated, the officers dragged him outside into the courtyard, formed a ring around him, and beat him until he "could neither see nor hear nor stand." Then, in a final act of indignity, each officer "gave him a cut" with a cowskin whip.[63]

The account published the next day in the *Gazette of the United States* justified the officers' assault, and Fenno (still active despite his recent farewell address) defended the chastisement of Citizen Duane as fitting punishment for a foreign "fugitive from justice," a United Irishman, and a man who had slandered the "great and good" George Washington. More wary and perhaps more sympathetic to his fellow editor, Cobbett ignored Duane's assault in *Porcupine's Gazette.* But the victim himself was not so reticent. In his account of the attack, under the headline "More of Good Order and Good Government!" Duane described his attackers as men who were as "equally disregardful of the *principles of honor* as of the *established laws.*" Their actions showed that Federalist support for law and order was a sham. If such violence were tolerated, argued "Nestor," "will not the bayonet soon become the test by which we are to be governed," and if the law were unable to protect a citizen from party violence, then what option did he have but to "turn warrior and defend himself?" A few days later, Duane answered this rhetorical question with a remarkable call to arms. Convinced that the law was "too feeble a barrier to restrain the licentiousness and outrage acted and meditated by men styling themselves '*the friends of order and good government*,'" he declared that Republicans must become "soldiers as well as citizens." "Arm and organize yourselves immediately," he instructed them, "make yourselves acquainted with military discipline, be ready, and you will be at peace.... To arms then, to arms."[64]

Using Federalist violence to justify the creation of Republican militias, Duane sought to harness the martial spirit of the late 1790s to his own cause. Announcing the formation of a new Republican militia company in the *Aurora*, he set out to challenge Federalist dominance of the militia in Philadelphia. Within days of Duane's editorial, Fenno was complaining about the "considerable accessions of strength" to Republican militias. During Fourth of July celebrations in Philadelphia in 1799, as Republican militias under Colonel Shee paraded separately from Federalists under General Macpherson, Captain Duane led his own company of Republican Greens, drawn from the strongly Irish and working-class areas of Southwark and the Northern Liberties, through the streets of the city. By late 1799, the Republican militias had established a powerful presence in Philadelphia, and by 1800 they had all but driven Federalists from the streets. This dominance was demonstrated at a militia review for the new governor, Thomas McKean, in May 1800. "The most beautiful military display that this city has exhibited since the retreat of the British from hence," wrote Duane, "all firm and steadfast Republicans, of the old whig principles of 1776, without a single trimmer." According to Duane, Republican militias had restored public order to the streets of Philadelphia, and by July 4, 1800, he announced with satisfaction, "the only uniform corps here now are the *Republicans*."[65]

The assault was a turning point for Duane and the Republicans in Pennsylvania, and in its aftermath, Duane (whose previous contributions to the *Aurora* had been anonymous) began to sign his editorials "William Duane" and to run the paper with a new flair and political aggressiveness. Alarmed by his success, Federalists tried to silence him by charging him with seditious libel, but when he threatened to involve John Adams in the trial, they backed off, reinforcing his image as a champion of free speech and a fearless opponent of Federalist repression. At the end of September 1799, Duane wrote a long editorial on "The Returning Sense of the Country," declaring an end to the period of "popular error" that had gripped the country for the previous eighteen months. Guided by the *Aurora*, he wrote, Americans had freed themselves from their "national infatuation" with Great Britain and reclaimed their independence and neutrality. The "satellites of Britain" had overplayed their hand by using "violence, insolence,

Aurora, Philadelphia, December 27, 1799. Published by William Duane, the front page announces the death of George Washington inside a black border. The irony would have been evident to all. Benjamin Bache, the newspaper's previous editor, had vilified Washington, and Duane's first publication in the United States was a pamphlet attacking Washington and his Farewell Address. By the time this notice appeared, however, Duane and the Republicans were scrambling to establish their political moderation and social respectability. Courtesy of the Library Company of Philadelphia.

slander, sophistry, falsehood, menace, and treachery" to advance their cause, and public opinion had turned against the "flagrant measures" of the Federalists. The "free American countenance," wrote Duane, "once more wears the softened lineaments of the independent and benevolent republican."[66]

Nothing epitomized this "change of public sentiment" more than the waning influence of William Cobbett. Duane's campaign against Cobbett was fascinating and reveals both his editorial courage and his political acumen. James Thomson Callender, who took a dim view of most Republican journalists, thought the *Aurora* under Duane had "got into the most excellent hands" and was thrilled by his willingness to confront Cobbett, who was still a force to be reckoned with despite his mounting legal and political difficulties. The two men were already well known to one another. Cobbett had attacked Duane and Lloyd when they ran the *Merchant's Daily Advertiser* for publishing "more news from Ireland than all the other papers put together," assuring them that stories of British brutality wouldn't prevent the Irish getting what they most deserved: the "ball and bayonet." And when Duane became editor of the *Aurora*, Cobbett renewed these attacks, assisted by his aide-de-camp John Ward Fenno. According to Fenno, the *Aurora* "must soon sink," and "revolutionary vermin" like Duane had to be extinguished or "America will ere long be converted into one vast store house of assassins." A few days later, he linked Duane directly to the "progress of that horrid plot forming in this city, under the name of the *United Irishmen*," publishing a list of Irishmen living in Philadelphia who were "disaffected to the government of the United States," which included Duane. According to Fenno, "every United Irishman ought to be hunted from the country."[67]

Fenno's attack on Duane as a dangerous Irish subversive was part of an anti-Irish campaign that Federalists had been waging since 1797. Cobbett, who according to Moreau de St. Mery "hated the Irish beyond words," was one of the leaders of this campaign. His attacks on the Irish and the United Irishmen dated back to *A Kick for a Bite* and *A Bone to Gnaw for the Democrats* in 1795. But Cobbett's stroke of genius was to link popular prejudice against the Irish to public fear about secret political societies and a French invasion. In early 1798, he published an exposé of the American Society of the United Irishmen, a secret fraternal organization founded in Philadelphia in August 1797 by a small group of radical Irish exiles that included Dr. James Reynolds, John Daly Burk, Matthew and James Carey, Matthew Lyon, and William Duane. According to Cobbett, the ASUI was an organization of "real, sincere, villainy" that had replaced the Democratic societies as the principal French ally in the United States. Its members (he claimed they numbered 1,500 in Philadelphia alone) awaited only the arrival of a French army to overthrow the government. Exploiting fears about the Haitian Revolution, Cobbett conjured up the prospect of an agreement among Irish radicals, "free negroes," and sympathetic southern slaveholders to release slaves and reduce the South to "bloodshed and rebellion." And with almost perfect political timing, he published his *Detection of a Conspiracy Formed by the United Irishmen with the Evident Intention of Aiding the Tyrants of France in Subverting the Government of the United States* just as news of the Irish Rebellion reached the United States in 1798, a rebellion planned to coincide with the French invasion of Ireland.[68]

Duane refused to let Cobbett intimidate him. When Cobbett greeted the revival of the *Aurora* by launching a savagely misogynist campaign against Margaret Bache and "Mother Bache's Gang," Duane denounced him as a coward for attacking a woman and refusing to confront "the man who alone is responsible for what appears in this paper." And when Cobbett and Fenno began to publicize his links to the United Irishmen, he refused to disown either the society or its cause. Making no secret of his hatred for the "tyranny and oppression of the British Empire," he announced that he owed too much to that "venerated and oppressed country," Ireland, "to say, I am not a United Irishman." But Duane did more than defy Cobbett; he turned the tables on him. Making the views of Cobbett and his auxiliary John Ward Fenno a central political issue, he condemned both men as agents of an alien power, Great Britain, and used their increasingly intemperate and anti-democratic writings to demonstrate the political bankruptcy of the Federalist Party.[69]

Realizing that the Federalist campaign against alien immigrants was a two-edged sword, Duane wielded it with a vengeance against Cobbett. When Cobbett was hauled before Chief Justice Thomas McKean as an alien menace in January 1799, Duane remained conspicuously silent, and by the end of the month he was editorializing about the dangers of "Foreign" and "British Influence." After Adams resumed negotiations with France in the spring, Duane launched a full-scale assault on Cobbett in the *Aurora*, condemning him as a "foreign emissary" who had "illiberally abused republican government, the people, congress, Mr. Adams, general Washington, B. Franklin, the free presses of the United States, and in short every thing important in this country." In league with the British minister, Robert Liston, Cobbett and Fenno had subverted the American press, reported Duane—the "English connexions of the *Gazette of the United States* are now well understood"—and tried to embroil the country in a disastrous war with France. Duane even claimed that Cobbett was a paid "English Spy" whose mission was to infiltrate the federal government, and he published Cobbett's 1793 letter of introduction to Thomas Jefferson to prove this charge. By the late summer of 1799, the *Aurora* was devoted almost entirely to Cobbett and the issue of "British Influence." "It is time," Duane declared loftily, "for virtuous and judicious men of all parties to concur in forcing the government and public agents of Great Britain" to disown "this insolent, immoral, and dangerous meddler."[70]

Chief Justice Thomas McKean's election as governor of Pennsylvania in October 1799 was a stunning political victory for Duane and the Republicans and sparked widespread celebrations in Philadelphia. The "Republican Triumph," announced Duane in the *Aurora*, would be marked by "A splendid pyrotechnical exhibition…to celebrate the TRIUMPH of the PUBLIC SUFFRAGE over FOREIGN INFLUENCE." According to him, this triumph was of more than local significance. "The Pennsylvania election," he reported, "has excited the liveliest interest in every part of the Union, and in truth must decide materially on the sentiments of the people—whether they are willing to be a republic, or become monarchists." During the election, Duane had constantly emphasized its national importance, and a crucial part of his strategy had been to focus public attention on Cobbett's support for the Federalist candidate, James Ross, and to portray the election as a struggle between the influence of Great Britain and Peter Porcupine and the republicanism of Thomas McKean, a signer of the Declaration of Independence. McKean's victory, he declared, represented a triumph for American independence and a revival of the spirit of 1776. In words that could easily have been written by John Fenno during the Genet crisis in 1793, Duane called on Americans to

> manfully disclaim and discard every cause of public jealousy—every matter or thing which by embarking our nation in European politics, or hostilities, may commit our peace, our freedom, and our fortunes, in quarrels from which our form of government and our situation should eternally separate us.[71]

By using Cobbett as a symbol of British influence, Duane was able to reclaim the issue of American neutrality and independence for Republicans. But Duane also used Cobbett to symbolize the personal and partisan animosity that had become such an alarming feature of public life, and after Cobbett turned against John Adams in 1798, Duane was quick to condemn his scurrilous attacks on the president. Cobbett's declining political fortunes, argued Duane, were evidence of a public "awakening" and "the aroused sense of the national mind." The people had finally realized that Republicans rather than Federalists were the best guardians of American independence and national character. *Porcupine's Gazette*, he wrote in November, had "sunk beneath that odium which the most abandoned abuse of decency, patriotism, the venerable dead, and the meritorious living drew down upon it." In contrast, respectable newspapers run on "democratical republican principles" had expanded rapidly throughout the country. In the recent past, argued Duane, "the United States could scarcely boast of six papers out of nearly 200, which maintained the principles of 1776." Now, there had arisen around the sun of the *Aurora* a "galaxy of republican prints, which unawed by power and devoted to the republican constitutions of these states, diffuse knowledge and truth, into all corners of the Union."[72]

By this time Duane and the Republicans had permanently usurped the language of moral indignation. While *Porcupine's Gazette* scandalized the public with its virulent personal attacks, the *Aurora* provided a model of political civility. Duane insisted that its pages "were never sullied by *indecency*—*vulgarity*—or any *violation* of domestic decorum; that public men and measures were boldly handled, with the magnanimous openness and love of truth alone, which is the character of the *true republican*." By the end of 1799, Duane was publishing editorial paragraphs in the *Aurora* expressing outrage about the attacks on officers of the United States by "Strangers." Apparently, the days of "Jasper Dwight" and his *Letter to George Washington* were long forgotten. Typical of this new Republican moralism was an address "To the Republicans of Pennsylvania," published in the *Aurora* during the Pennsylvania elections in October 1799. Defending the character of Thomas McKean against the slanders of the "Porcupine Junto," its authors blamed the corrupt influence of an "*alien monarchist*" for the "licentiousness of the press" in Pennsylvania:

> Perhaps a more extraordinary phenomenon never occurred in the political, or moral, history of a nation. We have seen gazettes, containing the most open and atrocious libels upon the revolution and the constitution…exciting domestic feuds.…We have seen the same gazettes rank and disgusting with falsehood, defamation and obscenity, become the amusement of men, who affect all the decencies, all the courtesies of private life.

Describing themselves as guardians of political civility who upheld the "principles of mutual deference and forbearance," the signatories of the address argued that the laws of the country had "surrendered the feelings and reputations of its citizens, as the legitimate prey of every intruding foreigner, and of every illiterate and unprincipled proprietor of a newspaper."[73]

In this contest between civility and scurrility, argued Duane, the "rising generation" of voters had learned a vital lesson. If McKean had been "an advocate of monarchy—a favorer of Aristocracy—an upholder of passive obedience and non-resistance—a friend of Toryism—an obsequious adulator of the British Treaty," he argued, all good Republicans would have repudiated him. But he was not, and his election therefore represented a triumph of principles over men and of ideas over the personal politics of Peter Porcupine. But Duane also interpreted McKean's success as a vindication for political character, both McKean's character and the character of the public. "Young men now perceive," he wrote, the importance of a "consistent and clear character," and they understood "that the majority of the people where they are free to act, will choose such characters—men of tried principles and unquestionable integrity." Despite the slanders circulated about McKean in *Porcupine's Gazette*, voters had "stood up like men and by choosing a man of '76, declared that—*a republic means something*." McKean's election thus represented both the triumph of principles over men and the triumph of good men over bad. In November 1799, Duane reported that Cobbett was leaving Philadelphia for New York, and in a New Year's Eve editorial on the "wonderful occurrences" of 1799, he included, among other important world events, "the complete destruction of that foreign, monarchical, diplomatic engine, the press of Porcupine. God save the People."[74]

Federalists worked hard in the 1790s to make the politics of character a central political issue, and one of the most important vehicles for this debate was the campaign against religious infidelity. This campaign was given new life by the revelations of the Reverend Jedediah Morse in the spring of 1798.[75] Morse's charge, that emissaries of a secret Masonic organization called the Order of the Bavarian Illuminati were at work in the United States, spreading radicalism and religious infidelity through their allies in the Republican press and the "self-created" Democratic societies, created an immediate sensation, quickly finding its way into print and into the sermons of other Federalist clergymen. The most important of these was the Reverend Timothy Dwight's *The Duty of Americans, at the Present Crisis*.[76]

Dwight, the president of Yale and author of the well-known poem *The Triumph of Infidelity*, had been warning for years about the growing influence of deist and atheist ideas in America. Although Dwight, like Morse, blamed the spread of infidelity on the machinations of the Illuminati (and their Republican allies), he also reminded readers of their own complicity, emphasizing the role of personal religious faith and character in public life. "Personal obedience and reformation is the foundation, and the sum, of all national worth," stated Dwight, and if each man conducted himself virtuously in private life, "the public state must be commendable and happy":

> *Individuals* are often apt to consider their own private conduct as of small importance to the public welfare. This opinion is wholly erroneous and highly mischievous. No man can adopt it, who believes, and remembers, the declarations of God.... the personal conduct of no individual can be insignificant to the safety and happiness of a nation.

Not all social ills could be blamed on French Illuminati, argued Dwight, who also blamed Americans themselves for the growth of atheism. Americans had become materialistic and self-regarding, forgetting how much the character of civic life depended on the private character of citizens. Infidel beliefs fed on this materialism and self-interest, and the only antidote to such ideas was Christianity. "Where religion prevails," he declared, "Illuminatism cannot make disciples, a French Directory cannot govern, a nation cannot be made slaves, nor villains, nor atheists, nor beasts." If Americans would only shun the corrupt influence of France and defend their government and the "religion of our fathers" against the "Antichristian empire," their freedom and independence could be preserved intact.[77]

Dwight's belief that the health of the body politic depended less on its formal Constitution than on its inherent character, the moral character of its citizens and the moral character of its leaders, was widely shared by the late 1790s. The federal Constitution was not after all a "machine that would go of itself," allowing Americans to dispense with the problem of public virtue as some members of the founding generation had hoped. Good government required good men, and in a society where rational political debate was drowned out by political hacks and intemperate scribblers, it was impossible to ensure the election of virtuous, disinterested men. To Dwight and other clergymen, this crisis of character justified their involvement in public life and gave them a central role in public debate. Far from being a private matter best left to the conscience of the individual, religion was an issue of public concern and importance. And it was the duty of the clergy to resist efforts to privatize religious life; they should remoralize public life, insist that private and public morality were closely intertwined, and preserve the foundations of a Christian republic.[78]

Federalist attacks on infidelity and "Illuminism" were thus framed within a language of moral crisis and virtue that made issues of character central to public debate, and not surprisingly, they quickly focused on the figure of Thomas Jefferson. In a Fourth of July oration in 1798, Theodore Dwight denounced Jefferson as "the very child of *modern illuminatism*, the foe of man, and the enemy of his country." As the presidential election loomed in 1800, the Federalist focus on Jefferson grew more urgent. Federalists, and especially Federalist clergymen, were appalled by the idea that a self-professed deist might become president of the United States. What would be the consequences for the United States, asked Abiel Abbott, "were our first magistrate an Illuminatus, a conspirator in league with the horde in Europe, the grand master of the demoralizers in America?" To prevent such a calamity, the Federalist press launched an unprecedented campaign of personal vilification against Jefferson, led by clerics like Jedediah Morse, Charles Osgood, and William Linn. "Should the infidel Jefferson be elected to the Presidency," wrote one hysterical correspondent to the *New England Palladium*, "the seal of death is that moment set on our holy religion, our churches will be prostrated, and some infamous prostitute under the title of the Goddess of Reason will preside in the sanctuaries devoted to the most High."[79]

Always reluctant to make public declarations about his beliefs, Jefferson refused to respond to Federalist charges of atheism and infidelity. His Republican supporters were not so complacent, and as they rushed into print to defend him, the issue of Jefferson's infidelity quickly came to dominate the campaign of 1800.

The Providential Detection. Unidentified artist, [1800?]. A letter that Jefferson wrote to his friend Philip Mazzei in 1796 referred to those "Samsons in the field and Solomons in the council" who have "had their heads shorn by the harlot England." Its publication by Noah Webster in 1797 caused a sensation. Here, God exposes Jefferson as an enemy of the Constitution and an agent of France and the devil. Among the works fueling the "Altar to Gallic Despotism" are Paine's *Age of Reason* and the *Aurora.* Courtesy of the Library Company of Philadelphia.

Some Republicans, loyal to the principle of a strict separation between religion and politics, defended Jefferson's public silence on the matter of religious faith. "What has the ensuing election to do with the work of *salvation?*" argued one writer in the *Aurora*, pointing out that Christ "never interfered in the *political* affairs of the world." "A President of the United States, *as such*, has nothing to do with religion," argued another commentator, "but he has much to do with our *Constitution*," and because the Constitution was more vulnerable to problems created by corruption than by irreligion, the election of a religious "Bigot" to public office was "much more dangerous than an Infidel."[80]

But such voices were rare. Few Republicans were brave enough to challenge Federalist arguments on principle and argue that Jefferson had no duty to reveal his religious beliefs or, even more controversially, no duty to be religious. Almost without exception, they fell back on Jefferson's authorship of the Virginia Statute of Religious Freedom and his well-known commitment to religious pluralism. The essays by Charles Pinckney in the *Aurora* in October and November 1800 exemplified this approach and the difficulties that confronted Jefferson's most articulate supporters. Religion, argued Pinckney, was a private affair "between God and our own souls," and he pointed out that Americans had never suffered religion "to mingle with public concerns." The Federalist attempt to impose a religious test on candidates for public office threatened political freedom and the vitality of American religion, and from this perspective, believed Pinckney, Jefferson was "the most valuable and the best friend" that true religion, and "particularly the doctrines of the *Christian religion*, ever had in the United States." The Virginia Statute of Religious Freedom, he claimed, had destroyed the "tyranny of religious establishments and emancipated from their fetters, the whole American church."[81]

But defending Jefferson's commitment to religious liberty failed to address the central issue raised by Federalists: the relationship between personal religious belief and political character. And it was precisely Jefferson's silence about his religious beliefs and his understanding of religion as private that disturbed his political and religious opponents. What did it mean to be a Christian if nobody could tell whether you were or not? Responding to this problem, most Republicans tried to make a case for Jefferson's Christianity. After arguing that Jefferson was the "truest friend of Christianity," Pinckney could not resist adding that he was also a "sincere, exemplary, practical Christian, in life and manners." But by arguing that Jefferson was a Christian Republican, writers in the *Aurora* implicitly ceded the main point of contention to Federalists: belief in Christianity was a requirement for public office. Slightly defensively and evasively, most Republican commentators found themselves defending not Jefferson's liberty of conscience but his conscientious Christianity.[82]

While the mainstream Republican defense of Jefferson mirrored the conservative drift of the party in 1799–1800, Duane adopted a much more uncompromising strategy, aligning the *Aurora* closely with the growing forces of radical Christianity. Not content to fill the newspaper with defensive Christian apologetics, he launched an aggressive campaign against what he dubbed the "New England Illuminati," warning the public that the religious doctrines and activities of the Federalists represented a fundamental threat to American Christianity. The genesis of this campaign was an article by John Cosens Ogden, an Episcopal minister from Connecticut, which was published in the *Aurora* in February 1799 shortly after Duane took over the newspaper. This article was written in response to Morse's pamphlet on the Bavarian Illuminati, and according to Duane, it was designed to "unmask the new sect of illuminati rule in New England." Turning

Morse's arguments upside down, Ogden's essay, which echoed his earlier pamphlet, *A View of the Calvinistical Clubs of the United States*, argued that there was indeed a conspiracy to undermine religious and political freedom in the United States, but it was organized by what he identified as the "ruling junto" of Connecticut, the "New England illuminati." At the head of this conspiracy was the Reverend Timothy Dwight, who had turned religion into a "political machine" and created a virtual "Union of Church and State" in Connecticut, using his power to "suppress the propagation of free sentiments among the people" and to advance the cause of clerical absolutism and monarchical government.[83]

Ogden's campaign against "Pope Dwight" and the Connecticut standing order played an important role in the New England elections of 1800, but Duane also put his ideas to work in Pennsylvania, publishing Ogden's views in the *Aurora* and arguing that the "alarming combination of priestcraft in the Eastern States" was part of a broader Jesuit conspiracy to establish papal domination throughout the world. Despite his Irish Catholic origins, Duane made anti-popery a constant theme in the *Aurora*. When Ogden published *A View of the New England Illuminati Who Are Indefatigably Engaged in Destroying the Religion and Government of the United States* in November 1799, Duane strongly recommended it to all those who were concerned about the "freedom, prosperity and morality of this country," emphasizing the nefarious coalition of Calvinist and Catholic "ecclesiastics" who had brought "serious evils to Connecticut." Attacks on the "New England Illuminati" referred constantly to "Pope Dwight" and "His Holiness of Yale," exploiting the fact that the same Presbyterian clergyman who had once welcomed the destruction of French Catholicism now prayed for "the pope and the re-establishment of the Romish religion."[84]

"Republicans," declared Duane, "are not enemies to order and religion" but its firmest friends, and he firmly rejected the notion that Republicanism had any connection whatsoever to deism, which flourished best under "kingly governments." As if to demonstrate his allegiance to Christianity, Duane even published a series of articles accusing the Federalist candidate for governor, James Ross, of being "in principle and practice a DEIST!" And in an election broadside published in early October, Duane compared the "devout Christian" Thomas McKean to the "avowed Deist" Ross. A few weeks later, he accused the new editors of the *Gazette of the United States*, Caleb Wayne and Joseph Dennie, of "Federal Atheism" for publishing the work of the "arch-infidel Voltaire" and for "using every means in their power to destroy the Christian religion." Once the barrage of attacks on Jefferson's infidelity began, Duane renewed his focus on the "Connecticut Illuminati," and by mid-1800 his campaign against Federalist religious tyranny was in full swing.[85]

The goal of this campaign was to show that Federalists were determined to establish a national church and religious uniformity in the United States. According to

Duane, this danger was symbolized by the power and influence of the Connecticut standing order, the government of the Presbyterian church in Connecticut, which he characterized as a church "directed by a *sovereign pontiff*, twelve *cardinals*, a *civil council* of nine, and about four hundred *parochial bishops.*" These men controlled not only the religious institutions of the state but also its political system, and they had seized control of the press "to destroy or bring into contempt those republican principles and sentiments which led us through the revolutionary war, and secured the independence of our country." Even more alarming, they sought to spread their pernicious doctrines beyond New England by infiltrating educational institutions and seminaries throughout the country and by organizing missionary work in league with the British Society for the Propagation of Religious Knowledge. An editorial by Duane in September 1800 on "Anglo-Federalism, British Influence and the New England Illuminati" brought these different conspiratorial strands together, emphasizing the close relationship between religious establishments and monarchical government and accusing Federalists of trying to introduce both to the United States. When Jefferson was elected, amid the many expressions of millennial joy that filled the *Aurora* was a paragraph predicting that "the friends of religion will rejoice—for the kingdom of the beast hath an end."[86]

Writing to Joseph Priestley after his inauguration, Jefferson expressed the view that religion had been the central issue of the recent election campaign: "What an effort…of bigotry in Politics & Religion have we gone through! The barbarians really flattered themselves they should be able to bring back the time of Vandalism, when ignorance put everything into the hands of power & priestcraft." His election had rescued the country from the Federalist assault on religious freedom and freedom of conscience. His defeated opponent, John Adams, also thought that religion had played a critical role in Jefferson's election, although he was predictably less happy about its consequences. Despite the many attacks on Jefferson's infidelity, he argued, religious issues had helped rather than hurt the Republican cause. "A general suspicion prevailed," he later confided to Benjamin Rush,

> that the Presbyterian Church was ambitious and aimed at an establishment as a national church. I was represented as a Presbyterian and at the head of this political and ecclesiastical project. The secret whisper ran through all the sects, "Let us have Jefferson, Madison, Burr, anybody, whether they be philosophers, Deists, or even atheists, rather than a Presbyterian President."

"Nothing," he added, "is more dreaded than the national government meddling with religion."[87]

The agents of these "secret whispers" were the gang of what Adams called "foreign liars" who ran the Republican press and whom Adams believed had "discomfited the education, the talents, the virtues, and the property of the country." According to Adams, Jefferson's election in 1800 signified the triumph of politics over political character, in which political journalists like William Duane, crude and interested peddlers of partisanship, had trampled underfoot the idea of a disinterested "natural" political elite. But Duane thought otherwise. On January 1, 1801, he announced "A New Day in America," and in an editorial called "The Eighteenth Century Terminated Yesterday," he celebrated the beginning of the new century and the nation's fortunate escape from "Gothic Tyranny" and "barbarism." Jefferson's election had decided the fate of democratic government in the United States, heralding a "return of public opinion to the old standard of 1776." "The Revolution of 1776," declared Duane, "is now and for the first time arrived at its completion."[88]

To Duane, the election of 1800 represented not only a return to the principles of 1776 but a return to the men of 1776. By turning out the Federalists, Americans had driven the "vicious and profligate" from public office and restored men of good character. "No man has been more calumniated than the man whom the American people have chosen for their first magistrate," declared Duane, but despite the charges of atheism trumpeted forth in "all the Federal papers on the continent," virtue and truth had emerged triumphant. Americans had seen through the haze of partisan lies and the press's misrepresentation, demonstrating their own political virtue and ensuring that candidates for public office would henceforth be judged according to their talents, truthfulness, and support for democratic government. Jefferson also interpreted his own election as a triumph for the national character:

> The order & good sense displayed in this recovery from delusion, and in the momentous crisis which lately arose, really bespeak a strength of character in our nation which augurs well for the durability of our Republic; & I am much better satisfied now of it's [*sic*] stability than I was before it was tried.

Duane was in full agreement. The Republican victory had restored a sense of order and harmony to American life. "What a contrast does the conduct of the republican exhibit in the present triumph with that of their adversaries," he observed, "no insults passing the streets—no rioting or breaking windows—no savage orgies as the streets exhibited four years ago." Instead, "peace and concord" reigned in the public sphere, while cries of war and sedition "no longer infest our firesides." The "reign of terror and corrupt government," Duane promised his readers, "is at an end."[89]

CONCLUSION

The Revenge of Respectability

When Thomas Jefferson delivered his first inaugural address to the U.S. Senate on March 4, 1801, he urged Americans to put the political divisions of the past behind them. The recent election campaign or, as he put it, "the contest of opinion through which we have passed" had been savage, a fitting climax to a decade of merciless partisan conflict. But now, he argued, it was time for Americans to "unite in common efforts for the common good." Political intolerance posed as much danger to the Republic as religious intolerance, he warned, and he struck a chord of approval with his listeners (and readers) when he urged them to "restore to social intercourse that harmony and affection without which liberty and even life itself are but dreary things." With all of the generosity of the victorious politician, Jefferson reminded his audience that "every difference of opinion is not a difference of principle. We have called by different names brethren of the same principle. We are all republicans—we are all federalists."[1]

This was a remarkable statement from the leader of a party that had spent most of the previous decade trying to convince Americans that just the opposite was true. One of the central themes of the recent Republican election campaign, the culmination of a campaign begun in 1791 by Freneau's *National Gazette*, had been the threat to republican government posed by the Federalists. Uttered a decade before, Jefferson's words would have been unremarkable, and only a few irreconcilable Anti-Federalists would have questioned his equation between republicanism and federalism. But by the mid-1790s, a Republican opposition had been formed, largely under the leadership of Jefferson himself, dedicated to portraying Federalists as an anti-republican elite that had corrupted American society and politics with its financial schemes, plundered the public purse, allied the country with its most dangerous adversary, Great Britain, and undermined the Constitution.

By 1800, enough Americans shared these beliefs to make Thomas Jefferson the third president of the United States, and his closely contested electoral

President Th. Jefferson, by Charles B. J. F. de Saint-Mémin, 1804. This is a portrait of President Thomas Jefferson near the end of his first term of office and at the height of his powers and popularity. Courtesy of the National Portrait Gallery, Smithsonian Institution; gift of Mr. and Mrs. Paul Mellon.

victory was immediately invested with cosmic political significance. To Republicans at the time, and to most historians ever since, Jefferson's election represented the culmination of the American Revolution: a triumph for the forces of egalitarian popular democracy unleashed by the Declaration of Independence over the forces of political reaction that struggled to contain and suppress them. The victory of the Republican Party in 1800 closed off the possibility of a Federalist counterrevolution, an American Thermidor, securing the revolutionary character of American politics and society on a permanent basis. In retrospect, the defeat of John Adams and the Federalists has assumed an aura of inevitability, and the steady decline of the Federalist Party after 1800 reinforced the belief that their defeat was the sad, unavoidable fate of a party ill adapted to the new democratic age. Jefferson's verdict, rendered almost twenty years after his victory, has become the definitive one: "The Revolution of 1800 was as real a revolution in the principles of our government as that of 1776 was in its form."[2]

But despite the millennial expectations of his supporters, such political triumphalism was not at all evident in Jefferson's inaugural. Although his speech was a clear attempt to advance his own partisan interests by forging a new politics of consensus around his presidency, it also expressed a genuine desire to restore a sense of civility to public life, and his sentiments were in tune with a broader conservative shift in American politics, a shift prefigured and encouraged by the Republican electoral campaigns of 1799–1800.[3] Although conducted by radical firebrands like William Duane, these campaigns had been remarkably conservative, and their success had depended not on the popular appeal of radical ideology but on the skill with which Republican journalists like Duane had co-opted a series of critical public issues—nationalism and independence, immigration and anti-alien sentiment, law and public safety, religion and moral order—that had been largely monopolized and controlled by Federalists during the 1790s.[4] Most historians have overlooked this development, failing to appreciate either the popular appeal of Federalism or the conservative appeal of Republicanism during the period from roughly 1797 to 1800.[5] This failure makes the politics of the late 1790s, for example the ascendancy (and subsequent decline) of the English expatriate and anti-Jacobin William Cobbett, almost incomprehensible. Assuming that Federalist policies were reactionary, anti-democratic, and deeply unpopular, historians have made Jefferson's victory in 1800 seem all but inevitable. But it was not. Far from relying on the obviously self-destructive policies of their Federalist opponents and the self-evident appeal of their own democratic ideas, journalists like Duane skillfully mobilized voters by appealing to the same sense of public anxiety about social change and political disorder that their Federalist opponents did their best to exploit against Republicans.

As we have seen already, one of the pivotal moments in this partisan battle was the passage of the Alien and Sedition Acts in 1798, around which swirled a fierce debate about the press and the politics of character. Conventionally, both acts have been regarded as a sign of the Federalists' inability to accept modern party politics and a more liberal understanding of the public sphere. But Federalist policies of press regulation and immigration restriction were popular, reflecting a very modern intolerance for political dissent (particularly during wartime) and an equally modern commitment to ideas of ethnic and racial nationalism. Anti-alien politics became a potent force in American politics during the 1790s and was exploited by Republicans like Duane as adeptly as by Federalists like John Fenno. A similar argument can be made about the popular response to the Sedition Act. Even by the standards of the 1790s, the Sedition Act aroused fierce political passions, and these passions have shaped historical interpretations of the legislation. After its passage in July 1798, Republicans denounced the measure as blatantly partisan, a "gag act" that violated the First Amendment and aimed, according to Jefferson, at "the suppression of the whig presses." Its subsequent enforcement against Republican journalists by the highly partisan secretary of state, Timothy Pickering, did nothing to dispel such claims.[6] But to simply echo Republican arguments against the Sedition Act and to view it as the "capstone" of a Federalist program of counterrevolution and political repression are mistakes.[7] Legally, the act was quite progressive, inscribing for the first time in statute the principles of the Zenger trial in 1735: the truth defense and the right of the jury to decide the question of libel as well as the fact of publication.[8]

Republican critics were well aware of this fact and less alarmed by the legal principles of the Sedition Act than by its "consolidating" influence, the power it gave to the federal government to initiate prosecutions for seditious libel in federal courts. They regarded this power as a violation of the First Amendment, arguing that prosecutions for seditious libel should be brought instead before state courts. Republican jurists like Thomas McKean, a proponent and practitioner of draconian restrictions on the press, opposed the Sedition Act on precisely these grounds, and Republicans opposed the act more often as an infringement of state sovereignty than as an infringement of press freedom.[9] Some Republicans even expressed support for the act's principles. James Sullivan, the Republican attorney general of Massachusetts, prosecuted the *Independent Chronicle* under the terms of the Sedition Act in 1799, and he supported the act's legal principles in his *Dissertation on the Constitutional Freedom of the Press*; and the publisher Matthew Carey, who opposed the act at the time, later described it as "a measure not merely defensible, but absolutely necessary and indispensable toward the support of government." Thomas Cooper, an English radical who was imprisoned under the Sedition Act, complained years later that states had still not adopted the legal framework established by the act, and it was Alexander Hamilton, acting for the Federalist Harry Croswell, editor of the Hudson *Wasp*, who first introduced its legal principles at the state level.[10]

Clearly, Federalists exploited popular hostility toward France, the reaction to the XYZ Affair, and the sudden popularity of John Adams to deliver a blow to the Republican press. But as these factors suggest, the Sedition Act was much more than a panic-stricken response to the rising tide of Jeffersonian democracy. Indeed, when Federalists passed the act in 1798, Republicans were in complete disarray, and the Sedition Act itself turned out to be the catalyst for their revival in 1799–1800.[11] Equally important, the Sedition Act has to be placed within the context of contemporary legal and political beliefs. Although hostility toward organized political opposition during this period has been exaggerated—Samuel Miller was not alone in thinking that the "natural and salutary collision of parties" was a good thing—suspicion of faction was a well-entrenched feature of Anglo-American political culture, and as we have seen, the formation of a government based on popular sovereignty reinforced this hostility and gave it a new form of democratic legitimacy.[12] After 1789, Federalists frequently argued that systematic opposition to the federal government represented a defiance of the popular will and was inherently subversive and anti-democratic. "From the very nature of republican government," insisted one Federalist writer, "the vote of the majority must constitute *law*." Although such arguments served clear partisan purposes, both Federalists and Republicans assumed that opposition to the will of the majority was anti-republican, and both continually questioned the political legitimacy of their opponents. While Federalists conflated popular sovereignty with the authority of the federal government they controlled, Republicans conflated popular sovereignty with the public opinion they claimed to represent. The idea that "the people" might be divided by legitimate conflicts of interest and opinion was rarely conceded by the members of either party.[13]

Such assumptions cut across party lines and shaped the evolution of public attitudes toward the press in the 1790s. The Constitution and the inauguration of the federal government had established a new framework for discussions of press freedom and had compelled Americans to reconsider their conventional understanding of the relationship between government and the press. In the past, they had regarded the press as a "representative" of the public interest and a censor of state power. But if the state embodied popular sovereignty and the *res publica*, then what role remained for the press? In colonial and revolutionary America, printers had been granted virtual immunity from prosecution for sedition when they represented popular authority against abuses of executive power, but those who challenged elected political assemblies were often arraigned for contempt or breach of privilege. And when conflict between competing claims to popular representation reemerged in the 1790s, many Americans sided with the federal government rather than with the opposition newspapers.[14]

We should not be too quick to belittle this support for the state. As the historian Richard Buel points out, contemporary Americans' support for unrestricted press freedom (and for the activities of organizations like political parties and protest groups) rests on a sense of confidence in the stability of the state that would have struck the founding generation as unrealistic. As they well knew, words could overturn governments. Members of the founding generation were political revolutionaries who lived in a revolutionary world, and it is crucial to realize how profoundly a sense of political fragility shaped their political views. As partisan conflict grew in the 1790s, protecting the elected leaders of a new and weak republican state against the actions of an increasingly influential and "irresponsible" press began to seem like common sense to many Americans. And it was in this context that proposals for press regulation found an increasingly receptive audience.[15]

The Sedition Act, in other words, was not only an effort to secure partisan advantage but a final, and ill-fated, effort to "civilize" the increasingly "uncivilized" tone of American political discourse. The public debate about the press from which it emerged and to which it contributed was not a theoretical exchange about freedom of expression and the First Amendment that pitted repressive Federalists against libertarian Republicans, but a direct public response to the partisan and iconoclastic political journalism of the 1790s and to journalists who challenged the conventional boundaries between liberty and license, public and private, the political and the personal, that had structured elite public discourse in the past. The success of these journalists eroded public faith in the free market of ideas and public consensus about self-regulation and led many Americans to regard formal, legal restraint of the press as unavoidable. Although Federalists were probably more likely than Republicans to favor press regulation (and to support the Sedition Act), there was no strong correlation between party affiliation and attitudes toward liberty of the press, which were shaped as much by politics as by legal principle. Republican opponents of the Sedition Act prosecuted Federalist advocates like Cobbett for libel and sedition without a word about press freedom appearing in Republican newspapers.

Moreover, when the Republicans took control of the federal government after 1800 and faced a barrage of Federalist abuse, they began to denounce the scurrility of the press with the same fervor as their opponents had in the past. Benjamin Austin, for example, attacked what was now the opposition press in a widely circulated and reprinted pamphlet, *Constitutional Republicanism*, and condemned Federalist newspapers for exciting "the hatred of the citizens against their constituted authorities" and attempting to dissolve the union. "What body of men," he demanded in language reminiscent of the late John Fenno, "have the privilege to contemn those, whom the citizens have approbated? Who have a license to calumniate, in terms the most opprobrious, those who are placed in the seats of government?" "Our national character," he declared, "has been sported with, by men who pretend to the honour of their country, with a wantonness that would disgrace a tribe of savages, or a horde of Hottentots."[16] Samuel Miller, an equally staunch Republican, rendered his judgment in more measured terms in *A Brief Retrospect of the Eighteenth Century*, published in 1803. But his verdict was similar. Astonished by the growth of the press in the 1790s, Miller described newspapers as "immense moral and political engines, closely connected with the welfare of the state." But he believed that they had been corrupted by the "slaves of interest" and the men of low character who edited them. Their licentiousness was so great, argued Miller, that self-regulation was no longer sufficient, and "we may anticipate the arrival of that crisis in which we must yield either to an abridgement of the liberty of the press, or to a disruption of every social bond." Even Thomas Paine felt compelled to remind Americans that, in France, the "clamours of anonymous scribblers," the growth of "faction," and the erosion of "civility and liberty" had ended in bloodshed. By the turn of the century, such views were commonplace, and while Republicans made no effort to revive the Sedition Act, they had few inhibitions about bringing seditious libel prosecutions or civil lawsuits for slander before state courts, exploiting existing laws to silence their political critics.[17]

By 1800, there was a new political mood in the air and a growing consensus about the scurrility of the partisan press, and the need to contain and limit the politics of character encouraged party leaders to banish the most partisan and polemical journalists of the 1790s to the political margins. By this time, most of the central figures in this book had already disappeared from public life. John Fenno and Benjamin Bache, two of the most tenacious and loyal partisan journalists of the period, both died of yellow fever in the epidemic that swept Philadelphia in 1798. Philip Freneau and Noah Webster, both of whom nursed more lofty literary ambitions and had always regarded the crude, combative world of partisan journalism with a degree of distaste, had retreated to their respective birthplaces in New Jersey and Connecticut. Cobbett had also returned home, although his public career had hardly yet begun. Welcomed back to England as the great American anti-Jacobin, he was quickly ushered into the highest circles of the English establishment. But within a few years, he had grown disillusioned with the English government, and after founding his famous *Political Register*, he went on to become the greatest radical journalist (and one of the greatest writers) in early nineteenth-century England. When he returned for a tour of the United States in 1819, he praised American democracy and even sought out the grave of his old enemy, "Citizen of the World" Thomas Paine, gathering up his bones to take home to their proper resting place in England.

Only William Duane remained. Widely regarded by fellow Republicans (and many less admiring Federalists) as the architect of Jefferson's triumph in 1800, he was at the peak of his political influence, "literally the toast of Republican America and a man of national influence." In August 1800, Republicans held a banquet in his honor at Lovett's Hotel in Philadelphia and toasted "William Duane—The Firm and enlightened editor of the Aurora; virtuous and undaunted in the worst of times, the friend of his country, and the scourge of her enemies."[18] An engraving by the French artist Charles Balthazar Julien Fevret de Saint-Mémin, executed in 1802, reveals an intense and forceful man (he was forty-two years of age), straining for public recognition and respectability. The election triumph had enhanced Duane's reputation, and it had also improved the circulation and profitability of the *Aurora*, which he now intended to move to the new federal capital in Washington, D.C., and to establish as the "head of American newspapers." Anything seemed possible, and it was even rumored that Duane might accept a position in the Jefferson administration, a rumor that prompted John Ward Fenno to quip that Duane had been appointed "Consul to CALCUTTA."[19]

But when he attended Jefferson's inaugural on March 4, 1801, it was not as a member of the Republican administration nor even as a privileged, well-connected insider, but as a bystander, and during the next six years that he spent in Washington, that is what he remained. After Jefferson's election, the new Republican establishment shunned Duane, refusing to grant the *Aurora* official party patronage and instead throwing their financial and political support behind Samuel Harrison Smith's respectable and staid *National Intelligencer*. Disappointed but still determined to turn the *Aurora* into a national newspaper, Duane set up shop in Washington, D.C., borrowed $22,000 to establish a printing office and bookshop, and began to lobby for printing contracts from the Jefferson administration and the new Republican Congress.[20] Again, he was disappointed. In May 1801, the new secretary of state, James Madison, refused his request for State Department patronage, the same patronage Jefferson had once extended to John Fenno's *Gazette of the United States*. But Duane remained optimistic. In August, he bought a small plot of land at the corner of Pennsylvania Avenue and Sixth Street, and in early December he announced plans to publish congressional debates in the *Aurora*, which he began to transform into an official paper of record. However, his fortunes took a turn for the worse when Congress awarded the official printing contract for the House of Representatives to his rival Samuel Harrison Smith. He was left, he lamented, with "only such part of the printing as Mr. Smith cannot execute," a situation that his fellow Republican and Pennsylvanian Albert Gallatin blamed on the clerk of the House, John Beckley.[21]

Shut out by the Jefferson administration, which fed news and official announcements as well as printing contracts to the *National Intelligencer*, Duane had to work hard just to stay afloat. And to add insult to injury, the Jefferson administration did almost nothing to halt the prosecutions against Duane that had been initiated under the Sedition Act from proceeding to trial, even after the act expired in March 1801. Indeed, some Republican leaders thought that he deserved prosecution. As a result, the man who had skillfully eluded and exploited the sedition prosecutions of the Federalists in 1799–1800 and become a Republican hero and martyr was stripped of his right to American citizenship and jailed for thirty days for contempt of the U.S. Senate.[22] When Duane finally wrote to complain about his treatment at the hands of the administration, Madison expressed sympathy and raised the issue directly with Jefferson. But characteristically, Jefferson kept his old political ally firmly at arm's length. Although he expressed admiration for Duane, Jefferson believed that the intensity of the editor's beliefs made him untrustworthy and "improper to be considered as speaking the sense of the government." Then he added, perhaps feeling a twinge of guilt, "Duane is honest, & well intentioned, but over zealous. These qualities harmonize with him a great portion of the republican body. He deserves therefore all the just & favorable attention which can properly be shown to him." Thus did the great man condescend to a tribune of the people.[23]

Jefferson was right though. Duane was "honest, & well intentioned, but over zealous" and not cut out to be a mouthpiece for the administration, to speak the "sense of the government." A natural ideologue and polemicist, he was never likely to be accepted by the discreet gentility of Jeffersonian Washington.[24] And in May 1807, after six unproductive and difficult years, he gave up trying and returned to his home in Philadelphia. There, he took up the political cudgels again, this time to do battle against the conservative Republican political establishment he had helped to bring to power under Governor Thomas McKean in 1799. Pushed to the political margins by the national leadership of the Republican party, he was also pushed to the political margins by the Republican leadership of his own city and state.[25]

In a sense, Duane was a victim of his own success. Having demonstrated that newspapers were an indispensable instrument of partisan conflict and party organization, he had ensured that they were too important to be left in the hands of independent artisan-intellectuals like himself. And having done more than anyone else to forge the new Jeffersonian coalition and to propel Republican political rhetoric in a more conservative direction, he was now cut loose as too inflammatory and partisan. Marginalized by the party he helped to create and increasingly estranged from a more organizationally disciplined, less ideologically creative, and in many ways less democratic and open political culture, he became a figure of largely local influence and significance and, eventually, a political curiosity from a more contentious and colorful age. He felt the slight acutely but made a merit of his neglect. Writing to fellow Republican Abraham Bishop in 1802, he declared:

> So at least I stand independent of favor. In fact I am under no obligation to any man in America in any way to control my opinion, or bias my judgment. If I depended upon anything but my own activity and principles, I should have been left in the *Slough of Party* long ago, trodden upon, and like my predecessor forgotten—my independence is my pride.[26]

The politics of character was not only politically contested terrain in the 1790s; like debates about national identity and national character, it also had a politics of its own, draining public attention away from issues of ideological conflict and focusing it instead on issues of personal moral corruption. In this sense, Duane's campaign in 1800 on behalf of Thomas Jefferson, a man who by "force of character and private virtue" had confounded his political enemies and "grown every way more and more in public opinion, and in general love and confidence," was exemplary, signaling the conservative drift of Republican and American politics after 1800.[27] But then as now, not all Americans embraced the politics of character. James Madison, for example, believed that the abstract and impersonal justice of the law could resolve the problems created by the absence of civic virtue, and Federalists like Noah Webster held similar views in the early 1790s as did cosmopolitan radicals, who insisted that measures, not men, were the central issue in public life. But as we have seen, this hostility toward character could easily fuel an iconoclastic politics of character assassination, and by the end of the 1790s both Webster and the majority of Republican radicals (including Duane) had largely abandoned their allegiance to a disembodied public sphere and their resistance to the politics of character. In 1800, Federalists participated fully in the iconoclastic politics they so frequently criticized by attacking Jefferson as an infidel, while Republicans who defended and eulogized Thomas Jefferson as a man of the people assumed their place as defenders of civic virtue and the "constituted authorities."[28]

But, as I hope this book has made clear, there was no golden age of American politics and no dark age of American partisan journalism. Scandal and political incivility have always been part of American public life, and Americans have always been troubled by their existence and by the great power of the press to inform and misinform us. And in this respect at least, the 1790s were not that different from our own time. The founding period was not an age of political giants, when great men agreed with one another about the purpose of public life and rose above their personal foibles and partisan interests to enact enduring measures for the public good. They lived in a time of political passion and intense partisan conflict. Like our own. And it was from this conflict that their own great acts of collective political creativity emerged: the Declaration of Independence, the founding of the American Republic, the establishment of the Constitution and the federal government, the Bill of Rights, the creation of the Supreme Court and the federal judiciary, and the invention of new institutions to express and organize public opinion, including political parties and a free press. Without such conflict, the political triumphs of the early Republic would have been impossible and even unimaginable.

We should remember this when we hear calls for the restoration of political civility and the election of men of character capable of rising above the ideological and partisan fray. Or when we hear calls for the restoration of an "impartial" and objective press. In fact, public debates about scandal and the rise of personal journalism in the 1790s directly mirror contemporary debates about advocacy journalism and the politics of personality, and the issues that most worried the public then, issues about the relationship between private and public life, men and measures, and where to draw the boundary line between the two, are with us still. Then as now, the public saw the excesses of the press corroding the basis for rational public discussion and fraying the bonds of civility that held the nation together. But present-day calls for a return to rational and civilized public discourse and denunciations of the relentlessly partisan and personal character of political life ignore the role that partisanship and political invective have played in opening up and democratizing American politics. As Americans today grapple with the problem of creating a democratic and publicly accountable media, they need to embrace political conflict and difference, the clash of divergent ideological perspectives, and the problems of political interpretation they impose on us all, not yearn for a simpler time when the press was "objective," when all honest, civic-minded people agreed, and when political differences could be resolved by the exercise of impartial rationality. Such a time never existed, and certainly it did not exist in the early American Republic. Americans in the 1790s fought about politics and political ideas because they believed they were central to their lives, and by portraying the founding period as an age of classical equipoise and social civility, we ignore the creativity and dynamism of a period in our history that has much to tell us about the connections between democracy and disagreement.

Notes

Abbreviations

AAS   American Antiquarian Society (Worcester, Mass.)
ADA   *American Daily Advertiser* (Philadelphia, Pa.)
AHR   *American Historical Review*
AM   *American Minerva* (Philadelphia, Pa.)
APS   American Philosophical Society (Philadelphia, Pa.)
CMHS   *Collections of the Massachusetts Historical Society*
DA   *Daily Advertiser* (New York, N.Y.)
DAB   *Dictionary of American Biography*
GA   *General Advertiser* (Philadelphia, Pa.)
GUS   *Gazette of the United States* (New York, N.Y., and Philadelphia, Pa.)
FG   *Federal Gazette* (Philadelphia, Pa.)
FJ   *Freeman's Journal* (Philadelphia, Pa.)
HSP   Historical Society of Pennsylvania (Philadelphia, Pa.)
JAH   *Journal of American History*
JMP   *Papers of James Madison*
LCS   London Corresponding Society (London, England)
LOC   Library of Congress (Washington, D.C.)
MHS   Massachusetts Historical Society
NG   *National Gazette* (Philadelphia, Pa.)
NYHS   New-York Historical Society (New York, N.Y.)
NYPL   New York Public Library (New York, N.Y.)
PAH   *The Papers of Alexander Hamilton*
PG   *Porcupine's Gazette* (Philadelphia, Pa.)
TJP   *The Papers of Thomas Jefferson*
WMQ   *William and Mary Quarterly*

Introduction

1. William Kristol, "Generation Obama? Perhaps Not," *New York Times*, Mar. 17, 2008.

2. The phrase "hermeneutics of suspicion" is from Paul Ricoeur, *Freud and Philosophy: An Essay on Interpretation* (New Haven, Conn.: Yale University Press, 1970).

3. Dror Wahrman, *The Making of the Modern Self: Identity and Culture in Eighteenth-Century England* (New Haven, Conn.: Yale University Press, 2004). Kristol's fascination with the character issue is commonplace. For a more skeptical treatment of the character issue from the other side of the political fence, see Paul Krugman, "A Question of Character," *New York Times*, Oct. 14, 2005. Character has been the focus of a number of popular political biographies; see, for example, Peggy Noonan, *When Character Was King: A Story of Ronald Reagan* (New York: Penguin, 2002); Chris Wallace, *Character: Profiles in Presidential Courage* (New York: Rugged Land, 2004); Ronald Kessler, *A Matter of Character: Inside the White House of George W. Bush* (New York: Sentinel, 2004), and in a slightly more scholarly vein, Doris Kearns Goodwin et al., *Character above All: Ten Presidents from FDR to Bush* (New York: Simon & Schuster, 1996). The issue of character appears to resonate more on the political Right, where it is usually defined as a personal, nonideological, and nonpartisan virtue; see, for example, William Bennett's speech to the National Symposium on Character in Politics (University of Virginia, Apr. 2000).

4. Professor Carey Cooper quoted in Graham Hill, "Sex and the White House," BBC Online Network, Sept. 9, 1998. http://news.bbc.co.uk/2/hi/events/clinton_under_fire/the_big_picture/167068.stm.

5. Robert Wiebe, *The Opening of American Society: From the Adoption of the Constitution to the Eve of Disunion* (New York: Knopf, 1984), 35–66; Gordon Wood, "Conspiracy and the Paranoid Style: Causality and Deceit in the Eighteenth Century," *WMQ*, 3rd ser., 39, no. 3 (July 1982): 402–411. For more recent work on the politics of character in the early Republic, see Jacob Katz Cogan, "The Reynolds Affair and the Politics of Character," *Journal of the Early Republic* 16, no. 3 (Autumn 1996): 389–417; David Waldstreicher, *In the Midst of Perpetual Fetes: The Making of American Nationalism, 1776–1820* (Chapel Hill: University of North Carolina Press, 1997); Christopher Grasso, *A Speaking Aristocracy: Transforming Public Discourse in Eighteenth-Century Connecticut* (Chapel Hill: University of North Carolina Press, 1999); Andrew S. Trees, *The Founding Fathers and the Politics of Character* (Princeton, N.J.: Princeton University Press, 2004); and Joanne Freeman, *Affairs of Honor: National Politics in the New Republic* (New Haven, Conn.: Yale University Press, 2001). More generally on this issue, see Richard Sennett, *The Fall of Public Man* (New York: Vintage, 1992), esp. 98–106.

6. For recent work by major historians that emphasizes the character of the founding fathers, see Gordon Wood, *Revolutionary Characters: What Made the Founders Different* (New York: Penguin, 2006); Bernard Bailyn, *To Begin the World Anew: The Genius and Ambiguities of the American Founders* (New York: Knopf, 2003); and the many works of Joseph J. Ellis, including *Founding Brothers: The Revolutionary Generation* (New York: Vintage, 2002). Wood's review of Ellis's *Founding Brothers*, "The Greatest Generation," *New York Review of Books* (Mar. 29, 2001), captures the general tone of these works. See also Roger Kennedy, *Burr, Hamilton, and Jefferson: A Study in Character* (New York: Oxford University Press, 1999); Thomas G. West, *Vindicating the Founders: Race, Sex, Class, and Justice in the Origins of America* (Lanham, Md.: Rowman & Littlefield, 1997), and the many biographies by Richard Brookhiser, including *What Would the Founders Do? Our Questions, Their Answers* (New York: Basic, 2006) and *Rediscovering George Washington, Founding Father* (New York: Free Press, 1996). Revealingly, Brookhiser has also edited George Washington's *Rules of Civility: The 110 Precepts That Guided Our First President* (Charlottesville: University of Virginia Press, 2003) and describes his study of Washington as a "moral biography." This emphasis on the exemplary character of Washington and other founding fathers is not entirely new; see the discussion of Parson Mason Locke Weems in Trees, *Founding Fathers*, 135–146. Trees places a "sharply personalized politics of character" at the center of the politics of the early Republic, arguing that the literary and rhetorical self-creation of men like Jefferson, Hamilton, Adams, Madison, and Washington was "profoundly intertwined with politics"; see Trees, *Founding Fathers*, xi–xiii, 1–11. Gordon Wood also approaches character as public and performative but misses its contested, political nature. Like us, eighteenth-century Americans never agreed about how to define "character," still less who possessed it. Interest

in the character of the founding fathers is part of a broader popular phenomenon dubbed "founders chic"; see Evan Thomas, "Founders Chic: Live from Philadelphia," *Newsweek*, July 9, 2001. Jeffrey Pasley calls it, in good partisan fashion, "Federalist Chic," *Common-Place* (Jan. 2002), www.common-place.org.

7. Thomas Paine, *A Letter to George Washington, President of the United States on Affairs Public and Private* (Philadelphia: Benjamin Franklin Bache, 1796); John Keane, *Tom Paine: A Political Life* (New York: Little, Brown, 1995), 457; Marshall Smelser, "The Federalist Period as an Age of Passion," *American Quarterly* 10, no. 4 (Winter 1958): 10. The expression of passion and emotion through speech and writing was central to what Jay Fliegelman calls the "elocutionary revolution" of the eighteenth century in *Declaring Independence: Jefferson, Natural Language & the Culture of Performance* (Stanford, Calif.: Stanford University Press, 1993), 28–35. The tone of the period is best captured in some of the older historical literature; see especially Smelser, "The Jacobin Phrenzy: The Menace of Monarchy, Plutocracy, and Anglophilia, 1789–1798," *Review of Politics* 21 (Jan. 1959): 1; Smelser, "The Jacobin Phrenzy: Federalism and the Menace of Liberty, Equality, and Fraternity," *Review of Politics* 13 (Oct. 1951): 4; Charles Warren, *Jacobin and Junto; or, Early American Politics as Viewed in the Diary of Dr. Nathaniel Ames 1758–1822* (New York: Benjamin Blom, 1968 [1931]); and Vernon Louis Parrington, *The Colonial Mind 1620–1800* (New York: Harcourt, Brace, 1927).

8. The political creativity of the founders is a central theme in Bailyn, *To Begin the World Anew*; see esp. chap. 1, "Politics and the Creative Imagination," although I would broaden Bailyn's understanding of collective as opposed to individual creativity to include not only members of the political elite but their more humble fellow citizens.

9. Gordon Wood, "The Democratization of Mind in the American Revolution," in *Leadership in the American Revolution* (Washington, D.C.: Library of Congress, 1974); Frank Luther Mott, *American Journalism: A History of Newspapers in the United States 1690–1940* (New York: Macmillan, 1941), 168–169. Donald Stewart's otherwise sympathetic *The Opposition Press of the Federalist Period* (Albany: State University of New York Press, 1969) apologizes for the failure of editors in the 1790s to meet modern standards of editorial responsibility and propriety. For a slightly more favorable assessment, see Thomas Leonard, *The Power of the Press* (New York: Oxford University Press, 1986). Jeffrey Pasley, *The Tyranny of Printers: Newspaper Politics in the Early American Republic* (Charlottesville: University of Virginia, 2001), is a welcome break from this approach, but old habits die hard. Although Eric Burns relishes the "rowdy" journalism of the 1790s, his book begins with a line adapted from Dickens, "It was the best of times, it was the worst of journalism," a judgment with which this book disagrees; see Burns, *Infamous Scribblers: The Founding Fathers and the Rowdy Beginnings of American Journalism* (New York: Public Affairs, 2006), 3.

10. This is my main disagreement with Jeffrey Pasley's otherwise outstanding *Tyranny of Printers*. Pasley does an excellent job establishing the central role that editors like William Duane played in the political life of the early Republic, but his vaguely Weberian emphasis on the role of editors as party activists and organizers leads him to neglect political ideas almost entirely, especially those of Federalists like Noah Webster (who doesn't even make the index) and William Cobbett, who challenge his rather conventional and celebratory approach to the rise of Jeffersonian democracy, for which see Pasley, "The Cheese and the Words: Popular Political Culture and Participatory Democracy in the Early American Republic," in Pasley, Andrew Robertson, and David Waldstreicher (eds.), *Beyond the Founders: New Approaches to the Political History of the Early American Republic* (Chapel Hill: University of North Carolina Press, 2004).

11. My emphasis on biography is inspired by the journalists of the 1790s and the work of Richard Cobb; see in particular "La Vie en Marge: Living on the Fringe of the Revolution," in Cobb, *Reactions to the French Revolution* (New York: Oxford University Press, 1972); and Robert Darnton, *The Literary Underground of the Old Regime* (Cambridge, Mass.: Harvard University Press, 1982). A few of the journalists of the 1790s have received able scholarly attention; see

James Tagg, *Benjamin Franklin Bache and the American Aurora* (Philadelphia: University of Pennsylvania Press, 1991); Jeffrey Smith, *Franklin and Bache: Envisioning the Enlightened Republic* (New York: Oxford University Press, 1990); and Michael Durey, *"With the Hammer of Truth": James Thomson Callender and America's Early National Heroes* (Charlottesville: University of Virginia, 1990). Robert Rosenfeld's homage to William Duane, *American Aurora: A Democratic Republican Returns: The Suppressed History of Our Nation's Beginnings and the Heroic Newspaper That Tried to Report It* (New York: St. Martin's, 1997), is also worthwhile but too long and, in the spirit of its central protagonist, too partisan. William Safire's lively historical novel *Scandalmongers* (New York: Simon & Schuster, 2000) also brings the key players of the political and publishing world of the 1790s sharply to life.

12. Samuel Miller, *A Brief Retrospect of the Eighteenth Century* (New York: T. & J. Swords, 1803), vol. 2, 249–253. David Hackett Fischer calculated there were 201 newspapers in the United States by 1800; see Fischer, *The Revolution of American Conservatism: The Federalist Party in the Era of Jeffersonian Democracy* (New York: Harper and Row, 1965), 131. But there were probably more; see "A List of the Whole Number of Newspapers Printed Weekly in the U. States" (1789), in Isaiah Thomas Papers, AAS; Isaiah Thomas, *The History of Printing in America* (New York: Burt Franklin, [1874]); Clarence Brigham (ed.), *History and Bibliography of American Newspapers, 1690–1820* (Worcester, Mass.: American Antiquarian Society, 1947). However, the influence of the press was not simply a function of numbers, and its rapid growth has to be explained rather than assumed in a way that addresses the qualitative changes in print culture discussed below. My thinking about the press and its formative influence has been strongly shaped by Roger Chartier's brilliant *The Cultural Origins of the French Revolution* (Durham, N.C.: Duke University Press, 1991); and Jeremy Popkin, *Revolutionary News: The Press in France, 1789–1799* (Durham, N.C.: Duke University Press, 1990).

13. Miller, *Brief Retrospect*, 251–252; Stephen Botein, "'Meer Mechanics' and an Open Press: The Business and Political Strategies of Colonial American Printers," *Perspectives in American History* 9 (1975): 127–228; and Botein, "Printers and the American Revolution," in Bernard Bailyn and John Hench (eds.), *The Press & the American Revolution* (Boston: Northeastern University Press, 1981).

14. The ideas expressed here reflect my understanding of David Hall, "The Uses of Literacy in New England 1600–1850," in William L. Joyce et al. (eds.), *Printing and Society in Early America* (Worcester, Mass.: American Antiquarian Society, 1983); Cathy N. Davidson, *Revolution and the Word: The Rise of the Novel in America* (New York: Oxford University Press, 1986); Michael Warner, *The Letters of the Republic: Publication and the Public Sphere in Eighteenth-Century America* (Cambridge, Mass.: Harvard University Press, 1990); Dan Schiller, *Objectivity and the News: The Public and the Rise of Commercial Journalism* (Philadelphia: University of Pennsylvania Press, 1981); and Raymond Williams, "The Press and Popular Culture: An Historical Perspective," in G. Boyce, J. Curran, and P. Wingate (eds.), *Newspaper History* (London: Constable, 1978).

15. The phrase "republican ideology of print" is from Warner, *Letters of the Republic*, 60–67, 107–108. As Warner makes clear, editorial impartiality was part of a much broader republican print culture. In his discussion of the influential Jeffersonian journalist and cleric the Reverend William Bentley, Richard D. Brown argues that "fundamental to Bentley's conception of the information system of a free republic was the ideal of non-partisan journalism"; see Brown, *Knowledge Is Power: The Diffusion of Information in Early America, 1700–1865* (New York: Oxford University Press, 1989), 214. During the Revolution, Patriot writers expressed what I would call a virtuous subjectivity, articulating a highly ideological and partisan political identity but one bounded by the interests of the revolutionary people and the new republican nation; see Botein, "Printers and the American Revolution," in Bailyn and Hench (eds.), *The Press & the American Revolution*; and Ann Fairfax Withington, *Toward a More Perfect Union: Virtue and the Formation of the American Republics* (New York: Oxford University Press, 1991).

16. *PG*, Mar. 4, 1797. A good illustration of the development of a more personal authorial style in the press is the fate of pseudonyms, which were used throughout the eighteenth century to disguise authorship. Previously viewed as a way to preserve the impersonality of public debate and the independence and legitimacy of political authors, pseudonyms were attacked in the late 1790s as a device that facilitated authorial irresponsibility, and their use went into permanent decline.

17. The politics of character is a central theme in Freeman's *Affairs of Honor*, and in its emphasis on political passion, the fragility of personal identity, and the obsessive concern with public reputation that marked the politics of the early Republic, her work has much in common with my own. But there are also important points of disagreement. In her view, the political culture of the early Republic was synonymous with a "culture of honor," a "way of life" for its elite participants that shaped every aspect of their belief system and political behavior. Her emphasis on the unitary and nonpartisan nature of this "honor culture" does move us beyond conventional binary descriptions of the 1790s as a "Manichean [*sic*] battle between right and wrong, true and false, us and them," and this is the best part of her book. But her larger argument fails. In Freeman's analysis, elite politics is a "national political game" played according to highly formal and fixed rules, rules defined by a strict code of personal honor. "National politics," she argues in an especially condensed and sweeping formulation of her central argument, "was personal." This argument would not have been out of place in the 1790s and reduces political conflict to an essentially nonideological clash of well-meaning, public-spirited men, a highly conservative and conventional view of the period. By reducing political to personal conflict, Freeman's arguments have the odd effect of producing a founding generation of unfathomable cynics. If she is right, parties were no more than social clubs and the clashes between them no more than undignified personal scraps. And although at moments she hesitates, her analysis tends inexorably in this direction. Ultimately, her emphasis on the personal nature of politics makes political conflict trivial and inexplicable. The reductio ad absurdum of her argument is reached, fittingly, in her handling of newspapers. Despite her emphasis on the "war of words" that raged throughout the 1790s, she pays hardly any attention to newspapers, ignoring both their content and their politics and emphasizing instead the way that "personal relationships" shaped their circulation. "Newspapers," she declares, were "a highly personal form of communication, grounded on reputation, status, and friendship as much as devotion to a cause." Not only is this political history with the politics left out, it is a "war of words" without words, unapologetically anti-intellectual and conservative in its approach to history. In the postscript to the book, her distaste for politics inspires a call for the revival of historical positivism, for an ethnographic history in which historians "to as great a degree as possible, assume nothing" and build their narratives around an objective examination of the evidence. To paraphrase the inimitable William Cobbett, such professions of impartiality are nonsense, especially when coming from a historian. Rather than placing the politics of character at the center of political culture in the early Republic, her work strips the debate about character of its politics. However, I disagree with David Waldstreicher, "Founders Chic as Culture War," *Radical History Review* 84 (Fall 2002): 185–194, who has accused her of reviving the ideas of Lewis Namier. Namier's work explained the struggle for political power in eighteenth-century England as a function of interest and basic psychological drives rather than formal political ideas. But power was central. Freeman's world is pure theater, as innocent of real emotion and power as it is of politics; see Lewis Namier, *The Structure of Politics at the Accession of George III* (London: Macmillan, 1929); and Linda Colley, *Lewis Namier* (New York: St. Martin's, 1989).

18. Wood, "Conspiracy and the Paranoid Style," 420–434. Albert Hirschman makes a similar point in *The Passions and the Interests: Political Arguments for Capitalism before Its Triumph* (Princeton, N.J.: Princeton University Press, 1977), dating the shift to the publication of Machiavelli's *Prince* and a new science of statecraft that purported to describe "man, as he really is," rather than as he ought to be. The classic analysis of conspiratorial thought in revolutionary

America is Bernard Bailyn, *The Ideological Origins of the American Revolution* (Cambridge, Mass.: Harvard University Press, 1967). Jay Fliegelman points out that, according to the *Oxford English Dictionary*, the noun "responsibility" makes its earliest appearance in print in the *Federalist* and reflects a "radical rethinking of the relationship of individuals to the making of history" during and after the American Revolution; *Declaring Independence*, 140–150.

19. Henry Fielding, "An Essay on the Knowledge of the Characters of Men," in Henry Knight Miller (ed.), *Wesleyan Edition of the Works of Henry Fielding* (Middletown, Conn.: Wesleyan University Press, 1972), vol. 1, 155, 175; Hirschman, *The Passions and the Interests*, 3–66. For a brilliant overview of the growth of ideas about a "natural aristocracy" in France and the United States, see John Carson, *The Measure of Merit: Talents, Intelligence, and Inequality in the French and American Republics, 1750–1940* (Princeton, N.J.: Princeton University Press, 2007).

20. The classic formulation of the eighteenth-century public sphere is Jurgen Habermas, *The Structural Transformation of the Public Sphere: An Inquiry into a Category of Bourgeois Society*, trans. Thomas Burger (Cambridge, Mass.: MIT Press, 1991), esp. chaps. 3–4. Habermas has had a profound influence on European and American historians; see Craig Calhoun (ed.), *Habermas and the Public Sphere* (Cambridge, Mass.: MIT Press, 1992). For works on eighteenth-century America that make creative use of Habermas and were especially useful for this book, see David S. Shields, *Civil Tongues & Polite Letters in British America* (Chapel Hill: University of North Carolina Press, 1997); Warner, *Letters of the Republic*; and Grasso, *A Speaking Aristocracy*. For discussions of the relevance of Habermas to this period, see John L. Brooke, "Consent, Civil Society, and the Public Sphere in the Age of Revolution and the Early American Republic," in Pasley, Robertson, and Waldstreicher (eds.), *Beyond the Founders*; and the essays by Brooke, Ruth Bloch, and David Waldstreicher in "Forum: Alternative Histories of the Public Sphere," *WMQ* (Jan. 2005) vol. 1: 93–112.

21. Wood, "Conspiracy and the Paranoid Style," 410–411. For a fascinating account of the growth of popular conspiratorial ideas in eighteenth-century France, see Arlette Farge and Jacques Revel, *The Vanishing Children of Paris: Rumor and Politics before the French Revolution*, trans. Claudia Mieville (Cambridge, Mass.: Harvard University Press, 1991). In a brilliant analysis of capitalist market relations in early modern England, Jean-Christophe Agnew argues that the anxiety created by anonymous market exchange was expressed in debates about theatrical representation in sixteenth- and seventeenth-century England. The transformation of the public sphere in the eighteenth century, which created a new audience for elite politics at the same time as it eroded the personal relationships upon which premodern politics was based, brought a similar anonymity to political life, and by the 1700s political rather than commercial discourse was saturated with metaphors of the stage; see Agnew, *Worlds Apart: The Market and the Theater in Anglo-American Thought, 1550–1750* (Cambridge: Cambridge University Press, 1986). See also Fliegelman, *Declaring Independence*, 79–94; and Jeffrey H. Richards, *Theater Enough: American Culture and the Metaphor of the World Stage, 1607–1789* (Durham, N.C.: Duke University Press, 1991), esp. 200–297.

22. Habermas, *Structural Transformation*, 49; Wahrman, *Making of the Modern Self*. In the last quarter of the eighteenth century, argues Wahrman, an "*ancien regime* of identity" in which ideas of the self were highly fluid and modern categories of collective identity like class, race, and gender were either nonexistent or much less rigidly and well defined was replaced by a "modern" conception of the self tied to increasingly rigid and scientific categories of collective identity; see also Roy Porter (ed.), *Rewriting the Self: Histories from the Renaissance to the Present* (London: Routledge, 1997). Although most scholars focus on the "rational-critical" nature of Habermas's public sphere, he himself puts great stress on the relationship between the growth of bourgeois "subjectivity" and the closely linked role of "publicity" in eighteenth-century public life, a relationship that merits more attention from historians. The classic analysis of the novel and society in the eighteenth century is Ian Watt, *The Rise of the Novel: Studies in Defoe, Richardson and Fielding* (Berkeley: University of California Press, 1957). See also Fliegelman, *Declaring Independence*, 58.

23. My thinking here has been influenced by Sarah Maza in *Private Lives and Public Affairs: The Cause Célèbres of Prerevolutionary France* (Berkeley: University of California Press, 1993), chap. 12 and introduction; and Lazar Ziff, who emphasizes the close links between literary and political representation in the eighteenth century in *Writing in the New Nation: Prose, Print and Politics in the Early United States* (New Haven, Conn.: Yale University Press, 1991), x–xi. Not coincidentally, the 1790s witnessed both an efflorescence of ad hominem political journalism and the publication of the first novels written in the United States; see Davidson, *Revolution and the Word*. Both drew heavily on the epistolary form, from which the novel derived many of its literary conventions. Letters and newsletters were closely linked in the eighteenth century. Newspapers were in some sense public letters, and private letters about public life were frequently circulated publicly and assumed a quasi-public status. As Peter Van Schaack wrote to his fellow Federalist Theodore Sedgwick in 1799, "I have read with great attention what you say about Publick matters and have shown your letter to some confidential friends"; Van Schaack to Sedgwick, Dec. 25, 1799, Sedgwick Letters, MHS. For a study of newspapers that links them to both the novel and other literary genres in the eighteenth century, see J. Paul Hunter, *Before Novels: The Cultural Context of Eighteenth-Century English Fiction* (New York: Norton, 1990). This issue is also discussed in Freeman, *Affairs of Honor*, chap. 3, esp. 141–158. Benedict Anderson describes newspapers as an "'extreme form' of the book…one day best-sellers" and compares reading them to "reading a novel whose author has abandoned any thought of a coherent plot." But editors like Cobbett and Freneau, who were authors, did assume control of the plot for their readers; see Anderson, *Imagined Communities: Reflections on the Origin and Spread of Nationalism* (London: Verso, 1983), 33–35.

24. For a good guide to the English Grub Street, see Pat Rogers, *Grub Street: Studies in a Subculture* (London: Methuen, 1972). For colonial literary and political satire, see David Shields, *Oracles of Empire: Poetry, Politics and Commerce in British America, 1690–1750* (Chicago: University of Chicago Press, 1990); Shields, *Civil Tongues & Polite Letters*; and William C. Dowling, *Poetry and Ideology in Revolutionary Connecticut* (Athens: University of Georgia Press, 1990). For the Revolution, see Bruce Granger, *Political Satire in the American Revolution* (Ithaca, N.Y.: Cornell University Press, 1960).

25. Wood, "Conspiracy and the Paranoid Style," 427; Fielding, "An Essay on the Knowledge of the Characters of Men," in Miller (ed.), *Works of Henry Fielding*, vol. 1, 152–156, 175. For an excellent discussion of the centrality of satire and invective to the 1790s and the hostility toward public artifice, see Nancy Isenberg, "The 'Little Emperor': Aaron Burr, Dandyism, and the Sexual Politics of Treason," in Pasley, Robertson, and Waldstreicher (eds.), *Beyond the Founders*.

26. Thomas Paine, *Common Sense*, in Philip S. Foner (ed.), *The Complete Writings of Thomas Paine* (New York: Citadel Press, 1945), vol. 1, 4; Thomas Jefferson to James Madison, May 19, 1793, in Julian P. Boyd (ed.), *The Papers of Thomas Jefferson* (Princeton, N.J.: Princeton University Press, 1950–), vol. 23; [John Adams], *The True Sentiments of America…and a Dissertation on the Canon and Feudal Law* (London: J. Almon, 1768); Fliegelman, *Declaring Independence*, 32–33, 120–140. The seminal study on the idea of transparency in the Enlightenment is Jean Starobinski, *Jean-Jacques Rousseau: Transparency and Obstruction*, trans. Arthur Goldhammer (Chicago: University of Chicago Press, 1988). As Karen Ordahl Kupperman argues, simplicity and transparency were also associated with the nakedness of Native Americans and the image of the "virtuous savage." Thomas Morton used words very similar to Paine's in the seventeenth century when he praised Native Americans for their simplicity and declared, "Cloaths are the badge of sinne." And Roger Williams reminded readers of his *Key to the Language of America* that both the Indians and the English would appear naked at the last judgment, when all things hidden would be revealed to God; see Kupperman, *Indians and English: Facing Off in Early America* (Ithaca, N.Y.: Cornell University Press, 2000), chap. 2.

27. For excellent discussions of elite anxiety and insecurity in colonial America, see Michael Zuckerman, "Identity in British America: Unease in Eden," in Nicholas Canny and Anthony

Pagden (eds.), *Colonial Identity in the Atlantic World, 1500–1800* (Princeton, N.J.: Princeton University Press, 1989); and Ronald Hoffman, Mechal Sobel, and Fredrika Teute, *Through a Glass Darkly: Reflections on Personal Identity in Early America* (Chapel Hill: University of North Carolina Press, 1997). Elite insecurity is a central theme in Bernard Bailyn's classic essay *The Origins of American Politics* (New York: Knopf, 1968) and also in Woody Holton, *Forced Founders: Indians, Debtors, Slaves & the Making of the American Revolution* (Chapel Hill: University of North Carolina Press, 1999), and Kathleen Brown, *Good Wives, Nasty Wenches & Anxious Patriarchs: Gender, Race, and Power in Colonial Virginia* (Chapel Hill: University of North Carolina Press, 1996).

28. Indeed, if Dror Wahrman is right and the American Revolution represented a sharp and radical break with what he calls an ancien régime of identity, it may have destabilized traditional signs of public identity just as new categories of identity were becoming more rigid and fixed, perhaps one reason that issues of personal identity were so highly charged in the postrevolutionary United States; see Wahrman, "The English Problem of Identity in the American Revolution," *AHR* 106, no. 4 (Oct. 2001): 1236–1262, and Wahrman, *Making of the Modern Self*, chap. 6. For a good case study of the anxiety that issues of public identity could cause in the early Republic, see Joanne Freeman's portrait of Senator William Maclay in *Affairs of Honor*, chap. 1.

29. Clinton Rossiter (ed.), *The Federalist Papers* (New York: Penguin Putnam, 1999), no. 10, 51 and 72; Norman Rosenberg, *Protecting the Best Men: An Interpretive History of the Law of Libel* (Chapel Hill: University of North Carolina Press, 1986); Hirschman, *The Passions and the Interests*, 28–30; Alan Taylor, "From Fathers to Friends of the People: Political Personas in the Early Republic," in Ralph D. Gray and Michael A. Morrison (eds.), *New Perspectives on the Early Republic, 1981–1991* (Urbana: University of Illinois Press, 1994).

30. Most Americans were deeply committed to a unitary understanding of the political nation and found it hard to conceive of partisan differences as anything other than a result of factional intrigue and organized self-interest; see Richard Hofstadter, *The Idea of a Party System: The Rise of Legitimate Opposition in the United States, 1780–1840* (Berkeley: University of California Press, 1969). As Waldstreicher argues, such political conflict challenged not only classical republican ideas about civic virtue and the public interest but also the culture of "sentimental nationalism" and "federal feeling" that reached its "high-water mark" in the 1780s and 1790s. According to these "sentimental nationalists," it was not republican rationality and civic virtue that held the political nation together but the "affective ties" of civility, sociability, and sensibility. This culture of sensibility, which has begun to receive a great deal of attention from historians, shaped ideas about personal authenticity and gentility as well as ideas about national character; see Waldstreicher, *In the Midst of Perpetual Fetes*, 52–107. On the importance of sensibility and sentiment in eighteenth-century America, see Andrew Burstein, *Sentimental Democracy: The Evolution of America's Romantic Self-Image* (New York: Hill and Wang, 1999); Sarah Knott, "Sensibility and the American War of Independence," *AHR* 109, no. 1 (Feb. 2004): 19–40; and Catherine O'Donnell Kaplan, *Men of Letters in the Early Republic: Cultivating Forums of Citizenship* (Chapel Hill: University of North Carolina Press, 2008). The "insensibility" of editors like William Cobbett and Benjamin Franklin Bache represented a challenge to these elite forms of sociability and politics, an eruption of plebian radicalism, manners, and masculinity in a period that David Shields describes as "obsessed with civility"; Shields, *Civil Tongues & Polite Letters*, xxi, chap. 9. In some respects, this book mirrors their challenge, reminding historians that the early Republic cannot be understood entirely in terms of a culture of sensibility and civility and that the effort to do so (which tends to focus historical attention on the writings and behavior of elite men and women) often reflects the class politics of its subjects and an equally problematic yearning for a more civil politics of our own.

31. I thus disagree with Gordon Wood's argument that, by the late eighteenth century, conspiratorial explanations for social change were in decline, retreating before a more modern

world view that emphasized not personal volition but the role of impersonal historical and social forces; Wood, "Conspiracy and the Paranoid Style," 337–441. It also seems to me too simple to conclude that a more privatized and liberal understanding of character was replacing a public understanding of character; see Cogan, "Reynolds Affair," 410–415. The relationships between private and public characters, and their very definitions, were always contested and remain so to the present day. For a slightly different point of view, see Shields, *Civil Tongues & Polite Letters*, xx–xxi. Conspiracy theories certainly didn't evaporate after 1800; see Richard Hofstadter, *The Paranoid Style in American Politics and Other Essays* (Cambridge, Mass.: Harvard University Press, 1952); David Brion Davis, *The Slave Power Conspiracy and the Paranoid Style* (Baton Rouge: Louisiana State University Press, 1970).

32. *PG*, June 22, 1797. The Lyon-Griswold affair is discussed in Aleine Austin, *Matthew Lyon: "New Man" of the Democratic Revolution, 1749–1822* (University Park: Pennsylvania State University Press, 1981), 95–102. Significantly, Lyon was infuriated by a story about his lack of military prowess during the American Revolution, which was circulating in William Cobbett's newspaper, *Porcupine's Gazette*. For Jefferson's remarks, see A. A. Lipscomb and A. E. Bergh (eds.), *The Writings of Thomas Jefferson* (Washington, D.C.: Thomas Jefferson Memorial Association, 1903–1904), vol. 9, 411.

33. James Madison, "Public Opinion," *NG*, Dec. 19, 1791. For an interesting discussion of this link between national integration and the press, see David Paul Nord, "Newspapers and American Nationhood, 1776–1826," in John B. Hench (ed.), *Three Hundred Years of the American Newspaper* (Worcester, Mass.: American Antiquarian Society, 1991).

34. *GUS*, Apr. 10, 1790. Only a few canonical religious books functioned similarly within popular reading culture, notably the Bible and John Bunyan's *Pilgrim's Progress*. For a discussion of some of the themes raised here, see William J. Gilmore, *Reading Becomes a Necessity of Life: Material and Cultural Life in Rural New England, 1780–1835* (Knoxville: University of Tennessee Press, 1989), chap. 6; Richard D. Brown, *Knowledge Is Power: The Diffusion of Information in Early America, 1700–1865* (New York: Oxford University Press, 1989), chap. 8; Thomas C. Leonard, *News for All: America's Coming-of-Age with the Press* (New York: Oxford University Press, 1995), chap. 1. For the circulation of newspapers in this period, see Richard B. Kielbowicz, "The Press, Post Office, and the Flow of News in the Early Republic," *Journal of the Early Republic* 3 (Fall 1983): 255–280; Richard R. John, *Spreading the News: The American Postal System from Franklin to Morse* (Cambridge, Mass.: Harvard University Press, 1995).

35. "The Lay Preacher," reprinted from Dennie's *Farmer's Weekly Museum* in the Hartford *American Mercury*, Aug. 7, 1797. See also the play by Samuel Low that begins with a satirical look at the popularity of "advertisers and intelligencers": [An American], *The Politician Out-Witted: A Comedy* (New York: W. Ross, 1788). Quotation by Andrews from the Stockbridge, Massachusetts, *Western Star*, reprinted in *GUS*, Dec. 12, 1789; and in the *Time-Piece and Literary Companion*, [Mar. 13, 1797].

36. Francis Wharton (ed.), *State Trials of the United States during the Administrations of Washington and Adams* (Philadelphia: Carey and Hart, 1849), 328; Miller, *Brief Retrospect*. For a fuller discussion of the Sedition Act and its relationship to popular concern about the licentiousness of the press, see the conclusion of this book.

37. See, for example, Robert A. Gross, "Politics, Printing, and the People," *Proceedings of the American Antiquarian Society* 99 (Oct. 1989): part 2; and the essays by Charles Clark, David Paul Nord, Gerald Baldasty, and Michael Schudson in Hench (ed.), *Three Hundred Years of the American Newspaper*.

38. This was not a mistake that people of the time made. They constantly blamed the scandalmongering of editors like Bache and Cobbett for the factionalism of American politics. Historians, however, have tended to treat the emergence of the first political parties as an organizational rather than an ideological problem; see, for example, Noble Cunningham, *The Jeffersonian Republicans: The Formation of a Party Organization, 1789–1801* (Chapel Hill:

University of North Carolina Press, 1957); and Stanley Elkins and Eric McKitrick, *The Age of Federalism: The Early American Republic, 1788–1800* (New York: Oxford University Press, 1993). This approach overlooks the critical role played by the press in the elaboration of political ideology and in the creation of a popular partisan consciousness. Even some of the most recent and innovative work on popular political culture, which does a superb job of recovering the political consciousness of the "inarticulate," implicitly equates (as does much social history) the use of printed words with elite culture, overlooking the articulation of popular political consciousness in the press; see, for example, Simon P. Newman, *Parades and the Politics of the Street: Festive Culture in the Early American Republic* (Philadelphia: University of Pennsylvania Press, 1997). For a brilliant example of the connections between print culture and popular political consciousness, see Michael Merrill and Sean Wilentz (eds.), *The Key of Liberty: The Life and Democratic Writings of William Manning, "A Laborer," 1747–1814* (Cambridge, Mass.: Harvard University Press, 1993).

39. From the late 1950s onward, scholars established in a succession of brilliant studies the importance of classical republican and civic humanist ideas in Anglo-American political thought, charting the complex history of American republican ideology in the eighteenth century; see Caroline Robbins, *The Eighteenth-Century Commonwealthman* (Cambridge, Mass.: Harvard University Press, 1959); Bailyn, *The Origins of American Politics*; Bailyn, *Ideological Origins of the American Revolution*; Gordon Wood, *The Creation of the American Republic, 1776–1787* (Chapel Hill: University of North Carolina Press, 1969); J. G. A. Pocock, *The Machiavellian Moment: Florentine Political Thought and the Atlantic Republican Tradition* (Princeton, N.J.: Princeton University Press, 1975). The direction of this work, with its emphasis on the transmission of ideas from the Old World to the New, signaled a decisive reorientation in the study of eighteenth-century American history. Ironically, however, by locating what Bailyn called the "origins of American politics" and Wood "the end of classical politics" in the revolutionary and immediate postrevolutionary period, their work deflected attention from the continuing influence of Europe on the development of American political culture. This neglect is especially problematic for the 1790s. Americans were astonishingly well informed about European politics during the 1790s, and it was easier, and probably more interesting, for them to follow events in the Batavian Republic than in Baltimore. This fact is reflected in older historical works; see R. R. Palmer, *The Age of Democratic Revolution: A Political History of Europe and America, 1760–1800* (Princeton, N.J.: Princeton University Press, 1964), 2 vols.; Warren, *Jacobin and Junto*; Charles Downer Hazen, *Contemporary American Opinion of the French Revolution* (Baltimore, Md.: Johns Hopkins University Press, 1897); Bernard Fay, *The Revolutionary Spirit in France and America* (New York: Harcourt, Brace, 1927). In *To Begin the World Anew*, Bailyn does explore the "Atlantic dimensions" of American thought, but in keeping with works like David Armitage's *The Declaration of Independence: A Global History* (Cambridge, Mass.: Harvard University Press, 2007), he focuses on the influence of American ideas rather than on the way these ideas were shaped by the broader history of the revolutionary Atlantic. The vibrant and radical cosmopolitan tradition recovered and explored by Seth Cotlar, however, is a reminder to historians that the transatlantic transmission of ideas and people did not come to a sudden halt in 1776, a point this book hopefully supports; see Cotlar, "In Paine's Absence: The Trans-Atlantic Dynamics of American Popular Political Thought, 1789–1804" (Ph.D. diss., Northwestern University, 2000), 1–65, and Cotlar, "Joseph Gales and the Making of the Jeffersonian Middle Class," in James Horn, Jan Lewis, and Peter Onuf (eds.), *The Revolution of 1800: Democracy, Race, and the New Republic* (Charlottesville: University of Virginia Press, 2002). For another antidote to the recent resurgence of American "exceptionalism," see Peter Linebaugh and Marcus Rediker, *The Many Headed Hydra: The Hidden History of the Revolutionary Atlantic* (Boston: Beacon, 2000).

40. For important works on the 1790s that make use of the republican paradigm, see Lance Banning, *The Jeffersonian Persuasion: Evolution of a Party Ideology* (Ithaca, N.Y.: Cornell

University Press, 1978); Banning, "Republican Ideology and the Triumph of the Constitution, 1789 to 1793," *WMQ* 31, no. 2 (Apr. 1974): 168–188; Banning, "Jeffersonian Ideology Revisited: Liberal and Classical Ideas in the New American Republic," *WMQ* 43, no. 1 (Jan. 1986): 4–19; Drew McCoy, *The Elusive Republic: Political Economy in Jeffersonian America* (Chapel Hill: University of North Carolina Press, 1980); John Murrin, "The Great Inversion; or, Court versus Country," in J. G. A. Pocock (ed.), *Three British Revolutions: 1641, 1688, 1776* (Princeton, N.J.: Princeton University Press, 1980); Richard Buel, *Securing the Revolution* (Ithaca, N.Y.: Cornell University Press, 1972). Critics of the republican paradigm, like Joyce Appleby, who had long insisted on the centrality of an older emphasis on American liberalism, were eventually joined by one of its originators, Gordon Wood; see Appleby, *Capitalism and the New Social Order* (New York: New York University Press, 1984); Appleby, "Republicanism in Old and New Contexts," *WMQ* 43, no. 1 (Jan. 1986): 20–34; and Wood, *The Radicalism of the American Revolution* (New York: Knopf, 1992). Paradigm shifts after all are only a matter of timing. For an effective coda to the debate about republicanism and liberalism, see Daniel Rodgers, "Republicanism: The Career of a Concept," *JAH* 79, no. 1 (June 1992): 11–38.

41. This is clear in Pocock's *The Machiavellian Moment*, which places American political culture in a kind of premodern prison house of the psyche where the bars are linguistic. Pocock's work was strongly influenced by Thomas Kuhn's seminal *The Structure of Scientific Revolutions* (Chicago: University of Chicago Press, 1962) and its concept of the "paradigm"; see Pocock, *Politics, Language and Time: Essays on Political Thought and History* (New York: Atheneum, 1971). Despite his efforts to historicize the study of political language, like many intellectual historians Pocock shows little regard for the political context within which words are used, and the abrasive, personal, and ephemeral language of the American press in the 1790s fits only jarringly into his linguistic paradigms. But this simply exposes their analytical inadequacy.

42. These ideas owe much to my reading of Michael Holquist (ed.), *The Dialogic Imagination: Four Essays by M. M. Bakhtin*, trans. Caryl Emerson and Michael Holquist (Austin: University of Texas Press, 1981), and to the example of Gareth Stedman Jones, *Languages of Class: Studies in English Working Class History, 1832–1982* (Cambridge: Cambridge University Press, 1983). David Waldstreicher's *In the Midst of Perpetual Fetes* takes a similar approach to language and the history of ideas, placing conflict and contested meaning at the center of his understanding of American political culture. To Waldstreicher, ideas about nationalism and national character are always part of a politically charged debate, and their partisan use reflects a broader political and rhetorical strategy that creates and defines what it only seems to describe: the nation. Although he pays little attention to particular partisan journalists, his work demonstrates the pivotal role that newspapers and their editors played in the construction and circulation of ideas about American nationalism. Waldstreicher's argument is strongly influenced by Benedict Anderson's emphasis on the role played by print culture and the newspaper in the formation of New World nationalism in *Imagined Communities*. For an approach that places more emphasis on the conservative nature of political language (and relies greatly on the work of Pocock and Quentin Skinner), see Andrew Robertson, *The Language of Democracy: Political Rhetoric in the United States and Britain, 1790–1900* (Ithaca, N.Y.: Cornell University Press, 1995).

43. See William Steirer, "Riding 'Everyman's Hobby Horse': Journalists in Philadelphia, 1764–1794," in G. Boyce, J. Curran, and P. Wingate (eds.), *Newspaper History from the Seventeenth Century to the Present Day* (London: Constable, 1978).

44. However, all communities, including political parties, are imagined; see Anderson, *Imagined Communities*. Ronald P. Formisano, "Deferential-Participant Politics: The Early Republic's Political Culture, 1789–1840," *American Political Science Review* 68, no. 2 (June 1974): 473–487, argues that political parties and a party system did not exist in the 1790s, a view endorsed by Wood, *Radicalism of the American Revolution*, 298–300. But efforts to assess party formation in the 1790s on the basis of models drawn from modern practice seem to

me fraught with problems, depending on assumptions about the legitimacy and stability of modern political parties that seem doubtful. Eighteenth-century Americans may have felt ambivalent about the legitimacy of political parties, but so do we, and it seems hard to pinpoint exactly when this hostility declined sufficiently to permit the development of modern political parties. Political parties in the 1790s were unstable coalitions because political parties are *always* unstable coalitions, particularly in the antebellum United States. Both institutionally and ideologically, parties and the electorate are always in flux, and "stable" party systems seem to me largely wishful thinking and/or a fiction of the political scientist's overly orderly imagination.

45. A Whiggish equation between Jeffersonianism and modernity is central to Gordon Wood's *Radicalism of the American Revolution*; see also Wood, "Interests and Disinterestedness in the Making of the Constitution," in Richard Beeman, Stephen Botein, and Edward C. Carter II (eds.), *Beyond Confederation: Origins of the Constitution and American National Identity* (Chapel Hill: University of North Carolina Press, 1987). Such an equation also shapes Elkins and McKitrick's *Age of Federalism*. Despite their sympathy for the Federalists, Elkins and McKitrick can't help regarding Federalism as a lost cause, and in this they agree with neo-Jeffersonians and even that old bugbear of Federalist history, Charles Beard; see his *An Economic Interpretation of the Constitution of the United States* (New York: Macmillan, 1960 [1913]) and *Economic Origins of Jeffersonian Democracy* (New York: Macmillan, 1915). Of course, Beard's belief that the clash between Republicans and Federalists represented a conflict between supporters of political and economic democracy and the members of a politically reactionary economic elite can be found in any Republican newspaper of the 1790s.

46. David Waldstreicher, "Two Cheers for the 'Public Sphere' and One for Historians' Skepticism," *WMQ* 62, no. 1 (Jan. 2005): 107–112.

Chapter 1

1. *GUS*, Apr. 15, 1789. Fenno subsequently moved his printing office to 9 Maiden Lane and then to 41 Broad Street in New York. In 1790, he moved to Philadelphia (the last New York issue of the paper appeared on Oct. 13), resuming publication at 69 Market Street on Nov. 3, 1790. He later moved to 34 North Street and then to 119 Chestnut Street. After his death on Sept. 14, 1798, his son, John Ward Fenno, took over the paper. He sold it to Caleb Wayne on May 28, 1800. See Brigham, *History and Bibliography of American Newspapers*.

2. Frederic Hudson, *Journalism in the United States, from 1690 to 1872* (Rpt., New York: Haskell House, 1968), 150. For the ratification process in New York, see Stephen L. Schecter (ed.), *The Reluctant Pillar: New York and the Adoption of the Federal Constitution* (Troy, N.Y.: Russell Sage, 1985); Linda Grant De Pauw, *The Eleventh Pillar: New York State and the Federal Constitution* (Ithaca, N.Y.: Cornell University Press, 1966).

3. For the political complexion of the press in New York City, see Edward C. Lathem, *Chronological Tables of American Newspapers, 1690–1820* (Worcester, Mass.: American Antiquarian Society, 1972). Because John Russell's brother, Benjamin Russell, was Fenno's former employer and the owner of the *Massachusetts Centinel*, it's possible that Fenno's arrival in New York was timed to coincide with Russell's departure; see Lewis G. Leary, *That Rascal Freneau: A Study in Literary Failure* (New Brunswick, N.J.: Rutgers University Press, 1941), 167; and John B. Hench (ed.), "Letters of John Fenno and John Ward Fenno, 1779–1800, Part 1: 1779–1790," *Proceedings of the American Antiquarian Society* 89, no. 2 (1980): 314 (hereafter "Fenno Letters, Part 1").

4. Hudson, *Journalism in the United States*, 144–145; Alfred F. Young, *The Democratic Republicans of New York: The Origins* (Chapel Hill: University of North Carolina Press, 1967), 120, 128; Robert Rutland, *The Newsmongers: Journalism in the Life of the Nation, 1690–1972* (New York: Dial, 1973), 61. For the attack on Greenleaf's printing office, see *New-York Journal*, July 24, 28, 31, Aug. 7, 21, 1788.

5. Fenno to Ward, Jan. 28, 1789, in Hench (ed.), "Fenno Letters, Part 1." Other editors had similar ideas. Andrew Brown launched his *Federal Gazette* in Philadelphia in 1788, just as Noah Webster established the *American Magazine* in collaboration with Ebeneezer Hazard, Jeremy Belknap, and Francis Childs, a venture that folded shortly before Fenno arrived in New York; see Richard Rollins, *The Long Journey of Noah Webster* (Philadelphia: University of Pennsylvania Press, 1980), 59; Noah Webster to Benjamin Rush, Feb. 10, 1788, in Harry Warfel (ed.), *Letters of Noah Webster* (New York: Library Publishers, 1953).

6. Douglas Southall Freeman, *George Washington: A Biography* (New York: Scribner's, 1948–1957), vol. 6, 195, and chap. 7. Garry Wills describes the "semi-deification" of Washington during the "parade of triumph taking him North to the presidency," in *Cincinnatus: George Washington and the Enlightenment* (Garden City, N.Y.: Doubleday, 1984), 23. The best account of this "sentimental nationalism" and its connection to ideas about national character is in Waldstreicher, *In the Midst of Perpetual Fetes*, chaps. 3–4.

7. *GUS*, Apr. 25, 1789.

8. *GUS*, Apr. 25, 1789. David Gelston, another observer of the day's events, was also struck by the intensity of public feeling, "the claps—the shouts—the huzzas exceeded all descriptions.... I never felt such strong emotions upon any public occasion." David Gelston to John Smith, Apr. 27, 1789, quoted in Young, *Democratic Republicans*, 149.

9. *GUS*, Apr. 25, 1789.

10. *GUS*, Apr. 25, 1789. For similar panegyric about Washington in other newspapers, see Freeman, *George Washington*, vol. 6, 183–184. Fenno's adulation was part of a cult of personality surrounding Washington that was well established by 1789; see Paul Longmore, *The Invention of George Washington* (Berkeley: University of California Press, 1988); Marcus Cunliffe, *George Washington: Man and Monument* (Boston: Little, Brown, 1958); Barry Schwartz, *George Washington: The Making of an American Symbol* (New York: Free Press, 1987).

11. *GUS*, Apr. 25, 1789.

12. On American ideas about revolutionary virtue, see Withington, *Toward a More Perfect Union*. The relationship between Fenno and Federalism is complex, but his emphasis on national consensus and character suggests caution about identifying him or Federalists in general with the Madisonian "liberalism" of the federal Constitution. Withington argues that members of the Constitutional Convention created a new form of republican government based on "the sovereignty of a people, not on their character—on balanced interests, not virtue," accepting and even exploiting the diverse and often jarring interests of American society. Her argument owes much to Gordon Wood's belief that the passage of the federal Constitution was a pivotal moment in the transition from a republican to a liberal political culture; see Wood, *Creation of the American Republic*. Madison's *Federalist*, no. 10, exemplified this new liberal emphasis on interest rather than virtue. Fenno, however, rejected the idea that interest alone could form a basis for national political union and placed much greater emphasis on the importance of personal character and public sentiment. In fact, Madison himself emphasized the need to ensure that public affairs remained in the hands of virtuous public men even in *Federalist*, no. 10.

13. *GUS*, Apr. 29, 1789.

14. *GUS*, Apr. 29, 15, July 4, Apr. 25, Sept. 8, 23, 26, 1789; Fenno to Joseph Ward, Aug. 5, 1789, in Hench (ed.), "Fenno Letters, Part 1."

15. The most important source for Fenno's life is the John Fenno Papers in the Joseph Ward Collection, Chicago Historical Society. These are edited and published in two parts in John B. Hench (ed.), "Letters of John Fenno and John Ward Fenno, 1779–1800," *Proceedings of the American Antiquarian Society* 89–90 (1980). See also "John Fenno, Orderly Book 1775," in Miscellaneous Manuscript Collection, LOC; William C. Kiessel, "The Family of John Fenno" (typescript, 1950); and "John Fenno," Printers File, both in the AAS; John Fenno to Joseph Dennie, Oct. 8, 1796, in Dennie Papers, Houghton Library, Harvard University; John Fenno to John Lamb, June 22, 1778, in Lamb Papers, NYHS. For useful printed sources, see Charles

R. King (ed.), *The Life and Correspondence of Rufus King* (New York: Putnam's, 1894–1900), vol. 1; "Belknap Papers, Part II," *CMHS*, 5th ser., 3 (1877); Dumas Malone (ed.), *DAB* (New York: Scribner's, 1928–1958), vol. 6, 325; J. Thomas Scarf and Thompson Westcott, *History of Philadelphia, 1609–1884* (Philadelphia: L. H. Everts, 1884), vol. 3; Brigham (ed.), *History and Bibliography of American Newspapers*; Freeman, *George Washington*, vol. 6, 393–413; Julian P. Boyd, *TJP*, vol. 16, 237–260.

16. John Fenno to Joseph Ward, July 5, 1789, in Hench (ed.), "Fenno Letters, Part 1." Ward taught briefly at Old South in 1769 and in 1772 announced his intention to start an "English grammar school" at the same time as Fenno advertised "a school for 20 scholars only"; see Robert Francis Seybolt, *The Private Schools of Colonial Boston* (Cambridge, Mass.: Harvard University Press, 1935), 31, 41, 66–69.

17. Colonel Joseph Ward was a secretary and aide-de-camp to General Artemas Ward, his second cousin once removed; see Hench (ed.), "Fenno Letters, Part 1," 303–304; "John Fenno, Orderly Book," LOC, June 17, 1775. His orderly book provides a fascinating glimpse into the organization of the colonial army and the discipline problems it experienced in its early days. Unfortunately, the last entry is on Sept. 6, 1775.

18. There are no further records of Fenno's service in the Continental army, but Colonel Joseph Ward remained on General Ward's staff until the latter retired in Mar. 1777, and Fenno may have served until then; see Hench (ed.), "Fenno Letters, Part 1," 302–303, 310; Fenno to John Lamb, June 22, 1778, in Lamb Papers, NYHS; "John Fenno, Orderly Book"; Kiessel, "Family of John Fenno"; Malone (ed.), *DAB*, vol. 6, 325; Fenno to Ward, Oct. 12, Nov. 15, 1789, in Hench (ed.), "Fenno Letters, Part 1"; Jeremy Belknap to Ebeneezer Hazard, May 8, 1789, in "Belknap Papers II."

19. John B. Hench, "The Newspaper in a Republic: Boston's 'Centinel' and 'Chronicle,' 1784–1801" (Ph.D. diss., Clark University, 1979), 42; Belknap to Hazard, May 2, [1789], "Belknap Papers II"; "An Address," Jan. 1, 1789; Fenno to Ward, Feb. 17, 1789, both in Hench (ed.), "Fenno Letters, Part 1."

20. Christopher Gore to Rufus King, Jan. 18, 1789, in King (ed.), *Life and Correspondence of Rufus King*, vol. 1, 357–358; "An Address," Jan. 1, 1789, in Hench (ed.), "Fenno Letters, Part 1." The support of Christopher Gore, a wealthy Boston lawyer with strong ties to the British mercantile community, was particularly crucial to Fenno. Gore was elected to the Massachusetts General Court in 1778, supported the passage of the federal Constitution in the Massachusetts Convention, and became U.S. district attorney for Massachusetts in 1789. A thoroughgoing economic nationalist, he speculated heavily in government securities in the 1780s and probably viewed the creation of the *Gazette of the United States* as a way to project his local political influence onto the national stage. Gore told speculator Andrew Craigie in Mar. 1789 that, although he'd like to come to New York, to do so "wou'd, though very unjustly, subject my political character at least, to many imputations, either of seeking preferment for myself or plotting some plans which wou'd be said unworthy," by which he meant the passage of Hamilton's funding bill. It was later claimed that his speculative ventures with Craigie, Duer, and others made him the richest lawyer in Massachusetts; see Helen R. Pinkney, *Christopher Gore: Federalist of Massachusetts, 1758–1827* (Waltham, Mass.: Gore Place Society, 1969), 9–43. By giving Fenno a letter of introduction to Rufus King, his contemporary and close friend at Harvard, Gore smoothed Fenno's way into the higher echelons of Federalist society in New York.

21. Belknap to Hazard, May 2, [1789], in "Belknap Papers, Part II"; Introduction and Fenno to Ward, Feb. 23, 1789, in Hench (ed.), "Fenno Letters, Part 1." Gore and eight other wealthy Bostonians, including Governor Bowdoin, loaned Fenno about £250, repayable in two years, to start his newspaper. There is no evidence that he ever repaid this loan. After he arrived in New York, Ward sent another £183, giving Fenno enough money to launch the *Gazette of the United States*. Both Ward and Gore later sent him more money; see Fenno, "An Address"; and Fenno to Ward, Jan. 28, Aug. 5, Oct. 9, Nov. 20, 1789, in Hench (ed.), "Fenno Letters, Part 1."

22. "An Address," Jan. 1, 1789, in Hench (ed.), "Fenno Letters, Part 1."

23. *GUS*, Apr. 15, 1789; Hazard to Belknap, May 28, 1789, in "Belknap Papers II." Fenno's decision not to accept advertising also emphasized the political rather than commercial character of his newspaper.

24. *GUS*, Apr. 15, 1789; "An Address," Jan. 1, 1789, in Hench (ed.), "Fenno Letters, Part 1."

25. "An Address," Jan. 1, 1789, in Hench (ed.), "Fenno Letters, Part 1."

26. *GUS*, Apr. 29, 1789.

27. Webster wrote for the *Gazette of the United States* in 1790, contributing a number of essays on language and politics; see Emily Ellsworth Ford Skeel (ed.), *A Bibliography of the Works of Noah Webster* (New York: New York Public Library, 1972), 443–444. For similarities between Webster's and Fenno's political nationalism, see chapter 4.

28. *GUS*, May 9, 1789.

29. *GUS*, Apr. 22, 1789.

30. *GUS*, Apr. 15, 1789.

31. The phrase "men of ideas" was used by Fenno in a letter to Joseph Ward on Nov. 28, 1789, in Hench (ed.), "Fenno Letters, Part 1."

32. *GUS*, Apr. 15, June 3, May 13, 1789. For a defense of "satirical animadversions," see *GUS*, Nov. 18, 1789, and on the importance of the censorial role of press, see *GUS*, Dec. 12, 1789, Nov. 11, 1791. For a contrary view, however, see *GUS*, June 13, 1789.

33. These essays were probably written by Noah Webster. See "The Tablet," *GUS*, Sept. 23, May 16, 20, June 6, Aug. 15, 1789. There is a strong defense of the utility of party conflict in "The Tablet: No. XCIV," *GUS*, Mar. 6, 1790.

34. *GUS*, Apr. 27, 1791.

35. *GUS*, June 13, Sept. 12, Oct. 21, 24, 1789. In an editorial published in Dec. 1790, Fenno mentioned that "with one solitary exception only, not a whisper of disapprobation [of the federal government] has been heard—and this is so confessedly partial and local, that it can hardly be supposed to have the smallest influence out of the limits of the state where it originated," a clear reference to Greenleaf and the *New-York Journal*; see *GUS*, Dec. 8, 1790.

36. *GUS*, Jan. 7, Apr. 11, May 2, 1792.

37. *GUS*, July 30, 1791, Sept. 15, 18, 4, 1790.

38. *GUS*, Aug. 26, June 6, 1789.

39. *GUS*, Aug. 26, 19, 22, 29, 1789.

40. *GUS*, Jan. 6, 1790, June 13, Oct. 28, 1789, Mar. 6, 1790.

41. *GUS*, Oct. 15, 1791, citing Edmund Burke, *A Letter to a Member of the National Assembly* (1791). The full quotation begins: "Men are qualified for civil liberty, in exact proportion to their disposition to put moral chains on their own appetites." This belief that freedom and restraint are self-negating and that excessive liberty leads to tyranny while restraint and self-restraint are a basis for true freedom was widespread in late eighteenth-century America.

42. *GUS*, Oct. 24, 1789.

43. *GUS*, Oct. 28, 1789, Jan. 6, 1790.

44. *GUS*, Apr. 3, 1790, Dec. 12, Oct. 14, 1789, Nov. 2, 1791, May 23, 1792, Jan. 30, 1790, Dec. 16, 1789.

45. *GUS*, Nov. 9, 1791.

46. *GUS*, Nov. 2, 1791, Mar. 7, 1792, Mar. 7, Jan. 15, 1791.

47. *GUS*, Jan. 2, 30, 1790, Oct. 28, 1789.

48. *GUS*, Apr. 25, 29, May 2, 13, 1789. Fenno did strike the odd courtly note in the *Gazette*. One early issue listed "the principal ladies" of New York ("The Lady of His Excellency the Governor…Lady Stirling, Lady Mary Watts, Lady Kitty Duer, La Marchioness de Brehan, the Ladies of the Most Hon. Mr. Langdon, and the Most Hon. M. Dalton, the Mayoress") in a way that was bound to offend the republican sensibilities of men like William Maclay, the Pennsylvania senator who spied monarchists lurking behind every public drapery. But such jarring references to the new federal "court" quickly disappeared from the paper; see Freeman,

George Washington, vol. 6, 212–213, 397–403. On public suspicion about monarchical precedents after 1789 and Maclay's suspicion in particular, see Freeman, *Affairs of Honor*, chap. 1.

49. *GUS*, May 6, 30, June 20, 1789. Privately, Fenno's position was probably closer to John Adams; see Fenno to Ward, July 26, 1789, in Hench (ed.), "Fenno Letters, Part 1," but in public, he eventually rejected the use of elaborate titles as unnecessary and outside the purview of the Constitution. For the views expressed in the *Gazette of the United States*, see "To the Printer," May 16, 1789; "Of Titles," June 3, 1789; "Argos," July 8, 1789; "New York, August 1, 1789," Aug. 1, 1789; "New York, August 12," Aug. 12, 1789; "The Tablet: No. XLI," Sept. 2, 1789; "New York, October 21," Oct. 21, 1789; "On Titles," Nov. 18, 1789. Changing forms of presidential address shed an interesting light on the rapidly changing politics of the period. "His Excellency" was a standard form of address for state governors and presidents of Congress in the 1780s and was used at first for President Washington as well but then fell out of favor. Thomas Paine, for example, addressed his letters to "His Excellency George Washington" until Feb. 13, 1792, at which point he abruptly changed his style of address to "George Washington, President of the United States"; see Philip S. Foner (ed.), *The Complete Writings of Thomas Paine* (New York: Citadel, 1945). The innovation after 1789 was not to adopt but to abandon honorific titles for public officers, and not for the last time John Adams was caught out of step with public opinion.

50. His allegiance, he declared, was to principles, not parties or persons: "The Constitution is the only ark of safety to the liberties of America," he wrote in the first issue of the *Gazette*, and "it will be pleasing to me, to enter into a hearty & spirited support of the administration so far as they appear to be influenced by its genuine Principles"; Fenno to Ward, Aug. 5, 1789; "An Address," Jan. 1, 1789; *GUS*, Apr. 15, 1789. Fenno made more fuss about Washington's tour of New England than his inauguration as president six months earlier; see Freeman, *George Washington*, 21; *GUS*, Aug. 22–29, Sept. 12, 23, 26, Oct. 20–31, Nov. 4–18, Dec. 9, 16, 1789.

51. *GUS*, Nov. 11, 18, 14, 1789. For an attack on the praise of public men, see Philip Freneau, "Rules on How to Compliment Great Men in a Proper Manner," in Philip M. Marsh (ed.), *The Prose of Philip Freneau* (New Brunswick, N.J.: Scarecrow, 1955), 262–264.

52. The best scholarly discussion of this theme is Douglass Adair's "Fame and the Founding Fathers," in Trevor Coulbourn (ed.), *Fame and the Founding Fathers: Essays by Douglas Adair* (New York: Norton, 1974); and Adair and John Schutz (eds.), *Fame Is the Spur: Dialogues of John Adams and Benjamin Rush, 1805–1813* (San Marino, Calif.: Huntington Library, 1966). Adams, of course, was particularly obsessed with the subject of fame, and his views may well have found a reflection in Fenno's. Fenno's use of this idea, however, was something of a vulgarization. Fame was usually linked to the judgment of posterity and defined as the antithesis of popularity. His use of the idea, however, was consistent with his desire to bolster popular support for the federal government. He discussed the concept of fame, "one of the most important springs of human nature," in the *Gazette of the United States* on Nov. 28, 1789.

53. *GUS*, Nov. 18, 1789

54. *GUS*, Feb. 17, 27, 1790, Mar. 2, 1791, Feb. 22, 25, 1792. Fenno's lack of enthusiasm for Washington's birthday contrasted greatly with his enthusiasm for July Fourth; see *GUS*, July 1, 4, 8, 25, 1789, July 7, 10, 17, 1790, July 4, 7, 25, 1792.

55. Fenno to Ward, Feb. 17, Apr. 5, Jan. 28, 1789, in Hench (ed.), "Fenno Letters, Part 1."

56. Fenno to Ward, Jan. 28, Feb. 17, 23, Mar. 11, Apr. 5, 1789, in Hench (ed.), "Fenno Letters, Part 1."

57. Fenno to Ward, July 26, 1789, in Hench (ed.), "Fenno Letters, Part 1."

58. Fenno to Ward, Aug. 5, Oct. 8, 1789, in Hench (ed.), "Fenno Letters, Part 1."

59. Fenno to Ward, Aug. 5, July 26, Oct. 8, Aug. 27, 1789, in Hench (ed.), "Fenno Letters, Part 1." Fenno was especially irritated by his failure to secure patronage from the treasury and the War Office; see Fenno to Ward, July 26, Nov. 28, Oct. 8, 9, 1789, in Hench (ed.), "Fenno Letters, Part 1." Greenleaf did printing work for the treasury and published the first official journal of the U.S. Senate; see Fenno to Ward, Feb. 23, 1789. Most government printing, however, was in

the hands of the New York printers Francis Childs and John Swaine, who referred to themselves as "Printers to the United States" and "Printers to the Congress of the United States." The patronage they enjoyed between 1789 and 1797 was funneled to them by John Beckley, clerk of the House of Representatives. When Beckley was defeated for reelection as clerk in 1797, their virtual monopoly of government printing was turned over to the Federalist printer James Ross. For their close relationship to Jefferson and their pivotal role in the establishment of Philip Freneau's *National Gazette* in 1791, see chapter 2.

60. Fenno to Ward, Nov. 28, 1789. Fenno estimated that he needed 1,500 subscribers to sustain himself and the paper. By July 1789, he had over 600, but a few months later this number had risen to only 650. Moreover, Fenno had collected only $500 of the subscription money owed to him; see Fenno to Ward, July 26, Oct. 9, 1789; *GUS*, Oct. 14, 1789. For his decision to run advertisements in *GUS*, see Fenno to Ward, Oct. 9, 1789; *GUS*, Nov. 28, 1789. On his mounting debts, see Fenno to Ward, Oct. 9–Nov. 28, 1789, in Hench (ed.), "Fenno Letters, Part 1."

61. Fenno to Ward, Nov. 28, 1789, Jan. 3, 31, Mar. 7, Apr. 11, 7, 1790, Apr. 30, Dec. 7, 1791, in Hench (ed.), "Fenno Letters, Part 1." During this difficult period, Fenno kept the *Gazette* afloat with financial help from Flint, Ward, Gore, and friends in the New York mercantile community; see Fenno to Ward, Oct. 9, Dec. 20, 1789, Jan. 10, 1790. His position as printer of the Senate journals, a position that Freneau later claimed was worth $2,500 a year, finally provided him with a steady source of income.

62. Fenno to Ward, July 5, 26, 1789, in Hench (ed.), "Fenno Letters, Part 1."

63. Fenno to Ward, Oct. 9, 10, 1789, in Hench (ed.), "Fenno Letters, Part 1"; Jefferson to George Gilmer, June 27, 1790, in Boyd (ed.), *TJP*, vol. 16, 574–575; Freeman, *George Washington*, 262; *GUS*, Apr. 15, 1789. Fenno was always keen to support national institutions. He endorsed plans for a national bank as a "spring to trade and commerce," supported the establishment of a "federal university" to train students in "the great objects of legislation and national jurisprudence," and even recommended the creation of a "domestic secretary," as an American equivalent to the British home secretary, to oversee domestic policy; see *GUS*, Apr. 25, May 30, Aug. 8, 12, 1789.

64. Hench, introduction to Hench (ed.), "Fenno Letters, Part 1," 305; *GUS*, Apr. 29, July 4, 1789; Fenno to Ward, Oct. 10, Nov. 28, 1789, in Hench (ed.), "Fenno Letters, Part 1."

65. "Americanus," *GUS*, Aug. 8, 1789. An editorial in the same issue supported the creation of a national bank. For Hamilton's report, see *Report Relative to a Provision for the Support of Public Credit*, in Harold C. Syrett (ed.), *The Papers of Alexander Hamilton* (New York: Columbia University Press, 1961–1979), vol. 6, 51–168; Elkins and McKitrick, *Age of Federalism*, 114–123.

66. *GUS*, Apr. 15, 25, Nov. 7, 1789, Apr. 24, 1790, July 4, Nov. 11, 21, 1789. Hamilton used the same argument in his report on public credit; see Syrett (ed.), *PAH*, vol. 6, 51–168; also see Banning, *Jeffersonian Persuasion*, 136–137.

67. Fenno to Ward, Jan. 17, 1790, in Hench (ed.), "Fenno Letters, Part 1." Fenno published Hamilton's report as a "Summary View of the Report of the Secretary of the Treasury" in the *Gazette of the United States* on Jan. 20, 1790, and at greater length in *GUS*, Jan. 27–Feb. 27, 1790. For discussion of the report in *GUS*, see Jan. 23, 27, Feb. 10, 13, 17, 24, Mar. 2, 3, 1790. For Fenno's pressure on Congress to act, see *GUS*, Nov. 7, 11, 21, Dec. 19, 23, 1789, Jan. 6, 9, 1790.

68. Fenno to Ward, Mar. 7, Apr. 9, 1790, in Hench (ed.), "Fenno Letters, Part 1." Fenno's response shows how little controversy Hamilton's plans generated in the *Gazette of the United States*. For his opposition to discrimination, see *GUS*, Jan. 23, 27, Feb. 2, 24, 1790.

69. Fenno to Ward, Jan. 17, May 16, 23, 27, June 3, 22, 1790, in Hench (ed.), "Fenno Letters, Part 1", *GUS*, Apr. 10, July 28, 1790. In the spring of 1790, the assumption bill got entangled in complex negotiations about the future site of the federal government, and Fenno had to wait for its passage until late July. James Madison led congressional opposition to Hamilton's policies, but according to Lance Banning there is no reason to think that at this time he saw "a deeper danger in the Treasury plan"; see Banning, *Jeffersonian Persuasion*, 150–153.

70. This little-known episode sheds interesting light on the reputation of the *Gazette* and Jefferson's relationship with the press. The only account of it is by Julian Boyd, who is an indefatigable scholar but tends to argue as counsel for Jefferson; see "Jefferson's Alliance with Fenno's Gazette of the United States," in Boyd (ed.), *TJP*, vol. 16, 237–247. It is given short shrift in almost all histories of the 1790s and is not mentioned at all by Jefferson's most thorough biographer, Dumas Malone, in his *Jefferson and the Ordeal of Liberty* (Boston: Little, Brown, 1962).

71. *GUS*, Apr. 7, 1790. See Culver H. Smith, *Press, Politics and Patronage: The American Government's Use of Newspapers, 1789–1875* (Athens: University of Georgia Press, 1977), 10–11; Boyd, "Jefferson's Alliance," in *TJP*, vol. 16, 240. Jefferson's request for editors to send their newspapers to the Department of State reads like a roll call of Federalist editors; see Henry Remsen to Editors, Sept. 10, 1790, in Boyd (ed.), *TJP*, vol. 17, 509. Jefferson was required to designate at least three newspapers in different states to print federal statutes. He eventually extended this privilege to five newspapers: those edited by Benjamin Russell, Childs and Swaine, Augustine Davis, Ann Timothy Boyd, and Andrew Brown, who was Fenno's replacement; see Remsen to Benjamin Russell et al., Nov. 23, 1790, in Boyd (ed.), *TJP*, vol. 18, 65–66. Interestingly, Benjamin Rush recommended Brown to Jefferson for his "zeal in promoting the adoption of the foederal [*sic*] constitution"; see Rush to Jefferson, Aug. 15, 1790, in Boyd (ed.), *TJP*, vol. 17, 391. For Jefferson's letters to printers during his tenure as secretary of state, see Jessie Ryon Lucke, "Some Correspondence with Thomas Jefferson Concerning the Public Printers," in *Papers of the Bibliographical Society, University of Virginia* (Charlottesville: University of Virginia Press, 1948), vol. 1, 27–37; J. H. Powell, *Books of a New Nation: United States Government Publications, 1774–1814* (Philadelphia: University of Pennsylvania Press, 1957), 88; W. A. Katz, "An Episode in Patronage: Federal Laws Published in the Newspapers," *American Journal of Legal History* 10 (July 1966): 214–223.

72. Boyd, "Jefferson's Alliance," in *TJP*, vol. 16, 238; Jefferson to Washington, Sept. 9, 1792, in Boyd (ed.), *TJP*, vol. 24, 351–359. Jefferson ignored the fact that most American editors relied on accounts from pro-revolutionary British newspapers like the *Morning Chronicle*, an issue that raises questions about his broader motives. On the political complexion and significance of the *Gazette de Leyde*, see Jeremy Popkin, *News and Politics in the Age of Revolution: Jean Luzac's "Gazette de Leyde"* (Ithaca, N.Y.: Cornell University Press, 1989).

73. Jefferson to George Washington, Sept. 9, 1792, in Boyd (ed.), *TJP*, vol. 24, 351–359; Dumas Malone, *Jefferson and the Rights of Man* (Boston: Little, Brown, 1951), 214–268. On the role of the press in the French Revolution, see Jeremy D. Popkin, *Revolutionary News: The Press in France, 1789–1799* (Durham, N.C.: Duke University Press, 1990); Roger Chartier, *The Cultural Origins of the French Revolution* (Durham, N.C.: Duke University Press, 1991).

74. *GUS*, Apr. 24, 1790; Jefferson to Martha Jefferson Randolph, Apr. 26, 1790, in Boyd (ed.), *TJP*, vol. 16; Margaret M. O'Dwyer, "A French Diplomat's View of Congress, 1790," *WMQ*, 3rd ser., 21, no. 3 (July 1964): 433. Otto was probably referring to John Pintard, the translator whom Jefferson employed in the Department of State. Jefferson to Washington, Sept. 9, 1792; "Jefferson's Alliance," in Boyd (ed.), *TJP*, vol. 16, 351–359, 242–243. For excerpts from the *Gazette de Leyde*, see *GUS*, Apr. 24–Aug. 4, 1790; Samuel Blackden to Jefferson, Dec. 25, 1789; John Brown Cutting to Jefferson, Mar. 20, 1790; "Extract from the Speech of Edmund Burke" [Feb. 9, 1790], all in Boyd (ed.), *TJP*, vol. 16, 247–262; *GUS*, Apr. 21, May 1, 1790. Jefferson probably also gave Fenno the excerpts from Brissot de Warville's "The French Patriot"; see *GUS*, Apr. 21, June 9, 1790.

75. Jefferson called the *Gazette of the United States* a paper "of pure Toryism, disseminating the doctrines of monarchy, aristocracy, and the exclusion of the influence of the people," claiming that the "aristocratical and monarchical principles" spread abroad by the "servile" Fenno had made it necessary for him to assist in the establishment of a "republican" rival to the *Gazette of the United States*, Philip Freneau's *National Gazette*; see Jefferson to George Washington, May 8, 1791; Jefferson to Mann Randolph, May 15, 1791; Jefferson to Madison, July 21, 1791; Jefferson to William Short, July 28, 1791; Jefferson to Thomas Paine, June 19, 1792; Jefferson to Washington, Sept. 9, 1792, all in Boyd (ed.), *TJP*, vols. 20, 24. This verdict has been damning and

enduring and explains why one of the most important and influential editors of the 1790s has been treated so dismissively by historians. The most definitive history of the period dispatches him in a few lines as a "large and somewhat ponderous man who deplored turmoil and was confused by it" (Elkins and McKitrick, *Age of Federalism*, 284), and most historians have simply recycled Jefferson's comments rather than read the newspaper.

76. The final extract from the *Gazette de Leyde* appeared on Aug. 4, 1790, and the essays on the French Revolution by John Courtenay appeared from Aug. 11 to Sept. 8, 1790. The short lapse of time between these two events leads Boyd to conclude that these essays precipitated Jefferson's break with Fenno; see Boyd, "Jefferson's Alliance," in *TJP*, vol. 16, 243–246; "Extract from the Speech of Edmund Burke," in Boyd (ed.), *TJP*, vol. 16, 260–262; *GUS*, May 1, 1790, Jan. 26, 1791. "Contempt is the best weapon against a madman like Mr. Burke," wrote Fenno (*GUS*, Feb. 5, 1791), whose treatment of Burke was almost completely hostile; see *GUS*, May 15, 1790. For a long, harshly critical attack on Burke on the front page, see *GUS*, Apr. 6, 1791; also see "The Beautiful and Sublime of Blackguardism," *GUS*, May 7, 1791; and an attack on Burke as a "Champion of Aristocracy," *GUS*, May 11, 1791. An article in *GUS*, May 14, 1791, declared that "were Mr. Burke to appear in Paris, the French would probably honor him with a *lantern*, for the *light* he has thrown on their revolution." For similar attacks, see *GUS*, May 18, 28, 1791. Fenno also printed Thomas Paine's response to Burke; see *GUS*, May 7, 11, 18, 1791, and the notes on Paine's *Rights of Man*, May 14, 1791. For a rare favorable reference to Burke reprinted "From the Colombian [*sic*] Centinel," see *GUS*, Oct. 21, 1791.

77. Boyd wrongly implies that Fenno's publication of the Courtenay articles was part of a more general opposition to the French Revolution; see Boyd, "Jefferson's Alliance," in *TJP*, vol. 16, 244; "A Sketch of the Political State of America: Number II," *GUS*, Apr. 29, 1789; "Story of Honestus and Constantia," *GUS*, May 23, 1789; "Illiberal Political Conduct of Britain towards America," *GUS*, July 22, 1789. For Fenno's comments on the need for a revolution in Great Britain, see *GUS*, Oct. 10, 1789, Apr. 3, May 1, 1790. In 1789, Fenno celebrated the alliance with "Our Allies," the French, and welcomed the French Revolution as the product of a spark of liberty created by the American Revolution; *GUS*, Nov. 18, Oct. 1, 28, 1789.

78. *GUS*, Sept. 26, Oct. 1, 28, 1789. On his reaction to the fall of the Bastille, see "Insurrection in France," *GUS*, Sept. 16, 1789; "Convulsions in France," *GUS*, Sept. 19, 1789; "Authentic Information," *GUS*, Sept. 26, 1789; "The Bastile [*sic*]," *GUS*, Sept. 30, 1789; "The Bastile," *GUS*, Oct. 14, 1789. For Fenno's earlier coverage of the Estates-General, see "Political State of France," *GUS*, Apr. 18, 1789; "His Most Christian Majesty's Speech to the States-General," *GUS*, July 29, 1789; "By Express from Paris," *GUS*, Aug. 19, 1789; "Foreign Miscellaneous Articles," *GUS*, Sept. 2, 1789; "New York, Sept. 5," *GUS*, Sept. 5, 1789.

79. *GUS*, Oct. 3, 1789. See also *GUS*, Oct. 7, 10, 1789. Like all good American Protestants, Fenno welcomed the revolution as a mortal blow to the Roman Catholic church; see "European Intelligence," *GUS*, Oct. 31, 1789.

80. "From the General Advertiser," *GUS*, June 1, 1791. For pro-French material, see "European Intelligence," *GUS*, Mar. 20, 1790; "Further Accounts from Europe," *GUS*, Mar. 24, 1790; "New York, Oct. 9," *GUS*, Oct. 9, 1790; "Philadelphia, Nov. 17," *GUS*, Nov. 17, 1790; "Philadelphia, Nov. 27," *GUS*, Nov. 27, 1790; "French Revolution," *GUS*, Mar. 16, 1791. In the *Gazette* for Apr. 21, 1790, Fenno published "Extract of Dr. Price's Revolution Sermon," Brissot de Warville's "French Patriot," a report on "Revolution in the Belgic States," and another from the French National Assembly. Privately, though, Fenno expressed reservations about the revolution: "What think you of French Matters, are they not democratically mad?" he wrote to Ward on Nov. 20, 1789; see Hench (ed.), "Fenno Letters, Part 1." For signs of this skepticism in the newspaper, see "The Present State of Europe," Mar. 27, 30, 1790; "Grand French Confederacy," Sept. 25, 1790; "Celebration of the Anniversary of French Freedom," Sept. 29, 1790; "Paris, August 8," Nov. 6, 1790; "An Authentic Statement of Affairs in France," Nov. 24, 1790.

81. *GUS*, Aug. 27, 1791; see also "France," *GUS*, Aug. 31, 1791.

82. "Elegant Impromptu of Mr. Barlow, Author of the 'Vision of Columbus,'" *GUS*, Oct. 8, 1791.

83. *GUS*, July 18, 20, 30, 1792.

84. Fenno published Jefferson's excerpts from the *Gazette de Leyde* regularly and promptly. The *Discourses on Davila* appeared in *GUS* from Apr. 27 to Dec. 4, 1790, and from Feb. 26 to Apr. 27, 1791. Fenno also published other work from Adams's pen during the same period; see *GUS*, Sept. 29, Oct. 2, 9, 13, 1790. The pamphlet by John Adams was *Twenty-Six Letters, upon Interesting Subjects Respecting the Revolution: Written in Holland in the Year M,DCCC,LXXX* (New York: John Fenno, 1789). First published in London in 1786, it was serialized by Fenno as "Letters Written in Holland," *GUS*, Oct. 17–Dec. 26, 1789. The pamphlet cost Fenno money; see Fenno to Ward, July 26, 1789, in Hench (ed.), "Fenno Letters, Part 1." For Fenno's use of the phrase "American Lycurgus," see Fenno to Ward, Feb. 23, 1794, in Hench (ed.), "Fenno Letters, Part 2." As far as I can tell, there is no extant correspondence between Fenno and Adams and virtually no information about their relationship in their letters to others. For Fenno's admiration of Adams, see the poem eulogizing him as a "giant in debate" and "Columbia's Safeguard, Glory, Boast and Pride"; *GUS*, Apr. 23, 1789.

85. Zoltan Haraszti, *John Adams & the Prophets of Progress* (Cambridge, Mass.: Harvard University Press, 1952), 47. Chapter 10 of Haraszti's book contains an excellent discussion of Adams's work, and there is a good summary of the *Discourses* in Page Smith, *John Adams, 1735–1826* (Garden City, N.Y.: Doubleday, 1962), vol. 2, 797–801. Henrico Davila's *Historia Delle Guerre Civili di Francia* was published in Venice in 1630 and was a history of the civil wars in sixteenth-century France.

86. Smith, *John Adams*, 797–801; Haraszti, *John Adams*, 165–179.

87. O'Dwyer, "A French Diplomat's View of Congress," 43; *GUS*, Apr. 27, 1791; C. F. Adams (ed.), *The Works of John Adams* (Boston: Little, Brown, 1850–1856), vol. 6, 272; Zoltan Haraszti, "The 32nd Discourse on Davila," *WMQ*, 3rd ser., 11, no. 1 (Jan. 1954): 89–92. The violent public response to Adams's remarks was partly shaped by the contemporaneous and closely linked controversy ignited by the American publication of Thomas Paine's *Rights of Man* and Jefferson's note on "political heresies"; see chapter 2 below, and Jefferson to Paine, July 29, 1791, in Boyd (ed.), *TJP*, vol. 20, 308–310.

88. Adams to Jefferson, July 29, 1791, in Boyd (ed.), *TJP*, vol. 20, 305–308; Adams Diary, quoted in Haraszti, *John Adams*, 179.

89. Hamilton to James Madison, Nov. 23, 1788, in Syrett (ed.), *PAH*, vol. 5, 236. For the debate about titles, see *Annals of Congress*, vol. 1, 332–337; Bowling and Veit (eds.), *Diary of William Maclay*, 1–3, 22–27, 63–137; James Hutson, "John Adams' Title Campaign," *New England Quarterly* 41 (1968): 30–39; Elkins and McKitrick, *Age of Federalism*, 46–47. [Anonymous], *The Dangerous Vice: A Fragment: Addressed to All Whom It May Concern* ([Boston]: n.p., 1789), was distributed in Boston and New York and is discussed in Fenno to Ward, Aug. 27, 1789, in Hench (ed.), "Fenno Letters, Part 1."

90. Freeman, *George Washington*, vol. 6, 231–232; Adams to James Warren, Jan. 9, 1787, quoted in Wood, *Creation of the American Republic*, 581; Benjamin Rush to Adams, Apr. 13, 1790, in L. H. Butterfield (ed.), *Letters of Benjamin Rush* (Princeton, N.J.: Princeton University Press, 1951), vol. 1, 546, 522; Adams to Rush, Apr. 18, 1790, in Adams Papers (microfilm reel 115); Jefferson to Washington, May 8, 1791; Jefferson to Adams, July 17, 1791; Adams to Jefferson, July 29, 1791, all in Boyd (ed.), *TJP*, vol. 20, 291–292, 302–303, 305–308.

91. *New-York Journal*, July 16, 1791, in Judith R. Hiltner (ed.), *The Newspaper Verse of Philip Freneau* (Troy, N.Y.: Whitston, 1986), 462–464.

92. The *Gazette of the United States* stopped publishing the laws of the United States "By Authority" on Sept. 15, 1790. Jefferson complained that the "unconstitutional doctrines" of the *Discourses on Davila* had "filled Fenno's papers for a twelvemonth, without contradiction"; see Jefferson to Thomas Mann Randolph, Jr., May 15, 1791; Jefferson to Washington, May 8, 1791,

both in Boyd (ed.), *TJP*, vol. 20, 414–416, 291–292. The taint of Adams's "monarchical" views proved impossible for Fenno to expunge and was exploited by Republican journalists for the rest of the decade. For a different interpretation of Fenno's relationship to Jefferson, see Boyd, "Jefferson's Alliance," in *TJP*, vol. 16, 246; and Michael Lienesch, "Thomas Jefferson and the American Democratic Experience: The Origins of the Partisan Press, Popular Political Parties, and Public Opinion," in Peter S. Onuf (ed.), *Jeffersonian Legacies* (Charlottesville: University of Virginia Press, 1993).

93. In Dec. 1790, Fenno temporarily suspended publication of the *Discourses*, and excerpts from the *Gazette de Leyde* appeared in the newspaper again, as well as some government printing "By Authority." When publication of the *Discourses* was finally brought to a halt in May 1791, Fenno published a flurry of official material for the Department of State, including Jefferson's *Report on Cod and Whale Fisheries*, which he also published as a pamphlet. The significance of all this is unclear. Fenno was not on Henry Remsen's list of official printers at the State Department. Did he continue to publish government documents unofficially or was his official patronage renewed at some point? The last item to appear "By Authority" was published in *GUS* on May 4, 1791. Fenno may have reprinted the excerpts from the *Gazette de Leyde* from Bache's *General Advertiser* or Brown's *Federal Gazette*; see *GUS*, Jan. 22, Mar. 19, 30, Apr. 16, 23, May 4, 1791. Whatever the cause, the political tone of the *Gazette* shifted noticeably in early 1791; see, for example, the hostile commentaries on Burke, *GUS*, Jan. 26, Feb. 5, 1791; the attack on the Bank of the United States, *GUS*, Feb. 5, 1791; the article on education by "A Mechanic," *GUS*, Jan. 15, 1791; and the positive coverage of the French Revolution in Mar.–Apr. 1791. For Jefferson's *Report on Fisheries*, see *GUS*, May 4–July 2, 1791, and *Report on Cod and Whale Fisheries* (Philadelphia: John Fenno, 1791).

94. *GUS*, Apr. 27, 1791.

95. Abigail Adams to Mary Cranch, Mar. 12, 1791, in Mitchell (ed.), *Letters of Abigail Adams*, 71; Fisher Ames to George Minot, Nov. 30, 1791, in Seth Ames (ed.), *Works of Fisher Ames* (Boston: Little, Brown, 1854), vol. 1, 105.

96. *GUS*, Dec. 7, 21, 1791, Apr. 18, May 19, Mar. 21, May 2, 1792. For Fenno's efforts to defend his republican credentials, see *GUS*, Apr. 28, May 2, 19, July 21, 25, 1792, and the series of essays by "A Republican" in *GUS* on Aug. 8 and Oct. 6–31, 1792.

97. "Philadelphia," *GUS*, May 5, 26, June 6, 20, 1792; "Original Communications," *GUS*, June 23, 27, 1792; "Crito," *GUS*, July 7, 1792. The letters by "T.L." accusing Freneau of being in the pay of Jefferson were published in *GUS* on July 25, Aug. 8, 11, 1792. See also " Detector," July 28, 1792; "An American," Aug. 4, 11, 1792; "Catullus," Sept. 15, 1792; "For the Gazette of the United States," Aug. 4, 1792; "The Nation's Gazette: A Parody," Aug. 25, 1792. For attacks on Jefferson, see "Catullus," *GUS*, Sept. 15, 19, 29, Oct. 17, 24, 1792; "Scourge," Sept. 23, 1792; "Metullus" and "Consistency," Oct. 24, 1792.

98. Fenno reprinted these articles at Dunlap's request; see *GUS*, Sept. 26, 29, Oct. 13, 24, Nov. 3, 10, Dec. 8, 1792, Jan. 5, 1793.

99. Fenno to Ward, May 23, 1790, in Hench (ed.), "Fenno Letters, Part 1"; Fenno to Ward, Apr. 6, 1793, in Hench (ed.), "Fenno Letters, Part 2." Fenno suspended publication of the *Gazette* in mid-Oct. 1790 and resumed publication at 69 Market Street in Philadelphia on Nov. 3. For the increase in subscribers, see *GUS*, Dec. 7, 1791. As late as Apr. 1791, the *Gazette* carried only two columns of advertisements. On delinquent subscribers, see *GUS*, Oct. 5, 1791. For Fenno's criticism of the French Revolution, see *GUS*, July 11, Sept. 1, Oct. 24, 1792, Jan. 26, 1793. For his continued support, see *GUS*, Jan. 5, 1793.

100. Fenno to Ward, Dec. 16, 1792, in Hench (ed.), "Fenno Letters, Part 2."

101. Fenno to Ward, Apr. 6, 1793, in Hench (ed.), "Fenno Letters, Part 2."

102. Fenno to Ward, Aug. 24, 1793, in Hench (ed.), "Fenno Letters, Part 2." For the Jacobin policy of de-Christianization, see F. A. Aulard, *Christianity and the French Revolution*, trans. Lady Frazer (London: E. Benn, 1927).

103. Fenno to Ward, Apr. 6, May 26, 1793, in Hench (ed.), "Fenno Letters, Part 2." For reports of civic celebrations, see *GUS*, Feb. 2, 6, 1793. On the Genet affair, see Harry Ammon, *The Genet Mission* (New York: Norton, 1973). The irony was that Genet, a member of the Girondin Party in France, was recalled after Robespierre and the Jacobin Party took power in 1793, but news of his recall took some time to reach the United States. Fearing for his life, Genet stayed in the United States, married the daughter of New York governor George Clinton, and settled on a farm on Long Island. For Republican efforts to politicize the French Revolution, see chapter 2.

104. Fenno to Ward, Aug. 24, Sept. 9, 12, Oct. 8, 17, 1793, in Hench (ed.), "Fenno Letters, Part 2."

105. Fenno to Ward, Nov. 14, Oct. 24, 1793, in Hench (ed.), "Fenno Letters, Part 2."

106. Fenno to Ward, Nov. 14, 1793, in Hench (ed.), "Fenno Letters, Part 2." Fenno calculated his debts at $2,000 even after Ward and other friends had forgiven their loans to him. In a letter to Hamilton dated Nov. 9, 1793, he calculated his debt at $2,500; see Syrett (ed.), *PAH*, vol. 15, 393–394. For Hamilton's intervention, see Fenno to Ward, Nov. 14, Dec. 18, 1793, July 21, Sept. 14, 1794; Fenno to Hamilton, Nov. 9, 1793; Hamilton to Rufus King, Nov. 11, 1793; Hamilton to John Kean, Nov. 29, 1793, all in Syrett (ed.), *PAH*, vol. 15, 393–394, 395–396, 418. Hamilton's loan was for $2,000, although he may have promised Fenno more, and in 1793–1794, Fenno also received far more federal patronage, second only to Childs and Swaine as a beneficiary of public printing contracts. Not coincidentally, Hamilton's quick response to Fenno's appeal coincided with a renewal of the controversy among Rufus King, John Jay, and Citizen Genet about his "Appeal to the People." See the editorial note in Syrett (ed.), *PAH*, vol. 15, 233–239.

107. Fenno to Ward, Feb. 23, 1794, in Hench (ed.), "Fenno Letters, Part 2." Madison's resolutions were a response to British attacks on American merchant shipping in early 1794. For the growth of the Democratic Republican societies, see Philip S. Foner (ed.), *The Democratic-Republican Societies, 1790–1800* (Westport, Conn.: Greenwood, 1976).

108. Fenno to Ward, Feb. 23, Sept. 14, 1794, in Hench (ed.), "Fenno Letters, Part 2." For discussions of the Democratic societies in *GUS*, see "Anarch," Jan. 10, 1795; "Thousands," Feb. 18, 1795; and the essay by William Willcocks on Feb. 7, 1795. The best history of the Whiskey Rebellion is Thomas Slaughter, *The Whiskey Rebellion: Frontier Epilogue to the American Revolution* (New York: Oxford University Press, 1986).

109. Fenno to Ward, Aug. 24, 1793, Sept. 14, 15, Feb. 23, 1794, in Hench (ed.), "Fenno Letters, Part 2."

110. Fenno to Ward, Sept. 14, 1794, in Hench (ed.), "Fenno Letters, Part 2."

111. It was the growth of this reactionary Federalist nationalism that gave William Cobbett his opening into American politics; see Rogers M. Smith, "Constructing American National Identity: Strategies of the Federalists," and Keith Arbour, "Benjamin Franklin as Weird Sister: William Cobbett and Federalist Philadelphia's Fear of Democracy," both in Doron S. Ben-Atar and Barbara B. Oberg (eds.), *Federalists Reconsidered* (Charlottesville: University of Virginia Press, 1998). The Republican version of this xenophobic nationalism linked the allegedly monarchical ideas of the Federalists to the corruption of European politics.

112. Fenno to Ward, Sept. 14, 1794, in Hench (ed.), "Fenno Letters, Part 2." The Treaty of Amity, Commerce and Navigation with Great Britain was signed by Chief Justice John Jay in Nov. 1794. It resolved outstanding differences between Britain and the United States and brought an end to British attacks on American shipping, but it proved deeply unpopular, provoking the first public expressions of hostility toward President George Washington. For more on this development, see chapter 3, and for the treaty more generally, see Jerald A. Combs, *The Jay Treaty: Political Battleground of the Founding Fathers* (Berkeley: University of California Press, 1970).

113. "No Jacobin," *GUS*, Mar. 10, 1796.

114. See chapter 5 for a discussion of Cobbett and the growth of American anti-Jacobinism.

115. On John Ward Fenno, see Hench (ed.), introduction to "Fenno Letters, Part 1," 303; Fenno to Ward, July 21, 1794, in Hench (ed.), "Fenno Letters, Part 2." Cobbett appears to have played an important role on the paper during the Jay Treaty debates. For his attacks on Bache

and the "Hollow Ware Company," see *GUS*, Apr. 22, 26, 30, May 4, 1796. For his attack on Gallatin, see *GUS*, Apr. 27, 1796. The newspaper had Peter Porcupine's paw prints all over it by Apr. 1796. For his distinctive trail, see "A Constant Reader," Jan. 15, 31, 1795; "Peter Porcupine," June 27, 1795; "Virtus Post Nummus," Nov. 20, 1795; "Surgo ut Prosim & Co.," Nov. 21, 24, 1795; "Philadelphia," Dec. 1, 1795; "From a Correspondent," Dec. 4, 1795; "A French Bone to Gnaw for American Democrats," Jan. 9, 1796; "Philadelphia," Jan. 23, 1796; "Philadelphia," Mar. 12, 17, Apr. 8, 1796; "For All Fool's Day," Mar. 31, 1796; "Hollow Ware Company," Mar. 7, 1796; "Firmness," Apr. 1, 1796; "Truth," Apr. 5, 1796; extract from *Bloody Buoy*, "For the Gazette of the United States," Apr. 12, 1796; "France: History of the Revolutionary Tribunal," Apr. 20, 1796.

116. Fenno to Ward, Oct. 26, 1795, Apr. 24, July 9, June 5, 1796, in Hench (ed.), "Fenno Letters, Part 2"; *GUS*, July 25, 1796. For his response to Republican attacks on George Washington, see "Lay Preacher," Jan. 14, 1796; "Virtus Post Nummus," Nov. 20, 1795; "Monitor," July 27, 1796; "Philadelphia" and "The Demoniac," Dec. 23, 1796; "Philadelphia," Dec. 14, 1796; "Detector," Dec. 20, 1796; "Gazette of the United States," Feb. 20, 1797. In general, Fenno treated these attacks with amused contempt.

117. *GUS*, June 29, Sept. 27, July 7, 23, 1796. Joseph Dennie's "Colon & Spondee" columns were reprinted regularly from his *Farmer's Weekly Museum* (Walpole, New Hampshire); see *GUS*, June 29, 30, July 7, 23, 25, Sept. 27, 1796. "Observer" accused Porcupine of enlisting American support for Great Britain in *GUS*, Aug. 30, 1796; and "Q." attacked both Paine and Cobbett as anti-Christian slanderers on June 8, 1796.

118. Fenno to Ward, July 9, 1796, Apr. 17, 1797, in Hench (ed.), "Fenno Letters, Part 2"; *GUS*, Apr. 24, May 1, 24, 1798; Fenno to Ward, June 17, July 22, 1797, in Hench (ed.), "Fenno Letters, Part 2."

119. Fenno to Ward, July 28, 1798, in Hench (ed.), "Fenno Letters, Part 2." For the public memorials to President Adams, see *GUS*, June–July 1798.

120. Fenno to Ward, Aug. 30, 1798, in Hench (ed.), "Fenno Letters, Part 2"; *GUS*, Sept. 17, 1798.

Chapter 2

1. "A Candid State of PARTIES," *NG*, Sept. 26, 1792.

2. Irving Brant, *James Madison* (Indianapolis, Ind.: Bobbs-Merrill, 1941–1961), vol. 3, 348. For Madison's authorship of this essay, see Robert Rutland (ed.), *The Papers of James Madison* (Charlottesville: University Press of Virginia, 1983), vol. 14, 110–112, 370–372. For a discussion of Madison's contributions to the *National Gazette*, see Elkins and McKitrick, *Age of Federalism*, 263–270; and Colleen Sheehan, "The Politics of Public Opinion: James Madison's 'Notes on Government,'" *WMQ*, 3rd ser., 49, no. 4 (Oct. 1992): 609–627.

3. Wood, *Radicalism of the American Revolution*, 240–243, 254–255; Aedanus Burke, *Considerations on the Order of the Society of the Cincinnati* (Philadelphia: n.p., 1783), quoted in Richard B. Morris, *The Forging of the Union* (New York: Harper and Row, 1987), 51–52. On the Society of the Cincinnati, see Wallace E. Davis, "The Society of Cincinnati in New England in 1783–1800," *WMQ*, 3rd ser., 5, no. 1 (Jan. 1948): 3–25; Minor Myers, *Liberty without Anarchy: A History of the Society of the Cincinnati* (Charlottesville: University of Virginia Press, 1983); Merrill Jensen, *The New Nation: A History of the United States during the Confederation, 1781–1789* (New York: Knopf, 1950), 261–265. For Anti-Federalist use of anti-aristocratic language, see Herbert J. Storing (ed.), *The Anti-Federalist* (Chicago: University of Chicago Press, 1981); Jackson Turner Main, *The Anti-Federalists: Critics of the Constitution, 1781–1788* (Chapel Hill: University of North Carolina Press, 1961); Saul Cornell, *The Other Founders: Anti-Federalism and the Dissenting Tradition in America, 1788–1828* (Chapel Hill: University of North Carolina Press, 1999); Cornell, "Aristocracy Assailed: The Ideology of Backcountry Anti-Federalism," *JAH* 76, no. 4 (Mar. 1990): 1148–1172; Louise Burnham Dunbar, *A Study of "Monarchical" Tendencies in the United States, from 1776 to 1801*, University of Illinois Studies in the Social Sciences, vol. 10 (Urbana: University of Illinois Press, 1922); Banning, *Jeffersonian Persuasion*, 109–113.

4. According to the most exhaustive study of the Republican press in this period, the charge that Federalists wished to impose a monarchical government on the United States was repeated "almost incessantly" after 1792; see Donald Stewart, *The Opposition Press of the Federalist Period* (Albany: State University of New York Press, 1969), 606. For work that recognizes the importance of anti-aristocratic rhetoric in the political discourse of the 1790s, see John Murrin, "Escaping Perfidious Albion: Federalism, Fear of Aristocracy, and the Democratization of Corruption in Postrevolutionary America," in Richard K. Matthews (ed.), *Virtue, Corruption, and Self-Interest: Political Values in the Eighteenth Century* (Bethlehem, Pa.: Lehigh University Press, 1994); Murrin, "Temptation, Loathing and Fear: The Problem of Monarchy in Early America" (unpublished paper, Princeton University, 1990); Smelser, "The Jacobin Phrenzy: Federalism and the Menace of Liberty, Equality, and Fraternity"; Smelser, "The Federalist Period as an Age of Passion"; Smelser, "The Jacobin Phrenzy: The Menace of Monarchy, Plutocracy, and Anglophilia"; John R. Howe, "Republican Thought and Political Violence of the 1790s," *American Quarterly* 19, no. 2 (Summer 1967): 147–165; Warren, *Jacobin and Junto*.

5. This is a complex issue that requires a nuanced approach to the language of class formation in postrevolutionary America, one that starts from a desire to explore rather than assume the nature of the relationship between radical language and social class. For historical treatments of some of the theoretical issues involved, see Jones, *Languages of Class*; and Dror Wahrman, *Imagining the Middle Class: The Political Representation of Class in Britain, c. 1780–1832* (Cambridge: Cambridge University Press, 1995).

6. Article I, section 9, of the Constitution of the United States reads: "No Title of Nobility shall be granted by the United States: And no person holding any Office of Profit or trust under them, shall, without the Consent of the Congress, accept of any present, Emolument, Office, or Title, of any kind whatever, from any King, Prince, or foreign State." The anecdotal tittle-tattle about aristocratic conspiracy contained in sources like Thomas Jefferson's *Anas* and William Maclay's well-known diary of the first federal Congress have been used much too uncritically by historians of this period. For a discussion of these sources, see Smelser, "The Jacobin Phrenzy: The Menace of Monarchy, Plutocracy, and Anglophilia," 240; Banning, *Jeffersonian Persuasion*, introduction and 117–119; and Freeman, *Affairs of Honor*, which treats these sources with real sensitivity and skepticism; see esp. 11–104. In contrast, Gordon Wood's *Radicalism of the American Revolution* treats anti-aristocratic language as an assault on the traditionalist ideology of an emergent American gentry. Interestingly, his emphasis on the struggle between aristocracy and democracy closely mirrors the great progressive historian Charles Beard, although the two men disagree completely about the relationship between democracy and capitalism; see Beard, *Economic Origins of Jeffersonian Democracy*.

7. Lance Banning, for example, argues that the pervasiveness of anti-aristocratic ideas reflected the persistence of British opposition ideology in the United States; see Banning, *Jeffersonian Persuasion*, 17. John Murrin also believes that the "British paradigm" that shaped eighteenth-century American political perceptions "almost guaranteed that fear of aristocracy would thrive after 1790," and its influence was reinforced by exiled British journalists like James Thomson Callender, James Carey, and William Duane; see Murrin, "Escaping Perfidious Albion," 23, 33; and Michael Durey, "Thomas Paine's Apostles: Radical Emigres and the Triumph of Jeffersonian Republicanism," *WMQ*, 3rd ser., 44, no. 4 (Oct. 1987): 662–688.

8. For the use of these terms in the French Revolution, see Palmer, *Age of Democratic Revolution*, vol. 2, 15.

9. For a somewhat similar account, see Jeffrey Pasley, "The Two National Gazettes: Newspapers and the Embodiment of American Political Parties," *Early American Literature* 35, no. 1 (2000): 51–86.

10. Pierre Fresneau, "Letter Book," Freneau Collection, Rutgers University Library. The literature on Freneau is voluminous but uneven. The standard biography is Leary, *That Rascal Freneau*, but Jacob Axelrad, *Philip Freneau: Champion of Democracy* (Austin: University of

Texas Press, 1967), is also useful and provides a fuller account of Freneau's political activity. In addition to these, see Malone (ed.), *DAB*, vol. 7, 27; Samuel E. Forman, *The Political Activities of Philip Freneau* (Baltimore, Md.: Johns Hopkins University Press, 1902); Philip M. Marsh, *Philip Freneau, Poet and Journalist* (Minneapolis, Minn.: Dillon, 1968); Marsh, *The Works of Philip Freneau: A Critical Study* (Metuchen, N.J.: Scarecrow, 1968); Marsh, "Freneau and Jefferson: The Poet-Editor Speaks for Himself about the *National Gazette* Episode," *American Literature* 8, no. 2 (May 1936): 180–189; Mary S. Austin, *Philip Freneau, the Poet of the Revolution* (New York: A. Wessels, 1901); Austin, "Notable Editors between 1776 and 1800," *Magazine of American History* 17, no. 2 (Feb. 1887): 122–127; Paul Leicester Ford, "Freneau's *National Gazette*," *Nation* 60, no. 1547 (Feb. 21, 1895): 143–144. For more specialized studies of Freneau, see Nelson F. Adkins, *Philip Freneau and the Cosmic Enigma: The Religious and Philosophical Speculations of an American Poet* (New York: New York University Press, 1949); Harry Hayden Clark, *The Literary Influences of Philip Freneau* (Chapel Hill: University of North Carolina Press, 1925); Kerry S. Walters, *The American Deists: Voices of Reason and Dissent in the Early Republic* (Lawrence: University of Kansas Press, 1992); Emory Elliot, *Revolutionary Writers: Literature and Authority in the New Republic, 1725–1810* (New York: Oxford University Press, 1982); Steven Watts, *The Republic Reborn: War and the Making of Liberal America, 1790–1820* (Baltimore, Md.: Johns Hopkins University Press, 1987). For Freneau's writings, see F. L. Pattee (ed.), *The Poems of Philip Freneau* (Princeton, N.J.: University Library, 1902–1907), 3 vols.; Judith Hiltner (ed.), *The Newspaper Verse of Philip Freneau* (Troy, N.Y.: Whitston, 1986); Philip M. Marsh, *Freneau's Published Prose: A Bibliography* (Metuchen, N.J.: Scarecrow, 1970); V. H. Paltsits, *A Bibliography of the Separate and Collected Works of Philip Freneau, Together with an Account of His Newspapers* (New York: Dodd, Mead, 1903).

11. For the curriculum at the College of New Jersey in this period, see John Witherspoon, *Address to the Inhabitants of Jamaica, and Other West-India Islands in Behalf of the College of New-Jersey* (Philadelphia: n.p., 1772); Lawrence Cremin, *American Education: The Colonial Experience, 1607–1783* (New York: Harper and Row, 1970), 298–301; Thomas Wertenbaker, *Princeton, 1746–1896* (Princeton, N.J.: Princeton University Press, 1932); Mark Noll, *Princeton and the Republic, 1768–1822: The Search for Christian Enlightenment in the Era of Samuel Stanhope Smith* (Princeton, N.J.: Princeton University Press, 1989).

12. [Philip Freneau and Hugh Henry Brackenridge], *A Poem, on the Rising Glory of America; Being an Exercise Delivered at the Public Commencement at Nassau Hall, September 25, 1771* (Philadelphia: Joseph Crukshank, 1772). Freneau's contribution to the commencement was an exploration of the question "Does Ancient Poetry Excel the Modern?" On Freneau's experience at Princeton, see Axelrad, *Philip Freneau*, 12–44; Leary, *That Rascal Freneau*, 18–36. For the Whig Society, see "Satires against the Tories. Written in the Last War between the Whigs & Cliosophian in Which the Former Obtained a Compleat Victory," in William Bradford Papers, HSP; Rutland (ed.), *JMP*, vol. 1, 61–68; Claude Newlin (ed.), *The Life and Writings of Hugh Henry Brackenridge* (Princeton, N.J.: Princeton University Press, 1932); Michael Davitt Bell (ed.), *Father Bombo's Pilgrimage to Mecca* (Princeton, N.J.: Princeton University Library, 1975).

13. Witherspoon, *Address to the Inhabitants of Jamaica*; L. H. Butterfield, *John Witherspoon Comes to America* (Princeton, N.J.: Princeton University Library, 1953), xiii; Axelrad, *Philip Freneau*, 34–35; James Madison to James Madison, Sr., July 23, 1770, in Rutland (ed.), *JMP*, vol. 1.

14. For Freneau's relationship to John Morin Scott, see Leary, *That Rascal Freneau*, 16, 66; Young, *Democratic Republicans*, 39. The Cliosophic Society, however, contained just as many future Patriots as did the Whig Society, including Aaron Burr and William Paterson; see Milton Lomask, *Aaron Burr: The Years from Princeton to Vice President 1756–1805* (New York: Farrar, Straus & Giroux, 1979), 28–29; Charles Richard Williams, *The Cliosophic Society* (Princeton, N.J.: Princeton University Press, 1916); Jacob N. Beam, *The American Whig Society* (Princeton, N.J.: American Whig Society, 1933).

15. [Freneau and Brackenridge], *A Poem, on the Rising Glory of America.*

16. Freneau to James Madison, Nov. 22, 1772, in Rutland (ed.), *JMP*, vol. 1; Leary, *That Rascal Freneau*, 49.

17. [Philip Freneau], *American Liberty: A Poem* (New York: J. Anderson, [1775]), in Pattee (ed.), *Poems of Philip Freneau*, vol. 1, 142–152; Axelrad, *Philip Freneau*, 62; Freneau, *The American Village* (New York: S. Inslee and A. Car, 1772). Published a year after *The Rising Glory* and inspired by Oliver Goldsmith's elegiac *The Deserted Village*, this poem shows how quickly Freneau's views were changing. Here, Freneau portrayed Europe as a source of corruption, not civilization, casting Native Americans as innocent victims of European conquest. For a discussion that places Freneau's changing views in a broader intellectual context, see Eve Kornfeld, "Encountering 'the Other': American Intellectuals and Indians in the 1790s," *WMQ*, 3rd ser., 52, no. 2 (Apr. 1995): 287–314.

18. [Philip Freneau], *A Voyage to Boston: A Poem* (New York: J. Anderson, 1775), in Pattee (ed.), *Poems*, vol. 1, 158–182. Freneau later changed the lines "But did I swear, I ask my heart again, / To fight for Britons against Englishmen?" to read: "In their base projects monarchs to maintain?" See *General Gage's Soliloquy* and *General Gage's Confession*, in Pattee (ed.), *Poems*, vol. 1, 153.

19. Freneau's impulse to retreat to "some lone island" was restrained only by a sense of honor that "checks my speed and bids me stay, / To try the fortune of the well fought day"; see [Freneau], *American Liberty*.

20. *MacSwiggen*, in Pattee (ed.), *Poems*, vol. 1, 206–211; Myles Cooper, *The Patriots of North America* (New York: n.p., 1775). As this poem shows, Freneau was deeply disturbed by the rupture with Britain; see *House of Night*, in Pattee (ed.), *Poems*, vol. 1, 212–239; and Leary, *That Rascal Freneau*, 67.

21. Freneau, *MacSwiggen* and *The Beauties of Santa Cruz*, both in Pattee (ed.), *Poems*, vol. 1, 249–268.

22. For Freneau's state of mind at this time, see [Philip Freneau], *The Travels of the Imagination: A True Journey from Newcastle to London: To Which Are Added, American Independence, an Everlasting Deliverance from British Tyranny: A Poem* (Philadelphia: Robert Bell, 1778), in Pattee (ed.), *Poems*, vol. 1, 271–282. Freneau served in the New Jersey militia until May 1, 1780, and was promoted to the rank of sergeant; see Leary, *That Rascal Freneau*, 73–74. Brackenridge started the *United States Magazine* in Jan. 1779 and Freneau's contributions date from then; see "Account of Some of the West-India Islands, by a Young American Philosopher and Bel Espirit," *United States Magazine* 1 (Jan. 1779). The magazine folded in Dec. 1779; see Newlin (ed.), *Life and Writings of Brackenridge*, 44–57; Frank Luther Mott, *A History of American Magazines* (Cambridge, Mass.: Harvard University Press, 1938), vol. 1, 27; Leary, *That Rascal Freneau*, bibliography, 422–424.

23. [Philip Freneau], *The British Prison Ship: A Poem in Four Cantos* (Philadelphia: Francis Bailey, 1781), in Pattee (ed.), *Poems*, vol. 2, 18–38; Freneau, "Pilgrim No. II," *FJ*, Nov. 28, 1781; "Some Account of the Capture of the Ship Aurora," Freneau Collection, Rutgers University Library; Leary, *That Rascal Freneau*, 82–83, 102; Philip Marsh, "Philip Freneau and His Circle," *Pennsylvania Magazine of History and Biography* 63, no. 2 (Jan. 1939): 43.

24. Freneau manuscripts, Pension Application (1832); Freneau to Madison, May 20, 1795, in Marsh (ed.), *Prose of Philip Freneau*, 483. Apparently Freneau was working on a play about Major Andre; see *The Spy*, in Pattee (ed.), *Poems*, vol. 2, 39–72. He probably met Francis Bailey, who published the *United States Magazine*, through his friend Hugh Brackenridge. Bailey had published *The British Prison Ship* (1781), *The Poems of Philip Freneau* (1786), and *The Miscellaneous Works of Mr. Philip Freneau* (1788) and opened the *Freeman's Journal* to Freneau's pen throughout the decade; see Leary, *That Rascal Freneau*, 86–87; Pattee (ed.), *Poems*, vol. 1, xxxiv–xxxv. On Bailey, who was the official printer for Congress and the state of Pennsylvania, see *DAB*, vol. 1, 494–495; Thomas, *History of Printing in America*, vol. 2, 423–425.

25. Pattee (ed.), *Poems*, vol. 1, xxxv. According to Pattee, the prospectus of the newspaper, which was published in the first issue on Apr. 25, 1781, was written by Freneau; see also Leary,

That Rascal Freneau, 86–87; *To His Excellency General Washington*, *FJ*, Sept. 5, 1781. Significantly, Freneau later altered the title of this poem to *An Address to the Commander-in-Chief, Officers, and Soldiers of the American Army*; see Pattee (ed.), *Poems*, vol. 2, 81–83. Freneau's annotated file of the *Freeman's Journal*, covering the period from Apr. 25, 1781, to Feb. 9, 1785, is in the New Jersey Historical Society; see Philip M. Marsh, "Philip Freneau's Personal File of the *Freeman's Journal*," *Proceedings of the New Jersey Historical Society* 57 (July 1939).

26. *FJ*, Apr. 25, 1781. For a sample of Freneau's writing on the Revolution, see "On the Fall of General Earl Cornwallis," *FJ*, Nov. 7, 1781; "Lord Dunmore's Petition to the Legislature of Virginia," *FJ*, Jan. 13, 1781; "A Speech That Should Have Been Spoken by the King of the Island of Britain to His Parliament," *FJ*, Feb. 20, 1782; "Sir Harry's Call," *FJ*, Apr. 17, 1782; "Sir Guy Carleton's Address to the Americans," *FJ*, June 5, 1782. For his attacks on Rivington, see "Rivington's Last Will and Testament," *FJ*, Feb. 27, 1782; "On Mr. Rivington's Engraved King's Arms to His Royal Gazette," *FJ*, Mar. 27, 1782; "Satan's Remonstrance: Occasioned by Mr. Rivington's Late Apology for Lying," *FJ*, Aug. 7, 1782; "Rivington's Confessions: Addressed to the Whigs of New York," *FJ*, Dec. 21, 1783, Jan. 7, 1784.

27. William Steirer, "Philadelphia Newspapers: Years of Revolution and Transition, 1764–1794" (Ph.D. diss., University of Pennsylvania, 1972), 137. For the background to this political conflict, see Robert L. Brunhouse, *The Counter-Revolution in Pennsylvania, 1776–1790* (New York: Octagon, 1971); and Wood, *Creation of the American Republic*, 438–446.

28. "Philosophical Reflections," *FJ*, July 17, 1782.

29. See, for example, "A Foe to Malice," *FJ*, Aug. 28, Sept. 4, 1782; "The Prophecy of King Tammany," *FJ*, Dec. 11, 1782. The Pilgrim essays were published in the *Freeman's Journal* from Nov. 21, 1781, to Aug. 4, 1782.

30. Brunhouse, *Counter-Revolution*, 123–125; George Hastings (ed.), *The Life and Works of Francis Hopkinson* (Chicago: University of Chicago Press, 1926), 115; A. H. Smyth (ed.), *The Writings of Benjamin Franklin* (New York: Macmillan, 1905–1907), vol. 8, 647.

31. Joseph Towne Wheeler, *The Maryland Press* (Baltimore: Maryland Historical Society, 1938), 19–36; Francis B. Heitman (ed.), *Historical Register of Officers in the Continental Army during the War of the Revolution* (Baltimore, Md.: Genealogical Publishing, 1982), 421. Oswald believed that newspaper editors should be active and aggressive advocates, not neutral arbiters of political debate; see *Independent Gazetteer*, Apr. 13, 1782. His abrasive journalism constantly provoked official and unofficial retaliation: he was arraigned for a libel on Francis Bailey in 1782, involved in the clubbing of Samuel Findlay in 1785, fought a duel with Mathew Carey in 1786, and was jailed for contempt by Pennsylvania chief justice Thomas McKean in 1788. In this respect, he followed closely in the footsteps of his mentor, William Goddard. Goddard, twice jailed for contempt by the Pennsylvania Assembly, was the prototype of the late eighteenth-century political editor: truculent, paranoid, self-righteous, and relentlessly polemical. As William Steirer argues, he constitutes an important link between the acrimonious newspaper debates in Philadelphia in the 1760s and those in the 1780s and 1790s. Like his later counterparts, Goddard moved effortlessly from serious political debate to interminable personal wrangling and invective; see Steirer, "Philadelphia Newspapers," 35–50; Leonard Levy, *Emergence of a Free Press* (New York: Oxford University Press, 1985), 206–207; Wood, *Creation of the American Republic*, 441–446.

32. *FJ*, Dec. 18, 1782; Abbé Robin, *New Travels through North-America: In a Series of Letters, Exhibiting the History of the Victorious Campaign of the Allied Armies, under His Excellency General Washington and the Count de Rochambeau in the Year 1781* (Philadelphia: Robert Bell, 1783); Leary, *That Rascal Freneau*, 129.

33. *DA*, Apr. 24, 1789. His later rival, the editor John Fenno, recorded Freneau's arrival: "Thursday arrived here the schooner Columbia, P. FRENEAU, in 8 days from Charleston.— Came passenger, Dr. KING, lately from South America, with a collection of natural curiosities, particularly a male Ourang Outan (or man of the woods) remarkable for its striking similarities to the human species." *GUS*, Apr. 25, 1789.

34. John Adams, *A Defence of the Constitutions of Government of the United States of America* (Philadelphia: Hall and Sellers, 1787). For the debate on titles, see chapter 1. Freneau had praised Washington extravagantly in the past, but now he declared that he dealt "neither in court sychophantism nor in sublime dedications," a clear jab at John Fenno; *DA*, Dec. 16, 1790. For Freneau's critical views on the matter of praising public men, see "Rules on how to compliment great Men in a proper manner," in Marsh (ed.), *Prose of Philip Freneau*, 262–264.

35. Thomas Jefferson, foreword to Thomas Paine, *Rights of Man: Being an Answer to Mr. Burke's Attack on the French Revolution* (Philadelphia: Samuel Harrison Smith, [1791]).

36. Thomas Paine, *Rights of Man* (Rpt., Harmondsworth, England: Penguin, 1984), 167; Boyd, "The Rights of Man," in *TJP*, vol. 20, 274. Paine dedicated the *Rights of Man* to President Washington and sent him fifty copies to distribute in the United States; see Paine to Washington, Feb. 21, July 21, 1791, in Foner (ed.), *Writings of Thomas Paine.*

37. Jefferson to Jonathan Bayard Smith, Apr. 26, 1791, in Boyd (ed.), *TJP*, vol. 20, 290; Paine, *Rights of Man* [1791], foreword. For a thorough discussion of the publication of this controversial note, see Boyd's "Rights of Man," in *TJP*, vol. 20, 268–290. Hamilton and Adams both thought that Jefferson was responsible for the publication of the foreword and interpreted it as a deliberate ploy to expose Adams to public censure; see "Catullus No. III," *GUS*, Sept. 29, 1792; Hamilton to Washington, Sept. 9, 1792, in Syrett (ed.), *PAH*, vol. 12, 347–350, 504–505; Joyce Appleby, "The Adams-Jefferson Rupture and the First French Translation of John Adams' Defence," *AHR* 73, no. 4 (Apr. 1968): 1084–1091. Jefferson disavowed any knowledge of the plan to publish his note; see Jefferson to Washington, May 8, 1791; Jefferson to Madison, May 9, 1791; Jefferson to Thomas Mann Randolph, July 3, 1791, all in Boyd (ed.), *TJP*, vol. 20.

38. John Adams to Jefferson, July 29, 1791, in Boyd (ed.), *TJP*, vol. 20. Jefferson's claim that his foreword "really had no effect" was therefore absurd; see Jefferson to Adams, Aug. 30, 1791. Jefferson admitted to others that he had in view the "doctrines of Davila" but was evasive to Adams himself; see Jefferson to Washington, May 8, 1791; Jefferson to Madison, May 9, 1791; Jefferson to Thomas Mann Randolph, July 3, 1791; Jefferson to James Monroe, July 10, 1791; Jefferson to Adams, July 17, Aug. 30, 1791, all in Boyd (ed.), *TJP*, vol. 20. After he was informed about the American response to the *Rights of Man*, Paine himself declared: "I had John Adams in my mind when I wrote the pamphlet and it has hit as I expected." But this seems unlikely; see Jefferson to Paine, July 29, 1791; Paine to William Short, Nov. 2, 1791, both in Foner (ed.), *Writings of Thomas Paine.*

39. Publicola quoted in Boyd, "Rights of Man," in *TJP*, vol. 20, 280–282. The essays were first published in Benjamin Russell's *Columbian Centinel*, June 8–June 27, 1791, and are reproduced in W. C. Ford (ed.), *Writings of John Quincy Adams* (New York: Macmillan, 1913–1917), vol. 1. Quincy Adams certainly criticized Paine (although he also criticized Edmund Burke's abuse of the French National Assembly), but his chief purpose was to vindicate the views of his father and to challenge the insinuations contained in Jefferson's foreword.

40. Jefferson to Paine, July 29, 1791, in Boyd (ed.), *TJP*, vol. 20; *Independent Chronicle*, July 21–Dec. 8, 1791; "Agricola," *GUS*, July 23, 1791; *FG*, July 11, 1791. More generally, see Boyd, "Rights of Man," in *TJP*, vol. 20, 282; and Hench, "The Newspaper in a Republic," 188–190.

41. "Publicola," *Columbian Centinel*, July 27, 1791; "Publicola," *GUS*, June 18–Aug. 3, 1791; "Philadelphia, July 27," *GUS*, July 27, 1791. For other defenses of Adams, see "Boston, July 13," *GUS*, July 27, 1791; "A Friend to Justice," *GUS*, July 30, 1791; "Gracchus," *GUS*, July 20, 1791; "New Light," *GUS*, Aug. 10, 1791. Fenno also published a series of attacks on Burke and a number of essays attacking Publicola; see "Extracts from the Answer to Mr. Burke, by Mr. Paine," *GUS*, May 7, 11, 18, 1791; "The Beautiful and Sublime of Blackguardism," *GUS*, May 7, 1791; "Boston, May 2," *GUS*, May 11, 1791; "London," *GUS*, May 14, 1791; "London, March 1," *GUS*, May 18, 1791; "Extract from an Address to Mr. Burke," *GUS*, May 28, 1791; "From the Poughkeepsie Journal," *GUS*, June 18, 1791; "Agricola," *GUS*, July 23, 1791; "Extract of a Letter from a Gentleman in Philadelphia," *GUS*, July 27, 1791; "Friend to Truth," *GUS*, Aug. 10, 1791. He also published an

excerpt from Paine's *Letter to the Abbe Sieyes* that defended republican government against a system of constitutional monarchy; see *GUS*, Sept. 17, 1791.

42. *Columbian Centinel*, July 2, 1791.

43. Edmund Randolph to James Madison, July 21, 1791, in Rutland (ed.), *JMP*, vol. 14; Madison to Jefferson, July 13, 1791; James Monroe to Jefferson, July 25, 1791, both in Boyd (ed.), *TJP*, vol. 20. Hamilton thought Adams had been imprudent "in having stirred the question" in the first place and later claimed that he restrained other Federalists from attacking Jefferson in an effort to contain the controversy; see Hamilton to Washington, Sept. 9, 1792, in Syrett (ed.), *PAH*, vol. 12. For evidence that anti-aristocratic rhetoric was beginning to be deployed against the federal government, see Banning, *Jeffersonian Persuasion*, 158–160.

44. Philip S. Klein (ed.), "Memoirs of a Senator from Pennsylvania: Jonathan Roberts, 1771–1854," *Pennsylvania Magazine of History and Biography* 62, no. 4 (Oct. 1938): 502–551. For another excellent example of Paine's influence on popular radicalism, see Merrill and Wilentz (eds.), *Key of Liberty*, 56–57.

45. Leary, *That Rascal Freneau*, 171–177; *DA*, May 27, 1791; "On the American and French Revolutions," *DA*, Mar. 6, 1790; Freneau, *Proposals for a Monmouth Newspaper…New York, February 15, 1791*. It was probably Freneau who published Paine's work in the *Daily Advertiser*. In a letter to Jefferson on May 1, 1791, Madison wrote from New York: "Paines answer has not yet been recd. here. The moment it can be got Freneau tells me it will be published in Childs' paper." In Rutland (ed.), *JMP*, vol. 14, 14–18.

46. Jefferson to Philip Freneau, Feb. 28, 1791, in Boyd (ed.), *TJP*, vol. 20. Freneau had probably been approached already by James Madison, who may have relied on information from Henry Lee and Aedanus Burke, all former Princeton classmates of Freneau. It's also possible that some role was played by John Pintard, the previous clerk of foreign languages, who was a friend of Freneau's and a contributor to the *Daily Advertiser*; see Marsh, "Philip Freneau and His Circle," 44–45.

47. This account of Freneau's reaction was related to Elias Boudinot by Francis Childs; see Boudinot to Alexander Hamilton, Aug. 16, 1792, in Syrett (ed.), *PAH*, vol. 12; Freneau to Jefferson, Mar. 5, 1791, in Boyd (ed.), *TJP*, vol. 20.

48. Jefferson's circumspection about the press is legendary; see Boyd's editorial note to Oct. 17, 1792, in *TJP*, vol. 24, and see vol. 20, 289–290, 722; Worthington C. Ford, "Jefferson and the Newspaper," *Records of the Columbia Historical Society* 8 (1905): 78–114. For a sampling of Jefferson's views, see Jefferson to Washington, Sept. 9, 1792; Jefferson to Randolph, Sept. 17, 1792; Jefferson to Adams, July 17, 1791, all in Boyd (ed.), *TJP*, vol. 20, 24. For his relations with Freneau, see Charleston *City Gazette*, Jan. 5, 1801, reprinted in Marsh, "Freneau and Jefferson"; *NG*, Oct. 20, 31, 1792; *GUS*, Aug. 8, 1792; Syrett (ed.), *PAH*, vol. 12, 188–189.

49. Boyd (ed.), *TJP*, vol. 20, 724; Jefferson to Washington, Sept. 9, 1792, in *TJP*, vol. 24. The two nationalist editors courted by Jefferson in 1790–1791, Benjamin Franklin Bache and Andrew Brown, broadly supported Hamilton's fiscal policies. Other newspapers, like those edited by Eleazar Oswald and Thomas Greenleaf, were tainted with Anti-Federalism. Moreover, none of these papers had a national circulation comparable to the *Gazette of the United States*.

50. Madison to Jefferson, May 1, 1791; Jefferson to Madison, May 9, 1791; Jefferson to Thomas Mann Randolph, May 15, 1791, all in Boyd (ed.), *TJP*, vol. 20. Jefferson and Madison met Freneau in New York (probably with Aaron Burr and Robert Livingston present) on May 20, 1791, a sign of the importance they attached to winning him over. Freneau referred to their discussion in a letter to Jefferson and made it clear that they talked about starting a newspaper, "the hint of which you, Sir, in conjunction with Mr Madison were pleased to mention to me in [M]ay last." Freneau to Jefferson, Aug. 4, 1791, in Boyd (ed.), *TJP*, vol. 20; Marsh, "Freneau and Jefferson," 185. Jefferson mentioned the meeting in a letter to Washington on Sept. 9, 1792, where he stated that he met Freneau but once "and that was at a public table, at breakfast at Mrs. Elsworth's." Dumas Malone makes much of their being "in public," arguing that Jefferson

confined his negotiations with Freneau to official matters; see *Jefferson and the Rights of Man*, 423–425, but there is no reason to think he is correct. This meeting created a buzz of political speculation, and Jefferson and Madison's "northern journey" has been the subject of much spilled ink. For a discussion of this controversy; see Julian Boyd, "The Northern Journey of Jefferson and Madison," in *TJP*, vol. 20. According to Boyd, the journey was political in only the broadest sense, and its only significant result was the meeting that led to the establishment of a new national newspaper. Alfred Young argues, I think correctly, that the first leg of Madison and Jefferson's trip to New York City was highly political; see Young, *Democratic Republicans*, 194–201. Interestingly, their journey was shadowed by the ubiquitous John Beckley, who mentioned in July that he had just returned from his "Eastern trip"; see Madison to Jefferson, July 13, 1791, in Boyd (ed.), *TJP*, vol. 20.

51. Madison to Jefferson, July 24, 1791; Beckley to Madison, Sept. 2, 1792, both in Rutland (ed.), *JMP*, vol. 14; Edmund Berkeley and Dorothy S. Berkeley, *John Beckley: Zealous Partisan in a Nation Divided* (Philadelphia: American Philosophical Society, 1973), 61–62; Freneau to Madison, July 25, 1791; Henry Lee to Madison, July 29, 1791; Madison to Jefferson, July 31, Aug. 1, 1791; Jefferson to Madison, Aug. 3, 1791, all in Rutland (ed.), *JMP*, vol. 14; Freneau to Jefferson, Aug. 4, 1791; editorial note, both in Boyd (ed.), *TJP*, vol. 20, 756; *DA*, Aug. 25, 1791.

52. Madison to Jefferson, July 10, 1791; Jefferson to Madison, July 21, 1791, both in Boyd (ed.), *TJP*, vol. 20; Freneau to Madison, July 25, 1791, in Rutland (ed.), *JMP*, vol. 20; Charleston *City Gazette*, Jan. 5, 1801. Freneau's relationship with Childs, who published the *Daily Advertiser*, is first mentioned by Madison in July 1791; see Madison to Jefferson, July 24, 1791, in Boyd (ed.), *TJP*, vol. 20.

53. Childs's business in Philadelphia (which included the *National Gazette*) may have cost him more than he anticipated; see J. Tillary to Alexander Hamilton, Mar. 6, 1792; Hamilton to Rufus King, July 25, 1792, both in Syrett (ed.), *PAH*, vol. 11, 12; Freeman, *George Washington*, vol. 6, 403–404; Malone, *Jefferson and the Rights of Man*, 425.

54. Freneau to Jefferson, Aug. 4, 1791, in Boyd (ed.), *TJP*, vol. 20; Charleston *City Gazette*, Jan. 5, 1801. Beckley was involved in the negotiations with Freneau in New York in July 1791, and as a confidant of Jefferson and clerk of the House of Representatives, he could have smoothed the way for an agreement with the two printers. The relationship among Freneau, Childs, Swaine, and the Jeffersonians was alluded to by "Candor" (possibly Hamilton) in *GUS*, Aug. 18, 1792; see Syrett (ed.), *PAH*, vol. 12, n. 225.

55. "To the Public," *NG*, Oct. 31, 1791; "To the Public," *NG*, Nov. 17, 1791.

56. Freeman argues that the *National Gazette* was "almost neutral" during its first few months; see *George Washington*, vol. 6, 404–405. See also Elkins and McKitrick, *Age of Federalism*, 271–272; "Thoughts on the Present Indian War. By H. H. Brackenridge," in *NG*, Feb. 2, 6, 1792. For articles critical of the Indian conflict, see "Boston, Dec. 22," *NG*, Jan. 2, 1792; "From the American Daily Advertiser," *NG*, Jan. 9, 1792; "Extract of a Letter from Princeton," *NG*, Jan. 19, 1792; "To the Editor of the National Gazette," *NG*, Feb. 6, 1792.

57. *GUS*, Dec. 7, 21, 1791.

58. "Consolidation," *NG*, Dec. 5, 1791. For Madison's authorship, see Rutland (ed.), *JMP*, vol. 14, 110–112, 137–139.

59. "Consolidation," *NG*, Dec. 5, 1791.

60. "Public Opinion," *NG*, Dec. 19, 1791; "Charters," *NG*, Jan. 19, 1792.

61. "Charters," *NG*, Jan. 19, 1792; "Government of the United States," *NG*, Feb. 6, 1792; "Spirit of Governments," *NG*, Feb. 20, 1792. Madison's emphasis on public opinion was inspired by his belief that this could play a critical role in the preservation of constitutional equilibrium by jealously watching over the maneuvers of the federal government. "Every citizen," he argued, should be "an ARGUS to espy, and an AEGEON to avenge."

62. "Caius," *NG*, Jan. 26, Feb. 6, Jan. 16, 1792. Freneau reprinted these essays from Dunlap's *American Daily Advertiser*, and they caused a stir. Fenno mentioned the public attacks on

Hamilton in the *Gazette of the United States* at the end of Jan. 1792, and a month later used the front page of his paper to denounce falsehoods about the government "which affront the reader by their grossness"; see *GUS*, Jan. 25, Feb. 8, 11, 22, 29, 1792. The Brutus essays appeared in the *National Gazette* from Mar. 15 to Apr. 9, 1792; see Leary, *That Rascal Freneau*, 199; Freeman, *George Washington*, 352; "Brutus, No. I," *NG*, Mar. 18, 1792; "Brutus, No. II," *NG*, Mar. 19, 1792.

63. "To the Public," *NG*, Oct. 31, 1791; "Observations on the Prospects of America," *NG*, Nov. 3, 1791; "The Interests of the Northern and Southern States Forever Inseparable," *NG*, Nov. 10, 1791; "Modern Explanation of a Few Terms Commonly Misunderstood," *NG*, Apr. 24, 1792.

64. "Caius," *NG*, Jan. 16, 1792; "Brutus, No. V," *NG*, Apr. 5, 1792; "On the Origin of Nobility," *NG*, Feb. 6, 1792. For Logan's essays, "To the Yeomanry of the United States," see *NG*, Mar. 1–Apr. 23, 1792. These were first published in Oswald's newspaper in Feb. 1792, and issued as *Five Letters Addressed to the Yeomanry of the United States: Containing Some Observations on the Dangerous Scheme of Governor Duer and Mr. Secretary Hamilton, to Establish National Manufactories: By a Farmer* (Philadelphia: Eleazar Oswald, 1792).

65. "Parties," *NG*, Jan. 1, 1792; Banning, *Jeffersonian Persuasion*, 167; Elkins and McKitrick, *Age of Federalism*, 266–267.

66. Robert A. East, *Business Enterprise in the American Revolutionary Era* (New York: Columbia University Press, 1938), 322–323; *Independent Chronicle*, Sept. 8, 1791; Madison to Jefferson, Aug. 8, 1791; Henry Lee to Madison, Aug. 24, 1791, both in Rutland (ed.), *JMP*, vol. 14.

67. Hamilton to Philip Livingston, Apr. 2, 1792. For more on Duer, see "Robert Duer," *DAB*, vol. 5, 486–487. For the subsequent panic and Hamilton's efforts to shore up financial markets, see Robert Troup to Hamilton, Mar. 19, 1792; Hamilton to Duer, Mar. 14, 1792; Hamilton to Adams, Mar. 20, 1792; William Seton to Hamilton, Mar. 21, 26, Apr. 11, 1792; Hamilton to Seton, Mar. 26, Apr. 4, 1792; Hamilton to the President and Directors of the Bank of New York, Apr. 12, 1792; "Meeting of the Commissioners of the Sinking Fund" [Mar. 26, Apr. 4, 12, 1792]; and editorial notes, all in Syrett (ed.), *PAH*, vol. 11, 127, 158–159, 258.

68. "Extract of a Letter from New-York, Apr. 10," *NG*, Apr. 16, 1792; "A Spectator," *NG*, Mar. 8, 1792. In mid-March, Freneau began to publish the Brutus essays, which, despite their limitations, were a forceful and bruising attack on Hamilton's economic policies. He also continued Logan's "Farmer" essays and published a series of lengthy (and rather pedantic) articles by William Findlay on Hamilton's usurpation of congressional authority and the injustice of the excise tax; see "Sidney," "On the Originating Revenue Bills by the Secretary," *NG*, Apr. 12, 16, 1792; "On the Secretary's Report on the Excise," *NG*, Apr. 23–May 3, 1792; "On the Injustice of the Excise Law and the Secretary's Report," *NG*, May 10–24, 1792. For Findlay's authorship, see *NG*, Sept. 22, 1792, and annotations to the copy of the *National Gazette* (Special Collections, Princeton University Library). See "The Union: Who Are Its Real Friends?" *NG*, Apr. 2, 1792. In this essay, Madison pointedly avoids using the term "consolidation," although he does refer to a "limited and republican system of government."

69. "Sentiments of a Republican," *NG*, Apr. 26, 1792.

70. "Chronology of Facts," *NG*, May 31, 1792.

71. "Caius, No. III," *NG*, Feb. 6, 1792; "A COMPARISON between the Promises and the Effects of the FUNDING SYSTEM, Submitted to the Serious Attention of the Citizens of the United States," by "A Citizen of Philadelphia," *NG*, May 24, 1792; "Cato," *NG*, Aug. 18, 1792; "Philadelphia," *NG*, May 24, June 28, 1792; "L.," *NG*, July 31, 1793; "Anthero," *NG*, Apr. 16, 1792. Freneau blamed the viciousness of the British penal system on the hardships of those "who are driven to desperation by extreme poverty"; see "Public Executions," *NG*, June 11, 1792.

72. "Rules for Changing a Limited Republican Government," *NG*, July 7, 1792; "Philadelphia," *NG*, Aug. 8, 1792; "Philadelphia," *NG*, May 17, 1792; "Encore," *NG*, May 10, 1792. On the same theme, see "A Citizen," *NG*, May 3, 1792; "A Spectator," *NG*, Mar. 8, 1792; "Philadelphia," *NG*, Apr. 16, 1792.

73. "Philadelphia, April 30, 1792," *NG*, Apr. 30, 1792; "Archimedes," *NG*, May 7, 1792. Although "Plan for a Nobility in the United States" was first published in Dunlap's *American*

Daily Advertiser, it was probably from Freneau's own pen; see Marsh (ed.), *Prose of Philip Freneau*, 535.

74. "Rules for Changing a Limited Republican Government," *NG*, July 4, 1792.

75. "Philadelphia, June 11, 1792," *NG*, June 11, 1792; "Sentiments of a Republican," *NG*, Apr. 26, 1792; "Chronology of Facts," *NG*, May 31, 1792.

76. Freeman, *George Washington*, vol. 6, 406; "Philadelphia," *GUS*, Mar. 14, 1792; "Philadelphia," *GUS*, Apr. 28, 1792. See also "Good Conscience" and "Viator," *GUS*, Mar. 21, 1792; "Philadelphia," *GUS*, Mar. 31, Apr. 11, May 2, 19, June 6, 1792.

77. Leary, *That Rascal Freneau*, 200; *NG*, Mar. 29, 1792; "Crito," *GUS*, July 7, 25, 1792; "Philadelphia," *GUS*, May 2, 5, June 6, 13, 1792. This quickly attracted the attention of Freneau, who had virtually ignored Fenno's *Gazette* until then; see "Communications," *NG*, Apr. 16, 1792; "Philadelphia," *NG*, Apr. 19, 1792; "To the Noblesse and Courtiers of the United States," *NG*, Jan. 5, 1792; "Encore" and "Dulce et Interdom Despere," *NG*, May 10, 1792; "Anti-Puff," *NG*, May 17, 1792; "Corrector," *NG*, May 24, 1792; "Original Communications," *NG*, June 27, 1792.

78. "Crito," *GUS*, July 7, 1792; "Communications," *GUS*, Aug. 25, 1792; "Crito," *GUS*, July 25, 1792; "Original Communications," *GUS*, July 21, 1792. See also "A Republican," *GUS*, Aug. 18, 1792.

79. "T.L.," *GUS*, July 25, 1792; Hamilton to Washington, Aug. 18, Sept. 9, 1792; Hamilton to Edward Carrington, May 26, 1792; Hamilton to John Adams, June 25, 1792; Hamilton to Rufus King, July 25, 1792, all in Syrett (ed.), *PAH*, vols. 11–12.

80. "Detector," *GUS*, July 28, 1792; "From the Gazette of the United States" and "Ode III," *NG*, July 28, 1792; "An American," *GUS*, Aug. 4, 1792. For Freneau's affidavit, see *NG*, Aug. 6, 1792, and for Hamilton's response, "An American," *GUS*, Aug. 11, 1792.

81. "An American," *GUS*, Aug. 4, 1792. See also "An American, No. II," *GUS*, Aug. 11, 1792, and "An American, No. III," *GUS*, Aug. 18, 1792; Edmund Randolph to Madison, Aug. 12, 1792; John Beckley to Madison, Sept. 2, 1792, both in *JMP*, vol. 14. Beckley was first into the breach, writing as "Mercator," and thereafter a steady stream of material appeared defending the secretary of state, denouncing the charges against him, and denigrating the political reputation of Alexander Hamilton; see "Aristides," *GUS*, Sept. 8, 1792; *NG*, Sept. 26, 1792; "For the National Gazette," *NG*, Sept. 8, 1792; "Defense of Mr. Jefferson's Political Character," *NG*, Sept. 26, 29, Oct. 13, 24, Nov. 3, 10, Dec. 8, 1792, Jan. 5, 1793; James Monroe to Madison, Oct. 9, 1792, *JMP*, vol. 14; Philip Marsh, "Madison's Defense of Freneau," *WMQ*, 3rd ser., 3, no. 2 (Apr. 1946): 269–274.

82. "Mutius," *NG*, Nov. 24, 1792; "Lucius," *NG*, Nov. 17, 24, 1792; Adams quoted in Axelrad, *Philip Freneau*, 244; "For the National Gazette," *NG*, Dec. 8, 1792; "Philadelphia," *NG*, Dec. 8, 12, 1792; "Franklin," *NG*, Feb. 20, 1792.

83. [William Loughton Smith], *The Politicks and Views of a Certain Party Displayed* (n.p., 1792). Madison prepared a point-by-point refutation of Smith's pamphlet; see "Notes on William Loughton Smith's Politicks and Views"; Madison to Madison Sr., Nov. 6, 1792, both in *JMP*, vol. 14, 396–402; John Beckley to Madison, Oct. 17, 1792, *JMP*, vol. 14. For Hamilton's contributions to this debate, see Syrett (ed.), *PAH*, vol. 12, 633–634; vols. 13 and 33, 393–395, 521–527.

84. Freeman, *George Washington*, vol. 6, 410. For a good discussion of the Reynolds affair, see Cogan, "Reynolds Affair." Hamilton disclosed his affair with Mrs. Maria Reynolds to Frederick Muhlenberg and James Monroe on Dec. 16, 1792 (Syrett [ed.], *PAH*, vol. 13, 330), and although the matter was not disclosed to the public, it quickly became an open secret in political circles; see the "Memorandum" by Thomas Jefferson, Dec. 17, 1792, in Boyd (ed.), *TJP*, vol. 23, 648–649.

85. "Aristides," *GUS*, Sept. 8, 1792; "For the National Gazette," *NG*, Sept. 8, 1792; "Catullus, No. III," *GUS*, Sept. 29, 1792; Monroe to Madison, Sept. 18, 1792, *JMP*, vol. 14. Jefferson's supporters may have blamed Hamilton for the decline in political civility, but they were only too eager to attack his personal character; see "Independent Federal Elector," *NG*, Aug. 15, 1792; "Aristides," *NG*, Sept. 26, 1792; "Defense of Mr. Jefferson's Political Character," *NG*, Sept. 26, 1792; "Z," *NG*, Oct. 3, 1792; "Medicus," *NG*, Oct. 24, 1792.

86. "A Candid Essay on Parties," *NG*, Sept. 26, 1792; "Philadelphia," *GUS*, July 28, 1792; "Brutus," *NG*, Sept. 1, 1792; "For the National Gazette," *NG*, Aug. 8, 1792; "A Republican Federalist," *NG*, Dec. 1, 1792; "A Uniform Federalist," "Strictures on Mr. Adam's [*sic*] Political Character," *NG*, Dec. 1, 5, 8, 1792; "Who Are the Best Keepers of the People's Liberties?" *NG*, Dec. 20, 1792.

87. Hamilton to William Short, Feb. 5, 1793, in Syrett (ed.), *PAH*, vol. 14, 7; Edward Thornton to James Bland Burges, Feb. 4, Mar. 5, 1793, in S. W. Jackman, "A Young Englishman Reports on the New Nation: Edward Thornton to James Bland Burges, 1791–1793," *WMQ*, 3rd ser., 18, no. 1 (Jan. 1961): 85–121.

88. Nineteenth-century historians like Charles Hazen thought that the influence of the French Revolution played a critical role in American party formation, while more recent historians, who generally locate the origins of partisan politics within American political culture, view party alignments as a determinant of attitudes toward the French Revolution. But whether they see the revolution as a source of partisan identity or as a symbol of party differentiation, most historians of the 1790s have assumed that attitudes toward the revolution coincided closely with domestic party divisions. See, for example, Hazen, *Contemporary American Opinion*; Fay, *Revolutionary Spirit*; Eugene P. Link, *Democratic-Republican Societies, 1790–1800* (New York: Columbia University Press, 1942); Cunningham, *Jeffersonian Republicans*; Buel, *Securing the Revolution*; Appleby, *Capitalism*; Newman, *Parades and the Politics of the Street*. For a more nuanced approach to the relationship between the revolution and party identity, see Gary Nash, "The American Clergy and the French Revolution," *WMQ*, 3rd ser., 22, no. 3 (July 1965): 392–412; and David Brion Davis, "American Equality and Foreign Revolutions," *JAH* 76, no. 3 (Dec. 1989): 729–752.

89. Davis, "American Equality and Foreign Revolutions," 731, 734; Nash, "American Clergy and the French Revolution"; Noah Webster, *The Revolution in France* (Philadelphia: n.p., 1794); Hazen, *Contemporary American Opinion*, 168–169; Palmer, *Age of Democratic Revolution*, vol. 2, 38–39; *Pennsylvania Gazette*, Mar. 9, 1796, quoted in Schwartz, *George Washington*, 83.

90. *NG*, Oct. 31, 1791; *NG*, May 11, 1793; "Philadelphus," "Cool Reflections Relative to the French Revolution," *NG*, June 19, 1793.

91. "William Tell," *NG*, June 29, 1793; "Philadelphus," *NG*, June 22, 8, 1793; "Aratus," *NG*, Nov. 14, 24, Dec. 12, 1791. Monroe's first essay was published in the *American Daily Advertiser*. For his authorship, see Harry Ammon, *James Monroe: The Quest for National Identity* (New York: McGraw-Hill, 1971), 87; Hazen, *Contemporary American Opinion*, 120–136.

92. Madison to George Nicholas, Mar. 15, 1793, *JMP*, vol. 14; Jefferson to Thomas Mann Randolph, Jan. 7, 1793, in Boyd (ed.), *TJP*, vol. 25; "Sidney," *NG*, Nov. 28, 1792; *NG*, Dec. 19, 1792.

93. "Brutus, No. IV," *NG*, Mar. 26, 1792; "Alcanor," *NG*, June 15, July 17, 1793; "A Citizen of Georgia," *NG*, June 29, 1793; "An Old Soldier," *NG*, May 8, 11, June 8, 1793; "J.D.W.," *NG*, Aug. 21, 1793; "Brutus," *NG*, July 4, 1792.

94. *NG*, Jan. 2, 1793; article reprinted from the *Connecticut Courant*, *NG*, Jan. 9, 1793.

95. *GUS*, Sept. 1, July 11, 1792, Jan. 26, 1793.

96. *The Tragedy of Louis Capet* (n.p., 1793). Aware that sympathy for Louis XVI might attract criticism, the author of this broadside announced that it was published "at the Request of many true Republicans"; see Jefferson to Joseph Fay, Mar. 18, 1793; Jefferson to Madison, [Mar. 25, 1793], both in Boyd (ed.), *TJP*, vol. 25; Edward Carrington to Hamilton, Apr. 26, 1793, in Syrett (ed.), *PAH*, vol. 14; Monroe to Jefferson, May 9, 1793; Madison to Jefferson, Apr. 12, 1793, both in *TJP*, vol. 25. News of the king's execution reached Philadelphia on Mar. 12, 1793, from London and was confirmed by news from Lisbon on Mar. 15. Nonetheless, the story was treated with skepticism. Earlier rumors of Louis's execution had proved unfounded; see Jefferson to Washington, May 23, 1792, in Boyd (ed.), *TJP*, vol. 23; *GUS*, Oct. 20, 1792. By Mar. 23, however, most Philadelphia newspapers had run the story, although Fenno held out until Mar. 30. Of the Philadelphia papers, Freneau's *National Gazette* and Bache's *General Advertiser* approved of the execution, the *Philadelphia Mail* and *Philadelphia Gazette* disapproved, and the remaining papers equivocated;

see *NG*, Mar. 23, 1793; *GA*, Mar. 18, 1793; *Philadelphia Mail*, Mar. 21, 1793; Steirer, "Philadelphia Newspapers," 400–402; Hazen, *Contemporary American Opinion*, 254–255.

97. "Philadelphia," *NG*, Dec. 22, 1792; "A Republican," *NG*, Mar. 20, 1793; "Louis CAPET Has Lost His CAPUT," *NG*, Apr. 20, 1793; "Cato," *NG*, Apr. 17, 1793; "Philadelphia," Mar. 20, 30, Apr. 20, 1793; "Philadelphus," *NG*, June 8, 1793; "Scevola," *NG*, Apr. 17, 1793; "An Old Soldier," *NG*, Apr. 20, 1793; "Freeman," *NG*, Apr. 23, 1793; "Correspondent," *NG*, Apr. 27, 1793. Similar essays appeared in the newspaper throughout the spring; see, for example, "To the Citizens of the United States," *NG*, May 11, 15, 1793; "Guillotine," *NG*, May 15, 1793. Interestingly, Freneau made no comment about Thomas Paine's plea for the king's life in the national convention, although he published Paine's speech; see *NG*, Apr. 10, 17, 1793.

98. "The Spirit of MDCCLXXVI," *NG*, Apr. 20, 1793; Jefferson to Monroe, May 5, 1793, in Boyd (ed.), *TJP*, vol. 25; "Freeman," *NG*, May 4, 1793; article reprinted from *Independent Chronicle*, *NG*, May 25, 1793; "A New Political Creed," *NG*, July 13, 1793; from *Independent Chronicle*, *NG*, Apr. 19, 1793; "Freeman," *NG*, May 4, 1793. Genet arrived in Charleston on Apr. 8, 1793, reaching Philadelphia on May 16; see Harry Ammon, *The Genet Mission* (New York: Norton, 1973). According to Alfred Young, the Genet mission posed the "stark question of monarchy versus republicanism" to Americans for the first time and transformed the French Revolution into a divisive, partisan issue; see Young, *Democratic Republicans*, 349.

99. The proclamation was published in *GUS* on Apr. 24, 1793. The term "neutrality" was in fact omitted from Washington's proclamation, apparently out of deference to Jefferson.

100. Jefferson to Madison, Apr. 28, 1793, in Boyd (ed.), *TJP*, vol. 25, illus. 400, 619–620; "Philadelphia," *NG*, Mar. 15, 1793; article reprinted from the *American Daily Advertiser*, *NG*, Mar. 16, 1793; "A Customer," *NG*, Apr. 13, 1793; *NG*, May 8, 1793. The arrival of Citizen Genet in the United States was noted in *NG* on Apr. 10, 1793, and a circular announcing the formation of the German Republican Society signed by its vice president, Henry Kammerer, appeared in *NG* on Apr. 13, 1793. The Patriotic French Society, headed by P. Barriere (president) and A. C. DuPlaine (secretary), was formed on Apr. 30, 1793; see "To the Public," *NG*, May 4, 15, 22, 1793. For the Democratic societies, see Foner (ed.), *Democratic-Republican Societies*, introduction. Freneau did publish a few essays defending the government's neutrality policy; see "A Friend to Peace," *NG*, June 15, 19, 22, 1793; "Observator," *NG*, June 19, 1793.

101. "Freeman," *NG*, Apr. 24, 1793. For Genet's reception in Philadelphia, see *NG*, May 18, 22, 25, 1793. For Pichon's poem, see "Philadelphia," *NG*, May 25, 1793. "An Old Soldier," *NG*, May 22, 1793; "An Old Soldier," New York *Time-Piece*, July 4, 1798; Marsh (ed.), *Prose of Philip Freneau*, 542–543. For another civic feast in Genet's honor held at Oeller's Hotel on June 1, see "Philadelphia," *NG*, June 5, 1793.

102. Axelrad, *Philip Freneau*, 255–258; Jefferson, "Notes of a Conversation with George Washington," May 23, 1793, in Boyd (ed.), *TJP*, vol. 26, 101–102.

103. "Veritas," *NG*, June 5, 8, 12, 26, 1793. See also "John Bull," *NG*, June 15, 1793; "Philo-Veritas," "A Brother Tory," *NG*, June 26, 1793.

104. *NG*, Aug. 31, 1793; "Reflections on Several Subjects," *NG*, Sept. 11, 1793. For an example of such simultaneous attacks on Washington and Louis XVI, see "Philadelphus" and "An Old Soldier," *NG*, June 8, 1793. There is a hint of Freneau's French Huguenot origins in the anti-Catholic undertones of these attacks.

105. "A Citizen of Georgia," *NG*, June 29, 1793.

106. No copy of the *Funeral Dirge* is extant, and I have not been able to locate this title in Charles Evans's catalog of eighteenth-century American imprints, but see Freeman, *George Washington*, vol. 7, 113; "Cabinet Meetings," in Syrett (ed.), *PAH*, vol. 15, 157–158; Jefferson, "Anas," Aug. 2, 1793, in P. L. Ford (ed.), *Writings of Jefferson* (New York: G. P. Putnam's Sons, 1892–1899) vol. 1, 253–254. For more references to the guillotine in the *National Gazette*, see "Patriotic Stanzas on the Anniversary of the Storming of the Bastille," *NG*, July 17, 1793; and "To Justice," *NG*, July 31, 1793.

107. Elkins and McKitrick, *Age of Federalism*, 350–352; Jefferson to Madison, July 7, 14, 1793; Jefferson, "Memorandum to George Washington," July 11, 1793, all in Boyd (ed.), *TJP*, vol. 25; "Cabinet Meetings: Proposals Concerning the Conduct of the French Minister," "Reasons for the Opinion of the Secretary of the Treasury and the Secretary of War Respecting the Brigantine *Little Sarah*," both in Syrett (ed.), *PAH*, vol. 15, 75, 157; Ford (ed.), *Writings of Jefferson*, vol. 1, 252–254.

108. Syrett (ed.), *PAH*, vol. 14, 267–269; "Pacificus," *GUS*, June 29, July 17, 1793; "An American," *FG*, July 23, 1793. For the rest of the Pacificus essays, see *GUS*, July 3–27, 1793.

109. Jefferson to Madison, July 7, 1793; Madison to Jefferson, July 22, 30, [Aug. 12], 20, 1793; "Madison's 'Helvidius' Essays," all in *JMP*, vol. 15. The essays were published in *GUS* from Aug. 24 to Sept. 18, 1793, and later republished as *Letters of Helvidius* (Philadelphia: Samuel Harrison Smith, 1796) during the Jay Treaty debates.

110. "Reasons for the Opinion of the Secretary of the Treasury and the Secretary of War Respecting the Brigantine *Little Sarah*," in Syrett (ed.), *PAH*, vol. 15, 75, 157; Jefferson to Madison, Aug. 11, 1793, in Boyd (ed.), *TJP*, vol. 25; "No Jacobin, No. 1," *ADA*, July 31, 1793; "No Jacobin, No. VIII," *ADA*, Aug. 26, 1793. For the rest of these essays, see *ADA*, Aug. 5–28, 1793. For a copy of the King-Jay letter, see Syrett (ed.), *PAH*, vol. 15, 233. This was published in the *Daily Advertiser* on Aug. 14, 1793, and reprinted in the *National Gazette* on Aug. 17, 1793. For a discussion of this entire episode, see the editorial note by Syrett in *PAH*, vol. 15, 233–239. For Genet's response, see Genet to Washington, Aug. 13, 1793, in Theodore J. Crackel (ed.), *The Papers of George Washington: Presidential Series* (Charlottesville: University of Virginia Press, 2007), vol. 13; Jefferson to Genet, Aug. 16, 1793, in Boyd (ed.), *TJP*, vol. 26; *New York Diary*, Aug. 21, 1793; *NG*, Aug. 28, 1793.

111. Jefferson to Madison, Aug. 3, 11, 25, 1793, *JMP*, vol. 15. See also Jefferson to Madison, Aug. 18, 1793, which described growing popular support for the president and his neutrality policy. On these events more generally, see the editorial note "Resolutions on the Franco-American Relations," *JMP*, vol. 15, 76–79; Harry Ammon, "The Genet Mission and the Development of American Political Parties," *JAH* 52, no. 4 (Mar. 1966): 725–741.

112. By "the people," Freneau seems to have meant Congress, which "emanates directly from the people," but even so this was radical stuff. See "Juba," *NG*, July 10, 1793; "An Anti-Gallican Federalist," "Queries to Messrs. Jay and King," *NG*, Aug. 24, 1793; "Juba," *NG*, Aug. 21, 1793. For Freneau's authorship of the Juba essays, see Marsh (ed.), *Prose of Philip Freneau*, 544–545. William Loughton Smith and Oliver Wolcott, Jr., attributed the essays to Freneau in "Phocion," *GUS*, Nov. 1, 1796.

113. P. L. Ford, "Freneau's *National Gazette*," *Nation*, Feb. 21, 1895. Freneau's resignation from the Department of State was marked "Rec'd. Nov. 7" by Jefferson, in Boyd (ed.), *TJP*, vol. 20, 759. For a discussion of their subsequent relationship, see 752–753; Freneau to Madison, May 20, 1795, quoted in Axelrad, *Philip Freneau*, 273.

114. Axelrad, *Philip Freneau*, 275–366. Freneau's Robert Slender letters were published in the *Aurora* from Mar. 29 to May 20, 1799, and republished as [Philip Freneau], *Letters on Various Interesting and Important Subjects: By Robert Slender, O. S. M.* (Philadelphia: D. Hogan, 1799); Philip Freneau to Seth Paine, June 26, 1801, Manuscripts Division, LOC.

115. "Lines Addressed to Mr. Jefferson, on His Retirement from the Presidency of the United States," in H. H. Clark (ed.), *Poems of Philip Freneau* (New York: Harcourt Brace, 1929), 170–173.

Chapter 3

1. *Aurora*, Dec. 23, 1796; John Prentiss, "Memoir," 4, "Recollections," 54, both in John Prentiss Papers, AAS.

2. Thomas Paine, *Common Sense*, in Bruce Kuklick (ed.), *Thomas Paine: Political Writings* (Cambridge: Cambridge University Press, 1989), 24, 28. The absence of a patricidal moment helps to account for the fact that, although a fierce civil war claimed the lives of thousands

in North America, the American Revolution nonetheless enjoys a reputation for political restraint and moderation; see Winthrop A. Jordan, "Familial Politics: Thomas Paine and the Killing of the King, 1776," *JAH* 60, no. 2 (Sept. 1973): 294–308. Jordan's article has not been fully appreciated by historians of the American Revolution, and its emphasis on the centrality of gender and political brotherhood prefigures the work of Lynn Hunt on the political culture of eighteenth-century France; see Hunt, *Politics, Culture and Class in the French Revolution* (Berkeley: University of California Press, 1989); Hunt, *The Family Romance of the French Revolution* (Berkeley: University of California Press, 1993).

3. Jordan, "Familial Politics," 301, 305; Paine, *Common Sense*, 28.

4. John Adams quoted in Wood, *Radicalism of the American Revolution*, 169. For two distinctive, incisive discussions of the politics of gender and the idea of revolutionary fraternity, see Carole Pateman, *The Sexual Contract* (Oxford: Polity, 1988); and Hunt, *Family Romance*. On the role of patriarchal ideology in Anglo-American political culture, see Gordon J. Schochet, *Patriarchalism in Political Thought* (New York: Basic, 1975); Melvin Yazawa, *From Colonies to Commonwealth: Familial Ideology and the Beginnings of the American Republic* (Baltimore, Md.: Johns Hopkins University Press, 1985); Jay Fliegelman, *Prodigals and Pilgrims: The American Revolt against Patriarchal Authority, 1750–1800* (New York: Cambridge University Press, 1982); Mary Beth Norton, *Founding Mothers and Fathers: Gendered Power and the Forming of American Society* (New York: Knopf, 1996); Edwin G. Burrows and Michael Wallace, "The American Revolution: The Ideology and Psychology of National Liberation," *Perspectives in American History* 6 (1972): 169–254.

5. Jordan, "Familial Politics," 308; Wills, *Cincinnatus*, xxi. According to Paul Longmore, the song "War and Washington" referred to the "God-like Washington" as early as 1776. Washington's birthday, which became a national celebration during the postrevolutionary period, was first observed at Valley Forge in the winter of 1778, and during the same year Washington was first referred to as the "father" of his country; see Longmore, *Invention of George Washington*, 200–205. See also Cunliffe, *George Washington*; Schwartz, *George Washington*; Simon Newman, "'Principles or Men?' George Washington and the Political Culture of National Leadership, 1776–1801," *Journal of the Early Republic* 12, no. 4 (Winter 1992): 477–507; Newman, *Parades and the Politics of the Street*; Jordan, "'Old Words' in 'New Circumstances,'" 491–513; Michael Gilmore, "Eulogy as Symbolic Biography: The Iconography of Revolutionary Leadership, 1776–1826," in Daniel Aaron (ed.), *Harvard English Studies* (Cambridge, Mass.: Harvard University Press, 1978), vol. 8.

6. John Adams quoted in Catherine Albanese, *Sons of the Fathers: The Civil Religion of the American Revolution* (Philadelphia: Temple University Press, 1976), 149. As Bernard Bailyn has shown, even before the Revolution, Americans viewed personal executive power with great suspicion, and they carried this suspicion over into the Revolution; see Bailyn, *The Origins of American Politics*. This skepticism influenced the creation of new state constitutions. The Pennsylvania Constitution of 1776, for example, established a plural executive drawn from the legislature and a rotating "presidency." In the Continental Congress prior to 1781, departments were controlled by standing committees. Congress then decided, against radical opposition, to place departments under the control of individuals appointed from outside Congress, a development that strengthened personal control over departments but further drained authority from the presiding president of Congress; see Morris, *Forging of the Union*, 106; Merrill Jensen, *The Articles of Confederation* (Madison: University of Wisconsin Press, 1940), 242–243; Jensen, *The New Nation*, 55–56.

7. Charles Thomson to Jacob Read, Sept. 27, 1784, quoted in Morris, *Forging of the Union*, 98; John Adams, *Discourses on Davila*, quoted in Schwartz, *George Washington*, 222. In the fifteen years from 1774 to 1789, fourteen men occupied the office of president. John Hancock was allowed to serve two nonconsecutive terms. Only in the Continental army was there any possibility that charismatic personal leadership and real power might converge, and there,

as the timidity and quick collapse of the Newburgh conspiracy showed, Washington himself was a decisive check; see Richard H. Kohn, "The Inside History of the Newburgh Conspiracy: America and the Coup d'Etat," *WMQ*, 3rd ser., 28, no. 2 (Apr. 1970): 187–220; Charles Royster, *A Revolutionary People at War: The Continental Army and American Character, 1775–1783* (Chapel Hill: University of North Carolina Press, 1979), chap. 8.

8. Stewart Mitchell (ed.), *New Letters of Abigail Adams, 1788–1801* (Boston: Houghton Mifflin, 1947), 35; George Washington to Edward Rutledge, May 5, 1789, in Dorothy Twohig (ed.), *Papers of George Washington* (Charlottesville: University of Virginia Press, 1987), vol. 2, 218. Michael Gilmore dates the use of the term "founding fathers" to the mid-1780s; see "Eulogy as Symbolic Biography." Distrust of personal executive power was expressed clearly at the Philadelphia Convention in William Paterson's New Jersey Plan, which proposed a plural executive of three men elected from the ranks of Congress.

9. For the widespread use of the term "monocrat" in the 1790s, see Warren, *Jacobin and Junto*. For Maclay's criticism of Washington's courtly style, see Kenneth Bowling and Helen Veit (eds.), *The Diary of William Maclay* (Baltimore, Md.: Johns Hopkins University Press, 1988). For Washington's conception of the presidency, see Longmore, *Invention of George Washington*; and Glenn A. Phelps, *George Washington and American Constitutionalism* (Lawrence: University of Kansas Press, 1993).

10. Mrs. E. D. Gillespie, *A Book of Remembrance* (Philadelphia: Lippincott, 1901), 18–20; Tagg, *Benjamin Franklin Bache*, 3–13. For additional material on Bache, see *DAB*, vol. 1, 462–463; Bernard Fay, *The Two Franklins: Fathers of American Democracy* (Boston: Little, Brown, 1933); Fay, "Benjamin Franklin Bache: A Democratic Leader of the Eighteenth Century," *Proceedings of the American Antiquarian Society* 40 (Oct. 1930): 277–304; Smith, *Franklin and Bache*.

11. Benjamin Franklin to Samuel Cooper, Dec. 9, 1780, in Smyth (ed.), *Writings of Franklin*, vol. 8, 348. Bache's parents probably wanted to get him away from Philadelphia and the impending war with Britain; see Claude-Anne Lopez and Eugenia W. Herbert, *The Private Franklin: The Man and His Family* (New York: Norton, 1975), 136–137, 216, 226–227. For the most thorough and insightful account of Bache's time in Geneva, see Tagg, *Benjamin Franklin Bache*, 29–42; see also "Diary of Benjamin Franklin Bache," in Bache Papers, APS; Fay, *Two Franklins*, 21–37; Lopez and Herbert, *The Private Franklin*, 220–232.

12. Sept. 13, 1785, "Bache Journal," in Bache Papers, APS; Lopez and Herbert, *The Private Franklin*, 234.

13. This strong sense of attachment to France is overlooked in many accounts of Bache's early life, which place more emphasis on Franklin's influence; see Tagg, *Benjamin Franklin Bache*, 47–49; Fay, *Two Franklins*, 21–118; Smith, *Franklin and Bache*, 45–82.

14. Franklin to Brillon, Apr. 19, 1788, in Smyth (ed.), *Writings of Franklin*, vol. 9, 644; Tagg, *Benjamin Franklin Bache*, 57–69.

15. Bache, "Melanges," in Bache Papers, APS. Bache had his own plans for self-improvement and, like Franklin, a tendency to tabulate and commit them to paper; see "Notebook of Resolutions and Plan for Self-Improvement" (1789), in "Melanges," in Bache Papers, APS.

16. For evidence that he did pay some attention to politics, see his "On the Rejection of the Federal Constitution by the State of North Carolina," in "Melanges"; Bache to Margaret Hartman Markoe, Mar. 20, 1790, and also Feb. 4, 1790, July 1, 1791, in Bache Papers, APS; Tagg, *Benjamin Franklin Bache*, 72–78; Fay, "Benjamin Franklin Bache," 283.

17. Bache to Margaret Hartman Markoe, May 2, 1790; Robert Morris to Bache, July 28, 1790, both in Bache Papers, APS. Bache to Jefferson, Aug. 20, 1790, in Boyd (ed.), *TJP*, vol. 17, 397.

18. Benjamin Franklin Bache, *Proposals for Publishing a News-Paper to be Entitled the Daily Advertiser, and Political, Commercial, Agricultural & Literary Journal* (Philadelphia: n.p., July 1790); William Bache to Benjamin Franklin Bache, July 25, 28, 1790; Benjamin Vaughan to Benjamin Franklin Bache, Sept. 1, 1790, all in Bache Papers, APS. Bache changed the name of the newspaper from "The Daily Advertiser" to "The General Advertiser" because he intended

to publish a weekly summary of events for rural subscribers. Bache's motto may have reflected the influence of Morris and his grandfather's dim view of the Philadelphia press; see Benjamin Franklin, "An Account of the Supremest Court of Judicature in Pennsylvania, viz. The Court of the Press," *FG*, Sept. 12, 1789.

19. *GA*, Oct. 2, 23, Nov. 5, 17, 27, 1790. For the theater controversy, see Nov. 11, 1790, Mar. 31, Apr. 15, 21, 1791. For similar paeans to the federal government and its officers, see *GA*, Oct. 15, 28, Nov. 19, 26, 28, Dec. 9, 1790, Feb. 22, 1791.

20. *GA*, July 4, 1790. Bache's father was a director of Robert Morris's Bank of North America from 1784 to 1792; see Tagg, *Benjamin Franklin Bache*, 11; *GA*, July 4, 1791. For Bache's support of Hamilton's *Report on the Bank of the United States*, see *GA*, Dec. 25, 29, 1790; for his support of Hamilton's *Report on the Mint*, see *GA*, Feb. 7, 1791; for his support of the assumption of state debts, see *GA*, Dec. 28, 1790, Feb. 2, 14, 1791; for his support of the excise tax, see *GA*, Jan. 20, 22, 24, 27, 1791. Hamilton's *Report on Manufactures* was published in the *General Advertiser* on Dec. 28, 1791, and Jan. 2, 1792. For Bache's positive assessment of the report and his previous support for domestic manufacturing, see *GA*, Jan. 16, 19, 1792, Oct. 2, 1790, Sept. 7, 1791. For his more general remarks on Hamilton, see *GA*, Aug. 10, 1791, Mar. 20, 1792.

21. *GA*, Jan. 16, 1792.

22. *GA*, Dec. 9, 1790, Nov. 7, 8, July 7, Aug. 30, 1791.

23. *GA*, Oct. 25, 1790. Good-naturedly, Bache printed the communication and remarked that the author "tells but one part of the story, and that he rather exaggerates." For a sampling of the articles Bache lifted from Fenno's *Gazette of the United States*, see *GA*, Oct. 15, Nov. 26, Dec. 9, 27, 1790, Jan. 24, 27, Feb. 17, 1791. These usually appeared in the editorial column of the newspaper headed "Philadelphia" and were not attributed to Fenno.

24. Tagg, *Benjamin Franklin Bache*, 43, 98; *GA*, Mar. 21–24, 1791. Bache and Jefferson were both members of the Pennsylvania Society for Mechanical Improvements and Philosophical Inquiries; see *GA*, Jan. 15, 1791. Jefferson later told Washington that Bache had reprinted extracts from the *Gazette de Leyde* for him, "but his being a dayly paper, did not circulate sufficiently in other states. He even tried at my request, the plan of a weekly paper of recapitulation from his daily paper, in hopes that that might go into the other States, but in this too we failed." If his recollection is correct, this may be a reference to Bache's weekly edition, which he dropped at the start of 1791. If so, Jefferson probably first approached Bache in Aug. or Sept. 1790; see Jefferson to Washington, Sept. 9, 1792, in Boyd (ed.), *TJP*, vol. 24. Interestingly, Bache continued to rely on British newspapers as well as the *Gazette de Leyde* and published a critique of those Americans (like Jefferson) who argued that no reliance could be placed on the British press, pointing out that British newspapers varied greatly and that the one on which he relied, the *Morning Chronicle*, was politically trustworthy; see *GA*, Apr. 1, 16, 25, 1791.

25. Jefferson to Bache, Apr. 22, 1791; Jefferson to Jonathan Bayard Smith, Apr. 26, 1791, both in Boyd (ed.), *TJP*, vol. 20, 246, 290. Bache advertised Paine's work in the *General Advertiser* on Apr. 22, 1791, and announced its publication by Smith on Apr. 29. It appeared on May 4 and was immediately extracted in the *General Advertiser*; see May 5, 1791, and following issues. Bache published attacks on John Adams's *Davila* essays, numerous extracts from Paine's work, articles assailing Burke, the essays of Publicola, and a long series of ripostes to these by Brutus. He also defended Jefferson against the aspersions of Publicola in the editorial columns of the newspaper; see "A French Citizen," *GA*, May 3, July 22, 1791; "Extract from Paine's Answer to Burke," May 5, 9–12, 1791; "Introductory Remarks" and "Letter by Thomas Paine," Oct. 10, 1791; "Advantages of the Republican over the Monarchical Form of Government," Dec. 6, 1791; "Thoughts on the Establishment of a Mint in the United States," Dec. 21, 22, 1791; "Boston, April 18," May 5, 1791; "Remarks on Mr. Burke's Philippic," May 12, 1791; "Remarks," Aug. 2, 1791; "Mr. Burke's Pamphlet," Oct. 24, 1791; "Brutus" and "Publicola," June 30–Aug. 4, 1791. For his defense of Jefferson, see *GA*, June 30, July 1, 1791; for his attack on titles, see May 16, June 4, 7, 10, July 23, 1791; and for his criticism of the public debt, see "Philadelphia," July 20, 1791.

26. Jefferson to Bache, Apr. 22, 1791, in Boyd (ed.), *TJP*, vol. 20, 246. However, Bache continued to publish extracts from the *Gazette de Leyde*; see *GA*, Apr. 14, 23, 25, July 23, Aug. 1, 1791. For the change of format, see "To the Public," *GA*, Oct. 4, 1790, Jan. 1, 1791. His decision may have been a response to Dunlap and Claypoole's *American Daily Advertiser*, which was advertised in the *General Advertiser* on Oct. 9, 1790, and launched on Jan. 1, 1791. Claypoole also launched a new evening paper in June, the Philadelphia *Mail*, which ran from June 1 to Sept. 30, 1793; see Bache to Margaret Hartman Markoe, May 9, 1791, in Bache Papers, APS.

27. Fenno's influence over Bache actually grew in late 1791 and early 1792. For material reprinted by Bache from the *Gazette of the United States*, see Jan. 4, Feb. 27, Mar. 1, 8, 15, 19, 20, 24, 1792. For Bache's marriage, see Bache to Richard Bache, Sept. 1, 20, 1791; Bache to Margaret Hartman Markoe, Oct. 4, 1791, all in Bache Papers, APS; Jefferson to Martha Jefferson Randolph, Nov. 13, 1791, in Boyd (ed.), *TJP*, vol. 22, 294.

28. *GA*, Apr. 19, 1792. Bache had earlier sounded warnings about the hazards of excessive financial speculation; see *GA*, Jan. 18, 23, Mar. 1, 20, 27, 1792. But he also published articles critical of these anti-speculative writings and continued to defend the federal government, and just days before Duer declared bankruptcy, he published a glowing tribute to members of the government and Hamilton in particular; see *GA*, Feb. 27, Mar. 1, 8, 15, 19, 23, 24, 29, 1792. For his tribute to Hamilton, see *GA*, Mar. 20, 1792. For criticism of Hamilton, however, see "Government of the United States," *GA*, Feb. 7, 1792; "From the National Gazette," Jan. 13, 1792; "The Downfall of Nobility," Jan. 20, 1792. The Sidney essays were published in the *National Gazette* from Apr. 5 to May 24, 1792, and reprinted in the *General Advertiser* from Apr. 16 to May 2, 1792. But shortly after their publication, Bache printed a paragraph from the *Gazette of the United States* acknowledging that, although "some part of the measures of the government may want wisdom…on the whole, no nation has prospered more, or enjoyed tranquility in a greater degree than the United States since the establishment of the present happy constitution"; *GA*, May 10, 1792. For continued criticism of the government, however, see *GA*, June 12, July 5, 27, Aug. 30, 1792.

29. *GA*, July 2, 17, 22, 1792, Aug. 22, 1791. For Bache's response to the Sept. massacres, see *GA*, Nov. 3, 1792; to the declaration of the French Republic, see *GA*, Nov. 29, Dec. 12, 1792; to revolutionary violence, see *GA*, Oct. 26, Nov. 1, 1792, Feb. 14, Mar. 9, 1793. In general, see Tagg, *Benjamin Franklin Bache*, 124–125, who also emphasizes the importance of the French Revolution to the evolution of Bache's political ideas.

30. *GA*, Dec. 1, 1792, Jan. 21, 1793, Dec. 16, 5, 21, 22, 1792. For a more detailed discussion of these developments, see Newman, *Parades and the Politics of the Street*, 120–185; and above, chapter 2.

31. Margaret M. O'Dwyer, "A French Diplomat's View of Congress, 1790," *WMQ*, 3rd ser., 21, no. 3 (July 1964): 413; *GA*, Nov. 27, Dec. 9, 1790, Feb. 24, 22, 27, 1792. "The day was marked," reported Bache on the occasion of Washington's birthday in 1791, "by universal demonstrations of the joy of a great and grateful people, who with his aid shook off the shackles of oppression, and are still by his assistance rapidly acquiring weight in the political scale of the universe"; *GA*, Feb. 24, 1791. For an extract from the *Gazette of the United States* attacking critics of Washington's birthday and other reports of birthday celebrations, see "New York, February 24: Birth Day Festival," *GA*, Feb. 27, 1792; "Charleston (S.C.) Feb. 14," *GA*, Mar. 6, 1792; "February 16," *GA*, Mar. 8, 1792; "Boston, February 22: President's Birth Day," *GA*, Mar. 8, 1792. The odd sour note about Washington's birthday did creep into Bache's newspaper, and at least one writer thought such celebrations contained "too strong a tincture of Monarchy to be adopted by Republicans," urging Americans to "let the Birth-Days of Presidents be blotted from the Calender of Feasts"; *GA*, Mar. 4, Apr. 23, 1791.

32. "Mirabeau," *GA*, Dec. 7, 1792. As James Tagg argues, Bache was now setting the pace for Freneau, who reprinted the Mirabeau essay in the *National Gazette* on Dec. 12, 1792; see Tagg, *Benjamin Franklin Bache*, 163.

33. "Mirabeau," *GA*, Dec. 7, 1792.

34. *GA*, Dec. 26, 1792. For a more general discussion of the relationship between gender and virtue in this period, see Ruth Bloch, "The Gendered Meanings of Virtue in Revolutionary America," *Signs 13* (Autumn 1987): 37–58; and Nancy Fraser and Linda Gordon, "A Geneaology of *Dependency*: Tracing a Keyword of the U.S. Welfare State," in Barbara Laslett (ed.), *Rethinking the Political: Gender, Resistance, and the State* (Chicago: University of Chicago Press, 1995).

35. *GA*, Jan. 21, 2, 26, 29, 1793. Whether American political culture really was characterized by the degree of deference attacked in these essays is a complex and, in my view, separate question. But it is wrong to assume, as Gordon Wood does in *The Radicalism of the American Revolution*, that anti-monarchical attitudes are evidence for the existence of a monarchical culture, or that this culture operated in the way its critics (and occasional apologists) described. Republicans obviously appealed to "manly independence" because independence was such a central value in American political culture, and discussions about the existence of deference in colonial and postcolonial America have been severely hampered by such conceptual confusions. Can any serious student of Edward Thompson's work on the rebellious and iconoclastic popular culture of eighteenth-century England, for example, accept the caricature of a deferential, monarchical prerevolutionary Anglo-American culture conjured up in Wood's work? See E. P. Thompson, *Customs in Common: Studies in Traditional Popular Culture* (New York: New Press, 1991). For a discussion of these issues, see the articles by Michael Zuckerman, Aaron Fogelman, John Murrin, Kathleen Brown, and Robert Gross in "Deference or Defiance in Eighteenth-Century America? A Roundtable," *JAH* 85, no. 1 (June 1998).

36. "Sidney," *GA*, Jan. 23, Feb. 4, 1793; see also "Mirabeau," Jan. 25, 1793, and "Sidney," Jan. 26, 1793; Oliver Wolcott quoted in George Gibbs, *Memoirs of the Administrations of Washington and John Adams* (New York: For the Subscribers, 1846), vol. 1, 85. In contrast, Freneau ridiculed the "monarchical farce of the birth day," although he found Washington's conduct at the inaugural commendably republican, prompting him to hope that "the simplicity that has heretofore marked your character" had been restored and that "every jealous republican spirit will be hushed into peace"; *NG*, Mar. 2, 13, 1793. Benjamin Franklin Bache to Richard Bache, Feb. 3, 1793, in Bache Papers, APS.

37. The execution of the French king, Louis XVI, took place on Jan. 21, 1793. For Bache's response, see Benjamin Bache to Richard Bache, Jan. 10, 1793, in Bache Papers, APS; *GA*, Jan. 1, 18, Mar. 18, 26, Apr. 3–16, 1793. For articles defending the decision of the national convention, see *GA*, Mar. 26, Apr. 3, 1793.

38. As Bache's activities showed, his support for France was not necessarily incompatible with support for the U.S. government's policy of neutrality. For Washington's proclamation, see *GA*, Apr. 23, 1793; Bache to Richard Bache, Jan. 10, 1793, in Bache Papers, APS; *GA*, Mar. 15, 22, 27, Apr. 25–26, May 17–22, 1793.

39. *NG*, Mar. 20–Apr. 17, 1793. The classic discussion of the king's two bodies, the one personal, corporeal, and mundane and the other impersonal, political, and sacred, is in Ernst H. Kantorowicz, *The King's Two Bodies: A Study in Mediaeval Political Theology* (Princeton, N.J.: Princeton University Press, 1957). For further discussion of Freneau's support for the execution of the French king and his campaign against Washington, see chapter 2.

40. *GA*, Jan. 2, 3, Feb. 8, 9, 12, 22, 1793. At a large civic festival in Boston, a more generous public tribute to Washington (accompanied by a thirteen-gun salute) expressed a similar sense of public uneasiness about the political influence of personality. After toasts to "The People" and "The Rights of Man," Citizen Charles Jarvis (a future Jeffersonian Republican firebrand) asked the gathering to toast "but one individual, and your hearts will tell you that this is WASHINGTON"; *GA*, Feb. 5, 1793.

41. *GA*, June 4, 1793; *NG*, June 5, 8, 1793.

42. *GA*, Aug. 16, 1793; see also *GA*, Aug. 15, 20, 24, 1793. For signs of a more critical response to government policies in this period, see *GA*, Aug. 15, 26, 1793; Bache to Richard Bache, Aug. 22, 1793, in Bache Papers, APS.

43. *GA*, Jan. 1, 1794.

44. See Tagg, *Benjamin Franklin Bache*, 8; *GA*, Feb. 6, Mar. 22, Apr. 3, May 27, 1794. On the rise of the Democratic societies, see Foner (ed.), *Democratic-Republican Societies*; and Link, *Democratic-Republican Societies*. Bache regularly advertised and reported meetings of the Democratic Society of Pennsylvania and other Democratic societies in the *General Advertiser*. For his defense of the societies, see *GA*, Jan. 20, Feb. 12, Apr. 16, May 16, 1794.

45. *GA*, Jan. 24, 25, 28, June 6, Feb. 12, 1794. On Robespierre, see *GA*, Oct. 8, 10, 20, 1794. On the rumors of Paine's execution, see *GA*, Oct. 10, 1794. His views on the French Revolution grew more abstract as he began to tailor them to the demands of domestic politics; see Tagg, *Benjamin Franklin Bache*, chap. 7; and Tagg, "The Limits of Republicanism: The Reverend Charles Nisbet, Benjamin Franklin Bache, and the French Revolution," *Pennsylvania Magazine of History and Biography* 112, no. 4 (Oct. 1988): 503–544.

46. At no point was this plainer than during the controversy created by the Giles resolutions in early 1793. Drafted by Jefferson and introduced to Congress by William Branch Giles, these resolutions censured Hamilton's management of public finances and were part of a public campaign to discredit the treasury secretary. In a letter to his father, Bache discussed the "danger of a moneyed interest" and mentioned the congressional campaign against Hamilton, arguing that "it is probable all is not as the friends of the treasury would wish to make it appear." But despite his sympathy for Hamilton's opponents, he paid little attention to the affair in the *General Advertiser*. For Bache's response to the Giles resolutions, see "An Observer," *GA*, Feb. 27, 1793; "Merlin," *GA*, Mar. 2, 1793; Bache to Richard Bache, Feb. 3, 1793, in Bache Papers, APS. The best treatment of the politics of the Giles resolutions is Eugene Sheridan, "Thomas Jefferson and the Giles Resolutions," *WMQ*, 3rd ser., 49, no. 4 (Oct. 1992): 589–608.

47. *GA*, Feb. 5, 1794; "Cato," Feb. 6, 1794; "From a Correspondent," Feb. 7, 1794. See, for example, "Philadelphia," *GA*, Mar. 24, 1794; "An American Sans-Culottes," *GA*, Apr. 3, 1794; "Philadelphia," *GA*, Apr. 12, 17, May 21, 1794; "At a Meeting of the Paper Noblemen," *GA*, Dec. 12, 1794. Bache also advertised for sale "A Definition of Parties; or the Political Effects of the Paper System, Considered," *GA*, May 3, 1794, and "A View of the Revenue System … by a Citizen"; *GA*, May 3, 1794. Callender's contribution to the more biting and astringent political style in the *General Advertiser* is unmistakable. For good examples, see the editorials published in the newspaper on May 8, 16, 1794. Although Callender worked for the Philadelphia editor of the *Federal Gazette*, Andrew Brown, until 1796, Michael Durey argues that he was responsible for much of the political commentary in Bache's newspaper from 1794 to 1798; see Durey, *With the Hammer of Truth*, 105–112. James Tagg makes no mention of this in his study of Bache.

48. *GA*, May 27, 1794.

49. *GA*, July 26, 1794; "Philadelphia," Aug. 16, 20, 1794. When Hamilton joined the militia sent to quash the Whiskey Rebellion, however, Bache attacked him mercilessly; see *GA*, Nov. 8, 10, 14, 1794. Bache had previously supported the excise tax and been critical of those who opposed its implementation; see *GA*, Jan. 22, 27, Feb. 19, July 11, Aug. 31, Sept. 5, 1791, Jan. 2, Mar. 8, 12, 19, Sept. 28, Nov. 13, 1792. For the meeting and resolutions of the Democratic Society of Pennsylvania, see *GA*, Aug. 7, 9, 12, 1794.

50. "Philadelphia," *GA*, Sept. 5, 6, 16, 1794. For McPherson's Blues, see "Liberty! Equality! Fraternity!" *GA*, Sept. 16, 17, 1794. For Bache's reports, see *GA*, Sept. 18, 23, 24, 1794. For his comments on liberty poles, see *GA*, Sept. 20, 1794. James Tagg plays down Bache's enthusiasm for the military campaign against the Whiskey rebels, describing him as vacillating and ambivalent, and exaggerates his subsequent "anti-administration stand." Although Bache criticized Washington and ridiculed Hamilton's military pretensions, he supported the government's general approach to the Whiskey Rebellion. His resentment about official attacks on the Democratic societies, like the attacks themselves, did not develop until early in 1795, after the Whiskey Rebellion had been extinguished; see Tagg, *Benjamin Franklin Bache*, 215–216.

51. *GA*, Sept. 13, Dec. 13, 1794. The controversial third resolution was first passed by a vote of 30–29. In response, President Blair McClenachan and 28 other dissidents marched out of the meeting. Bache then took the chair, and after further debate the resolution was withdrawn by a vote of 30–0. This leaves no doubt that Bache was in the initial majority that supported the harsher resolution, a fact left ambiguous in Tagg's account; see *Benjamin Franklin Bache*, 218; Foner (ed.), *Democratic-Republican Societies*, 30.

52. Noah Webster, *The Revolution in France*, reprinted in Ellis Sandoz (ed.), *Political Sermons of the American Founding Era, 1730–1805* (Indianapolis, Ind.: Liberty, 1991), 1290 (hereafter, this will be the edition cited); Adams to Abigail Adams, Jan. 2, 1794, in Charles Francis Adams (ed.), *Letters of John Adams* (Boston: C. C. Little and J. Brown, 1841), vol. 2, 134.

53. *GA*, July 27, 1792, Mar. 9, 1793; *Aurora*, Mar. 2, 1795. For examples of Republican criticism of Washington's birthday, see *GA*, Dec. 5, 1792, Jan. 2, 21, Feb. 16, 18, July 2, 1793, June 30, July 4, 8, 1794. For Bache's views, see *GA*, Feb. 5–28, Mar. 5, 1794; Tagg, *Benjamin Franklin Bache*, 222–223. For other examples of such nonpartisan celebrations, see *GA*, July 18, 1791, Feb. 24, July 17, 21, 25, 1792, Feb. 21, July 6, 13, 17, 1793, July 8, 9, 1794; *Aurora*, July 7, 8, 10, 14, 1795. For a perspective that places greater emphasis on the partisan nature of these popular celebrations even earlier in the 1790s, see Newman, *Parades and the Politics of the Street*, 44–119.

54. *New-York Journal & Patriotic Register*, Nov. 20, 23, 1793. Greenleaf claimed that the article attacking Washington had been published by mistake; see *New-York Journal*, Dec. 7, 11, 14, 1793; Benjamin Strong, Dec. 10, 1793, in Strong Family Papers, NYHS; *AM*, Dec. 11, 13, 1793; *GA*, Dec. 26, 1793. A resolution defending Greenleaf and freedom of the press was passed by supporters at Corre's Hotel; see *New-York Journal*, Dec. 25, 1793.

55. This was a point of view shared by the French, who began to attack American neutral shipping in retaliation. The classic study of the Jay Treaty is by Samuel Flagg Bemis, *Jay's Treaty: A Study in Commerce and Diplomacy* (New York: Macmillan, 1923). More useful on its relationship to domestic politics is Jerald A. Combs, *The Jay Treaty: Political Battle Ground of the Founding Fathers* (Berkeley: University of California Press, 1970).

56. *GA*, Mar. 31, Apr. 19, May 27, Apr. 27, 1794. Jay was appointed on Apr. 15, and his appointment was confirmed by the Senate on Apr. 19. For the first notice and criticism of this in the *General Advertiser*, see Apr. 17, 19, 29, 1794. Republicans despised Jay for his involvement in the press campaign against Citizen Genet in late 1793, and Madison believed that his appointment was a serious political blunder; see Elkins and McKitrick, *Age of Federalism*, 395.

57. *GA*, May 9, June 2, May 21, 1794, Jan. 31, 1795; Fisher Ames, Feb. 3, 1795, in Seth Ames (ed.), *Works of Fisher Ames* (New York: Da Capo, 1969), vol. 1, 166. Much of the criticism of executive excess was clearly Callender's work; see *GA*, June 11, 30, July 5, 19, 21, 31, 1794.

58. [James Madison], *Political Observations* (Philadelphia: n.p., 1795), 13; "Franklin," *Aurora*, Mar. 24, Apr. 24, Mar. 27, Apr. 20, 1795. Madison's essays appeared in the *Aurora*, May 6, 7, 30, June 3, 4, 5, 1795. The essays of "Franklin," usually attributed to Alexander James Dallas, were the first major Republican response to the Jay Treaty and were published in Eleazar Oswald's *Independent Gazetteer* and reprinted in the *Aurora*, Mar. 19–May 19, 1795. They were reprinted as *The Letters of Franklin* (Philadelphia: Eleazar Oswald, 1795). Although the details of the Jay Treaty were not yet known, critics like "Franklin" regarded the mere existence of a treaty with Great Britain as a betrayal of the French alliance and a source of monarchical infection and corruption.

59. *Aurora*, Apr. 13, May 26, June 18, 19, 20, 22, 23, 1795; Feb. 10, 1796.

60. *Aurora*, June 29, July 1, July 4, 1795. While the "authentic" copy of the treaty came from Senator Mason, the abstract probably came from the French minister, Pierre Adet, who claimed credit for it in his dispatches of July 3, 1795; see Freeman, *George Washington*, vol. 7, 256 nn102–103; Tagg, *Benjamin Franklin Bache*, 246–247; Frederick J. Turner (ed.), "Correspondence of the French Ministers to the United States, 1791–1797," *Annual Report of the American Historical Association* 2 (1904): 741–742.

61. Bache to Margaret Bache, July 3, 8, 15, 1795. For his journey to Boston, see Bache to Margaret Bache, July 3 (morning and evening), 15, 1795, in Bache Papers, APS. The meeting at Boston was reported in the *Independent Chronicle*, July 13, 1795; *Aurora*, July 18, 21, 22, 1795; and see also Warren, *Jacobin and Junto*, 59.

62. *Aurora*, Aug. 14, 1795. For Fourth of July protests in Philadelphia, see *Aurora*, July 7, 8, 9, 14, 1795; Freeman, *George Washington*, vol. 7, 258; *Independent Gazetteer*, July 8, 1795. For New York, see Young, *Democratic Republicans*, 449–454. Bache also attended the meeting in New York, which he described as "glorious"; see Bache to Margaret Bache, July 18, 21, 1795, in Bache Papers, APS; *Aurora*, July 22, 23, 28, 1795. For the petitioning campaign, see *Aurora*, July 14–Aug. 15, 1795; Freeman, *George Washington*, vol. 7, 291n119.

63. Bache to Margaret Bache, July 8, 1795, in Bache Papers, APS; *Aurora*, July 9, 10, Sept. 9, July 21, 1795.

64. Freeman, *George Washington*, vol. 7, 291; *Aurora*, Aug. 27, 21, 22, 19, 1795. For additional attacks on Washington's contempt for public opinion, see *Aurora*, Aug. 29, Sept. 1–12, 1795. Bache discounted rumors of Washington's signature a few days earlier, denouncing such rumors as a "false and most scandalous libel" on the president on the day he signed the treaty. When Fenno's *Gazette of the United States* reported that the treaty had been signed, doubt was no longer possible, and Bache turned on Washington; see *Aurora*, Aug. 15, 18, 19, 21, 1795. The first installment by Hancock was published on Aug. 21, 1795.

65. *Aurora*, Aug. 21, Sept. 18, 21, 1795. See the other articles by Hancock and Atticus in the *Aurora*, Aug. 24, 27, Sept. 3, 8, 26, 1795.

66. *Aurora*, Aug. 21, 22, Sept. 9, 17, 21, 1795.

67. *Aurora*, Sept. 11, 15, 21, 22, 25, 27, Oct. 1, 1795.

68. *Aurora*, Sept. 11, 21, 24, 26, 30, Oct. 1, 5, 1795.

69. *Aurora*, Oct. 8, 19, 21, Nov. 13, 1795; *Letters from General Washington to Several of His Friends, in June and July 1776* (Philadelphia: Republished at the Federal Press [Benjamin Franklin Bache], 1795). Washington's official letters were edited by John Carey and published as *Official Letters to the Honorable American Congress... by His Excellency George Washington* (London: Cadell Junior, 1795). For the original edition of the forgeries, see *Letters from General Washington to Several of His Friends in the Year 1776* ([New York]: James Rivington, 1778).

70. "Casca," *Aurora*, Oct. 16, 1795. For earlier calls for Washington's impeachment, see *Aurora*, Aug. 19, 21, Sept. 21, 1795.

71. *Aurora*, Oct. 23, 1795; *GA*, June 11, 1794. Congressional Republicans suggested that the president's pay should be cut to $12,000 a year; see *GA*, July 5, June 30, 1794. For attacks on executive extravagance, see *GA*, May 21, June 11, July 19, 21, 31, 1794; *Aurora*, Jan. 20, 24, 28, 1795.

72. *Aurora*, Oct. 23–29, Nov. 3, 5, 18, 26, 12, 20, 1795. See also *Aurora*, Oct. 30, 31, Nov. 2, 1795.

73. *Aurora*, Oct. 16, 1795. See also "Tammany Society," *Aurora*, May 14, 1796; *Aurora*, June 19, July 7, 1795; Paine, *Letter from Thomas Paine to George Washington* (Philadelphia: [Benjamin Franklin Bache], 1797); Paine to James Madison, Sept. 24, 1795, in Foner (ed.), *Writings of Thomas Paine*. The toast of the county brigade was received with "3 cheers." The resolutions of the Virginia Assembly demanded that the House of Representatives be given the power to ratify foreign treaties, that powers of impeachment be vested in a tribunal other than the Senate, that Senate terms be reduced to three years, and that judges of the United States be excluded from all other official appointments and offices. For a discussion of these resolutions, see Malone, *Jefferson and the Ordeal of Liberty*, 252–253; Stephen G. Kurtz, *The Presidency of John Adams: The Collapse of Federalism, 1795–1800* (Philadelphia: University of Pennsylvania Press, 1957), chap. 1. These resolutions clearly foreshadowed the more famous Virginia and Kentucky resolutions of 1798.

74. [John Beckley], *Remarks Occasioned by the Late Conduct of Mr. Washington as President of the United States* (Philadelphia: Benjamin Franklin Bache, 1797).

75. *Aurora*, Nov. 16, 1795; John Fenno to Joseph Ward, Oct. 26, 1795, in Hench (ed.), "Fenno Letters, Part 2"; Elias Boudinot to Samuel Bayard, Dec. 14, 1795, in Everett Papers, MHS; *Aurora*,

Jan. 19, 1796. For Hamilton's defense of Washington against A Calm Observer, see *Aurora*, Nov. 18–21, 1795. These essays revived opposition attacks on Hamilton; see *Aurora*, Nov. 21, 23, 28, Dec. 7, 1795. For continued attacks on Washington in the *Aurora*, see "Valerius," Dec. 1, 9, 11, 1795, and "Pittachus," Dec. 15, 1795. Edmund Randolph's *Vindication*, published in late Dec. 1795, further dampened attacks on the president by revealing Washington's dislike for the Jay Treaty and his reluctance to sign it. The publication of Randolph's *Vindication* by Samuel Harrison Smith was announced in the *Aurora* on Dec. 29, 1795; see the response from Pittachus, *Aurora*, Jan. 1, 9, 12, 13, 1796.

76. *Aurora*, Dec. 7, 1795, Mar. 3, 9, 11, 14, 15, 17, 29, Apr. 1, 2, 4, 5, 6, 11, 14, 16, 1796. See also *Aurora*, Jan. 12, 19, Mar. 3, 4, 1796.

77. *Aurora*, Apr. 7, 19, 22, 23, 26, 28, 29, May 5, 1796.

78. *Aurora*, May 24, 1796; see also May 3, 1796. For Bache's continued attacks on Washington, see the essays of "Paulding," which ran in the *Aurora* from May 24, 1796, until Aug. 1796. The attacks on Cobbett took up so much space in the newspaper by Aug. 1796 that one reader complained, to no avail; see *Aurora*, Aug. 11, July 2, Sept. 5, Oct. 7, 1796. See also *Aurora*, June 30, July 29, 1796. For rumors of Washington's retirement, see *Aurora*, June 24, 1796. Bache also printed Washington's Farewell Address in the *Aurora* on Sept. 20–21, 1796, without critical comment; see also *Aurora*, Oct. 7, 1796.

79. *Aurora*, Dec. 23, 1796. This was the last in a series of three articles attacking Washington; see *Aurora*, Dec. 20, 21, 23, 1796. Paine, *Letter to George Washington*; [Beckley], *Remarks Occasioned by the Late Conduct of Mr. Washington*; [William Duane], *A Letter to George Washington, President of the United States: Containing Strictures on His Address of the Seventeenth of September 1796…by Jasper Dwight of Vermont* (Philadelphia: Benjamin Franklin Bache, 1796). For the publication of these, see *Aurora*, Dec. 6, 8, 1796.

80. See Isaac Weld, *Travels through the States of North America* (London: J. Stockdale, 1807), vol. 1, 107–109; Fisher Ames to Oliver Wolcott, Nov. 14, 1796, quoted in Warren, *Jacobin and Junto*, 66–67; *Aurora*, Apr. 19, 22, 23, 26, 28, May 5, 1796; Schwartz, *George Washington*, 74–77; Newman, *Parades and the Politics of the Street*, 68–74; *GUS* and *Aurora*, Dec. 27, 1799; *City Gazette*, Jan. 10, 15, 1800.

81. See Nathan Hatch, *The Democratization of American Christianity* (New Haven, Conn.: Yale University Press, 1989); *Aurora*, Apr. 7, Sept. 7, 8, 17, 23, Oct. 7, Nov. 17, 1796. The publication of Paine's *Age of Reason* and Federalist attacks on French irreligion and Jefferson's religious beliefs provoked an upsurge in public discussion about religion in the second half of the 1790s; see chapter 6. An interesting issue arises here about the place of the Constitution in American political culture. In many respects, the impersonal and abstract authority of the Constitution replaced the personal authority of Washington as the sacred center of American politics in the 1790s, although, as I have argued, many radical Republicans did not see the Constitution as a "sacred" text, and Jefferson's belief that the "earth belongs to the living" was inherently hostile to the sacralization of the Constitution; see Michael G. Kammen, *A Machine That Would Go of Itself: The Constitution in American Culture* (New York: Knopf, 1986).

82. *Aurora*, Oct. 1, 1795.

Chapter 4

1. Sir Charles Lyell (1797–1875) was the author of *Principles of Geology* (1830–1833), which had considerable influence on Charles Darwin. The brief account of his meeting with Webster is in his *Travels in North America, in the Years 1841–1842* (New York: n.p., 1845), vol. 1, 53. See also Emily Ellsworth Fowler Ford (ed.), *Notes on the Life of Noah Webster* (New York: Burt Franklin, 1912), vol. 1, n. 382. Ironically, the one word "invented" by this tireless advocate of linguistic and cultural nationalism was of French origin.

2. On the origin of the word "demoralize," see *Oxford English Dictionary*, 2nd ed., vol. 4 (Oxford: Clarendon, 1989); Robert K. Barnhart (ed.), *The Barnhart Dictionary of Etymology*

(Bronx, N.Y.: H. W. Wilson, 1988). Webster included the word in *A Compendious Dictionary of the English Language* (New Haven, Conn.: Hudson and Goodwin, 1806), where he defined *demoralize* as "to corrupt, undermine or destroy moral principles" and *demoralization* as simply "the destruction of morality." The words were given a similar definition in Webster's *An American Dictionary of the English Language* (New York: S. Converse, 1828).

3. "Memoir of Noah Webster, LL.D.," in Richard M. Rollins (ed.), *The Autobiographies of Noah Webster* (Columbia: University of South Carolina Press, 1989), 133. For an interesting discussion of this "Memoir," see Rollins, *Autobiographies*, 35–57. Webster's account may also, as Richard Rollins has argued, provide evidence of a rift between Webster and his father; see Rollins, *Autobiographies*, 19–21; Rollins, *Long Journey*, 19.

4. On the importance of the "self-made man" in the early Republic, see Steven Watts, *The Republic Reborn: War and the Making of Liberal America, 1790–1820* (Baltimore, Md.: Johns Hopkins University Press, 1987). Rollins emphasizes the anti-patriarchal nature of Webster's ideas, arguing that his break with his father led him toward Rousseau and contract theory. Rollins, however, exaggerates Webster's alienation from his father and his break with patriarchal thought. I prefer to see Webster as conflicted about these issues and to see his patriarchal impulses reemerging after he reaches middle age. In his writings, however, he often defends the independence of children and attacks authoritarian methods of education; see *GUS*, Jan. 9, 13, 16, 1790. For his remarks on "free sons" and Rollins's discussion of these issues, see Rollins, *Long Journey*, 25–27.

5. "Memoir," 131. See also Webster to Thomas Dawes, Dec. 20, 1808, in which Webster describes "being educated in a religious family, under pious parents"; Warfel (ed.), *Letters*. For information on the ancestry of Noah Webster, Jr., see "Memoir," 129–131; Rollins, *Long Journey*, 8; K. Alan Snyder, *Defining Noah Webster: Mind and Morals in the Early Republic* (Lanham, Md.: University Press of America, 1990), 9–10. Noah Webster was descended from Governor John Webster, who left for western Massachusetts with the Reverend John Russel, Jr., of the Hartford church after Thomas Hooker's death in 1659, a schism precipitated by disagreement about infant baptism. John Webster died in 1661. His eldest son, Robert, chose to remain in Hartford, where he owned "large tracts of land" at the end of the seventeenth century. Noah Webster's paternal grandfather, Daniel, was one of the first settlers of West Hartford and "commanded a military company" in King George's War. His father, however, was less well off than his forebears, although he was a respectable member of the local community in West Hartford. He was a deacon of the Fourth Church and was elected a justice of the peace continuously from 1781 to 1796, which entitled him to be called Deacon or Squire Webster.

6. "Memoir," 131. For Webster's schooldays, see his letter to Henry Barnard in 1840 in Rollins (ed.), *Autobiographies*, 116; and Rollins, *Long Journey*, 12; also see Snyder, *Defining Noah Webster*, 14–15; "Tablet," *GUS*, Jan. 9, 13, 16, 1790, which are attributed to Webster in Rollins, *Long Journey*, 149n62; and Emily Ellsworth Ford Skeel, *A Bibliography of the Writings of Noah Webster*, ed. Edwin H. Carpenter, Jr. (New York: New York Public Library, 1958). The Reverend Nathan Perkins (1727–1843) served as pastor of the Fourth Church of Hartford from the 1770s onward; see Nathan Perkins, *A Half Century Sermon*, cited in Rollins, *Long Journey*, 11; Rollins (ed.), *Autobiographies*, 183; Snyder, *Defining Noah Webster*, 10. According to one historian, the Great Awakening exerted the most influence in the eastern part of Connecticut, and Old Light orthodoxy remained dominant in the area where Webster grew up. Among other things, the Awakening involved an attack on the external aspects of orthodox religiosity and a reemphasis on the importance of God's grace. Neither moral rectitude nor simple obedience were guarantees of salvation. As one revivalist put it, "Civility and external Acts belonging to Morality are no Part of the Essence of the Religion of Christ"; see Richard L. Bushman, *From Puritan to Yankee: Character and the Social Order in Connecticut, 1690–1765* (New York: Norton, 1970), 193–195. Perkins, *The Benign Influence of Religion on Civil Government and National Happiness* (Hartford, Conn.: n.p., 1808), is discussed in Ruth Bloch, *Visionary Republic: Millennial Themes in American Thought, 1756–1800* (New York: Cambridge University Press, 1985), 224; Rollins (ed.), *Autobiographies*, 183.

7. Brooks Mather Kelley, *Yale: A History* (New Haven, Conn.: Yale University Press, 1974), 53, 71–79, 80–82. For the schism that led to the founding of the College of New Jersey in 1746, see T. J. Wertenbaker, *Princeton 1746–1896* (Princeton, N.J.: Princeton University Press, 1946), 18. Clap closed the college altogether in 1742 when he felt students were becoming infected by the new religious doctrines and in 1745 issued a declaration condemning the preaching of evangelist George Whitefield; see Kelley, *Yale*, 49, 60–63. In his 1754 pamphlet, *The Religious Constitutions of Colleges*, Clap wrote that "Colleges are Religious Societies…for training up persons for the work of the Ministry." The best discussion of Clap and eighteenth-century Connecticut is in Grasso, *A Speaking Aristocracy*, chap. 3.

8. Rollins, *Long Journey*, 14–16, 18. Webster recounts "falling into vicious company at college" and losing his early impressions of Christian teaching in a letter to Thomas Dawes, Dec. 20, 1808, in Warfel (ed.), *Letters*. He may also have been influenced by his tutor Joseph Buckminster, who placed a strong emphasis on the importance of rational religion; see Arthur Lewis Ford, *Joel Barlow* (New York: Twayne, 1971), 15, 18. There can be no doubt that Webster was deeply influenced by scientific rationalism and specifically by Lockean ideas at Yale. Locke's *Essay Concerning Human Understanding* (as well as Wollaston's *The Religion of Nature Delineated*) was required reading for seniors at the college at this time as they pondered the problem of how to reconcile religion and reason; see Kelley, *Yale*, 80. Rollins also points to Webster's essay "A Short View of the Origin and Progress of the Science of Natural Philosophy," which praises Copernicus, Galileo, Descartes, and Newton and was written shortly after he left Yale; Rollins, *Long Journey*, 15. The essay was reprinted in the *New York Magazine and Literary Repository* in 1790. Locke's ideas certainly show up in Webster's writings, and his belief that we "come into the world with minds totally unfurnished with ideas; but, like white paper, capable of receiving and retaining any notions, good or bad, which education or accident happens to impress" was the basis for his early interest in education; see *GUS*, Jan. 9, 1790; and "On the Education of Youth in America," *American Magazine*, Dec. 1787.

9. Snyder, *Defining Noah Webster*, 18–22. Snyder emphasizes the theological moderation of Yale at this time and makes a good case for the influence of Scottish commonsense philosophy on Webster. For a discussion of religion at Yale that places it at a distance from both the Arminianism of Boston and the New Light theology of Jonathan Edwards, see Henry F. May, *The Enlightenment in America* (New York: Oxford University Press, 1976), chap. 1, 185–187. On the influence of Scottish commonsense philosophy more generally, see Garry Wills, *Inventing America: Jefferson's Declaration of Independence* (Garden City, N.Y.: Doubleday, 1978), part 3.

10. "Memoir," 132–133; Kelley, *Yale*, 84–88; Rollins, *Long Journey*, 17–18; Snyder, *Defining Noah Webster*, 25–27. Even collecting their diplomas was not so easy as public commencements were suspended from 1775 to 1781. During 1776 and 1777, classes were disrupted by the threat of war and the difficulty of providing provisions for students; see Ford, *Notes*, vol. 1, 20, 25. Webster's class included Joel Barlow, Josiah Meigs, Uriah Tracy, Zephaniah Swift, Abraham Bishop, and Oliver Wolcott, Jr.

11. For Barlow, see James Woodress, *A Yankee Odyssey: The Life of Joel Barlow* (Philadelphia: Lippincott, 1958). Like Webster, Barlow was from a humble Connecticut farm family, and despite their later political differences the two remained lifelong friends. Barlow encouraged Webster's early literary efforts, helped to find a publisher for the English grammar, and loaned him money. Woodress's biography contains an interesting account of Yale in the mid-1770s. See also Ford, *Barlow*, 17. Even before Lexington and Concord, students had formed their own militia and begun to drill in the college yard, and when news of the first clash with British troops arrived, they set out for Boston under the command of Captain Benedict Arnold. When Generals George Washington and Charles Lee led the new Continental army through New Haven in June 1775, Yale students mustered to greet them and accompanied them through the town with great fanfare led by, among others, Noah Webster, Jr. President Daggett was said to be a man of fierce political convictions and an ardent supporter of the Patriot cause. See

Snyder, *Defining Noah Webster*, 22–23. The comment by the Tory graduate is from Kelley, *Yale*, 89. On student radicalism and the formation of a militia at Yale, see Kelley, *Yale*, 83–84. For the reference to Arnold, see Rollins, *Long Journey*, 17. For the account of Washington and Lee's arrival in New Haven, see Ford, *Notes*, vol. 1, 16–18; Rollins (ed.), *Autobiographies*, 118. See also E. S. Thomas, *Reminiscences of the Last Sixty Five Years* (Hartford, Conn.: For the Author, 1840). In later years, Webster liked to exaggerate his participation in the struggle for independence and claimed that he "bore arms to defend independence" and that he offered to "hazard my life" to protect American liberties; *AM*, Mar. 21, 1797; "To the Editor of the American Palladium," in Rollins (ed.), *Autobiographies*, 113. In 1776, Webster did accompany his brother Abraham north to Canada to join the Continental forces encamped there. For his experiences during the Revolution, see Ford, *Notes*, vol. 1, 20–28; and Rollins (ed.), *Autobiographies*, 118–133.

12. Joseph Buckminster to Noah Webster, Oct. 30, 1779, in Webster Papers, NYPL. For the removal of Daggett, see Rollins, *Long Journey*, 18, who also reports that the senior class refused to be drafted into the Continental army, making them the first college draft resisters in American history. They also refused to gather in New Haven during the winter of 1777–1778, and in 1777 decamped from College Chapel to protest the punishment of two classmates; see "Memoir" and "Class Confession," both in Rollins (ed.), *Autobiographies*, 133, 67–68. See also Joel Barlow's satirical poem attacking Naphtali Daggett in Ford, *Barlow*, 17.

13. This was first published as "The Tablet, Nos. CXIX–CXXIII," *GUS*, June 2–16, 1790. There is a good discussion of this essay in Snyder, *Defining Noah Webster*, 32–34.

14. Webster to John Canfield, Jan. 6, 1783, in Warfel (ed.), *Letters*; Noah Webster, *A Grammatical Institute of the English Language* (Hartford, Conn.: Hudson and Goodwin, 1783), [part 1], 12; *American Magazine*, Jan. 1788, 80–81; Snyder, *Defining Noah Webster*, 59–62.

15. Webster to John Canfield, Jan. 6, 1783, in Warfel (ed.), *Letters*; Ford, *Notes*, vol. 1, 61; Webster, *Grammatical Institute*, [part 1].

16. Webster to Thomas Dawes, Dec. 20, 1808, in Warfel (ed.), *Letters*; "Memoir," 133–134. For Johnson's *Rambler* essays, see W. J. Bate and Albrecht B. Strauss (eds.), *The Yale Edition of the Works of Samuel Johnson* (New Haven, Conn.: Yale University Press, 1969–), vols. 3–5. For Webster's reading of the *Rambler* essays, see Rollins (ed.), *Autobiographies*, 133–134. Webster's father lost the family farm as a result of his mortgage; see Ford, *Notes*, vol. 1, 38. Contrary to the Freudian analysis offered in Rollins, *Long Journey*, there is no evidence that Webster resented his father's inability to help him after his graduation from Yale, nor is there any evidence that his father ever held this financial debacle against his son. Indeed, most evidence points the other way. Webster returned to his father's home in 1780 after a period of "distressing nervous affliction" and kept in close touch with other family members. He spent Thanksgiving in 1784 at his father's house "as usual," sent his father money, and corresponded with him; see Ford, *Notes*, vol. 1, 40, 56, 87, 173–176, 230, 270. See especially his father's friendly letter to him dated July 28, 1787, in Ford, *Notes*, vol. 1, 173–174. The reports of their breach are greatly exaggerated.

17. Webster later declared, "[B]ooks & business will ever be my principal pleasure. I must write—it is a happiness I cannot sacrifice." Webster to George Washington, Dec. 18, 1785, in Warfel (ed.), *Letters*; Samuel Johnson, *Rambler*, no. 8, in *Works of Samuel Johnson*, vol. 3, 42. For Webster's emphasis on self-control, see the letter from his former Yale tutor Joseph Buckminster, Oct. 30, 1779, in Webster Papers, NYPL.

18. For a discussion of this in relation to Locke, see P. A. Alkorn, *Samuel Johnson and Moral Discipline* (Evanston, Ill.: Northwestern University Press, 1967), 11–12; Johnson, *Rambler*, no. 8, in *Works of Samuel Johnson*, vol. 3, 7. This discussion is indebted to Alkorn, who describes Johnson's moral essays as characterized by "their harmonious acceptance of Lockean descriptive psychology within a broader framework of ethical concern"; Alkorn, *Samuel Johnson*, 86, chap. 3. For more on Locke's influence, see Jean H. Hagstrum, *Samuel Johnson's Literary Criticism* (Chicago: University of Chicago Press, 1952); and Donald J. Greene, *The Politics of Samuel Johnson* (New Haven, Conn.: Yale University Press, 1960). For the influence of Mandeville on

Johnson, see Alkorn, *Samuel Johnson*, 32n34. Clearly, the ideas of the Scottish Enlightenment are significant here as well.

19. See Alkorn, *Samuel Johnson*, 4–23.

20. Alkorn, *Samuel Johnson*, 4, 144–154. Johnson stated that "self-confidence is the first requisite to great undertakings," a lesson Webster certainly took to heart. Donald Greene characterizes Johnson's political thought as a belief that the aim of politics should be to make "political power work as well as it can for the greatest happiness of the greatest number of individual human beings"; see Greene, *Politics of Samuel Johnson*, 148–149. For a similar statement by Webster in the *American Magazine*, see Rollins, *Long Journey*, 56. Although he regarded himself as a Christian moralist whose ideas were "conformable to the precepts of Christianity," Johnson's approach to religion in the *Rambler* essays was eminently practical and rational. He expressed hope that rational men would follow a life of faith, "regulated not by our senses but by belief," but for those who would not, belief in the afterlife was an indispensable sanction for good behavior, part of a theological calculus. In fact, like Webster, Johnson avoided specific references to Christianity and most often spoke of God as the Supreme Being, "Infinite Goodness," or "Omnipotent Goodness" rather than as Christ. God represents compassion and forgiveness, a position echoed in Webster's phrase "God is Love." For a discussion of Johnson's understanding of the relationship between reason and religion, see Alkorn, *Samuel Johnson*, 40–55, chap. 2.

21. "Memoir," 134–136; Ford, *Notes*, vol. 1, 40–46. Webster began his legal career by boarding with Oliver Ellsworth, a future chief justice of the Supreme Court, in Hartford in 1779, but his "nervous afflictions" prevented him from continuing. In 1781, following the advice of Titus Hosmer, a well-known Connecticut jurist and a native of West Hartford, he took a position with Jedediah Strong, the registrar of deeds in Litchfield, and continued to study law. After failing to qualify for the bar in Litchfield in 1781, he was admitted to practice by the county court in Hartford that same year. After opening his school in Sharon, Connecticut, he continued to read law under the guidance of John Canfield, whom he described as a "jurist of talents and of uncommon philanthropy."

22. Webster, *Grammatical Institute*; Rollins, *Long Journey*, 34–36. Webster's speller has some claim to be called the bestselling political tract in the early Republic, and it may have rivaled Paine's *Common Sense* in its timeliness and influence. Webster intended to call the work "The American Instructor" and then "The American Spelling Book and Grammar" but on the advice of Ezra Stiles adopted the title *Grammatical Institute* instead; see "To the General Assembly of Connecticut, Hartford, October 24, 1782," and "Memorial to the Legislature of New York, Goshen, New York, January 18, 1783," both in Warfel (ed.), *Letters*. He altered the title to *The American Spelling Book* later in the 1780s; see Snyder, *Defining Noah Webster*, 49–50. The first edition of the work numbered 5,000 and was priced at fourteen pence, or ten shillings a dozen; see Emily Ellsworth Ford Skeel, *A Bibliography of the Writings of Noah Webster* (New York: New York Public Library, 1958). In the spring of 1783, Webster returned home to Hartford to secure its publication, but no printer would touch the work. Determined to publish it, Webster financed the speller himself with aid from his friend and former Yale classmate Joel Barlow, who loaned him $500; see Ford, *Notes*, vol. 1, 59. It proved a wise investment, although Webster himself did not profit much at first. The speller appeared just as the war with Great Britain came to a conclusion and American schools were beginning to reestablish themselves. According to Rollins, the book was "the most widely read secular book in eighteenth- and nineteenth-century America," and by 1818 Webster estimated its sales at about 5 million; see the preface to *The American Spelling Book* (Rpt., New York: Columbia University Press, 1962). For its publication history, see Rollins, *Long Journey*, 34–36; and E. Jennifer Monaghan, *A Common Heritage: Noah Webster's Blue-Back Speller* (Hamden, Conn.: Archon, 1983).

23. *American Magazine*, Mar. 1788; Webster to Canfield, Jan. 6, 1783; "To the General Assembly of Connecticut," and "Memorial to the Legislature of New York," all in Warfel (ed.), *Letters*.

24. "To Dilworth's Ghost," Feb. 15, 1785, in Warfel (ed.), *Letters*; Webster to Timothy Pickering, in Ford, *Notes*, vol. 1, 156–157. In July 1784, Webster announced his intention to study law with John Trumbull in Hartford, and in Aug. he "read a little law and some poetry" and attended the local law courts. He was even involved in a few suits, although he confessed to his diary that he divided his time between "the Ladies and the books" and, when time was short, exclusively to the former; see Ford, *Notes*, vol. 1, 79–87. Noah Webster, *A Grammatical Institute...Part II* (Hartford, Conn.: Hudson and Goodwin, 1784); *A Grammatical Institute... Part III* (Hartford, Conn.: Barlow and Babcock, 1785). His opposition to the use of Latin grammar was revolutionary for the time, although neither of these two works sold as well as the speller. Like the speller, Webster's reader was full of patriotic essays. It was reissued later in the 1780s in enlarged form as *An American Selection of Lessons in Reading and Speaking* (Philadelphia: Young and M'Culloch, 1787).

25. For synopses of these lectures, which were revised and published as *Dissertations on the English Language* (Boston: Isaiah Thomas, 1789), see Ford, *Notes*, vol. 1, 160–161. They were of varying success. After a lecture in Petersburg, Virginia, Webster recorded the word "Disappointed" in his diary. In Williamsburg, he drew an audience of only 6, and in Alexandria 10. Virginians, he commented, had an "amazing fondness for Dissipation." Apparently, it didn't occur to Webster that southerners might resent the instruction of a New England schoolteacher in the finer points of their own native tongue. In Annapolis, Maryland, he managed to corral 30 members of the state assembly for his first lecture, but his subsequent performance attracted only 14. In Wilmington, Delaware, however, he read his lectures to a "crouded audience, whose applause is flattering." In New York, he claimed, over 200 people attended his final lecture, and in Philadelphia, he attracted well over 100 listeners and "great applause." A lecture at Princeton, however, mustered only 16 students and was cancelled, a showing Webster blamed on impending examinations. Fittingly, his warmest reception was in New Haven; see Ford, *Notes*, vol. 1, 143–159.

26. Ford, *Notes*, vol. 1, 114. Webster's emphasis on uniformity opened him to charges of linguistic coercion. And indeed, there is no question that the idea of a national language was a coercive one, designed to obliterate provincial distinctions. The objective of the *Institute*, as he made clear in his "Memorial to the Legislature of New York," was to render pronunciation "accurate and uniform by demolishing those odious distinctions of provincial dialects which are the subject of reciprocal ridicule in different states." See Warfel (ed.), *Letters*; and the preface to *Dissertations on the English Language*. At the same time, Webster defended popular usage and idiomatic expressions. His conception of a national language was thus somewhat unclear. Was he describing a language already in existence or a language that had to be created? At times, he seems to suggest that the gradual "americanization" of the English language is part of an inevitable, organic process, "necessary and unavoidable," and that his own role in this process was basically conservative and documentary; see in particular the preface to his *Dissertations*, 22. "My principal aim," Webster stated in the *American Magazine* (Aug. 30, 1790), "has been to check innovations, and bring the language back to its purity and original simplicity." But at other times, Webster presents himself as a linguistic innovator with an active and prescriptive role to play in the establishment of a national language; see especially his *A Collection of Essays and Fugitiv Writings* (Boston: I. Thomas and E. T. Andrews, 1790). Webster confronts this issue directly in his preface to *Dissertations*; see esp. 22–29, where he argues that he seeks neither to establish a prescriptive grammar/lexicon nor to simply document variable and fluctuating local usage but to base his standard on national practice. The tension between conservatism and innovation in Webster's linguistic theory reflects a more general tension between freedom and coercion, democracy and elitism, optimism and pessimism in his writings of the 1780s.

27. "To the General Assembly of Connecticut," in Warfel (ed.), *Letters*; preface, *Dissertations*, 20.

28. Noah Webster, *An Examination into the Leading Principles of the Constitution* (Philadelphia: Prichard & Hall, 1787), 29, 46.

29. "Memoir," 142. Warfel states that Webster was unquestionably "the father of copyright legislation in America"; see Harry Warfel, *Noah Webster: Schoolmaster to America* (New York: Octagon, 1967), 54–58, as does Henry Steele Commager in his introductory essay to *Noah Webster's American Spelling Book* (Rpt., New York: Columbia University Press, 1962), 3. For Webster's own account of his campaign for copyright, see his "Memoir," 136–138. James Madison, whom Webster had already met in Philadelphia, introduced the copyright motion to the Congress. For Webster's arguments about copyright protection, see "To the General Assembly of Connecticut"; Webster to Canfield, Jan. 6, 1783; "Memorial to the Legislature of New York," all in Warfel (ed.), *Letters*. As Joel Barlow pointed out, whatever the intrinsic merits of Webster's speller, it had to be published and circulated in large numbers at low cost if it were to compete with existing textbooks, like Dilworth's, and the absence of copyright laws made it highly vulnerable to literary piracy; Barlow to Webster in Ford, *Notes*, vol. 1, 54–55.

30. "Memoir," 141. Webster's first political essays were "Observations on the Revolution of America," *New York Packet*, Jan. 17, 31, Feb. 7, 1782. These were reprinted with three additional essays in the *Freeman's Chronicle* on Sept. 22, 29, Oct. 6, 20, 27, Nov. 3, 10, 1783. For the background to the Middletown Convention, see Richard Buel, *Dear Liberty: Connecticut's Mobilization for the Revolutionary War* (Middletown, Conn.: Wesleyan University Press, 1980), 297–318; Grasso, *A Speaking Aristocracy*, 425–431. For Webster's contributions to this debate, see Ford, *Notes*, vol. 1, 73–75; "Memoir," 139–141; Webster to James Kent, Oct. 20, 1804, in Rollins (ed.), *Autobiographies*, 89–93. For the Honorius essays, see *Connecticut Courant*, Aug. 26, Sept. 2, 9, 16, 30, Oct. 14, 21, 1783, Jan. 27, 1784. The first article is unsigned. For Webster's authorship, see Skeel (ed.), *Bibliography*, 435. Marked copies of the articles in Webster's hand are extant in the NYPL. For "The Policy of Connecticut," see *Connecticut Courant*, Feb. 24, Mar. 2, 9, 16, May 18, 25, 1784. Reprinted in the *Connecticut Gazette*, Mar. 26–June 4, 1784. According to Webster, the leaders of the Middletown Convention were no more than former Tories who wished to foment anarchy and civil war. Apparently, there was some basis for Webster's belief; see Buel, *Dear Liberty*, 311–312. In any case, Webster's arguments contributed to a shift in public opinion, and in May 1784 the Connecticut Assembly passed legislation to support commutation; see Buel, *Dear Liberty*, 318. For Webster's generous assessment of his own influence, see "Memoir," 140–141.

31. Webster, *Sketches of American Policy* (Hartford, Conn.: Hudson and Goodwin, 1785). The immediate occasion for *Sketches* was a debate on "the great question What are the means of improving & establishing the Union of the States," held in Hartford on Jan. 25, 1785. Webster began *Sketches* in mid-Feb. and, with his usual alacrity, finished the book by the end of the month; see Ford, *Notes*, vol. 1, 124–126; and appendix VIII, in Ford, *Notes*, vol. 2, 453–454. For the influence of Rousseau and Price, see "Memoir," 141–142; Webster to James Kent, Oct. 20, 1804, in Rollins (ed.), *Autobiographies*, 89–93; Rollins, *Long Journey*, chap. 2. Webster claimed that he was introduced to Rousseau and other radical Enlightenment thinkers by the Reverend John Peter Tetard, a Genevan and "a learned and pious clergyman," who taught him French in the early 1780s while he was living in Sharon, Connecticut; see Ford, *Notes*, vol. 1, 44–45; Rollins, *Long Journey*, 21; "Memoir," 135. For the influence of Richard Price, see Webster, *Sketches*, 2; and Price to Webster, Aug. 29, 1785, in Webster Papers, NYPL. For Rousseau's influence on American thought during this period, see May, *Enlightenment in America*, 165–167; and Paul Merrill Spurling, *Rousseau in America 1760–1809* (Tuscaloosa: University of Alabama Press, 1969).

32. Webster, *Sketches*, 3–4, 42–43, 31–32, 11.

33. Webster, *Sketches*, 31–48.

34. Webster, *Sketches*, 10–18, 24–26, 46. Webster supported the confiscation and sale of large estates as a step toward the destruction of aristocratic ideas, arguing that "the great fundamental principle on which alone a free government can be founded and by which alone the freedom of a nation can be rendered permanent, is an equal distribution of property" (18). The best testimony to Webster's early radicalism is his own. His copy of *Sketches* in the New York Public Library, annotated in later life, includes remarks like "many of these notions...are found to

be chimerical," and "these ideas are too democratic and not just. Experience does not warrant them"; see Harry Warfel's introduction to *Sketches of American Policy* (New York: Scholars' Facsimiles & Reprints, 1937), ii.

35. Webster, *Sketches*, 30, 12–13, 19–21; *Freeman's Chronicle*, Nov. 3, 1783, cited in Rollins, *Long Journey*, 31; Webster, *Sketches*, 27. His views went well beyond simple religious "toleration" and recall this statement in the speller, "Let sacred things be appropriated to sacred purposes"; Webster, *Grammatical Institute*, [part 1], 12. His views may have caused his father some concern; see the letter he wrote to his son on Dec. 16, 1782, admonishing him to "so live as to obtain the favor of Almighty God & his grace in this world & a Saving interest in the merits of Jesus Christ, without which no man can be happy"; Ford, *Notes*, vol. 1, 56. For Webster's later views on religion, see below.

36. Webster, *Sketches*, 24, 29, 3, 8.

37. Webster, *Examination*, 57–63; Webster, "Essay No. VII," "Essay No. IV," in *Collection of Essays*, 46–51, 82. Webster's arguments about government in his *Collection of Essays and Fugitiv Writings* are fascinating. On the one hand, they are clearly reactionary, constructing a rationale for state power that is designed to limit the role of direct popular participation in political life. On the other hand, Webster's belief that the ingrained hostility of Anti-Federalists to state power was an anachronism in a representative democracy had some validity, and his insistence on the right of the people's representatives to legislate, subject to democratic election, had radical implications. His view that constitutions were provisional documents came very close to Jefferson's belief that "the earth belongs to the living." And at one point in his volume, Webster takes Jefferson to task for supporting the inviolability of the Virginia Constitution and chastises him (with highly Jeffersonian logic) as a supporter of "unalterable constitutions." His position rested on faith in the American people. "Why should we be so anxious to guard the future rights of a nation?" he asked. "For my part, I believe that the people and their Representatives, two or three centuries hence, will be as honest, as wise, as faithful to themselves, and will understand their rights as well, and be as able to defend them, as the people are at this period" (61–63). All of these arguments, of course, were designed to undermine support for a Bill of Rights and need to be understood in this context. For a slightly different perspective on this period in Webster's life, see Rollins, *Long Journey*, 50–51; Snyder, *Defining Noah Webster*, 94–96. Webster's views and language did grow more conservative in the late 1780s. One interesting sign of this was his emphasis on the need for children to be under the control of their elders and betters, a position that contrasted starkly with his earlier insistence on youthful independence; see *American Magazine*, Feb. 1788, 159, cited in Snyder, *Defining Noah Webster*, 112.

38. Webster was close to Benjamin Franklin, who shared his interest in language reform, was acquainted with Washington (who called on him on May 26, 1787), and moved freely in nationalist circles, dining with Timothy Pickering and visiting James Madison, Benjamin Rush, and Rufus King; see Ford, *Notes*, vol. 1, 215, 218, 208–224; "Memoir," 146–149; Ford, *Notes*, vol. 1, 219–222. The *American Magazine* was founded to promote "literary intercourse" between citizens of the new nation and more immediately to rally support for the ratification of the federal Constitution. Webster arranged for the printer Samuel Loudon to publish the magazine in New York in Nov. 1787, and by the end of the year, the first issue, dated Jan. 1, 1788, was ready for distribution; see Ford, *Notes*, vol. 1, 223, 225. It was not a financial success, and after an effort to save the magazine by creating a broader partnership, Webster abandoned it; see "Memoir," 149–150; Ford, *Notes*, vol. 1, 179, 237–239, and vol. 2, 407–408. Webster later claimed that *Sketches of American Policy* "contained the first public proposition" of the need to establish a "National Constitution," a statement supported by his biographer; see *AM*, July 19, 1796; Warfel, *Noah Webster*, 166; appendix VIII in Ford, *Notes*, vol. 2, 453–454; and "Memoir," 142. This was an exaggeration as Webster himself acknowledged in a letter to James Kent written in 1804. There, he described his role more humbly, acknowledging the precedence of Pelatiah Webster's *A Dissertation on the Political Union and Constitution of the Thirteen United States*

of North America (1783) and George Washington's famous "Circular Address to the Governors of the Several States" in the same year; see Webster to Kent, Oct. 20, 1804, in Rollins (ed.), *Autobiographies*, 89–93. However, Webster's *Sketches* was important. He took copies with him on his tour of the United States in 1785–1786, distributing them to men of importance, including Washington (who thought them "beneficial") and Madison, up and down the eastern seaboard; see Ford, *Notes*, vol. 1, 104, 109. They were also reprinted in the *Maryland Gazette* in late 1785 to early 1786, shortly before the Annapolis Convention; see Ford, *Notes*, vol. 1, 66–68, 111.

39. *DA*, Aug. 2, 1788, cited in Warfel, *Noah Webster*, 186. See also Ford, *Notes*, vol. 1, 232–233, 184. Appropriately, it was Webster who took it upon himself to "draw up an account of the proceedings" for publication; see "Memoir," 150. He joined the "Society for promoting a knowledge of the English Language" in Mar. 1788 and recorded a meeting to "form a Constitution for the Philological Society" in Apr.; see Ford, *Notes*, vol. 1, 227–228. The society included William Dunlap, Samuel Latham Mitchell, and Charles Brockden Brown and was formed for the purpose of "ascertaining the force and beauty of our own language" and "improving the American tongue." It later evolved into the Friendly Club; see Warfel, *Noah Webster*, 185–187. Ebeneezer Hazard, who disliked Webster, referred to him as the "Monarch" of the Philological Society; Ford, *Notes*, vol. 1, 185.

40. Ford, *Notes*, vol. 1, 236; Webster to James Greenleaf, Feb. 1, 15, 1789, in Warfel (ed.), *Letters*. In Nov. 1788, Webster recorded, "busy trying to form a Society for publishing the American Magazine & Universal register. succeed." On Dec. 6, he announced that he had signed an agreement with Francis Childs for the publication of the magazine in New York, but while in Boston in early 1789 he devised another plan to merge the magazine with Isaiah Thomas's *Massachusetts Magazine*. None of this came to anything, and in early 1789 he wrote, "There is a company formed for carrying on the magazine in New York; but I am doubtful of its success—& not very anxious about it." Webster to James Greenleaf, Feb. 1, 1789, in Warfel (ed.), *Letters*. For a full account of these negotiations, see Skeel (ed.), *Bibliography*, 395–397. For the publication of *Dissertations*, see Ford, *Notes*, vol. 1, 191–192. Webster later confessed to Timothy Pickering, "My dissertations, which cost me a large sum of money, lie on hand, and must be sold for wrapping paper"; Ford, *Notes*, vol. 1, 308–309. Webster estimated his loss at £250; see Webster to James Greenleaf, Feb. 1, 1789, in Warfel (ed.), *Letters*. Webster met Rebecca Greenleaf in Philadelphia in Mar. 1788 and quickly fell in love. They were married in Boston in Oct. 1789; see Ford, *Notes*, vol. 1, 172–173, 213, 207.

41. Webster believed that his prospects as a lawyer were good, "as several old attorneys have left practice lately, I shall stand a chance for a share of business." But John Trumbull's assessment proved to be more accurate: "In the present decay of business in our profession," he wrote to Oliver Wolcott in Oct. 1789, Webster would find it hard to "keep up the style he sets out with. I fear he will breakfast upon Institutes, dine upon Dissertations, and go to bed supperless"; see Ford, *Notes*, vol. 1, 269, 295; vol. 2, 411–412. Webster was forced to borrow repeatedly from his brother-in-law James Greenleaf; see Ford, *Notes*, vol. 1, 185–188; vol. 2, 415–418, 420–422; and Warfel, *Noah Webster*, 194, 197. He felt this dependence grievously. "I have not influence enough," he wrote to Greenleaf in Oct. 1791. "[M]oney gives that influence. This circumstance gives me more mortification than any regard to property from other motives"; Webster to Greenleaf, Oct. 13, 1791, in Ford, *Notes*, vol. 2, 420–422. According to his own accounts, in July 1793, he was still in debt to the sum of $1,815 (although owed $680) and had repaid none of the loans advanced by Greenleaf; see Webster to Greenleaf, July 8, 1793, in Ford, *Notes*, vol. 2, 423–425.

42. Webster to Greenleaf, June 6, 1789, in Ford, *Notes*, vol. 2, 411–412. See also Webster to George Washington, Sept. 1790, in Ford, *Notes*, vol. 1, 288–289. His diary in 1789–1792 reveals a man who spent more time dining and entertaining than practicing law but who was deeply involved in the public affairs of his community; see Ford, *Notes*, vol. 1, 341–364; "Memoir," 150–157. For the poetry of the Hartford Wits, see Warfel, *Noah Webster*, 200; and more generally Leon Howard, *The Connecticut Wits* (Chicago: University of Chicago Press, 1943); [Noah

Webster], *Attention! or, New Thoughts on a Serious Subject: Being an Inquiry into the Excise Laws of Connecticut: Addressed to the Freemen of the State: By a Private Citizen* (Hartford, Conn.: Hudson and Goodwin, 1789); Webster, *Collection of Essays.* In this collection, Webster used the radical orthography that earned him such public ridicule. See Noah Webster (ed.), *A Journal of the Transactions and Occurrences in the Settlement of Massachusetts and the Other New-England Colonies, from the Year 1630 to 1644: Written by John Winthrop, Esq* (Hartford, Conn.: Elisha Babcock, 1790). The anonymous Prompter essays were published in the *Connecticut Courant,* Dec. 6, 1790–June 13, 1791, and subsequently republished as *The Prompter; or, A Commentary on Common Saying[s] and Objects* (Hartford, Conn.: Hudson and Goodwin, 1791). They were highly successful and showed Webster's ability to write humorous, ironic prose. In one essay, he even poked fun at a "learned wordmonger"; see Skeel (ed.), *Bibliography,* 271–290, 444–445; *AM,* Jan. 16, 1796. For the rest of his journalism in this period, see Skeel (ed.), *Bibliography,* 443–448.

43. Webster to Greenleaf, June 24, July 8, Oct. 16, 1793, in Ford, *Notes,* vol. 2, 423–430; Ford, *Notes,* vol. 1, 366, 443, 442, 364. In his "Memoir," Webster claimed that he learned about the "project of establishing a newspaper for the purpose of defending the measure of Gen. Washington, particularly his proclamation of neutrality" only after his arrival in New York. This may be true, but Webster arrived in the city on Aug. 12, dined with John Jay on Aug. 16, James Watson on Aug. 21, and Rufus King on Aug. 24, and he left on Aug. 27 having already worked out an agreement to publish the newspaper with the printer George Bunce; see Ford, *Notes,* vol. 1, 442–443; and Webster to Greenleaf, Sept. 2, 1793, in Ford, *Notes,* vol. 2, 428. Given the efficiency of these negotiations, it seems likely that Webster came to New York to meet with Federalists about the creation of a newspaper.

44. Ford, *Notes,* vol. 1, 364, 442–445, 373–377. According to Webster, there were twelve people involved in the agreement, which would have produced a total of $1,800; see "Memoir," 159. However, in a letter to James Greenleaf a short while later, Webster said that he had received $2,000 from his "patrons" of which he had already used $1,200 to cover his personal debts and the expenses of his family. And there may have been more. In the same letter, he declares his hopes to receive more money from some gentlemen in New York, although "I am not certain of it," and warns Greenleaf that the newspaper "will no more bear its own weight, the first 6 months—& very little more, the first year," and would require another $1,500 to keep it afloat; see Webster to Greenleaf, [Sept.] 2, 1793, in Ford, *Notes,* vol. 2, 430–432. The full name of the newspaper was the *American Minerva, Patroness of Peace, Commerce and the Liberal Arts,* a clear indication of its position on the question of neutrality. It was priced at $6 per annum. An abbreviated semi-weekly edition, the *Herald,* intended "for country subscribers," appeared in June 1794; see "Memoir," 159–160. The newspaper in the 1790s underwent several name changes, which chart its slow evolution from political to commercial daily. In Mar. 1794, it became the *American Minerva and the New-York (Evening) Advertiser,* which was shortened to the *American Minerva: An Evening Advertiser* in May 1795. After Webster dissolved his partnership with George Bunce in Apr. 1796, the paper became the *Minerva & Mercantile Evening Advertiser,* the name under which it continued until Sept. 1797, when it was renamed the *Commercial Advertiser.* Webster finally relinquished control of the newspaper in 1803.

45. Webster had already declared his support for Washington's Proclamation of Neutrality, joining John Trumbull and Chauncy Goodrich in drafting an "Address from the Inhabitants of Hartford to the President of the United States," which assured Washington of their support for his neutrality policy and warned against "the insidious designs of those persons, if there be any so deluded, who may wish to subject the country to foreign influence, and involve it in the horrors of war." Dated August 2, this appeared in the *Connecticut Courant* on Aug. 19, 1793; see Skeel (ed.), *Bibliography,* 522; Webster, "Diary," July and Aug. 1793, in Ford, *Notes,* vol. 1, 441–442. Newspapers, argued Webster, were "the heralds of truth" and the "common instruments of social intercourse, by which the Citizens of this vast Republic constantly discourse and debate with each other on subjects of public concern." To them was due the good sense of the

American people. But newspapers were not only vehicles of rational public discourse, they were also agents of social solidarity. "In no country on earth," he observed, "are Newspapers so generally circulated among the body of the people as in America," and it was to this "facility of spreading knowledge" that he attributed "that *civility of manners,* that *love of peace and good order,* and that *propriety of public conduct,* which characterize the substantial body of Citizens in the United States." *AM,* Dec. 9, 1793. His optimism about the press did not survive the 1790s.

46. Webster, *Grammatical Institute…Part III,* 21; *AM,* Dec. 9, 1793, Jan. 24, 1795.

47. *AM,* Dec. 11, 1793, Dec. 5, Feb. 12, 1795, Dec. 21, 1793, Apr. 20, 1795.

48. *AM,* Dec. 5, 1794, Dec. 11, 1793.

49. *AM,* Feb. 12, Apr. 20, Jan. 24, 1795, Dec. 25, 16, 1793, Jan. 24, 1795.

50. Webster, *Revolution in France,* 1297; *AM,* Dec. 26, 1793, Apr. 11, 1794, Apr. 27, 1795. Webster was quick to refute charges that he was pro-British. For his support of British radicals and reformers, see *AM,* July 17, Sept. 29, Nov. 4, 1794. For the trial of Horne Tooke, see *AM,* July 30, Sept. 10, 1794. For the trial of Thomas Muir, see *AM,* Sept. 29–30, 1794. For the campaign against habeas corpus, see *AM,* Nov. 1, 1794. For reaction to Thomas Hardy's acquittal, see *AM,* Jan. 13, 1795, and for the acquittal of Thelwall and Tooke, see *AM,* Feb. 18, 1795. For an attack from the London *Morning Chronicle* on Dundas, see *AM,* Mar. 13, 1795. Webster's distaste for Great Britain was evident from his earliest writings and, as his later feud with the British journalist William Cobbett would show, was quite genuine.

51. *AM,* Dec. 26, 1793; Webster, *Effects of Slavery, on Morals and Industry* (Hartford, Conn.: Hudson and Goodwin, 1793), 30; *AM,* Apr. 27, 1795; Webster to Washington, Apr. 20, 1794, in Warfel (ed.), *Letters,* 117–118; Noah Webster, *The Revolution in France, Considered in Respect to Its Progress and Effects: By an* AMERICAN (New York: George Bunce, 1794). Webster advertised the work in the *American Minerva* on Apr. 19, 1794, as "just published." Webster was no poet, but his fraternal feelings for the French are left in no doubt by the following verse, written for the *Gazette of the United States* in 1790:

> Fair Liberty, whose gentle sway
> First blest these shores, has cross'd the sea
> To visit Gallia, and inflame
> Her sons their ancient rights to claim.
> From realm to realm she still shall fly,
> As lightening [*sic*] shoots across the sky,
> And tyrants her just empire own,
> And at her feet submit their crown.

Warfel, *Noah Webster,* 200. Before 1793, this enthusiasm was undiminished. His praise for the revolution as the "most interesting spectacle ever exhibited in the theater of this earth" comes from an oration on slavery delivered to the Abolition Society in Hartford, Connecticut, on May 9, 1793, and published later that year. He blamed the political violence of the revolution squarely on "perfidious domestic foes" and the threat posed by the combined powers. Such calamities, he wrote, were "inseparable from such great changes and events"; see *Effects of Slavery,* 31, and his writings in the *Connecticut Courant,* both in Warfel, *Noah Webster,* 215–216. Although he criticized the execution of Marie Antoinette privately to Timothy Pickering ("Quem Deus vult perdere, prius dementat!" he wrote), his attitude in the *American Minerva* was more equivocal, and he admitted that the execution of Louis XVI may have been "expedient and necessary"; see *AM,* Jan. 9, 11, 20, 29, Nov. 15, 1794. Moreover, he blamed the combined powers for the ascendancy of the Jacobin Party and welcomed news of French victories against them; see *AM,* Dec. 26, 1793, Jan. 2, 14, 20, Feb. 6, 24, Mar. 11, 1794. His attacks on Citizen Genet and his remarks on the revolution in early 1794 distinguished carefully between the current leadership of the revolution and the revolution itself. Not all critics of Genet, he argued, were "enemies of the French Revolution," which was "glorious in its principles, and *unhappy* in its progress"; *AM,*

Dec. 26, 1793. Once the Jacobin dictatorship fell, his support for the progress as well as the principles of the revolution revived.

52. Webster, *Revolution in France*, 1239–1240.

53. Webster, *Revolution in France*, 1240, 1268–1270. Although there are interesting comparisons to be made between Webster and Burke, nothing can be more ridiculous than to equate the two. Even in his later, more conservative phase, Webster referred to "that arch fanatic Burke, the pensioned traitor to the Rights of Man"; *AM*, Nov. 1, 1796. Webster was greatly impressed by the "union and vigor" that the Jacobin government had imparted to the people of France—"The present efforts of the French nation," he stated, "astonish even reflecting men"—predicting, with accuracy, that they would eventually turn back the armies of the combined powers and launch their own "offensive" campaign; see Webster, *Revolution in France*, 1240–1247. For his optimism about the effects of the revolution on French agriculture, commerce, manufactures, arts, and science, see 1248–1251; for his admiration of the Jacobin government and his confidence in the revolutionary process, see 1240, 1244–1246, 1249, 1266, 1270–1271.

54. Webster, *Revolution in France*, 1239–1242, 1262–1269.

55. Webster, *Revolution in France*, 1270–1280. For Webster's discussion of political party and faction, see 1271–1299, and his lengthy appendix "On Faction." Webster distinguished his hostility toward faction from hostility toward political opposition, a hostility he ascribed to the Jacobins. In a remarkable passage, he argued that their intolerance was inspired by a conception of truth and a sense of their own intellectual infallibility that was idolatrous and had its source not in reason but in "the passions of the mind." Webster rejected such an absolute definition of truth and defended instead the use of reason and reflection to arrive at an "imaginary truth." "That this reason is not truth itself nor an infallible standard of truth, is obvious," he explained, "for no two men agree what it is, what its nature, extent or limits." This intellectual uncertainty formed the indispensable basis for political cooperation and cohesion. "While each man and each society is freely indulged in his own opinion, and that opinion is mere speculation," wrote Webster, "there is peace, harmony and good understanding." Social unity thus depended on the toleration of political difference while faction sought to impose uniformity; see 1255–1257, 1275. Ironically, the triumph of faction laid the groundwork for the destruction of political opposition and was inimical to a liberal vision of political tolerance. Webster's vision of political society was not so much pluralist as radically individualist, a political order in which all men struggled to restrain their passions and to transform themselves into rational, self-governing, and independent citizens. One of his chief objections to political parties was that they infringed on personal autonomy and the rights of individual conscience.

56. Webster, *Revolution in France*, 1279. Webster's view was not just the product of political paranoia and opportunism, although it contained elements of both. Political committees of the kind Webster had in mind formed the vanguard of revolution in both America and France, and the temptation of contemporary historians to see organizations like the Democratic societies of the 1790s as simply electoral organizations and therefore as proto-parties heralding the arrival of a liberal, democratic party system obscures their contemporary significance. This is not to argue that the objectives of organizations like the Democratic societies were revolutionary, only that they invoked revolutionary precedents and, indeed, the revolutionary present. Webster discusses the role of party in the American Revolution on 1284–1285, and his attitude toward the role of party in the French Revolution is surprisingly equivocal. Although he denounced the Jacobin societies, he admitted that they may have been necessary to "exterminate the remains of royalty and nobility"; see 1271–1272.

57. Webster, *Revolution in France*, 1277, 1272, 12/8, 1286, 1299. In many respects, Webster's essay was an extension of the polemic against the Democratic societies that had filled the *American Minerva* since the start of 1794. For his discussion of the Democratic societies, see 1271–1299. These societies sprang up in the wake of the Genet mission, played an important part in organizing public opposition to British attacks on American shipping, and provided

support for Madison's commercial resolutions against Great Britain. Webster first discussed them in the *American Minerva* in Dec. 1794 and began to criticize them in late Jan. 1795; see *AM*, Dec. 19, 20, 1794, Jan. 16, 24, 25, Feb. 8, 19, 24, 25, Mar. 4, 5, 1795.

58. For the efforts of Philip Freneau and other Republicans to appropriate the French Revolution, see chapter 2. Nothing shows more clearly Webster's consciousness of this rhetorical and political battle over the domestic political uses of the French Revolution than his use of the term "aristocracy" to describe the Democratic societies; see "Of Aristocracy," in Webster, *Revolution in France*, 1288–1291. His efforts to identify the societies with Jacobinism had the same objective and became more explicit as public opposition to the Jay Treaty mounted in 1795, opposition he blamed on the influence of the Democratic societies; see *AM*, Aug. 5, Sept. 2, 15, Oct. 1, 6, 19, 1795. At this point, Webster began to use the term Jacobins routinely to refer to the political opposition; see *AM*, Sept. 2, 7, 15, 16, Oct. 1, 5, 20, 21, 22, 1795. Interestingly, this coincided with his renewed support for the revolution following the execution of Robespierre and the suppression of the Jacobin clubs, a development he greeted with elation; see *AM*, Jan. 6, 9, Sept. 14, 1795, Jan. 26, 1796. The demise of Jacobinism enabled Webster to attack the political societies, and he was supported by the example of the new revolutionary government in France, which had recently proscribed political clubs; see his call for the suppression of the Democratic societies in the *Minerva*, Sept. 15, Oct. 19, 20, 21, 1795. He was even able to use Thomas Paine's attacks on the Jacobins; see *AM*, Dec. 12, 15, 1795. The irony was that Webster himself warned constantly against the use of "odious names" to disguise political reality and mislead the public; see *AM*, Oct. 20, 1795.

59. "Republicanism is founded in self-interest," wrote Webster; *AM*, May 15, 1795. For a good discussion of this issue, see *AM*, May 13–15, 1795.

60. Webster, *Revolution in France*, 1251–1252, 1239. Webster was especially scornful about the cult of Reason; see 1251–1264. For American attitudes toward the religious policies of the French Revolution, see Nash, "American Clergy and the French Revolution," 392–412; and Bloch, *Visionary Republic*. For the campaign of de-Christianization in France, see A. Aulard, *Christianity and the French Revolution* (London: E. Benn, 1927). This defense of Christianity was a departure for Webster and probably indicated a shift away from his earlier deism. But it was not without ambiguity. His hostility toward Jacobin religious policy was still predicated on his belief in "rational religion," and what disturbed him most about the Jacobins was their revival of a spirit of religious zealotry (Catholic in its origins) with its attendant evils of superstition, idolatry, and fanaticism. Webster's arguments retained a deist tone, and in a short statement of his intellectual credo, he expressed belief in a "Supreme Intelligence" but said nothing about Jesus Christ. In general, his attitude toward religion was dictated by utilitarian rather than spiritual or even ethical considerations. The purpose of religion (together with law and education) was to "restrain and direct the passions to the purposes of social happiness." Its function was not to create good men but to prevent the creation of bad ones. "Religion," he stated blandly, "has an excellent effect in repressing vices, in softening the manners of men, and consoling them under the pressure of calamities"; Webster, *Revolution in France*, 1267–1268. "The business of ministers of religion," he later wrote, "is to make their hearers *wiser* and *better* by teaching them *practical truths* and *duty*. Conjectures have nothing to do with morality and religion"; *AM*, May 20, 1796. Perhaps Webster was not so far from the Old Light religion of his childhood after all.

61. Webster, *Revolution in France*, 1261–1267. Webster, however, believed that the people of France would eventually "embrace a rational religion"; see 1266, 1270. Ironically, his concern about the moral vacuum created by the disestablishment of the French church was shared by Robespierre, whose cult of Reason was designed to fill this spiritual vacuum with a new civil religion, and by Thomas Paine, who set out to remoralize the French with his *Age of Reason* at about the same time.

62. *AM*, Oct. 30–31, 1794. The excesses of the French Revolution, argued Webster, were at least partly the result of a neglect of age and experience in the political leadership. "An old respected citizen has a thousand opportunities of correcting the opinions, settling the quarrels,

and restraining the passions of his neighbors," and where such influence does not exist, "society is distracted with quarrels and parties, which produce an uncommon depravity of morals"; Webster, *Revolution in France*, 1290. For a revealing tirade against the "young men of America," see *AM*, Mar. 27, 1795.

63. "Constantius," *AM*, Apr. 20, 1795; Webster to Oliver Wolcott, Jr., July 30, 1795, in Warfel (ed.), *Letters*. Webster also began to idealize the patriarchal order of his native Connecticut, "the most free, as well as the most happy state in America"; *AM*, Oct. 31, 1794. Webster first referred to the importance of patriarchal government in the context of a discussion of George Washington, whose "personal influence," he argued, had restrained "the violence of parties" and held the union together. "Americans," he wrote, "rally round the man and it is a problem to be solved, after his leaving the office, what energy, or force really exists in the executive authority itself"; Webster, *Revolution in France*, 1290. Webster also began to emphasize the importance of personal executive authority, attacking the French Republic as a "hydra of many heads" and Republican proposals for a plural executive; see *AM*, Nov. 3, 15, 1794, May 20, Sept. 14, 1795, Sept. 1, 1796; Webster, *Revolution in France*, 1267. Only when Republican journalists led by Benjamin Franklin Bache launched a ferocious campaign against the personal prestige and political legitimacy of Washington did Webster's campaign of support for the Jay Treaty reveal a sense of genuine urgency and outrage. For the Republican campaign against Washington in 1795–1796, see chapter 3; for Webster's response, see *AM*, Dec. 9, 1794, Sept. 2, 15, Oct. 6, 10, 28, 29, 30, Nov. 21, 23, 27, Dec. 8, 1795, Jan. 1, 9, 1796.

64. Webster blamed the rise of personal politics on political factions, which he believed had an irresistible tendency to displace rational discourse with acrimonious personal abuse; see Webster, *Revolution in France*, 1273; *AM*, Dec. 11, 12, 1793, Apr. 28, Dec. 5, 1794. See also Constantius, who argued that parties inevitably "degenerate from the REAL to the PERSONAL" and that "when parties become wholly personal: then indeed is liberty far in her decline," in *AM*, Apr. 20, 1795. Webster viewed the Democratic societies, which he believed had orchestrated the vicious personal attacks on Washington, as agents of political intolerance and personal calumny. I hope that the irony of Webster's transformation is evident. The increasing personalization of politics led Webster to place more emphasis on the importance of character and personality than he had before. This development illustrates the symbiotic relationship between Republican and Federalist political rhetoric in the 1790s. The personalization of American politics proceeded as a process that involved and implicated all political actors, not as a simple clash between radicals who supported measures, not men, and traditionalists who favored men rather than measures. While Republicans expressed their belief in measures rather than men and accused Federalists of the opposite, they developed a politics of exposure that was highly personal. Federalists, on the other hand, accused Republicans of slavishly following men like Robespierre and Jefferson, trumpeted their allegiance to the impersonal rule of law, but were also drawn inexorably into the politics of private character.

65. *AM*, Jan. 9, Oct. 21, 1795. When Pierre Adet, the French minister to the United States, presented a tricolor flag to Congress in token of the renewed friendship between the United States and France in Jan. 1796, Webster welcomed the gesture warmly, assuring readers that "the effusions of federal Republicans" were once more evident in support of the French cause; see *AM*, Jan. 8, 9, 1796. Webster's renewed enthusiasm for the French Republic was shared by many Federalists after the fall of Robespierre; see, for example, the toast offered to "The Republic of France" at a dinner held for Alexander Hamilton by a group of Philadelphia merchants in Feb. 1795; *AM*, Feb. 23, 1795. For similar sentiments at other Federalist gatherings, see *AM*, Jan. 9, May 29, June 23, July 1, 10, 1795, Jan. 7, 1796.

66. *AM*, Feb. 4, 24, 1796. When debate on the Jay Treaty began in earnest in July 1795, Webster sprang at once to its defense but privately expressed disappointment in the treaty and even admitted in public that it was "less favorable than many people expected"; see Webster to Oliver Wolcott, Jr., July 30, 1795, in Warfel (ed.), *Letters*; *AM*, July 10, 1795. From early on,

however, Webster believed that the public would rally behind the president; see *AM*, July 30, 31, Sept. 3, 15, 17, 1795.

67. *AM*, July 4, 1796, Feb. 13, Mar. 8, 10, 1797.

68. *PG*, Mar. 8, 1797; *AM*, Jan. 28, 1797; *PG*, Mar. 3, 1797; *AM*, Mar. 21, 1797; Webster to Rufus King, May 30, 1797, in Warfel (ed.), *Letters*, 149–150. Cobbett's proposals were published in the *Minerva* on Feb. 9, 1797, and his newspaper appeared on Mar. 1, 1797, a week before this first contretemps with Webster. For Webster's response, see *AM*, Mar. 11, 1797. Webster had attacked Cobbett's first (anonymous) pamphlet, *Observations on the Emigration of Dr. Joseph Priestley* (Philadelphia: Thomas Bradford, 1794), as an effort to "prejudice the minds of Americans against the French Republic" but since then had treated Peter Porcupine favorably; see *AM*, June 18, Aug. 2, Sept. 7, 1795, Jan. 8, 15, Feb. 29, Apr. 16, 29, May 3, 27, June 8, Aug. 16, 19, 1796. Webster, however, was sensitive to any suggestion that Cobbett played a critical role in the Federalist Party, and when Bache stated in late 1796 that Cobbett was the "head of the federal faction," Webster dismissed the idea with a tirade against foreign "upstarts"; see *AM*, Sept. 16, 1796. He may also have felt that Cobbett was trying to poach his readers by advertising in New York and launching a country edition to rival the *Herald*. In a revealing letter to Webster on Feb. 6, 1797, Cobbett expressed respect for Webster and urged a united front: "It is not only necessary that the friends of order be attached to each other, they must let the world see that they are so"; Ford, *Notes*, vol. 1, 417–418.

69. This was despite Webster's complete disillusionment with the revolution in France. For his support of John Adams, see *AM*, May 19, 23, June 10, 23, Sept. 8, 1797.

70. For Webster's attacks on French policy, see *AM*, Jan. 21, 22, 23, Feb. 3, Nov. 11, 16, Dec. 8, 1796, Jan. 9, Feb. 23, Mar. 1, 6, Apr. 6, 7, May 8, 10, 1797. For a series of essays on French political machinations in the United States, see *AM*, Dec. 14, 1796–Mar. 1, 1797. But even after France began to seize American merchant ships in early 1796, Webster's disillusionment with the revolution was not complete. In a letter to the Comte de Volney in July 1796, he wrote: "I congratulate you, Sir, on the late important revolution in France; an event that will result in immense advantages to the French people; & which seems to be but a prelude to a general regeneration in Europe....The *mad work* which factions make with free governments, both in Europe and America, much of which has fallen under my own observation, has somewhat abated the ardor of my enthusiasm. But I cannot withdraw my confidence from a republican form of gov't" (Webster to Volney, July 10, 1796, in Webster Papers, NYPL). Webster, who had consistently defended the right of the French people to self-determination (a principle he regarded as the foundation of a republican international order), was appalled to see the French trampling this right underfoot. Bonaparte, he observed savagely, was no more than an "audacious conqueror, who is disgracing the name of a republican," and France was now a "mere military nation" whose imperial ambitions would "render republicanism odious, and retard its progress in the world." See *AM*, Sept. 10, 23, Oct. 13, 24, 1796. He continued, however, to denounce the monarchical coalition against France and to declare his support for republican revolution and an end to "the monstrous fabrick of king-craft and priest-craft in Europe and Asia"; see *AM*, Nov. 1, Oct. 7, 1796, Mar. 1, 1797. He also foresaw the final act. "Weary with discord and insecurity," he predicted, the French people would rally to the most popular military commander, "some Buonaparte or Pichegru," and "seek repose under a THRONE"; *AM*, Sept. 22, 1797. Remarkably, the coup d'état of 18 Fructidor (Sept. 4) that cleared the way for Napoleon's rise to power occurred just before Webster made this statement and could not yet have been known in the United States.

71. *AM*, Sept. 10–Nov. 8, June 13, Sept. 21, 1796. Webster indicted France as a "nation without morals" and believed that the adoption of a policy of military conquest and imperial expansion was the natural result of the fanaticism and intolerance that had characterized French politics since 1792.

72. Webster, *An Oration: Pronounced before the Citizens of New Haven, on the Anniversary of American Independence, July 1802* (New Haven, Conn.: William W. Morse, 1802); *AM*, Sept. 27,

1796. For Webster's repudiation of the French Revolution, see the series of articles "To the People of the United States" in *AM*, Dec. 14, 1796–Mar. 1, 1797, which argued that the French had harbored plans for an invasion of the United States since 1793. See also Webster to Pickering, Nov. 24, Dec. 8, 1796; "To the Public," Mar. 4, 1797; Webster to Barlow, Nov. 16, 1798, all in Warfel (ed.), *Letters*. Republican theorists, argued Webster, had ignored the "nature of man" and taken no account of the need to preserve self-restraint and self-government; see *AM*, Sept. 1, 1796, Aug. 14, 1797.

73. Webster to Jedediah Morse, May 15, 1797, in Warfel (ed.), *Letters*; *AM*, Aug. 26, Sept. 5, 9, 26, 1797; Webster to Pickering, July 7, 1797, in Ford, *Notes*, vol. 1, 422; *AM*, July 12, 1797. Webster observed wearily in Sept. 1797 that there were now three parties in the United States, "one blindly devoted to Great Britain—another to France" and a third "consisting of principled Americans"; *AM*, Sept. 9, 1797. The "perpetual stream of slander which issues from the presses in the interest of the French and the English," he wrote, threatened to "corrupt and debase the moral character of our citizens." "Their daring and wanton attacks on private characters" destroyed public respect for the political order but, perhaps even more important, abuse and calumny destroyed respect "for private character and virtue" and rent the social fabric by undermining "men's natural respect for each other"; *AM*, Aug. 26; see also *AM*, Sept. 5, 7, 21, 1797.

74. See Webster to Rufus King, May 30, 1797; Webster to Timothy Pickering, July 7, 1797, and Apr. 13, 1798, all in Ford, *Notes*, vol. 1, 420–422, 434; Webster to William Cranch, June 26, 1797, in Cranch Papers, MHS. One sign of Webster's disillusionment with his role as a political editor was his decision to change the name of the *Minerva* to the *Commercial Advertiser* in Oct. 1797. He abandoned the newspaper just as it reached the zenith of its commercial success. In Jan. 1797, Webster claimed a circulation of 1,700 and reckoned the paper made $5,000 a year in clear profit. He had also been granted a contract for federal printing, presumably after the ejection of John Beckley as clerk of the House of Representatives in 1797; see *AM*, Jan. 30, 1797; Webster to Cranch, June 26, 1797, in Cranch Papers, MHS. His chief interest after late 1797 was in the history of epidemic diseases; see letters to Dr. William Currie in *AM*, Oct. 26–Dec. 20, 1797; Benjamin Rush to Webster, Nov. 27, 1797; Webster to Jeremy Belknap, Jan. 4, 1798, all in Ford, *Notes*, vol. 1, 456–457, 461; Webster to Benjamin Rush, Dec. 2, 1797; "Proposal for the Publication by Subscription of an Inquiry into the Origin of Epidemic Diseases," Mar. 17, 1797, both in Warfel (ed.), *Letters*. Webster began to collect materials for this study in late 1797; see "Memoir," 163–164; and "Diary," Apr. 10, 1798, in Ford, *Notes*, vol. 1, 485. On Webster's removal to New Haven, see "Memoir," 164–165; "Diary," Apr. 1, 1798, in Ford, *Notes*, vol. 1, 450–451, 485; Webster to Elijah Waddington, July 6, 1798, in Warfel (ed.), *Letters*.

75. Webster to Timothy Pickering, July 17, 1798, in Warfel (ed.), *Letters*; Webster, *An Oration: Pronounced before the Citizens of New Haven* (New Haven, Conn.: T. & S. Green, 1798).

76. On the issue of yellow fever, Webster was an environmentalist like his friend Benjamin Rush, whose side he took in the acrimonious public controversy between Rush and Cobbett; see Webster to Rush, Dec. 2, 1797, in Warfel (ed.), *Letters*. For the publication of his study, see Webster to Rush, Feb. 15, 27, Nov. 26, 1799, Feb. 18, 1800, in Warfel (ed.), *Letters*. Webster reckoned he lost $700–800 on the American edition; see Webster to Rush, Sept. 11, 1801, in Warfel (ed.), *Letters*. The *Commercial Advertiser*, now under the editorial control of Webster's nephew Ebeneezer Belden, gave dutiful but uninspired support to President John Adams. Webster contributed to the newspaper sporadically and published two biting pamphlets attacking Joseph Priestley and the Connecticut Republican Abraham Bishop; see Noah Webster, *Ten Letters to Dr. Joseph Priestley* (New Haven, Conn.: Read & Morse, 1800); [Noah Webster], *A Rod for a Fool's Back* (New Haven, Conn.: n.p., 1800). Both of Webster's pamphlets were narrow and parochial in outlook, and neither engaged effectively with the broader political debate.

77. While it may be true that Webster remained a republican (see Snyder, *Defining Noah Webster*, n. 182), he did not remain a democrat, even by his own lights. This repudiation of democratic ideology and rhetoric, which had been fiercely contested in the recent past, must be judged one of the most striking political follies of Federalism at the end of the 1790s, confirming

Republican charges at just the moment they had become most damaging; see Webster, *Ten Letters*; [Webster], *A Rod for a Fool's Back*; Webster to Benjamin Rush, Dec. 15, 1800; Webster to Wolcott, Sept. 17, 1800, both in Warfel (ed.), *Letters*; Webster, *Miscellaneous Papers on Political and Commercial Subjects* (New York: E. Belden, 1802).

78. Webster to Benjamin Rush, Dec. 15, 1800, in Warfel (ed.), *Letters*. "The characters of public officers," argued Webster, "are of more importance than those of private citizens, because they represent the laws. A portion of the respect which men have for the laws, is inseparably attached to the personal character of the man; and a degradation of the man is always followed, in a greater or lesser degree, with contempt for the laws" (Webster, *Ten Letters*, letter VI). For Webster's legal position on the Alien and Sedition Acts, see letter V; and for further comment, see Webster to Charles Holt, June 3, 1799; Webster to Oliver Wolcott, June 23, 1800, both in Warfel (ed.), *Letters*.

79. Webster, *An Oration...July 1802*. This speech was delivered as the Connecticut Assembly was considering a measure to extend the political franchise, a measure Webster firmly opposed. For Webster's growing emphasis on the virtues of capitalist accumulation, see the letter to his old friend Joel Barlow in 1798 in which he accused Republicans of encouraging the "unlettered mass of citizens...to undertake the work of plundering the more wealthy citizens of their property and their influence"; Webster to Barlow, Nov. 16, 1798, in Warfel (ed.), *Letters*. In his *Ten Letters*, Webster praised commerce as the "parent of civilization and humanity, as well as wealth." Although he had always supported commerce as a civilizing influence and ridiculed republican concern about luxury, this praise of wealth was new and eroded Webster's commitment to representative democracy. In a speech to the Connecticut Assembly in Nov. 1802, he argued that extending the vote "prostrates the wealth of individuals to the rapaciousness of a malicious gang who have nothing to lose, and will delight in plundering their neighbors"; *American Mercury*, Dec. 2, 1802, cited in Warfel, *Noah Webster*, 280–281. The political context for all of this was crucial. Webster not only wanted to stop the poor from plundering the rich, but Republicans from overturning the Federalists. On Sept. 17, 1800, he wrote to Oliver Wolcott, Jr., stating that "the principles of corruption are spreading fast in Connecticut, and the *last stronghold of republicanism* is so violently assaulted that its fate is uncertain"; Warfel (ed.), *Letters*.

80. Webster seems to have believed (encouraged no doubt by the sentiments of Jefferson's inaugural address) that Jefferson's election might be a harbinger of party reconciliation. He firmly opposed Federalist schemes to throw the election to Burr and chastised the Federalist press for its vilification of the president. "It is the duty of good citizens to acquiesce in the election and be tranquil. It is proper that Mr. Jefferson be made Chief Magistrate....Let us have the experiment"; Warfel, *Noah Webster*, 269–270. See also Webster to Madison, July 18, 1801, and Webster to Wolcott, Oct. 1, 1801, both in Warfel (ed.), *Letters*; [Webster], *A Letter to General Hamilton Occasioned by His Letter to President Adams: By a Federalist* [1800]. This was, of course, a response to Hamilton's *Letter Concerning the Public Conduct and Character of John Adams* (New York: John Lang, 1800). In his reply, Webster identified Hamilton as the head of a pro-British faction (inspired by the British agent William Cobbett) that had tried to secure an alliance with Great Britain. Although Webster did not believe that Hamilton himself had sought such an alliance, he held him responsible for efforts to raise a standing army designed to overawe the domestic political opposition. Raising briefly the issue of the Reynolds affair, he called Hamilton's *Letter* the "most indiscrete of all your indiscrete conduct," predicting, quite correctly, that it would be judged "little short of insanity."

81. Webster to Rush, Sept. 11, 1801, in Warfel (ed.), *Letters*; Webster, *Miscellaneous Papers*, 11. Webster was particularly infuriated by the appointment of Samuel Bishop to the post of collector of the port of New Haven. Bishop replaced Elizur Goodrich, a former Federalist member of Congress, but he was largely a proxy for his son, Abraham Bishop, with whom Webster had already crossed swords. According to Webster, both *père et fils* were unfit and unqualified for the post. Webster wrote to Madison, asking him to raise the matter with the president but received no reply; see "Remonstrance of the New Haven Merchants" (1801) and

Jefferson's reply. Webster's *Letter to the President* appeared in the *Minerva* from Sept. 30 to Nov. 7, 1801, and was republished as a pamphlet in 1802; see Webster to Rufus King, June 12, 1801; Webster to Madison, July 18, 1801, both in Warfel (ed.), *Letters*; Jefferson to Madison, Aug. 12, 1801 in Paul Leicester Ford (ed.), *The Works of Thomas Jefferson* (New York: G. P. Putnam's Sons, 1904–1905), vol. 9; Webster, *Miscellaneous Papers*, 17–23; Ford, *Notes*, vol. 1, 515–529; Warfel, *Noah Webster*, 273–274; Henry Adams, *History of the United States during the Administration of Jefferson and Madison* (New York: Scribner's, 1896–1904), vol. 1, 226.

82. Webster, *Miscellaneous Papers*, cited in Warfel, *Noah Webster*, 273–274; Webster, *Miscellaneous Papers*, 11–12.

83. See Webster to Rush, Sept. 11, 1801, in Warfel (ed.), *Letters*; Samuel Bayard to Webster, Sept. 21 and Oct. 13, 1801, both in Ford, *Notes*, vol. 1, 498–500, 507; Webster to Wolcott, Oct. 1 and Oct. 13, 1801, both in Ford, *Notes*, vol. 1, 481–482, 522–523; James Kent to Webster, May 14, 1802, in Ford, *Notes*, vol. 1, 508; Webster to Stephen Twining, Jan. 22, 1802; Webster to Samuel Bayard, Mar. 2, 1802, both in Warfel (ed.), *Letters*. Coleman definitely had it in for Webster, whom he called "that pedant and something infinitely worse.... I can never forgive this man for his infamous & unprincipled attack on the great & good Hamilton"; Coleman to Harry Croswell, Jan. 20, 1803, in Ford, *Notes*, vol. 1, n. 503. By 1803, Webster's income from the *Minerva* had fallen off sharply and he was forced to sell; see Webster to Wolcott, Apr. 13, 1803, in Ford, *Notes*, vol. 1, 530, 508. Webster was also ridiculed mercilessly by other Federalist writers, notably William Dutton of the *New England Palladium* and Joseph Dennie, editor of the *Gazette of the United States* and the *Port Folio*. These men were ardent Anglophiles who resented both Webster's politics and his literary pretensions. They found the idea of an American dictionary of the English language especially amusing; see Webster to New England Palladium, Nov. 10, 1801; Webster to Samuel Bayard, Mar. 2, 1802, both in Warfel (ed.), *Letters*; Warfel, *Noah Webster*, 290–298.

84. Noah Webster, Sr., to Noah Webster, Jr., Dec. 16, 1782, in Ford, *Notes*, vol. 1, 56. "Let reason go before every enterprise," wrote Webster in the introduction to the *Grammatical Institute...Part III*, 1. In a letter to his brother-in-law Nathaniel Appleton, he wrote that he was "happy that my opinions of certain supposed Doctrines of the Christian Religion accord so well with yours. When Revelation was made manifest, our benevolent Parent never designed that we should extinguish Reason, that noblest gift of heaven to Man"; Ford, *Notes*, vol. 1, 190–191. Webster later recalled that, at this time, he had lost the religious "impressions" of his youth; Webster to Thomas Dawes, Dec. 20, 1808, in Warfel (ed.), *Letters*. Ford describes him as an "independent thinker and investigator of religious creeds" and states baldly, "of religious conviction he had none"; Ford, *Notes*, vol. 2, 34. He was probably a deist.

85. Webster, *An Oration...July 1802*. Webster thought that the state should take responsibility for the maintenance of religious institutions, but he was careful to make clear that everyone had "the right of adopting his own particular tenets and of attaching himself to any external rites, ceremonies, modes of worship, which he shall conscientiously feel." This shift in his position was probably in response to Baptist and Methodist challenges to the Congregational church in Connecticut; see Warfel, *Noah Webster*, 282.

86. Webster to Thomas Dawes, Dec. 20, 1808, in Warfel (ed.), *Letters*.

87. Webster to Dawes, Dec. 20, 1808. There is another account of Webster's conversion in his "Memoir," but it is simply a slightly sensationalized and later rewriting of the Dawes letter; see Ford, *Notes*, vol. 2, 35–49.

88. Webster to Dawes, Dec. 20, 1808; Snyder, *Defining Noah Webster*, 225. Snyder's work contains by far the best and most sensitive account of Webster's religious views and conversion; Webster, *Value of the Bible* (1834), cited in Snyder, *Defining Noah Webster*, 260; Webster, *A Collection of Papers on Political, Literary and Moral Subjects* (New York: Webster and Clark, 1843), 337; Webster, "Speech to the Connecticut Historical Society" (1840), cited in Snyder, *Defining Noah Webster*, 258.

89. Webster to Dawes, Dec. 20, 1808.

Chapter 5

1. *PG*, Mar. 4, 1797. For the role of British journalists in the formation and development of Jeffersonian ideology, see Durey, "Thomas Paine's Apostles"; Durey, "Transatlantic Patriotism: Political Exiles and America in the Age of Revolutions," in Clive Emsley and James Walvin (eds.), *Artisans, Peasants and Proletarians, 1760–1860: Essays Presented to Gwyn A. Williams* (London: Croom Helm, 1985). See also Richard Twomey, "Jacobins and Jeffersonians: Anglo-American Radical Ideology, 1790–1810," in Margaret Jacob and James Jacob (eds.), *The Origins of Anglo American Radicalism* (London: Allen & Unwin, 1984); Edward C. Carter, "A Wild Irishman under Every Federalist's Bed," *Pennsylvania Magazine of History and Biography* 94 (1970): 331–346. For an interesting discussion of the French refugee community in this period, see Francis Childs, *French Refugee Life in the United States, 1790–1800* (Baltimore, Md.: Johns Hopkins University Press, 1940); and K. Roberts and A. M. Roberts (eds.), *Moreau de St. Mery's American Journey [1793–1798]* (Garden City, N.Y.: Doubleday, 1947).

2. *Herald of Vermont*, June 25, 1792. For an important discussion of authorial impersonality, which treats this as the defining characteristic of republican print culture in eighteenth-century America, see Warner, *Letters of the Republic*.

3. *PG*, Mar. 4, 1797. Cobbett articulated more explicitly and boldly the same ideological motives that inspired many other partisan journalists of the period, and by the late 1790s, the rhetoric of editorial impartiality was wearing thin; see Donald H. Stewart, *Opposition Press of the Federalist Period* (Albany: State University of New York Press, 1969), 28–30.

4. [Cobbett], *Observations on the Emigration of Dr. Joseph Priestley*, preface; Ray Boston, "The Impact of 'Foreign Liars' on the American Press (1790–1800)," *Journalism Quarterly* 50 (Winter 1973): 725–726.

5. Despite its unreliability, the best source for Cobbett's life is still his own autobiography, [William Cobbett], *The Life and Adventures of Peter Porcupine, with a Full and Fair Account of All His Authoring Transactions; Being a Sure and Infallible Guide for All Enterprising Young Men Who Wish to Make a Fortune by Writing Pamphlets* (Philadelphia: William Cobbett, 1796). Cobbett revised this account throughout his long political and literary career in *Cobbett's Weekly Political Register*; see esp. Oct. 5, 1805, June 17, 1809, June 23, 1832, and Dec. 28, 1833. His autobiographical writings are conveniently collected and edited in William Reitzel (ed.), *The Progress of a Plough-Boy to a Seat in Parliament* (London: Faber and Faber, 1933). The best biographies of Cobbett are G. D. H. Cole, *The Life of William Cobbett* (New York: Harcourt, 1924); Daniel Green, *Great Cobbett: The Noblest Agitator* (Oxford: Oxford University Press, 1985); and George Spater, *William Cobbett: The Poor Man's Friend* (Cambridge: Cambridge University Press, 1982), 2 vols. But see also Raymond Williams, *Cobbett* (New York: Oxford University Press, 1983); and Ian Dyck, *William Cobbett and Rural Popular Culture* (Cambridge: Cambridge University Press, 1992). On Cobbett's American career, see David A. Wilson, *Paine and Cobbett: The Transatlantic Connection* (Montreal: McGill-Queen's University Press, 1988); the lengthy introduction to Wilson (ed.), *Peter Porcupine in America: Pamphlets on Republicanism and Revolution* (Ithaca, N.Y.: Cornell University Press, 1994), 1–49; William Reitzel, "William Cobbett and Philadelphia Journalism, 1794–1800," in Edwin H. Ford and Edwin Emery (eds.), *Highlights in the History of the American Press* (Minneapolis: University of Minnesota Press, 1954); Pierce W. Gaines, *William Cobbett and the United States, 1792–1835: A Bibliography with Notes and Extracts* (Worcester, Mass.: American Antiquarian Society, 1971); Mary Elizabeth Clark, *Peter Porcupine in America: The Career of William Cobbett, 1792–1800* (Philadelphia, n.p., 1939); C. Rexford Davis, "William Cobbett: Philadelphia Bookseller and Publisher," *Journal of the Rutgers University Library* 16 (Dec. 1952); Karen K. List, "The Role of William Cobbett in Philadelphia's Party Press" (Ph.D. diss., University of Wisconsin, 1980); Ruth N. Dowling, "William Cobbett: His Trials and Tribulations as an Alien Journalist, 1794–1800" (Ph.D. diss., Southern Illinois University, 1973).

6. Reitzel (ed.), *Progress of a Plough-Boy*, 3–23. For a wonderful description of the habits that made Cobbett a first-rate soldier, see 28–30. One of the books that Cobbett read during his first year in the army was Robert Lowth's *A Short Introduction to English Grammar*, first published in 1762, which he copied and committed to heart. He had read Jonathan Swift's *Tale of a Tub* as a young boy; see Spater, *William Cobbett*, vol. 1, 18–21; Wilson, *Paine and Cobbett*, 101–103.

7. Reitzel (ed.), *Progress of a Plough-Boy*, 24, 5, 28. David Wilson argues convincingly that Cobbett supported the popular side against both the local elites and British officers in the bitterly divided Loyalist community of St. John's during the late 1780s and that his experiences there "predisposed him towards some form of political radicalism before he returned to England in Nov. 1791"; see Wilson, *Paine and Cobbett*, 104–105. For Cobbett's drafting of the report of the Loyalist Claims Commission, see Reitzel (ed.), *Progress of a Plough-Boy*, 32–35; and Wilson, *Paine and Cobbett*, 102. The long and rather wistful passage of his autobiography that describes his love affair with the daughter of an American Loyalist family has been overlooked by almost all of Cobbett's biographers; see Reitzel (ed.), *Progress of a Plough-Boy*, 39–44; and Green, *Great Cobbett*, 73–78.

8. *The Soldier's Friend; or, Considerations on the Late Pretended Augmentation of the Subsistence of Private Soldiers* (London: n.p., 1792). This pamphlet was published after his departure from England in March 1792. Although there is no direct proof of Cobbett's authorship, all of his biographers attribute the work to him. Michael Durey, however, argues that he was not the sole author of the pamphlet, which contained ideas too radical to be ascribed to Cobbett alone. Durey's skepticism is worth bearing in mind, and it's possible that Cobbett's case was exploited by more radical political figures, but his case against Cobbett's authorship is not entirely convincing. Although Cobbett was understandably circumspect about his role in the production of the pamphlet, he also stated that he "most heartily approved of every word of it"; see Michael Durey, "William Cobbett, Military Corruption and London Radicalism in the Early 1790s," *Proceedings of the American Philosophical Society* 131, no. 4 (Dec. 1987): 348–366. For accounts that place more emphasis on Cobbett's radicalism, see Spater, *William Cobbett*, vol. 1, 30–36; Wilson, *Paine and Cobbett*, 105–110. For Cobbett's own account of this episode, see Reitzel (ed.), *Progress of a Plough-Boy*, 48–56.

9. William Cobbett, *The Life of William Cobbett, Author of the Political Register* (London: n.p., 1816), 9. Cobbett had begun to learn French while in the army and planned to spend a year in France partly to "perfect myself in the language." He loved France, where he was "met everywhere with civility, and even hospitality, in a degree that I had never been accustomed to"; Reitzel (ed.), *Progress of a Plough-Boy*, 57–60. As David Wilson points out, Cobbett's positive view of the United States was shaped not only by the French writer Abbé Raynal's *History of the Two Indies* but also by Thomas Paine's *Rights of Man*, part 2; see Wilson, *Paine and Cobbett*, 110.

10. Reitzel (ed.), *Progress of a Plough-Boy*, 58–60; *PG*, Aug. 12, 1799. Cobbett's letter of introduction was from the American minister to the Hague, William Short, and was supplied to him at the request of a "gentleman in the family of the English Ambassador here, and acquainted with Mr. Cobbett"; see William Cobbett to Thomas Jefferson, Nov. 2, 1792; Jefferson to William Cobbett, Nov. 5, 1792, both in John Catanzareti (ed.), *The Papers of Thomas Jefferson* (Princeton, N.J.: Princeton University Press, 1990), vol. 24, 554–555, 580–581. For speculation about how Cobbett procured such a letter of introduction, see Spater, *William Cobbett*, 41–42.

11. Reitzel (ed.), *Progress of a Plough-Boy*, 57; William Cobbett, *Le Tuteur Anglais; ou, Grammaire Reguliere de la Langue Anglaise en Deux Parties* (Philadelphia: Thomas Bradford, 1795). According to Samuel Bradford, Cobbett received a "considerable sum of money" for this work; see [Samuel F. Bradford], *The Imposter Detected; or, A Review of Some of the Writings of "Peter Porcupine"* (Philadelphia: Thomas Bradford, 1796); Cobbett to Rachel Smithers, July 6, 1794, in Cobbett Papers, HSP.

12. William Cobbett to James Mathieu, July 19, 1793, in Cobbett Papers, HSP.

13. [Cobbett], *Observations on the Emigration of Dr. Joseph Priestley*. The work was advertised in Dunlap and Claypoole's *ADA*, July 25, 1794. Cobbett wanted to call the pamphlet "The Tartuffe Detected; or Observations, &c." but Bradford discouraged him from doing so as he feared it would "endanger his windows." Cobbett, *The Life of William Cobbett* (London: n.p., 1816), 11; *Cobbett's Weekly Political Register*, Sept. 29, 1804, 450–451. For the public response to Priestley's arrival, see "Address of the Democratic Society of New York" and the addresses (with Priestley's replies) from the Tammany Society, the Associated Teachers of the City of New York, the Medical Society, the Republican Natives of Great Britain and Ireland, and the American Philosophical Society, all in Philadelphia *GA*, June 10, 13–23, 1794.

14. *Cobbett's Weekly Political Register*, Sept. 29, 1804, 454–455; Reitzel (ed.), *Progress of a Plough-Boy*, 73–74; Roberts and Roberts (eds.), *Moreau de St. Mery's American Journey*, 211. Cobbett's image received a great deal of reinforcement from his Republican enemies, who were only too eager to portray him as a loyal son of Britain. For an interesting analysis of how Cobbett's patriotic persona served his political purposes in the early 1800s, see Leonora Nattrass, *William Cobbett: The Politics of Style* (Cambridge: Cambridge University Press, 1995), 89–96. The insistence on calling Cobbett a "Tory" rather than a "Federalist" is odd but ubiquitous, and its function is to marginalize, and avoid the need to explore or explain, his contribution to American politics in the 1790s; see, for example, David Wilson, who describes him as a "born-again English Tory rather than as an American Federalist," and Michael Durey, who argues that "Cobbett was never a Federalist, nor their propagandist; he remained an English ultra-tory patriot who happened to be fighting his battles against his country's enemies on the wrong side of the Atlantic"; Wilson, *Paine and Cobbett*, 121; Michael Durey, *Transatlantic Radicals and the Early American Republic* (Lawrence: University of Kansas Press, 1997), 242. But dismissing Cobbett as an English Tory creates some real problems. Most important, it assumes an absurdly restrictive and unhelpful definition of Federalism. Should we also exclude other English-born Anglophiles? Or Americans who favored Great Britain over republican France? Or native-born crypto-monarchists like Joseph Dennie? Or perhaps all those who expressed reservations about republican government? Jefferson and other Republicans believed that such men dominated the Federalist Party in the 1790s, and such a narrow definition of Federalism would also exclude the West Indies native, instinctive Anglophile, republican skeptic, and Federalist par excellence Alexander Hamilton.

15. [Cobbett], *Life and Adventures of Peter Porcupine*, 12–13.

16. *Cobbett's Weekly Political Register*, Sept. 29, 1804, 456. For Cobbett's self-presentation as a yeoman farmer, his identification with the land, and his appeal to small producers, see Dyck, *William Cobbett*, 1–14, 45–75; E. P. Thompson, *Making of the English Working Class* (New York: Pantheon, 1964), 758–759.

17. *Cobbett's Weekly Political Register*, Oct. 12, 1805. One way to explain Cobbett's radical apostasy is to emphasize the conservatism of his politics prior to his arrival in America; see Durey, "William Cobbett, Military Corruption and London Radicalism." As we have seen, Durey argues that *The Soldier's Friend* was too radical to be the product of Cobbett's pen, although he also points out (somewhat contradictorily) that its ideas were classical republican rather than Paineite and not necessarily hostile to a reformed constitutional monarchy. But in England in the early 1790s, the boundary between reform and revolution was extremely fluid, both the friends and enemies of parliamentary reform frequently characterized its supporters as "republicans," and enthusiasm for Paine's anti-monarchical ideas was not confined to self-conscious revolutionaries. It is interesting to note, however, that Cobbett's departure from revolutionary France, where he had been extremely happy, coincided with the overthrow of the constitutional monarchy and the imprisonment of Louis XVI. David Wilson's emphasis on Cobbett's disillusionment with republican government in the United States is characteristic of all the accounts of his political transformation with which I am familiar; see Wilson (ed.), *Peter Porcupine in America*, 8–13.

18. Cobbett considered moving to the West Indies in 1794; see Cobbett to Rachel Smithers, July 6, 1794, in Cobbett Papers, HSP. His early writings show a high degree of familiarity with events in Santo Domingo, and his *Observations on the Emigration of Dr. Joseph Priestley* expresses outrage about the slave revolts there and the plight of white colonists. For a discussion of the French émigré community in the 1790s, see Childs, *French Refugee Life in the United States.* Many of the French newspapers published in the United States were violently anti-Jacobin and politically conservative. The *American Star,* for example, edited by C. C. Tanguy de la Boissiere in Philadelphia, deplored the fate of Santo Domingo, attacked the French government as "enemies and persecutors of the unhappy white colonists," and denounced Citizen Genet and his supporters as "revolutionary moles, who work underground to overturn the edifice erected by the Wisdom of America's legislators"; see *American Star,* Feb. 4, 11, 1794; William Cobbett, *Impeachment of Mr. Lafayette* (Philadelphia: John Parker, 1793). The introduction to this promised "the most scrupulous impartiality" and was signed "William Cobbett, Wilmington Feb. 19, 1793." Its publication was announced in the *National Gazette* on Jan. 30, 1793. Parker also published *The Trial of Louis XVI, Late King of France … Translated from the French* (Philadelphia: John Parker, 1793), which appeared two months later, and lamented the execution of "the unfortunate Louis" as a "generous friend and ally of the United States." Parker also owned the *Courier de l'Amerique,* which he discontinued in early 1793, and he may have been an important link between Cobbett and anti-revolutionary propagandists and journalists in Philadelphia. Cobbett himself later translated Moreau de St. Mery's idealized account of colonial society in Santo Domingo; see Médéric-Louis-Elie Moreau de Saint-Méry, *A Topographical and Political Description of the Spanish Part of Saint-Domingo* (Philadelphia: By the Author, 1796). For a discussion of Moreau de St. Mery's work, see Doris Garraway, *The Libertine Colony: Creolization in the Early French Caribbean* (Durham, N.C.: Duke University Press, 2005).

19. [William Cobbett], *The Republican Judge; or, The American Liberty of the Press* (London: n.p., 1798), 9. It would be useful to know what Cobbett had been reading since his arrival in the United States. One clue is provided in *Observations on the Emigration of Dr. Joseph Priestley,* which echoes, as David Wilson astutely observes, Burke's attack on Richard Price in his *Reflections on the Revolution in France.* Price, like Priestley, was a radical dissenter and closely associated with Priestley; see Wilson (ed.), *Peter Porcupine in America,* 25, 261, 63. Not much has been written on the importance of Cobbett's religious views, but they may have shaped his response to the French Revolution and his reading of the Irish crypto-Catholic Burke. He shared Burke's hostility toward religious dissent and his sympathy for Roman Catholicism, a sympathy he later expressed in his eccentric *History of the Protestant "Reformation" in England and Ireland* (London: n.p., 1821). *Observations* also reveals his familiarity with the work of another Irishman, Jonathan Swift, and shares Swift's contempt for science. Priestley was widely regarded for his experiments on oxygen or what he called "dephlogisticated air," but Cobbett accused him of bottling his farts and "selling them for superfine inflammable air." America, he argued, would be better off with a few more cobblers and mechanics than a "dozen philosophi-theologi-politi-cal empiriks with all their boasted apparatus"; see Wilson (ed.), *Peter Porcupine in America,* 86, 82, 57–58. For a brilliant analysis of Burke's religious views, see Conor Cruise O'Brien, *The Great Melody: A Thematic Biography* (Chicago : University of Chicago Press, 1992).

20. [Cobbett], *Observations on the Emigration of Dr. Joseph Priestley.* There are striking similarities between the political imaginations of James Gillray, the English anti-revolutionary cartoonist, and Cobbett, a kinship that Gillray acknowledged in a series of cartoons designed to illustrate "The Life of William Cobbett" (1809). For a discussion of Gillray, see Ronald Paulson, "James Gillray, Political Caricature and the Grotesque," in Paulson, *Representations of Revolution: 1789–1820* (New Haven, Conn.: Yale University Press, 1983).

21. The genesis of his pamphlet on Priestley was not nearly as spontaneous as Cobbett later claimed. As he admitted, he had "long felt a becoming indignation at the atrocious slander that was continually vomited forth against Great Britain" in the popular press, and he was

also aware that the anti-British character of the American press left "room for such as have a mind to write on the other side." It seems likely he had been looking for an opportunity to get involved in partisan debate for some time, and Priestley's arrival gave him an ideal opportunity; see [Cobbett], *Republican Judge*, 8–9; [Cobbett], *Life and Adventures of Peter Porcupine*, 37.

22. [Cobbett], *Observations on the Emigration of Dr. Joseph Priestley*. Cobbett's father supported the American cause in the 1770s and his son's admiration for George Washington appears to have been genuine; see [Cobbett], *Life and Adventures of Peter Porcupine*, 14. Until 1798, Cobbett had every reason to support the policies of the federal government, and it's important not to assume that his support for the British monarchy somehow made it impossible for him to support a republican government in the United States. Cobbett always compared himself favorably to those British émigrés who joined the Jeffersonian opposition after their arrival in the United States, while he remained loyal to the American government.

23. For an argument that runs parallel to my own but also places Cobbett at the center of American politics in the late 1790s, see Seth Cotlar, "The Federalists' Transatlantic Cultural Offensive of 1798 and the Moderation of American Political Discourse," in Pasley, Robertson, and Waldstreicher (eds.), *Beyond the Founders*.

24. Reitzel (ed.), *Progress of a Plough-Boy*, 72; William Cobbett, *Porcupine's Works* (London: Cobbett and Morgan, 1801), vol. 8, 320; "William Cobbett Account Book," AAS. Cobbett published 25,000 copies of *The Cannibal's Progress* in August 1798 and reckoned "about as many more have issued, by my permission, from the German and other presses in the States"; Cobbett to Edward Thornton, Aug. 27, 1798, in G. D. H. Cole (ed.), *Letters from William Cobbett to Edward Thornton* (Oxford: Oxford University Press, 1937). Cobbett's dealings with English booksellers enabled him to establish a ready-made network of patronage after his return to England in 1800. John Wright, for example, who began to publish John Gifford's *Anti-Jacobin Review* in 1797–1798, was closely linked to major political figures like William Pitt and George Canning. He helped to publicize Cobbett's work and helped to produce an English edition of his writings; see Cole (ed.), *Letters from William Cobbett*, 12–13. Cobbett also published works by American authors, including John Adams's *Defence of the Constitutions of the United States* (Philadelphia: Budd & Bartram for William Cobbett, 1797); John Lowell's *The Antigallican; or, The Lover of His Own Country...by a Citizen of New England* (Philadelphia: William Cobbett, 1797); William Loughton Smith's *The Pretensions of Thomas Jefferson to the Presidency Examined* (Philadelphia: William Cobbett, 1796); and Robert Goodloe Harper's *Observations on the Dispute between the United States and France* (Philadelphia: William Cobbett, 1798), circulating books to and exchanging books with booksellers and printers throughout the United States, Canada, and even Jamaica; see "Cobbett Account Book," AAS. For a summary of his account book and a listing of his American imprints, see Gaines (ed.), *William Cobbett*, 299–302, 159–173. For Cobbett's publishing activities in general, see Reitzel, "William Cobbett and Philadelphia Journalism."

25. [William Cobbett], *A Bone to Gnaw for the Democrats; or, Observations on a Pamphlet, Entitled "The Political Progress of Britain"* (Philadelphia: For the Purchasers, 1795), 5, 11, 35, 16, 33, 27. The preface to this pamphlet is dated Jan. 10, 1795, and it was advertised in the *Gazette of the United States* on Jan. 16, 1795. For Callender's work, see [James Thomson Callender], *The Political Progress of Britain: or, An Impartial History of the Abuses in the Government of the British Empire, in Europe, Asia and America* (Philadelphia: Richard Folwell, 1795). This was first published in London and Edinburgh in 1792 and precipitated Callender's flight to the United States; see Durey, *With the Hammer of Truth*.

26. [William Cobbett], *A Kick for a Bite; or, Review upon Review: With a Critical Essay on the Works of Mrs. S. Rowson...by Peter Porcupine* (Philadelphia: Thomas Bradford, [Mar. 6], 1795). Susanna Rowson, republican, feminist, novelist, playwright, and actress, was the author of the novels *Rebecca; or, The Fille de Chambre* and *Charlotte Temple*. Her play *Slaves in Algiers*, which Cobbett attacked in his pamphlet, opened at the New Theatre in Philadelphia in June 1794. She had also written a play called *The Volunteers* about the Whiskey Rebellion; see Clark, *Peter*

Porcupine, 29–30. For Cobbett's account of the destruction of Lyons, see [William Cobbett], *Part II. A Bone to Gnaw, for the Democrats...by Peter Porcupine* (Philadelphia: Thomas Bradford, [May 28], 1795), 23–42. Also see [William Cobbett], *The Bloody Buoy Thrown Out as a Warning to the Political Pilots of America; or, A Faithful Revelation of a Multitude of Acts of Horrid Barbarity, Such as the Eye Never Witnessed, the Tongue Never Expressed or the Imagination Conceived, until the Commencement of the French Revolution...by Peter Porcupine* (Philadelphia: Benjamin Davies, 1796); Anthony Aufrere, *The Cannibal's Progress; or, The Dreadful Horrors of French Invasion, as Displayed by the Republican Officers and Soldiers, in Their Perfidy, Rapacity, Ferociousness and Brutality* (Philadelphia: William Cobbett, [1798]). Cobbett's account of the attack on Lyons was reprinted for the English market as *Democratic Principles Illustrated by Example...by Peter Porcupine* (London: John Wright, 1798).

27. [Cobbett], *Bloody Buoy*, 139; [William Cobbett], *History of American Jacobinism, Commonly Denominated Democrats by Peter Porcupine* (Philadelphia: William Cobbett, 1796), 43–46. This work was originally published as an appendix to William Playfair's *The History of Jacobinism, Its Crimes, Cruelties and Perfidies* (Philadelphia: William Cobbett, 1796). For similar passages in Cobbett's other writings, see *A Little Plain English Addressed to the People of the United States on the Treaty Negotiated with His Brittanic [sic] Majesty...by Peter Porcupine* (Philadelphia: Thomas Bradford, 1795), 52–53, 109–110; [Cobbett], *Part II. A Bone to Gnaw*, 47–57; [Cobbett], *A Bone to Gnaw*, 35–39.

28. [Cobbett], *Part II. A Bone to Gnaw*, 44; [Cobbett], *History of American Jacobinism*, 47; [William Cobbett], *The Political Censor; or, Monthly Review of the Most Interesting Occurrences, Relative to the United States of America: By Peter Porcupine* (Philadelphia: Benjamin Davies, 1796), Mar. 1796, 9; Apr. 1796, 115–120, 164; May 1796, 231–239.

29. [Cobbett], *Bloody Buoy*, 155; [Cobbett], *History of American Jacobinism*, 47. In his preface to Playfair's *History of Jacobinism*, Cobbett openly defended limited monarchy, and in Sept. 1796 he launched an offensive against Thomas Paine in the *Political Censor*, which was included in *An Antidote for Tom Paine's Theological and Political Poison* (Philadelphia: William Cobbett, 1796). He also reprinted Henry MacKenzie's *An Answer to Paine's Rights of Man...to Which Is Added a Letter from P. Porcupine to Citizen John Swanwick, an Englishman, the Son of a British Wagon-Master, and Member of Congress for the City of Philadelphia* (Philadelphia: William Cobbett, 1796), declaring in his introduction that hereditary monarchy was "the only pledge of peace to a people." In Mar. 1796, however, he also declared: "More has been accomplished in the short space of seven years, under the federal government than was accomplished in an age, under any other government in the world"; *Political Censor* (Mar. 1796), 33.

30. William Cobbett, *The Carriers of Porcupine's Gazette* (broadside published for the "commencement of the year 1798"). In addition to launching *Porcupine's Gazette*, during this short period Cobbett wrote twenty-one pamphlets, most of which he published himself, published several new editions of his own work, translated Georg Friedrich von Martens's *Summary of the Laws of Nations* and Moreau de St. Mery's *Topographical and Political Description*, and published a number of new works by other authors; see Gaines (ed.), *William Cobbett*.

31. [Cobbett], *A Little Plain English*, 6; [Cobbett], *A Bone to Gnaw*, 66. After his return to England in 1800, Cobbett became one of the great leaders of the English radical movement, and many characteristic features of this later radicalism were already evident in the prose of Peter Porcupine. For more on Cobbett's demotic style, see Nattrass, *William Cobbett*.

32. [Cobbett], *Life and Adventures of Peter Porcupine*, 9, 11; Harold Bloom (ed.), *The Spirit of the Age, or Contemporary Portraits by William Hazlitt* (New York: Chelsea House, 1983), 293. The allusion is, of course, to Swift's satirical attacks on Laputan science in *Gulliver's Travels*. Such ridicule became a standard part of the Federalist political repertoire after 1800, fueled by Anglophile Federalist writers like Joseph Dennie who established themselves during Cobbett's brief reign of influence; see chapter 1, "Journey to Laputa: The Federalist Era as an

Augustan Age," in Linda Kerber, *Federalists in Dissent: Imagery and Ideology in Jeffersonian America* (Ithaca, N.Y.: Cornell University Press, 1970). Inexplicably, Kerber doesn't mention Cobbett. Cobbett also played a critical role in what Andrew Robertson calls the development of the hortatory style in American political rhetoric; see "Oral Speech on the Printed Page," in Robertson, *Language of Democracy*, chap. 2.

33. *FG*, Jan. 5, 1798; William Loughton Smith to Ralph Izard, May 23, 1797, in Ullrich B. Phillips (ed.), "South Carolina Federalist Correspondence II," *AHR* 14, no. 4 (July 1909): 788; [Cobbett], *A Kick for a Bite*, 13. Of course, these judgments betray the class assumptions of both men and their belief that Cobbett's style was very different from the conventional discourse of the political elite. Cobbett also claimed that his writing reflected the rough-and-ready speech of ordinary Americans; see *Rush-Light*, no. 6, 280. For his thoughts on writing in general, which emphasized the importance of writing spontaneously and clearly, see his *A Grammar of the English Language* (New York: n.p., 1818) and his critical remarks in *A Kick for a Bite* on the prose and grammar of Samuel Harrison Smith. For E. P. Thompson's judgment and his characteristically incisive and sympathetic discussion of Cobbett's influence on English culture, see *Making of the English Working Class*, 746–762.

34. According to Jay Fliegelman, the "simple voice was implicitly antiaristocratic" and closely linked to new and powerful ideas about natural eloquence and a natural language in the eighteenth century; *Declaring Independence*, 42–65.

35. Quoted in Wilson (ed.), *Peter Porcupine in America*, 217; [Anonymous], *The Philadelphia Jockey Club; or, Mercantile Influence Weighed* (Philadelphia: n.p., 1795). *Observations on the Emigration of Dr. Joseph Priestley* (1794), for example, accused Priestley of having "an understanding little superior to that of an idiot" and "the heart of a *Marat*." *A Bone to Gnaw for the Democrats* (1795) began as an attack on the Scottish radical journalist James Thomson Callender, "a cur howling at the moon," but quickly deteriorated into a succession of sly personal attacks on Jefferson; Joel Barlow; the governor of Pennsylvania, Thomas Mifflin; the editor of the *Philadelphia Gazette*, Andrew Brown; and Philadelphia congressman John Swanwick. *A Kick for a Bite* (1795) ridiculed the prose style of Samuel Harrison Smith and the politics of Susanna Rowson, and *A New Year's Gift to the Democrats* (1795) heaped scorn on the "precious confessions" of the disgraced former secretary of state, Edmund Randolph.

36. James Thomson Callender, *The History of the United States for 1796* (Philadelphia: Snowden & M'Corkle, 1797), 39. On the evolution of American law and attitudes toward press censorship, see Harold L. Nelson, "Seditious Libel in Colonial America," *American Journal of Legal History* 3 (1959): 160–172; Richard Buel, "Freedom of the Press in Revolutionary America: The Evolution of Libertarianism, 1760–1820," in Bernard Bailyn and John B. Hench (eds.), *The Press & the American Revolution* (Worcester, Mass.: American Antiquarian Society, 1980); Levy, *Emergence of a Free Press*; Jeffrey Smith, *Printers and Press Freedom: The Ideology of Early American Journalism* (New York: Oxford University Press, 1988). Although the trial of John Peter Zenger in 1735 was a cause célèbre, its significance has been exaggerated. Even before the Zenger trial, prosecutions for seditious libel were rare and defendants were generally acquitted. Harold Nelson has discovered only four other trials for seditious libel in the American colonies before 1735, and only one resulted in a conviction. Although there were probably more prosecutions, they were neither commonplace nor assured of success. One reason for this was the role of the jury. Andrew Hamilton's famous defense of Zenger was based on two major arguments—that truth was a legitimate defense against an accusation of libel and that the jury could rightfully consider the issue of libel as well as the fact of publication—and has been treated as a departure from existing law. But in fact it was based on existing legal practice in both Britain and America; see Nelson, "Seditious Libel," 165–166. Although neither the truth defense nor the right of the jury to deliberate on the legal definition of libel were established by statute in Britain before the passage of Fox's Libel Act in 1792, both ideas were well established in legal practice long before this, and government efforts to reassert a rigorous doctrine of seditious libel in the eighteenth

century, for example in the trial of Richard Francklin in England in 1731, met with great resistance from members of both the jury and the public. Of the four known prosecutions for seditious libel in colonial America before 1735, the jury considered the issue of libel as well as the fact of publication in at least two of the cases, and in only one did members of the jury leave this task to the presiding judge. Not surprisingly, this was the only trial that ended in a conviction; see Thomas A. Green, "The Jury, Seditious Libel and the Criminal Law," in R. A. Helmholz and Thomas A. Green, *Juries, Libel & Justice: The Role of English Juries in Seventeenth- and Eighteenth-Century Trials for Libel and Slander* (Los Angeles: William Andrews Clark Library, 1984).

37. Smith, *Printers and Press Freedom*, 11; Buel, "Freedom of the Press," 59. On the issue of support for press censorship in eighteenth-century America, see Leonard Levy's classic *Legacy of Suppression* (Cambridge, Mass.: Harvard University Press, 1960). Norman Rosenberg, who generally supports the argument of Levy's controversial work, believes that although the American press enjoyed immunity from legal prosecution after 1735, Americans remained committed to a restricted, albeit not strictly Blackstonian, understanding of press freedom until well into the nineteenth century; see his *Protecting the Best Men*.

38. Benjamin Rush to Andrew Brown, Oct. 1, 1788, in Butterfield (ed.), *Letters of Benjamin Rush*, vol. 1, 487–488; Smith, *Printers and Press Freedom*, 11, 74–77.

39. Benjamin Franklin, "An Account of the Supremest Court of Judicature in Pennsylvania, viz. the Court of the Press," in Smyth (ed.), *Writings of Franklin*, vol. 10, 36–40. Franklin's article appeared in Andrew Brown's *Federal Gazette* on Sept. 12, 1789.

40. [Cobbett], *A Bone to Gnaw*, preface. For evidence of his female readers, see Elaine Forman Crane (ed.), *The Diary of Elizabeth Drinker* (Boston: Northeastern University Press, 1991), vol. 2. See Cobbett's reaction to the death of his first son in Cobbett to Rachel Smithers, July 6, 1794, in Cobbett Papers, HSP: "Oh Miss Smithers! I hope you will never experience a calamity like this—All I ever felt before was nothing—nothing, nothing at all to this. The dearest, sweetest, beautifullest little fellow that ever was seen." For this and his comments on his wife's superlative housekeeping, see Reitzel (ed.), *Progress of a Plough-Boy*, 65–66.

41. [Cobbett], *A Kick for a Bite*, 20–31. The connection between women's equality and the French Revolution was clearly spelled out for readers in *A Bone to Gnaw*, where Cobbett argued that "Democrats, in their rage for equality, may, one of these days, attempt to reduce them [women] to a level with their sable 'property'"; see 54–55. Susan Branson discusses both Cobbett and Rowson in her study of women and issues of gender in the political discourse of the 1790s; see *These Fiery, Frenchified Dames: Women and Political Culture in Early National Philadelphia* (Philadelphia: University of Pennsylvania Press, 2001). See also Arbour, "Benjamin Franklin as Weird Sister," 191–193. Rowson's *Charlotte Temple* was published in England in 1791 and republished in Philadelphia in 1794. It outsold all other contemporary works of fiction. For a brilliant discussion of the gender politics of this novel and other contemporary novels, see Davidson, *Revolution and the Word. Slaves in Algiers* is reprinted in Amelia Howe Kritzer (ed.), *Plays by Early American Women, 1775–1850* (Ann Arbor: University of Michigan Press, 1995). For Rowson herself, see Dorothy Weil, *In Defense of Women: Susanna Rowson, 1762–1824* (University Park: Pennsylvania State University Press, 1976); and Patricia L. Parker, *Susanna Rowson* (Boston: Twayne, 1986).

42. [John Swanwick], *A Rub from Snub* (Philadelphia: Printed for the Purchasers, 1795), 17. The phrase is borrowed from Richard Polwhele's *The Unsex'd Females* (New York: William Cobbett, 1800).

43. [Cobbett], *A Bone to Gnaw*, 56; *Porcupine's Political Censor* (Apr. 1796), 146–148; (May 1796), 191. For a similar attack on Swanwick's masculinity, see [Cobbett], *A New Year's Gift*, 66. Cobbett also published an open letter to Swanwick during the congressional elections of 1796, accusing him of political corruption and electoral fraud on a scale that surpassed even that "Alma Mater of election charity and munificence," the English borough election; see MacKenzie, *An Answer to Paine's Rights of Man*, 93–96.

44. *Political Censor* (Nov. 1796), 68; [Cobbett], *A Bone to Gnaw*, 26; [Cobbett], *Part II. A Bone to Gnaw*, preface; [Cobbett], *A Little Plain English*, preface. Cobbett identified "Tom the Tinker" as Governor Mifflin in a note to an edition of this last work published in London in 1795; see Gaines (ed.), *William Cobbett*, 25.

45. [Cobbett], *Life and Adventures of Peter Porcupine*, 38–44; *Political Censor* (Sept. 1796), 61–79; (Mar. 1796), 109–114. Thomas Bradford published all of Cobbett's writings prior to early 1796, at which stage the two men quarreled and Cobbett left to start his own bookselling and printing business. Bradford then refused to sell him the copyrights to his own writings and threatened to sue him for breach of contract. Cobbett was outraged and attacked Bradford in *The Life and Adventures of Peter Porcupine*. Bradford's son, Samuel Bradford, then retaliated in *The Imposter Detected*, accusing Cobbett of working secretly for the British government and writing puffs, anonymous self-promotional paragraphs, of his own work. Cobbett lashed back furiously, calling Samuel Bradford a "lump of walking tallow streaked with lampblack" and a "sooty fisted son of ink and urine, whose heart is as black and foul as the liquid in which he dabbles," although the charge that Cobbett had written a puff attacking the second part of his *Bone to Gnaw* and sent it to Benjamin Franklin Bache, who refused to print it, was true. Cobbett argued that his self-promoting tactics had good literary antecedents; see *Political Censor* (Sept. 1796), 61–79.

46. [Cobbett], *Life and Adventures of Peter Porcupine*, 37. The original title was rejected by Cobbett's printer, Thomas Bradford, as dangerously provocative.

47. [James Thomson Callender], *British Honour and Humanity; or, The Wonders of American Patience, as Exemplified in the Modest Publications, and Universal Applause of Mr. William Cobbet[t]* (Philadelphia: Robert Campbell, 1796); [John Swanwick], *A Rub from Snub; or, A Cursory Analytical Epistle: Addressed to Peter Porcupine, Author of the Bone to Gnaw, Kick for a Bite, &c &c. Containing, Glad Tidings for the Democrats, and a Word of Comfort to Mrs. S. Rowson* (Philadelphia: For the Purchasers, 1795).

48. [Anonymous], *A Twig of Birch for a Butting Calf* (New York: J. Buel, 1795); [Samuel Bradford], *The Imposter Detected*; [James Carey], *A Pill for Porcupine: Being a Specific for an Obstinate Itching Which That Hireling Has Long Contracted for Lying and Calumny* (Philadelphia: [Stewart and Cochran] For the Author, 1796); [Joseph Hopkinson], *A Congratulatory Epistle to the Redoubtable "Peter Porcupine"…by Peter Grievous* (Philadelphia: Thomas Bradford, 1796); [Santiago Felipe Puglia], *The Blue Shop; or, Impartial and Humorous Observations on the Life and Adventures of Peter Porcupine…by James Quicksilver* (Philadelphia: Moreau de St. Mery, 1796); Mathew Carey, *The Porcupiniad: A Hudibrastic Poem…Addressed to William Cobbett* (Philadelphia: For the Author, 1799). See also [Puglia], *The Political Massacre…by James Quicksilver* (Philadelphia: Moreau de St. Mery, 1796); [John Swanwick], *A Roaster; or, A Check to the Progress of Political Blasphemy: Intended as a Brief Reply to Peter Porcupine* (Philadelphia: J. Johnson, 1796); [James Thomson Callender], *The American Annual Register* (Philadelphia: Bioren & Madan, 1797); [Anonymous], *The Last Confession and Dying Speech of Peter Porcupine, with an Account of His Dissection* (Philadelphia: [William Palmer], 1797); [James Carey], *The Life of Skunk Peter Porcupine* ("Printed at Constantinople," 1798); Mathew Carey, *A Plum Pudding for the Humane, Chaste, Valiant, Enlightened Peter Porcupine* (Philadelphia: For the Author, 1799). For a complete list of these and other titles, see Gaines (ed.), *William Cobbett*, 174–204; and Clark, *Peter Porcupine*, 66–75, 189–191.

49. Gaines (ed.), *William Cobbett*, 186. Published by Moreau de St. Mery, this was one of the few well-executed political cartoons printed in the United States in the 1790s. Its caption read "See Porcupine in Coulours Just Portray'd Urg'd by Old Nick to Drive his Dirty Trade"; see *Political Censor* (Sept. 1796).

50. Cobbett, *Cobbett's Political Register* (London: Cox and Baylis, 1804), vol. 5, 452; [Cobbett], *Part II. A Bone to Gnaw*, preface. Stanley Elkins and Eric McKitrick's lengthy political history of the period gives Cobbett only a brief mention, and Jeffrey Pasley's otherwise excellent history of partisan journalism in the 1790s argues that Cobbett "had little to do with party politics" and

devotes only a dismissive footnote to his influence; see Elkins and McKitrick, *Age of Federalism*, 518, 555, 698–699; Pasley, *Tyranny of Printers*, 100, 102–104, 429. Cobbett is not mentioned at all in Wood's *Radicalism of the American Revolution*. The figures for Cobbett's pamphlets do not include English editions; see Gaines (ed.), *William Cobbett*, 3–158. Collected editions, of course, were not necessarily a good gauge of popularity and were often used by publishers to dispose of surplus pamphlets. However, Thomas Bradford's refusal to part with the copyrights and Cobbett's own reprinting of these works suggest their market appeal. Cobbett also created an impressive distribution network for his publications, selling and exchanging books with over thirty booksellers between 1797 and 1799. These included James Wright of Boston, who had transactions with Cobbett totaling about $2,000; George Price of Baltimore, who had accounts of almost $3,000; and William Young of Charleston, who did almost $1,000 worth of business with Cobbett in this period; see "Cobbett Account Book," AAS.

51. [Cobbett], *Die Blut-Fahne Ausgertecket zur Warnung Politischer Wegweiser in America* (Reading, Pa.: Gottlob Jungmann, 1797); Jacob Cox Parsons (ed.), *Extracts from the Diary of Jacob Hiltzheimer* (Philadelphia: n.p., 1893), 257; *PG*, July 13, 1797. Of Aufrere's work, Cobbett reckoned "about as many more have issued, by my permission, from the German and other presses in the States"; see Cole (ed.), *Letters from William Cobbett*, 4. For the German edition, see Anthony Aufrere, *Der Fortgang der Menschenfresser* (Philadelphia: Henrich Schweitzer, 1798); Davis, "William Cobbett," 23–25; "Cobbett Account Book," AAS. This records sales of 7,185 copies by mid-1798. Cobbett later claimed "upwards of a hundred thousand copies" of *The Cannibal's Progress* had been printed and sold in the United States; see Cobbett, *Porcupine's Works*, vol. 8, 320.

52. Cobbett, *Cobbett's Political Register*, vol. 5, 451. This total does not include his publication and distribution of works by other authors; see William Cobbett, *Proposals for Publishing by Subscription an Edition of Porcupine's Works* (Philadelphia: n.p., 1799), in William L. Clements Library, University of Michigan.

53. Clark, *Peter Porcupine*, 95; *PG*, Apr. 24, Nov. 2, 1797. The Philadelphia printer Mathew Carey, no novice and no friend of Cobbett's, estimated the circulation of *Porcupine's Gazette* at 2,000 in 1799; see Carey, *A Plum Pudding for…Porcupine*, 8. But this was after Cobbett's influence reached its zenith. There was also a German version of *Porcupine's Gazette* published weekly as *Der Deutsche Porcupein und Lancaster Anzeigs-Nachricten* by Johann Albrecht in Lancaster, Pennsylvania, from Jan. 1798 to Dec. 1799, although its connection with Cobbett is unclear; see Gaines (ed.), *William Cobbett*, 77.

54. *Charleston State Gazette*, Sept. 13, 1797. Other southern states mustered only a fraction of this number, although these figures may not tell the whole story. "A Subscription List of Country Subscribers to Peter Porcupine's Gazette," NYHS, shows *Porcupine's Gazette* (or possibly the *Country Porcupine*) had about 600 subscribers in the following states: Virginia (295), Maryland (162), Delaware (4), Pennsylvania (109), Kentucky (11), Tennessee (13), North Carolina (3), and New Jersey (4). Unfortunately, this list is undated and clearly incomplete. It gives no figures for South Carolina or Georgia, for example, and only covers western Pennsylvania. It is also hard to believe that the *Gazette* had only 8 readers total in Delaware and New Jersey, both strongly Federalist states, suggesting that this list may date from early in the life of *Porcupine's Gazette*. Nonetheless, it provides a useful baseline for the circulation of the newspaper in the southern and western states.

55. *Political Censor* (Mar. 1797), 100; Noah Webster to Joseph Priestley, Jan. 20, 1800, in Warfel (ed.), *Letters*, 206; William Branch Giles, speech to the U.S. House of Representatives, reported in the *Newburyport Herald and Country Gazette*, Apr. 13, 1798; Cobbett, *Proposals*.

56. [Callender], *British Honour and Humanity*, 17; Joseph Priestley, *Letters to the Inhabitants of Northumberland* (Northumberland, Pa.: Andrew Kennedy, 1799); Rush to Jefferson, Mar. 12, 1801, in Butterfield (ed.), *Letters of Benjamin Rush*, vol. 2, 831–833; Benjamin Austin, *Constitutional Republicanism* (Boston: n.p., 1803), 146.

57. Wood, "Conspiracy and the Paranoid Style," 425. Wood's essay challenges Richard Hofstadter's emphasis on the irrationality of conspiratorial thinking in his classic *Paranoid Style in American Politics*.

58. See Habermas, *Structural Transformation*; Wood, "Conspiracy and the Paranoid Style," 410, 423. My emphasis on personal satire and the politics of exposure conflicts with the emphasis that Habermas and (in the American context) Michael Warner place on the role of a rational-critical discourse in the political public sphere. Oddly, both Habermas and Warner almost completely neglect the influence of satire in eighteenth-century Anglo-American literary culture; see Shields, *Civil Tongues & Polite Letters*; Warner, *Letters of the Republic*.

59. [Ezra Sampson], *The Sham Patriot Unmasked; or, An Exposition of the Fatally Successful Arts of Demagogues, to Exalt Themselves by Flattering and Swindling the People* (Hudson, N.Y.: Sampson, Crittenden and Croswell, 1802), 80, 27.

60. [Sampson], *Sham Patriot Unmasked*, 2, 45–46, 139.

61. *Political Censor* (Nov. 1796), 61; [Cobbett] *A Kick for a Bite*, 31. "*Liberty*, according to the Democratic Dictionary," wrote Cobbett, "does not mean *freedom from oppression*; it is a very comprehensive term, signifying, among other things, *slavery, robbery, murder*, and *blasphemy*"; [Cobbett], *A Bone to Gnaw*, 95 n. Of the rights of man (and woman), he had this to say: "The author of the *rights of man*, and the authoress of the *rights of women*, are at this moment starving in a dirty dungeon, not a hundred paces from the *sanctum sanctorum* of liberty and equality; and the poor unfortunate Goddess herself is guillotined! So much for liberty and the rights of man" ([Cobbett], *Observations on the Emigration of Dr. Joseph Priestley*). Cobbett ridiculed the republicans' fashion for renaming and their obsession with forms of address, which he viewed as the triumph of form over content; see, for example, [Cobbett], *History of American Jacobinism*, 23–29.

62. *Political Censor* (Jan. 1797), 44; [Cobbett], *Part II. A Bone to Gnaw*, 23–42; *Political Censor* (Nov. 1796), 13; (May 1796), 229; (Dec. 1796), 229; [Cobbett], *Bloody Buoy*, 234–236.

63. Henry Fielding, "An Essay on the Knowledge of the Characters of Men," in Miller (ed.), *Works of Henry Fielding*, vol. 1, 155, 175.

64. Edmund Burke, *Reflections on the Revolution in France* (Rpt., Harmondsworth, England: Penguin, [1969]), 16, 135, 170–172, 156. This paragraph draws on Ronald Paulson's brilliant essay "Burke, Paine and Wollstonecraft: The Sublime and the Beautiful," in his *Representations of Revolution: 1789–1820* (New Haven, Conn.: Yale University Press, 1983). For a discussion of similar themes in Burke's writing, see Isaac Kramnick, *The Rage of Edmund Burke* (New York: Basic, 1977); and Linda M. G. Zerilli, *Signifying Woman: Culture and Chaos in Rousseau, Burke and Mill* (Ithaca, N.Y.: Cornell University Press, 1994).

65. Wilson (ed.), *Peter Porcupine in America*, 24–29; Burke, *Reflections*, 90. One of Cobbett's legacies to American politics was his transmission and popularization of Burke. Cobbett published Burke's *A Letter from the Rt. Honourable Edmund Burke to a Noble Lord… The First American Edition with a Preface by Peter Porcupine* (Philadelphia: Benjamin Davies, H. & P. Rice, and Ormrod, [1796]) and *Two Letters Addressed to a Member of the Present Parliament on the Proposals for Peace with the Regicide Directory of France* (Philadelphia: William Cobbett and J. Ormrod, 1797). The phrase "family romance" is from Lynn Hunt's *Family Romance of the French Revolution*; and Sigmund Freud, *Totem and Taboo: Resemblances between the Psychic Lives of Savages and Neurotics*, trans. A. A. Brill (New York: Vintage, 1946).

66. *Political Censor* (Dec. 1796), 10; (Sept. 1796), 10–11, 20. For Cobbett's campaign against Paine, see also his preface to Playfair's *History of Jacobinism*; *Porcupine's Political Censor* (Nov. 1796, Dec. 1796); *An Antidote for Tom Paine's Theological and Political Poison* (Philadelphia: William Cobbett, 1796); [Cobbett], *A Letter to the Infamous Tom Paine, in Answer to a Letter Written by Him to General Washington by Peter Porcupine* [Philadelphia: William Cobbett, 1797]; MacKenzie, *An Answer to Paine's Rights of Man*; Patrick Kennedy, *An Answer to Paine's Letter to Washington* (Philadelphia: William Cobbett, 1798).

67. *Political Censor* (Nov. 1796), 31; [Cobbett], *Observations on the Emigration of Dr. Joseph Priestley*, 13. Responding to Benjamin Franklin's famous aphorism "Where liberty dwells, there is my country," Paine, the quintessential political cosmopolitan, declared: "Where liberty is not, there is my country." I don't want to push psychological explanations too far, but Cobbett's animus toward Paine and other émigré Englishmen suggests that he may have found in the writings of Burke a theory of connection—to place, to his past, to people—that addressed his own sense of displacement, detecting and responding to the emotional passion that resulted from Burke's own sense of marginality; see O'Brien, *Great Melody*, and his introduction to the Penguin edition of *Reflections*.

68. *Political Censor* (Nov. 1796), 33; Playfair, *History of Jacobinism*, 11.

69. Cobbett reprinted this charge from the *Boston Mercury* in *Porcupine's Gazette*; see *PG*, May 9, 1797; *Commercial Advertiser*, Oct. 6, 1797; *Norfolk Herald*, July 22, 1797 quoted in *PG*, Aug. 3, 1797; [Anonymous], *Twig of Birch*, 26; Pattee (ed.), *Poems*, vol. 3, 186; Carey, *Porcupiniad*, quoted in Wilson (ed.), *Peter Porcupine in America*, 38.

70. Noah Webster to Jedediah Morse, May 15, 1797; Webster to Timothy Pickering, July 17, 1798, both in Warfel (ed.), *Letters*, 148, 182–184; quoted in Butterfield (ed.), *Letters of Benjamin Rush*, vol. 2, 1214; *Newburyport Herald & Country Gazette*, June 8, 1798; Robert Liston to Grenville, June 25, 1798, quoted in B. Perkins, *The First Rapprochement* (Berkeley: University of California Press, 1967), 9; Abigail Adams to Mary Cranch, Mar. 13, 1798, in Mitchell (ed.), *Letters of Abigail Adams*, 142–144; *FG*, Jan. 5, 1798.

71. Miller, *Brief Retrospect*, vol. 2, 255. The phrase "masters of scurrility" is Charles Warren's; see Warren, *Jacobin and Junto*, 90–95.

72. William Linn, *A Discourse, Delivered on the 26th of November, 1795* (New York: T. and J. Swords, 1795). The best discussion of fame is Douglas Adair, "Fame and the Founding Fathers," in Trevor Coulbourn (ed.), *Fame and the Founding Fathers: Essays by Douglas Adair* (New York: Norton 1974). But for a more recent analysis that places the idea of public honor at the center of an analysis of political life in the early Republic, see Freeman, *Affairs of Honor*. Whether or not fame rather than self-interest really was the dominant concern of the founding generation is less important for the purposes of this argument than its function within a republican conception of political leadership.

73. *Newburyport Herald*, Mar. 30, 1798. When Alexander Addison considered reforms in libel law in Pennsylvania during the mid-1790s, one of his primary concerns was to protect the reputations of public men; see Norman Rosenberg, "Alexander Addison and the Pennsylvania Origins of the Federalist First Amendment," *Pennsylvania Magazine of History and Biography* 108, no. 4 (Oct. 1, 1984): 410–412. As Rosenberg argues, libel law had definite social objectives: to preserve the reputations of the "best men"; Rosenberg, *Protecting the Best Men*.

74. Wharton (ed.), *State Trials of the United States*, 670–677; Miller, *Brief Retrospect*, vol. 2, 255; *PG*, Sept. 28, 1797; reprinted from the *Courier Francois* (Philadelphia) in the *Newburyport Herald*, Oct. 31, 1797.

75. Article from the *Boston Mercury* reprinted in the Boston *Commercial Advertiser*, Oct. 6, 1797. The newspapers referred to were Thomas and Abijah Adams's *Independent Chronicle* (Boston), Thomas Greenleaf's New York *Argus*, and Benjamin Bache's *Aurora* (Philadelphia), all staunchly Republican newspapers.

76. Butterfield (ed.), *Letters of Benjamin Rush*, vol. 2, 806–807; Adams, "Address to the Young Men of Boston," *Boston Centinel*, May 30, 1798. See also Adams (ed.), *Works of John Adams*, vol. 9, 194.

77. Henry Van Schaack to Theodore Sedgwick, Jan. 30, 1797, in Sedgwick Papers, MHS. For threats of violence toward Cobbett, see [Cobbett], *The Scare-Crow: Being an Infamous Letter, Sent to Mr. John Olden, Threatening Destruction to His House, and Violence to His Tenant, William Cobbett* (Philadelphia: William Cobbett, 1796); *PG*, Apr. 6–10, 1797. John Beckley apparently threatened to "horsewhip" Cobbett, who had dubbed him the "DISCARDED CLERK"; see *PG*, May

17, 1797. Cobbett's persecution adds an important dimension to discussions of press freedom in the 1790s, which have revolved almost entirely around the Federalists and the Sedition Act. Although Cobbett's case strengthens his overall argument, Leonard Levy mentions him only briefly in *Legacy of Suppression*, 206–207, and adds nothing to this in his revised version of the same work, *Emergence of a Free Press* (New York: Oxford University Press, 1985), 212–213. In both standard accounts of the Alien and Sedition Acts, Cobbett is presented as a belligerent advocate of repression, and his own travails are largely ignored; see John C. Miller, *Crisis in Freedom: The Alien and Sedition Acts* (Boston: Little, Brown, 1951), 51, 55n66, 229; and James Morton Smith, *Freedom's Fetters: The Alien and Sedition Laws and American Civil Liberties* (Ithaca, N.Y.: Cornell University Press, 1956), 175.

78. Cobbett was only the second newspaper editor to be prosecuted for seditious libel since the end of the American Revolution. Eleazar Oswald, editor of the *Independent Gazetteer*, was hauled before the Supreme Court of Pennsylvania in 1782 but acquitted by a grand jury. Arrested again in 1788, he was convicted and sentenced to a month in prison and a fine of £10. His persecutor was Chief Justice Thomas McKean, who also played a key role in Cobbett's various trials; see Levy, *Emergence of a Free Press*, 206–211. Cobbett's predicament was not entirely novel. In March 1796, William Keteltas was charged with seditious contempt for publishing articles critical of the New York Assembly and jailed. In 1795, the editor of the *New-York Journal*, Thomas Greenleaf, was indicted in federal court for criminal libel, but the charges were dropped. In May 1797, the case was renewed, and Greenleaf was found guilty and fined $700. Noah Webster was also threatened with a civil lawsuit for libel in mid-1797 by the Republican lawyer Alexander James Dallas, who also played a role in Cobbett's denouement, but it's unclear whether or not this case was ever brought. In early 1798, before the passage of the Sedition Act, the federal government brought charges of seditious libel against Benjamin Franklin Bache and John Daly Burk, but Bache died and Burk fled before he could be brought to trial; see Levy, *Emergence of a Free Press*, 276–277, 294–296; *PG*, May 24, 1797; New York *Argus*, May 8, 1797. Such episodes need more investigation, but Cobbett's trials are the first important test of press freedom in the overheated partisan climate of the late 1790s.

79. *PG*, May 27, June 13, 17, July 10, 12–15, 17, 1797. Pickering was terrified that Spanish Louisiana and Florida would become a sphere of French influence and possibly even a launching pad for a French invasion. D'Yrujo, on the other hand, justified his efforts to stall the progress of Pinckney's Treaty by invoking the threat of a British invasion from American territory, fears that seemed justified by the discovery of British involvement in the Blount conspiracy in 1797. The best account of these complex developments is Gerald Clarfield, *Timothy Pickering and American Diplomacy, 1795–1800* (Columbia: University of Missouri Press, 1969), chap. 7. But for a more recent and sympathetic assessment of Pickering's diplomacy and politics, see Garry Wills, *Negro President: Jefferson and the Slave Power* (Boston: Houghton Mifflin, 2003).

80. *PG*, Aug. 9, 11, 1797; Pickering to d'Yrujo, Aug. 10, 1797; Rawle to Pickering, Apr. 12, 1798, both in Pickering Papers (MHS,). The speed with which the government decided to prosecute Cobbett was astonishing, especially as relations with d'Yrujo were so strained. The culprit was probably John Adams, who disliked Cobbett immensely and who had already considered deporting him under the Alien Act. Pickering informed d'Yrujo that the prosecution had been set in motion "by direction of the President of the United States," and it's hard to believe that Pickering, who despised d'Yrujo and shared Cobbett's "violent anti-Gallican" feelings, would have agreed to the prosecution without strong pressure from Adams. Adams later appointed Cobbett's nemesis, Dr. Benjamin Rush, to the post of treasurer of the U.S. Mint; see John Adams to Abigail Adams, Feb. 22, 1799, in Adams (ed.), *Works of John Adams*, vol. 1, 545; Smith, *Freedom's Fetters*, 164–176; Pickering to d'Yrujo, July 24, 1797; Pickering to Rawle, July 29, 1797; Pickering to d'Yrujo, Aug. 2, 1797, all in Pickering Papers (MHS).

81. *PG*, Aug. 8, 29, 1797; G. S. Rowe, *Thomas McKean: The Shaping of an American Republican* (Boulder: Colorado University Press, 1978), 295–300; Pickering to d'Yrujo, Aug. 2, 10, 1797,

in Pickering Papers (MHS). For Cobbett's description of these legal maneuvers and copies of McKean's bill of arrest and the indictment, see [Cobbett], *The Democratic Judge; or, The Equal Liberty of the Press, as Exhibited, and Exposed, in the Prosecution of William Cobbett, for a Pretended Libel against the King of Spain and His Embassador, before Thomas M'Kean, Chief Justice of the State of Pennsylvania* (Philadelphia: William Cobbett, 1798).

82. Charge to the jury by Thomas McKean in Wharton (ed.), *State Trials of the United States*, 322–326. For McKean's persecution of Oswald, see Levy, *Emergence of a Free Press*, 206–211; Dwight Teeter, "The Printer and the Chief Justice: Seditious Libel in 1782–83," *Journalism Quarterly*, vol. 45 (Summer 1968): 235–242. Cobbett accused McKean on a number of occasions of degrading his position as chief justice. Commenting that one such "instance of dirty meanness" by McKean was "hardly to be equaled in the annals of democracy," he declared: "A Chief Justice! Good Heaven, preserve me from his clutches: I would almost as soon, God forgive me, fall under those of his wife"; see *PG*, July 27, 1797; *Political Censor* (Jan. 1797), 39; *PG*, July 5, 18, 1797.

83. Levy, *Emergence of a Free Press*, 213; Wharton (ed.), *State Trials of the United States*, 328. It is worth pointing out that the same man who delivered this charge also condemned the Alien and Sedition Acts as "unnecessary, nay injurious and provoking, unaccompanied with any possible advantages to the United States." "Trial by Jury," he argued, "and the Sovereignty of the respective States [would] be prostrated" by these "extraordinary acts of Congress"; see Rowe, *Thomas McKean*, 293. McKean's opposition to the Sedition Act was clearly inspired by its federal character rather than its assault on press freedom. For a clear exposition of his reasoning about state jurisdiction and the limitations of federal authority, see "Respublica versus Cobbett," in A. J. Dallas (ed.), *Reports of Cases Ruled and Adjudged in the Several Courts of the United States and of Pennsylvania* (Philadelphia: n.p., 1799), 467–476.

84. Rush announced his legal action against Cobbett in Andrew Brown's *Philadelphia Gazette*, Oct. 2, 1797. Cobbett treated this with contempt and declared his defiance; *PG*, Oct. 3, 1797. For reports of the cases, see Jasper Yeates (ed.), *Reports of Cases Adjudged in the Supreme Court of Pennsylvania* (Philadelphia: n.p., 1818), vol. 2, 275–276. For Cobbett's discussion of the reasons for McKean's delay and the petition for the removal of his case to the federal courts, see *Rush-Light*, Mar. 31, 1800. For his remorseless and hilarious campaign against Rush, whom he dubbed "our Modern Sangrado" and the "Master Bleeder," see *Political Censor* (Jan. 1797), 34; *PG*, Aug. 23–29, Sept. 19–26, Oct. 3–24, 1797; "The Cobbett-Rush Feud," appendix III in Butterfield (ed.), *Letters of Benjamin Rush*, vol. 2, 1213–1218; George W. Corner (ed.), *The Autobiography of Benjamin Rush* (Princeton, N.J.: Princeton University Press, 1948), 1–2, 95–104.

85. Cobbett was charged as a "common libeler" who was responsible for publications intended to "slanderously and maliciously defame the government of the *United States*, the officers and the good citizens thereof, as well as the government of this commonwealth, his excellency the governor, and others the good officers and citizens thereof." The sweeping nature of these charges is testimony to the arbitrary character of the entire legal proceedings; see "Respublica against William Cobbett," in Yeates (ed.), *Reports*, vol. 2, 352–363; "Respublica versus Cobbett," in Dallas (ed.), *Reports*, vol. 3, 467–476; Wharton (ed.), *State Trials of the United States*, 322; "Respublica against William Cobbett" and "Respublica against Benjamin Davies," in Yeates (ed.), *Reports*, vol. 3, 93–101, 128–131; *Rush-Light*, Apr. 30, 1800. Cobbett was still trying to wring justice and his $2,000 out of the Pennsylvania legislature when he returned to the United States in 1817; see Clark, *Peter Porcupine*, chap. 9.

86. *PG*, Oct. 5, 6, 1797; [Cobbett], *Democratic Judge*, 22–23. Cobbett wished to distinguish here not only between legal rights and practice but between a negative understanding of legal right, which prevented legal restraint of the press, and a more positive understanding of legal right, which provided protection for those who chose to exercise the liberty of the press. "For where is the difference to the printer," he asked, "whether the law itself restrains his press or suffers it to be restrained?" [Cobbett], *Democratic Judge*, 37, 6, 18.

87. [Cobbett], *Democratic Judge*, 6, 18, 89, 56, 90–91.

88. Levy, *Emergence of a Free Press*, 297, chap. 9. For an interpretation of the English political press that emphasizes a similar dissolution of the boundary between public and private, see Eckhart Hellmuth, "'The Palladium of All Other English Liberties': Reflections on the Liberty of the Press in England during the 1760s and 1770s," in Hellmuth (ed.), *The Transformation of Political Culture: England and Germany in the Late Eighteenth Century* (Oxford: Oxford University Press, 1990); and John Brewer, *Party Ideology and Popular Politics at the Accession of George III* (Cambridge: Cambridge University Press, 1976), 163–200, 219–239.

89. William Rawle to Pickering, Apr. 12, 1798, in Pickering Papers (MHS); Cobbett, *Porcupine's Works*, 10, 190–191; Clark, *Peter Porcupine*, 150–152. The election of McKean, wrote Cobbett, "has, in my opinion *decided* the fate of what has been called Federalism"; *PG*, Oct. 12–19, 1799; Cobbett to Thornton, Nov. 18, 1799, in Cole (ed.), *Letters from William Cobbett*; Cobbett to Edward Tilghman, Dec. 9, 1799, in Cobbett Papers, HSP.

90. Cobbett himself declared: "The oppressive, the unprecedented, the abominable decision against me at Philadelphia has been ascribed to party spirit; but justice to those whom I long combated, demands from me the acknowledgement, that the Democrats were not only perfectly innocent of the deed, but that they expressed, and still do express, their horror at it. The insidious and malignant prosecutor is an officer under the Federal Government, the Judge, the Jury, the lawyers of Rush, and, am sorry to add, my own lawyers, were all Federalists to a man!" (*Rush-Light*, Apr. 30, 1800). One of Rush's lawyers was Joseph Hopkinson, the Federalist author of "Hail Columbia" and future defender of Justice Samuel Chase; see *A Report of an Action for a Libel, Brought by Dr. Benjamin Rush, against William Cobbett* (Philadelphia: W. W. Woodward, 1800); Clark, *Peter Porcupine*, 153–157; Burton Alva Konkle, *Joseph Hopkinson, 1770–1842* (Philadelphia: University of Pennsylvania Press, 1931), chaps. 7–8; Spater, *William Cobbett*, vol. 1, 104. For Cobbett's unhappiness with his legal counsel, see Cobbett to Edward Tilghman, Dec. 18, 1799; Cobbett to Robert Goodloe Harper, Jan. 20, 1800, both in Cobbett Papers, HSP. For an indication of how he would have defended himself against Rush's charges, see *Rush-Light*, Mar. 15, 31, 1800.

91. Cobbett to Wright, Jan. 4, 1800; Cobbett to Tilghman, Dec. 30, 1799, both in Cobbett Papers, HSP; Cobbett to Thornton, Dec. 25, 1799, Jan. 20, Mar. 14, 1800, in Cole (ed.), *Letters from William Cobbett*; *Rush-Light*, Apr. 30, 1800; Spater, *William Cobbett*, vol. 1, 108. Cobbett's one reference to the elections of 1800 was in a letter to Edward Thornton written just before his departure to England. Commenting on the crucial contest in New York, he wrote: "[P]arties run high, great efforts are making on both sides, and it is said, that the result is of no less importance than the decision of the question;—who shall be President?" This sounds like the remark of a political ingenue rather than a seasoned partisan, and it seems unlikely that Cobbett any longer cared who became president; see Cobbett to Thornton, Apr. 29, 1800, in Cole (ed.), *Letters from William Cobbett*.

Chapter 6

1. *Aurora*, Nov. 3, 1802. For accounts of Paine's homecoming, see Keane, *Tom Paine*, chap. 12; Jerry Knudsen, *Jefferson and the Press: Crucible of Liberty* (Columbia: University of South Carolina Press, 2006), chap. 5. For Paine's changing reputation in the United States, see Alfred F. Young, "Common Sense and the Rights of Man in America: The Celebration and Damnation of Thomas Paine," in K. Gavroglu (ed.), *Science, Mind, and Art* (Amsterdam: Kluwer Academic, 1995).

2. *Aurora*, July 14, 1801, Nov. 8, 1802. Duane tried to deter Paine from attacking Christianity in the United States; see Worthington Chauncy Ford (ed.), "Letters of William Duane, 1800–1834," *Proceedings of the Massachusetts Historical Society*, 2nd ser., 20 (1906–1907): 279.

3. *Port Folio*, July 18, 1801. Federalist attacks on Paine linked his alleged character failings to his heterodox religious ideas; see Keane, *Tom Paine*, 460–462.

4. Thomas Jefferson to Messrs. Nehemiah Dodge, Ephraim Robbins, and Stephen S. Nelson, a Committee of the Danbury Baptist Association, Jan. 1, 1802 (Jefferson Papers, Manuscript Division, LOC); James Hutson, "Thomas Jefferson's Letter to the Danbury Baptists: A Controversy Rejoined," *WMQ*, 3rd ser., 56, no. 4 (Oct. 1999): 775–790; Benjamin Rush to Thomas Jefferson, Aug. 22, 1800, May 5, 1803, both in Butterfield (ed.), *Letters of Benjamin Rush*, vol. 2, 819–820, 863–865; Jefferson to Rush, Apr. 21, 1803, in Ford (ed.), *Works of Thomas Jefferson*, vol. 9, 457.

5. John Mitchell Mason, *The Voice of Warning to Christians* (1800), in Ellis Sandoz (ed.), *Political Sermons of the Founding Era, 1730–1805* (Indianapolis, Ind.: Liberty, 1991).

6. On the issue of public transparency, see Fliegelman, *Declaring Independence*.

7. *Aurora*, May 18, 1799. The best and fullest account of Duane's life is by Kim Tousley Phillips, *William Duane: Radical Journalist in the Age of Jefferson* (New York: Garland, 1989), but see also Pasley, *Tyranny of Printers*, esp. chaps. 8, 12; Rosenfeld, *American Aurora*; Durey, *Transatlantic Radicals*, 181–182, 247–257; Andrew Shankman, *Crucible of Democracy: The Struggle to Fuse Egalitarianism & Capitalism in Jeffersonian Pennsylvania* (Lawrence: University of Kansas Press, 2004), chap. 2; Smith, *Freedom's Fetters*, 277–306. For useful older accounts of his life, see Allan C. Clark, "William Duane," in *Records of the Columbia Historical Society* (Washington D.C.: Published by the Society, 1906); and [William John Duane], *Biographical Memoir of William J. Duane* (Philadelphia: Claxton, Remsen and Haffelfinger, 1868).

8. *Aurora*, May 18, 1799; Duane to Stephen Bradley, Nov. 10, 1808, in Clark, "William Duane," 57; Durey, *Transatlantic Radicals*, 80–92.

9. [Duane], *Biographical Memoir*, 1; Horace Walpole to Sir Horace Mann, Dec. 4, 1781, in W. S. Lewis (ed.), *The Yale Edition of Horace Walpole's Correspondence* (New Haven, Conn.: Yale University Press, 1971), vol. 25, 216; *DAB*, vol. 6, 76. For John Almon's links to Horace Walpole, see Robert R. Rea, "John Almon: Bookseller to John Wilkes," *Indiana Quarterly for Bookmen* 4 (1948): 111.

10. Phillips, *William Duane*, 9–11; Lucyle Werkmeister, *A Newspaper History of England, 1792–1793* (Lincoln: University of Nebraska Press, 1967), 38, 60, 197; Rea, "John Almon"; Robert Rea, *The English Press in Politics, 1760–1774* (Lincoln: University of Nebraska Press, 1963); John Almon, *Memoirs of John Almon, Bookseller* (London: n.p., 1790), 125–146, 167–238; Brewer, *Party Ideology and Popular Politics*, 48, 60–61, 167–172, 204, 215, 227.

11. Frederick S. Siebert, *Freedom of the Press in England: The Rise and Decline of Government Controls, 1476–1776* (Urbana: University of Illinois, 1952), 356–363; Arthur Aspinall, *Politics and the Press, c. 1780–1850* (London: Home and Van Thal, [1949]), 35–36.

12. *Aurora*, Feb. 7, 1800. Phillips suggests the connection to Pitt's prosecution of Almon in *William Duane*, 11–12, but although Almon was found guilty of libel and ordered to pay about £300 in damages, this was not a ruinous sum; see Almon, *Memoirs*, 125–146, 167–238; P. J. Marshall, "The British in Asia: Trade to Dominion, 1700–1765"; Rajat Kanta Ray, "Indian Society and the Establishment of British Supremacy, 1765–1818"; H. V. Bowen, "British India, 1765–1813: The Metropolitan Context," all in P. J. Marshall (ed.), *Oxford History of the British Empire: The Eighteenth Century* (Oxford: Oxford University Press, 1998), vol. 2.

13. *Aurora*, June 22, 1795; John Kelly [to Mathew Carey], Jan. 23, 1795, in Lea & Febiger Papers, HSP; *Aurora*, Sept. 23, 30, 1800; Phillips, *William Duane*, 12–15; Sunit Ghosh, *Modern History of the Indian Press* (New Delhi: Cosmo, 1998), 22–23; Mrinal Kanti Chandra, *A History of the British Press in Bengal, 1780–1857* (Calcutta: Bagchi, 1987), 11–12; *Aurora*, May 18, 1799; Y. J. Taraporewala (ed.), *Fort William–India House Correspondence*: vol. 17, 1792–1795 (Delhi: National Archives of India, 1955), 521, 402, 409; and Syed Hasan Askari (ed.), *Fort William–India House Correspondence*: vol. 16, 1787–1791 (Delhi: National Archives of India, 1976), lix, lx.

14. Askari (ed.), *Fort William–India House Correspondence*, vol. 16, 409; Taraporewala (ed.), *Fort William–India House Correspondence*, vol. 17, 32, 48–49; Ghosh, *Modern History of the Indian Press*, 22–23; Phillips, *William Duane*, 21–27; Chandra, *History of the British Press in*

Bengal, 23–24; Brijendra Mohan Sankhdher, *Press, Politics and Public Opinion in India* (New Delhi: Deep & Deep, 1984), 33–38.

15. Duane expressed the same desire to the Governor's Council, stating that he wished only to leave India and to "spend my life in my native country"; see William Duane, "Memorial," Aug. 26, 1795, in Duane Family Papers, APS; Sir John Shore to Henry Dundas, Mar. 10, Aug. 25, 1794, in Holden Furber (ed.), *The Private Record of an Indian Governor-Generalship: The Correspondence of Sir John Shore, Governor-General, with Henry Dundas, President of the Board of Control 1793–1798* (Cambridge, Mass.: Harvard University Press, 1933); Phillips, *William Duane*, 27–28; Ghosh, *Modern History of the Indian Press*, 23–24; Sankhdher, *Press, Politics and Public Opinion*, 38–42; Chandra, *History of the British Press in Bengal*, 23–24.

16. [William Duane] to I. E. Hay, [Dec. 1794]; Duane, "Memorial," Aug. 26, 1795, both in Duane Family Papers, APS; Sir John Shore to Henry Dundas, Dec. 31, 1794, in Furber (ed.), *Correspondence of Sir John Shore*; Phillips, *William Duane*, 29–31; Pasley, *Tyranny of Printers*, 179–180.

17. Duane, "Memorial," Aug. 26, 1795; E. Shaw to William Duane, [Dec. 30, 1794]; [Duane] to I. E. Hay, [Dec. 1794], all in Duane Family Papers, APS; Phillips, *William Duane*, 32–33; Duane, "Appeal to the Governor of St. Helena" [1795]; Duane to Governor of St. Helena [1795], both in Duane Family Papers, APS.

18. Thompson, *Making of the English Working Class*, 99, 102–185; Peter Linebaugh and Marcus Rediker, *The Many Headed Hydra: Sailors, Slaves, Commoners, and the Hidden History of the Revolutionary Atlantic* (Boston: Beacon, 2000), 239–354; Keane, *Tom Paine*, 308.

19. Paine, *Rights of Man* (1984), 262; Thompson, *Making of the English Working Class*, 93–94, 107–111; Keane, *Tom Paine*, 308–309; Paine to George Washington, July 21, 1791, in Foner (ed.), *Writings of Thomas Paine*; Robert Burns, "The Rights of Woman: An Occasional Address, Spoken by Miss Fontenelle on Her Benefit Night, Dumfries, Nov. 26, 1792," in *The Complete Poems & Songs of Robert Burns* (Glasgow: HarperCollins, 1995); Durey, *Transatlantic Radicals*, 47.

20. Thompson describes Paine's *Rights of Man* as the "foundation-text of the English working class movement." See Thompson, *Making of the English Working Class*, 90–94, chap. 1; [John Binns], *Recollections of the Life of John Binns: Twenty Nine Years in Europe and Fifty Three in the United States* (Philadelphia: n.p., 1854), 41–46. Binns estimated the membership of the LCS at 18–20,000 in 1795–1796, while the more moderate and cautious Francis Place estimated active membership at about 2,000. Thompson's estimate of about 10,000 seems plausible; see *Making of the English Working Class*, 152–154.

21. [Binns], *Recollections*, 196, 41–43; Durey, *Transatlantic Radicals*, 39.

22. For a list of Citizen Richard Lee's works, see *Account of the Proceedings of a Meeting of the People* (London: Printed for Citizen Richard Lee, at the Tree of Liberty, 1795). These included *The Happy Reign of George the Last: An Address to the Little Tradesmen and Labouring Poor of England, Citizen Guillotine; or, A Cure for the King's Evil, King Killing,* and *The Reign of the English Robespierre.* On Duane and Lee, see Twomey, "Jacobins and Jeffersonians," 24–27; [Binns], *Recollections*, 53–56; [Duane], *Biographical Memoir*, 4; Phillips, *William Duane*, 40–43; Thompson, *Making of the English Working Class*, 144–146; [Citizen Richard Lee], *The History of the Two Acts* (London: n.p., 1796), 15.

23. Thompson, *Making of the English Working Class*, 145–148; *Account of the Proceedings*; Phillips, *William Duane*, 43–44.

24. The first part of the *Age of Reason* was translated by Lanthenas from a manuscript that Paine gave to the American Joel Barlow before his arrest and was published as *Le Siècle de la Raison* in Paris in Jan. 1794. The first English edition was printed by the London radical printer Daniel Isaac Eaton in the spring of 1794. The second part of the *Age of Reason* was published in late 1795 at about the time Duane arrived back in England. Paine probably wrote part 2 in the house of James Monroe, the American ambassador to France; see Thomas Clio Rickman, *The Life of Thomas Paine* (London: n.p., 1819), 164; Moncur Conway, *Life of Thomas Paine* (New York: Putnam's, 1892), vol. 2, 208, 227; Paine to Samuel Adams, Jan. 1, 1803, in Foner (ed.), *Writings of*

Thomas Paine, 1434–1438; Paine, *Age of Reason*, parts 1 and 2, in Foner (ed.), *Writings of Thomas Paine*, 464, 497, 514. For Paine's use of Christianity in his earlier work, see *Common Sense* in Isaac Kramnick and Michael Foot (eds.), *Thomas Paine Reader* (Harmondsworth, England: Penguin, 1987), 73–75, 104; Paine, *Rights of Man* (1984), 87, 268–271; the quotation is from 268.

25. Paine, *Age of Reason*, in Foner (ed.), *Writings of Thomas Paine*, 512, 487, 464–466, 599–600.

26. Paine to Samuel Adams, Jan. 1, 1803; *Age of Reason*, part 2, 521; Paine to Gilbert Wakefield, Nov. 19, 1795, all in Foner (ed.), *Writings of Thomas Paine*; Richard Watson, *An Apology for the Bible in a Series of Letters, Addressed to Thomas Paine* (London: William Young, 1796), 3–4, 167, 130–131; W. H. Reid, *The Rise and Dissolution of the Infidel Societies in the Metropolis… from the Publication of Paine's Age of Reason till the Present Period* (London: n.p., 1800), 34, iii, 1–4, 9; Mary Thale (ed.), *The Autobiography of Francis Place* (Cambridge: Cambridge University Press, 1972), 126, 197 n; Thale (ed.), *Selections from the Papers of the London Corresponding Society, 1792–1799* (Cambridge: Cambridge University Press, 1983), 306–307 n.

27. Richard Brothers, *Revealed Knowledge of the Prophecies and Times* (London: n.p., 1794). On Brothers's influence, see Thompson, *Making of the English Working Class*, 117 and chap. 2, "Christian and Appollyon"; Bloch, *Visionary Republic*, 163–168; [Binns], *Recollections*, 48–50. On religion in the LCS, see Thale (ed.), *Autobiography of Francis Place*, 197–198; Thale (ed.), *LCS Papers*, 31 n, 306–312; Reid, *Infidel Societies*, 5–6. On Lee, see Durey, *Transatlantic Radicals*, 43. According to Gwyn Williams, the most striking feature of 1796–1797 was the growth of deism and free thought in British radical circles; see *Artisans and Sansculottes: Popular Movements in France and Britain during the French Revolution* (London: Edward Arnold, 1968), 109.

28. Reid, *Infidel Societies*, 10–12, 22–25.

29. Clark, "William Duane," 21; Phillips, *William Duane*, 46–47; *Aurora*, July 22, 1796, May 18, 1799. On Lloyd, see Marion Tinling, "Thomas Lloyd's Reports of the First Federal Congress," *William and Mary Quarterly*, 3rd ser., 18, no. 4 (Oct. 1961): 519–545; Durey, *Transatlantic Radicals*, 182; Twomey, "Jacobins and Jeffersonians," 44–46. Duane and Lloyd were part of an exodus of British radicals in the 1790s that helped to transform the character of American political life; see Durey, *Transatlantic Radicals*, 220–288; Durey, "Thomas Paine's Apostles," 661–688; Durey, "Transatlantic Patriotism"; Twomey, "Jacobins and Jeffersonians."

30. *Aurora*, June 22, 1795. This was an extract of a letter from John Kelly to Mathew Carey, Jan. 23, 1795, in Lea & Febiger Papers, HSP, and must have been passed along from Carey to Bache. For other signs of his connection to Bache, see *Aurora*, Jan. 20, 23, Mar. 9, Aug. 8, 1796. Duane's work for Stewart was eventually published as part of John Gifford, *The History of France, from the Earliest Times till the Death of Louis Sixteenth… and Continued from the Above Period until the Conclusion of the Present War: By a Citizen of the United States* (Philadelphia: John Stewart, 1796–1798), 4 vols. Later, it was published separately as William Duane, *A History of the French Revolution from Its Commencement to the Complete Establishment of the Republic* (Philadelphia: Stewart & Rowson, 1798). Also see "Diary of William Wood Thackara, 1791–1815," in Diaries and Letterbooks, HSP; Carey, *Autobiographical Sketches* (Rpr., New York: Arno, 1970), 39.

31. Washington's Farewell Address was issued on Sept. 17, 1796, and published in the *Aurora* on Sept. 20, 21, 1796. Duane's response appeared two months later as Jasper Dwight of Vermont, *A Letter to George Washington*. The pamphlet was advertised in the *Aurora* on Dec. 6, 1796, for twenty-five cents, and although Bache printed it, he kept his name off the title page.

32. [Duane], *Letter to George Washington*, 17–22, 32, 443–444.

33. New York *Time-Piece*, Mar. 22, 1797; [Thomas Williams], *The Age of Infidelity: In Answer to Thomas Paine's Age of Reason* (Boston: Manning and Loring, 1794); Gilbert Wakefield, *An Examination of the Age of Reason* (Boston: David West, 1794); Jeremy Belknap, *Dissertations on the Age of Reason* (Boston: Joseph Belknap, 1795); Elhanan Winchester, *Ten Letters Addressed to Mr. Paine* (New York: Samuel Campbell, 1795); Hannah More, *An Estimate of the Religion of the Fashionable World* (Philadelphia: William Young, 1795); Watson, *An Apology for the Bible*; Joseph Priestley, *An Answer to Mr. Paine's Age of Reason Being a Continuation of Letters to the*

Philosophers and Politicians of France (Northumberland, England: n.p., 1794); Elias Boudinot, *The Age of Revelation; or, The Age of Reason Shown to Be an Age of Infidelity* (Philadelphia: Asbury Dickens, 1801). My estimate is drawn from a review of Charles Evans (ed.), *American Bibliography* (New York: P. Smith, 1941–1959). This review did not include sermons and other less easily identifiable pamphlets on Paine's work and excluded material published in the periodical press.

34. Nine American editions of part 1 were published in 1794 and six more in 1795; see Evans (ed.), *American Bibliography*. Part 2 was published in 1796 by Bache; see *Aurora*, Jan. 20, Apr. 7, 1796. On the impact of the *Age of Reason* in the United States, see May, *Enlightenment in America*, 174–176, 184, 226, 233–234, 263–264; Herbert M. Morais, *Deism in Eighteenth-Century America* (New York: Russell & Russell, 1960), 168–169.

35. Thomas Paine, *Age of Reason: Part the Second* (Philadelphia: B. F. Bache, 1795); *GA*, May 28, 1794; *Aurora*, Jan. 20, Apr. 7, 1796; *Political Censor* (May 1796); May, *Enlightenment in America*, 232. Palmer's keenest supporters were drawn from the ranks of the British and Irish radical exiles who brought their deist beliefs with them to the United States, men like James Cheetham, later the editor of the New York *American Citizen*, who, according to Richard Twomey, as a member of the Manchester Corresponding Society had rushed "from tavern to tavern and from brothel to brothel with the *Rights of Man* in one hand and *Age of Reason* in the other"; Twomey, "Jacobins and Jeffersonians," 29–30; Durey, *Transatlantic Radicals*, 195–196; Sean Wilentz, *Chants Democratic: New York City & the Rise of the American Working Class, 1788–1850* (New York: Oxford University Press, 1984), 77–79; Roderick S. French, "Elihu Palmer, Radical Deist, Radical Republican: A Reconsideration of American Freethought," *Studies in Eighteenth-Century Culture*, no. 8 (1979): 87–108; Eric Foner, *Tom Paine and Revolutionary America* (New York: Oxford University Press, 1976), 258–259.

36. Ebeneezer Bradford, *Mr. Thomas Paine's Trial* (Boston: Isaiah Thomas, 1795), quoted in May, *Enlightenment in America*, 264; New York *Argus*, Mar. 1, June 6, 7, 1798. Even Bache didn't reprint the *Age of Reason* in the *Aurora*, and although James Carey included it in an edition of Paine's writings published in 1797, he also included an antidote, Watson's *Apology for the Bible*; see *Aurora*, Sept. 8, 22, 1796, Jan. 5, 6, 1797. When Dennis Driscoll began to publish the *Temple of Reason* in 1800, his feisty attacks on Christianity weren't appreciated by fellow Republicans (including Duane) who were struggling to establish the Christian credentials of their presidential candidate, Thomas Jefferson; see Durey, *Transatlantic Radicals*, 195–196; Twomey, "Jacobins and Jeffersonians," 73.

37. Nash, "American Clergy and the French Revolution"; Davis, "American Equality," 739–743. Views like this were typical of the "francophilic millennialism" that dominated American religion during this period; see Bloch, *Visionary Republic*, chap. 7; May, *Enlightenment in America*, 264–265.

38. One violent exception was the Reverend David Osgood who, in a controversial Thanksgiving Day sermon in 1794, denounced the French Revolution and "those excesses and cruelties which chill all humane minds with horror." See David Osgood, *The Wonderful Works of God Are to Be Remembered: A Sermon Delivered on the Day of Annual Thanksgiving, November 20, 1794* (Boston: Samuel Hall, 1794); Nash, "American Clergy and the French Revolution," 393.

39. Fisher Ames to Christopher Gore, quoted in May, *Enlightenment in America*, 258; *Aurora*, Sept. 23, 1796.

40. *GUS*, May 2, 1792.

41. The phrase "Citizen Ego" was used by the Washington *Federalist* in 1802; see Constance B. Schulz, "'Of Bigotry in Politics and Religion': Jefferson's Religion, the Federalist Press, and the Syllabus," *Virginia Magazine of History and Biography* 91, no. 1 (1983): 79. Even Christian radicals like Joseph Priestley made this point. Because deism or natural religion, argued Priestley, could offer no proof for the existence of an afterlife, its adherents were free to abandon themselves "without restraint to sensual gratifications" and the indulgence of the "natural passions." The

only rational basis for their conduct was present rather than future happiness, and "to this they will, and must refer everything; and their love of others, of their country, and of mankind, will be no farther regarded by them than as it tends to their own happiness"; Priestley, *Observations on the Increase of Infidelity* (Philadelphia: n.p., 1797), 16–17.

42. *Aurora*, May 3, 1799. For Duane's response to Green's sermon, see *Aurora*, May 7, 11, 1799.

43. *DA*, Apr. 20, 1797. One writer called the press the "priesthood of liberty"; *AM*, Feb. 24, 1794. For an excellent discussion of this issue, see Grasso, *A Speaking Aristocracy*, 285–460.

44. Phillips, *William Duane*, 52–58; Durey, *Transatlantic Radicals*, 181–182, 247, 682–683; *Merchant's Daily Advertiser*, July 24, 1797; *Carey's Daily Advertiser*, July 24, 1797; *DA*, Feb. 7, 8, 1797. For a hilarious account of this by William Cobbett, see *PG*, July 21, 1797. On the expiration of the *Daily Advertiser*, see *PG*, Sept. 14, 1797; Duane to [James] Thackera, June 5, 7, 1797 (Duane Family Papers, APS). As Callender later complained to Jefferson, he and Bache had fallen out over poor treatment and the censorship of his work; see Callender to Thomas Jefferson, Sept. 22, Oct. 26, 1798, in Barbara Oberg (ed.), *The Papers of Thomas Jefferson* (Princeton, N.J.: Princeton University Press, 2003), vol. 30. Duane continued this vendetta and refused to republish articles from Callender's Richmond *Examiner* in the *Aurora*; see Callender to Jefferson, Aug. 10, 1799, in Oberg (ed.), *TJP*, vol. 31.

45. *Carey's Daily Advertiser*, July 24, 1797; Fisher Ames to Timothy Pickering, June 4, 1798, quoted in Warren, *Jacobin and Junto*, 74. On the conflict with France, see Alexander DeConde, *The Quasi-War: The Politics and Diplomacy of the Undeclared War with France, 1797–1801* (New York: Scribner's, 1966).

46. *Aurora*, Aug. 1, 1798.

47. Theodore Sedgwick to Henry Van Schaack, Apr. 21, 1798, in Sedgwick Papers, MHS; *Aurora*, June 5, Aug. 23, Mar. 12, 30, Apr. 10–11, 1798; *GUS*, Apr. 10, 1798; *Aurora*, May 29, June 7, 1798.

48. *Aurora*, May 2–12, June 16, 25–30, Aug. 10–11, 23, Sept. 4, 7, 1798. In his last moments, he dictated a confidential memorandum to Tench Coxe, asking him to ensure the survival of the *Aurora*; see Coxe to Margaret Bache, Sept. 13, 1798, in Coxe Papers, HSP; William Duane to Richard Bache, Sept. 11, 1798 (Duane Family Papers, APS). Although Duane later claimed that Bache appointed him as editor in his will, Bache's will did not mention him becoming the editor of the newspaper; see *Aurora*, May 12, 1800.

49. New York *Argus*, June 23, 26, Aug. 1, 1798; *Aurora*, May 2, 9, 14, 1798.

50. *Aurora*, Aug. 1, 1798; New York *Argus*, Dec. 6, 1798.

51. New York *Argus*, Aug. 3, 6, 1798; *Aurora*, Apr. 30, Aug. 27, 1798.

52. *Aurora*, July 21, Aug. 22, 23, 1798.

53. *GUS*, Aug. 2, 1798; *Aurora*, Aug. 13, July 21, 18, 1798. One interesting sign of this new political strategy was the republication of an essay entitled "The Union: Who Are Its Real Friends?" from Freneau's *National Gazette*.

54. The *Aurora* remained under the nominal direction of Margaret Bache; see Duane [to Tench Coxe], n.d., Duane to Coxe, Oct. 15, 1798, Duane [to Coxe], Sept. 14, 28, 1798, all in Tench Coxe Papers, HSP. For Coxe's role in the newspaper, see Jacob Cooke, *Tench Coxe and the Early Republic* (Chapel Hill: University of North Carolina Press, 1978), 345.

55. *Aurora*, July 6, 1797.

56. The phrase "Order and Good Government" appeared in an editorial in the *Aurora* on Apr. 24, 1799; also see William Duane, *A Report of the Extraordinary Transactions Which Took Place at Philadelphia, in February 1799* (Philadelphia: Office of the Aurora, 1799); *Aurora*, Feb. 22, 1799; Phillips, *William Duane*, 66–70; Clark, "William Duane," 26; *PG*, Feb. 12, 14, 1799; Carey, *Autobiography*, 39–40; Durey, *Transatlantic Radicals*, 253; Wharton (ed.), *State Trials of the United States*. The petition reminded John Adams of his own "Address to the People of Ireland" in 1775, which asked the Irish to support the American struggle against British imperialism; see David Wilson, *United Irishmen, United States: Immigrant Radicals in the Early Republic* (Ithaca, N.Y.: Cornell University Press, 1998), 47–55.

57. Duane, *Extraordinary Transactions*, 41; *GUS*, Feb. 11, 1799.

58. *Aurora*, Feb. 22, 1799.

59. See the extract from *Porcupine's Gazette* in the *Aurora*, Feb. 22, 1799. Not all Federalists were so gloomy. Theodore Sedgwick thought that the Federalists were still in a strong political position and but for the "*faux pas* of the great man we should have hardly anything to regret." And he may have been right. Despite public controversy about the Alien and Sedition Acts, Republicans actually lost ground in the congressional elections of 1798–1799, especially in the South; see Sedgwick to Henry Van Schaack, Mar. 4, 1799, in Sedgwick Papers, MHS; Cunningham, *Jeffersonian Republicans*, 134.

60. *GUS*, Mar. 4, 1799. Duane published the essay in the *Aurora* on Mar. 5, 1799, and it was later published as a full-length pamphlet, [John Ward Fenno], *Desultory Reflections on the New Political Aspects of Public Affairs in the United States of America* (New York: n.p., 1800). In *The Revolution of American Conservatism*, David Hackett Fischer argues that younger Federalists adapted better to democratic politics than did their elders, but the violent Anglophilia and anti-democratic rantings of John Ward Fenno suggest that the opposite may also have been true; see, for example, the circle around Joseph Dennie (another admirer of Cobbett) and the *Port Folio*; Kerber, *Federalists in Dissent*; Kaplan, *Men of Letters*; and William C. Dowling, *Literary Federalism in the Age of Jefferson: Joseph Dennie and the Port Folio, 1801–1812* (Columbia: University of South Carolina Press, 1999).

61. [John Ward Fenno], *Desultory Reflections*.

62. *Aurora*, Feb. 20–21, Apr. 10, Mar. 6–13, 1799.

63. *Minutes of Examination, Taken in Short Notes—on the Trial of the Rioters for a Riot and Assault on William Duane* (Philadelphia: n.p., 1799); *Aurora*, May 16–18, 1799; Duane to Stephen R. Bradley, Nov. 10, 1808, in Clark, "William Duane," 58, 26–27; Phillips, *William Duane*, 70–71; [Duane], *Biographical Memoir*, 7; Durey, *Transatlantic Radicals*, 255.

64. *GUS*, May 16, 1799; *Aurora*, May 17, 21, 23, 1799.

65. *GUS*, May 23, 1799; *Aurora*, July 4–5, 1799, Apr. 22, May 3, June 14, 1800; Duane to Ephraim Kirby, July 3, 1800, in Kirby Papers, Duke University Library; *PG*, July 9, 1799; Phillips, *William Duane*, 75–76; Wilson, *United Irishmen*, 55.

66. *Aurora*, May 16, July 31, Oct. 11, 22, Sept. 21, 1799; Phillips, *William Duane*, 77–83; Timothy Pickering to John Adams, July 24, 1799; Adams to Pickering, Aug. 1, 1799, both in Adams (ed.), *Works of John Adams*, vol. 9, 4–5.

67. James Thomson Callender to Thomas Jefferson, Nov. 19, 1798, in Oberg (ed.), *TJP*, vol. 30; *PG*, Apr. 20, July 11, 1797; *GUS*, Nov. 12, 26, Dec. 4, 18, 20, 1798.

68. Roberts and Roberts, *Moreau de St. Mery's American Journey*, 211; [Cobbett], *A Kick for a Bite*; [Cobbett], *Part II. A Bone to Gnaw*; Cobbett, *Detection of a Conspiracy Formed by the United Irishmen* (Philadelphia: William Cobbett, 1798); Wilson, *United Irishmen*, 43–53; Durey, *Transatlantic Radicals*, 250–251; Edward C. Carter III, "A Wild Irishman under Every Federalist's Bed: Naturalization in Philadelphia, 1789–1806," *Pennsylvania Magazine of History and Biography* 94, no. 3 (1970): 331–346.

69. *Aurora*, Nov. 5, 8, 14, 1798, May 18, 1799. Duane also quietly dropped Margaret Bache's name from the masthead of the newspaper and replaced her name with "Published for the Heirs of Benjamin Franklin Bache"; see *Aurora*, Nov. 14, 1798.

70. *Aurora*, Jan. 23, Feb. 9, Apr. 19, 21, 26, 30, May 1, 4, 22, 28, July 16–17, 26, 30, Aug. 6, 13–14, Sept. 6, 9, 10, 1799. Duane was not the first to exploit Cobbett's alien status. Writing in the *Aurora* in May 1798, "Humanitas" attacked foreigners for stirring up trouble in Philadelphia and singled Cobbett out for his advocacy of the black cockade; *Aurora*, May 14, 1798. Noah Webster had also been attacking Cobbett's alien influence for some time, and James Carey's *Daily Advertiser*, which Duane had worked for in 1797, constantly attacked Cobbett as a "foreigner" and the "hireling of a British Ministry"; *Carey's Daily Advertiser*, May 3, 1797. Cobbett attacked this "distinction between foreigners and Americans," asserting the right of foreigners to free

speech and liberty of the press; see [Cobbett], *Life and Adventures of Peter Porcupine*, 54; and *Political Censor* (Sept. 1796), 57–61. His support for the Alien and Sedition Acts, of course, puts these statements in their proper political perspective.

71. *Aurora*, Oct. 7, 22, 23, 1799.

72. *Aurora*, Nov. 23, Sept. 21, 1799.

73. The address was signed by Alexander James Dallas, Tench Coxe, Michael Leib, and Peter Muhlenberg; see *Aurora*, Sept. 24, 27, Oct. 5, 1799.

74. *Aurora*, Oct. 18, Dec. 28, 1799.

75. Jedediah Morse, *A Sermon: Delivered at the New North Church in Boston...May 9th, 1798* (Boston: n.p., 1798), 21–25; Vernon Stauffer, *New England and the Bavarian Illuminati* (New York: Russell & Russell, 1918), 235–237. One of the stranger episodes of the 1790s, the Illuminati controversy had great influence in New England, where it became a focus for some of the central religious and political issues of the day. The Order of the Bavarian Illuminati was a Masonic organization founded in Bavaria in 1776 and later suppressed by authorities for its radical views. According to John Robison, author of *Proofs of a Conspiracy against All Religions and Governments of Europe, Carried on in the Secret Meetings of the Free Masons, Illuminati, and Reading Societies* (Philadelphia: T. Dobson for W. Cobbett, 1798), this secret organization spread its "detestable doctrines" of atheism, republicanism, and libertinism through Masonic lodges that were dedicated to "ROOTING OUT ALL THE RELIGIOUS ESTABLISHMENTS, AND OVERTURNING ALL THE EXISTING GOVERNMENTS OF EUROPE." According to Robison, they had played a leading role in the French Revolution. Morse was careful not to imply that American Masonic lodges had been taken over by the Illuminati, but his attack reawakened anxiety about the danger of "self-created societies," echoed Cobbett's simultaneous campaign against the United Irishmen, and played on real concerns about the religious heterodoxy, secrecy, and exclusivity of Masonic societies, especially in a country like the United States, where transparency and inclusivity were becoming the hallmarks of a new democratic political culture. As Alan Taylor points out, the politics of anti-Masonry had popular resonance in a frontier society where Masonic organizations were closely identified with an acquisitive and commercially successful middle class; see Taylor, *William Cooper's Town: Power and Persuasion on the Frontier of the Early American Republic* (New York: Knopf, 1995), 210–213, 262–277; and, more generally, Stephen Bullock, *Freemasonry and the Transformation of the American Social Order, 1730–1840* (Chapel Hill: University of North Carolina Press, 1996), esp. chap. 5.

76. Timothy Dwight, *The Duty of Americans, at the Present Crisis, Illustrated in a Discourse, Preached on the Fourth of July, 1798* (New Haven, Conn.: Thomas and Samuel Green, 1798). Dwight's oration was delivered at the meeting house in New Haven before a large crowd of clergymen, university members, and "respectable inhabitants," including Noah Webster, who also delivered an oration; see Stauffer, *New England and the Bavarian Illuminati*, 238–246, 252–260. For a discussion of Dwight's place in the religious and print culture of late eighteenth-century Connecticut, see Grasso, *A Speaking Aristocracy*, chap. 7.

77. Dwight, *Duty of Americans*; Timothy Dwight, *The Triumph of Infidelity: A Poem* ("Printed in the World," 1788). Dwight was also responsible for introducing Americans to another advocate of the European counterrevolution, the Abbe Barruel, a French Jesuit who also blamed the French Revolution on a secret "ANTICHRISTIAN CONSPIRACY" organized through the Masonic societies. Morse used Barruel to support his claim that the Illuminati had already established themselves in the United States; see Abbe Barruel, *Memoirs of the History of Jacobinism* (London: n.p., 1797–1798), 4 vols. (first published as *Memoires pour servir a l'histoire du Jacobinisme*), xiv–xv, 493–551; Stauffer, *New England and the Bavarian Illuminati*, 214–228.

78. Jonathan Sassi, *The Republic of Righteousness: The Public Christianity of the Post-Revolutionary New England Clergy* (New York: Oxford University Press, 2001), 3–83; Waldstreicher, *In the Midst of Perpetual Fetes*, 145–155; Grasso, *A Speaking Aristocracy*, 351–374. As Grasso argues, by the end of the eighteenth century, clergymen like Morse and Dwight were on

the defensive even in pious New England. Once part of a "speaking aristocracy" that dominated American life, the clergy were being challenged by new claimants to public attention, especially newspaper editors. As influence shifted from the pulpit to the press, and from speech to print culture, clergymen tried to reassert their former authority by participating more actively in print culture and disseminating their views to a growing reading public. At stake here was a larger issue of control over what Grasso calls "meaning and moral order." To earlier Americans, it seemed self-evident that men of religious leaning and piety should act as arbiters of public meaning, but such faith in the disinterested mediation of elite men had dissipated by the end of the century, and the right of the clergy to speak on public affairs was coming under strong public attack. Grasso, *A Speaking Aristocracy*, 1–23.

79. Theodore Dwight, *An Oration Spoken at Hartford, in the State of Connecticut, on the Anniversary of American Independence, July 4th, 1798* (Hartford, Conn.: n.p., 1798); Stauffer, *New England and the Bavarian Illuminati*, 253–254, 283, 273; Warren, *Jacobin and Junto*, 293; William Linn, *Serious Considerations on the Election of the President* (New York: John Furman, 1800). According to Noble Cunningham, "few issues in the campaign provoked a wider hearing"; Cunningham, *Jeffersonian Republicans*, 227.

80. "As to the calumny of Atheism," Jefferson wrote in May 1800, "I am so broken to calumnies of every kind…that I entirely disregard it." Jefferson to Monroe, May 26, 1800, in Oberg (ed.), *TJP*, vol. 32; *Aurora*, Sept. 1, Oct. 14, 1800.

81. *Aurora*, Oct. 27, Nov. 11, 13–14, 1800.

82. *Aurora*, Nov. 14, 1800. One sign of this was the endless Republican assertions that Jefferson believed in God, as of course did all deists, including the notorious infidel Thomas Paine.

83. *Aurora*, July 25, 1798, Feb. 5, 1799; [John Cosens Ogden], *A View of the Calvinistic Clubs in the United States* (Litchfield, Conn.: Thomas Collier, 1799). For Duane's campaign, see Alan V. Briceland, "The Philadelphia *Aurora*, the New England Illuminati, and the Election of 1800," *Pennsylvania Magazine of History and Biography* 100, no. 1 (Jan. 1976): 3–36.

84. [John Cosens Ogden], *A View of the New England Illuminati Who Are Indefatigably Engaged in Destroying the Religion and Government of the United States under a Feigned Regard for Their Safety—and under an Impious Abuse of True Religion* (Philadelphia: James Carey, 1799); *Aurora*, Nov. 6, 1799, July 11, Aug. 1, 1800; [Philip Freneau], *Letters on Various Interesting and Important Subjects: By Robert Slender, O. S. M.* (Philadelphia: D. Hogan, 1799), 72. Ogden had earlier published an attack on Dwight and the Connecticut standing order; see *An Appeal to the Candid, upon the Present State of Religion and Politics in Connecticut* [New Haven, Conn.: 1798?]; see Grasso, *A Speaking Aristocracy*, 377–381.

85. *Aurora*, Sept. 2, 16, 24, Oct. 1, 5, 8, 19, 1799.

86. *Aurora*, Mar. 31, Apr. 9–10, 17, 21, Aug. 22–23, Sept. 2, 6, 11–12, Dec. 27, 1800.

87. Jefferson to Joseph Priestley, Mar. 21, 1801, in Oberg (ed.), *TJP*, vol. 33; John Adams to Benjamin Rush, June 12, 1812, in John Schutz and Douglas Adair (eds.), *The Spur of Fame: Dialogues of John Adams and Benjamin Rush, 1805–1813* (San Marino, Calif.: Huntington Library, 1966).

88. John Adams to Benjamin Stoddert, Mar. 31, 1801, in Adams (ed.), *Works of John Adams*, vol. 9, 582; *Aurora*, Dec. 6, 1800, Jan. 1, 1801. See also Duane's discussion of political character in the *Aurora*, Aug. 21, 28, Oct. 25, 27, 29, Nov. 3, 1800.

89. *Aurora*, Dec. 17, 15, 1800, Jan. 3, Feb. 20, 1801; Jefferson to Joseph Priestley, Mar. 21, 1801, in Oberg (ed.), *TJP*, vol. 33.

Conclusion

1. Thomas Jefferson, "First Inaugural Address," in Merrill D. Peterson (ed.), *The Portable Thomas Jefferson* (Harmondsworth, England: Penguin, 1975). For an interesting discussion of antipartisanship as a disguise for the "worst kinds of partisan cant," see Waldstreicher, *In the Midst of Perpetual Fetes*, 201–207.

2. While it is true that Jefferson's famous assessment of the election of 1800 was not delivered until almost twenty years after the event, as we have seen already Republicans at the time also invested the election with millennial significance; see Thomas Jefferson to Spencer Roane, Sept. 6, 1819, in Andrew A. Lipscomb and Albert E. Bergh (eds.), *The Writings of Thomas Jefferson* (Washington, D.C.: Thomas Jefferson Memorial Association, 1903), vol. 15, 212. For a discussion of the phrase "revolution of 1800" and the historiographical tradition it represents, which is somewhat different from mine, see Daniel Sisson's *The Revolution of 1800* (New York: Knopf, 1974), 3–22. For a more recent recapitulation of this interpretive tradition, see John Ferling, *Adams vs. Jefferson: The Tumultuous Election of 1800* (New York: Oxford University Press, 2004); and Susan Dunn, *Jefferson's Second Revolution: The Election Crisis of 1800 and the Triumph of Republicanism* (New York: Houghton Mifflin, 2004).

3. The most important aspect of this conservatism was the exclusion of women and African Americans from public life, an exclusion that represented a significant ideological retreat from the 1790s. Most discussions of the revolution of 1800 still ignore these inconvenient truths. In this respect, it might be fruitful to explore Benedict Anderson's suggestion that New World nationalism was not driven by the entry of the lower classes into political life, as in Europe, but by the fears of largely agrarian slaveholders about Indian uprisings and slave revolts in a liberalizing imperial system; Anderson, *Imagined Communities*, 48–49.

4. For a good discussion of this conservative shift, see Cotlar, "In Paine's Absence," 66–120; and Cotlar, "Federalists' Transatlantic Cultural Offensive." Waldstreicher also suggests a narrowing in the range of political discourse after 1800 and remarks, "partisan practice clarified the meanings and goals of nationalism, but not without ultimately narrowing the political"; Waldstreicher, *In the Midst of Perpetual Fetes*, 244, chap. 4. This conservative shift began well before 1800, and nothing illustrates it better than public debates about nationalism and personal character. As Waldstreicher recognizes, although ideas about nationalism are always contested, the nation is not just a subject of contestation, an old wine bottle into which new ideological content can be poured. Nationalism also has a form and politics of its own, a point that Seth Cotlar makes clear in his work on popular cosmopolitanism and internationalism in the 1790s. Inspired by the French Revolution and Thomas Paine's *Rights of Man*, many Americans in the 1790s saw themselves not only as Americans but also as "citizens of the world." Cotlar's work rightly emphasizes the extraordinary openness to ideas about women's equality and the equality of nonwhites, for example, that characterized the cosmopolitan radicalism of the 1790s. As he points out, the partisan struggle to appropriate the mantle of American nationalism intensified just as Jeffersonian radicals abandoned popular cosmopolitanism in the late 1790s, signaling a sharp and decisive conservative turn in the political culture, a shift borne out by my analysis of Republican political rhetoric and Duane's role in the elections of 1800. Waldstreicher makes the same point, identifying 1793 as a critical turning point, after which Republicans began to fold American nationalism into their own partisan cause. The fierce public debate about American nationalism, in other words, was partly predicated on a retreat from the politics of internationalism inspired by Paine, a retreat that left the country more insular and parochial in its political sympathies and ideas.

5. See Waldstreicher's comment that "it is easy to forget that the reactionary nationalism of 1798 succeeded less through legal fiat or disembodied fear than through mobilizing people"; Waldstreicher, *In the Midst of Perpetual Fetes*, 172, 155–173.

6. For a full account of the background to the Sedition Act and its subsequent history, see Smith, *Freedom's Fetters*; James Morton Smith, "The Sedition Law, Free Speech, and the American Political Process," *WMQ* 9, no. 4 (Oct. 1952): 497–511; Miller, *Crisis in Freedom*; Buel, "Freedom of the Press"; Levy, *Emergence of a Free Press*; Rosenberg, *Protecting the Best Men*.

7. James Morton Smith's *Freedom's Fetters* is still the most authoritative and influential work to date on the Alien and Sedition Acts. Writing from the perspective of the early 1950s, Smith was deeply influenced by the repressive climate created by McCarthyism and the hearings

of the House Un-American Activities Committee, and he interpreted the Sedition Act as an early manifestation of the same political paranoia and intolerance. In his view, the Alien and Sedition Acts were a panic-stricken attempt by Federalists to check the inexorable growth of popular support for the Republicans and a systematic effort to silence Republican editors by subjecting them to an anticonstitutional, anti-republican doctrine of seditious libel derived from the English common law. Smith's interpretation of the act has proved to be remarkably tenacious. Whether viewed as an aberration in a robust libertarian tradition or as the last gasp of an older legacy of suppression, most historians have accepted Smith's verdict on the act, a verdict that bears a close resemblance to Republican verdicts at the time.

8. However politically inept, the act represented an attempt to frame a law of seditious libel suitable for a republican form of government and was not, as James Morton Smith argued, a restatement of William Blackstone's doctrine of seditious libel. Indeed, the Sedition Act marked an emphatic break with Blackstone's understanding of libel law, and its relationship to English common law was quite complex. In the first place, it is important to distinguish between Blackstone's *Commentaries* and the practice of English common law. As I have argued, English libel law was more complicated and less repressive in practice than it was in theory. Moreover, this law was radically transformed by the passage of Charles James Fox's celebrated Libel Act in 1792. This act, which gave the truth defense statutory definition for the first time and expanded the power of the jury to rule on the question of libel, was the true model for the Sedition Act, not the repressive British Sedition Act of 1795; see Smith, *Freedom's Fetters*, 147; Smith, "Sedition Law," 499, 506. Manning Dauer mistakenly compares the Sedition Act to its British namesake in *The Adams Federalists* (Baltimore, Md.: Johns Hopkins University Press, 1953), 157–159.

9. See Walter Berns, "Freedom of the Press and the Alien and Sedition Laws: A Reappraisal," in Philip B. Kurland (ed.), *The Supreme Court Review 1970* (Chicago: University of Chicago Press, 1970), 111–121; Buel, "Freedom of the Press," 87–88; Dallas (ed.), *Reports*, 467–476; Rowe, *Thomas McKean*, 293; Levy, *Emergence of a Free Press*, 213.

10. James Sullivan, *Dissertation on the Constitutional Freedom of the Press* (Boston: n.p., 1801); Buel, "Freedom of the Press," 86; Mathew Carey, *The Olive Branch* (1814), cited in Warren, *Jacobin and Junto*, 113; Thomas Cooper, *A Treatise on Libel and the Liberty of the Press* (New York: n.p., 1830), 109; "Harry Croswell v. People of New York State" (1804), cited in Berns, "Freedom of the Press," 151–158.

11. Far from silencing the Republican press, the prosecution of Republican journalists in 1798–1799 sparked a dramatic resurgence of opposition throughout the country, symbolized by the Virginia and Kentucky resolutions, and galvanized public support for the Republican Party and Thomas Jefferson in the elections of 1800; see Pasley, *Tyranny of Printers*, chap. 5. To project Jefferson's subsequent electoral victory back into the events of the late 1790s seriously distorts our perception and understanding of events.

12. Miller, *Brief Retrospect*, vol. 2, 254. For American attitudes toward the legitimacy of political parties and political opposition, see Richard Hofstadter, *The Idea of a Party System: The Rise of Legitimate Opposition in the United States, 1780–1840* (Berkeley: University of California Press, 1969); Pocock, *The Machiavellian Moment*; Banning, *Jeffersonian Persuasion*; Murrin, "The Great Inversion," in Pocock (ed.), *Three British Revolutions*.

13. This notion of political legitimacy informed Federalist attacks on the Democratic Republican societies in the mid-1790s. The political character of these self-constituted societies was viewed as a direct challenge to the properly constituted authority of the federal government; see Link, *Democratic-Republican Societies*, chap. 8.

14. After the trial of John Peter Zenger in 1735, seditious libel was dealt with primarily by legislatures as a breach of legislative privilege or contempt, and printers were called before the bar of the legislative body to answer for "affronts" and "indignities." The chief legal threat to colonial printers after 1735 came from the popular branches of colonial government. Richard Buel believes that prosecutions by the lower houses of the assembly and arguments for the legal

restraint of press licentiousness had considerable popular support. See Buel, "Freedom of the Press," 74; and Nelson, "Seditious Libel," 163–172.

15. Buel, "Freedom of the Press," 63.

16. Austin, *Constitutional Republicanism*, 3–6.

17. Miller, *Brief Retrospect*, vol. 2, 253–255; New York *Time-Piece*, Aug. 11, 1797; Keane, *Tom Paine*, 468–469. For Republican efforts to prosecute Federalist journalists for libel after 1800, see Pasley, *Tyranny of Printers*, chap. 11. Pasley tries to refute the argument that "Republicans and Federalists allegedly exchanged positions on press freedom" (449n46)—unsuccessfully in my view.

18. Pasley, *Tyranny of Printers*, 188, 286–299.

19. *Aurora*, May 12, Aug. 8, Dec. 20, 1800; Duane to Ephraim Kirby, July 3, 1800, in Kirby Papers, Duke University Library; *GUS*, Feb. 16, 1801.

20. In what must have been an irritation to Duane, Smith advertised the *National Intelligencer and Washington Advertiser* in the *Aurora*, Aug. 31, 1800, as "a Newspaper conducted on national principles." In their emphasis on national rather than republican principles, Smith's proposals were strikingly similar to those published by John Fenno in the *Gazette of the United States* in 1789 and a stark contrast to the proposals for the short-lived *National Magazine*, which was edited by Duane's fellow radical James Lyons in Richmond, Virginia, in 1799–1800, and which was designed to "Ellect, preserve, and disseminate the most valuable productions of the Republican pen, in all parts of the Union." Lyons also denounced the "pretended impartiality of Printers" as a "delusion" and announced his refusal to avoid issues of private character: "It is difficult in pursuing a course of scrutiny into the measures of the government and designs of men in office, to draw a line of demarkation between legal plunder and personal villainy, public rapine, and private intrigue; whenever the nature of inquiry will admit of it, personal weakness and folly ought to be lightly touched, but when an officer of government, connecting public fraud with private vice, at the same time, is wallowing in the lap of infamy and reveling in the peculation of the national treasury, the regard for personal character ought to be sacrificed to public justice." See *Aurora*, May 4, 1799. For the *National Intelligencer*, see William Ames, *A History of the "National Intelligencer"* (Chapel Hill: University of North Carolina Press, 1972), 1–67; Frank Luther Mott, *Jefferson and the Press* (Baton Rouge: Louisiana State University Press, 1943), 47–88; Gailard Hunt (ed.), *The First Forty Years of Washington Society, Portrayed by the Family Letters of Mrs. Samuel Harrison Smith* (New York: Scribner's, 1906), 9. Smith had previously edited the *New World; or, the Morning and Evening Gazette* (1796–1797) and the *Universal Gazette* (1797–1800) in Philadelphia, was a graduate of the University of Pennsylvania, and was a former secretary of the American Philosophical Society. Widely regarded as a "gentleman, and a scholar," he was not well regarded as a newspaper editor, and battle-hardened radicals like James Thomson Callender referred to him as "Miss Smith"; see Durey, *Transatlantic Radicals*, 265; Phillips, *William Duane*, 101.

21. Jefferson's reluctance to aid Duane was not entirely personal; other stalwart Republican editors, like Charles Holt, were also passed over for government patronage, and newspaper editors were generally excluded from government office, even "their traditional niche in the postal service"; see Pasley, *Tyranny of Printers*, 297–298. Duane's situation failed to improve after 1801, and by the end of Jefferson's first term, he had lost all of his official patronage and a considerable amount of money; see Duane to Gallatin, Dec. 13, 1801, in Gallatin Papers, NYHS; Gallatin to Jefferson, Dec. 15, 1801, in Jefferson Papers, LOC; Phillips, *William Duane*, 130–134; Clark, "William Duane," 28; [Duane], *Biographical Memoir*, 7.

22. Jefferson to Duane, May 23, 1801; Duane to Jefferson, June 10, 1801, Oberg (ed.), *TJP*, vol. 34. Jefferson apparently decided not to pardon him; see Robert Livingston to Jefferson, May 31, 1801, in Oberg (ed.), *TJP*, vol. 34; Phillips, *William Duane*, 116–130; Pasley, *Tyranny of Printers*, 288–290.

23. Jefferson to Madison, Aug. 13, 29, 1803; Madison to Jefferson, Aug. 21, 1803, both in Jefferson Papers, LOC. Jefferson believed that editors like Duane threatened the "coalition of sentiments" he wished to encourage in public opinion; see Jefferson to Elbridge Gerry, Mar. 29,

1801, in Oberg (ed.), *TJP*, vol. 34. For growing tensions between Jefferson and Duane over the administration's appointments policy, see Pasley, *Tyranny of Printers*, 293–299. For Jefferson's generally dim view of newspapers, which he believed filled the popular mind with "falsehoods & errors," see Pasley, *Tyranny of Printers*, 258–259. Jefferson was more than willing to prosecute newspaper editors for libel; see Leonard Levy, *Jefferson and Civil Liberties: The Darker Side* (Cambridge, Mass.: Belknap Press of Harvard University Press, 1963).

24. Duane was fascinated by the change of style that accompanied the new administration and thought that Jefferson himself was a model of democratic simplicity and republican austerity; see Clark, "William Duane," 31–32. For President Jefferson's ideas about etiquette, or rather the elaborate etiquette of non-etiquette, see Fliegelman, *Declaring Independence*, 113–114.

25. For Duane's subsequent career and his political battles against McKean and the conservative Pennsylvania Quids (the Society of Independent Republicans), see Durey, *Transatlantic Radicals*, 269–288; Phillips, *William Duane*, 158–185; Pasley, *Tyranny of Printers*, 285–319; and Shankman, *Crucible of Democracy*, chaps. 3–5.

26. William Duane to Abraham Bishop, Aug. 28, 1802, in Ford (ed.), "Letters of William Duane," 257–394.

27. *Aurora*, Oct. 29, 1800; see also Duane's attack on "Federal Characters" in the *Aurora*, Aug. 21, 1800. The flip side of Duane's defense of Jefferson's "character" was his dogged campaign against the personal corruption of Federalist office holders. On the theme of personal corruption in American politics during this period, see Murrin, "Escaping Perfidious Albion."

28. Andrew Trees argues that Madison's ideas expressed his "desire to escape the politics of character"; see Trees, *Founding Fathers*, 11, chap. 4; Cotlar, "In Paine's Absence." On this theme, see also Newman, "Principles or Men?"

Index

7672146R00223

Printed in Great Britain
by Amazon.co.uk, Ltd.,
Marston Gate.